FORD | PICK-UPS AND EXPEDITION/NAVIGATOR 1997-00 REPAIR MANUAL

CHILTON'S

CEO	Rick Van Dalen
President	Dean F. Morgantini, S.A.E.
Vice President–Finance	Barry L. Beck
Vice President–Sales	Glenn D. Potere
Executive Editor	Kevin M. G. Maher, A.S.E.
Manager–Consumer Automotive	Richard Schwartz, A.S.E.
Manager–Professional Automotive	Richard J. Rivele
Manager–Marine/Recreation	James R. Marotta, A.S.E.
Production Specialist	Melinda Possinger
Project Managers	Tim Crain, A.S.E., Thomas A. Mellon, A.S.E., S.A.E., Eric Michael Mihalyi, A.S.E., S.T.S., S.A.E., Christine L. Sheeky, S.A.E., Richard T. Smith, Ron Webb
Schematics Editors	Christopher G. Ritchie, A.S.E., S.A.E., S.T.S., Stephanie A. Spunt
Editor	Eric Michael Mihalyi, A.S.E., S.A.E., S.T.S.

CHILTON *Automotive Books*

PUBLISHED BY **W. G. NICHOLS, INC.**

Manufactured in USA
© 1999 W. G. Nichols, Inc.
1025 Andrew Drive
West Chester, PA 19380
ISBN 0-8019-9119-6
Library of Congress Catalog Card No. 99-072304
4567890123 0987654321

Contents

Contents

7 DRIVE TRAIN

8 SUSPENSION AND STEERING

9 BRAKES

10 BODY AND TRIM

GLOSSARY

MASTER INDEX

See last page for information on additional titles

SAFETY NOTICE

Proper service and repair procedures are vital to the safe, reliable operation of all motor vehicles, as well as the personal safety of those performing repairs. This manual outlines procedures for servicing and repairing vehicles using safe, effective methods. The procedures contain many NOTES, CAUTIONS and WARNINGS which should be followed, along with standard procedures to eliminate the possibility of personal injury or improper service which could damage the vehicle or compromise its safety.

It is important to note that repair procedures and techniques, tools and parts for servicing motor vehicles, as well as the skill and experience of the individual performing the work vary widely. It is not possible to anticipate all of the conceivable ways or conditions under which vehicles may be serviced, or to provide cautions as to all possible hazards that may result. Standard and accepted safety precautions and equipment should be used when handling toxic or flammable fluids, and safety goggles or other protection should be used during cutting, grinding, chiseling, prying, or any other process that can cause material removal or projectiles.

Some procedures require the use of tools specially designed for a specific purpose. Before substituting another tool or procedure, you must be completely satisfied that neither your personal safety, nor the performance of the vehicle will be endangered.

Although information in this manual is based on industry sources and is complete as possible at the time of publication, the possibility exists that some car manufacturers made later changes which could not be included here. While striving for total accuracy, Nichols Publishing cannot assume responsibility for any errors, changes or omissions that may occur in the compilation of this data.

PART NUMBERS

Part numbers listed in this reference are not recommendations by Nichols Publishing for any product brand name. They are references that can be used with interchange manuals and aftermarket supplier catalogs to locate each brand supplier's discrete part number.

SPECIAL TOOLS

Special tools are recommended by the vehicle manufacturer to perform their specific job. Use has been kept to a minimum, but where absolutely necessary, they are referred to in the text by the part number of the tool manufacturer. These tools can be purchased, under the appropriate part number, from your local dealer or regional distributor, or an equivalent tool can be purchased locally from a tool supplier or parts outlet. Before substituting any tool for the one recommended, read the SAFETY NOTICE at the top of this page.

ACKNOWLEDGMENTS

This publication contains material that is reproduced and distributed under a license from Ford Motor Company. No further reproduction or distribution of the Ford Motor Company material is allowed without the express written permission from Ford Motor Company.

Nichols Publishing would like to express thanks to all of the fine companies who participate in the production of our books:
- Hand tools supplied by Craftsman are used during all phases of our vehicle teardown and photography.
- Many of the fine specialty tools used in our procedures were provided courtesy of Lisle Corporation.
- Lincoln Automotive Products (1 Lincoln Way, St. Louis, MO 63120) has provided their industrial shop equipment, including jacks (engine, transmission and floor), engine stands, fluid and lubrication tools, as well as shop presses.
- Rotary Lifts (1-800-640-5438 or www.Rotary-Lift.com), the largest automobile lift manufacturer in the world, offering the biggest variety of surface and in-ground lifts available, has fulfilled our shop's lift needs.
- Much of our shop's electronic testing equipment was supplied by Universal Enterprises Inc. (UEI).
- Safety-Kleen Systems Inc. has provided parts cleaning stations and assistance with environmentally sound disposal of residual wastes.
- United Gilsonite Laboratories (UGL), manufacturer of Drylok® concrete floor paint, has provided materials and expertise for the coating and protection of our shop floor.

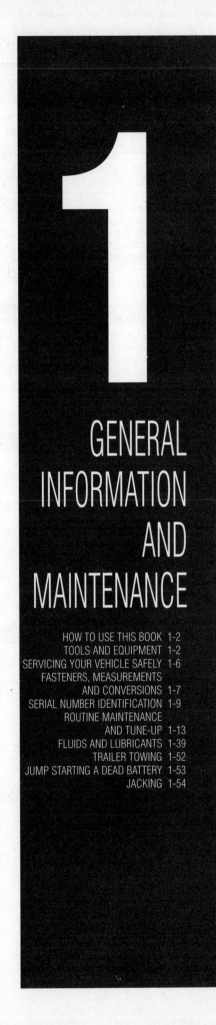

1

GENERAL INFORMATION AND MAINTENANCE

HOW TO USE THIS BOOK

Chilton's Total Car Care manual for 1997–00 Ford F-series Trucks, Ford Expedition and the Lincoln Navigator is intended to help you learn more about the inner workings of your vehicle while saving you money on its upkeep and operation.

The beginning of the book will likely be referred to the most, since that is where you will find information for maintenance and tune-up. The other sections deal with the more complex systems of your vehicle. Systems (from engine through brakes) are covered to the extent that the average do-it-yourselfer can attempt. This book will not explain such things as rebuilding a differential because the expertise required and the special tools necessary make this uneconomical. It will, however, give you detailed instructions to help you change your own brake pads and shoes, replace spark plugs, and perform many more jobs that can save you money and help avoid expensive problems.

A secondary purpose of this book is a reference for owners who want to understand their vehicle and/or their mechanics better.

Where to Begin

Before removing any bolts, read through the entire procedure. This will give you the overall view of what tools and supplies will be required. So read ahead and plan ahead. Each operation should be approached logically and all procedures thoroughly understood before attempting any work.

If repair of a component is not considered practical, we tell you how to remove the part and then how to install the new or rebuilt replacement. In this way, you at least save labor costs.

Avoiding Trouble

Many procedures in this book require you to "label and disconnect . . ." a group of lines, hoses or wires. Don't be think you can remember where everything goes—you won't. If you hook up vacuum or fuel lines incorrectly, the vehicle may run poorly, if at all. If you hook up electrical wiring incorrectly, you may instantly learn a very expensive lesson.

You don't need to know the proper name for each hose or line. A piece of masking tape on the hose and a piece on its fitting will allow you to assign your own label. As long as you remember your own code, the lines can be reconnected by matching your tags. Remember that tape will dissolve in gasoline or solvents; if a part is to be washed or cleaned, use another method of identification. A permanent felt-tipped marker or a metal scribe can be very handy for marking metal parts. Remove any tape or paper labels after assembly.

Maintenance or Repair?

Maintenance includes routine inspections, adjustments, and replacement of parts which show signs of normal wear. Maintenance compensates for wear or deterioration. Repair implies that something has broken or is not working. A need for a repair is often caused by lack of maintenance. for example: draining and refilling automatic transmission fluid is maintenance recommended at specific intervals. Failure to do this can shorten the life of the transmission/transaxle, requiring very expensive repairs. While no maintenance program can prevent items from eventually breaking or wearing out, a general rule is true: MAINTENANCE IS CHEAPER THAN REPAIR.

Two basic mechanic's rules should be mentioned here. First, whenever the left side of the vehicle or engine is referred to, it means the driver's side. Conversely, the right side of the vehicle means the passenger's side. Second, screws and bolts are removed by turning counterclockwise, and tightened by turning clockwise unless specifically noted.

Safety is always the most important rule. Constantly be aware of the dangers involved in working on an automobile and take the proper precautions. Please refer to the information in this section regarding SERVICING YOUR VEHICLE SAFELY and the SAFETY NOTICE on the acknowledgment page.

Avoiding the Most Common Mistakes

Pay attention to the instructions provided. There are 3 common mistakes in mechanical work:

1. Incorrect order of assembly, disassembly or adjustment. When taking something apart or putting it together, performing steps in the wrong order usually just costs you extra time; however, it CAN break something. Read the entire procedure before beginning. Perform everything in the order in which the instructions say you should, even if you can't see a reason for it. When you're taking apart something that is very intricate, you might want to draw a picture of how it looks when assembled in order to make sure you get everything back in its proper position. When making adjustments, perform them in the proper order. One adjustment possibly will affect another.

2. Overtorquing (or undertorquing). While it is more common for overtorquing to cause damage, undertorquing may allow a fastener to vibrate loose causing serious damage. Especially when dealing with aluminum parts, pay attention to torque specifications and utilize a torque wrench in assembly. If a torque figure is not available, remember that if you are using the right tool to perform the job, you will probably not have to strain yourself to get a fastener tight enough. The pitch of most threads is so slight that the tension you put on the wrench will be multiplied many times in actual force on what you are tightening.

There are many commercial products available for ensuring that fasteners won't come loose, even if they are not torqued just right (a very common brand is Loctite®. If you're worried about getting something together tight enough to hold, but loose enough to avoid mechanical damage during assembly, one of these products might offer substantial insurance. Before choosing a threadlocking compound, read the label on the package and make sure the product is compatible with the materials, fluids, etc. involved.

3. Crossthreading. This occurs when a part such as a bolt is screwed into a nut or casting at the wrong angle and forced. Crossthreading is more likely to occur if access is difficult. It helps to clean and lubricate fasteners, then to start threading the bolt, spark plug, etc. with your fingers. If you encounter resistance, unscrew the part and start over again at a different angle until it can be inserted and turned several times without much effort. Keep in mind that many parts have tapered threads, so that gentle turning will automatically bring the part you're threading to the proper angle. Don't put a wrench on the part until it's been tightened a couple of turns by hand. If you suddenly encounter resistance, and the part has not seated fully, don't force it. Pull it back out to make sure it's clean and threading properly.

Be sure to take your time and be patient, and always plan ahead. Allow yourself ample time to perform repairs and maintenance.

TOOLS AND EQUIPMENT

▶ **See Figures 1 thru 15**

Without the proper tools and equipment it is impossible to properly service your vehicle. It would be virtually impossible to catalog every tool that you would need to perform all of the operations in this book. It would be unwise for the amateur to rush out and buy an expensive set of tools on the theory that he/she may need one or more of them at some time.

The best approach is to proceed slowly, gathering a good quality set of those tools that are used most frequently. Don't be misled by the low cost of bargain tools. It is far better to spend a little more for better quality. Forged wrenches, 6 or 12-point sockets and fine tooth ratchets are by far preferable to their less expensive counterparts. As any good mechanic can tell you, there are few worse experiences than trying to work on a vehicle with bad tools. Your monetary savings will be far outweighed by frustration and mangled knuckles.

Begin accumulating those tools that are used most frequently: those associated with routine maintenance and tune-up. In addition to the normal assortment of screwdrivers and pliers, you should have the following tools:

• Wrenches/sockets and combination open end/box end wrenches in sizes from 1/8 –3/4 in. or 3–19mm, as well as a 13/16 in. or 5/8 in. spark plug socket (depending on plug type).

➡ **If possible, buy various length socket drive extensions. Universal-joint and wobble extensions can be extremely useful, but be careful when using them, as they can change the amount of torque applied to the socket.**

• Jackstands for support.
• Oil filter wrench.
• Spout or funnel for pouring fluids.

Fig. 1 All but the most basic procedures will require an assortment of ratchets and sockets

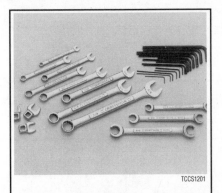

Fig. 2 In addition to ratchets, a good set of wrenches and hex keys will be necessary

Fig. 3 A hydraulic floor jack and a set of jackstands are essential for lifting and supporting the vehicle

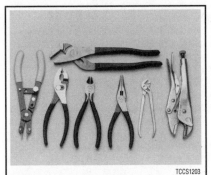

Fig. 4 An assortment of pliers, grippers and cutters will be handy for old rusted parts and stripped bolt heads

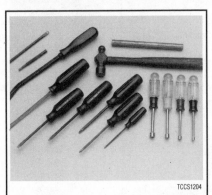

Fig. 5 Various drivers, chisels and prybars are great tools to have in your toolbox

Fig. 6 Many repairs will require the use of a torque wrench to assure the components are properly fastened

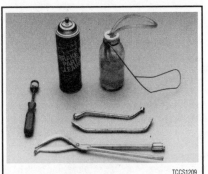

Fig. 7 Although not always necessary, using specialized brake tools will save time

Fig. 8 A few inexpensive lubrication tools will make maintenance easier

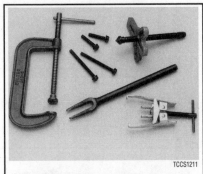

Fig. 9 Various pullers, clamps and separator tools are needed for many larger, more complicated repairs

Fig. 10 A variety of tools and gauges should be used for spark plug gapping and installation

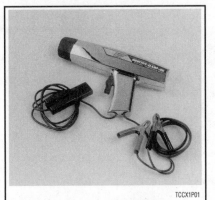

Fig. 11 Inductive type timing light

Fig. 12 A screw-in type compression gauge is recommended for compression testing

TCCX1P03

Fig. 13 A vacuum/pressure tester is necessary for many testing procedures

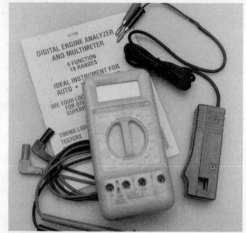

TCCX1P06

Fig. 14 Most modern automotive multimeters incorporate many helpful features

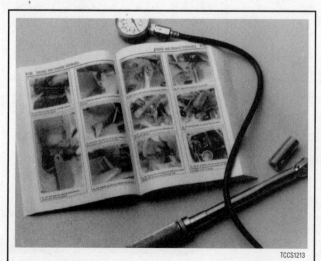

TCCS1213

Fig. 15 Proper information is vital, so always have a Chilton Total Car Care manual handy

- Grease gun for chassis lubrication (unless your vehicle is not equipped with any grease fittings)
- Hydrometer for checking the battery (unless equipped with a sealed, maintenance-free battery).
- A container for draining oil and other fluids.
- Rags for wiping up the inevitable mess.

In addition to the above items there are several others that are not absolutely necessary, but handy to have around. These include an equivalent oil absorbent gravel, like cat litter, and the usual supply of lubricants, antifreeze and fluids. This is a basic list for routine maintenance, but only your personal needs and desire can accurately determine your list of tools.

After performing a few projects on the vehicle, you'll be amazed at the other tools and non-tools on your workbench. Some useful household items are: a large turkey baster or siphon, empty coffee cans and ice trays (to store parts), a ball of twine, electrical tape for wiring, small rolls of colored tape for tagging lines or hoses, markers and pens, a note pad, golf tees (for plugging vacuum lines), metal coat hangers or a roll of mechanic's wire (to hold things out of the way), dental pick or similar long, pointed probe, a strong magnet, and a small mirror (to see into recesses and under manifolds).

A more advanced set of tools, suitable for tune-up work, can be drawn up easily. While the tools are slightly more sophisticated, they need not be outrageously expensive. There are several inexpensive tach/dwell meters on the market that are every bit as good for the average mechanic as a professional model. Just be sure that it goes to a least 1200–1500 rpm on the tach scale and that it works on 4, 6 and 8-cylinder engines. The key to these purchases is to make them with an eye towards adaptability and wide range. A basic list of tune-up tools could include:

- Tach/dwell meter.
- Spark plug wrench and gapping tool.
- Feeler gauges for valve adjustment.
- Timing light.

The choice of a timing light should be made carefully. A light which works on the DC current supplied by the vehicle's battery is the best choice; it should have a xenon tube for brightness. On any vehicle with an electronic ignition system, a timing light with an inductive pickup that clamps around the No. 1 spark plug cable is preferred.

In addition to these basic tools, there are several other tools and gauges you may find useful. These include:

- Compression gauge. The screw-in type is slower to use, but eliminates the possibility of a faulty reading due to escaping pressure.
- Manifold vacuum gauge.
- 12V test light.
- A combination volt/ohmmeter
- Induction Ammeter. This is used for determining whether or not there is current in a wire. These are handy for use if a wire is broken somewhere in a wiring harness.

As a final note, you will probably find a torque wrench necessary for all but the most basic work. The beam type models are perfectly adequate, although the newer click types (breakaway) are easier to use. The click type torque wrenches tend to be more expensive. Also keep in mind that all types of torque wrenches should be periodically checked and/or recalibrated. You will have to decide for yourself which better fits your pocketbook, and purpose.

Special Tools

Normally, the use of special factory tools is avoided for repair procedures, since these are not readily available for the do-it-yourself mechanic. When it is possible to perform the job with more commonly available tools, it will be pointed out, but occasionally, a special tool was designed to perform a specific function and should be used. Before substituting another tool, you should be convinced that neither your safety nor the performance of the vehicle will be compromised.

Special tools can usually be purchased from an automotive parts store or from your dealer. In some cases special tools may be available directly from the tool manufacturer.

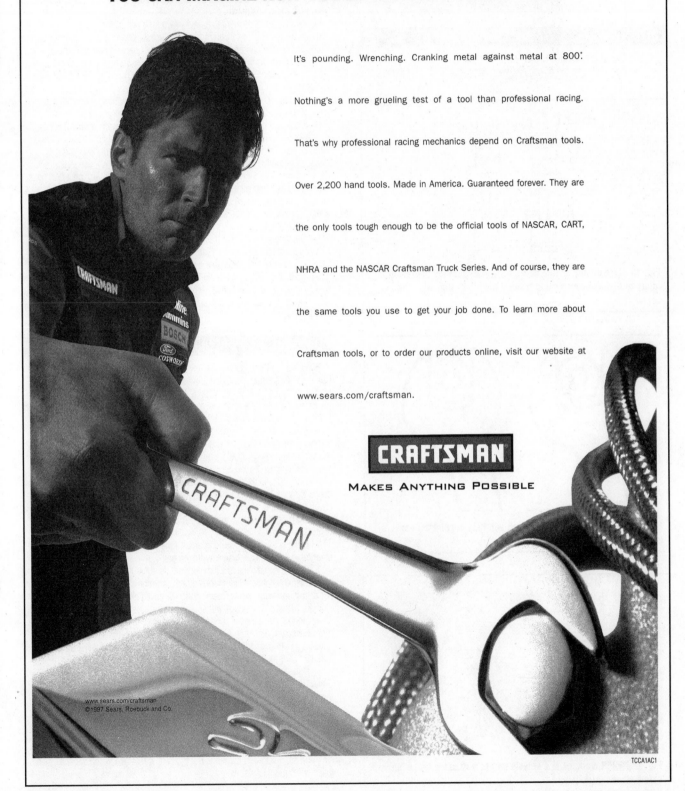

TCCA1AC1

SERVICING YOUR VEHICLE SAFELY

▶ **See Figures 16, 17 and 18**

It is virtually impossible to anticipate all of the hazards involved with automotive maintenance and service, but care and common sense will prevent most accidents.

The rules of safety for mechanics range from "don't smoke around gasoline," to "use the proper tool(s) for the job." The trick to avoiding injuries is to develop safe work habits and to take every possible precaution.

Do's

- Do keep a fire extinguisher and first aid kit handy.
- Do wear safety glasses or goggles when cutting, drilling, grinding or prying, even if you have 20–20 vision. If you wear glasses for the sake of vision, wear safety goggles over your regular glasses.
- Do shield your eyes whenever you work around the battery. Batteries contain sulfuric acid. In case of contact with, flush the area with water or a mixture of water and baking soda, then seek immediate medical attention.
- Do use safety stands (jackstands) for any undervehicle service. Jacks are for raising vehicles; jackstands are for making sure the vehicle stays raised until you want it to come down.
- Do use adequate ventilation when working with any chemicals or hazardous materials. Like carbon monoxide, the asbestos dust resulting from some brake lining wear can be hazardous in sufficient quantities.
- Do disconnect the negative battery cable when working on the electrical system. The secondary ignition system contains EXTREMELY HIGH VOLTAGE. In some cases it can even exceed 50,000 volts.
- Do follow manufacturer's directions whenever working with potentially hazardous materials. Most chemicals and fluids are poisonous.
- Do properly maintain your tools. Loose hammerheads, mushroomed punches and chisels, frayed or poorly grounded electrical cords, excessively worn screwdrivers, spread wrenches (open end), cracked sockets, slipping ratchets, or faulty droplight sockets can cause accidents.
- Likewise, keep your tools clean; a greasy wrench can slip off a bolt head, ruining the bolt and often harming your knuckles in the process.
- Do use the proper size and type of tool for the job at hand. Do select a wrench or socket that fits the nut or bolt. The wrench or socket should sit straight, not cocked.
- Do, when possible, pull on a wrench handle rather than push on it, and adjust your stance to prevent a fall.
- Do be sure that adjustable wrenches are tightly closed on the nut or bolt and pulled so that the force is on the side of the fixed jaw.
- Do strike squarely with a hammer; avoid glancing blows.
- Do set the parking brake and block the drive wheels if the work requires a running engine.

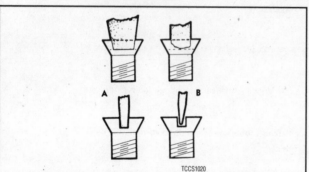

Fig. 16 Screwdrivers should be kept in good condition to prevent injury or damage which could result if the blade slips from the screw

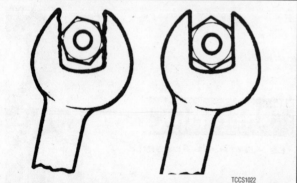

Fig. 17 Using the correct size wrench will help prevent the possibility of rounding off a nut

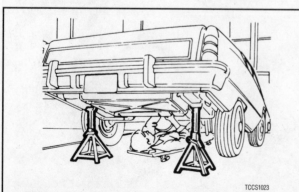

Fig. 18 NEVER work under a vehicle unless it is supported using safety stands (jackstands)

Don'ts

- Don't run the engine in a garage or anywhere else without proper ventilation—EVER! Carbon monoxide is poisonous; it takes a long time to leave the human body and you can build up a deadly supply of it in your system by simply breathing in a little at a time. You may not realize you are slowly poisoning yourself. Always use power vents, windows, fans and/or open the garage door.
- Don't work around moving parts while wearing loose clothing. Short sleeves are much safer than long, loose sleeves. Hard-toed shoes with neoprene soles protect your toes and give a better grip on slippery surfaces. Watches and jewelry is not safe working around a vehicle. Long hair should be tied back under a hat or cap.
- Don't use pockets for toolboxes. A fall or bump can drive a screwdriver deep into your body. Even a rag hanging from your back pocket can wrap around a spinning shaft or fan.
- Don't smoke when working around gasoline, cleaning solvent or other flammable material.
- Don't smoke when working around the battery. When the battery is being charged, it gives off explosive hydrogen gas.
- Don't use gasoline to wash your hands; there are excellent soaps available. Gasoline contains dangerous additives which can enter the body through a cut or through your pores. Gasoline also removes all the natural oils from the skin so that bone dry hands will suck up oil and grease.
- Don't service the air conditioning system unless you are equipped with the necessary tools and training. When liquid or compressed gas refrigerant is released to atmospheric pressure it will absorb heat from whatever it contacts. This will chill or freeze anything it touches.
- Don't use screwdrivers for anything other than driving screws! A screwdriver used as an prying tool can snap when you least expect it, causing injuries. At the very least, you'll ruin a good screwdriver.
- Don't use an emergency jack (that little ratchet, scissors, or pantograph jack supplied with the vehicle) for anything other than changing a flat! These jacks are only intended for emergency use out on the road; they are NOT designed as a maintenance tool. If you are serious about maintaining your vehicle yourself, invest in a hydraulic floor jack of at least a 1½ ton capacity, and at least two sturdy jackstands.

FASTENERS, MEASUREMENTS AND CONVERSIONS

Bolts, Nuts and Other Threaded Retainers

▶ See Figures 19 and 20

Although there are a great variety of fasteners found in the modern car or truck, the most commonly used retainer is the threaded fastener (nuts, bolts, screws, studs, etc.). Most threaded retainers may be reused, provided that they are not damaged in use or during the repair. Some retainers (such as stretch bolts or torque prevailing nuts) are designed to deform when tightened or in use and should not be reinstalled.

Whenever possible, we will note any special retainers which should be replaced during a procedure. But you should always inspect the condition of a retainer when it is removed and replace any that show signs of damage. Check all threads for rust or corrosion which can increase the torque necessary to achieve the desired clamp load for which that fastener was originally selected. Additionally, be sure that the driver surface of the fastener has not been compromised by rounding or other damage. In some cases a driver surface may become only partially rounded, allowing the driver to catch in only one direction. In many of these occurrences, a fastener may be installed and tightened, but the driver would not be able to grip and loosen the fastener again.

If you must replace a fastener, whether due to design or damage, you must ALWAYS be sure to use the proper replacement. In all cases, a retainer of the same design, material and strength should be used. Markings on the heads of most bolts will help determine the proper strength of the fastener. The same material, thread and pitch must be selected to assure proper installation and safe operation of the vehicle afterwards.

Thread gauges are available to help measure a bolt or stud's thread. Most automotive and hardware stores keep gauges available to help you select the proper size. In a pinch, you can use another nut or bolt for a thread gauge. If the bolt you are replacing is not too badly damaged, you can select a match by finding another bolt which will thread in its place. If you find a nut which threads properly onto the damaged bolt, then use that nut to help select the replacement bolt.

✳✳ WARNING

Be aware that when you find a bolt with damaged threads, you may also find the nut or drilled hole it was threaded into has also been damaged. If this is the case, you may have to drill and tap the hole, replace the nut or otherwise repair the threads. NEVER try to force a replacement bolt to fit into the damaged threads.

Torque

Torque is defined as the measurement of resistance to turning or rotating. It tends to twist a body about an axis of rotation. A common example of this would be tightening a threaded retainer such as a nut, bolt or screw. Measuring torque is one of the most common ways to help assure that a threaded retainer has been properly fastened.

When tightening a threaded fastener, torque is applied in three distinct areas, the head, the bearing surface and the clamp load. About 50 percent of the measured torque is used in overcoming bearing friction. This is the friction between the bearing surface of the bolt head, screw head or nut face and the base material or washer (the surface on which the fastener is rotating). Approximately 40 percent of the applied torque is used in overcoming thread friction. This leaves only about 10 percent of the applied torque to develop a useful clamp load (the force which holds a joint together). This means that friction can account for as much as 90 percent of the applied torque on a fastener.

TORQUE WRENCHES

▶ See Figure 21

In most applications, a torque wrench can be used to assure proper installation of a fastener. Torque wrenches come in various designs and most automotive supply stores will carry a variety to suit your needs. A torque wrench should be used any time we supply a specific torque value for a fastener. Again, the general rule of "if you are using the right tool for the job, you should not have to strain to tighten a fastener" applies here.

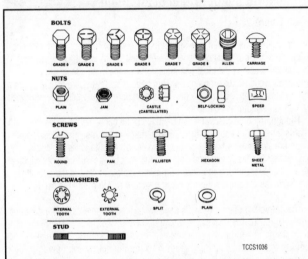

TCCS1036

Fig. 19 There are many different types of threaded retainers found on vehicles

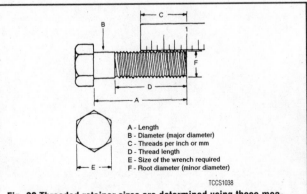

A - Length
B - Diameter (major diameter)
C - Threads per inch or mm
D - Thread length
E - Size of the wrench required
F - Root diameter (minor diameter)

TCCS1038

Fig. 20 Threaded retainer sizes are determined using these measurements

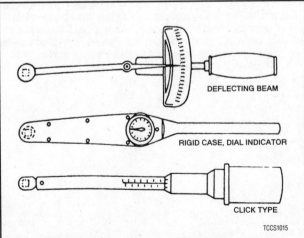

TCCS1015

Fig. 21 Various styles of torque wrenches are usually available at your local automotive supply store

Beam Type

The beam type torque wrench is one of the most popular types. It consists of a pointer attached to the head that runs the length of the flexible beam (shaft) to a scale located near the handle. As the wrench is pulled, the beam bends and the pointer indicates the torque using the scale.

Click (Breakaway) Type

Another popular design of torque wrench is the click type. To use the click type wrench you pre-adjust it to a torque setting. Once the torque is reached, the wrench has a reflex signaling feature that causes a momentary breakaway of the torque wrench body, sending an impulse to the operator's hand.

Pivot Head Type

♦ See Figure 22

Some torque wrenches (usually of the click type) may be equipped with a pivot head which can allow it to be used in areas of limited access. BUT, it must be used properly. To hold a pivot head wrench, grasp the handle lightly, and as you pull on the handle, it should be floated on the pivot point. If the handle comes in contact with the yoke extension during the process of pulling, there is a very good chance the torque readings will be inaccurate because this could alter the wrench loading point. The design of the handle is usually such as to make it inconvenient to deliberately misuse the wrench.

➡ **It should be mentioned that the use of any U-joint, wobble or extension will have an effect on the torque readings, no matter what type of wrench you are using. For the most accurate readings, install the socket directly on the wrench driver. If necessary, straight extensions (which hold a socket directly under the wrench driver) will have the least effect on the torque reading. Avoid any extension that alters the length of the wrench from the handle to the head/driving point (such as a crow's foot). U-joint or wobble extensions can greatly affect the readings; avoid their use at all times.**

Rigid Case (Direct Reading)

A rigid case or direct reading torque wrench is equipped with a dial indicator to show torque values. One advantage of these wrenches is that they can be held at any position on the wrench without affecting accuracy. These wrenches are often preferred because they tend to be compact, easy to read and have a great degree of accuracy.

TORQUE ANGLE METERS

Because the frictional characteristics of each fastener or threaded hole will vary, clamp loads which are based strictly on torque will vary as well. In most applications, this variance is not significant enough to cause worry. But, in certain applications, a manufacturer's engineers may determine that more precise clamp loads are necessary (such is the case with many aluminum cylinder heads). In these cases, a torque angle method of installation would be specified. When installing fasteners which are torque angle tightened, a predetermined seating torque and standard torque wrench are usually used first to remove any compliance from the joint. The fastener is then tightened the specified additional portion of a turn measured in degrees. A torque angle gauge (mechanical protractor) is used for these applications.

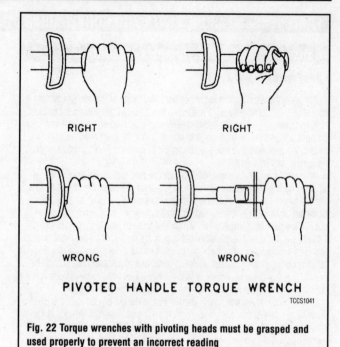

Fig. 22 Torque wrenches with pivoting heads must be grasped and used properly to prevent an incorrect reading

Standard and Metric Measurements

♦ See Figure 23

Throughout this manual, specifications are given to help you determine the condition of various components on your vehicle, or to assist you in their installation. Some of the most common measurements include length (in. or cm/mm), torque (ft. lbs., inch lbs. or Nm) and pressure (psi, in. Hg, kPa or mm Hg). In most cases, we strive to provide the proper measurement as determined by the manufacturer's engineers.

Though, in some cases, that value may not be conveniently measured with what is available in your toolbox. Luckily, many of the measuring devices which are available today will have two scales so the Standard or Metric measurements may easily be taken. If any of the various measuring tools which are available to you do not contain the same scale as listed in the specifications, use the accompanying conversion factors to determine the proper value.

The conversion factor chart is used by taking the given specification and multiplying it by the necessary conversion factor. For instance, looking at the first line, if you have a measurement in inches such as "free-play should be 2 in." but your ruler reads only in millimeters, multiply 2 in. by the conversion factor of 25.4 to get the metric equivalent of 50.8mm. Likewise, if the specification was given only in a Metric measurement, for example in Newton Meters (Nm), then look at the center column first. If the measurement is 100 Nm, multiply it by the conversion factor of 0.738 to get 73.8 ft. lbs.

CONVERSION FACTORS

LENGTH–DISTANCE

Inches (in.)	x 25.4	= Millimeters (mm)	x .0394	= Inches
Feet (ft.)	x .305	= Meters (m)	x 3.281	= Feet
Miles	x 1.609	= Kilometers (km)	x .0621	= Miles

VOLUME

Cubic Inches (in3)	x 16.387	= Cubic Centimeters	x .061	= in3
IMP Pints (IMP pt.)	x .568	= Liters (L)	x 1.76	= IMP pt.
IMP Quarts (IMP qt.)	x 1.137	= Liters (L)	x .88	= IMP qt.
IMP Gallons (IMP gal.)	x 4.546	= Liters (L)	x .22	= IMP gal.
IMP Quarts (IMP qt.)	x 1.201	= US Quarts (US qt.)	x .833	= IMP qt.
IMP Gallons (IMP gal.)	x 1.201	= US Gallons (US gal.)	x .833	= IMP gal.
Fl. Ounces	x 29.573	= Milliliters	x .034	= Ounces
US Pints (US pt.)	x .473	= Liters (L)	x 2.113	= Pints
US Quarts (US qt.)	x .946	= Liters (L)	x 1.057	= Quarts
US Gallons (US gal.)	x 3.785	= Liters (L)	x .264	= Gallons

MASS–WEIGHT

Ounces (oz.)	x 28.35	= Grams (g)	x .035	= Ounces
Pounds (lb.)	x .454	= Kilograms (kg)	x 2.205	= Pounds

PRESSURE

Pounds Per Sq. In. (psi)	x 6.895	= Kilopascals (kPa)	x .145	= psi
Inches of Mercury (Hg)	x .4912	= psi	x 2.036	= Hg
Inches of Mercury (Hg)	x 3.377	= Kilopascals (kPa)	x .2961	= Hg
Inches of Water (H_2O)	x .07355	= Inches of Mercury	x 13.783	= H_2O
Inches of Water (H_2O)	x .03613	= psi	x 27.684	= H_2O
Inches of Water (H_2O)	x .248	= Kilopascals (kPa)	x 4.026	= H_2O

TORQUE

Pounds–Force Inches (in–lb)	x .113	= Newton Meters (N·m)	x 8.85	= in–lb
Pounds–Force Feet (ft–lb)	x 1.356	= Newton Meters (N·m)	x .738	= ft–lb

VELOCITY

Miles Per Hour (MPH)	x 1.609	= Kilometers Per Hour (KPH)	x .621	= MPH

POWER

Horsepower (Hp)	x .745	= Kilowatts	x 1.34	= Horsepower

FUEL CONSUMPTION*

Miles Per Gallon IMP (MPG)	x .354	= Kilometers Per Liter (Km/L)
Kilometers Per Liter (Km/L)	x 2.352	= IMP MPG
Miles Per Gallon US (MPG)	x .425	= Kilometers Per Liter (Km/L)
Kilometers Per Liter (Km/L)	x 2.352	= US MPG

*It is common to covert from miles per gallon (mpg) to liters/100 kilometers (1/100 km), where mpg (IMP) x 1/100 km = 282 and mpg (US) x 1/100 km = 235.

TEMPERATURE

Degree Fahrenheit (°F)	= (°C x 1.8) + 32
Degree Celsius (°C)	= (°F – 32) x .56

TCCS1044

Fig. 23 Standard and metric conversion factors chart

SERIAL NUMBER IDENTIFICATION

Vehicle

VEHICLE IDENTIFICATION NUMBER

▶ **See Figure 24**

The Vehicle Identification Number (VIN) is stamped onto a metal tag mounted in the upper left-hand corner of the instrument panel, visible through the windshield from the outside of the vehicle. The VIN is also presented on various other labels and identifiers found throughout the vehicle.

The VIN is an identification code comprised of a seventeen-digit combination of numbers and letters. Each letter, number or combination represents different items, such as manufacturer, type of restraint system, line, series and body type, engine, model year and consecutive unit number.

The last six digits of the VIN indicate the assembly plant production sequence number of each individual vehicle manufactured at the factory. The last six digits are alphanumeric and begin with A00001, after A99999, the next number would be B00001.

Refer to the accompanying specifications chart and illustrations for VIN breakdown.

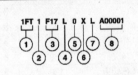

Item	Description
1	World manufacturer identifier
2	Brake type and gross vehicle weight rating (GVWR)
3	Vehicle line, series, body type
4	Engine type
5	Check digit
6	Model year
7	Assembly plant
8	Production sequence number

91191G01

Fig. 24 Breakdown of the VIN number sequence

VEHICLE CERTIFICATION LABEL

▶ **See Figure 25**

The vehicle certification label is affixed to the driver's side door pillar. The vehicle certification label displays various, important information regarding your particular vehicle, such as the following:

- Name of the manufacturer
- Month and year of manufacture
- Gross Vehicle Weight Rating (GVWR)
- Gross Axle Weight Rating (GAWR)
- Tire sizes
- Rim sizes
- Tire cold psi
- Vehicle Identification Number (VIN)
- Front axle accessory reserve capacity in pounds
- Suspension identification including auxiliary/optional components
- Spring identification
- Vehicle body type
- Brake type
- Moulding option (if applicable)
- Tape stripe or paint stripe option (if applicable)
- Interior trim/seat/cab style type
- Exterior paint code(s)
- Axle ratio identification
- Model type
- Transmission identification
- District sales office
- Special order codes
- Date of manufacture

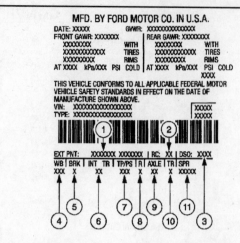

Item	Description
1	Exterior paint code
2	Region code
3	Domestic special order code
4	Wheel base code
5	Brake code
6	Interior trim code
7	Tape/paint pinstripe code
8	Radio code
9	Axle code
10	Transmission code
11	Spring code

91191G02

Fig. 25 Location of various codes on the vehicle certification label

ENGINE AND VEHICLE IDENTIFICATION

Engine							Model Year	
Code ①	Liters (cc)	Cu. In.	Cyl.	Fuel Sys.	Type	Eng. Mfg.	Code ②	Year
A	5.4 (5409)	330	8	SFI	DOHC	Ford	V	1997
2	4.2 (4195)	256	6	EFI	OHV	Ford	W	1998
3	5.4 (5409)	330	8	SFI	SOHC	Ford	X	1999
5	6.8 (6802)	415	10	EFI	SOHC	Ford	Y	2000
6	4.6 (4588)	280	8	EFI	SOHC	Ford		
F	7.3 (7292)	445	8	DIT	OHV	Navistar		
G	7.5 (7538)	460	8	EFI	OHV	Ford		
H	5.8 (5752)	351	8	EFI	OHV	Ford		
L	5.4 (5409)	330	8	EFI	SOHC	Ford		
M	5.4 (5409)	330	8	EFI ③	SOHC	Ford		
W	4.6 (4588)	280	8	EFI	SOHC	Ford		
Z	5.4 (5409)	330	8	EFI ④	SOHC	Ford		

EFI - Electronic Fuel Injection
SFI - Sequential Fuel Injection
DIT - Direct Injection Turbo (Diesel)
OHV- Overhead Valve
SOHC- Single Overhead Camshaft
DOHC- Dual Overhead Camshaft
① 8th digit of the Vehicle Identification Number (VIN)
② 10th digit of the Vehicle Identification Number (VIN)
③ Natural Gas Vehicle (NGV)
④ Bi-fuel Vehicle (Natural Gas/Propane)

91191C01

Engine

▶ See Figure 26

There are several ways to determine engine type supplied with the vehicle. The Vehicle Emission Control Information (VECI) decal mounted under the hood is perhaps the simplest way to identify the vehicle's engine. Another way is to refer to the 10th digit of the VIN along with the necessary chart to determine the meaning of that digit (engine code). In addition to those labels, there is also a specific engine identification label (or tag) attached to the engine.

The engine identification tag identifies the cubic inch displacement of the engine, the model year, the year and month in which the engine was built, where it was built and the change level number. The change level is usually the number one (1), unless there are parts on the engine that will not be completely interchangeable and will require minor modification.

The engine identification tag is typically located on one of the valve covers, usually the driver's side except on the 7.3L diesel engine. The diesel engine I.D. number is stamped on the front of the block, in front of the left cylinder head.

Fig. 26 The engine identification label is typically located on the valve cover

GENERAL ENGINE SPECIFICATIONS

Year	Model	Engine Displacement Liters (cc)	Engine Series (ID/VIN)	Fuel System Type	Net Horsepower @ rpm	Net Torque @ rpm (ft. lbs.)	Bore x Stroke (in.)	Compression Ratio	Oil Pressure @ rpm
1997	Expedition	4.6 (4588)	6/W	EFI	210@4400	290@3250	3.55x3.54	9.0:1	20-45@1500
	Expedition	5.4 (5409)	L	EFI	235@4250	330@3000	3.55X4.17	9.0:1	40-70@1500
	F-150	4.2 (4195)	2	EFI	205@4400	255@3000	3.81x3.74	9.3:1	50@2000
	F-150	4.6 (4588)	6/W	EFI	210@4400	290@3250	3.55x3.54	9.0:1	20-45@1500
	F-150	5.4 (5409)	L	EFI	235@4250	330@3000	3.55X4.17	9.0:1	40-70@1500
	F-250	4.6 (4588)	6/W	EFI	210@4400	290@3250	3.55x3.54	9.0:1	20-45@1500
	F-250	5.4 (5409)	L	EFI	235@4250	330@3000	3.55X4.17	9.0:1	40-70@1500
	F-250HD	5.8 (5752)	H	EFI	210@3600	325@2800	4.00x3.50	8.8:1	40-65@2000
	F-250HD	7.3 (7292)	F	DIT	210@3000	425@2000	4.11x4.18	17.5:1	40-70@3000
	F-250HD	7.5 (7538)	G	EFI	245@4000	400@2200	4.36x3.85	8.5:1	40-88@2000
	F-350	5.8 (5752)	H	EFI	210@3600	325@2800	4.00x3.50	8.8:1	40-65@2000
	F-350	7.3 (7292)	F	DIT	210@3000	425@2000	4.11x4.18	17.5:1	40-70@3000
	F-350	7.5 (7538)	G	EFI	245@4000	400@2200	4.36x3.85	8.5:1	40-88@2000
	F-Super Duty	5.8 (5752)	H	EFI	210@3600	325@2800	4.00x3.50	8.8:1	40-65@2000
	F-Super Duty	7.3 (7292)	F	DIT	210@3000	425@2000	4.11x4.18	17.5:1	40-70@3000
	F-Super Duty	7.5 (7538)	G	EFI	245@4000	400@2200	4.36x3.85	8.5:1	40-88@2000
1998	Expedition	4.6 (4588)	6/W	EFI	210@4400	290@3250	3.55x3.54	9.0:1	20-45@1500
	Expedition	5.4 (5409)	L	EFI	235@4250	330@3000	3.55X4.17	9.0:1	40-70@1500
	F-150	4.2 (4195)	2	EFI	205@4400	255@3000	3.81x3.74	9.3:1	50@2000
	F-150	4.6 (4588)	6/W	EFI	210@4400	290@3250	3.55x3.54	9.0:1	20-45@1500
	F-150	5.4 (5409)	L	EFI	235@4250	330@3000	3.55X4.17	9.0:1	40-70@1500
	F-150	5.4 (5409)	M①	EFI	235@4250	330@3000	3.55X4.17	9.0:1	40-70@1500
	F-250	4.6 (4588)	6/W	EFI	210@4400	290@3250	3.55x3.54	9.0:1	20-45@1500
	F-250	5.4 (5409)	L	EFI	235@4250	330@3000	3.55X4.17	9.0:1	40-70@1500
	F-250	5.4 (5409)	M①	EFI	235@4250	330@3000	3.55X4.17	9.0:1	40-70@1500
	F-250HD	5.8 (5752)	H	EFI	210@3600	325@2800	4.00x3.50	8.8:1	40-65@2000
	F-250HD	7.3 (7292)	F	DIT	210@3000	425@2000	4.11x4.18	17.5:1	40-70@3000
	F-250HD	7.5 (7538)	G	EFI	245@4000	400@2200	4.36x3.85	8.5:1	40-88@2000
	F-350	5.8 (5752)	H	EFI	210@3600	325@2800	4.00x3.50	8.8:1	40-65@2000
	F-350	7.3 (7292)	F	DIT	210@3000	425@2000	4.11x4.18	17.5:1	40-70@3000
	F-350	7.5 (7538)	G	EFI	245@4000	400@2200	4.36x3.85	8.5:1	40-88@2000
	F-Super Duty	5.8 (5752)	H	EFI	210@3600	325@2800	4.00x3.50	8.8:1	40-65@2000
	F-Super Duty	7.3 (7292)	F	DIT	210@3000	425@2000	4.11x4.18	17.5:1	40-70@3000
	F-Super Duty	7.5 (7538)	G	EFI	245@4000	400@2200	4.36x3.85	8.5:1	40-88@2000
	Navigator	5.4 (5409)	L	EFI	235@4250	330@3000	3.55X4.17	9.0:1	40-70@1500
1999	Expedition	4.6 (4588)	6/W	EFI	240@4400	290@3250	3.55x3.54	9.0:1	20-45@1500
	Expedition	5.4 (5409)	L	EFI	260@4750	345@3000	3.55X4.17	9.0:1	40-70@1500
	Expedition	5.4 (5409)	A	EFI	300@3750	330@3000	3.55X4.17	9.0:1	40-70@1500
	F-150	4.2 (4195)	2	EFI	205@4400	255@3000	3.81x3.74	9.3:1	50@2000
	F-150	4.6 (4588)	6/W	EFI	220@4400	290@3250	3.55x3.54	9.0:1	20-45@1500
	F-150	5.4 (5409)	L/M/Z	EFI	260@4500	345@2300	3.55X4.17	9.0:1	40-70@1500
	F-150 ①	5.4 (5409)	3	EFI	360@4750	440@3000	3.55X4.17	8.4:1	40-70@1500
	F-250	4.6 (4588)	6/W	EFI	210@4400	290@3250	3.55x3.54	9.0:1	20-45@1500
	F-250	5.4 (5409)	L/M/Z	EFI	235@4250	330@3000	3.55X4.17	9.0:1	40-70@1500
	F-Super Duty ②	5.4 (5409)	L	EFI	235@4250	330@3000	3.55X4.17	9.0:1	40-70@1500
	F-Super Duty ②	6.8 (6802)	5	EFI	265@4250	410@2750	3.55X4.17	9.0:1	40-70@1500
	F-Super Duty ②	7.3 (7292)	F	DIT	235@2700	500@1600	4.11x4.18	17.5:1	40-70@3000
	Navigator	5.4 (5409)	L	EFI	260@4750	345@3000	3.55X4.17	9.0:1	40-70@1500
	Navigator	5.4 (5409)	A	EFI	300@3750	345@3000	3.55X4.17	9.0:1	40-70@1500

91191C02

GENERAL ENGINE SPECIFICATIONS

Year	Model		Engine Displacement Liters (cc)	Engine Series (ID/VIN)	Fuel System Type	Net Horsepower @ rpm	Net Torque @ rpm (ft. lbs.)	Bore x Stroke (in.)	Compression Ratio	Oil Pressure @ rpm
2000	Expedition		4.6 (4588)	6/W	EFI	240@4400	290@3250	3.55x3.54	9.0:1	20-45@1500
	Expedition		5.4 (5409)	L	EFI	260@4750	345@3000	3.55X4.17	9.0:1	40-70@1500
	Expedition		5.4 (5409)	A	EFI	300@3750	345@3000	3.55X4.17	9.0:1	40-70@1500
	F-150		4.2 (4195)	2	EFI	205@4400	255@3000	3.81x3.74	9.3:1	50@2000
	F-150		4.6 (4588)	6/W	EFI	220@4400	290@3250	3.55x3.54	9.0:1	20-45@1500
	F-150		5.4 (5409)	L/M/Z	EFI	260@4500	345@2300	3.55X4.17	9.0:1	40-70@1500
	F-150	①	5.4 (5409)	3	EFI	360@4750	440@3000	3.55X4.17	8.4:1	40-70@1500
	F-250		4.6 (4588)	6/W	EFI	210@4400	290@3250	3.55x3.54	9.0:1	20-45@1500
	F-250		5.4 (5409)	L/M/Z	EFI	235@4250	330@3000	3.55X4.17	9.0:1	40-70@1500
	F-Super Duty	②	5.4 (5409)	L	EFI	235@4250	330@3000	3.55X4.17	9.0:1	40-70@1500
	F-Super Duty	②	6.8 (6802)	5	EFI	265@4250	410@2750	3.55X4.17	9.0:1	40-70@1500
	F-Super Duty	②	7.3 (7292)	F	DIT	235@2700	500@1600	4.11x4.18	17.5:1	40-70@3000
	Navigator		5.4 (5409)	L	EFI	260@4750	345@3000	3.55X4.17	9.0:1	40-70@1500
	Navigator		5.4 (5409)	A	EFI	300@3750	345@3000	3.55X4.17	9.0:1	40-70@1500

EFI - Electronic Fuel Injection
DIT - Direct Injection Turbo (Diesel)
① Lightning Pickup Model
② F-Super Duty models 1999-00 include the F-250 Super Duty and above

91191C03

Transmission

▶ See Figure 27

An identification tag is located on the transmission case, typically on the left side rearward of the transmission range (TR) sensor on automatic transmissions and on the side of the case on a manual transmission. A transmission code is also located on the vehicle certification label, however it is alphanumeric code and only identifies the model of the transmission and cannot be used for parts ordering or application.

Drive Axle

▶ See Figures 28 and 29

The drive axle code is found stamped on a flat surface on the axle support arm or on the axle tube next to the differential housing. Also, and more easily

found, is a tag secured by one of the differential housing cover bolts. The axle tag has several identifying codes on it including manufacturer, axle ratio, ring gear diameter and date of manufacture. The axle code is also listed on the certification label, however, this is a code is not the axle ratio, but a two digit code (4 X 2 only) and three digit code (4 X 4 only) with the third digit being the front axle identifying code.

Transfer Case

A tag is affixed to the case mounting bolts, usually where the case splits. The information on the tag is needed when ordering service parts. If the tag is removed for any reason, make sure it is reinstalled.

1. Assembly Part Number Prefix and Suffix
2. Transmission Model
3. Serial
4. Build Date (Year, Month, and Day).

91191G03

Fig. 27 Typical breakdown of a transmission identification label

91191P59

Fig. 28 The axle identification tag is typically attached to one of the axle cover bolts

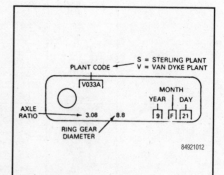

84921012

Fig. 29 Differential identification label. Limited slip units have a separate tag secured by a cover bolt

ROUTINE MAINTENANCE AND TUNE-UP

UNDERHOOD MAINTENANCE COMPONENT LOCATIONS—4.2L ENGINE

1) Windshield washer solvent reservoir
2) Spark plugs (3 on each side)
3) Battery
4) Automatic transmission dipstick
5) PCV valve
6) Spark plug wires
7) Drive belt
8) Power steering pump reservoir (below A/C compressor)
9) Engine oil fill cap
10) Engine oil dipstick
11) Brake master cylinder reservoir
12) Engine compartment fusebox
13) Air cleaner assembly
14) Coolant recovery tank

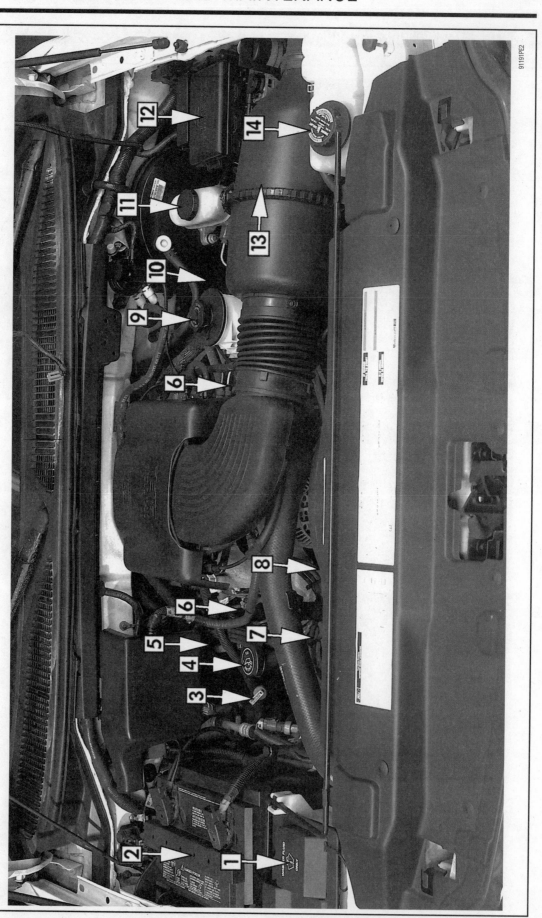

UNDERHOOD MAINTENANCE COMPONENT LOCATIONS—4.6L ENGINE

1) Windshield washer solvent reservoir
2) Battery
3) Automatic transmission dipstick
4) Engine oil fill cap
5) PCV valve
6) Spark plugs (4 on each side)
7) Spark plug wires
8) Drive belt
9) Power steering pump reservoir
10) Engine oil dipstick
11) Brake master cylinder reservoir
12) Engine compartment fusebox
13) Air cleaner assembly
14) Coolant recovery tank

UNDERHOOD MAINTENANCE COMPONENT LOCATIONS—5.4L ENGINE

1) Windshield washer solvent reservoir
2) Battery
3) Automatic transmission dipstick
4) PCV valve
5) Spark plugs and ignition coils (4 on each side)
6) Drive belt
7) Engine oil fill cap
8) Power steering pump reservoir
9) Brake master cylinder reservoir
10) Engine compartment fusebox
11) Air cleaner assembly
12) Coolant recovery tank

UNDERHOOD MAINTENANCE COMPONENT LOCATIONS—6.8L ENGINE

1) Battery
2) Coolant recovery tank
3) Engine oil fill cap
4) PCV valve
5) Spark plugs and ignition coils (5 on each side)
6) Engine oil dipstick
7) Air cleaner assembly
8) Clutch fluid reservoir
9) Brake master cylinder reservoir
10) Engine compartment fusebox
11) Power steering pump reservoir
12) Drive belt

91191P E4

UNDERHOOD MAINTENANCE COMPONENT LOCATIONS—5.8/7.5L ENGINE

1) Battery
2) Spark plugs and plug wires (4 on each side)
3) PCV valve
4) Distributor cap & rotor
5) Drive belt
6) Engine oil fill cap
7) Engine oil dipstick
8) Clutch master cylinder
9) Brake master cylinder
10) Engine compartment fusebox
11) Air cleaner assembly
12) Coolant recovery tank

91191PE5

UNDERHOOD MAINTENANCE COMPONENT LOCATIONS—7.3L DIESEL ENGINE

1) Windshield washer solvent reservoir
2) Battery
3) Coolant recovery tank
4) Engine oil dipstick
5) Engine oil fill cap
6) Drive belt
7) Clutch master cylinder
8) Brake master cylinder
9) Air cleaner assembly
10) Engine compartment fusebox

Proper maintenance and tune-up is the key to long and trouble-free vehicle life, and the work can yield its own rewards. Studies have shown that a properly tuned and maintained vehicle can achieve better gas mileage than an out-of-tune vehicle. As a conscientious owner and driver, set aside a Saturday morning, say once a month, to check or replace items which could cause major problems later. Keep your own personal log to jot down which services you performed, how much the parts cost you, the date, and the exact odometer reading at the time. Keep all receipts for such items as engine oil and filters, so that they may be referred to in case of related problems or to determine operating expenses. As a do-it-yourselfer, these receipts are the only proof you have that the required maintenance was performed. In the event of a warranty problem, these receipts will be invaluable.

The literature provided with your vehicle when it was originally delivered includes the factory recommended maintenance schedule. If you no longer have this literature, replacement copies are usually available from the dealer. A maintenance schedule is provided later in this section, in case you do not have the factory literature.

Air Cleaner (Element)

REMOVAL & INSTALLATION

Except 1997–98 Super Duty and All Diesel

▶ See Figures 30, 31, 32 and 33

1. Disconnect the negative battery cable.
2. Remove the outlet tube clamp from around the air cleaner element housing and remove the tube from the air cleaner housing. Position the tube out of the way.

3. Remove the air cleaner element from the air cleaner housing.
4. Installation is the reverse of removal.

1997–98 Super Duty

1. Disconnect the negative battery cable.
2. Remove the outlet tube clamps from the air cleaner housing and remove the tubes from the housing and secure out of the way.
3. Remove the screws securing the air cleaner cover and remove the cover.
4. Remove the air cleaner element from the air cleaner housing.
5. Installation is the reverse of removal.

7.3L Diesel Engine

▶ See Figure 34

➡ The 7.3L engine is equipped with a air restriction gauge also referred to as a "filter minder". This device alerts the operator, or person performing the maintenance, of the condition of the filter element. When the "filter minder" reaches the YELLOW band in the gauge, it is time to replace the filter. The gauge can be reset by pushing the button on the end of the gauge.

1. Disconnect the negative battery cable.
2. Remove the air cleaner outlet tube-to-radiator support retaining screw.
3. Remove the air cleaner outlet tube clamps and remove the outlet duct.
4. Loosen the clamp retaining the engine air cleaner-to-air cleaner outlet tube adapter.
5. Loosen the nuts retaining the upper air cleaner housing to the lower air cleaner housing and remove the upper housing.

Fig. 30 Detach the outlet tube clamp and . . .

Fig. 31 . . . carefully pull the tube and lid from the air cleaner housing

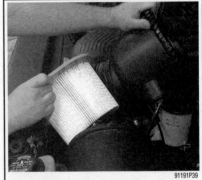

Fig. 32 Remove the air cleaner element from the air cleaner housing

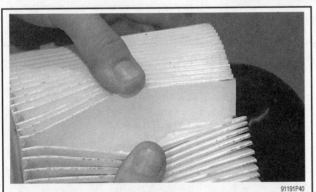

Fig. 33 Inspect the condition of the air cleaner element and replace as necessary

6. Remove the air cleaner element from the housing.
To install:
7. Before installing a new element, inspect the following:
   a. The housing gasket surfaces must be clean and un-damaged.
   b. The water drain tube should be free of obstructions.
   c. The housing should be free of dents, ruptures and holes.

✳✳ WARNING

A special filtering element is used on the 7.3L diesel engine. Use only a specific Ford filter element for replacement. Use of other elements can result in serious engine damage. Do not attempt to clean the element, replace it only.

8. The balance of the installation is the reverse of removal.

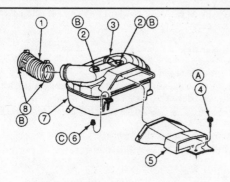

Item	Description
1	Engine Air Cleaner Duct Tube Adapter
2	Nut
3	Restriction Gauge
4	Screw
5	Engine Air Cleaner Intake Tube
6	Nut and Washer
7	Engine Air Cleaner Assy
8	Engine Air Cleaner Duct Tube Adapter Clamp (Part of 9B676)
A	Tighten to 7-9 N·m (62-80 Lb-In)
B	Tighten to 2-3 N·m (18-27 Lb-In)
C	Tighten to 5-7 N·m (44-62 Lb-In)

91191G04

Fig. 34 The air cleaner assembly—7.3L diesel engine

Fuel Filter

REMOVAL & INSTALLATION

▶ **See Figures 35, 36, 37, 38 and 39**

➡The fuel filter is located along the frame rail under the vehicle and is accessible only from underneath the vehicle.

✳✳ CAUTION

Observe all applicable safety precautions when working around fuel. Whenever servicing the fuel system, always work in a well ventilated area. Do not allow fuel spray or vapors to come in contact with a spark or open flame. Keep a dry chemical fire extinguisher near the work area. Always keep fuel in a container specifically designed for fuel storage; also, always properly seal fuel containers to avoid the possibility of fire or explosion.

1. Disconnect the negative battery cable.
2. Properly relieve the fuel system pressure.
3. Raise and safely support the vehicle securely on jackstands.
4. Remove the fitting safety clips by gently prying them off. Usually they are held to the fuel lines by small retaining straps, however take care not to lose them.
5. Insert fuel line disconnect tool T90T-9550-S into the quick-connect fittings on the fuel lines.
6. Push the tool into the spring lock coupling and release the garter spring and separate the fitting.

➡Twisting the line sometimes aid in releasing stubborn connections.

✳✳ CAUTION

Fuel will most likely run out of the line after it is removed from the filter.

91191P97

Fig. 35 Remove the safety retaining clip from the fuel lines

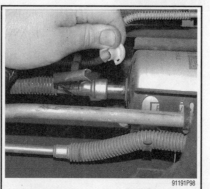

91191P98

Fig. 36 Spread the special release tool open and . . .

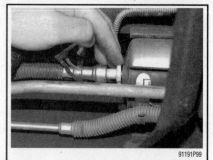

91191P99

Fig. 37 . . . place the tool on the filter inlet/outlet tube and carefully press the tool inward to release the garter spring on the spring lock coupling

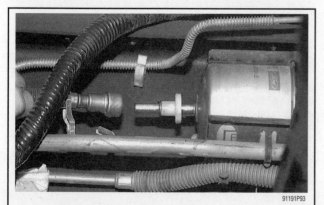

91191P93

Fig. 38 Remove the fuel line from the filter

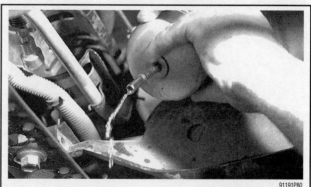

91191P80

Fig. 39 Now remove the filter from the clamp by pulling it straight out

7. Repeat the procedure for the other fuel line.

8. Grasp the fuel filter and carefully pull it straight out of the retaining clamp.

To install:

9. Push the filter into the retaining clamp aligning the front lip on the filter into the groove.

10. Attach the fuel lines to the filter until an audible click is heard from the connection. Sometimes the click is very quiet, so test the fitting by gently pulling on the line to see if it comes loose.

11. Attach the fitting safety clips by snapping them into place over the fittings.

12. Lower the vehicle

13. Connect the negative battery cable.

14. Start the vehicle and check the filter and lines for leaks.

Fuel/Water Separator

DRAINING

The 7.3L diesel engine is equipped with a fuel/water separator in the fuel supply line. A "Water in Fuel" indicator light is provided on the instrument panel to alert the driver. The light should glow when the ignition switch is in the **start** position to indicate proper light and water sensor function. If the light glows continuously while the engine is running, the water must be drained from the separator as soon as possible to prevent damage to the fuel injection system.

1. Shut off the engine. Failure to shut the engine **OFF** before draining the separator will cause air to enter the system.

2. Place an appropriate container under the drain valve on the water separator.

3. Manually open the drain valve, and allow the valve to remain open for approximately 15 seconds, or until clear water-free diesel fuel flows out.

4. After the water is completely drained, close the water drain valve.

5. Start the engine and check the "Water in Fuel" indicator light; it should not be lit. If it is lit and continues to stay so, there is a problem somewhere else in the fuel system.

REMOVAL & INSTALLATION

▶ See Figures 40, 41, 42 and 43

1. Disconnect both battery ground cables.

2. Open the fuel filter/water separator drain valve to release the fuel pressure. Completely drain the fuel filter/water separator assembly.

3. Disconnect the fuel supply and fuel return lines.

4. Disconnect the two cylinder head fuel supply lines.

5. Disconnect the electrical connector from the fuel filter/water separator.

6. Remove the fuel filter/water separator from the vehicle.

7. Disconnect the exhaust back pressure sensor electrical connector.

8. Remove the fuel filter/water separator retaining bolts.

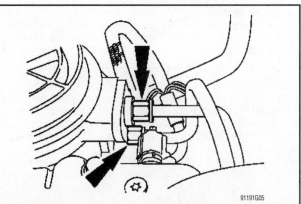

Fig. 40 Disconnect the fuel supply and return lines from the separator assembly

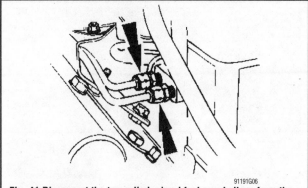

Fig. 41 Disconnect the two cylinder head fuel supply lines from the separator assembly

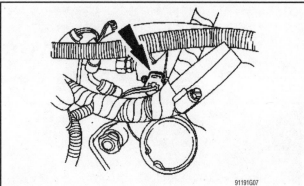

Fig. 42 Unplug the electrical connector from the fuel filter/water separator

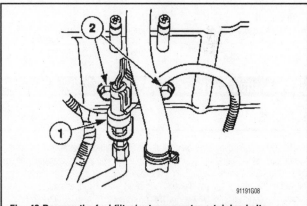

Fig. 43 Remove the fuel filter/water separator retaining bolts

✳✳ WARNING

Clean all the fuel residue from the engine compartment. Failure to do so can cause personal injury or damage to the vehicle.

9. Installation is the reverse of removal.

PCV Valve

REMOVAL & INSTALLATION

▶ See Figures 44 and 45

1. Disconnect the oil separator hose from the PCV valve.

2. Remove the PCV valve from the grommet in the crankcase.

Fig. 44 Grasp the valve and gently remove it from the grommet in the passenger side valve cover

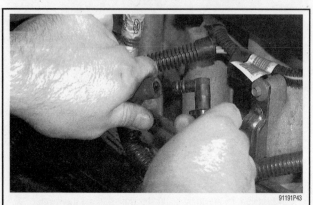

Fig. 45 Remove the valve from the hose by carefully twisting it out

3. Inspect the grommet for deterioration.
To install:
4. If necessary, replace the crankcase grommet.
5. Install the PCV valve.
6. Install the hose.

Evaporative Canister

SERVICING

The fuel evaporative emission control canister should be inspected for damage or leaks at the hose fittings every 24,000 miles. Repair or replace any old or cracked hoses. Replace the canister if it is damaged in any way. The canister is located in the engine compartment on all F250HD/SD, F350, and all Super Duty trucks. The canister is located on the rear crossmember on all F150, F250, Expedition and Navigator models.

For more detailed canister service, see Section 4.

Battery

PRECAUTIONS

Always use caution when working on or near the battery. Never allow a tool to bridge the gap between the negative and positive battery terminals. Also, be careful not to allow a tool to provide a ground between the positive cable/terminal and any metal component on the vehicle. Either of these conditions will cause a short circuit, leading to sparks and possible personal injury.

Do not smoke, have an open flame or create sparks near a battery; the gases contained in the battery are very explosive and, if ignited, could cause severe injury or death.

All batteries, regardless of type, should be carefully secured by a battery hold-down device. If this is not done, the battery terminals or casing may crack from stress applied to the battery during vehicle operation. A battery which is not secured may allow acid to leak out, making it discharge faster; such leaking corrosive acid can also eat away at components under the hood.

Always visually inspect the battery case for cracks, leakage and corrosion. A white corrosive substance on the battery case or on nearby components would indicate a leaking or cracked battery. If the battery is cracked, it should be replaced immediately.

GENERAL MAINTENANCE

▶ **See Figure 46**

A battery that is not sealed must be checked periodically for electrolyte level. You cannot add water to a sealed maintenance-free battery (though not all maintenance-free batteries are sealed); however, a sealed battery must also be checked for proper electrolyte level, as indicated by the color of the built-in hydrometer "eye."

Always keep the battery cables and terminals free of corrosion. Check these components about once a year. Refer to the removal, installation and cleaning procedures outlined in this section.

Keep the top of the battery clean, as a film of dirt can help completely discharge a battery that is not used for long periods. A solution of baking soda and water may be used for cleaning, but be careful to flush this off with clear water. DO NOT let any of the solution into the filler holes. Baking soda neutralizes battery acid and will de-activate a battery cell.

Batteries in vehicles which are not operated on a regular basis can fall victim to parasitic loads (small current drains which are constantly drawing current from the battery). Normal parasitic loads may drain a battery on a vehicle that is in storage and not used for 6–8 weeks. Vehicles that have additional accessories such as a cellular phone, an alarm system or other devices that increase parasitic load may discharge a battery sooner. If the vehicle is to be stored for 6–8 weeks in a secure area and the alarm system, if present, is not necessary, the negative battery cable should be disconnected at the onset of storage to protect the battery charge.

Remember that constantly discharging and recharging will shorten battery life. Take care not to allow a battery to be needlessly discharged.

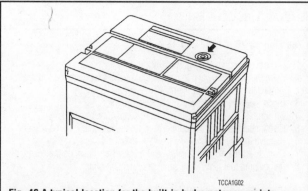

Fig. 46 A typical location for the built-in hydrometer on maintenance-free batteries

BATTERY FLUID

Check the battery electrolyte level at least once a month, or more often in hot weather or during periods of extended vehicle operation. On non-sealed batteries, the level can be checked either through the case on translucent batteries or by removing the cell caps on opaque-cased types. The electrolyte level in each cell should be kept filled to the split ring inside each cell, or the line marked on the outside of the case.

If the level is low, add only distilled water through the opening until the level is correct. Each cell is separate from the others, so each must be checked and filled individually. Distilled water should be used, because the chemicals and minerals found in most drinking water are harmful to the battery and could significantly shorten its life.

If water is added in freezing weather, the vehicle should be driven several miles to allow the water to mix with the electrolyte. Otherwise, the battery could freeze.

Although some maintenance-free batteries have removable cell caps for access to the electrolyte, the electrolyte condition and level on all sealed maintenance-free batteries must be checked using the built-in hydrometer "eye." The exact type of eye varies between battery manufacturers, but most apply a sticker to the battery itself explaining the possible readings. When in doubt, refer to the battery manufacturer's instructions to interpret battery condition using the built-in hydrometer.

➡**Although the readings from built-in hydrometers found in sealed batteries may vary, a green eye usually indicates a properly charged battery with sufficient fluid level. A dark eye is normally an indicator of a battery with sufficient fluid, but one which may be low in charge. And a light or yellow eye is usually an indication that electrolyte supply has dropped below the necessary level for battery (and hydrometer) operation. In this last case, sealed batteries with an insufficient electrolyte level must usually be discarded.**

Checking the Specific Gravity

▶ **See Figures 47, 48 and 49**

A hydrometer is required to check the specific gravity on all batteries that are not maintenance-free. On batteries that are maintenance-free, the specific gravity is checked by observing the built-in hydrometer "eye" on the top of the battery case. Check with your battery's manufacturer for proper interpretation of its built-in hydrometer readings.

✷✷ CAUTION

Battery electrolyte contains sulfuric acid. If you should splash any on your skin or in your eyes, flush the affected area with plenty of clear water. If it lands in your eyes, get medical help immediately.

The fluid (sulfuric acid solution) contained in the battery cells will tell you many things about the condition of the battery. Because the cell plates must be kept submerged below the fluid level in order to operate, maintaining the fluid level is extremely important. And, because the specific gravity of the acid is an indication of electrical charge, testing the fluid can be an aid in determining if the battery must be replaced. A battery in a vehicle with a properly operating charging system should require little maintenance, but careful, periodic inspection should reveal problems before they leave you stranded.

As stated earlier, the specific gravity of a battery's electrolyte level can be used as an indication of battery charge. At least once a year, check the specific gravity of the battery. It should be between 1.20 and 1.26 on the gravity scale. Most auto supply stores carry a variety of inexpensive battery testing hydrometers. These can be used on any non-sealed battery to test the specific gravity in each cell.

The battery testing hydrometer has a squeeze bulb at one end and a nozzle at the other. Battery electrolyte is sucked into the hydrometer until the float is lifted from its seat. The specific gravity is then read by noting the position of the float. If gravity is low in one or more cells, the battery should be slowly charged and checked again to see if the gravity has come up. Generally, if after charging, the specific gravity between any two cells varies more than 50 points (0.50), the battery should be replaced, as it can no longer produce sufficient voltage to guarantee proper operation.

CABLES

▶ **See Figures 50, 51, 52, 53 and 54**

Once a year (or as necessary), the battery terminals and the cable clamps should be cleaned. Loosen the clamps and remove the cables, negative cable first. On batteries with posts on top, the use of a puller specially made for this purpose is recommended. These are inexpensive and available in most auto parts stores. Side terminal battery cables are secured with a small bolt.

Clean the cable clamps and the battery terminal with a wire brush, until all corrosion, grease, etc., is removed and the metal is shiny. It is especially important to clean the inside of the clamp thoroughly (an old knife is useful here), since a small deposit of foreign material or oxidation there will prevent a sound

Fig. 47 On non-maintenance-free batteries, the fluid level can be checked through the case on translucent models; the cell caps must be removed on other models

Fig. 48 If the fluid level is low, add only distilled water through the opening until the level is correct

Fig. 49 Check the specific gravity of the battery's electrolyte with a hydrometer

Fig. 50 Maintenance is performed with household items and with special tools like this post cleaner

Fig. 51 The underside of this special battery tool has a wire brush to clean post terminals

Fig. 52 Place the tool over the battery posts and twist to clean until the metal is shiny

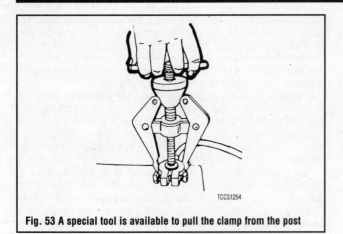

Fig. 53 A special tool is available to pull the clamp from the post

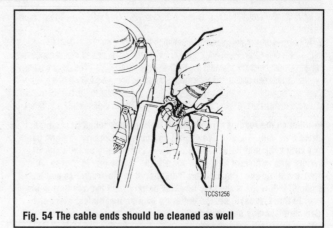

Fig. 54 The cable ends should be cleaned as well

electrical connection and inhibit either starting or charging. Special tools are available for cleaning these parts, one type for conventional top post batteries and another type for side terminal batteries. It is also a good idea to apply some dielectric grease to the terminal, as this will aid in the prevention of corrosion.

After the clamps and terminals are clean, reinstall the cables, negative cable last; DO NOT hammer the clamps onto battery posts. Tighten the clamps securely, but do not distort them. Give the clamps and terminals a thin external coating of grease after installation, to retard corrosion.

Check the cables at the same time that the terminals are cleaned. If the cable insulation is cracked or broken, or if the ends are frayed, the cable should be replaced with a new cable of the same length and gauge.

CHARGING

✳✳ CAUTION

The chemical reaction which takes place in all batteries generates explosive hydrogen gas. A spark can cause the battery to explode and splash acid. To avoid serious personal injury, be sure there is proper ventilation and take appropriate fire safety precautions when connecting, disconnecting, or charging a battery and when using jumper cables.

A battery should be charged at a slow rate to keep the plates inside from getting too hot. However, if some maintenance-free batteries are allowed to discharge until they are almost "dead," they may have to be charged at a high rate to bring them back to "life." Always follow the charger manufacturer's instructions on charging the battery.

REPLACEMENT

When it becomes necessary to replace the battery, select one with an amperage rating equal to or greater than the battery originally installed. Deterioration

and just plain aging of the battery cables, starter motor, and associated wires makes the battery's job harder in successive years. The slow increase in electrical resistance over time makes it prudent to install a new battery with a greater capacity than the old.

Belts

INSPECTION

▶ See Figures 55, 56, 57 and 58

Inspect the belts for signs of glazing or cracking. A glazed belt will be perfectly smooth from slippage, while a good belt will have a slight texture of fabric visible. Cracks will usually start at the inner edge of the belt and run outward. All worn or damaged drive belts should be replaced immediately. It is best to replace all drive belts at one time, as a preventive maintenance measure, during this service operation.

ADJUSTMENT

▶ See Figures 59 thru 67

All engines use an automatic drive belt tensioner. On the 7.5L engine, there are two belts, one uses the automatic tensioner, while the alternator belt requires periodic tensioning. On all belts using an automatic tensioner, no adjustment is necessary because the tensioner adjusts for belt wear. To adjust the tension on the 7.5L engine alternator belt, loosen the adjusting bolts and rotate the alternator until the proper tension is on the drive belt and tighten the adjusting bolts. It is recommended that the belt tension indicator mark be inspected with the engine **OFF** at 60,000 mile (96,000 km) intervals. If the wear indicator mark is out of specification, the drive belt is worn or an incorrect drive belt has been installed.

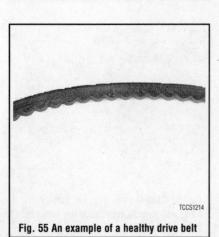

Fig. 55 An example of a healthy drive belt

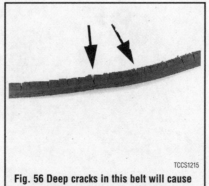

Fig. 56 Deep cracks in this belt will cause flex, building up heat that will eventually lead to belt failure

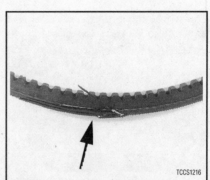

Fig. 57 The cover of this belt is worn, exposing the critical reinforcing cords to excessive wear

Fig. 58 Installing too wide a belt can result in serious belt wear and/or breakage

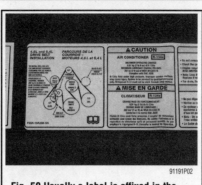

Fig. 59 Usually a label is affixed in the engine compartment with the proper belt routing on it

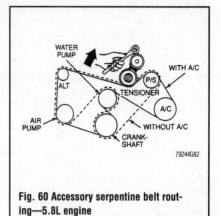

Fig. 60 Accessory serpentine belt routing—5.8L engine

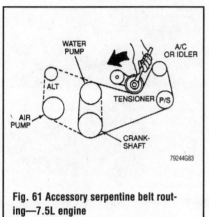

Fig. 61 Accessory serpentine belt routing—7.5L engine

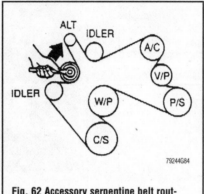

Fig. 62 Accessory serpentine belt routing—7.3L turbo diesel engine

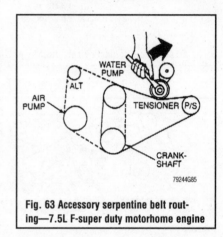

Fig. 63 Accessory serpentine belt routing—7.5L F-super duty motorhome engine

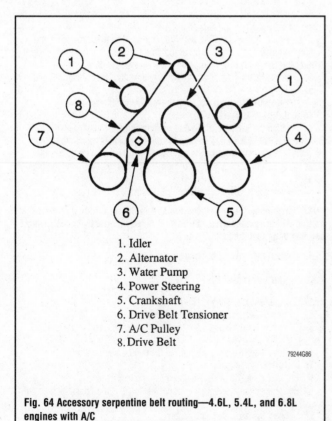

1. Idler
2. Alternator
3. Water Pump
4. Power Steering
5. Crankshaft
6. Drive Belt Tensioner
7. A/C Pulley
8. Drive Belt

Fig. 64 Accessory serpentine belt routing—4.6L, 5.4L, and 6.8L engines with A/C

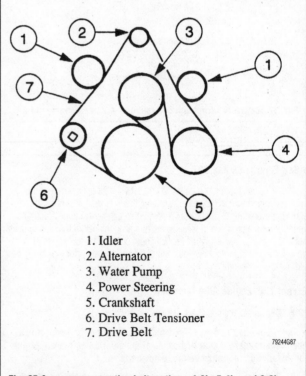

1. Idler
2. Alternator
3. Water Pump
4. Power Steering
5. Crankshaft
6. Drive Belt Tensioner
7. Drive Belt

Fig. 65 Accessory serpentine belt routing—4.6L, 5.4L, and 6.8L engines without A/C

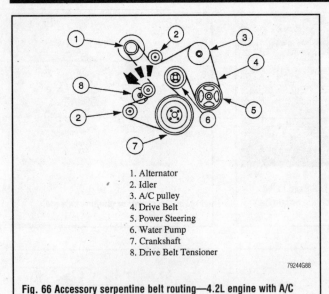

1. Alternator
2. Idler
3. A/C pulley
4. Drive Belt
5. Power Steering
6. Water Pump
7. Crankshaft
8. Drive Belt Tensioner

79244G88

Fig. 66 Accessory serpentine belt routing—4.2L engine with A/C

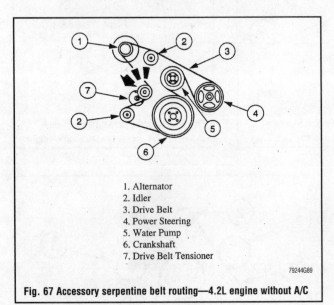

1. Alternator
2. Idler
3. Drive Belt
4. Power Steering
5. Water Pump
6. Crankshaft
7. Drive Belt Tensioner

79244G89

Fig. 67 Accessory serpentine belt routing—4.2L engine without A/C

REMOVAL & INSTALLATION

▶ See Figures 68 and 69

The drive belt routing can be found on a label under the hood or in the engine compartment. If the label is missing, there are diagrams of all the engines covered in this manual. However, be sure to verify the belt routing on your engine matches one of these before removing the belt. If the routing does not match one of our diagrams, the belt could possibly be routed wrong. A good idea is to draw your own diagram of the belt routing prior to removing the old belt from the engine.

Except 7.5L Engine Alternator Belt

1. Disconnect the negative battery cable.

➥The proper belt routing is included in this section, however, it is a good idea to make a simple drawing of the belt routing of your engine for installation reference before removing the belt.

2. Rotate the drive belt tensioner to relieve the belt tension. The procedure is as follows:
   a. On the 4.6L, 5.4L and 6.8L engines, use a ½ drive tool or a special

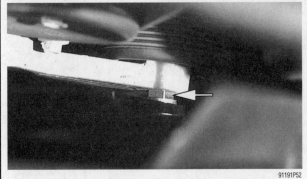

91191P52

Fig. 68 The tensioner on the 4.6L engine requires a ⅜ inch drive tool to rotate the tensioner

91191P53

Fig. 69 Rotate the tensioner and remove the drive belt from around one of the pulleys

belt removal tool to rotate the tensioner in the proper direction as directed by the rotation arrow on the tensioner.
   b. On the 4.2L, 5.8L, 7.5L and 7.3L engines, use a 16mm socket and drive tool or a special belt removal tool to rotate the tensioner in the proper direction as directed by the rotation arrow on the tensioner.
   c. While holding the tensioner back, remove the belt from around one pulley.

3. Remove the belt from around the remaining pulleys.

To install:

4. Position the belt around the pulleys in the proper routing with the exception of one pulley. It is easiest to keep the belt off of the easiest pulley to access. Hold the belt tight with your hands and using the proper tool for your engine, rotate the tensioner in the correct direction and place the belt around the final pulley.

5. Release the tensioner slowly until it sits firmly against the belt.

➥If the tensioner does not touch the belt or the wear indicator marks are not within specification, the belt is routed incorrectly or the wrong belt has been installed.

6. Connect the negative battery cable.

7.5L Engine Alternator Belt

1. Disconnect the negative battery cable.
2. Loosen the adjusting bolts on the alternator.
3. Carefully rotate the alternator to relieve the tension on the drive belt.
4. Remove the drive belt from around the pulleys and remove.

To install:

5. Properly route the drive belt around the pulleys.
6. Rotate the alternator until the proper tension is achieved and tighten the adjusting bolts.
7. Connect the negative battery cable.

Hoses

INSPECTION

▶ See Figures 70, 71, 72 and 73

Upper and lower radiator hoses, along with the heater hoses, should be checked for deterioration, leaks and loose hose clamps at least every 15,000 miles (24,000 km). It is also wise to check the hoses periodically in early spring and at the beginning of the fall or winter when you are performing other maintenance. A quick visual inspection could discover a weakened hose which might have left you stranded if it had remained unrepaired.

Whenever you are checking the hoses, make sure the engine and cooling system are cold. Visually inspect for cracking, rotting or collapsed hoses, and replace as necessary. Run your hand along the length of the hose. If a weak or swollen spot is noted when squeezing the hose wall, the hose should be replaced.

REMOVAL & INSTALLATION

1. Remove the radiator pressure cap.

✴✴ CAUTION

Never remove the pressure cap while the engine is running, or personal injury from scalding hot coolant or steam may result. If possible, wait until the engine has cooled to remove the pressure cap. If this is not possible, wrap a thick cloth around the pressure cap and turn it slowly to the stop. Step back while the pressure is released from the cooling system. When you are sure all the pressure has been released, use the cloth to turn and remove the cap.

2. Position a clean container under the radiator and/or engine draincock or plug, then open the drain and allow the cooling system to drain to an appropriate level. For some upper hoses, only a little coolant must be drained. To remove hoses positioned lower on the engine, such as a lower radiator hose, the entire cooling system must be emptied.

✴✴ CAUTION

When draining coolant, keep in mind that cats and dogs are attracted by ethylene glycol antifreeze, and are quite likely to drink any that is left in an uncovered container or in puddles on the ground. This will prove fatal in sufficient quantity. Always drain coolant into a sealable container. Coolant may be reused unless it is contaminated or several years old.

3. Loosen the hose clamps at each end of the hose requiring replacement. Clamps are usually either of the spring tension type (which require pliers to squeeze the tabs and loosen) or of the screw tension type (which require screw or hex drivers to loosen). Pull the clamps back on the hose away from the connection.

4. Twist, pull and slide the hose off the fitting, taking care not to damage the neck of the component from which the hose is being removed.

➡If the hose is stuck at the connection, do not try to insert a screwdriver or other sharp tool under the hose end in an effort to free it, as the connection and/or hose may become damaged. Heater connections especially may be easily damaged by such a procedure. If the hose is to be replaced, use a single-edged razor blade to make a slice along the portion of the hose which is stuck on the connection, perpendicular to the end of the hose. Do not cut deep so as to prevent damaging the connection. The hose can then be peeled from the connection and discarded.

5. Clean both hose mounting connections. Inspect the condition of the hose clamps and replace them, if necessary.

To install:

6. Dip the ends of the new hose into clean engine coolant to ease installation.

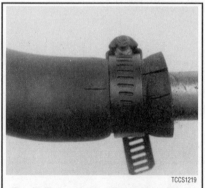

Fig. 70 The cracks developing along this hose are a result of age-related hardening

TCCS1219

Fig. 71 A hose clamp that is too tight can cause older hoses to separate and tear on either side of the clamp

TCCS1220

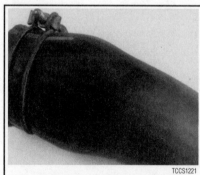

Fig. 72 A soft spongy hose (identifiable by the swollen section) will eventually burst and should be replaced

TCCS1221

Fig. 73 Hoses are likely to deteriorate from the inside if the cooling system is not periodically flushed

TCCS1222

7. Slide the clamps over the replacement hose, then slide the hose ends over the connections into position.

8. Position and secure the clamps at least ¼ in. (6.35mm) from the ends of the hose. Make sure they are located beyond the raised bead of the connector.

9. Close the radiator or engine drains and properly refill the cooling system with the clean drained engine coolant or a suitable mixture of ethylene glycol coolant and water.

10. If available, install a pressure tester and check for leaks. If a pressure tester is not available, run the engine until normal operating temperature is reached (allowing the system to naturally pressurize), then check for leaks.

✴✴ CAUTION

If you are checking for leaks with the system at normal operating temperature, BE EXTREMELY CAREFUL not to touch any moving or hot engine parts. Once temperature has been reached, shut the

engine OFF, and check for leaks around the hose fittings and connections which were removed earlier.

CV-Boots

INSPECTION

▶ See Figures 74 and 75

The CV (Constant Velocity) boots should be checked for damage each time the oil is changed and any other time the vehicle is raised for service. These boots keep water, grime, dirt and other damaging matter from entering the CV-joints. Any of these could cause early CV-joint failure which can be expensive to repair. Heavy grease thrown around the inside of the front wheel(s) and on the brake caliper/drum can be an indication of a torn boot. Thoroughly check the boots for missing clamps and tears. If the boot is damaged, it should be replaced immediately. Please refer to Section 7 for procedures.

Spark Plugs

▶ See Figure 76

A typical spark plug consists of a metal shell surrounding a ceramic insulator. A metal electrode extends downward through the center of the insulator and protrudes a small distance. Located at the end of the plug and attached to the side of the outer metal shell is the side electrode. The side electrode bends in at a 90° angle so that its tip is just past and parallel to the tip of the center electrode. The distance between these two electrodes (measured in thousandths of an inch or hundredths of a millimeter) is called the spark plug gap.

The spark plug does not produce a spark, but instead provides a gap across which the current can arc. The coil produces anywhere from 20,000 to 50,000 volts (depending on the type and application) which travels through the wires to the spark plugs. The current passes along the center electrode and jumps the gap to the side electrode, and in doing so, ignites the air/fuel mixture in the combustion chamber.

SPARK PLUG HEAT RANGE

▶ See Figure 77

Spark plug heat range is the ability of the plug to dissipate heat. The longer the insulator (or the farther it extends into the engine), the hotter the plug will operate; the shorter the insulator (the closer the electrode is to the block's cooling passages) the cooler it will operate. A plug that absorbs little heat and remains too cool will quickly accumulate deposits of oil and carbon since it is not hot enough to burn them off. This leads to plug fouling and consequently to misfiring. A plug that absorbs too much heat will have no deposits but, due to the excessive heat, the electrodes will burn away quickly and might possibly lead to preignition or other ignition problems. Preignition takes place when plug tips get so hot that they glow sufficiently to ignite the air/fuel mixture before the actual spark occurs. This early ignition will usually cause a pinging during low speeds and heavy loads.

The general rule of thumb for choosing the correct heat range when picking a spark plug is: if most of your driving is long distance, high speed travel, use a colder plug; if most of your driving is stop and go, use a hotter plug. Original equipment plugs are generally a good compromise between the 2 styles and most people never have the need to change their plugs from the factory-recommended heat range.

Fig. 74 CV-boots must be inspected periodically for damage

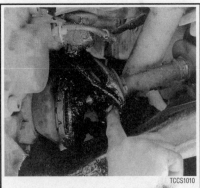

Fig. 75 A torn boot should be replaced immediately

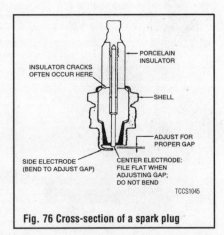

Fig. 76 Cross-section of a spark plug

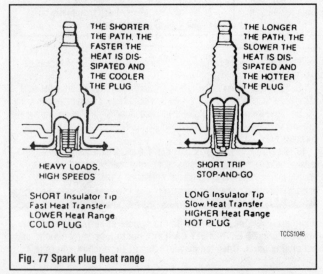

Fig. 77 Spark plug heat range

REMOVAL & INSTALLATION

▶ See Figures 78 thru 86

A set of spark plugs usually requires replacement after about 20,000–30,000 miles (32,000–48,000 km), depending on your style of driving. In normal operation plug gap increases about 0.001 in. (0.025mm) for every 2500 miles (4000 km). As the gap increases, the plug's voltage requirement also increases. It requires a greater voltage to jump the wider gap and about two to three times as much voltage to fire the plug at high speeds than at idle. The improved air/fuel ratio control of modern fuel injection combined with the higher voltage output of modern ignition systems will often allow an engine to run significantly longer on a set of standard spark plugs, but keep in mind that efficiency will drop as the gap widens (along with fuel economy and power).

When you're removing spark plugs, work on one at a time. Don't start by removing the plug wires all at once, because, unless you number them, they may become mixed up. Take a minute before you begin and number the wires with tape.

1. Disconnect the negative battery cable, and if the vehicle has been run recently, allow the engine to thoroughly cool.

2. Except on the 5.4L and 6.8L engines, carefully twist the spark plug wire

boot to loosen it, then pull upward and remove the boot from the spark plug. Be sure to pull on the boot and not on the wire, otherwise the connector located inside the boot may become separated.

3. On the 5.4L and 6.8L engines, unplug the electrical connector on the individual cylinder ignition coil and remove the retaining screw. Remove the coil from the cylinder head, taking care in removing it from the spark plug.

4. Using compressed air, blow any water or debris from the spark plug well to assure that no harmful contaminants are allowed to enter the combustion chamber when the spark plug is removed. If compressed air is not available, use a rag or a brush to clean the area.

➡Remove the spark plugs when the engine is cold, if possible, to prevent damage to the threads. If removal of the plugs is difficult, apply a few drops of penetrating oil or silicone spray to the area around the base of the plug, and allow it a few minutes to work.

5. Using a spark plug socket that is equipped with a rubber insert to properly hold the plug, turn the spark plug counterclockwise to loosen and remove the spark plug from the bore.

✲✲ WARNING

Be sure not to use a flexible extension on the socket. Use of a flexible extension may allow a shear force to be applied to the plug. A shear force could break the plug off in the cylinder head, leading to costly and frustrating repairs.

To install:

6. Inspect the spark plug boot for tears or damage. If a damaged boot is found, the spark plug wire must be replaced.

7. Using a wire feeler gauge, check and adjust the spark plug gap. When using a gauge, the proper size should pass between the electrodes with a slight drag. The next larger size should not be able to pass while the next smaller size should pass freely.

8. Carefully thread the plug into the bore by hand. If resistance is felt before the plug is almost completely threaded, back the plug out and begin threading again. In small, hard to reach areas, an old spark plug wire and boot could be used as a threading tool. The boot will hold the plug while you twist the end of the wire and the wire is supple enough to twist before it would allow the plug to crossthread.

✲✲ WARNING

Do not use the spark plug socket to thread the plugs. Always carefully thread the plug by hand or using an old plug wire to prevent the possibility of crossthreading and damaging the cylinder head bore.

9. Carefully tighten the spark plug. If the plug you are installing is equipped with a crush washer, seat the plug, then tighten about ¼ turn to crush the washer. If you are installing a tapered seat plug, tighten the plug to specifications provided by the vehicle or plug manufacturer.

10. Except for the 5.4L and 6.8L engines, apply a small amount of silicone dielectric compound to the end of the spark plug lead or inside the spark plug boot to prevent sticking, then install the boot to the spark plug and push until it clicks into place. The click may be felt or heard, then gently pull back on the boot to assure proper contact.

11. On the 5.4L and 6.8L engines, slide the coil into the cylinder head and engage the coil onto the spark plug. Tighten the retaining screw and attach the electrical connector.

12. Connect the negative battery cable.

Fig. 78 Grasp the plug wire and carefully twist the wire to release the retainer from the spark plug

Fig. 79 If the plug wire is stubborn, a pair of special removal pliers is recommended to remove the wires from the plugs

Fig. 80 Carefully remove the plug wire from the cylinder head

Fig. 81 A special spark plug socket with a rubber insert is needed to remove the spark plugs. Typically the spark plugs on engines covered by this manual require a ⅝ socket

Fig. 82 Using a suitable drive tool and the special socket, loosen the spark plug and . . .

Fig. 83 . . . remove the spark plug from the engine

Fig. 84 Clean out the spark plug bore and threads before installing the new spark plug

Fig. 85 An inspection of the old spark plugs will give a general idea of the condition of the motor, compare the spark plugs to the chart in this section

Fig. 86 A piece of fuel line or a small hose is useful in installing the spark plugs to avoid stripping the threads

INSPECTION & GAPPING

▶ **See Figures 87, 88, 89, 90 and 91**

Check the plugs for deposits and wear. If they are not going to be replaced, clean the plugs thoroughly. Remember that any kind of deposit will decrease the efficiency of the plug. Plugs can be cleaned on a spark plug cleaning machine, which can sometimes be found in service stations, or you can do an acceptable job of cleaning with a stiff brush. If the plugs are cleaned, the electrodes must be filed flat. Use an ignition points file, not an emery board or the like, which will leave deposits. The electrodes must be filed perfectly flat with sharp edges; rounded edges reduce the spark plug voltage by as much as 50%.

Check spark plug gap before installation. The ground electrode (the L-shaped one connected to the body of the plug) must be parallel to the center electrode and the specified size wire gauge (please refer to the Tune-Up Specifications chart for details) must pass between the electrodes with a slight drag.

A normally worn spark plug should have light tan or gray deposits on the firing tip.

A carbon fouled plug, identified by soft, sooty, black deposits, may indicate an improperly tuned vehicle. Check the air cleaner, ignition components and engine control system.

This spark plug has been **left in the engine too long,** as evidenced by the extreme gap- Plugs with such an extreme gap can cause misfiring and stumbling accompanied by a noticeable lack of power.

An oil fouled spark plug indicates an engine with worn poston rings and/or bad valve seals allowing excessive oil to enter the chamber.

A physically damaged spark plug may be evidence of severe detonation in that cylinder. Watch that cylinder carefully between services, as a continued detonation will not only damage the plug, but could also damage the engine.

A bridged or almost bridged spark plug, identified by a build-up between the electrodes caused by excessive carbon or oil build-up on the plug.

Fig. 87 Inspect the spark plug to determine engine running conditions

Fig. 88 A variety of tools and gauges are needed for spark plug service

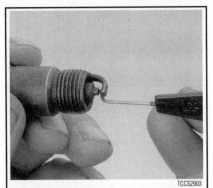

Fig. 89 Checking the spark plug gap with a feeler gauge

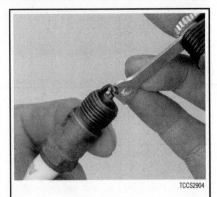

Fig. 90 Adjusting the spark plug gap

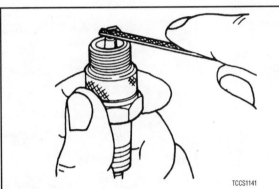

Fig. 91 If the standard plug is in good condition, the electrode may be filed flat—WARNING: do not file platinum plugs

Fig. 92 Checking individual plug wire resistance with a digital ohmmeter

➡**NEVER adjust the gap on a used platinum type spark plug.**

Always check the gap on new plugs as they are not always set correctly at the factory. Do not use a flat feeler gauge when measuring the gap on a used plug, because the reading may be inaccurate. A round-wire type gapping tool is the best way to check the gap. The correct gauge should pass through the electrode gap with a slight drag. If you're in doubt, try one size smaller and one larger. The smaller gauge should go through easily, while the larger one shouldn't go through at all. Wire gapping tools usually have a bending tool attached. Use that to adjust the side electrode until the proper distance is obtained. Absolutely never attempt to bend the center electrode. Also, be careful not to bend the side electrode too far or too often as it may weaken and break off within the engine, requiring removal of the cylinder head to retrieve it.

Spark Plug Wires

TESTING

▶ **See Figure 92**

➡The 5.4L, 6.8L and 7.3L engines do not utilize spark plug wires. The 5.4L and 6.8L engines use a direct ignition or "coil over plug" type ignition in which each individual cylinder has itís own coil attached to a boot that fits on the spark plug. The 7.3L engine is a diesel, and as anyone familiar with diesels is aware, diesel engines do not utilize an ignition system. They instead rely on high compression ratios and the extreme cylinder temperatures, as well as a glow plug system used on cold starts to fire the fuel/air mixture.

At every tune-up/inspection, visually check the spark plug cables for burns cuts, or breaks in the insulation. Check the boots and the nipples on the distributor cap and/or coil. Replace any damaged wiring.

Every 50,000 miles (80,000 km) or 60 months, the resistance of the wires should be checked with an ohmmeter. Wires with excessive resistance will cause misfiring, and may make the engine difficult to start in damp weather.

To check resistance, an ohmmeter should be used on each wire to test resistance between the end connectors. Remove and install/replace the wires in order, one-by-one.

Resistance on these wires should be 4,000–6,000 ohms per foot. To properly measure this, remove the wires from the plugs and the coil pack. Do not pierce any ignition wire for any reason. Measure only from the two ends. Take the length and multiply it by 6,000 to achieve the maximum resistance allowable in each wire, resistance should not exceed this value. If resistance does exceed this value, replace the wire.

➡**Whenever the high tension wires are removed from the plugs, coil, or distributor, silicone grease must be applied to the boot before reconnection. Coat the entire interior surface with Ford silicone grease D7AZ-19A331-A or its equivalent.**

REMOVAL & INSTALLATION

▶ **See Figures 93 thru 98**

1. Label each spark plug wire and make a note of its routing.

➡**Don't rely on wiring diagrams or sketches for spark plug wire routing. Improper arrangement of spark plug wires will induce voltage between wires, causing misfiring and surging. Be careful to arrange spark plug wires properly.**

2. Starting with the longest wire, disconnect the spark plug wire from the spark plug and then from the coil pack or the distributor cap.
3. Disconnect the ignition wire from the coil pack, if equipped, by squeezing the locking tabs and twisting while pulling upward.
4. Disconnect the ignition wire from the distributor cap, if equipped, by gently twisting and pulling upward on the wire.
To install:
5. If replacing the spark plug wires, match the old wire with an appropriately sized wire in the new set.
6. Lubricate the boots and terminals with dielectric grease and install the

Fig. 93 Grasp the plug wire and carefully twist the wire to release the retainer from the spark plug

Fig. 94 If the plug wire is stubborn, a pair of special removal pliers is recommended to remove the wires from the plugs

Fig. 95 Carefully remove the plug wire from the cylinder head

Fig. 96 Remove the plug wires from the ignition coil by squeezing the retaining tabs and carefully lifting the wires up

Fig. 97 Disconnect the plug wire retaining clips from the wires and . . .

Fig. 98 . . . remove the plug wires from the engine

wire on the coil pack or distributor cap. Make sure the wire snaps into place.

7. Route the wire in the exact path as the original and connect the wire to the spark plug.

8. Repeat the process for each remaining wire, working from the longest wire to the shortest.

Distributor Cap and Rotor

REMOVAL & INSTALLATION

1. Disconnect the negative battery cable.
2. Label and disconnect the spark plug wires from the distributor cap.

➡Depending on the reason for removing the distributor cap, it may make more sense to leave the spark plug wires attached. This is handy if you are testing spark plug wires, or if removal is necessary to access other components, and wire length allows you to reposition the cap out of the way.

3. Detach the two spring clips that secure the cap to the distributor.
4. Remove the cap from the distributor.

➡The rotor is press fit onto the distributor shaft.

5. Pull the rotor straight up to remove.

To install:

6. Inspect the cap and rotor as described below.
7. Align the rotor locating boss on the distributor shaft and install by pressing into place.
8. Align the distributor cap on the distributor and secure the spring clips.
9. Connect the spark plug wires to their proper terminals.
10. Connect the negative battery cable.

INSPECTION

▶ See Figures 99 and 100

After removing the distributor cap and rotor, clean the components (both inside and outside of the cap) using soap and water. If compressed air is available, carefully dry the components (wearing safety goggles) or allow the parts to air dry. You can dry them with a clean, soft cloth, but don't leave any lint or moisture behind.

Once the cap and rotor have been thoroughly cleaned, check for cracks, carbon tracks, burns or other physical damage. Make sure the distributor cap's center button is free of damage. Check the cap terminals for dirt or corrosion. Always check the rotor blade and spring closely for damage. Replace any components where damage is found.

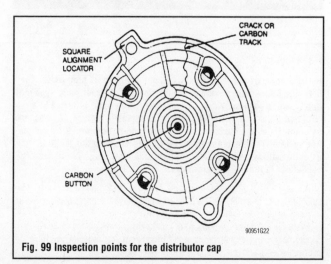

Fig. 99 Inspection points for the distributor cap

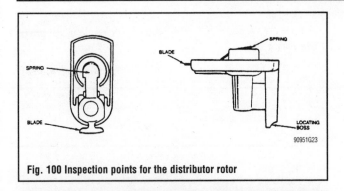

Fig. 100 Inspection points for the distributor rotor

Ignition Timing

GENERAL INFORMATION

Periodic adjustment of the ignition timing is not necessary for any engine covered by this manual. If ignition timing is not within specification, there is a fault in the engine control system. Diagnose and repair the problem as necessary.

Ignition timing is the measurement, in degrees of crankshaft rotation, of the point at which the spark plugs fire in each of the cylinders. It is measured in degrees before or after Top Dead Center (TDC) of the compression stroke.

Ideally, the air/fuel mixture in the cylinder will be ignited by the spark plug just as the piston passes TDC of the compression stroke. If this happens, the piston will be at the beginning of the power stroke just as the compressed and ignited air/fuel mixture forces the piston down and turns the crankshaft. Because it takes a fraction of a second for the spark plug to ignite the mixture in the cylinder, the spark plug must fire a little before the piston reaches TDC. Otherwise, the mixture will not be completely ignited as the piston passes TDC and the full power of the explosion will not be used by the engine.

The timing measurement is given in degrees of crankshaft rotation before the piston reaches TDC (BTDC). If the setting for the ignition timing is 10 BTDC, each spark plug must fire 10 degrees before each piston reaches TDC. This only holds true, however, when the engine is at idle speed. The combustion process must be complete by 23° ATDC to maintain proper engine performance, fuel mileage, and low emissions.

As the engine speed increases, the pistons go faster. The spark plugs have to ignite the fuel even sooner if it is to be completely ignited when the piston reaches TDC. On all engines covered in this manual, spark timing changes are accomplished electronically by the Powertrain Control Module (PCM), based on input from engine sensors.

If the ignition is set too far advanced (BTDC), the ignition and expansion of the fuel in the cylinder will occur too soon and tend to force the piston down while it is still traveling up. This causes pre ignition or "knocking and pinging". If the ignition spark is set too far retarded, or after TDC (ATDC), the piston will have already started on its way down when the fuel is ignited. The piston will be forced down for only a portion of its travel, resulting in poor engine performance and lack of power.

Timing marks or scales can be found on the rim of the crankshaft pulley and the timing cover. The marks on the pulley correspond to the position of the piston in the No. 1 cylinder. A stroboscopic (dynamic) timing light is hooked onto the No. 1 cylinder spark plug wire. Every time the spark plug fires, the timing light flashes. By aiming the light at the timing marks while the engine is running, the exact position of the piston within the cylinder can be easily read (the flash of light makes the mark on the pulley appear to be standing still). Proper timing is indicated when the mark and scale are in specified alignment.

☀☀ WARNING

When checking timing with the engine running, take care not to get the timing light wires tangled in the fan blades and/or drive belts.

INSPECTION

1. Place the vehicle in **P** or **N** with the parking brake applied and the drive wheels blocked.

2. Connect a suitable tachometer and timing light to the engine, as per the manufacturerís instructions.

3. Remove the **SPOUT** (Spark Output) connector.

4. Start the engine and allow it reach normal operating temperature. Make sure all accessories are off.

5. Check that the idle speed is within the specified rpm range.

6. Following the timing light manufacturerís instructions, aim the timing light and check the ignition timing. As the light flashes, note the position of the mark on the crankshaft pulley against the scale on the timing cover. Timing should be 8–12 degrees BTDC.

7. If the ignition timing is not within specification, refer to ADJUSTMENT, in this Section.

8. Install the **SPOUT** connector.

9. Stop the engine and remove the tachometer and timing light.

ADJUSTMENT

5.8L and 7.5L Engines

If the ignition timing is not within specification, loosen the distributor hold-down bolt and carefully rotate the distributor in the correct direction to achieve the desired advance/retard required to correct the timing. Recheck the timing as you rotate the distributor and when the desired timing is reached, tighten the hold-down bolt.

Except For 5.8L, 6.8L and 7.3L Engines

If the ignition timing is not within specification, there is a fault in the engine control system. Diagnose and repair the problem as necessary.

Valve Lash

ADJUSTMENT

The only engines requiring a valve lash adjustment are the 5.8L and 7.5L engines. All other engines are contain hydraulic self-adjusting lifters or other devices.

5.8L Engine

▶ See Figures 101 and 102

1. Rotate the crankshaft by hand so that No. 1 piston is at TDC of the compression stroke. Make a chalk mark on the damper at that point, then, make 2 more chalk marks about 90° apart in a clockwise direction.

2. With No. 1 at TDC, slowly apply pressure, using Lifter Bleed-down wrench T70P-6513-A, or equivalent, to completely bottom the lifter, on the following valves:

- No. 1 intake and exhaust
- No. 4 intake
- No. 3 exhaust
- No. 8 intake
- No. 7 exhaust

Take care to avoid excessive pressure that might bend the pushrod. Hold the lifter in this position and check the clearance between the rocker arm and the valve stem tip. Allowable clearance is 2.5–5.0mm (0.098–0.198 in.) with a desired clearance of 3.1–4.4mm (0.123–0.173 in.).

3. If the clearance is less than specified, install a shorter pushrod. If the clearance is greater than specified, install a longer pushrod.

4. Rotate the crankshaft clockwise—viewed from the front—180°, until the next chalk mark is aligned with the timing pointer. Repeat the procedure for:

- No. 3 intake
- No. 2 exhaust
- No. 7 intake
- No. 6 exhaust

5. Rotate the crankshaft to the next chalk mark—90°—and repeat the procedure for:

- No. 2 intake
- No. 4 exhaust
- No. 5 intake and exhaust
- No. 6 intake
- No. 8 exhaust

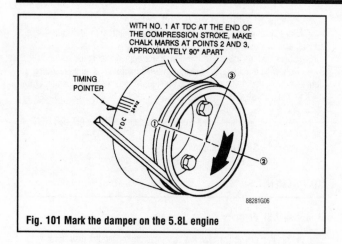

Fig. 101 Mark the damper on the 5.8L engine

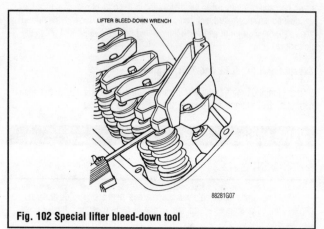

Fig. 102 Special lifter bleed-down tool

7.5L ENGINE

▶ **See Figure 102**

1. Rotate the crankshaft by hand so that No. 1 piston is at TDC of the compression stroke. Make a chalk mark on the damper at that point.

2. With No. 1 at TDC, slowly apply pressure, using Lifter Bleed-down wrench T70P-6513-A, or equivalent, to completely bottom the lifter, on the following valves:
- No. 1 intake and exhaust
- No. 3 intake
- No. 4 exhaust
- No. 7 intake
- No. 5 exhaust
- No. 8 intake and exhaust

Take care to avoid excessive pressure that might bend the pushrod. Hold the lifter in this position and check the clearance between the rocker arm and the valve stem tip. Allowable clearance is 1.9–4.4mm (0.075–0.175 in.) with a desired clearance of 2.5–3.8mm (0.100-0.150 in.).

3. If the clearance is less than specified, install a shorter pushrod. If the clearance is greater than specified, install a longer pushrod.

4. Rotate the crankshaft clockwise—viewed from the front—360°, until the chalk mark is once again aligned with the timing pointer. Repeat the procedure for:
- No. 2 intake and exhaust
- No. 4 intake
- No. 3 exhaust
- No. 5 intake
- No. 7 exhaust
- No. 6 intake and exhaust

Idle Speed and Mixture Adjustments

The engines covered by this manual utilize sophisticated fuel injection systems in which an engine control computer utilizes information from various sensors to control idle speed and air/fuel mixtures. No periodic adjustments are either necessary or possible on these systems. If a problem is suspected, please refer to Sections 4 of this manual for more information on electronic engine controls and fuel injection.

GASOLINE ENGINE TUNE-UP SPECIFICATIONS

Year	Engine Displacement Liters (cc)	Engine ID/VIN	Spark Plug Gap (in.)	Ignition Timing (deg.) MT	Ignition Timing (deg.) AT	Fuel Pump (psi)	Idle Speed (rpm) MT	Idle Speed (rpm) AT	Valve Clearance In.	Valve Clearance Ex.
1997	4.2 (4195)	2	0.052-0.056	10B ②	10B ②	30-45	①	①	HYD	HYD
	4.6 (4588)	6/W	0.052-0.056	8-12B ②	8-12B ②	30-45	①	①	HYD	HYD
	5.4 (5409)	L	0.052-0.056	10B ②	10B ②	28-45	①	①	HYD	HYD
	5.8 (5752)	H	0.042-0.046	10B	10B	35-45	①	①	HYD	HYD
	7.5 (7538)	G	0.042-0.046	10B	10B	35-45	①	①	HYD	HYD
1998	4.2 (4195)	2	0.052-0.056	10B ②	10B ②	30-45	①	①	HYD	HYD
	4.6 (4588)	6/W	0.052-0.056	8-12B ②	8-12B ②	30-45	①	①	HYD	HYD
	5.4 (5409)	L	0.052-0.056	10B ②	10B ②	28-45	①	①	HYD	HYD
	5.8 (5752)	H	0.042-0.046	10B	10B	35-45	①	①	HYD	HYD
	7.5 (7538)	G	0.042-0.046	10B	10B	35-45	①	①	HYD	HYD
1999	4.2 (4195)	2	0.052-0.056	10B ②	10B ②	30-45	①	①	HYD	HYD
	4.6 (4588)	6/W	0.052-0.056	8-12B ②	8-12B ②	30-45	①	①	HYD	HYD
	5.4 (5409)	L/M/Z/A	0.052-0.056	10B ②	10B ②	28-45	①	①	HYD	HYD
	5.4 (5409)	3	0.052-0.056	10B ②	10B ②	28-45	①	①	HYD	HYD
	6.8 (6802)	5	0.052-0.055	10B ②	10B ②	28-45	①	①	HYD	HYD
2000	4.2 (4195)	2	0.052-0.056	10B ②	10B ②	30-45	①	①	HYD	HYD
	4.6 (4588)	6/W	0.052-0.056	8-12B ②	8-12B ②	30-45	①	①	HYD	HYD
	5.4 (5409)	L/M/Z/A	0.052-0.056	10B ②	10B ②	28-45	①	①	HYD	HYD
	5.4 (5409)	3	0.052-0.056	10B ②	10B ②	28-45	①	①	HYD	HYD
	6.8 (6802)	5	0.052-0.055	10B ②	10B ②	28-45	①	①	HYD	HYD

NOTE: The Vehicle Emission Control Information label often reflects specification changes changes made during production. The label figures must be used if they differ from those in this chart.

B - Before top dead center

HYD - Hydraulic

NA - Not Available

① Idle speed is electronically controlled and cannot be adjusted

② Ignition timing is preset and cannot be adjusted

91191C04

DIESEL ENGINE TUNE-UP SPECIFICATIONS

Year	Engine ID/VIN	Engine Displacement cu. in. (cc)	Valve Clearance Intake (in.)	Valve Clearance Exhaust (in.)	Intake Valve Opens (deg.)	Injection Pump Setting (deg.)	Injection Nozzle Pressure (psi) New	Injection Nozzle Pressure (psi) Used	Idle Speed (rpm)	Cranking Compression Pressure (psi)
1997	F	7.3 (7292)	HYD	HYD	—	①	1875	1425	②	③
1998	F	7.3 (7292)	HYD	HYD	—	①	1875	1425	②	③
1999	F	7.3 (7292)	HYD	HYD	—	①	1875	1425	②	③
2000	F	7.3 (7292)	HYD	HYD	—	①	1875	1425	②	③

NOTE: The Vehicle Emission Control Information label often reflects specification changes made during production. The label figures must be used if they differ from those in this chart

HYD - Hydraulic

B - Before top dead center

NA - Not Available

① PCM controlled

② See underhood emission label

③ Compression pressure in the lowest cylinder must be at least 75%
   of the highest cylinder
   Minimum pressure: 195 psi
   Maximum pressure: 440 psi

91191C05

Air Conditioning System

SYSTEM SERVICE & REPAIR

➡ **It is recommended that the A/C system be serviced by an EPA Section 609 certified automotive technician utilizing a refrigerant recovery/recycling machine.**

The do-it-yourselfer should not service his/her own vehicle's A/C system for many reasons, including legal concerns, personal injury, environmental damage and cost. The following are some of the reasons why you may decide not to service your own vehicle's A/C system.

According to the U.S. Clean Air Act, it is a federal crime to service or repair (involving the refrigerant) a Motor Vehicle Air Conditioning (MVAC) system for money without being EPA certified. It is also illegal to vent R-134a refrigerant into the atmosphere.

State and/or local laws may be more strict than the federal regulations, so be sure to check with your state and/or local authorities for further information. For further federal information on the legality of servicing your A/C system, call the EPA Stratospheric Ozone Hotline.

➡ **Federal law dictates that a fine of up to $25,000 may be levied on people convicted of venting refrigerant into the atmosphere. Additionally, the EPA may pay up to $10,000 for information or services leading to a criminal conviction of the violation of these laws.**

When servicing an A/C system you run the risk of handling or coming in contact with refrigerant, which may result in skin or eye irritation or frostbite. Although low in toxicity (due to chemical stability), inhalation of concentrated refrigerant fumes is dangerous and can result in death; cases of fatal cardiac arrhythmia have been reported in people accidentally subjected to high levels of refrigerant. Some early symptoms include loss of concentration and drowsiness.

Also, refrigerants can decompose at high temperatures (near gas heaters or open flame), which may result in hydrofluoric acid, hydrochloric acid and phosgene (a fatal nerve gas).

R-134a refrigerant is a greenhouse gas which, if allowed to vent into the atmosphere, will contribute to global warming (the Greenhouse Effect).

It is usually more economically feasible to have a certified MVAC automotive technician perform A/C system service to your vehicle. While it is illegal to service an A/C system without the proper equipment, the home mechanic would have to purchase an expensive refrigerant recovery/recycling machine to service his/her own vehicle.

PREVENTIVE MAINTENANCE

Although the A/C system should not be serviced by the do-it-yourselfer, preventive maintenance can be practiced and A/C system inspections can be performed to help maintain the efficiency of the vehicle's A/C system. For preventive maintenance, perform the following:

• The easiest and most important preventive maintenance for your A/C system is to be sure that it is used on a regular basis. Running the system for five minutes each month (no matter what the season) will help ensure that the seals and all internal components remain lubricated.

➡ **Some newer vehicles automatically operate the A/C system compressor whenever the windshield defroster is activated. When running, the compressor lubricates the A/C system components; therefore, the A/C system would not need to be operated each month.**

• In order to prevent heater core freeze-up during A/C operation, it is necessary to maintain a proper antifreeze protection. Use a hand-held coolant tester (hydrometer) to periodically check the condition of the antifreeze in your engine's cooling system.

➡ **Antifreeze should not be used longer than the manufacturer specifies.**

• For efficient operation of an air conditioned vehicle's cooling system, the radiator cap should have a holding pressure which meets manufacturer's specifications. A cap which fails to hold these pressures should be replaced.

• Any obstruction of or damage to the condenser configuration will restrict air flow which is essential to its efficient operation. It is, therefore, a good rule to keep this unit clean and in proper physical shape.

➡ **Bug screens which are mounted in front of the condenser (unless they are original equipment) are regarded as obstructions.**

• The condensation drain tube expels any water, which accumulates on the bottom of the evaporator housing, into the engine compartment. If this tube is obstructed, the air conditioning performance can be restricted and condensation buildup can spill over onto the vehicle's floor.

SYSTEM INSPECTION

Although the A/C system should not be serviced by the do-it-yourselfer, preventive maintenance can be practiced and A/C system inspections can be performed to help maintain the efficiency of the vehicle's A/C system. For A/C system inspection, perform the following:

The easiest and often most important check for the air conditioning system consists of a visual inspection of the system components. Visually inspect the air conditioning system for refrigerant leaks, damaged compressor clutch, abnormal compressor drive belt tension and/or condition, plugged evaporator drain tube, blocked condenser fins, disconnected or broken wires, blown fuses, corroded connections and poor insulation.

A refrigerant leak will usually appear as an oily residue at the leakage point in the system. The oily residue soon picks up dust or dirt particles from the surrounding air and appears greasy. Through time, this will build up and appear to be a heavy dirt impregnated grease.

For a thorough visual and operational inspection, check the following:
• Check the surface of the radiator and condenser for dirt, leaves or other material which might block air flow.
• Check for kinks in hoses and lines. Check the system for leaks.
• Make sure the drive belt is properly tensioned. When the air conditioning is operating, make sure the drive belt is free of noise or slippage.
• Make sure the blower motor operates at all appropriate positions, then check for distribution of the air from all outlets with the blower on **HIGH** or **MAX**.

➡**Keep in mind that under conditions of high humidity, air discharged from the A/C vents may not feel as cold as expected, even if the system is working properly. This is because vaporized moisture in humid air retains heat more effectively than dry air, thereby making humid air more difficult to cool.**

• Make sure the air passage selection lever is operating correctly. Start the engine and warm it to normal operating temperature, then make sure the temperature selection lever is operating correctly.

Windshield Wipers

ELEMENT (REFILL) CARE & REPLACEMENT

▶ **See Figures 103, 104 and 105**

For maximum effectiveness and longest element life, the windshield and wiper blades should be kept clean. Dirt, tree sap, road tar and so on will cause streaking, smearing and blade deterioration if left on the glass. It is advisable to wash the windshield carefully with a commercial glass cleaner at least once a month. Wipe off the rubber blades with the wet rag afterwards. Do not attempt to move wipers across the windshield by hand; damage to the motor and drive mechanism will result.

To inspect and/or replace the wiper blade elements, place the wiper switch in the **LOW** speed position and the ignition switch in the **ACC** position. When the wiper blades are approximately vertical on the windshield, turn the ignition switch to **OFF**.

Examine the wiper blade elements. If they are found to be cracked, broken or torn, they should be replaced immediately. Replacement intervals will vary with usage, although ozone deterioration usually limits element life to about one year. If the wiper pattern is smeared or streaked, or if the blade chatters across

the glass, the elements should be replaced. It is easiest and most sensible to replace the elements in pairs.

If your vehicle is equipped with aftermarket blades, there are several different types of refills and your vehicle might have any kind. Aftermarket blades and arms rarely use the exact same type blade or refill as the original equipment.

Regardless of the type of refill used, be sure to follow the part manufacturer's instructions closely. Make sure that all of the frame jaws are engaged as the refill is pushed into place and locked. If the metal blade holder and frame are allowed to touch the glass during wiper operation, the glass will be scratched.

Tires and Wheels

Common sense and good driving habits will afford maximum tire life. Make sure that you don't overload the vehicle or run with incorrect pressure in the tires. Either of these will increase tread wear. Fast starts, sudden stops and sharp cornering are hard on tires and will shorten their useful life span.

➡**For optimum tire life, keep the tires properly inflated, rotate them often and have the wheel alignment checked periodically.**

Inspect your tires frequently. Be especially careful to watch for bubbles in the tread or sidewall, deep cuts or underinflation. Replace any tires with bubbles in the sidewall. If cuts are so deep that they penetrate to the cords, discard the tire. Any cut in the sidewall of a radial tire renders it unsafe. Also look for uneven tread wear patterns that may indicate the front end is out of alignment or that the tires are out of balance.

TIRE ROTATION

▶ **See Figure 106**

Tires must be rotated periodically to equalize wear patterns that vary with a tire's position on the vehicle. Tires will also wear in an uneven way as the front steering/suspension system wears to the point where the alignment should be reset.

Rotating the tires will ensure maximum life for the tires as a set, so you will not have to discard a tire early due to wear on only part of the tread. Regular rotation is required to equalize wear.

When rotating "unidirectional tires," make sure that they always roll in the same direction. This means that a tire used on the left side of the vehicle must not be switched to the right side and vice-versa. Such tires should only be rotated front-to-rear or rear-to-front, while always remaining on the same side of the vehicle. These tires are marked on the sidewall as to the direction of rotation; observe the marks when reinstalling the tire(s).

Some styled or "mag" wheels may have different offsets front to rear. In these cases, the rear wheels must not be used up front and vice-versa. Furthermore, if these wheels are equipped with unidirectional tires, they cannot be rotated unless the tire is remounted for the proper direction of rotation.

➡**The compact or space-saver spare is strictly for emergency use. It must never be included in the tire rotation or placed on the vehicle for everyday use.**

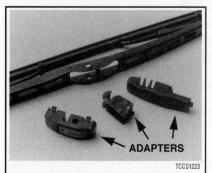

TCCS1223

Fig. 103 Most aftermarket blades are available with multiple adapters to fit different vehicles

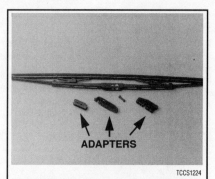

TCCS1224

Fig. 104 Choose a blade which will fit your vehicle, and that will be readily available next time you need blades

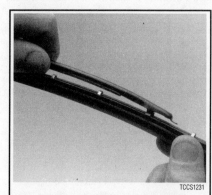

TCCS1231

Fig. 105 When installed, be certain the blade is fully inserted into the backing

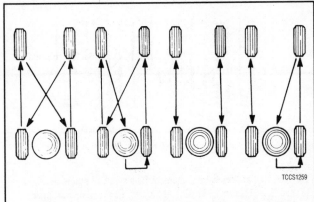

Fig. 106 Common tire rotation patterns for 4 and 5-wheel rotations

TIRE DESIGN

▶ **See Figure 107**

For maximum satisfaction, tires should be used in sets of four. Mixing of different brands or types (radial, bias-belted, fiberglass belted) should be avoided. In most cases, the vehicle manufacturer has designated a type of tire on which the vehicle will perform best. Your first choice when replacing tires should be to use the same type of tire that the manufacturer recommends.

When radial tires are used, tire sizes and wheel diameters should be selected to maintain ground clearance and tire load capacity equivalent to the original specified tire. Radial tires should always be used in sets of four.

❊❊ CAUTION

Radial tires should never be used on only the front axle.

When selecting tires, pay attention to the original size as marked on the tire. Most tires are described using an industry size code sometimes referred to as P-Metric. This allows the exact identification of the tire specifications, regardless of the manufacturer. If selecting a different tire size or brand, remember to check the installed tire for any sign of interference with the body or suspension while the vehicle is stopping, turning sharply or heavily loaded.

Snow Tires

Good radial tires can produce a big advantage in slippery weather, but in snow, a street radial tire does not have sufficient tread to provide traction and control. The small grooves of a street tire quickly pack with snow and the tire

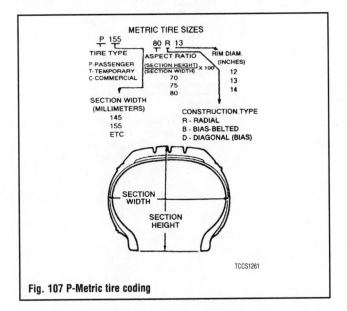

Fig. 107 P-Metric tire coding

behaves like a billiard ball on a marble floor. The more open, chunky tread of a snow tire will self-clean as the tire turns, providing much better grip on snowy surfaces.

To satisfy municipalities requiring snow tires during weather emergencies, most snow tires carry either an M + S designation after the tire size stamped on the sidewall, or the designation "all-season." In general, no change in tire size is necessary when buying snow tires.

Most manufacturers strongly recommend the use of 4 snow tires on their vehicles for reasons of stability. If snow tires are fitted only to the drive wheels, the opposite end of the vehicle may become very unstable when braking or turning on slippery surfaces. This instability can lead to unpleasant endings if the driver can't counteract the slide in time.

Note that snow tires, whether 2 or 4, will affect vehicle handling in all non-snow situations. The stiffer, heavier snow tires will noticeably change the turning and braking characteristics of the vehicle. Once the snow tires are installed, you must re-learn the behavior of the vehicle and drive accordingly.

➡**Consider buying extra wheels on which to mount the snow tires. Once done, the "snow wheels" can be installed and removed as needed. This eliminates the potential damage to tires or wheels from seasonal removal and installation. Even if your vehicle has styled wheels, see if inexpensive steel wheels are available. Although the look of the vehicle will change, the expensive wheels will be protected from salt, curb hits and pothole damage.**

TIRE STORAGE

If they are mounted on wheels, store the tires at proper inflation pressure. All tires should be kept in a cool, dry place. If they are stored in the garage or basement, do not let them stand on a concrete floor; set them on strips of wood, a mat or a large stack of newspaper. Keeping them away from direct moisture is of paramount importance. Tires should not be stored upright, but in a flat position.

INFLATION & INSPECTION

▶ **See Figures 108 thru 113**

The importance of proper tire inflation cannot be overemphasized. A tire employs air as part of its structure. It is designed around the supporting strength of the air at a specified pressure. For this reason, improper inflation drastically reduces the tire's ability to perform as intended. A tire will lose some air in day-to-day use; having to add a few pounds of air periodically is not necessarily a sign of a leaking tire.

Two items should be a permanent fixture in every glove compartment: an accurate tire pressure gauge and a tread depth gauge. Check the tire pressure (including the spare) regularly with a pocket type gauge. Too often, the gauge on the end of the air hose at your corner garage is not accurate because it suffers too much abuse. Always check tire pressure when the tires are cold, as pressure increases with temperature. If you must move the vehicle to check the tire inflation, do not drive more than a mile before checking. A cold tire is generally one that has not been driven for more than three hours.

A plate or sticker is normally provided somewhere in the vehicle (door post, hood, tailgate or trunk lid) which shows the proper pressure for the tires. Never counteract excessive pressure build-up by bleeding off air pressure (letting some air out). This will cause the tire to run hotter and wear quicker.

❊❊ CAUTION

Never exceed the maximum tire pressure embossed on the tire! This is the pressure to be used when the tire is at maximum loading, but it is rarely the correct pressure for everyday driving. Consult the owner's manual or the tire pressure sticker for the correct tire pressure.

Once you've maintained the correct tire pressures for several weeks, you'll be familiar with the vehicle's braking and handling personality. Slight adjustments in tire pressures can fine-tune these characteristics, but never change the cold pressure specification by more than 2 psi. A slightly softer tire pressure will give a softer ride but also yield lower fuel mileage. A slightly harder tire will give crisper dry road handling but can cause skidding on wet surfaces. Unless you're fully attuned to the vehicle, stick to the recommended inflation pressures.

All automotive tires have built-in tread wear indicator bars that show up as

Fig. 108 Tires with deep cuts, or cuts which bulge, should be replaced immediately

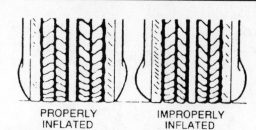

Fig. 109 Radial tires have a characteristic sidewall bulge; don't try to measure pressure by looking at the tire. Use a quality air pressure gauge

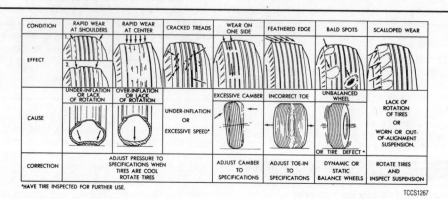

Fig. 110 Common tire wear patterns and causes

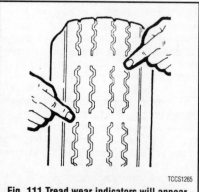

Fig. 111 Tread wear indicators will appear when the tire is worn

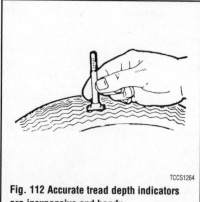

Fig. 112 Accurate tread depth indicators are inexpensive and handy

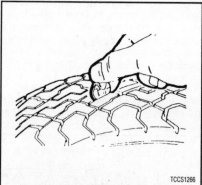

Fig. 113 A penny works well for a quick check of tread depth

½ in. (13mm) wide smooth bands across the tire when 1/16 in. (1.5mm) of tread remains. The appearance of tread wear indicators means that the tires should be replaced. In fact, many states have laws prohibiting the use of tires with less than this amount of tread.

You can check your own tread depth with an inexpensive gauge or by using a Lincoln head penny. Slip the Lincoln penny (with Lincoln's head upside-down)

into several tread grooves. If you can see the top of Lincoln's head in 2 adjacent grooves, the tire has less than 1/16 in. (1.5mm) tread left and should be replaced. You can measure snow tires in the same manner by using the "tails" side of the Lincoln penny. If you can see the top of the Lincoln memorial, it's time to replace the snow tire(s).

FLUIDS AND LUBRICANTS

Fluid Disposal

Used fluids such as engine oil, transmission fluid, antifreeze and brake fluid are hazardous wastes and must be disposed of properly. Before draining any fluids, consult with your local authorities; in many areas, waste oil, antifreeze, etc. is being accepted as a part of recycling programs. A number of service stations and auto parts stores are also accepting waste fluids for recycling.

Be sure of the recycling center's policies before draining any fluids, as many will not accept different fluids that have been mixed together

Fuel and Engine Oil Recommendations

GASOLINE ENGINES

Fuel

All 1997–00 Ford F-Series, Expedition and Lincoln Navigators must use lead-free gasoline with an (R+M)/2 minimum anti-knock index rating of at least 87. The Lightning Pick-up engine requires 91 octane due to the fact that it is high-performance and the engine is supercharged. Use of gasoline with an anti-knock index rating lower than specified can cause persistent, heavy spark knock which can lead to engine damage.

Oil

▶ See Figures 114 and 115

➡Ford recommends that SAE 5W-30 viscosity engine oil should be used for all climate conditions, however, SAE 10W-30 is acceptable for vehicles operated in moderate-to-hot climates.

When adding oil to the crankcase or changing the oil or filter, it is important that oil of an equal quality to original equipment be used in your truck. The use of inferior oils may void the warranty, damage your engine, or both.

The SAE (Society of Automotive Engineers) grade number of oil indicates the viscosity of the oil (its ability to lubricate at a given temperature). The lower the SAE number, the lighter the oil; the lower the viscosity, the easier it is to crank the engine in cold weather but the less the oil will lubricate and protect the engine in high temperatures. This number is marked on every oil container.

Oil viscosityís should be chosen from those oils recommended for the lowest anticipated temperatures during the oil change interval. Due to the need for an oil that embodies both good lubrication at high temperatures and easy cranking in cold weather, multigrade oils have been developed. Basically, a multigrade oil is thinner at low temperatures and thicker at high temperatures. For example, a 10W-40 oil (the W stands for winter) exhibits the characteristics of a 10 weight (SAE 10) oil when the truck is first started and the oil is cold. Its lighter weight allows it to travel to the lubricating surfaces quicker and offer less resistance to starter motor cranking than, say, a straight 30 weight (SAE 30) oil. But after the engine reaches operating temperature, the 10W-40 oil begins acting like straight

Fig. 115 Look for the API oil identification label when choosing your engine oil

40 weight (SAE 40) oil, its heavier weight providing greater lubrication with less chance of foaming than a straight 30 weight oil.

The API (American Petroleum Institute) designations, also found on the oil container, indicates the classification of engine oil used under certain given operating conditions. Only oils designated for use Service SG heavy duty detergent should be used in your truck. Oils of the SG type perform many functions inside the engine besides their basic lubrication. Through a balanced system of metallic detergents and polymeric dispersants, the oil prevents high and low temperature deposits and also keeps sludge and dirt particles in suspension. Acids, particularly sulfuric acid, as well as other by-products of engine combustion are neutralized by the oil. If these acids are allowed to concentrate, they can cause corrosion and rapid wear of the internal engine parts.

✳✳ CAUTION

Non-detergent motor oils or straight mineral oils should not be used in your Ford gasoline engine.

Synthetic Oil

There are many excellent synthetic and fuel-efficient oils currently available that can provide better gas mileage, longer service life and, in some cases, better engine protection. These benefits do not come without a few hitches, however; the main one being the price of synthetic oil, which is significantly more expensive than conventional oil.

Synthetic oil is not for every truck and every type of driving, so you should consider your engine's condition and your type of driving. Also, check your truck's warranty conditions regarding the use of synthetic oils.

DIESEL ENGINES

Diesel Fuel

Fuel makers produce two grades of diesel fuel, No. 1 and No. 2, for use in automotive diesel engines. Generally speaking, No. 2 fuel is recommended over No. 1 for driving in temperatures above 20°F (–7°C). In fact, in many areas, No. 2 diesel is the only fuel available. By comparison, No. 2 diesel fuel is less volatile than No. 1 fuel, and gives better fuel economy. No. 2 fuel is also a better injection pump lubricant.

Two important characteristics of diesel fuel are its cetane number and its viscosity.

The cetane number of a diesel fuel refers to the ease with which a diesel fuel ignites. High cetane numbers mean that the fuel will ignite with relative ease or that it ignites well at low temperatures. Naturally, the lower the cetane number, the higher the temperature must be to ignite the fuel. Most commercial fuels have cetane numbers that range from 35 to 65. No. 1 diesel fuel generally has a higher cetane rating than No. 2 fuel.

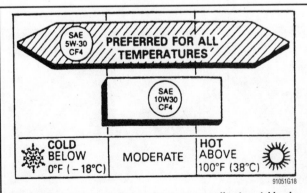

Fig. 114 Recommended oil viscosity usage according to outside air temperature

Viscosity is the ability of a liquid, in this case diesel fuel, to flow. Using straight No. 2 diesel fuel below 20°F (–7°C) can cause problems, because this fuel tends to become cloudy, meaning wax crystals begin forming in the fuel. 20°F (–7°C) is often call the cloud point for No. 2 fuel. In extremely cold weather, No. 2 fuel can stop flowing altogether. In either case, fuel flow is restricted, which can result in no start condition or poor engine performance. Fuel manufacturers often winterize No. 2 diesel fuel by using various fuel additives and blends (no. 1 diesel fuel, kerosene, etc.) to lower its winter time viscosity. Generally speaking, though, No. 1 diesel fuel is more satisfactory in extremely cold weather.

➡No. 1 and No. 2 diesel fuels will mix and burn with no ill effects, although the engine manufacturer recommends one or the other. Consult the owner's manual for information.

Depending on local climate, most fuel manufacturers make winterized No. 2 fuel available seasonally.

Many automobile manufacturers publish pamphlets giving the locations of diesel fuel stations nationwide. Contact the local dealer for information.

Do not substitute home heating oil for automotive diesel fuel. While in some cases, home heating oil refinement levels equal those of diesel fuel, many times they are far below diesel engine requirements. The result of using dirty home heating oil will be a clogged fuel system, in which case the entire system may have to be dismantled and cleaned.

One more word on diesel fuels. Don't thin diesel fuel with gasoline in cold weather. The lighter gasoline, which is more explosive, will cause rough running at the very least, and may cause extensive damage to the fuel system if enough is used.

Engine Oil

Diesel engines require different engine oil from those used in gasoline engines. Besides doing the things gasoline engine oil does, diesel oil must also deal with increased engine heat and the diesel blow-by gases, which create sulfuric acid, a high corrosive.

Under the American Petroleum Institute (API) classifications, gasoline engine oil codes begin with an **S**, and diesel engine oil codes begin with a **C**. This first letter designation is followed by a second letter code which explains what type of service (heavy, moderate, light) the oil is meant for. For example, the top of a typical oil can will include: API SERVICES SH, CD. This means the oil in the can is a superior, heavy duty engine oil when used in a diesel engine.

Many diesel manufacturers recommend an oil with both gasoline and diesel engine API classifications.

➡Ford specifies the use of an engine oil conforming to API service categories of both SH and CD. DO NOT use oils labeled as only SH or only CD as they could cause engine damage.

OPERATION IN FOREIGN COUNTRIES

If you plan to drive your truck outside the United States or Canada, there is a possibility that fuels will be too low in anti-knock quality and could produce engine damage. It is wise to consult with local authorities upon arrival in a foreign country to determine the best fuels available.

Engine

OIL LEVEL CHECK

▶ See Figures 116 thru 122

❊❊ CAUTION

The EPA warns that prolonged contact with used engine oil may cause a number of skin disorders, including cancer! You should make every effort to minimize your exposure to used engine oil. Protective gloves should be worn when changing the oil. Wash your hands and any other exposed skin areas as soon as possible after

Fig. 116 Grasp the engine oil dipstick and . . .

Fig. 117 . . . pull the dipstick out of the tube

Fig. 118 Wipe the dipstick clean and replace it into the tube to inspect the oil level

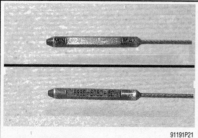

Fig. 119 The dipstick has two sides, one has the MIN and MAX markings, and the other has the part number of the dipstick, ensure that the oil level is between the MIN and MAX lines

Fig. 120 To remove the oil fill cap, grasp the cap and turn it counter-clockwise until . . .

Fig. 121 . . . the cap unscrews from the valve cover. Be sure to place the oil cap in a safe place so as not to lose it

Fig. 122 Place a funnel directly into the oil fill port and pour oil into the engine

exposure to used engine oil. Soap and water, or waterless hand cleaner should be used.

The engine oil dipstick is located on the driverís side of the engine near that sideís exhaust manifold, with the exception of the 7.3L diesel which is on the passenger side.

Engine oil level should be checked every time you put fuel in the vehicle or are under the hood performing other maintenance.

1. Park the vehicle on a level surface.

2. The engine may be either hot or cold when checking oil level. However, if it is hot, wait a few minutes after the engine has been turned **OFF** to allow the oil to drain back into the crankcase. If the engine is cold, do not start it before checking the oil level.

3. Open the hood and locate the engine oil dipstick. Pull the dipstick from its tube, wipe it clean, and reinsert it. Make sure the dipstick is fully inserted.

4. Pull the dipstick from its tube again. Holding it horizontally, read the oil level. The oil should be between the MIN and MAX mark. If the oil is below the MIN mark, add oil of the proper viscosity through the capped opening of the valve cover.

5. Replace the dipstick, and check the level again after adding any oil. Be careful not to overfill the crankcase. Approximately one quart of oil will raise the level from the low mark to the high mark. Excess oil will generally be consumed at an accelerated rate even if no damage to the engine seals occurs.

OIL & FILTER CHANGE

▶ **See Figures 123 thru 129**

The oil and filter should be changed every 5,000 miles (8,000 km) under normal service and every 3,000 miles (5,000 km) under severe service.

✳✳ CAUTION

The EPA warns that prolonged contact with used engine oil may cause a number of skin disorders, including cancer! You should make every effort to minimize your exposure to used engine oil. Protective gloves should be worn when changing the oil. Wash your hands and any other exposed skin areas as soon as possible after exposure to used engine oil. Soap and water, or waterless hand cleaner should be used.

➡The engine oil and oil filter should be changed at the recommended intervals on the Maintenance Chart. Though some manufacturers have at times recommended changing the filter only at every other oil change, Chilton recommends that you always change the filter with the oil. The benefit of fresh oil is quickly lost if the old filter is clogged and unable to do its job. Also, leaving the old filter in place leaves a significant amount of dirty oil in the system.

The oil should be changed more frequently if the vehicle is being operated in a very dusty area. Before draining the oil, make sure that the engine is at operat-

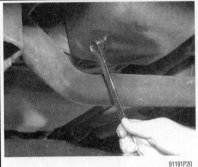

Fig. 123 Loosen the engine oil drain plug. Typically the oil drain plug requires a 16mm wrench

Fig. 124 Loosen the drain plug but do not remove it from the oil pan, make sure to keep constant inward pressure on the drain plug because . . .

Fig. 125 . . . the oil drains out rather fast when the drain plug is removed

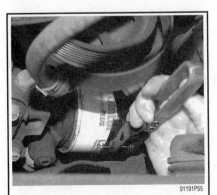

Fig. 126 Loosen the oil filter using a suitable oil filter wrench

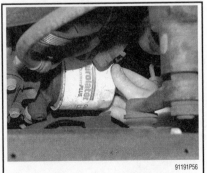

Fig. 127 After the filter is sufficiently loose, carefully unscrew it using hand power and . . .

Fig. 128 . . . remove the filter from the engine

Fig. 129 Before installing a new oil filter, lightly coat the rubber gasket with clean oil

ing temperature. Hot oil will hold more impurities in suspension and will flow better, allowing the removal of more oil and dirt.

It is a good idea to warm the engine oil first so it will flow better. This can be accomplished by 15–20 miles of highway driving. Fluid which is warmed to normal operating temperature will flow faster, drain more completely and remove more contaminants from the engine.

1. Raise and support the vehicle safely on jackstands.
2. If necessary, remove the skid plate or splash shield.
3. Make sure the oil drain plug is at the lowest point on the oil pan. If not, you may have to raise the vehicle slightly higher on one jackstand (side) than the other.
4. Before you crawl under the vehicle, take a look at where you will be working and gather all the necessary tools, such as a few wrenches or a ratchet and strip of sockets, the drain pan, some clean rags and, if the oil filter is more accessible from underneath the vehicle, you will also want to grab a bottle of oil, the new filter and a filter wrench at this time.
5. Position the drain pan beneath the oil pan drain plug. Keep in mind that the fast flowing oil, which will spill out as you pull the plug from the pan, will flow with enough force that it could miss the pan. Position the drain pan accordingly and be ready to move the pan more directly beneath the plug as the oil flow lessens to a trickle.

➡ **Typically the engine oil drain plug requires a 16mm drive tool.**

6. Loosen the drain plug with a wrench (or socket and driver), then carefully unscrew the plug with your fingers. Use a rag to shield your fingers from the heat. Push in on the plug as you unscrew it so you can feel when all of the screw threads are out of the hole (and so you will keep the oil from seeping past the threads until you are ready to remove the plug). You can then remove the plug quickly to avoid having hot oil run down your arm. This will also help assure that have the plug in your hand, not in the bottom of a pan of hot oil.

�֎ CAUTION

Be careful of the oil; when at operating temperature, it is hot enough to cause a severe burn.

7. Allow the oil to drain until nothing but a few drops come out of the drain hole. Check the drain plug to make sure the threads and sealing surface are not damaged. Carefully thread the plug into position and tighten it with a torque wrench to 9–11 ft. lbs. (11–16 Nm). If a torque wrench is not available, snug the drain plug and give a slight additional turn. You don't want the plug to fall out (as you would quickly become stranded), but the pan threads are EASILY stripped from overtightening (and this can be time consuming and/or costly to fix).

8. To remove the filter, you may need an oil filter wrench since the filter may have been fitted too tightly and/or the heat from the engine may have made it even tighter. A filter wrench can be obtained at any auto parts store and is well-worth the investment. Loosen the filter with the filter wrench. With a rag wrapped around the filter, unscrew the filter from the boss on the side of the engine. Be careful of hot oil that will run down the side of the filter. Make sure that your drain pan is under the filter before you start to remove it from the engine; should some of the hot oil happen to get on you, there will be a place to

dump the filter in a hurry and the filter will usually spill a good bit of dirty oil as it is removed.

9. Wipe the base of the mounting boss with a clean, dry cloth. When you install the new filter, smear a small amount of fresh oil on the gasket with your finger, just enough to coat the entire contact surface. When you tighten the filter, rotate it about a quarter-turn after it contacts the mounting boss (or follow any instructions which are provided on the filter or parts box).

10. Install the skid plate or splash shield as necessary.

✷✷ WARNING

Operating the engine without the proper amount and type of engine oil will result in severe engine damage.

11. Remove the jackstands and carefully lower the vehicle, then IMMEDIATELY refill the engine crankcase with the proper amount of oil. DO NOT WAIT TO DO THIS because if you forget and someone tries to start the vehicle, severe engine damage will occur.

12. Refill the engine crankcase slowly, checking the level often. You may notice that it usually takes less than the amount of oil listed in the capacity chart to refill the crankcase. But, that is only until the engine is run and the oil filter is filled with oil. To make sure the proper level is obtained, run the engine to normal operating temperature, shut the engine **OFF**, allow the oil to drain back into the oil pan, and recheck the level. Top off the oil at this time to the fill mark.

➡ **If the vehicle is not resting on level ground, the oil level reading on the dipstick may be slightly off. Be sure to check the level only when the vehicle is sitting level.**

13. Drain your used oil in a suitable container for recycling.

Manual Transmission

FLUID RECOMMENDATIONS

Ford recommends using Motorcraft Mercon ATF (Automatic Transmission Fluid) XT-2-QDX or equivalent Mercon ATF fluid (Dexron Mercon III) in the M5OD manual transmission and ZF 5-speed or 6-speed when used in all models except for those with the 6.8L V-10 gasoline or 7.3L diesel engines.

Ford recommends using Motorcraft Mercon synthetic ATF (Automatic Transmission Fluid) or equivalent in the ZF 5-speed or 6-speed when used in conjunction with the 6.8L V-10 gasoline or 7.3L diesel engines due to the enormous amount of torque these engines creates.

LEVEL CHECK

◆ **See Figure 130**

1. Park the truck on a level surface, turn off the engine, apply the parking brake and block the wheels.
2. Remove the filler plug from the side of the transmission case with a proper size wrench. The fluid level should be even with the bottom of the filler hole.

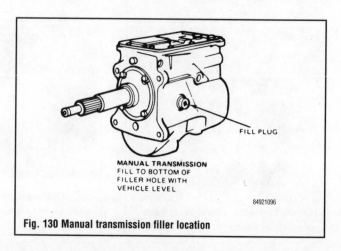

Fig. 130 Manual transmission filler location

3. If additional fluid is necessary, add it through the filler hole using a siphon pump or squeeze bottle.

4. Replace the filler plug; do not overtighten.

DRAIN & REFILL

▶ **See Figure 131**

1. Place a suitable drain pan under the transmission.
2. Remove the drain plug and allow the fluid to drain out.
3. Replace the drain plug, remove the filler plug and fill the transmission to the proper level with the required fluid.
4. Reinstall the filler plug.

Fig. 131 This manual transmission has its drain plug clearly marked

Automatic Transmission

FLUID RECOMMENDATIONS

Ford recommends using Motorcraft Mercon ATF (Automatic Transmission Fluid) XT-2-QDX or equivalent Mercon ATF fluid (Dexron Mercon III).

LEVEL CHECK

▶ **See Figures 132 thru 138**

The transmission dipstick is typically located near the back of the engine, towards the firewall.

1. Park the vehicle on a level surface.
2. The transmission should be at normal operating temperature when checking fluid level. To ensure the fluid is at normal operating temperature, drive the vehicle at least 10 miles.
3. With the selector lever in **P** and the parking brake applied, start the engine.
4. Open the hood and locate the transmission fluid dipstick. Pull the dipstick from its tube, wipe it clean, and reinsert it. Make sure the dipstick is fully inserted.
5. Pull the dipstick from its tube again. Holding it horizontally, read the fluid level. The fluid should be between the MIN and MAX mark. If the fluid is below the MIN mark, add fluid through the dipstick tube.
6. Insert the dipstick, and check the level again after adding any fluid. Be careful not to overfill the transmission.

Fig. 132 Grasp the dipstick and . . .

Fig. 133 . . . remove the dipstick from the tube

Fig. 134 Wipe the dipstick clean and insert the dipstick into the tube and remove the dipstick again

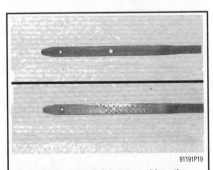

Fig. 135 The dipstick has two sides, the level should be checked on the side with the cross-hatches. If the level is in the cross-hatched area, do not add fluid

Fig. 136 Fluid is added directly into the dipstick tube

Fig. 137 Place a suitable funnel into the dipstick tube and . . .

Fig. 138 . . . pour the proper fluid into the transmission

PAN & FILTER SERVICE

▶ **See Figures 139 thru 151**

The fluid should be changed according to the schedule in the Maintenance Intervals chart. If the car is normally used in severe service, such as stop and start driving, trailer towing, or the like, the interval should be halved. If the car is driven under especially nasty conditions, such as in heavy city traffic where the temperature normally reaches 90°F (32°C), or in very hilly or mountainous areas, or in police, taxi, or delivery service, the fluid should be changed according to the severe service schedule.

The fluid must be hot before it is drained; a 20 minute drive should accomplish this.

1. To drain the automatic transmission fluid, the fluid pan must be removed. Raise and safely support the vehicle. Place a drain pan underneath the transmission pan, then remove the pan attaching bolts except on the four corners of the pan.

2. Loosen the four attaching bolts on the corners approximately four turns each, but do not remove them.

3. Very carefully pry the pan loose on one corner. You can use a small pry-bar for this if you work CAREFULLY. Do not distort the pan flange, or score the mating surface of the transmission case. You'll be very sorry later if you do. As the pan is pried loose, all of the fluid is going to come pouring out.

4. Carefully break the other corners loose until fluid is flowing steadily from the entire pan.

➡ **If the drained fluid is discolored (brown or black), thick, or smells burnt, serious transmission troubles, probably due to overheating, should be suspected. Your car's transmission should be inspected by a reliable transmission specialist to determine the problem.**

5. After the fluid is down flowing, remove one corner bolt and attempt to drain any remaining fluid. Remove the remaining bolts and remove the pan and gasket.

➡ **The transmission pan gasket is reusable, do no throw it away.**

6. Clean the pan with solvent and allow it to air dry. If you use a rag to wipe out the pan, you risk leaving bits of lint behind, which will clog the dinky hydraulic passages in the transmission.

7. Remove and discard the filter and the O-ring seal if applicable.
   To install:
8. Install a new filter and O-ring, if applicable.
9. Position the gasket on the pan, then install the pan. Tighten the bolts evenly and in rotation to 10 ft. lbs. (13 Nm.). Do not overtighten.
10. Add the recommended automatic transmission fluid to the transmission through the dipstick tube. You will need a long necked funnel, or a funnel and tube to do this. A quick check of the capacities chart later in this Section will reveal the capacity of the transmission in your vehicle. On a first fill after removing the pan and filter, this number should cut into a ⅓ and checked on the dipstick before refilling.
11. With the transmission in **P**, put on the parking brake, block the front wheels, start the engine and let it idle. DO NOT RACE THE ENGINE. DO NOT MOVE THE LEVER THROUGH ITS RANGES.

Fig. 139 The transmission pan is held to the transmission case by retaining bolts. Typically the retaining bolts require a 10mm socket

Fig. 140 Remove the retaining bolts on the transmission pan except . . .

Fig. 141 . . . for the bolts on the four corners of the pan

Fig. 142 Slowly loosen the four corner bolts and lower the pan

Fig. 143 As the pan is lowered fluid will begin to pour out

Fig. 144 After the fluid is drained out, remove the pan from the transmission

Fig. 145 Remove the transmission filter by gently pulling it out of the valve body. Make sure that the O-ring on the filter nipple is removed from the valve body

Fig. 146 You may find this piece in your transmission pan upon removal, it is a dipstick tube plug that is knocked out on the assembly line

Fig. 147 Remove the transmission pan gasket from the pan and place it in a safe place, the gasket is reusable

Fig. 148 Remove the transmission pan magnets from the pan and . . .

Fig. 149 . . . wipe the magnets clean before installing them back into the pan

Fig. 150 Thoroughly clean the mating surfaces of the pan and . . .

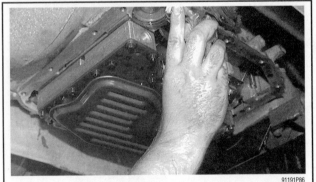

Fig. 151 . . . the transmission case before installing the gasket and pan onto the case

12. With the lever in Park, check the fluid level. If it's OK, take the car out for a short drive, park on a level surface, and check the level again, as outlined earlier in this section. Add more fluid if necessary. Be careful not to overfill, which will cause foaming and fluid loss.

Transfer Case

FLUID RECOMMENDATIONS

Ford recommends using Motorcraft Mercon ATF (Automatic Transmission Fluid) XT-2-QDX or equivalent Mercon ATF fluid (Dexron Mercon III).

LEVEL CHECK

▶ See Figure 152

1. Park the truck on a level surface, turn off the engine, apply the parking brake and block the wheels.
2. Remove the check/fill plug from the side of the transfer case with a proper size wrench. The fluid level should be even with the bottom of the check/fill hole.
3. If additional fluid is necessary, add it through the check/fill hole using a siphon pump or squeeze bottle.
4. Reinstall the check/fill plug; do not overtighten.

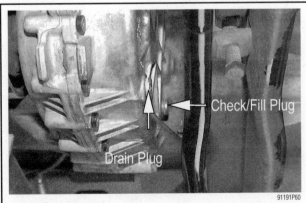

Fig. 152 The check/fill and drain plug locations on a typical transfer case

DRAIN & REFILL

▶ **See Figures 152 and 153**

1. Place a suitable drain pan under the transfer case.
2. Remove the drain plug and allow the fluid to drain out.
3. Replace the drain plug, remove the check/fill plug and fill the transfer case to the proper level with the required fluid.
4. Reinstall the check/fill plug.

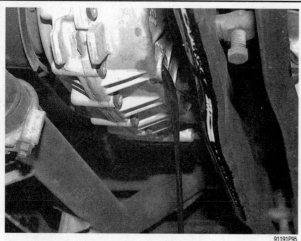

Fig. 153 Remove the drain plug to drain the fluid out of the transfer case

Drive Axles

FLUID RECOMMENDATIONS

Use hypoid gear lubricant SAE 80W90. If the differential is of the limited slip type, be sure and use special limited slip differential additive Ford Friction Modifier C8AZ-19B546-A or equivalent.

LEVEL CHECK

▶ **See Figures 154 thru 159**

Clean the area around the fill plug, which is located in the housing cover, before removing the plug. The lubricant level should be maintained to the bottom of the fill hole with the axle in its normal running position. If lubricant does not appear at the hole when the plug is removed, additional lubricant should be added.

➡ **If the differential is of the limited slip type, be sure and use special limited slip differential additive.**

DRAIN & REFILL

▶ **See Figures 160 thru 168**

Drain and refill the front and rear axle housing every 24,000 miles, or anytime the vehicle is operated in deep water. Typically front axles have a drain plug located on the cover. Be sure and clean the area around the drain plug before removing the plug.

The best way to drain a Ford or Dana rear axle is to remove the cover. If desired, you may also remove the oil with a suction gun. Refill the axle housings with the proper oil.

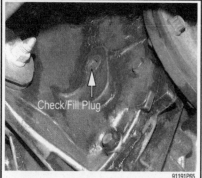

Fig. 154 The check/fill plug location—front axle (4 X 4 only)

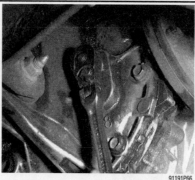

Fig. 155 Loosen the check/fill plug with a ⅜ drive tool and . . .

Fig. 156 . . . remove the plug from the axle—front axle (4 X 4 only)

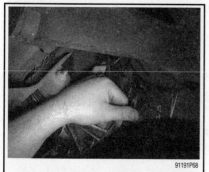

Fig. 157 Place a finger into the check/fill plug hole to measure the amount of fluid in the differential—front axle (4 X 4 only)

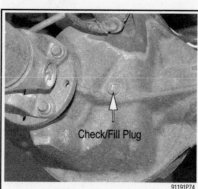

Fig. 158 The check/fill plug location—rear axle

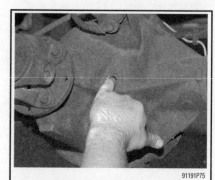

Fig. 159 Remove the check/fill plug and check the fluid level by placing a finger into the hole—rear axle

Fig. 160 The drain plug location—front axle (4 X 4 only)

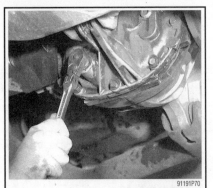

Fig. 161 Loosen the drain plug with a ⅜ drive tool and . . .

Fig. 162 . . . remove the plug from the axle—front axle (4 X 4 only)

Fig. 163 Once the drain plug is removed the axle fluid will begin to flow out

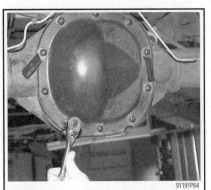

Fig. 164 Remove the axle cover retaining bolts—rear axle

Fig. 165 After the cover bolts are removed, carefully pry the cover loose and . . .

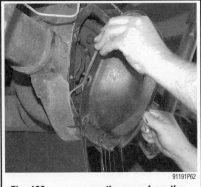

Fig. 166 . . . remove the cover from the axle—rear axle

Fig. 167 Thoroughly clean the axle housing and cover mating surfaces before reinstalling the cover—rear axle

Fig. 168 Fluid is added directly into the rear axle check/fill plug

Cooling System

FLUID RECOMMENDATIONS

Ford recommends a good quality ethylene glycol based or other aluminum compatible antifreeze for use in the vehicles covered by this Manual. It is best to add a ⁵⁰/₅₀ mix of antifreeze and distilled water to avoid diluting the coolant in the system.

LEVEL CHECK

♦ **See Figure 169**

The coolant recovery tank is located in the engine compartment on the inside fenderwells, along the radiator support behind the headlamps, or between the engine and the radiator on some Super-Duty models.

The proper coolant level is slightly above the **FULL COLD** marking on the recovery tank when the engine is cold. Top off the cooling system using the recovery tank and its marking as a guideline.

➡**Never overfill the recovery tank.**

A coolant level that consistently drops is usually a sign of a small, hard to detect leak, although in the worst case it could be a sign of an internal engine leak. In most cases, you will be able to trace the leak to a loose fitting or damaged hose.

Evaporating ethylene glycol antifreeze will have a sweet smell and leave small, white (salt-like) deposits, which can be helpful in tracing a leak.

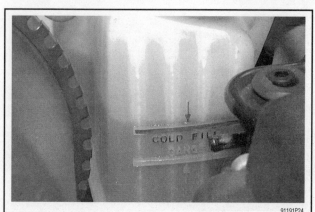

Fig. 169 The coolant level should be up to the COLD FILL mark with the engine off and cold

✳✳ CAUTION

Never open, service or drain the radiator or cooling system when hot; serious burns can occur from the steam and hot coolant. Also, when draining engine coolant, keep in mind that cats and dogs are attracted to ethylene glycol antifreeze and could drink any that is left in an uncovered container or in puddles on the ground. This will prove fatal in sufficient quantities. Always drain coolant into a sealable container. Coolant should be reused unless it is contaminated or is several years old.

DRAIN & REFILL

▶ See Figures 170, 171, 172, 173 and 174

Ensure that the engine is completely cool prior to starting this service.

✳✳ CAUTION

Never open, service or drain the radiator or cooling system when hot; serious burns can occur from the steam and hot coolant. Also, when draining engine coolant, keep in mind that cats and dogs are attracted to ethylene glycol antifreeze and could drink any that is left in an uncovered container or in puddles on the ground. This will prove fatal in sufficient quantities. Always drain coolant into a sealable container. Coolant should be reused unless it is contaminated or is several years old.

1. Remove the recovery tank or radiator cap.
2. Raise and support the vehicle.
3. Place a drain pan of sufficient capacity under the radiator and open the petcock (drain) on the radiator.

➡ Plastic petcocks easily bind. Before opening a plastic radiator petcock, spray it with some penetrating lubricant.

4. Drain the cooling system completely.
5. Close the petcock.
6. Remove the drain pan.
7. Lower the vehicle.
8. Determine the capacity of the cooling system, then properly refill the system with a 50/50 mixture of fresh coolant and distilled water.
9. Leave the recovery tank or radiator cap off to aid in bleeding the system.
10. Start the engine and allow it to idle until the thermostat opens (the upper

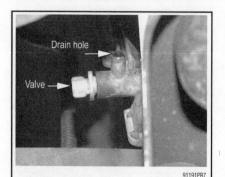

Fig. 170 Open the valve on the petcock until the coolant begins to flow out of the drain hole

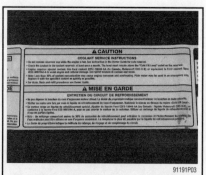

Fig. 171 Follow any instructions about coolant system service found on labels in the engine compartment

Fig. 172 Grasp the recovery tank cap and turn it counterclockwise to . . .

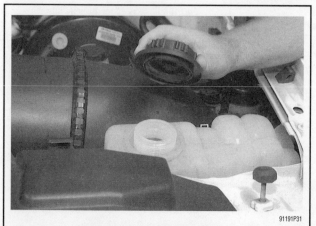

Fig. 173 . . . remove it from the recovery tank

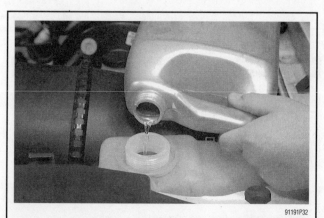

Fig. 174 Pour the proper coolant to water mixture directly into the recovery tank

radiator hose will become hot). The coolant level should go down, this is normal as the system bleeds the air pockets out of the system.

11. Refill the system with coolant to the proper level.
12. Turn the engine **OFF** and check for leaks.

FLUSHING & CLEANING THE SYSTEM

▶ **See Figure 175**

1. Drain the cooling system completely as described earlier.
2. Close the petcock and fill the system with a cooling system flush (clean water may also be used, but is not as efficient).
3. Idle the engine until the upper radiator hose gets hot.
4. Allow the engine to cool completely and drain the system again.
5. Repeat this process until the drained water is clear and free of scale.
6. Flush the recovery tank with water and leave empty.

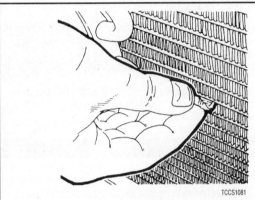

TCCS1081

Fig. 175 Periodically remove all debris from the radiator fins

✳ CAUTION

Never open, service or drain the radiator or cooling system when hot; serious burns can occur from the steam and hot coolant. Also, when draining engine coolant, keep in mind that cats and dogs are attracted to ethylene glycol antifreeze and could drink any that is left in an uncovered container or in puddles on the ground. This will prove fatal in sufficient quantities. Always drain coolant into a sealable container. Coolant should be reused unless it is contaminated or is several years old.

7. Fill and bleed the cooling system as described earlier.

Brake Master Cylinder

The brake master cylinder reservoir is located under the hood, attached to the brake booster and firewall on the driver's side of the engine compartment.

FLUID RECOMMENDATIONS

✳ CAUTION

Brake fluid contains polyglycol ethers and polyglycols. Avoid contact with the eyes and wash your hands thoroughly after handling brake fluid. If you do get brake fluid in your eyes, flush your eyes with clean, running water for 15 minutes. If eye irritation persists, or if you have taken brake fluid internally, IMMEDIATELY seek medical assistance.

✳ WARNING

Clean, high quality brake fluid is essential to the safe and proper operation of the brake system. You should always buy the highest quality brake fluid that is available. If the brake fluid becomes contaminated, drain and flush the system, then refill the master cylinder with new fluid. Never reuse any brake fluid. Any brake fluid that is removed from the system should be discarded. Also, do not allow any brake fluid to come in contact with a painted surface; it will damage the paint.

When adding fluid to the system, ONLY use fresh DOT 3 brake fluid from a sealed container. DOT 3 brake fluid will absorb moisture when it is exposed to the atmosphere, which will lower its boiling point. A container that has been opened once, closed and placed on a shelf will allow enough moisture to enter over time to contaminate the fluid within. If your brake fluid is contaminated with water, you could boil the brake fluid under hard braking conditions and lose all or some braking ability. Don't take the risk, buy fresh brake fluid whenever you must add to the system.

LEVEL CHECK

▶ **See Figures 176, 177, 178 and 179**

✳ CAUTION

Brake fluid contains polyglycol ethers and polyglycols. Avoid contact with the eyes and wash your hands thoroughly after handling brake fluid. If you do get brake fluid in your eyes, flush your eyes with clean, running water for 15 minutes. If eye irritation persists, or if you have taken brake fluid internally, IMMEDIATELY seek medical assistance.

Observe the fluid level indicators on the master cylinder; the fluid level should be between the **MIN** and **MAX** lines.

Before removing the master cylinder reservoir cap, make sure the vehicle is resting on level ground and clean all dirt away from the top of the master cylinder. Unscrew the cap and fill the master cylinder until the level is between the **MIN** and **MAX** lines.

If the level of the brake fluid is less than half the volume of the reservoir, it is advised that you check the brake system for leaks. Leaks in a hydraulic brake system most commonly occur at the wheel cylinder and brake line junction points.

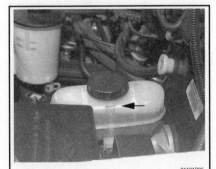

91191P25

Fig. 176 The brake fluid level should not be above the MAX line on the side of the reservoir

91191P30

Fig. 177 Wipe the master cylinder reservoir clean before . . .

91191P28

Fig. 178 . . . removing the reservoir cap

Fig. 179 Pour brake fluid from a sealed container directly into the reservoir

Clutch Master Cylinder

FLUID RECOMMENDATIONS

Keep the reservoir topped up with Ford Heavy-Duty Brake fluid Ford specification No. ESA–M6C25–A, or equivalent; do not overfill.

LEVEL CHECK

▸ See Figure 180

The hydraulic fluid reservoirs on these systems are mounted on the firewall. Fluid level checks are performed like those on the brake hydraulic system. The proper fluid level is indicated by a step on the reservoir.

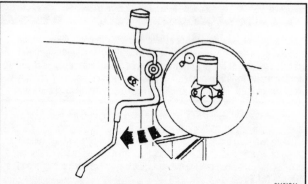

Fig. 180 The clutch master cylinder is located just to the right of the brake master cylinder along the firewall

---

✳✳ CAUTION

Carefully clean the top and sides of the reservoir before opening, to prevent contamination of the system with dirt, etc. Remove the reservoir diaphragm before adding fluid, and replace after filling.

Power Steering Pump

FLUID RECOMMENDATIONS

Ford recommends using Motorcraft Mercon ATF (Automatic Transmission Fluid) XT-2-QDX or equivalent Mercon ATF fluid (Dexron Mercon III).

LEVEL CHECK

▸ See Figures 181, 182 and 183

1. Start the engine and let id idle for 2 or 3 minutes.
2. Turn the steering wheel all the way to the right and left several times to help warm the fluid and force it circulate.
3. Check the fluid level in the reservoir. It should be at the **FULL COLD** mark.
4. If the level is low, fill the reservoir up to the **FULL COLD** mark with the appropriate fluid, but do not overfill the system or problems in the system can occur.

Chassis Greasing

▸ See Figure 184

There are several components in the front end and steering that require periodic lubrication. Typically these components include the tie rod ends, ball joints, pitman arm, and several other components in the steering system such as an idler arm or center link that vary by model. Any greaseable item will be identifiable by a grease or Zerk® fitting on the component.

Some components are permanently lubricated during manufacture and do not need periodic maintenance. These components can be identified by the lack of a grease fitting.

Inspect each component to be lubricated. Replace components with torn/ruptured seals. Damaged seals will eventually leak grease or allow contaminates to enter and eventually cause component failure and/or seizure.

Body Lubrication and Maintenance

LUBRICATION OF HINGES, LATCHES & LOCKS

Periodically it is recommended that the hinges, latches and locks be lubricated with a suitable grease. A quality white lithium grease is the best choice to lubricate these components. White lithium grease can be bought in a spray can with a long application tube for reaching into latches, locks, and hinges to avoid

---

Fig. 181 The power steering pump reservoir is marked with a MIN and MAX line on the side. The fluid level should be between these marks

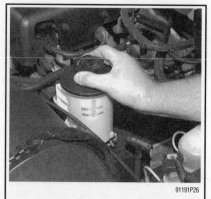

Fig. 182 Remove the reservoir cap and . . .

Fig. 183 . . . pour the proper fluid directly into the reservoir, but make sure you do not overfill the reservoir

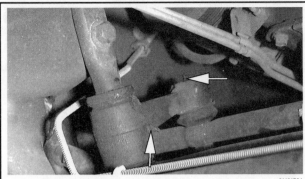

91191P84

Fig. 184 On 4 X 4 F-150 models, the only component that requires greasing is the idler arm

getting the grease all over the place. A good time to accomplish this task is on every oil change.

VEHICLE WASHING

The vehicle should be washed at regular intervals to remove dirt, dust, insects, and tar and other possibly damaging stains that can adhere to the paint and may cause damage. Proper exterior maintenance also helps in the resale value of the vehicle by maintaining its like-new appearance.

→**It is particularly important to frequently wash the vehicle in the wintertime to prevent corrosion, when salt has been used on the roads.**

There are many precautions and tips on washing, including the following:
• When washing the vehicle, do not expose it do direct sunlight.
• Use lukewarm water to soften the dirt before you wash with a sponge, and plenty of water, to avoid scratching.
• A detergent can be used to facilitate the softening of dirt and oil.
• A water-soluble grease solvent may be used in cases of sticky dirt. However, use a washplace with a drainage separator.
• Dry the vehicle with a clean chamois and remember to clean the drain holes in the doors and rocker panels.
• If equipped with a power radio antenna, it must be dried after washing.

❊❊ CAUTION

Never clean the bumpers with gasoline or paint thinner, always use the same agent as used on the painted surfaces of the vehicle.

• Tar spots can be removed with tar remover or kerosene after the vehicle has been washed.
• A stiff-bristle brush and lukewarm soapy water can be used to clean the wiper blades. Frequent cleaning improves visibility when using the wipers considerably.
• Wash off the dirt from the underside (wheel housings, fenders, etc.).
• In areas of high industrial fallout, more frequent washing is recommended.

❊❊ CAUTION

During high pressure washing the spray nozzle must never be closer to the vehicle than 13 inches (30 cm). Do not spray into the locks.

• When washing or steam cleaning the engine, avoid spraying water or steam directly on the electrical components or near the distributor or ignition components. After cleaning the engine, the spark plug wells should be inspected for water and blown dry if necessary.
• Special vehicle washing detergent is the best to use. Liquid dishwashing detergent can remove wax and leave the vehicle's paint unprotected and in addition some liquid detergents contains abrasives which can scratch the paint.
• Bird droppings should be removed from the paintwork as soon as possible, otherwise the finish may be permanently stained.

❊❊ WARNING

When the vehicle is driven immediately after being washed, apply the brakes several times in order to remove any moisture from the braking surfaces.

❊❊ WARNING

Engine cleaning agents should not be used when the engine is warm, a fire risk is present as most engine cleaning agents are highly flammable.

Automatic vehicle washing is a simple and quick way to clean your vehicle, but it is worth remembering that it is not as thorough as when you yourself clean the vehicle. Keeping the underbody clean is vitally important, and some automatic washers do not contain equipment for washing the underside of the vehicle.

When driving into an automatic was, make sure the following precautions have been taken:
• Make sure all windows are up, and no objects that you do not want to get wet are exposed.
• In some cases, rotating the side view mirrors in can help to avoid possible damage.
• If your vehicle is equipped with a power antenna, lower it. If your vehicle has a solid mounted, non-power antenna, it is best to remove it, but this is not always practical. Inspect the surroundings to reduce the risk of possible damage, and check to see if the antenna can be manually lowered.

❊❊ WARNING

Most manufacturers do not recommend automatic vehicle washing in the first six months due to the possibility of insufficient paint curing; a safe bet is to wait until after six months of ownership (when purchased new) to use an automatic vehicle wash.

WAXING

→**Before applying wax, the vehicle must be washed and thoroughly dried.**

Waxing a vehicle can help to preserve the appearance of your vehicle. A wide range of polymer-based vehicle waxes are available today. These waxes are easy to use and produce a long-lasting, high gloss finish that protects the body and paint against oxidation, road dirt, and fading.

Sometimes, waxing a neglected vehicle, or one that has sustained chemical or natural element damage (such as acid rain) require more than waxing, and a light-duty compound can be applied. For severely damaged surfaces, it is best to consult a professional to see what would be required to repair the damage.

Waxing procedures differ according to manufacturer, type, and ingredients, so it is best to consult the directions on the wax and/or polish purchased.

INTERIOR CLEANING

Upholstery

Fabric can usually be cleaned with soapy water or a proper detergent. For more difficult spots caused by oil, ice cream, soda, etc., use a fabric cleaner available at most parts stores. Be sure when purchasing the cleaner to read the label to ensure it is safe to use on your type of fabric. A safe method of testing the cleaner is to apply a small amount to an area usually unseen, such as under a seat, or other areas. Wait a while, perhaps even a day to check the spot for fading, discoloring, etc., as some cleaners will only cause these problems after they have dried.

Leather upholstery requires special care, it can be cleaned with a mild soap and a soft cloth. It is recommended that a special leather cleaner be used to clean but also treat the leather surfaces in your vehicle. Leather surfaces can age quickly and can crack if not properly taken care of, so it is vital that the leather surfaces be maintained.

Floor Mats and Carpet

The floor mats and carpet should be vacuumed or brushed regularly. They can be cleaned with a mild soap and water. Special cleaners are available to clean the carpeted surfaces of your vehicle, but take care in choosing them, and again it is best to test them in a usually unseen spot.

Dashboard, Console, Door Panels, Etc.

The dashboard, console, door panels, and other plastic, vinyl, or wood surfaces can be cleaned using a mild soap and water. Caution must be taken to keep water out of electronic accessories and controls to avoid shorts or ruining the components. Again special cleaners are available to clean these surfaces, as with other cleaners care must taken in purchasing and using such cleaners.

There are protectants available which can treat the various surfaces in your vehicle giving them a "shiny new look", however some of these protectants can cause more harm than good in the long run. The shine that is placed on your dashboard attracts sunlight accelerating the aging, fading and possibly even cracking the surfaces. These protectants also attract more dust to stick to the surfaces they treat, increasing the cleaning you must do to maintain the appearance of your vehicle. Personal discretion is advised here.

Wheel Bearings

REPACKING

➥Sodium based grease is not compatible with lithium based grease. Read the package labels and be careful not to mix the two types. If there is any doubt as to the type of grease used, completely clean the old grease from the bearing and hub before replacing.

Before handling the bearings, there are a few things that you should remember to do and not to do.
DO the following:
- Remove all outside dirt from the housing before exposing the bearing.
- Treat a used bearing as gently as you would a new one.
- Work with clean tools in clean surroundings.
- Use clean, dry gloves, or at least clean, dry hands.
- Clean solvents and flushing fluids are a must.
- Use clean paper when laying out the bearings to dry.
- Protect disassembled bearings from rust and dirt. Cover them up.

- Use clean, lint-free rags to wipe the bearings.
- Keep the bearings in oil-proof paper when they are to be stored or are not in use.
- Clean the inside of the housing before replacing the bearing.
Do NOT do the following:
- Do not work in dirty surroundings.
- Do not use dirty, chipped or damaged tools.
- Do not work on wooden work benches or use wooden mallets.
- Do not handle bearings with dirty or moist hands.
- Do not use gasoline for cleaning. Use a safe solvent.
- Do not spin dry bearings with compressed air. They will be damaged.
- Do not use cotton waste or dirty cloths to wipe bearings.
- Do not scratch or nick bearing surfaces.
- Do not allow the bearing to come in contact with dirt or rust at any time.

The front wheel bearings require periodic maintenance. A premium high melting point grease meeting Ford specification ESA-M1C75-B or equivalent must be used. Long fiber type greases must not be used. This service is recommended every 90,000 miles (144,000 km) for normal maintenance and every 30,000 miles (48,000 km) for severe service.

➥For information on Wheel Bearing removal and installation, refer to Section 8 of this manual.

1. Remove the wheel bearing.
2. Clean all parts in a non-flammable solvent and let them air dry.

➥Only use lint-free rags to dry the bearings. Never spin-dry a bearing with compressed air, as this will damage the rollers.

3. Check for excessive wear and damage. Replace the bearing as necessary.

➥Packing wheel bearings with grease is best accomplished by using a wheel bearing packer (available at most automotive parts stores).

4. If a wheel bearing packer is not available, the bearings may be packed by hand.
   a. Place a "healthy" glob of grease in the palm of one hand.
   b. Force the edge of the bearing into the grease so that the grease fills the space between the rollers and the bearing cage.
   c. Keep rotating the bearing while continuing to push the grease through.
   d. Continue until the grease is forced out the other side of the bearing.
5. Place the packed bearing on a clean surface and cover it until it is time for installation.
6. Install the wheel bearing.

TRAILER TOWING

General Recommendations

Your vehicle was primarily designed to carry passengers and cargo. It is important to remember that towing a trailer will place additional loads on your vehicles engine, drive train, steering, braking and other systems. However, if you decide to tow a trailer, using the prior equipment is a must.

Local laws may require specific equipment such as trailer brakes or fender mounted mirrors. Check your local laws.

Trailer Weight

The weight of the trailer is the most important factor. A good weight-to-horsepower ratio is about 35:1, 35 lbs. of Gross Combined Weight (GCW) for every horsepower your engine develops. Multiply the engine's rated horsepower by 35 and subtract the weight of the vehicle passengers and luggage. The number remaining is the approximate ideal maximum weight you should tow, although a numerically higher axle ratio can help compensate for heavier weight.

Hitch (Tongue) Weight

◗ See Figure 185

Calculate the hitch weight in order to select a proper hitch. The weight of the hitch is usually 9–11% of the trailer gross weight and should be measured with the trailer loaded. Hitches fall into various categories: those that mount on the frame and rear bumper, the bolt-on type, or the weld-on distribution type used

for larger trailers. Axle mounted or clamp-on bumper hitches should never be used.

Check the gross weight rating of your trailer. Tongue weight is usually figured as 10% of gross trailer weight. Therefore, a trailer with a maximum gross weight of 2000 lbs. will have a maximum tongue weight of 200 lbs. Class I trailers fall into this category. Class II trailers are those with a gross weight rating of 2000–3000 lbs., while Class III trailers fall into the 3500–6000 lbs. category.

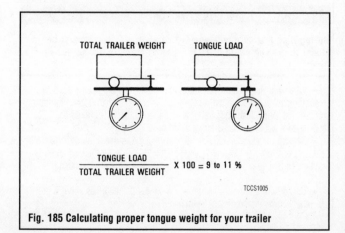

Fig. 185 Calculating proper tongue weight for your trailer

Class IV trailers are those over 6000 lbs. and are for use with fifth wheel trucks, only.

When you've determined the hitch that you'll need, follow the manufacturer's installation instructions, exactly, especially when it comes to fastener torques. The hitch will subjected to a lot of stress and good hitches come with hardened bolts. Never substitute an inferior bolt for a hardened bolt.

Engine

One of the most common, if not THE most common, problems associated with trailer towing is engine overheating. If you have a cooling system without an expansion tank, you'll definitely need to get an aftermarket expansion tank kit, preferably one with at least a 2 quart capacity. These kits are easily installed on the radiator's overflow hose, and come with a pressure cap designed for expansion tanks.

Aftermarket engine oil coolers are helpful for prolonging engine oil life and reducing overall engine temperatures. Both of these factors increase engine life. While not absolutely necessary in towing Class I and some Class II trailers, they are recommended for heavier Class II and all Class III towing. Engine oil cooler systems usually consist of an adapter, screwed on in place of the oil filter, a remote filter mounting and a multi-tube, finned heat exchanger, which is mounted in front of the radiator or air conditioning condenser.

Transmission

An automatic transmission is usually recommended for trailer towing. Modern automatics have proven reliable and, of course, easy to operate, in trailer towing. The increased load of a trailer, however, causes an increase in the temperature of the automatic transmission fluid. Heat is the worst enemy of an automatic transmission. As the temperature of the fluid increases, the life of the fluid decreases.

It is essential, therefore, that you install an automatic transmission cooler. The cooler, which consists of a multi-tube, finned heat exchanger, is usually installed in front of the radiator or air conditioning compressor, and hooked in-line with the transmission cooler tank inlet line. Follow the cooler manufacturer's installation instructions.

Select a cooler of at least adequate capacity, based upon the combined gross weights of the vehicle and trailer.

Cooler manufacturers recommend that you use an aftermarket cooler in addition to, and not instead of, the present cooling tank in your radiator. If you do want to use it in place of the radiator cooling tank, get a cooler at least two sizes larger than normally necessary.

➡A transmission cooler can, sometimes, cause slow or harsh shifting in the transmission during cold weather, until the fluid has a chance to come up to normal operating temperature. Some coolers can be purchased with or retrofitted with a temperature bypass valve which will allow fluid flow through the cooler only when the fluid has reached above a certain operating temperature.

Handling a Trailer

Towing a trailer with ease and safety requires a certain amount of experience. It's a good idea to learn the feel of a trailer by practicing turning, stopping and backing in an open area such as an empty parking lot.

JUMP STARTING A DEAD BATTERY

▶ See Figure 186

Whenever a vehicle is jump started, precautions must be followed in order to prevent the possibility of personal injury. Remember that batteries contain a small amount of explosive hydrogen gas which is a by-product of battery charging. Sparks should always be avoided when working around batteries, especially when attaching jumper cables. To minimize the possibility of accidental sparks, follow the procedure carefully.

☀ CAUTION

NEVER hook the batteries up in a series circuit or the entire electrical system will go up in smoke, including the starter!

Vehicles equipped with a diesel engine may utilize two 12 volt batteries. If so, the batteries are connected in a parallel circuit (positive terminal to positive terminal, negative terminal to negative terminal). Hooking the batteries up in parallel circuit increases battery cranking power without increasing total battery voltage output. Output remains at 12 volts. On the other hand, hooking two 12 volt batteries up in a series circuit (positive terminal to negative terminal, positive terminal to negative terminal) increases total battery output to 24 volts (12 volts plus 12 volts).

Jump Starting Precautions

- Be sure that both batteries are of the same voltage. Vehicles covered by this manual and most vehicles on the road today utilize a 12 volt charging system.
- Be sure that both batteries are of the same polarity (have the same terminal, in most cases NEGATIVE grounded).
- Be sure that the vehicles are not touching or a short could occur.
- On serviceable batteries, be sure the vent cap holes are not obstructed.
- Do not smoke or allow sparks anywhere near the batteries.
- In cold weather, make sure the battery electrolyte is not frozen. This can occur more readily in a battery that has been in a state of discharge.
- Do not allow electrolyte to contact your skin or clothing.

Jump Starting Procedure

1. Make sure that the voltages of the 2 batteries are the same. Most batteries and charging systems are of the 12 volt variety.
2. Pull the jumping vehicle (with the good battery) into a position so the jumper cables can reach the dead battery and that vehicle's engine. Make sure that the vehicles do NOT touch.
3. Place the transmissions/transaxles of both vehicles in **Neutral** (MT) or **P** (AT), as applicable, then firmly set their parking brakes.

➡If necessary for safety reasons, the hazard lights on both vehicles may be operated throughout the entire procedure without significantly increasing the difficulty of jumping the dead battery.

4. Turn all lights and accessories OFF on both vehicles. Make sure the ignition switches on both vehicles are turned to the **OFF** position.
5. Cover the battery cell caps with a rag, but do not cover the terminals.
6. Make sure the terminals on both batteries are clean and free of corrosion or proper electrical connection will be impeded. If necessary, clean the battery terminals before proceeding.
7. Identify the positive (+) and negative (-) terminals on both batteries.

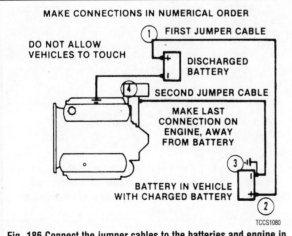

MAKE CONNECTIONS IN NUMERICAL ORDER

DO NOT ALLOW VEHICLES TO TOUCH

① FIRST JUMPER CABLE

DISCHARGED BATTERY

SECOND JUMPER CABLE

MAKE LAST CONNECTION ON ENGINE, AWAY FROM BATTERY

BATTERY IN VEHICLE WITH CHARGED BATTERY

TCCS1080

Fig. 186 Connect the jumper cables to the batteries and engine in the order shown

8. Connect the first jumper cable to the positive (+) terminal of the dead battery, then connect the other end of that cable to the positive (+) terminal of the booster (good) battery.

9. Connect one end of the other jumper cable to the negative (-) terminal on the booster battery and the final cable clamp to an engine bolt head, alternator bracket or other solid, metallic point on the engine with the dead battery. Try to pick a ground on the engine that is positioned away from the battery in order to minimize the possibility of the 2 clamps touching should one loosen during the procedure. DO NOT connect this clamp to the negative (–) terminal of the bad battery.

✳ CAUTION

Be very careful to keep the jumper cables away from moving parts (cooling fan, belts, etc.) on both engines.

10. Check to make sure that the cables are routed away from any moving parts, then start the donor vehicle's engine. Run the engine at moderate speed for several minutes to allow the dead battery a chance to receive some initial charge.

11. With the donor vehicle's engine still running slightly above idle, try to start the vehicle with the dead battery. Crank the engine for no more than 10 seconds at a time and let the starter cool for at least 20 seconds between tries. If the vehicle does not start in 3 tries, it is likely that something else is also wrong or that the battery needs additional time to charge.

12. Once the vehicle is started, allow it to run at idle for a few seconds to make sure that it is operating properly.

13. Turn ON the headlights, heater blower and, if equipped, the rear defroster of both vehicles in order to reduce the severity of voltage spikes and subsequent risk of damage to the vehicles' electrical systems when the cables are disconnected. This step is especially important to any vehicle equipped with computer control modules.

14. Carefully disconnect the cables in the reverse order of connection. Start with the negative cable that is attached to the engine ground, then the negative cable on the donor battery. Disconnect the positive cable from the donor battery and finally, disconnect the positive cable from the formerly dead battery. Be careful when disconnecting the cables from the positive terminals not to allow the alligator clips to touch any metal on either vehicle or a short and sparks will occur.

JACKING

♦ See Figures 187, 188, 189, 190 and 191

Your vehicle was supplied with a jack for emergency road repairs. This jack is fine for changing a flat tire or other short term procedures not requiring you to go beneath the vehicle. If it is used in an emergency situation, carefully follow the instructions provided either with the jack or in your owner's manual. Do not attempt to use the jack on any portions of the vehicle other than specified by the vehicle manufacturer. Always block the diagonally opposite wheel when using a jack.

A more convenient way of jacking is the use of a garage or floor jack. You may use the floor jack under the differential as well as the axle tubes in the rear. To raise the front of the vehicle, there are several options based on model and whether or not it is a 4 X 4 or not. On a 1997–98 F-250HD, F-350 and Super Duty 4 X 2 you may lift the vehicle by placing the jack under the I-beam on a flat spot or in the middle of the torsion bar. On 1997–98 F-250HD, F-350 and Super Duty 4 X 4 you may lift the vehicle by placing the jack under the front axle. On all F-150, F-250, Expedition and Navigator models you may places a jack under a bracket welded to the frame on a 4 X 2 model and under a raised boss located on the lower suspension arm or the front crossmember on a 4 X 4 model. On a 1999–00 Super Duty 4 X 4 you may place the jack under the front axle. On a 1999–00 Super Duty 4 X 2 you may place the jack under the radius arm.

Never place the jack under the radiator, engine or transmission components. Severe and expensive damage will result when the jack is raised. Additionally, never jack under the floorpan or bodywork; the metal will deform.

Whenever you plan to work under the vehicle, you must support it on jackstands or ramps. Never use cinder blocks or stacks of wood to support the vehi-

cle, even if you're only going to be under it for a few minutes. Never crawl under the vehicle when it is supported only by the tire-changing jack or other floor jack.

➡**Always position a block of wood or small rubber pad on top of the jack or jackstand to protect the lifting point's finish when lifting or supporting the vehicle.**

Small hydraulic, screw, or scissors jacks are satisfactory for raising the vehicle. Drive-on trestles or ramps are also a handy and safe way to both raise and support the vehicle. Be careful though, some ramps may be too steep to drive your vehicle onto without scraping the front bottom panels. Never support the vehicle on any suspension member (unless specifically instructed to do so by a repair manual) or by an underbody panel.

Jacking Precautions

The following safety points cannot be overemphasized:
• Always block the opposite wheel or wheels to keep the vehicle from rolling off the jack.
• When raising the front of the vehicle, firmly apply the parking brake.
• When the drive wheels are to remain on the ground, leave the vehicle in gear to help prevent it from rolling.
• Always use jackstands to support the vehicle when you are working underneath. Place the stands beneath the vehicle's jacking brackets. Before climbing underneath, rock the vehicle a bit to make sure it is firmly supported.

91191PB2

Fig. 187 Place a suitable jack under the rear differential and raise the rear of the vehicle up

91191PB1

Fig. 188 Place jackstands under the rear axle tubes to support the rear of the vehicle

91191PB4

Fig. 189 On 4 X 4 F-150, F-250, Expedition and Navigator models, the front crossmember is a good place to raise the front of the vehicle

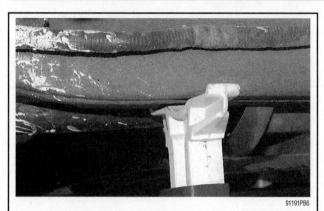

Fig. 190 Place jackstands under the framerails on . . .

Fig. 191 . . . both sides to support the front of the vehicle

1997-00 SCHEDULED MAINTENANCE INTERVALS
(FORD F-150, LIGHT-DUTY F-250, EXPEDITION & NAVIGATOR)

TO BE SERVICED	TYPE OF SERVICE	VEHICLE MILEAGE INTERVAL (x1000)																							
		5	10	15	20	25	30	35	40	45	50	55	60	65	70	75	80	85	90	95	100	105	110	115	120
Accessory drive belt	S/I												✓												✓
Air cleaner filter ①	R						✓						✓						✓			✓			✓
Automatic transmission fluid	R						✓						✓						✓			✓			✓
Automatic transmission shift linkage	S/I & L	✓	✓	✓	✓	✓	✓	✓	✓	✓	✓	✓	✓	✓	✓	✓	✓	✓	✓	✓	✓	✓	✓	✓	✓
Brake caliper slide rails	L			✓			✓			✓			✓			✓			✓			✓			✓
Brake system, hoses & lines	S/I			✓			✓			✓			✓			✓			✓			✓			✓
Clutch reservoir fluid level	S/I	✓	✓	✓	✓	✓	✓	✓	✓	✓	✓	✓	✓	✓	✓	✓	✓	✓	✓	✓	✓	✓	✓	✓	✓
Engine coolant ②	R										✓						✓						✓		
Engine cooling system hoses, clamps & coolant	S/I			✓			✓			✓			✓			✓			✓			✓			✓
Engine oil & filter	R	✓	✓	✓	✓	✓	✓	✓	✓	✓	✓	✓	✓	✓	✓	✓	✓	✓	✓	✓	✓	✓	✓	✓	✓
Exhaust system	S/I	✓	✓	✓	✓	✓	✓	✓	✓	✓	✓	✓	✓	✓	✓	✓	✓	✓	✓	✓	✓	✓	✓	✓	✓
Front wheel bearings	S/I & L						✓						✓						✓						✓
Front/rear axle driveshaft slip yoke	L						✓						✓						✓						✓
Front/rear axle fluid ③	R																				✓				
Fuel filter	R			✓						✓			✓									✓			✓
Manual transmission fluid	R												✓												✓
Parking brake system	S/I						✓						✓						✓						✓
PCV valve	R												✓												✓
Rotate tires	S/I	✓	✓	✓	✓	✓	✓	✓	✓	✓	✓	✓	✓	✓	✓	✓	✓	✓	✓	✓	✓	✓	✓	✓	✓
Spark plugs	R																				✓				
Steering linkage, suspension, driveshaft U-joints	S/I & L	✓	✓	✓	✓	✓	✓	✓	✓	✓	✓	✓	✓	✓	✓	✓	✓	✓	✓	✓	✓	✓	✓	✓	✓

① Perform this at the mileage shown or every 30 months, whichever occurs first.

② Drain, flush and refill the cooling system initially at 50,000 miles or 48 months, whichever occurs first, then every 30,000 miles or 30 months thereafter.

③ The axle lubricant must be replaced every 100,000 miles or if the axle has been submerged under water. Otherwise the lube should not be checked or changed unless a repair is required.

R - Replace   S/I - Inspect and service, if needed   L - Lubricate   A - Adjust   C - Clean

FREQUENT OPERATION MAINTENANCE (SEVERE SERVICE)

If a vehicle is operated under any of the following conditions it is considered severe service:

- Towing a trailer or using a camper or car-top carrier.
- Repeated short trips of less than 5 miles in temperatures below freezing, or trips of less than 10 miles in any temperature.
- Extensive idling or low-speed driving for long distances as in heavy commercial use, such as delivery, taxi or police cars.
- Operating on rough, muddy or salt-covered roads.
- Operating on unpaved or dusty roads.
- Driving in extremely hot (over 90°) conditions.

91191C06

1997-00 SCHEDULED MAINTENANCE INTERVALS
(FORD F-150, LIGHT-DUTY F-250, EXPEDITION & NAVIGATOR)

FREQUENT OPERATION MAINTENANCE (SEVERE SERVICE)—continued

Engine oil & filter - replace every 3,000 miles.
Tires - rotate and inspect every 6,000 miles.
Clutch reservoir fluid level - inspect every 6,000 miles.
Automatic transmission shift linkage - lubricate every 6,000 miles.
Steering linkage, suspension, U-joints - lubricate every 6,000 miles.
Exhaust system - inspect for leaks or damage every 6,000 miles.
Fuel filter - replace every 15,000 miles.
Automatic transmission fluid - change every 21,000 miles.
Crankcase emission air filter - replace every 60,000 miles.
PCV valve - replace every 60,000 miles.
Accessory drive belt - inspect every 60,000 miles.
Spark plugs - replace every 99,000 miles.

1997-00 SCHEDULED MAINTENANCE INTERVALS
(HEAVY-DUTY F-250, F-350, AND SUPER-DUTY)

FREQUENT OPERATION MAINTENANCE (SEVERE SERVICE)

If a vehicle is operated under any of the following conditions it is considered severe service:
- Towing a trailer or using a camper or car-top carrier.
- Repeated short trips of less than 5 miles in temperatures below freezing, or trips of less than 10 miles in any temperature.
- Extensive idling or low-speed driving for long distances as in heavy commercial use, such as delivery, taxi or police cars.
- Operating on rough, muddy or salt-covered roads.
- Operating on unpaved or dusty roads.
- Driving in extremely hot (over 90°) conditions.

Engine oil & filter - replace every 3,000 miles.
Tires - rotate and inspect every 6,000 miles.
Steering linkage, suspension, U-joints - lubricate every 6,000 miles.
Exhaust system - inspect for leaks or damage every 12,000 miles.
Fuel filter - replace every 15,000 miles.
Automatic transmission fluid - change every 21,000 miles.
Front wheel bearings (2WD) - inspect and repack every 30,000 miles.
PCV valve - replace every 60,000 miles.
Accessory drive belt - inspect every 60,000 miles.

91191C08

1997-00 SCHEDULED MAINTENANCE INTERVALS
(HEAVY-DUTY F-250, F-350, AND SUPER-DUTY)

TO BE SERVICED	TYPE OF SERVICE	VEHICLE MILEAGE INTERVAL (x1000)																		
		5	10	15	20	25	30	35	40	45	50	55	60	65	70	75	80	85	90	95	100
Accessory drive belt	S/I																				✓
Air cleaner filter ①②	R						✓						✓						✓		
Automatic transmission fluid ③	R						✓						✓						✓		
Engine coolant ④⑤	R									✓						✓					
Engine cooling system hoses, clamps & coolant ⑥	S/I			✓					✓				✓			✓			✓		
Engine oil & filter	R	✓	✓	✓	✓	✓	✓	✓	✓	✓	✓	✓	✓	✓	✓	✓	✓	✓	✓	✓	✓
Exhaust system	S/I		✓	✓					✓				✓			✓			✓		
Front wheel bearings	S/I & L																				
Front/rear axle lubricant ⑦	R						✓						✓						✓		✓
Fuel filter ⑧	R			✓			✓			✓			✓			✓			✓		✓
PCV valve	R												Every 120,000 miles								
Rotate tires	S/I		✓	✓	✓	✓	✓	✓	✓	✓	✓	✓	✓	✓	✓	✓	✓	✓	✓	✓	✓
Spark plugs	R																				✓
Steering linkage, suspension, driveshaft U-joints	S/I & L	✓	✓	✓	✓	✓	✓	✓	✓	✓	✓	✓	✓	✓	✓	✓	✓	✓	✓	✓	✓

①Perform this at the mileage shown or every 30 months, whichever occurs first.
②7.3L DIT Diesel engine: the air filter should be replaced when the restriction gauge is in the red zone.
③Except the E40D transmission.
④Drain, flush and refill the cooling system initially at 50,000 miles or 48 months, whichever occurs first, then every 30,000 miles or 30 months thereafter.
⑤7.3L DIT Diesel engine: add 4 pints of FW-15 each time the coolant is replaced.
⑥7.3L DIT Diesel engine: add 8-10 oz. of FW-15 to the engine coolant every 15,000 miles.
⑦The axle lubricant must be replaced every 100,000 miles or if the axle has been submerged under water. Otherwise the lube should not be checked or changed unless a repair is required.
⑧7.3L DIT Diesel engine: the fuel filter should be replaced when the restriction lamp is illuminated.

R - Replace   S/I - Inspect and service, if needed   L - Lubricate   A - Adjust   C - Clean

91191C07

CAPACITIES — 2000

91191C10

Year	Model	Engine Displacement Liters (cc)	Engine ID/VIN	Engine Oil with Filter (qts.)	Transmission (pts.) Manual	Transmission (pts.) Auto.	Transfer Case (pts.)	Drive Axle Front (pts.)	Drive Axle Rear (pts.)	Fuel Tank (gal.)	Cooling System (qts.)
2000	Expedition	4.6 (4588)	6/W	6.0	—	②	4.0	3.7	5.5	⑨	19.4
	Expedition	5.4 (5409)	L/A	7.0	—	②	4.0	3.7	5.5	⑨	19.4
	F-150	4.2 (4195)	2	6.0	5.6	②	4.0	3.7	5.5	⑨	17.3
	F-150	4.6 (4588)	6/W	6.0	5.6	②	4.0	3.7	5.5	⑨	19.4
	F-150	5.4 (5409)	L/M/Z/3	7.0	5.6	②	4.0	3.7	5.5	⑨	19.4
	F-250	4.6 (4588)	6/W	6.0	5.6	②	4.0	3.7	5.5	⑪	19.4
	F-250	5.4 (5409)	L/W/Z	7.0	5.6	②	4.0	3.7	5.5	⑪	19.4
	F-Super Duty ①	5.4 (5409)	L	7.0	②	②		6.0	6.0 ④	⑪	19.4
	F-Super Duty ①	6.8 (6802)	5	7.0	②	②		6.0	6.0 ④	⑪	23.0
	F-Super Duty ①	7.3 (7292)	F	14.0	②	②		6.0	6.0 ④	⑪	23.0
	Navigator	5.4 (5409)	L/A	7.0	—	②	4.0	3.7	5.5	30.0	19.4

NOTE: All capacities are approximate. Add fluid gradually and check to be sure a proper fluid level is obtained.

① F-Super Duty models 1999-00 include the F-250 Super Duty and above
② Without PTO: 8.0 pts. With PTO: 12.0 pts.
③ 4X2 with 4R70W: 28.0 pts. 4X4 with 4R70W: 30.0 pts. 4R100 with 4R70W: 28.0 pts.
④ 4X2 with 4R70W: 28.0 pts. 4X4 with 4R70W: 30.0 pts. 4R100 with 20 plate fluid cooler: 34.0 pts. 4R100 with 26 plate fluid cooler: 35.2 pts.
⑤ 4X2 with E40D: 32.0 pts. 4X4 with E40D: 33.0 pts.
⑥ 10.25 inch rear: 7.5 pts.
⑦ 25.0 gallon tank on short bed, 30 gallon tank on long bed
⑧ 4X2 models 25.0 gallon tank, 4X4 models 30 gallon tank
⑨ Without PTO: 4.0 pts. With PTO: 12.0 pts.
⑩ Manual trans. with standard cooling: 15.0 qts. Automatic trans. with standard cooling: 16.4 qts. Manual/automatic trans. with A.C. 16.4 qts. Man/auto trans. with supercooling and A.C.: 18.0 qts.

(right column notes)

② 402 with 4R70W: 28.0 pts. 4X4 with 4R70W: 30.0 pts.
⑨ F250 Heavy Duty 4X2 regular cab midship tank 19.0, aft axle tank 18.2
F250 Heavy Duty 4X2 super cab midship tank 19.0, aft axle tank 18.2
F250 Heavy Duty 4X2 regular cab midship tank 19.0, aft axle tank 18.2
F250 Heavy Duty 4X4 midship tank 19.0, aft axle tank 18.2
F350 chassis cab 4X2 and 4X4 without E4OD trans. midship tank 18.2, aft axle tank 19.0
F350 chassis cab 4X2 and 4X4 with E4OD trans. midship tank 19.0, aft axle tank 19.0
F350 chassis cab 4X4 midship tank 19.0, aft axle tank 15.2
F-super duty motorhome chassis 75.0
⑪ Midship tank 29.0 on F250/350 with standard wheelbase
Midship tank 38.0 on F250/350 with long wheelbase
Aft axle tank 38.0 on standard chassis cab
Optional 19.0 tank in place of 36.0 tank on chassis cab

CAPACITIES — 1997–1999

91191C09

Year	Model	Engine Displacement Liters (cc)	Engine ID/VIN	Engine Oil with Filter (qts.)	Transmission (pts.) Manual	Transmission (pts.) Auto.	Transfer Case (pts.)	Drive Axle Front (pts.)	Drive Axle Rear (pts.)	Fuel Tank (gal.)	Cooling System (qts.)
1997	Expedition	4.6 (4588)	6/W	6.0	—	⑩	2.5	3.7	5.5	⑧	19.4
	Expedition	5.4 (5409)	L	7.0	—	⑩	2.5	3.7	5.5	⑧	19.4
	F-150	4.2 (4195)	2	6.0	5.6	⑩	2.5	3.7	5.5	⑧	17.3
	F-150	4.6 (4588)	6/W	6.0	5.6	⑩	2.5	3.7	5.5	⑧	19.4
	F-150	5.4 (5409)	L	7.0	5.6	⑩	2.5	3.7	5.5	⑧	19.4
	F-250	4.6 (4588)	6/W	6.0	5.6	⑩	2.5	3.7	5.5	⑧	19.4
	F-250	5.4 (5409)	L	7.0	5.6	⑩	2.5	3.7	5.5	⑧	19.4
	F-250HD	5.8 (5752)	H	6.0	②	⑩	②	6.0	6.0	⑧	19.4
	F-250HD	7.3 (7292)	F	14.0	②	⑩	②	6.0	6.0	⑧	23.0
	F-250HD	7.5 (7538)	H	6.0	②	⑩	②	6.0	6.0	⑧	18.0
	F-350	7.3 (7292)	F	14.0	②	⑩	②	6.0	7.5	⑧	23.0
	F-350	7.5 (7538)	H	6.0	②	⑩	②	6.0	7.5	⑧	18.0
	F-Super Duty	5.8 (5758)	R	6.0	②	⑩	②	6.0	7.5	⑧	23.0
	F-Super Duty	7.3 (7292)	F	14.0	②	⑩	②	6.0	7.5	⑧	18.0
	F-Super Duty	7.5 (7538)	G	6.0	②	⑩	②	6.0	7.5	⑧	⑧
1998	Expedition	4.6 (4588)	6/W	6.0	—	⑩	2.5	3.7	5.5	⑧	19.4
	Expedition	5.4 (5409)	L	7.0	—	⑩	2.5	3.7	5.5	⑧	19.4
	F-150	4.2 (4195)	2	6.0	5.6	⑩	2.5	3.7	5.5	⑧	17.3
	F-150	4.6 (4588)	6/W	6.0	5.6	⑩	2.5	3.7	5.5	⑧	19.4
	F-150	5.4 (5409)	L/M	7.0	5.6	⑩	2.5	3.7	5.5	⑧	19.4
	F-250	4.6 (4588)	6/W	6.0	5.6	⑩	2.5	3.7	5.5	⑧	19.4
	F-250	5.4 (5409)	L/M	7.0	5.6	⑩	2.5	3.7	5.5	⑧	19.4
	F-250HD	5.8 (5752)	H	6.0	②	⑩	②	6.0	6.0	⑧	19.4
	F-250HD	7.3 (7292)	F	14.0	②	⑩	②	6.0	6.0	⑧	23.0
	F-250HD	7.5 (7538)	L	6.0	②	⑩	②	6.0	6.0	⑧	18.0
	F-350	5.8 (5752)	R	6.0	②	⑩	②	6.0	7.5	⑧	23.0
	F-350	7.3 (7292)	G	14.0	②	⑩	②	6.0	7.5	⑧	18.0
	F-Super Duty	5.8 (5758)	R	6.0	②	⑩	②	6.0	7.5	⑧	23.0
	F-Super Duty	7.3 (7292)	F	14.0	②	⑩	②	6.0	7.5	⑧	18.0
	F-Super Duty	7.5 (7538)	G	6.0	②	⑩	②	6.0	7.5	⑧	⑧
1999	Expedition	4.6 (4588)	6/W	6.0	—	⑩	4.0	3.7	5.5	⑧	19.4
	Expedition	5.4 (5409)	L/A	7.0	—	⑩	4.0	3.7	5.5	⑧	19.4
	F-150	4.2 (4195)	2	6.0	5.6	⑩	4.0	3.7	5.5	⑧	17.3
	F-150	4.6 (4588)	6/W	6.0	5.6	⑩	4.0	3.7	5.5	⑧	19.4
	F-150	5.4 (5409)	L/M/Z/3	7.0	5.6	⑩	4.0	3.7	5.5	⑧	19.4
	F-250	4.6 (4588)	6/W	6.0	5.6	⑩	4.0	3.7	5.5	⑧	19.4
	F-250	5.4 (5409)	L/M/Z	7.0	5.6	⑩	4.0	3.7	5.5	⑧	19.4
	F-Super Duty ①	5.4 (5409)	L	7.0	②	⑩	⑦	6.0	6.0 ④	⑧	19.4
	F-Super Duty ①	6.8 (6802)	5	7.0	②	⑩	⑦	6.0	6.0 ④	⑧	19.4
	F-Super Duty ①	7.3 (7292)	F	14.0	②	⑩	⑦	6.0	6.0 ④	⑧	23.0
	Navigator	5.4 (5409)	L/A	7.0	—	②	4.0	3.7	5.5	30.0	19.4

ENGLISH TO METRIC CONVERSION: MASS (WEIGHT)

Current **mass** measurement is expressed in pounds and ounces (lbs. & ozs.). The metric unit of mass (or weight) is the kilogram (kg). Even although this table does not show conversion of masses (weights) larger than 15 lbs, it is easy to calculate larger units by following the data immediately below.

To convert ounces (oz.) to grams (g): multiply th number of ozs. by 28
To convert grams (g) to ounces (oz.): multiply the number of grams by .035

To convert pounds (lbs.) to kilograms (kg): multiply the number of lbs. by .45
To convert kilograms (kg) to pounds (lbs.): multiply the number of kilograms by 2.2

lbs	kg	lbs	kg	oz	kg	oz	kg
0.1	0.04	0.9	0.41	0.1	0.003	0.9	0.024
0.2	0.09	1	0.4	0.2	0.005	1	0.03
0.3	0.14	2	0.9	0.3	0.008	2	0.06
0.4	0.18	3	1.4	0.4	0.011	3	0.08
0.5	0.23	4	1.8	0.5	0.014	4	0.11
0.6	0.27	5	2.3	0.6	0.017	5	0.14
0.7	0.32	10	4.5	0.7	0.020	10	0.28
0.8	0.36	15	6.8	0.8	0.023	15	0.42

ENGLISH TO METRIC CONVERSION: TEMPERATURE

To convert Fahrenheit (°F) to Celsius (°C): take number of °F and subtract 32; multiply result by 5; divide result by 9

To convert Celsius (°C) to Fahrenheit (°F): take number of °C and multiply by 9; divide result by 5; add 32 to total

Fahrenheit (F)		Celsius (C)		Fahrenheit (F)		Celsius (C)		Fahrenheit (F)		Celsius (C)	
°F	°C	°C	°F	°F	°C	°C	°F	°F	°C	°C	°F
−40	−40	−38	−36.4	80	26.7	18	64.4	215	101.7	80	176
−35	−37.2	−36	−32.8	85	29.4	20	68	220	104.4	85	185
−30	−34.4	−34	−29.2	90	32.2	22	71.6	225	107.2	90	194
−25	−31.7	−32	−25.6	95	35.0	24	75.2	230	110.0	95	202
−20	−28.9	−30	−22	100	37.8	26	78.8	235	112.8	100	212
−15	−26.1	−28	−18.4	105	40.6	28	82.4	240	115.6	105	221
−10	−23.3	−26	−14.8	110	43.3	30	86	245	118.3	110	230
−5	−20.6	−24	−11.2	115	46.1	32	89.6	250	121.1	115	239
0	−17.8	−22	−7.6	120	48.9	34	93.2	255	123.9	120	248
1	−17.2	−20	−4	125	51.7	36	96.8	260	126.6	125	257
2	−16.7	−18	−0.4	130	54.4	38	100.4	265	129.4	130	266
3	−16.1	−16	3.2	135	57.2	40	104	270	132.2	135	275
4	−15.6	−14	6.8	140	60.0	42	107.6	275	135.0	140	284
5	−15.0	−12	10.4	145	62.8	44	112.2	280	137.8	145	293
10	−12.2	−10	14	150	65.6	46	114.8	285	140.6	150	302
15	−9.4	−8	17.6	155	68.3	48	118.4	290	143.3	155	311
20	−6.7	−6	21.2	160	71.1	50	122	295	146.1	160	320
25	−3.9	−4	24.8	165	73.9	52	125.6	300	148.9	165	329
30	−1.1	−2	28.4	170	76.7	54	129.2	305	151.7	170	338
35	1.7	0	32	175	79.4	56	132.8	310	154.4	175	347
40	4.4	2	35.6	180	82.2	58	136.4	315	157.2	180	356
45	7.2	4	39.2	185	85.0	60	140	320	160.0	185	365
50	10.0	6	42.8	190	87.8	62	143.6	325	162.8	190	374
55	12.8	8	46.4	195	90.6	64	147.2	330	165.6	195	383
60	15.6	10	50	200	93.3	66	150.8	335	168.3	200	392
65	18.3	12	53.6	205	96.1	68	154.4	340	171.1	205	401
70	21.1	14	57.2	210	98.9	70	158	345	173.9	210	410
75	23.9	16	60.8	212	100.0	75	167	350	176.7	215	414

TCCS1C01

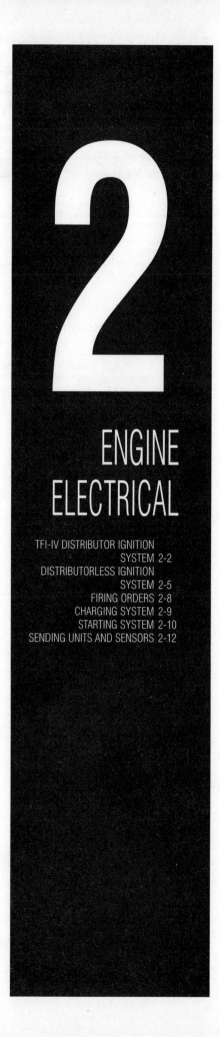

2

ENGINE
ELECTRICAL

TFI-IV DISTRIBUTOR IGNITION SYSTEM

➡For information on understanding electricity and troubleshooting electrical circuits, please refer to Section 6 of this manual.

General Information

♦ See Figure 1

The Thick Film Integrated (TFI-IV) ignition system uses a camshaft driven distributor with no centrifugal or vacuum advance. The distributor has a diecast base, incorporating a Hall effect stator assembly. The TFI-IV system module is mounted on the distributor base, it has 6 pins and uses an E-Core ignition coil, named after the shape of the laminations making up the core.

The TFI-IV module supplies voltage to the Profile Ignition Pick-up (PIP) sensor, which sends the crankshaft position information to the TFI-IV module. The TFI-IV module then sends this information to the EEC-IV module, which determines the spark timing and sends an electronic signal to the TFI-IV ignition module to turn off the coil and produce a spark to fire the spark plug.

The operation of the universal distributor is accomplished through the Hall effect stator assembly, causing the ignition coil to be switched off and on by the EEC-IV computer and TFI-IV modules. The vane switch is an encapsulated package consisting of a Hall sensor on one side and a permanent magnet on the other side.

A rotary vane cup, made of ferrous metal, is used to trigger the Hall effect switch. When the window of the vane cup is between the magnet and the Hall effect device, a magnetic flux field is completed from the magnet through the Hall effect device back to the magnet. As the vane passes through the opening, the flux lines are shunted through the vane and back to the magnet. A voltage is produced while the vane passes through the opening. When the vane clears the opening, the window causes the signal to go to 0 volts. The signal is then used

by the EEC-IV system for crankshaft position sensing and the computation of the desired spark advance based on the engine demand and calibration. The voltage distribution is accomplished through a conventional rotor, cap and ignition wires.

Diagnosis and Testing

SECONDARY SPARK TEST

♦ See Figures 2, 3, 4 and 5

The best way to perform this procedure is to use a spark tester (available at most automotive parts stores). Three types of spark testers are commonly available. The Neon Bulb type is connected to the spark plug wire and flashes with each ignition pulse. The Air Gap type must be adjusted to the individual spark plug gap specified for the engine. The last type of spark plug tester looks like a spark plug with a grounding clip on the side, but there is no side electrode for the spark to jump to. The last two types of testers allows the user to not only detect the presence of spark, but also the intensity (orange/yellow is weak, blue is strong).

1. Disconnect a spark plug wire at the spark plug end.
2. Connect the plug wire to the spark tester and ground the tester to an appropriate location on the engine.
3. Crank the engine and check for spark at the tester.
4. If spark exists at the tester, the ignition system is functioning properly.
5. If spark does not exist at the spark plug wire, perform diagnosis of the ignition system using individual component diagnosis procedures.

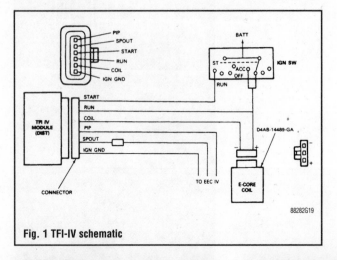

Fig. 1 TFI-IV schematic

Fig. 2 This spark tester looks just like a spark plug, attach the clip to ground and crank the engine to check for spark

Fig. 3 This spark tester has an adjustable air-gap for measuring spark strength and testing different voltage ignition systems

Fig. 4 Attach the clip to ground and crank the engine to check for spark

Fig. 5 This spark tester is the easiest to use just place it on a plug wire and the spark voltage is detected and the bulb on the top will flash with each pulse

CYLINDER DROP TEST

♦ See Figures 6, 7 and 8

The cylinder drop test is performed when an engine misfire is evident. This test helps determine which cylinder is not contributing the proper power. The easiest way to perform this test is to remove the plug wires one at a time from the cylinders with the engine running.

1. Place the transmission in **P**, engage the emergency brake, and start the engine and let it idle.
2. Using a spark plug wire removing tool, preferably, the plier type, carefully remove the boot from one of the cylinders.

❈❈ WARNING

Make sure your body is free from touching any part of the car which is metal. The secondary voltage in the ignition system is high and although it cannot kill you, it will shock you and it does hurt.

3. The engine will sputter, run worse, and possibly nearly stall. If this happens reinstall the plug wire and move to the next cylinder. If the engine runs no differently, or the difference is minimal, shut the engine off and inspect the spark plug wire, spark plug, and if necessary, perform component diagnostics as covered in this section. Perform the test on all cylinders to verify the which cylinders are suspect.

Adjustments

The only adjustment available on the TFI-IV system is the timing. Refer to Section 1 for Timing inspection and adjustment.

Ignition Coil

TESTING

Primary Coil

♦ See Figures 9, 10 and 11

The first check of the primary ignition coil is to verify that there is battery voltage at the **BATT** terminal on the coil. A DVOM is recommended to test for voltage. Turn the ignition switch to the **RUN** position and connect the negative lead of the DVOM to a ground or the negative post/cable clamp on the battery. Connect the other lead of the DVOM to the **BATT** terminal on the coil. The voltage measured should be within 1 volt of the battery voltage as measure across the posts of the battery.

After verifying there is battery voltage present, the next check is to verify the operation of the coil primary ground which is received at the coil from the ICM (Ignition Control Module). This check is accomplished using a test lamp and connecting the lead of the test lamp to the ground or the battery negative post/cable clamp. Connect the test lamp to the ground side of the coil (the connection opposite the **BATT** terminal on the coil on the other side of the coil tower) and crank the engine. The light should blink on and off repeatedly as long as the engine cranks or runs. If the light does not blink the problem is either in the ICM or the **PIP** signal generated by the sensor inside the distributor.

The final check of the primary coil is to check the resistance of the coil. This is accomplished by using a DVOM and probing the **BATT** terminal and the coil ground terminal. Measure the resistance between the two terminals. If the resistance is between 0.3 and 1.0 ohm, the primary ignition coil is within specifications. If the reading differs from this specification, replace the coil and retest.

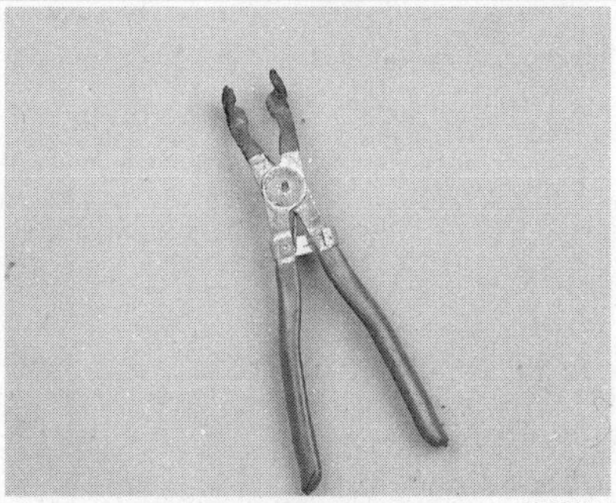

91052P14

Fig. 6 These pliers are insulated and help protect the user from shock as well as the plug wires from being damaged

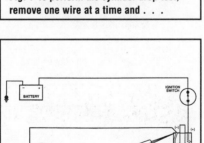

91052P15

Fig. 7 To perform the cylinder drop test, remove one wire at a time and . . .

91052P16

Fig. 8 . . . note the idle speed and idle characteristics of the engine. The cylinder(s) with the least drop is the non-contributing cylinder(s)

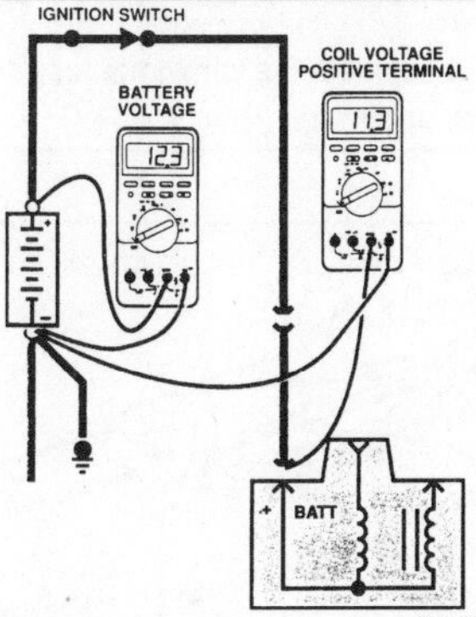

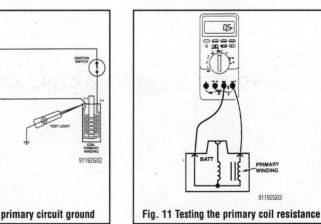

91192G01

Fig. 9 Testing the coil supply voltage

91192G02

Fig. 10 Testing the primary circuit ground

91192G03

Fig. 11 Testing the primary coil resistance

Secondary Windings

◗ **See Figure 12**

The coil secondary resistance is the final check of the ignition coil. Use a DVOM to measure the resistance between the **BATT** terminal to the high voltage terminal of the ignition coil. If the reading is between 6,500–11,500 ohms, the ignition coil is OK. If the reading is less than 6,500 or more than 11,500 ohms, replace the ignition coil. If the secondary windings are within specifications and the primary circuit also tests within specifications, inspect and test the spark plug wires and the spark plugs, refer to Section 1.

REMOVAL & INSTALLATION

◗ **See Figures 13, 14, 15 and 16**

1. Pulling on the connector boot, disconnect the high tension lead at the coil.
2. Disconnect the wiring at the ignition coil.
3. Remove the ignition coil-to-bracket attaching screws, then remove the coil.
To install:
4. Install the coil, tightening the screws to 25–35 inch lbs. (3–4 Nm).
5. Connect the ignition coil wiring harness and the high tension lead.

Ignition Module

REMOVAL & INSTALLATION

◗ **See Figure 17**

➡ **The ignition module is located on the driver's side fender apron.**

1. Disconnect the negative battery cable.
2. Detach the module harness connector.
3. Remove the heat sink-to-fender retaining screws and remove the heat sink and module from the vehicle.

4. Remove the TFI module-to-heat sink retaining screws and remove the module from the heat sink.
To install:
5. Coat the TFI module baseplate with a thin layer of dielectric grease (FD7AZ–19A331–A or its equivalent).
6. Place the TFI module on the heat sink.
7. Tighten the TFI module-to-heat sink retaining screws to 11–16 inch lbs. (1.2–1.8 Nm).
8. Install the heat sink onto the fender and tighten the heat sink-to-fender retaining screws to 80–124 inch lbs. (9–14 Nm).
9. Attach the module harness connector.
10. Connect the negative battery cable.

Distributor

REMOVAL

◗ **See Figures 18 and 19**

1. Disengage the primary wiring connector from the distributor.
2. Mark the position of the cap's No. 1 terminal on the distributor base.
3. Unclip and remove the cap. Remove the adapter.
4. Remove the rotor.
5. Remove the TFI connector.
6. Matchmark the distributor base and engine for installation reference.
7. Remove the hold-down bolt and lift out the distributor.

INSTALLATION

Timing Not Disturbed

1. Visually inspect the distributor. The O-ring should fit tightly onto the housing and be free of cuts. The drive gear should be free of nicks, cracks or

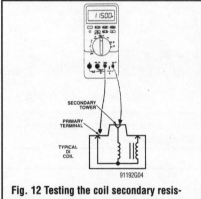

Fig. 12 Testing the coil secondary resistance

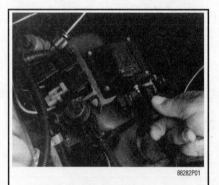

Fig. 13 Disengage the high tension wire by pulling on the connector boot

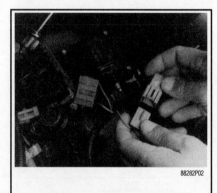

Fig. 14 Separate the wiring harness connection at the coil

Fig. 15 Unscrew the coil from its bracket mount

Fig. 16 Remove the coil from the engine

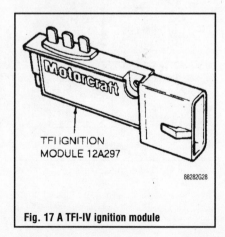

Fig. 17 A TFI-IV ignition module

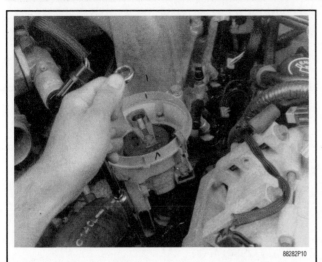

Fig. 18 Remove the hold-down bolt to the distributor—fuel injected engine shown

Fig. 19 Remove the distributor from the engine

excessive wear. The distributor shaft should rotate freely, without any binding.

2. Lubricate the distributor gear teeth with a coating of engine assembly lubricant, such as Ford D9AZ-19579-D, or with fresh motor oil meeting Ford specification ESR-M99C80-A.

3. Align the locating boss and fully seat the distributor rotor on the distributor shaft, if removed.

4. Rotate the distributor shaft so that the distributor rotor blade points toward the marked position on the distributor base adapter.

5. Install the distributor assembly into the engine block with a slight side-to-side twist.

➡ If the vane and vane switch assembly cannot be kept on the leading edge after installation, remove the distributor from the cylinder block by pulling upward enough for the distributor gear to disengage the distributor gear from the camshaft gear. Rotate the distributor rotor enough so that the gear will align on the next tooth of the camshaft gear.

6. Install the distributor hold-down clamp and bolt; leave it snug.

7. Position the adapter base in place, then install the attaching bolts.

8. Attach the electrical connector to the distributor.

9. Install the distributor cap. If the spark plug wires were removed from the distributor cap, install them in their proper position, as marked during the removal procedure.

10. Connect the negative battery cable. Check the initial timing according to the proper procedure.

11. Adjust the timing, as necessary, then tighten the distributor hold-down bolt to 17–25 ft. lbs. (23–34 Nm).

Timing Disturbed

1. Disconnect the No. 1 spark plug wire and remove the No. 1 spark plug.

2. Place a finger over the spark plug hole and crank the engine slowly until compression is felt.

3. Align the TDC mark on the crankshaft pulley with the pointer on the timing cover. This places the No. 1 cylinder at TDC on the compression stroke.

4. Turn the distributor shaft until the rotor points to the No. 1 spark plug tower on the cap.

5. Install the distributor assembly into the engine block with a slight side-to-side twist.

➡ If the vane and vane switch assembly cannot be kept on the leading edge after installation, remove the distributor from the cylinder block by pulling upward enough for the distributor gear to disengage the distributor gear from the camshaft gear. Rotate the distributor rotor enough so that the gear will align on the next tooth of the camshaft gear.

6. Install the distributor hold-down clamp and bolt; leave it snug.

7. Position the adapter base in place, then install the attaching bolts.

8. Attach the electrical connector to the distributor.

9. Install the distributor cap. If the spark plug wires were removed from the distributor cap, install them in their proper position, as marked during the removal procedure.

10. Connect the negative battery cable.

11. Check the initial timing according to the proper procedure.

12. Adjust the timing, as necessary, then tighten the distributor hold-down bolt to 17–25 ft. lbs. (23–34 Nm).

Crankshaft Position Sensor

For procedures on the crankshaft position sensor, please refer to Section 4 in this manual.

DISTRIBUTORLESS IGNITION SYSTEM

General Information

The ignition system used on the 4.2L, 4.6L, 5.4L and 6.8L engine is an electronic distributorless ignition system known as the High Data Rate ignition system. These engines utilize what is known as an integrated ignition system in which the Powertrain Control Module (PCM) performs all the control functions and the Ignition control Module (ICM) is eliminated.

The integrated ignition system consists of the PCM, crankshaft position sensor (CKP), CKP trigger wheel, and a coil pack(s) on the 4.2L and 4.6L engines and individual coils known as "coil over plug" on the 5.4L and 6.8L engines. The system operates as follows: The CKP sensor produces a signal generated from the induced voltage created as the trigger wheel on the crankshaft or fly-wheel passes the sensor. This signal is received at the PCM as a Profile Ignition Pickup (PIP) signal. The PCM processes the PIP signal along with signals received from other sensors on engine speed, engine temperature, and engine load, and determines the correct ignition timing and grounds the proper ignition coils in the coil pack or the individual coils. When the ignition coil is grounded, an Ignition Diagnostic Monitor (IDM) signal is sent to the PCM. This signal provides the PCM with diagnostic information and confirms that the coil fired and is also used to operate the vehicle's tachometer (if equipped).

Diagnosis and Testing

Refer to Diagnosis and Testing under TFI-IV Distributor Ignition in this section.

Adjustments

Base timing for distributorless engines is set from the factory at 10 degrees BTDC and is not adjustable.

Ignition Coil Pack

TESTING

4.2L Engine

PRIMARY WINDING RESISTANCE

▶ **See Figure 20**

1. Turn the ignition **OFF**.
2. Disconnect the negative battery cable.
3. Disconnect the wiring harness from the ignition coil.
4. Check for dirt, corrosion or damage on the terminals and repair as necessary.
5. Measure coil primary resistance between ignition coil pin 4 (B+) and pins 1 (coil 1), 2 (coil 3) and 3 (coil 2).
6. Resistance should be 0.3–1.0 ohms. If resistance is out of specifications, replace the coil pack. If resistance is within specifications, proceed to secondary windings testing.

SECONDARY WINDING RESISTANCE

1. Measure coil secondary resistance between the corresponding spark plug wire towers on the coil.
   - Coil 1—cylinders 1 and 5
   - Coil 2—cylinders 3 and 4
   - Coil 3—cylinders 2 and 6
2. Resistance should be 12.8–13.1 kilohms. If secondary resistance is not within specification, replace the coil pack.

4.6L Engine

PRIMARY WINDING RESISTANCE

▶ **See Figure 21**

1. Turn the ignition **OFF**.
2. Disconnect the negative battery cable.
3. Disconnect the wiring harness from the ignition coil.
4. Check for dirt, corrosion or damage on the terminals and repair as necessary.
5. Measure coil primary resistance between ignition coil pin 2 (B+) and pins 1 (coil 2), 2 (coil 3) and 3 (coil 1).
6. Resistance should be 0.3–1.0 ohms. If resistance is out of specifications, replace the coil pack. If resistance is within specifications, proceed to secondary windings testing.

SECONDARY WINDING RESISTANCE

▶ **See Figure 22**

1. Measure coil secondary resistance between the corresponding spark plug wire towers on the coil.
   - Coil 1—cylinders 1 and 6
   - Coil 2—cylinders 3 and 5
   - Coil 3—cylinders 4 and 7
   - Coil 4—cylinders 2 and 8
2. Resistance should be 12.8–13.1 kilohms. If secondary resistance is not within specification, replace the coil pack.

5.4L and 6.8L Engines

1. Remove the suspect coil from the engine.
2. Measure across the pins of the coil.
3. Resistance should be between 4 and 10 kohms.
4. If resistance is out of range, replace the coil and retest.

REMOVAL & INSTALLATION

4.2L Engine

1. Disconnect the negative battery cable.
2. Disconnect the ignition coil and radio ignition interference capacitor electrical harness connectors.
3. Tag the ignition wires and note their location on the coil pack before removing. Remove the ignition wires by squeezing the locking tabs to release the coil boot retainers and twisting while pulling upward.
4. Remove the accelerator cable nut and bolt and remove the bracket. Position the bracket aside.
5. Remove 2 ignition coil retaining nuts and 1 stud bolt and remove the ignition coil.
6. If replacing the ignition coil, save the radio capacitor for installation on the new ignition coil.
   To install:
7. Place the ignition coil on the mounting bracket.
8. Install 2 ignition coil nuts and 1 stud bolt. Tighten to 84 inch lbs. (10 Nm).
9. Place the accelerator cable bracket and install the nut and bolt. Tighten to 84 inch lbs. (10 Nm).
10. Install the ignition wires to their proper terminals on the ignition coil. Apply silicone dielectric compound to the ignition wire boots prior to installation.
11. Connect the electrical harness connectors to the ignition coil and the radio ignition interference capacitor.
12. Connect the negative battery cable.
13. Road test the vehicle and check for proper engine operation.

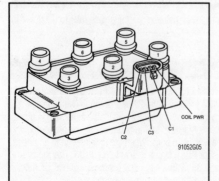

Fig. 20 4.2L engine coil pack pin location and coil towers

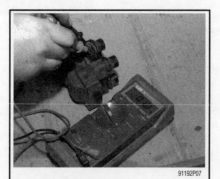

Fig. 21 Testing the primary ignition coil resistance—4.6L engine

Fig. 22 Testing the secondary ignition coil resistance—4.6L engine

Fig. 23 Remove the ignition wires from the coil pack by squeezing the retaining tabs and carefully lifting up

Fig. 24 Detach the connector for the coil pack

Fig. 25 Remove the four coil pack retaining screws and . . .

Fig. 26 . . . remove the coil pack from the bracket

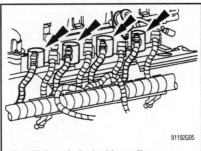

Fig. 27 Detach the ignition coil connector(s)

Fig. 28 Remove the bolt(s) retaining the coil(s) to the engine

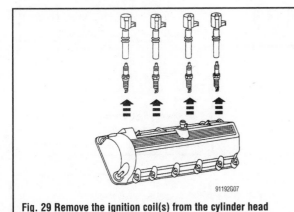

Fig. 29 Remove the ignition coil(s) from the cylinder head

4.6L Engine

▶ See Figures 23, 24, 25 and 26

➡Two ignition coil packs are used, one for each bank of cylinders. This procedure is for removing 1 ignition coil pack, but the procedure remains the same for either side.

1. Disconnect the negative battery cable.
2. Disconnect the ignition coil and radio ignition interference capacitor electrical harness connectors.
3. Tag the ignition wires and note their location on the coil pack before removing. Remove the ignition wires by squeezing the locking tabs to release the coil boot retainers and twisting while pulling upward.
4. Remove 4 ignition coil retaining screws and remove the ignition coil and radio capacitor.
5. If replacing the ignition coil, save the radio capacitor for installation on the new ignition coil.

To install:

6. Place the ignition coil and radio capacitor on the mounting bracket.
7. Install 4 retaining screws and tighten to 40–61 inch lbs. (5–7 Nm).

8. Install the ignition wires to their proper terminals on the ignition coil. Apply silicone dielectric compound to the ignition wire boots prior to installation.
9. Connect the electrical harness connectors to the ignition coil and the radio ignition interference capacitor.
10. Connect the negative battery cable.
11. Road test the vehicle and check for proper engine operation.

5.4L and 6.8L Engines

▶ See Figures 27, 28 and 29

➡The 5.4L and 6.8L engines have individual coils on each spark plug.

1. Disconnect the negative battery cable.
2. Detach the connector for the ignition coil.
3. Remove the retaining screw for the ignition coil.
4. Carefully grasp the ignition coil and gently remove it from the cylinder.

To install:

5. Apply dielectric grease D7AZ-19A331-A or equivalent to the inside of the coil boot that sits on the spark plug.
6. Gently push the coil onto the spark plug. An audible click can usually be heard.
7. Tighten the retaining screw to 40–62 inch lbs. (5–7 Nm).
8. Attach the connector for the ignition coil.
9. Connect the negative battery cable.

Ignition Module

REMOVAL & INSTALLATION

The ignition module is integrated into the PCM. For PCM removal and installation, refer to Section 4.

Crankshaft and Camshaft Position Sensors

For procedures on the position sensors, please refer to Section 4 in this manual.

FIRING ORDERS

▶ See Figures 30 thru 36

➡To avoid confusion, remove and tag the spark plug wires one at a time, for replacement.

If a distributor is not keyed for installation with only one orientation, it could have been removed previously and rewired. The resultant wiring would hold the correct firing order, but could change the relative placement of the plug towers in relation to the engine. For this reason it is imperative that you label all wires before disconnecting any of them. Also, before removal, compare the current wiring with the accompanying illustrations. If the current wiring does not match, make notes in your book to reflect how your engine is wired.

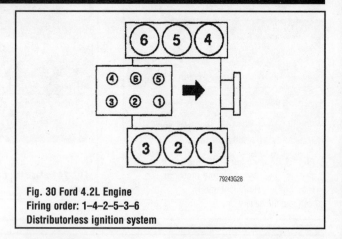

Fig. 30 Ford 4.2L Engine
Firing order: 1–4–2–5–3–6
Distributorless ignition system

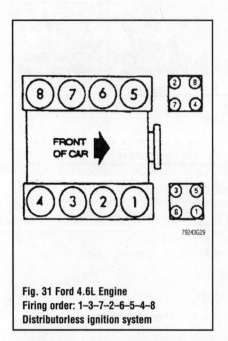

Fig. 31 Ford 4.6L Engine
Firing order: 1–3–7–2–6–5–4–8
Distributorless ignition system

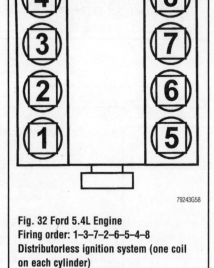

Fig. 32 Ford 5.4L Engine
Firing order: 1–3–7–2–6–5–4–8
Distributorless ignition system (one coil on each cylinder)

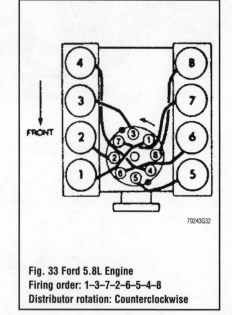

Fig. 33 Ford 5.8L Engine
Firing order: 1–3–7–2–6–5–4–8
Distributor rotation: Counterclockwise

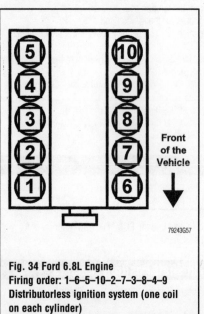

Fig. 34 Ford 6.8L Engine
Firing order: 1–6–5–10–2–7–3–8–4–9
Distributorless ignition system (one coil on each cylinder)

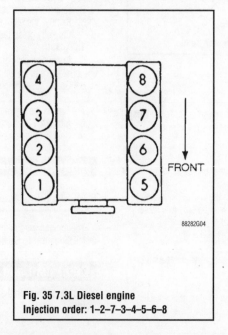

Fig. 35 7.3L Diesel engine
Injection order: 1–2–7–3–4–5–6–8

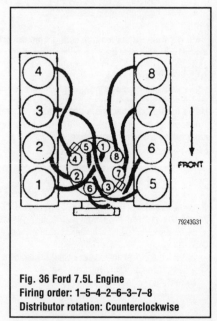

Fig. 36 Ford 7.5L Engine
Firing order: 1–5–4–2–6–3–7–8
Distributor rotation: Counterclockwise

CHARGING SYSTEM

General Information

The automobile charging system provides electrical power for operation of the vehicle's ignition and starting systems and all the electrical accessories. The battery serves as an electrical surge or storage tank, storing (in chemical form) the energy originally produced by the engine driven alternator. The system also provides a means of regulating generator output to protect the battery from being overcharged and to avoid excessive voltage to the accessories.

The storage battery is a chemical device incorporating parallel lead plates in a tank containing a sulfuric acid/water solution. Adjacent plates are slightly dissimilar, and the chemical reaction of the 2 dissimilar plates produces electrical energy when the battery is connected to a load such as the starter motor. The chemical reaction is reversible, so that when the generator is producing a voltage (electrical pressure) greater than that produced by the battery, electricity is forced into the battery, and the battery is returned to its fully charged state.

The vehicle's alternator is driven mechanically, by a belt(s) that is driven by the engine crankshaft. In an alternator, the field rotates while all the current produced passes only through the stator winding. The brushes bear against continuous slip rings rather than a commutator. This causes the current produced to periodically reverse the direction of its flow creating alternating current (A/C). Diodes (electrical one-way switches) block the flow of current from traveling in the wrong direction. A series of diodes is wired together to permit the alternating flow of the stator to be converted to a pulsating, but unidirectional flow at the alternator output. The alternator's field is wired in series with the voltage regulator.

The regulator consists of several circuits. Each circuit has a core, or magnetic coil of wire, which operates a switch. Each switch is connected to ground through one or more resistors. The coil of wire responds directly to system voltage. When the voltage reaches the required level, the magnetic field created by the winding of wire closes the switch and inserts a resistance into the generator field circuit, thus reducing the output. The contacts of the switch cycle open and close many times each second to precisely control voltage.

Alternator Precautions

Several precautions must be observed when performing work on alternator equipment.

- If the battery is removed for any reason, make sure that it is reconnected with the correct polarity. Reversing the battery connections may result in damage to the one-way rectifiers.
- Never operate the alternator with the main circuit broken. Make sure that the battery, alternator, and regulator leads are not disconnected while the engine is running.
- Never attempt to polarize an alternator.
- When charging a battery that is installed in the vehicle, disconnect the negative battery cable.
- When utilizing a booster battery as a starting aid, always connect it in parallel; negative to negative, and positive to positive.
- When arc (electric) welding is to be performed on any part of the vehicle, disconnect the negative battery cable and alternator leads.
- Never unplug the PCM while the engine is running or with the ignition in the **ON** position. Severe and expensive damage may result within the solid state equipment.

Alternator

TESTING

Voltage Test

1. Make sure the engine is **OFF**, and turn the headlights on for 15–20 seconds to remove any surface charge from the battery.
2. Using a DVOM set to volts DC, probe across the battery terminals.
3. Measure the battery voltage.
4. Write down the voltage reading and proceed to the next test.

No-Load Test

1. Connect a tachometer to the engine.

✴✳✴ CAUTION

Ensure that the transmission is in PARK and the emergency brake is set. Blocking a wheel is optional and an added safety measure.

2. Turn off all electrical loads (radio, blower motor, wipers, etc.)
3. Start the engine and increase engine speed to approximately 1500 rpm.
4. Measure the voltage reading at the battery with the engine holding a steady 1500 rpm. Voltage should have raised at least 0.5 volts, but no more than 2.5 volts.
5. If the voltage does not go up more than 0.5 volts, the alternator is not charging. If the voltage goes up more than 2.5 volts, the alternator is overcharging.

➡**Usually under and overcharging is caused by a defective alternator, or its related parts (regulator), and replacement will fix the problem; however, faulty wiring and other problems can cause the charging system to malfunction. Further testing, which is not covered by this book, will reveal the exact component failure. Many automotive parts stores have alternator bench testers available for use by customers. An alternator bench test is the most definitive way to determine the condition of your alternator.**

6. If the voltage is within specifications, proceed to the next test.

Load Test

1. With the engine running, turn on the blower motor and the high beams (or other electrical accessories to place a load on the charging system).
2. Increase and hold engine speed to 2000 rpm.
3. Measure the voltage reading at the battery.
4. The voltage should increase at least 0.5 volts from the voltage test. If the voltage does not meet specifications, the charging system is malfunctioning.

➡**Usually under and overcharging is caused by a defective alternator, or its related parts (regulator), and replacement will fix the problem; however, faulty wiring and other problems can cause the charging system to malfunction. Further testing, which is not covered by this book, will reveal the exact component failure. Many automotive parts stores have alternator bench testers available for use by customers. An alternator bench test is the most definitive way to determine the condition of your alternator.**

REMOVAL & INSTALLATION

4.2L Engine

1. Disconnect the negative battery cable.
2. Disconnect 2 alternator and voltage regulator electrical harness connectors at the alternator. To disconnect push-on type terminals, depress the lock tab and pull straight off.
3. Remove the positive battery cable nut and remove the positive battery cable at the alternator.
4. Rotate the drive belt tensioner away from the drive belt and remove the drive belt from the alternator pulley.
5. Remove 3 alternator retaining bolts and remove the alternator.
   To install:
6. Place the alternator on the engine and install 3 alternator retaining bolts. Tighten the bolts to 18–22 ft. lbs. (20–30 Nm).
7. Rotate the drive belt tensioner away from the drive belt and install the drive belt on the alternator pulley.
8. Connect 2 alternator and voltage regulator electrical harness connectors.
9. Connect the positive battery cable to the alternator and install the nut and washer. Tighten the nut to 84 inch lbs. (10 Nm).
10. Connect the negative battery cable.
11. Start the engine and check for proper charging system operation.

Fig. 37 Detach the connectors from the alternator

Fig. 38 Remove the nut and the battery cable from the post on the rear of the

Fig. 39 Remove the 2 front alternator mounting bolts

Fig. 40 Remove the alternator from the engine by carefully lifting it up and . . .

Fig. 41 . . . out of the engine compartment

4.6L, 5.4L and 6.8L Engines

▶ **See Figures 37, 38, 39, 40 and 41**

1. Disconnect the negative battery cable.
2. Rotate the drive belt tensioner away from the drive belt and remove the drive belt from the alternator pulley.
3. Detach the electrical harness connectors at the alternator assembly.
4. Disconnect the positive battery cable and remove the nut and washer.
5. Remove 2 front alternator bolts.
6. Remove the rear alternator support bracket retaining bolts and the support bracket.
7. Remove the alternator from the vehicle.

To install:

8. Place the alternator in position and loosely install 2 front alternator retaining bolts.
9. Install the alternator bracket and 3 alternator bracket bolts. Tighten to 84 inch lbs. (10 Nm).
10. Tighten 2 front alternator retaining bolts to 19 ft. lbs. (26 Nm).
11. Connect 2 electrical harness connectors to the alternator assembly.

12. Connect the positive battery cable and install the nut and washer. Tighten the nut to 72 inch lbs. (8 Nm).
13. Rotate the drive belt tensioner away from the drive belt and install the drive belt on the alternator pulley.
14. Connect the negative battery cable.
15. Start the engine and check for proper charging system operation.

5.8L and 7.5L Gasoline Engines and 7.3L Diesel Engine

1. Disconnect the battery ground cable.
2. Label and detach the connectors from the alternator.
3. Release the tensioner and remove the drive belt from the alternator pulley.
4. Remove the alternator retaining bolts.
5. Remove the alternator from the vehicle.

To install:

6. Position the alternator and install the retaining bolts. Tighten the retaining bolts to 15–21 ft. lbs. (21–29 Nm).
7. Install the drive belt.
8. Attach the alternator connectors.
9. Connect the battery ground cable.

STARTING SYSTEM

General Information

The starting system includes the battery, starter motor, solenoid, ignition switch, circuit protection and wiring connecting the components. An inhibitor switch located in the Transmission Range (TR) sensor is included in the starting system to prevent the vehicle from being started with the vehicle in gear.

When the ignition key is turned to the **START** position, current flows and energizes the starter's solenoid coil. The solenoid plunger and clutch shift lever are activated and the clutch pinion engages the ring gear on the flywheel. The switch contacts close and the starter cranks the engine until it starts.

To prevent damage caused by excessive starter armature rotation when the engine starts, the starter incorporates an over-running clutch in the pinion gear.

Starter

TESTING

Voltage Drop Test

➡The battery must be in good condition and fully charged prior to performing this test.

1. Disable the ignition system. Verify that the vehicle will not start.
2. Connect a voltmeter between the positive terminal of the battery and the starter **B+** circuit.
3. Turn the ignition key to the **START** position and note the voltage on the meter.
4. If voltage reads 0.5 volts or more, there is high resistance in the starter cables or the cable ground, repair as necessary. If the voltage reading is ok proceed to the next step.
5. Connect a voltmeter between the positive terminal of the battery and the starter **M** circuit.
6. Turn the ignition key to the **START** position and note the voltage on the meter.
7. If voltage reads 0.5 volts or more, there is high resistance in the starter. Repair or replace the starter as necessary.

➡Many automotive parts stores have starter bench testers available for use by customers. A starter bench test is the most definitive way to determine the condition of your starter.

REMOVAL & INSTALLATION

4.2L, 4.6L, 5.4L and 6.8L Engines

♦ See Figures 42, 43, 44, 45 and 46

1. Disconnect the negative battery cable.
2. Raise and safely support the vehicle.

3. Remove the starter terminal cover.
4. Remove the terminal nut and separate the battery starter cable from the starter motor.
5. Disconnect the solenoid **S** terminal connector, if equipped with a starter mounted solenoid.

➡To disconnect the hard-shell connector from the solenoid S terminal, grasp the plastic shell and pull off; do not pull on the wire. Pull straight off to prevent damage to the connector and S terminal.

6. Remove the starter motor retaining bolts.
7. Remove the starter motor from the vehicle.
To install:
8. Place the starter motor in position and install the starter motor retaining bolts. Tighten the bolts to 15–20 ft. lbs. (20–27 Nm).
9. Install the battery starter cable and a terminal nut to the starter motor. Tighten the terminal nuts to 79 inch lbs. (9 Nm).
10. Connect the solenoid **S** terminal connector, if equipped with a starter mounted solenoid.
11. Install the starter solenoid safety cap, if equipped.
12. Lower the vehicle.
13. Connect the negative battery cable.
14. Start the engine several times to check starter motor operation.

5.8L and 7.5L Engines

1. Disconnect the negative battery cable.
2. Raise and safely support the vehicle securely on jackstands.
3. Remove the starter cable heat shield(s).
4. Disconnect the wiring at the starter.
5. Remove the starter mounting bolts and remove the starter.
To install:
6. Install the starter and tighten the retaining bolts 15–20 ft. lbs. (20–27 Nm).
7. Attach the wiring and install the heat shield(s).
8. Lower the vehicle and connect the negative battery cable.
9. Check for proper operation.

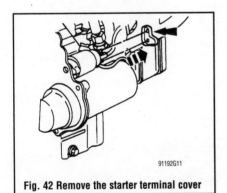

Fig. 42 Remove the starter terminal cover

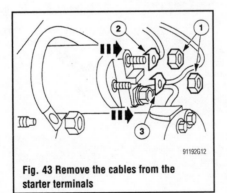

Fig. 43 Remove the cables from the starter terminals

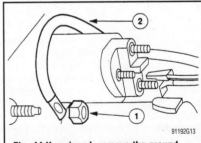

Fig. 44 If equipped, remove the ground cable retaining nut from the stud and remove the ground cable

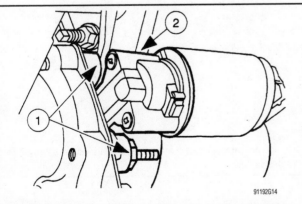

Fig. 45 Remove the two starter retaining bolts—4.2L engine shown

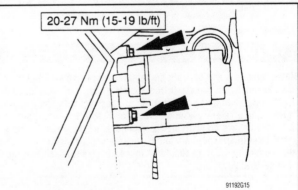

Fig. 46 Remove the two starter retaining bolts—4.6L engine shown, 5.4L and 6.8L engines similar

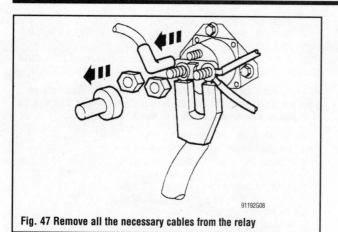

Fig. 47 Remove all the necessary cables from the relay

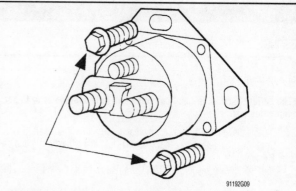

Fig. 48 Remove the two relay retaining bolts and remove the relay from the vehicle

7.3L Diesel Engine

1. Disconnect the negative battery cable.
2. Raise the front of the truck and install jackstands beneath the frame. Firmly apply the parking brake and place blocks in back of the rear wheels.
3. Label and detach the wiring from the starter motor terminals.
4. Loosen the starter motor retaining bolts.
5. Remove the starter retaining bolts while supporting the starter motor and remove the starter from the vehicle.

To install:

6. The installation is the reverse of removal. Tighten the starter retaining bolts to 15–20 ft. lbs. (20–27 Nm)

RELAY REPLACEMENT

♦ **See Figures 47 and 48**

1. Disconnect the negative battery cable from the battery.
2. Remove the nut securing the positive battery cable to the relay.
3. Remove the positive cable and any other wiring under that cable.
4. Label and remove the push-on wires from the front of the relay.
5. Remove the nut and disconnect the cable from the starter side of the relay.
6. Remove the relay mounting bolts and remove the relay.

To install:

7. Install the relay and mounting bolts. Tighten the mounting bolts until snug.
8. Attach all wiring to the relay.
9. Connect the negative battery cable.

SENDING UNITS AND SENSORS

➡This section describes the operating principles of sending units, warning lights and gauges. Sensors which provide information to the Electronic Control Module (ECM) are covered in Section 4 of this manual.

Instrument panels contain a number of indicating devices (gauges and warning lights). These devices are composed of two separate components. One is the sending unit, mounted on the engine or other remote part of the vehicle, and the other is the actual gauge or light in the instrument panel.

Several types of sending units exist, however most can be characterized as being either a pressure type or a resistance type. Pressure type sending units convert liquid pressure into an electrical signal which is sent to the gauge. Resistance type sending units are most often used to measure temperature and use variable resistance to control the current flow back to the indicating device. Both types of sending units are connected in series by a wire to the battery (through the ignition switch). When the ignition is turned **ON**, current flows from the battery through the indicating device and on to the sending unit.

Temperature Gauge Sending Unit

The sending unit is located in the front section of the intake manifold in the vicinity of the thermostat.

✳✳ CAUTION

Never open, service or drain the radiator or cooling system when hot; serious burns can occur from the steam and hot coolant. Also, when draining engine coolant, keep in mind that cats and dogs are attracted to ethylene glycol antifreeze and could drink any that is left in an uncovered container or in puddles on the ground. This will prove fatal in sufficient quantities. Always drain coolant into a sealable container. Coolant should be reused unless it is contaminated or is several years old.

TESTING

♦ **See Figures 49 and 50**

1. Check the appropriate fuse before attempting any other diagnostics.
2. Disconnect the sending unit electrical harness.
3. Remove the radiator cap and place a mechanic's thermometer in the coolant.
4. Using an ohmmeter, check the resistance between the sending unit terminals.

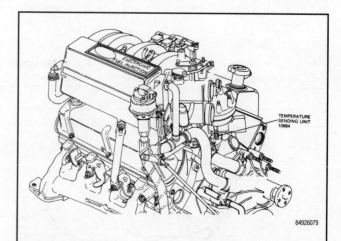

Fig. 49 Coolant temperature sending unit—5.8L engine shown, 7.5L engine similar

Fig. 50 The temperature gauge sending unit is located in the front section of the intake manifold, just to the right of the alternator—4.6L engine, 5.4L and 6.8L similar

Fig. 51 Detach the connector for the temperature sending unit

Fig. 52 Using a suitable size socket and drive tool, remove the sending unit from the intake manifold

5. Resistance should be high (74 ohms) with engine coolant cold and low (9.7 ohms) with engine coolant hot.

➡️It is best to check resistance with the engine cool, then start the engine and watch the resistance change as the engine warms.

6. If resistance does not drop as engine temperature rises, the sending unit is faulty.

REMOVAL & INSTALLATION

▶ **See Figures 51 and 52**

1. Disconnect the negative battery cable.
2. Detach the sending unit electrical push on connector.
3. Drain the engine coolant below the level of the sending unit.
4. Remove the sending unit from the engine using the proper size socket (Usually an 11⁄16 inch or 17mm).

To install:

5. Coat the new sending unit with Teflon® tape or electrically conductive sealer.
6. Install the sending unit and tighten to 10–14 ft. lbs. (13–20 Nm).
7. Attach the sending unit's electrical connector.
8. Fill the engine with coolant.
9. Start the engine, allow it to reach operating temperature ,bleed the cooling system and check for leaks.
10. Check for proper sending unit operation.

Oil Pressure Sensor

TESTING

1. Test and verify the engine oil pressure. See Section 3 for more information. If no or insufficient pressure exists, oil pressure problem exists and gauge and sensor are operational, repair oil pressure problem.

2. Check the appropriate fuse before attempting any other diagnostics.
3. Unplug the sensor electrical harness.
4. Using an ohmmeter, check continuity between the sensor terminals.
5. With the engine stopped, continuity should not exist.

➡️The switch inside the oil pressure sensor opens at 6 psi or less of pressure.

6. With the engine running, continuity should exist.
7. If continuity does not exist as stated, the sensor is faulty.

REMOVAL & INSTALLATION

▶ **See Figures 53, 54 and 55**

✳️✳️ CAUTION

The EPA warns that prolonged contact with used engine oil may cause a number of skin disorders, including cancer! You should make every effort to minimize your exposure to used engine oil. Protective gloves should be worn when changing the oil. Wash your hands and any other exposed skin areas as soon as possible after exposure to used engine oil. Soap and water, or waterless hand cleaner should be used.

1. Disconnect the sensor electrical harness.
2. Unfasten and remove the sensor from the engine.

To install:

3. Coat the new sensor with Teflon® tape or electrically conductive sealer.
4. Install the sensor and tighten to 11–15 ft. lbs. (15–20 Nm).
5. Attach the sensor's electrical connector.
6. Start the engine, allow it to reach operating temperature and check for leaks.
7. Check for proper sensor operation.

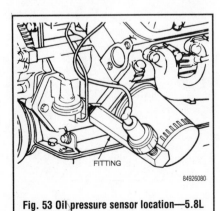

Fig. 53 Oil pressure sensor location—5.8L engines

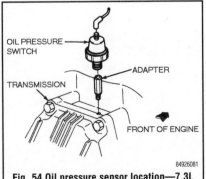

Fig. 54 Oil pressure sensor location—7.3L diesel and 7.5L gasoline engines (adapter is for 7.3L only)

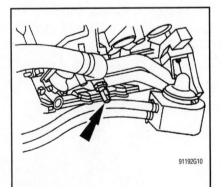

Fig. 55 Oil pressure sensor location—4.6L engine, 5.4L and 6.8L similar

Fuel Level Sending Unit

The fuel level sending unit is located on the fuel pump inside the fuel tank.

TESTING

✳ CAUTION

Observe all applicable safety precautions when working around fuel. Whenever servicing the fuel system, always work in a well ventilated area. Do not allow fuel spray or vapors to come in contact with a spark or open flame. Keep a dry chemical fire extinguisher near the work area. Always keep fuel in a container specifically designed for fuel storage; also, always properly seal fuel containers to avoid the possibility of fire or explosion.

➥**An assistant is recommended and extremely helpful for this testing procedure.**

1. Check the appropriate fuse before attempting any other diagnostics.
2. Raise and support the vehicle.
3. Unplug the fuel level sending unit connector from the top of the fuel tank.
4. Insert the leads of the Rotunda gauge tester number 021-00055 or equivalent into the fuel level sender connector and set the scale to 145 ohms.

➥**Although a gauge tester is recommended for the testing of the fuel level sending unit, you can purchase resistors of the equivalent value at any electrical store and form your own tool.**

5. Turn the ignition to the **ON** position and verify that the fuel gauge reads **EMPTY**. If the gauge reads **EMPTY**, proceed to the next step, if it does not, repair gauge and/or wiring as necessary.

➥**It may take as long as 60 seconds for the gauge to move.**

6. Slowly turn the resistance level on the gauge tester to 22 ohms and verify that the gauge reading moves to **FULL**. If the gauges moves to **FULL**, the gauge and wiring are operating as designed, most likely the sending unit is faulty, repair as necessary. If the gauge does not read **FULL**, repair gauge and/or wiring as necessary.

An alternative method requiring no special testers is to remove the fuel pump from the tank. Connect the wiring to the pump and sending unit and manually operate the sending unit arm while an assistant observes the gauge.

REMOVAL & INSTALLATION

The fuel level sending unit is attached to the fuel pump. Refer to Section 5 and the fuel pump removal and installation procedure.

3

ENGINE
AND
ENGINE
OVERHAUL

ENGINE MECHANICAL

4.2L ENGINE MECHANICAL SPECIFICATIONS

Description	English Specifications	Metric Specifications
General Information		
Type	Liquid Cooled, Overhead Valve	
Displacement	256 cid	
Number of cylinders	6	
Bore	3.81 in.	96.83mm
Stroke	3.74 in.	95.0mm
Compression ratio	9.3:1	
Firing order	1-4-2-5-3-6	
Oil Pressure	40-125 psi @ 2500 RPM (engine hot)	
Cylinder Head and Valve Train		
Valve guide bore diameter	0.3443-0.3433 in.	8.745-8.720
Valve seat width (intake and exhaust)	0.06-0.08 in.	1.5-2.0mm
Valve seat angle	44.75 degrees	
Valve seat run-out	0.003 in.	0.076mm
Valve stem-to-guide clearance		
Intake	0.00079-0.00272 in.	0.020-0.069mm
Exhaust	0.00177-0.00374 in.	0.045-0.095mm
Valve head diameter		
Intake	1.86 in.	47.27mm
Exhaust	1.46 in.	37.1mm
Valve face run-out limit	0.001 in.	0.05mm
Valve face angle	45.675 degrees	
Valve stem diameter		
Intake	0.3423-0.3415 in.	8.694-8.674mm
Exhaust	0.3418-0.3410 in.	8.682-8.662mm
Free length		
Intake	1.99 in.	50.5mm
Exhaust	1.99 in.	50.5mm
Valve spring assembled length	1.566-1.637 in.	39.8-41.6mm
Camshaft		
Lobe lift		
Intake	0.245 in.	6.22mm
Exhaust	0.259 in.	6.57mm
Lobe wear limit (all)	0.005 in.	0.127mm
End-play wear limit	0.001-0.006 in.	0.025-0.150mm
Bearing-to-journal clearance	0.0001-0.0006 in.	0.025-0.150mm
Journal diameter	2.0515-2.0505 in.	52.108-52.082mm
Run-out	0.002 in.	0.05mm
Out-of-round limit	0.001 in.	0.025mm
Cylinder Block		
Cylinder bore diameter		
Standard	3.81 in.	96.80mm
Out-of-round	0.002 in.	0.050mm
Taper limit	0.002 in.	0.050mm
Cylinder head gasket surface flatness per 0.003 in. (0.08mm)	6.0 in.	152.00mm
Crankshaft		
Main bearing journal diameter (standard)	2.5190-2.5198 in.	62.968-62.992mm
Main bearing journal diameter (0.010 in. (0.25mm) undersize)	2.5182-2.5190 in.	62.963-62.983mm
Main bearing journal taper limit	0.0006 in.	0.016mm
Main bearing journal out-of-round limit	0.0012 in.	0.3mm
Main bearing journal run-out limit	0.002 in.	0.05mm
Crankshaft free end-play	0.00003-0.00787 in.	0.007-0.20mm
Connecting Rod		
Connecting rod bearing journal diameter (standard)	2.3103-2.3111 in.	58.682-58.702mm
Connecting rod bearing journal diameter (0.010 in. (0.25mm) undersize)	2.3095-2.3103 in.	58.662-58.682mm
Connecting rod bearing journal diameter (0.020 in. (0.50mm) undersize)	2.3083-2.3091 in.	58.632-58.652mm
Connecting rod bearing journal taper limit	0.0006 in.	0.016mm
Connecting rod bearing journal out-of-round limit	0.0012 in.	0.3mm
Bend for each 1.97 in. (25mm)	0.04 in.	
Side clearance (max)	0.0047-0.01929 in.	0.11-0.49mm
Pistons		
Piston diameter	3.81 in.	96.795mm
Piston-to-bore clearance	0.000709-0.00173 in.	0.018-0.044mm
Piston ring side clearance (all)	0.00122-0.00315 in.	0.030-0.080mm
Piston ring gap		
Upper compression ring	0.00098-0.00161 in.	0.25-0.41mm
Lower compression ring	0.00149-0.0025 in.	0.38-0.64mm
Oil control ring	0.0059-0.0064 in.	0.15-0.65mm
Oil Pump		
Oil pump gear radial clearance (idler and drive)	0.0055-0.002 in.	0.125-0.050mm
Oil pump gear end height (extends below the housing)	0.0033-0.0004 in.	0.085-0.010mm

91193C01

4.6L ENGINE MECHANICAL SPECIFICATIONS

Description	English Specifications	Metric Specifications
General Information		
Type	Liquid Cooled, Overhead Camshaft	
Displacement	280 cid	
Number of cylinders	8	
Bore	3.55 in.	90.2mm
Stroke	3.54 in.	90.0mm
Compression ratio	9.0:1	
Firing order	1-3-7-2-6-5-4-8	
Oil Pressure	20-45 psi @ 1500 RPM (engine hot)	
Cylinder Head and Valve Train		
Valve guide bore diameter	0.3443-0.3433 in.	8.745-8.720
Valve seat width		
Intake	0.074-0.083 in.	1.9-2.1mm
Exhaust	0.074-0.083 in.	1.9-2.1mm
Valve seat angle	45 degrees	
Valve seat run-out	0.00094 in.	0.025mm
Valve stem-to-guide clearance		
Intake	0.00079-0.00272 in.	0.020-0.069mm
Exhaust	0.018-0.0037 in.	0.046-0.095mm
Valve guide inner diameter	0.2773-0.2762 in.	7.044-7.015mm
Valve head diameter		
Intake	1.75 in.	44.5mm
Exhaust	1.34 in.	34.0mm
Valve face run-out limit	0.001 in.	0.05mm
Valve face angle	45.5 degrees	
Valve stem diameter		
Intake	0.275-0.2746 in.	6.995-6.975mm
Exhaust	0.274-0.2736 in.	6.970-6.949mm
Free length		
Intake	1.976 in.	50.2mm
Exhaust	1.976 in.	50.2mm
Valve spring assembled length	1.566-1.637 in.	39.8-41.6mm
Rocker arm ratio	1.75:1	
Valve tappet diameter	0.63-0.629 in.	16.0-15.98mm
Valve tappet-to-bore clearance	0.00071-0.00272 in.	0.018-0.069mm
Valve tappet service limit	0.00063 in.	0.016mm
Valve tappet leakdown rate	5-25 seconds	
Valve tappet collapsed tappet gap (desired)	0.0335-0.0177 in.	0.85-0.45mm
Camshaft		
Lobe lift		
Intake	0.2594 in.	6.59mm
Exhaust	0.2594 in.	6.59mm
Lobe wear limit (all)	0.005 in.	0.127mm
Theoretical valve lift @ zero lash (all)	0.472 in.	12.0mm
End-play	0.00098-0.0065 in.	0.025-0.165mm
End-play wear limit	0.0075 in.	0.190mm
Bearing-to-journal clearance	0.00098-0.003 in.	0.025-0.076mm
Bearing-to-journal clearance service limit	0.0048 in.	0.121mm
Journal diameter	1.061-1.060 in.	26.962-26.936mm
Bearing journal inside diameter	1.063-1.0625 in.	27.012-26.987mm
Run-out	0.002 in.	0.05mm
Cylinder Block		
Cylinder bore diameter	0.0006 in.	0.015mm
Out-of-round	0.00079 in.	0.020mm
Out-of-round (service limit)	0.00023 in.	0.006mm
Taper limit		
Main bearing bore	2.85-2.851 in.	72.402-72.422mm
Crankshaft		
Main bearing journal diameter	2.65-2.657 in.	67.483-67.503mm
Main bearing journal taper	0.0007 in.	0.02mm
Main bearing journal run-out	0.0011-0.0026 in.	0.027-0.065mm
Bearing wall thickness	0.075-0.076 in.	1.920-1.928mm
Connecting rod bearing journal diameter	2.087-2.867 in.	52.988-53.003mm
Crankshaft free end-play	0.130-0.301 in.	0.0051-0.012mm
Crankshaft runout-to-rear face of the block	0.002 in.	0.05mm
Connecting Rod		
Connecting rod bearing-to-crankshaft clearance	0.001-0.0027 in.	0.027-0.069mm
Connecting rod bearing wall thickness	0.096-0.0965 in.	2.444-2.452mm
Connecting rod main bearing bore diameter	2.234-2.24 in.	56.756-56.876mm
Connecting rod length (center-to-center)	5.93 in.	150.7mm

91193C02

4.6L ENGINE MECHANICAL SPECIFICATIONS

Description	English Specifications	Metric Specifications
Connecting Rod (cont'd)		
Connecting rod-to-crank side clearance (standard)	0.0006-0.0177 in.	0.015-0.45mm
Connecting rod-to-crank side clearance (maximum)	0.02 in.	0.5mm
Connecting rod main bearing journal taper	0.0005 in.	0.015 mm
Pistons		
Piston diameter		
Coded red	3.550-3.551 in.	90.177-90.197mm
Coded blue	3.5507-3.5515 in.	90.190-90.210mm
Coded yellow	3.5513-3.5521 in.	90.203-90.223mm
Piston-to-bore clearance	0.0005-0.001 in.	0.012-0.026mm
Piston pin bore diameter	0.864-0.865 in.	21.959-21.979mm
Piston pin bore length	2.44-2.443 in.	61.99-62.05mm
Piston pin-to-rod clearance	0.0006-0.00157 in.	0.015-0.040mm
Piston pin-to-piston clearance	0.0002-0.0004 in.	0.005-0.010mm
Piston ring side clearance		
Upper compression ring	0.0016-0.0035 in.	0.040-0.090mm
Lower compression ring	0.0012-0.0031 in.	0.030-0.080mm
Oil control ring	0.05 in.	1.25mm
Piston ring groove width		
Upper compression ring	0.060-0.0610 in.	1.530-1.550mm
Lower compression ring	0.060-0.0620 in.	1.520-1.530mm
Oil control ring	0.2750-0.2844 in.	6.996-7.224mm
Piston ring gap		
Upper compression ring	0.01-0.02 in.	0.23-0.49mm
Lower compression ring	0.01-0.02 in.	0.23-0.49mm
Oil control ring	0.006-0.026 in.	0.15-0.66mm
Oil Pump		
Oil pump gear radial clearance (idler and drive)	0.0055-0.002 in.	0.125-0.050mm
Oil pump gear end height (extends below the housing)	0.0033-0.0004 in.	0.085-0.010mm

5.4L SOHC ENGINE MECHANICAL SPECIFICATIONS

Description	English Specifications	Metric Specifications
General Information		
Type	Liquid Cooled, Overhead Camshaft	
Displacement	330 cid	5.4L
Number of cylinders	8	8
Bore	3.55 in.	90.2mm
Stroke	4.17 in.	105.8mm
Compression ratio	9.0:1	
Firing order	1-3-7-2-6-5-4-8	
Oil Pressure	40-70 psi @ 1500 RPM (engine hot)	
Cylinder Head and Valve Train		
Valve guide bore diameter	0.3443-0.3433 in.	8.745-8.720
Valve seat width		
Intake	0.074-0.083 in.	1.9-2.1mm
Exhaust	0.074-0.083 in.	1.9-2.1mm
Valve seat angle	45 degrees	
Valve seat run-out	0.00094 in.	0.025mm
Valve stem-to-guide clearance		
Intake	0.00079-0.00272 in.	0.020-0.069mm
Exhaust	0.018-0.0037 in.	0.046-0.095mm
Valve guide inner diameter	0.2773-0.2762	7.044-7.015mm
Valve head diameter		
Intake	1.75 in.	44.5mm
Exhaust	1.34 in.	34.0mm
Valve face run-out limit	0.001 in.	0.05mm
Valve face angle	45.25-45.75 degrees	
Valve stem diameter		
Intake	0.275-0.2746 in.	6.995-6.975mm
Exhaust	0.274-0.2736 in.	6.970-6.949mm
Free length		
Intake	1.976 in.	50.2mm
Exhaust	1.976 in.	50.2mm
Valve spring assembled length	1.566-1.637 in.	39.8-41.6mm
Rocker arm ratio	1.75:1	
Valve tappet diameter	0.63-0.629 in.	16.0-15.98mm
Valve tappet-to-bore clearance	0.00071-0.00272 in.	0.018-0.069mm
Valve tappet service limit	0.00063 in.	0.016mm
Valve tappet leakdown rate	5-25 seconds	
Valve tappet collapsed tappet gap (desired)	0.0335-0.0177 in.	0.85-0.45mm

91193C03

5.4L SOHC ENGINE MECHANICAL SPECIFICATIONS

Description	English Specifications	Metric Specifications
Camshaft		
Lobe lift		
Intake	0.2594 in.	6.59mm
Exhaust	0.2594 in.	6.59mm
Lobe wear limit (all)	0.005 in.	0.127mm
Theoretical valve lift @ zero lash (all)	0.472 in.	12.0mm
End-play	0.00098-0.0065 in.	0.027-0.190mm
End-play wear limit	0.0075 in.	0.190mm
Bearing-to-journal clearance	0.00099-0.003 in.	0.025-0.076mm
Bearing-to-journal clearance service limit	0.003 in.	0.076mm
Journal diameter	1.061-1.060 in.	26.962-26.936mm
Bearing journal inside diameter	1.063-1.0625 in.	27.012-26.987mm
Run-out	0.004 in.	0.09mm
Cylinder Block		
Cylinder bore diameter		
Grade 1	3.5512-3.5516 in.	90.20-90.21mm
Grade 2	3.5516-3.5520 in.	90.21-90.22mm
Grade 3	3.5520-3.5524 in.	90.22-90.23mm
Out-of-round	0.0006 in.	0.015mm
Out-of-round (service limit)	0.00079 in.	0.020mm
Taper limit	0.00023 in.	0.006mm
Main bearing bore	2.85-2.851 in.	72.400-72.424mm
Crankshaft		
Main bearing journal diameter	2.65-2.657 in.	67.483-67.503mm
Main bearing journal taper	0.0007 in.	0.02mm
Main bearing journal run-out	0.002 in.	0.05mm
Main bearing-to-crankshaft clearance	0.0011-0.0025 in.	0.027-0.065mm
Bearing wall thickness	0.095-0.10 in.	2.436-2.545mm
Connecting rod bearing journal diameter	2.087-2.867 in.	52.988-53.003mm
Crankshaft free end-play	0.130-0.301 in.	0.075-0.377mm
Crankshaft runout-to-rear face of the block	0.002 in.	0.05mm
Connecting Rod		
Connecting rod bearing-to-crankshaft clearance	0.001-0.0027 in.	0.027-0.069mm
Connecting rod bearing wall thickness	0.096-0.0965 in.	2.444-2.452mm
Connecting rod main bearing bore diameter	2.234-2.24 in.	56.756-56.876mm
Connecting rod length (center-to-center)	6.65 in.	169.1mm
Connecting rod-to-crank side clearance (standard)	0.0006-0.0177 in.	0.015-0.45mm
Connecting rod-to-crank side clearance (maximum)	0.02 in.	0.5mm
Connecting rod main bearing journal taper	0.0005 in.	0.015 mm
Pistons		
Piston diameter	3.550 in.	90.180mm +/- 0.005mm
Piston-to-bore clearance	0.0005-0.001 in.	0.012-0.026mm
Piston pin bore diameter	0.864-0.865 in.	22.015-22.04mm
Piston pin bore length	2.44-2.443 in.	61.93-62.05mm
Piston pin-to-rod clearance	0.0006-0.00157 in.	0.015-0.040mm
Piston ring side clearance	0.0002-0.0004 in.	0.005-0.010mm
Upper compression ring	0.0012-0.0031 in.	0.030-0.080mm
Lower compression ring	0.0012-0.0031 in.	0.030-0.080mm
Oil control ring	0.0010-0.0077 in.	0.027-0.196mm
Piston ring groove width		
Upper compression ring	0.060-0.0610 in.	1.530-1.550mm
Lower compression ring	0.060-0.0602 in.	1.520-1.530mm
Oil control ring	0.1192-0.1201 in.	3.030-3.050mm
Piston ring gap		
Upper compression ring	0.005-0.011 in.	0.13-0.28mm
Lower compression ring	0.01-0.02 in.	0.23-0.49mm
Oil control ring	0.006-0.026 in.	0.15-0.66mm

5.4L DOHC ENGINE MECHANICAL SPECIFICATIONS

Description	English Specifications	Metric Specifications
General Information		
Type	Liquid Cooled, Overhead Camshafts	
Displacement	330 cid	5.4L
Number of cylinders	8	8
Bore	3.55 in.	90.2mm
Stroke	4.17 in.	105.8mm
Compression ratio	9.0:1	
Firing order	1-3-7-2-6-5-4-8	
Oil Pressure	40-70 psi @ 1500 RPM (engine hot)	

91193C04

5.4L DOHC ENGINE MECHANICAL SPECIFICATIONS

Description	English Specifications	Metric Specifications
Cylinder Head and Valve Train		
Valve guide bore diameter	0.3443-0.3443 in.	8.745-8.720
Valve seat width		
Intake	0.074-0.083 in.	1.9-2.1mm
Exhaust	0.074-0.083 in.	1.9-2.1mm
Valve seat angle	45 degrees	
Valve seat run-out	0.00094 in.	0.025mm
Valve stem-to-guide clearance		
Intake	0.00079-0.00272 in.	0.020-0.069mm
Exhaust	0.018-0.0037 in.	0.046-0.095mm
Valve guide inner diameter	0.2773-0.2762	7.044-7.015mm
Valve head diameter		
Intake	1.75 in.	44.5mm
Exhaust	1.34 in.	34.0mm
Valve face run-out limit	0.001 in.	0.05mm
Valve face angle	45.25-45.75 degrees	
Valve stem diameter		
Intake	0.275-0.2746 in.	6.995-6.975mm
Exhaust	0.274-0.2736 in.	6.970-6.949mm
Free length		
Intake	1.976 in.	50.2mm
Exhaust	1.976 in.	50.2mm
Rocker arm ratio	1.75:1	
Valve tappet diameter	1.566-1.637 in.	39.8-41.6mm
Valve tappet-to-bore clearance	0.63-0.629 in.	16.0-15.98mm
Valve tappet service limit	0.00071-0.00272 in.	0.018-0.069mm
Valve tappet leakdown rate	0.00063 in.	0.016mm
Valve tappet collapsed tappet gap (desired)	0.0335-0.0177 in. (5-25 seconds)	0.85-0.45mm
Camshaft		
Lobe lift		
Intake	0.2594 in.	6.59mm
Exhaust	0.2594 in.	6.59mm
Lobe wear limit (all)	0.005 in.	0.127mm
Theoretical valve lift @ zero lash (all)	0.472 in.	12.0mm
End-play	0.00098-0.0065 in.	0.027-0.190mm
End-play wear limit	0.0075 in.	0.025-0.076mm
Bearing-to-journal clearance	0.00098-0.003 in.	0.076mm
Bearing-to-journal clearance service limit	0.003 in.	0.076mm
Journal diameter	1.061-1.060 in.	26.962-26.936mm
Bearing journal inside diameter	1.063-1.0625 in.	27.012-26.987mm
Run-out	0.004 in.	0.09mm
Cylinder Block		
Cylinder bore diameter		
Grade 1	3.5512-3.5516 in.	90.20-90.21mm
Grade 2	3.5516-3.5520 in.	90.21-90.22mm
Grade 3	3.5520-3.5524 in.	90.22-90.23mm
Out-of-round	0.0006 in.	0.015mm
Out-of-round (service limit)	0.00079 in.	0.020mm
Taper limit	0.00023 in.	0.006mm
Main bearing bore	2.85-2.851 in.	72.400-72.424mm
Crankshaft		
Main bearing journal diameter	2.65-2.657 in.	67.483-67.503mm
Main bearing journal taper	0.0007 in.	0.02mm
Main bearing journal run-out	0.002 in.	0.05mm
Main bearing-to-crankshaft clearance	0.0011-0.0026 in.	0.027-0.065mm
Bearing wall thickness	0.095-0.10 in.	2.436-2.545mm
Connecting rod bearing journal diameter	2.087-2.867 in.	52.988-53.003mm
Crankshaft free end-play	0.130-0.301 in.	0.075-0.377mm
Crankshaft runout-to-rear face of the block	0.002 in.	0.05mm
Connecting Rod		
Connecting rod bearing-to-crankshaft clearance	0.001-0.0027 in.	0.027-0.069mm
Connecting rod bearing wall thickness	0.096-0.0965 in.	2.444-2.452mm
Connecting rod main bearing bore diameter	2.234-2.24 in.	56.756-56.876mm
Connecting rod length (center-to-center)	6.65 in.	169.1mm
Connecting rod-to-crank side clearance (standard)	0.0006-0.0177 in.	0.015-0.45mm
Connecting rod-to-crank side clearance (maximum)	0.02 in.	0.5 mm
Pistons		
Piston diameter	3.550 in.	90.180mm +/- 0.005mm
Piston-to-bore clearance	0.0005-0.001 in.	0.012-0.028mm

91193C05

5.4L DOHC ENGINE MECHANICAL SPECIFICATIONS

Description	English Specifications	Metric Specifications
Pistons (cont'd)		
Piston pin bore diameter	0.864-0.865 in.	22.008-22.015mm
Piston pin bore length	2.44-2.443 in.	61.93-62.05mm
Piston pin-to-rod clearance	0.0006-0.00157 in.	0.015-0.040mm
Piston pin-to-piston clearance	0.0002-0.0004 in.	0.005-0.010mm
Piston ring side clearance		
Upper compression ring	0.0012-0.0031 in.	0.030-0.080mm
Lower compression ring	0.0012-0.0031 in.	0.030-0.080mm
Oil control ring	0.0010-0.0077 in.	0.027-0.196mm
Piston ring groove width		
Upper compression ring	0.060-0.0610 in.	1.530-1.550mm
Lower compression ring	0.060-0.0602 in.	1.520-1.540mm
Oil control ring	0.1192-0.1201 in.	3.030-3.050mm
Piston ring gap		
Upper compression ring	0.005-0.011 in.	0.13-0.28mm
Lower compression ring	0.01-0.02 in.	0.25-0.40mm
Oil control ring	0.006-0.026 in.	0.15-0.65mm

5.8L ENGINE MECHANICAL SPECIFICATIONS

Description	Footnotes	English Specifications (in.)	Metric Specifications (mm)
Cylinder Block			
Cylinder bore			
Standard size:		4.0000-4.0048	101.600-101.722
Maximum out-of-round:		0.0015	0.0381
Maximum taper:		0.0100	0.2540
Main bearing			
Bore diameter:		3.1922-3.1930	81.08-81.10
Crankshaft-to-rear face of block runout (TIR max.):		0.0050	0.1270
Distributor shaft bearing bore diameter:		.5155-.5170	13.09-13.13
Head gasket surface flatness:			
Overall:		0.0060	0.1524
In any 6 in. (152.4mm):		0.0030	0.0080
Head gasket Surface finish (RMS):		60-150	60-150
Tappet bore diameter:		0.8752-0.8767	22.23-22.69
Cylinder Head			
Combustion chamber volume	2	3.70-3.88 cid	60.6-63.6 cc
Valve guide bore diameter			
Intake:		0.3433-0.3443	8.719-8.745
Exhaust:		0.3433-0.3443	8.719-8.745
Valve seat	3		
Maximum runout:		0.0020	0.0051
Gasket surface flatness			
Overall:		0.0060	0.1524
In any 6 in. (152.4mm):		0.0030	0.0762
Valve Rocker Arm Shaft, Pushrods and Tappets			
Rocker arm lift ratio to 1:		1.59	
Pushrod runout TIR maximum:		0.0150	0.3810
Valve tappet or lifter			
Standard diameter:	4	0.8740-0.8745	22.199-22.212
Clearance to bore:		0.0007-0.0027	0.0178-0.0068
Hydraulic lifter leakdown rate:	5	10 to 50 seconds for 1/16 travel	
Collapsed tappet gap			
Allowable:		0.092-0.192	2.337-4.876
Desired:		0.112-0.172	2.845-4.369
Valves			
Valve stem to guide clearance			
Intake:		0.0010-0.0027	0.00254-0.0686
Exhaust:		0.0015-0.0032	0.0381-0.0813
Valve head diameter			
Intake:		1.770-1.794	44.958-45.567
Exhaust:		1.453-1.468	36.906-37.287
Maximum valve face runout:		0.0020	0.0508
Valve springs			
Valve spring compression pressure @ specified height	6		
Intake:		74-82 lbs. @ 1.78 in.; 190-210 lbs. @ 1.20 in.	33.57-37.19 kg @ 45.21mm; 86.18-95.25 kg @ 30.48mm
Exhaust:		76-84 lbs. @ 1.6 in.; 190-210 lbs. @ 1.20 in.	34.47-38.10 kg @ 40.64mm; 86.18-95.25 kg @ 30.48mm

91193C06

5.8L ENGINE MECHANICAL SPECIFICATIONS

Description	English Specifications	Metric Specifications
Valve springs (cont'd)		
Free length (approx.):		
Intake:	2.0600	52.3200
Exhaust:	1.8800	47.7500
Valve spring assembled height		
Intake:	1.75-1.81	44.45-45.97
Exhaust:	1.58-1.64	40.13-41.66
Valve spring out of square:	5/64 (0.078)	1.9900
Valve Stem Diameter		
Standard		
Intake:	0.3415-0.3423	8.67-8.69
Exhaust:	0.3410-0.3418	8.66-8.68
0.015 Oversize		
Intake:	0.3565-0.3573	9.06-9.08
Exhaust:	0.3561-0.3568	9.04-9.06
0.030 Oversize		
Intake:	0.3715-0.3723	9.44-9.46
Exhaust:	0.3711-0.3718	9.43-9.44
Crankshaft and Flywheel		
Main bearing journals		
Diameter: [7]	2.9994-3.0002	76.185-76.205
TIR Maximum runout:	0.0020	0.0508
Maximum out of round:	0.0006	0.0152
Thrust face runout TIR maximum:	0.0010	0.0254
Maximum taper per inch/mm:	0.0005	0.0127
Thrust bearing journal length:	1.137-1.139	28.88-28.93
Main and rod bearing journal Finish RMS maximum: 12		
Main bearing thrust face Finish RMS maximum: 25 front/20 rear		
Connecting rod journal		
Diameter:	2.3103-2.3111	58.6816-58.7019
Taper per inch/cm maximum:	0.0006	0.0152
Crankshaft free end-play:	0.004-0.008	0.102-0.203
Flywheel clutch face run-out:	0.0100	0.2540
Crankshaft Bearings		
Connecting rod bearing to crankshaft clearance selective fit		
Desired:	0.0008-0.0015	0.020-0.038
Allowable:	0.0008-0.0025	0.0203-0.0635
Bearing wall thickness		
Standard:	0.572-0.577	14.53-14.66
0.002 undersize:	0.573-0.578	14.55-14.68
Main bearing to crankshaft selective fit		
Desired:		
No. 1 bearing:	0.0008-0.0015	0.0200-0.0381
All other bearings:	0.0001-0.0015	0.00254-0.0381
Allowable:	0.0005-0.0015	0.0127-0.0381
No. 1 bearing:	1.0008-1.0026	1.020-1.066
All other bearings:	1.0001-1.0020	1.00254-1.0508
No. 1 bearing:	1.0005-1.0024	1.0127-1.0609
Bearing wall thickness		
Standard		
No. 1 upper bearing:	0.0957-0.0960	2.430-2.438
All other bearings:	0.0961-0.0966	2.441-2.454
0.002 undersize		
No. 1 upper bearing:	0.0957-0.0962	2.431-2.443
All other bearings:	0.0958-0.0962	2.433-2.443
	0.0958-0.0963	2.433-2.446
Connecting rods		
Piston pin bore or bushing I.D.:	0.9097-0.9112	23.106-23.144
Rod bearing bore I.D.:	2.4265-2.4273	61.633-61.653
Connecting rod bore max. out of round:	0.0004	0.0102
Rod length center to center:	5.9545-5.9575	151.244-151.321
Connecting rod alignment maximum total difference		
Twist: [8]	0.0240	3.1500
Service limit:	0.0230	0.5840
Bend:	0.0120	0.3048
Rod to crankshaft assembled side clearance:	0.010-0.020	0.254-0.508
Service limit:	0.0230	0.5840

91193C07

5.8L ENGINE MECHANICAL SPECIFICATIONS

Description	English Specifications	Metric Specifications
Pistons		
Diameter [9]		
Coded red:	3.9978-3.9984	101.544-101.560
Coded blue:	3.9990-3.9996	101.575-101.590
.003 oversize:	4.0002-4.0008	101.605-101.620
Piston to bore clearance selective fit		
Standard engine:	0.0018-0.0026	0.0457-0.0660
Lightning engine:	0.0015-0.0023	0.0381-0.0584
Piston pin bore diameter:	0.9123-0.9126	23.172-23.180
Ring groove width with compression		
Top:	0.080-0.081	2.032-2.057
Bottom:	0.080-0.081	2.032-2.057
Oil:	0.188-0.189	4.775-4.801
Piston pins		
Length:	3.010-3.040	76.45-77.21
Diameter		
Standard:	0.9119-0.9124	23.162-23.174
.001 oversize:	0.9130-0.9133	23.190-23.197
.002 oversize:	0.9140-0.9143	23.215-23.223
To piston pin bore clearance (selective fit):	0.0003-0.0005	0.0076-0.0127
To connecting rod bushing clearance: interference fit		
Piston rings		
Ring width [10]		
Top Compression:	0.077-0.087	1.9558-2.2098
Bottom compression:	0.077-0.087	1.9558-2.2098
Side clearance		
Piston rings (cont'd)		
Top compression:	0.002-0.004	0.051-0.102
Bottom compression:	0.002-0.004	0.051-0.102
Oil: snug		
Ring gap		
Top compression:	0.010-0.020	0.254-0.508
Bottom compression:	0.010-0.020	0.254-0.508
Oil (steel rail):	0.015-0.040	0.381-1.016
Camshaft		
Lobe lift [11]		
Intake:	0.2780	7.0610
Exhaust:	0.2830	7.1880
End-play		
Standard:	0.001-0.007	0.0254-0.178
Maximum:	0.0090	0.2280
Camshaft journal to bearing clearance [12]:	0.001-0.003	0.0254-0.076
Camshaft drive		
Journal diameter (standard) [13]		
No. 1:	2.0815	52.8700
No. 2:	2.0655	52.4600
No. 3:	2.0515	51.1810
No. 4:	2.0365	51.7270
No. 5:	2.0215	51.3460
Bearing inside diameter		
No. 1:	2.0835	52.9210
No. 2:	2.0685	52.5400
No. 3:	2.0535	52.1590
No. 4:	2.0385	51.7780
No. 5:	2.0235	51.3970
Camshaft front bearing location [14]:	0.005-0.020	0.127-0.508
Oil pump and oil capacity		
Relief valve spring pressure @ specified length:	18.2-20.2 lbs. @ 2.49 in.	8.26-9.16 kg @ 63.25mm
Driveshaft to housing clearance:	0.0015-0.003	0.0381-0.076
Relief valve to housing clearance:	0.0015-0.003	0.0381-0.076
Rotor assembly end clearance:	0.004 maximum	0.100 maximum
Outer race to housing clearance:	0.001-0.003	0.0254-0.0762
Engine oil capacity		
U.S. quarts: 5		
Imperial quarts: 4.2		
Litres: 4.7		

1 Unless otherwise specified with a different measurement (for example, psi, kPa, lbs., N, etc.)
2 Compression pressure (PSI) of the lowest cylinder must be at least 75 percent of the highest to be within specification
3 Valve seat angle: 45 degrees
4 Service limit: 0.005 in. (0.127mm)
5 Time required for plunger to leak down 0.625 in. (15.87mm) under load of 50 lbs. (22.5 kg) using leak down fluid in tappet

91193C08

5.8L ENGINE MECHANICAL SPECIFICATIONS

Description	English Specifications	Metric Specifications

6 Service limit: 10 percent loss pressure
7 Service limit: 0.005 in. (0.127mm)
8 Pin bushing and crankshaft bore must be parallel and in the same vertical plane with specified total difference when measured at the ends of an
   8-inch long bar, 4 inches on each side of the rod centerline
9 Measured at the piston pin bore centerline at 90 degrees to the pin
10 Service limit: 0.002 in. (.0508mm) maximum increase in clearance
11 Maximum allowable lift loss: 0.005 in. (0.127mm)
12 Service limit: 0.006 in. (0.1524mm)
13 Camshaft journal runout of 0.005 in. (0.127mm) TIR maximum
14 Distance in inches/millimeters that the front edge of the bearing is installed below the front face of the cylinder block

6.8L ENGINE MECHANICAL SPECIFICATIONS

Description	English Specifications	Metric Specifications
General Information		
Type	Liquid Cooled, Overhead Camshaft	
Displacement	415 cid	6.8L
Number of cylinders	10	
Bore	3.55 in.	90.2mm
Stroke	4.17 in.	105.8mm
Compression ratio	9.0:1	
Firing order	1-6-5-10-2-7-3-8-4-9	
Oil Pressure	40-70 psi @ 1500 RPM (engine hot)	
Cylinder Head and Valve Train		
Valve guide bore diameter	0.3443-0.3433 in.	8.745-8.720
Valve seat width		
Intake	0.074-0.083 in.	1.9-2.1mm
Exhaust	0.074-0.083 in.	1.9-2.1mm
Valve seat angle	45 degrees	
Valve seat run-out	0.00094 in.	0.025mm
Valve stem-to-guide clearance		
Intake	0.00079-0.00272 in.	0.020-0.069mm
Exhaust	0.018-0.0037 in.	0.046-0.095mm
Valve guide inner diameter	0.2773-0.2762	7.044-7.015mm
Valve head diameter		
Intake	1.75 in.	44.5mm
Exhaust	1.34 in.	34.0mm
Valve face run-out limit	0.001 in.	0.05mm
Valve face angle	45.25-45.75 degrees	
Valve stem diameter		
Intake	0.275-0.2746 in.	6.995-6.975mm
Exhaust	0.274-0.2736 in.	6.970-6.949mm
Free length		
Intake	1.976 in.	50.2mm
Exhaust	1.976 in.	50.2mm
Valve spring assembled length	1.566-1.637 in.	39.8-41.6mm
Rocker arm ratio	1.75:1	
Valve tappet diameter	0.63-0.629 in.	16.0-15.98mm
Valve tappet-to-bore clearance	0.00071-0.00272 in.	0.018-0.069mm
Valve tappet service limit	0.00063 in.	0.016mm
Valve tappet leakdown rate	5-25 seconds	
Valve tappet collapsed tappet gap (desired)	0.0235-0.0177 in.	0.85-0.45mm
Camshaft		
Lobe lift		
Intake	0.2594 in.	6.59mm
Exhaust	0.2594 in.	6.59mm
Lobe wear limit (all)	0.005 in.	0.127mm
Theoretical valve lift @ zero lash (all)	0.472 in.	12.0mm
End-play	0.00098-0.0065 in.	0.027-0.190mm
End-play wear limit	0.0075 in.	0.190mm
Bearing-to-journal clearance	0.00098-0.003 in.	0.025-0.076mm
Bearing-to-journal clearance service limit	0.003 in.	0.076mm
Journal diameter	1.061-1.060 in.	26.962-26.936mm
Bearing journal inside diameter	1.063-1.0625 in.	27.012-26.987mm
Run-out	0.004 in.	0.09mm
Cylinder Block		
Cylinder bore diameter		
Grade 1	3.5512-3.5516 in.	90.20-90.21mm
Grade 2	3.5516-3.5520 in.	90.21-90.22mm
Grade 3	3.5520-3.5524 in.	90.22-90.23mm
Out-of-round	0.0006 in.	0.015mm

91193C09

6.8L ENGINE MECHANICAL SPECIFICATIONS

Description	English Specifications	Metric Specifications
Cylinder Block (cont'd)		
Out-of-round (service limit)	0.00079 in.	0.020mm
Taper limit	0.00023 in.	0.006mm
Main bearing bore	2.85-2.851 in.	72.400-72.424mm
Crankshaft		
Main bearing journal diameter	2.65-2.657 in.	67.483-67.503mm
Main bearing journal taper	0.0007 in.	0.02mm
Main bearing journal run-out	0.002 in.	0.05mm
Main bearing-to-crankshaft clearance	0.0011-0.0026 in.	0.027-0.065mm
Bearing wall thickness	0.095-0.10 in.	2.436-2.545mm
Connecting rod bearing journal diameter	2.087-2.867 in.	52.988-53.003mm
Crankshaft free end-play	0.130-0.301 in.	0.075-0.377mm
Crankshaft runout-to-rear face of the block	0.002 in.	0.05mm
Connecting Rod		
Connecting rod bearing-to-crankshaft clearance	0.001-0.0027 in.	0.027-0.069mm
Connecting rod bearing wall thickness	0.096-0.0965 in.	2.444-2.452mm
Connecting rod main bearing bore diameter	2.234-2.24 in.	56.756-56.876mm
Connecting rod length (center-to-center)	6.65 in.	169.1mm
Connecting rod-to-crank side clearance (standard)	0.0006-0.0177 in.	0.015-0.45mm
Connecting rod-to-crank side clearance (maximum)	0.02 in.	0.5mm
Connecting rod main bearing journal taper	0.0005 in.	0.015mm
Pistons		
Piston diameter	3.550 in.	90.160mm +/- 0.005mm
Piston-to-bore clearance	0.0005-0.001 in.	0.012-0.026mm
Piston pin bore diameter	0.864-0.865 in.	22.015-22.04mm
Piston pin bore length	2.44-2.443 in.	61.93-62.05mm
Piston pin-to-rod clearance	0.0006-0.00157 in.	0.015-0.040mm
Piston pin-to-piston clearance	0.0002-0.0004 in.	0.005-0.010mm
Piston ring side clearance		
Upper compression ring	0.0012-0.0031 in.	0.030-0.080mm
Lower compression ring	0.0012-0.0031 in.	0.030-0.080mm
Oil control ring	0.0010-0.0077 in.	0.027-0.196mm
Piston ring groove width		
Upper compression ring	0.060-0.0610 in.	1.530-1.550mm
Lower compression ring	0.060-0.0602 in.	1.520-1.530mm
Oil control ring	0.1192-0.1201 in.	3.030-3.050mm
Piston ring gap		
Upper compression ring	0.005-0.011 in.	0.13-0.28mm
Lower compression ring	0.01-0.02 in.	0.23-0.49mm
Oil control ring	0.006-0.026 in.	0.15-0.66mm
Balance Shaft System		
Balance shaft journal diameter	1.062-1.061 in.	26.962-26.936mm
Balance shaft journal-to-cylinder head clearance	0.00098-0.003 in.	0.025-0.076mm
Cylinder head balance shaft journal clearance	1.063-1.062 in.	27.012-26.987mm
Gear backlash	0.0031-0.0050 in.	0.0076-0.1295mm
Balance shaft end-play	0.00157-0.00709 in.	0.04-0.18mm
Alignment (bore-to-bore max. twist)		
Bore-to-bore max. twist	0.002 in. +/-	0.05mm +/-
Bore-to-bore max. bend	0.00142 in. +/-	0.038mm +/-
Side-play		
Standard	0.016 +/- 0.010 in.	0.410 +/- 0.26mm
Max.	0.026 in.	0.670mm

Max. - Maximum
Min. - Minimum

7.3L DIESEL ENGINE MECHANICAL SPECIFICATIONS

Description	Footnotes	English Specifications (in.)	Metric Specifications (mm)
Cylinder Block			
Cylinder bore			
Standard size:		4.1096-4.1103	104.384-104.402
Oversize			
.010 (.254mm):		4.1143	104.5020
.020 (.508mm):		4.1243	104.7560
.030 (.762mm):		4.1343	105.0100
Maximum out-of-round:		0.0020	0.0508
Maximum taper:		0.0020	0.0508
Main bearing			
Bore diameter:	2	3.3152-3.3162	84.21-84.23
Head gasket surface flatness:			

91193C10

7.3L DIESEL ENGINE MECHANICAL SPECIFICATIONS

Description		English Specifications	Metric Specifications
Cylinder Block (cont'd)			
Overall:		0.0060	0.1524
In any 6 in.(152.4mm):		0.0030	0.0762
Head gasket Surface finish (RMS):		63-125	-
Cylinder Head			
Valve guide bore diameter			
Intake:		0.3141-0.3151	7.978-8.004
Exhaust:		0.3141-0.3151	7.978-8.004
Valve seat width	3		
Intake:		0.065-0.095	1.651-2.413
Exhaust:		0.065-0.095	1.651-2.413
Maximum runout:		0.0020	0.0051
Gasket surface flatness			
Overall:		0.0060	0.1524
In any 6 in. (152.4mm):		0.0030	0.0762
Valve Rocker Arm Shaft, Pushrods and Tappets			
Pushrod runout TIR maximum:		0.0200	0.5000
Valve tappet or lifter			
Standard diameter:		0.9209-0.9217	23.391-23.411
Clearance to bore:	4	0.0011-0.0034	00279-00864
Hydraulic lifter leakdown rate:	5	18 to 90 seconds for 0.125 in. (3.175mm) travel	
Collapsed tappet gap (clearance):	6	0.1850	4.6990
Valves			
Valve stem to guide clearance			
Intake:		0.0055	0.1397
Exhaust:		0.0055	0.1397
Valve face angle			
Intaki 30 degrees			
Exha 37.5 degrees			
Maximum valve face runout:		0.0020	0.0508
Minimum valve face margin			
Intake valves:		0.0660	1.6764
Exhaust valves:		0.0540	1.3716
Valve springs			
Valve spring compression pressure @ specified height	7		
Intake:		71-79 lbs. @ 1.833 in.	32.2-35.8 @ 46.56mm
Exhaust:		71-79 lbs. @ 1.833 in.	32.2-35.8 @ 46.56mm
Free length (approx.):			
Intake:		1.925-2.225	48.905-56.505
Exhaust:		1.925-2.225	48.905-56.505
Assembled height			
Intake:		1.7670	44.8818
Exhaust:		1.8330	46.5582
Valve spring out of square (max.):		5/64 (0.078)	1.9800
Valve Stem Diameter			
Standard:		0.31185-0.31255	7.921-7.939
Valve head recession relative to deck surface			
Intake:		0.046-0.058	1.168-1.473
Exhaust:		0.052-0.064	1.321-1.626
Crankshaft and Flywheel			
Main bearing journals			
Diameter			
Standard:		3.1228-3.1236	79.319-79.340
Undersize			
0.01:		3.1128-3.1136	79.065-79.085
0.02:		3.1028-3.1036	78.811-78.831
0.03:		3.0928-3.0936	78.557-78.577
TIR Maximum runout:		0.0020	0.05080
Maximum out of round:		0.0002	0.00508
Thrust face runout TIR maximum:		0.0010	0.02540
Maximum taper per inch/mm:		0.0015	0.03810
Thrust bearing journal width:		1.1325-1.1355	28.766-28.842
Main and rod bearing journal			
Finish RMS maximum: 10			
Main bearing thrust face			
Finish RMS maximum: 20			
Connecting rod journal			
Diameter:	8		
Standard		2.4980-2.4990	63.3492-63.4746
Undersize			
0.01:		2.488-2.489	63.1952-63.2206

7.3L DIESEL ENGINE MECHANICAL SPECIFICATIONS

Description		English Specifications	Metric Specifications
Crankshaft and Flywheel (cont'd)			
0.02:		2.478-2.479	62.9412-62.9666
0.03:		2.468-2.469	62.6872-62.7126
Taper per inch/mm maximum:		0.00026	0.0066
Crankshaft end-play:		0.0025-0.0085	0.063-0.216
Flywheel and ring gear runout:		0.0080	0.2032
Flywheel and ring gear concentricity:		0.0080	0.2032
Crankshaft Bearings			
Connecting rod bearing to crankshaft clearance selective fit			
Desired:		0.0015-0.0045	0.0381-0.1140
Allowable:		0.0011-0.0036	0.0279-0.09144
Main bearing to crankshaft selective fit			
Desired:		0.0018-0.0036	0.0457-0.0914
Allowable:		0.0018-0.0046	0.0457-0.1168
Connecting rods			
Piston pin bushing bore I.D.:		1.432-1.433	36.373-36.398
Rod bearing bore I.D.:	9	2.5005-2.5025	63.513-63.564
Connecting rod bore max. out of round:		0.0005	0.0127
Connecting rod bore max. taper:		0.0005	0.0127
Connecting rod alignment maximum total difference			
Twist:	10	0.0020	0.0508
Bend:	10	0.0020	0.0508
Rod to crankshaft assembled side clearance:		0.012-0.024	0.3048-0.6096
Crankpin bearing bore diameter:		2.6905-2.6915	68.339-68.364
Pistons			
Diameter	11		
Standard piston:		4.1045-4.1050	104.2543-104.2670
Piston to bore clearance selective fit:		0.0044-0.0057	0.112-0.149
Piston pin bore diameter:		1.3075-1.3095	33.2105-33.2613
Piston height above crankcase:		0.010-0.031	0.254-0.787
Oversize			
0.01:		4.1148	104.5146
0.02:		4.1248	104.7686
0.03:		4.1348	105.0226
Piston pins			
Length:		2.99-3.00	75.94-76.20
Diameter:		1.3079-1.3081	33.220-33.226
To piston pin bore clearance (selective fit):		0.0003-0.0007	0.00762-0.01778
To connecting rod bushing clearance:		0.0004-0.0009	0.0102-0.0229
Piston rings			
Side clearance (2nd ring only):		0.002-0.004	0.0508-0.1016
Ring gap			
Top compression:		0.014-0.024	0.35-0.61
Bottom compression:		0.062-0.072	1.57-1.83
Oil:		0.012-0.024	0.305-0.610
Oversize			
0.01:		4.1200	104.6480
0.02:		4.1300	104.9020
0.03:		4.1400	105.1560
Exhaust manifold			
Maximum allowable warpage			
Between ports:		0.0050	0.1300
Total:		0.0100	0.2500
Maximum allowable removal of material:		0.0100	0.2500
Camshaft			
End-play:		0.002-0.008	0.051-0.203
Camshaft journal to bearing clearance:		0.002-0.006	0.051-0.165
Lobe lift	12		
Intake:		0.2535	6.4390
Exhaust:		0.2531	6.4290
Camshaft front bearing location:		0.0020-0.0500	0.508-1.270
Gear backlash:		0.0055-0.010	0.140-0.256
Camshaft drive			
Bearing inside diameter	13		
No. 1:		2.102-2.105	53.39-53.48
No. 2:		2.102-2.105	53.39-53.48
No. 3:		2.102-2.105	53.39-53.48
No. 4:		2.102-2.105	53.39-53.48
No. 5:		2.102-2.105	53.39-53.48
Camshaft front bearing location:	14	0.020-0.050	0.508-1.270
Gear backlash:		0.0055-0.0100	0.140-0.256

7.3L DIESEL ENGINE MECHANICAL SPECIFICATIONS

Description	English Specifications	Metric Specifications
Oil pump, oil cooler and oil capacity		
Oil pump pressures		
Curb idle:	10 psi	69 kPa
3300 rpm:	40-70 psi	276-483 kPa
Engine oil capacity		
U.S. quarts: 14		
Litres: 13.2		
Imperial quarts: 11.6		
Oil pump drive gear radial clearance:	0.012-0.032	0.305-0.813
Oil pump drive gear end clearance:	0.001-0.003	0.025-0.0762

1 Unless otherwise specified with a different measurement (for example, psi, kPa, lbs., N, etc.)
2 With bearing caps tightened in place
3 Valve seat angle: intake: 30 degrees, exhaust: 37.5 degrees
4 Service limit: 0.005 in. (0.127mm)
5 Time required for plunger to leak down 0.125 in. (3.175mm) under load of 50 lbs. (22.5 kg) using leak down fluid in tappet
6 Measured at the valve tip to rocker arm
7 Service limit: 10 percent loss pressure
8 Service limit: 0.005 in. (0.127mm)
9 With bearing caps tightened in place
10 Pin bushing and crankshaft bore must be parallel and in the same vertical plane with specified total difference when measured at at the ends of an 8-inch long bar, 4 inches on each side of the rod centerline
11 Measured at 90 degrees to the pin, at 1.25 in. (31.75mm) below the oil ring groove
12 Service limit: 0.002 in. (0.0508mm) maximum increase in clearance
13 Distance in inches/millimeters that the front edge of the bearing is installed below the front face of the cylinder block
14 All camshaft journals are 2.099-2.100 in. (53.315-53.340mm)

7.5L ENGINE MECHANICAL SPECIFICATIONS

Description	Footnotes	English Specifications (in.)	Metric Specifications (mm)
Cylinder Block			
Cylinder bore			
Standard size:		4.360-4.364	110.744-110.846
Maximum out-of-round:		0.00150	0.03810
Maximum taper:		0.01000	0.25400
Main bearing			
Bore diameter:		3.1922-3.1934	81.082-81.112
Distributor shaft bearing bore diameter:		0.5160-0.5175	13.106-13.145
Head gasket surface flatness:			
Overall:		0.00600	0.15240
In any 6 in. (152.4mm):		0.00300	0.07620
Head gasket Surface finish (RMS):		90-150	
Tappet bore diameter:		0.8752-0.8767	22.230-22.690
Cylinder Head			
Combustion chamber volume	2	5.84-6.02 cid	95.70-98.70 cc
Valve guide bore diameter			
Intake:		0.3433-0.3443	8.719-8.745
Exhaust:		0.3433-0.3443	8.719-8.745
Valve seat			
Maximum runout:	3	0.00200	0.00508
Gasket surface finish (RMS):		60-150	
Width			
Intake:		0.060-0.080	1.524-2.032
Exhaust:		0.060-0.080	1.524-2.032
Gasket surface flatness:			
Overall:		0.00600	0.15240
In any 6 in. (152.4mm):		0.00300	0.07620
Valve Rocker Arm Shaft, Pushrods and Tappets			
Rocker arm ratio to 1:1.73			
Pushrod runout TIR maximum:		0.01500	0.38100
Valve tappet or lifter			
Standard diameter:	4	0.8740-0.8745	22.1990-22.2120
Clearance to bore:		0.0007-0.0027	0.0178-0.0068
Hydraulic lifter leakdown rate:	5	10 to 50 seconds for 1/16 travel	
Collapsed tappet gap			
Allowable:		0.075-0.175	1.905-4.445
Desired:		0.100-0.150	2.540-3.810
Valves			
Valve stem to guide clearance			
Intake:		0.0010-0.0027	0.00254-0.0686
Exhaust:		0.0010-0.0027	0.00254-0.0686

7.5L ENGINE MECHANICAL SPECIFICATIONS

Description		English Specifications	Metric Specifications
Valves (cont'd)			
Valve head diameter			
Intake:		1.965-1.989	49.911-50.521
Exhaust:		1.646-1.661	41.808-42.189
Maximum valve face runout:		0.00200	0.05080
Valve springs			
Valve spring compression pressure @ specified height	6		
Intake:		76-84 lbs. @ 1.81 in.	34.47-38.10 kg @ 45.97mm
		218-240 lbs. @ 1.33 in.	98.89-108.86 kg. @ 33.78mm
Exhaust:		76-84 lbs. @ 1.81 in.	34.47-38.10 kg @ 45.97mm
		218-240 lbs. @ 1.33 in.	98.89-108.86 kg. @ 33.78mm
Free length (approx.)			
Intake:		2.06000	52.32400
Exhaust:		2.06000	52.32400
Valve spring assembled height			
Intake:		1.790-1.830	45.466-46.482
Exhaust:		1.790-1.830	45.466-46.482
Valve spring out of square:		5/64 (0.078)	1.98000
Valve Stem Diameter			
Standard			
Intake:		0.3415-0.3423	8.68-8.69
Exhaust:		0.3415-0.3423	8.68-8.69
0.015 Oversize			
Intake:		0.3565-0.3573	9.06-9.08
Exhaust:		0.3565-0.3573	9.06-9.08
0.030 Oversize			
Intake:		0.3715-0.3723	9.44-9.46
Exhaust:		0.3715-0.3723	9.44-9.46
Crankshaft and Flywheel			
Main bearing journals			
Diameter:		2.9994-3.0002	76.1847-76.2051
TIR Maximum runout:	7	0.00200	0.05080
Maximum out-of-round:		0.00060	0.01524
Thrust face runout TIR maximum:		0.00100	0.02540
Maximum taper per inch/mm:		0.00050	0.01270
Thrust bearing journal length:		1.124-1.126	28.5496-28.6004
Main and rod bearing journal			
Finish RMS maximum: 12			
Main bearing thrust face			
Finish RMS maximum: 25 front/23 rear			
Connecting rod journal			
Diameter:		2.4992-2.5000	63.4797-63.5000
Taper per inch/mm maximum:		0.00060	0.01520
Crankshaft free end-play:		0.0040-0.0080	0.1020-0.2030
Crankshaft Bearings			
Connecting rod bearing to crankshaft clearance selective fit			
Desired:		0.0008-0.0015	0.020-0.038
Allowable:		0.0007-0.0025	0.0178-0.0635
Bearing wall thickness			
Standard:		0.0757-0.0762	1.923-1.935
0.002 undersize:		0.0767-0.0772	1.948-1.961
Main bearing to crankshaft selective fit			
Desired:		0.0008-0.0015	0.020-0.038
Allowable:		.0008-.0026	0.020-0.0660
Bearing wall thickness			
Standard:		0.0955-0.0960	2.426-2.38
0.002 undersize:		0.0965-0.0970	2.451-2.464
Connecting rods			
Piston pin bore or bushing I.D.:		1.0386-1.0393	26.380-26.398
Rod bearing bore I.D.:		2.2390-2.2398	56.87-56.89
Connecting rod bore max. out of round:		0.00040	0.01016
Rod length center to center:		6.6035-6.6065	168.529-169.291
Connecting rod alignment maximum total difference			
Twist:	8	0.02400	0.61000
Bend:	8	0.01200	0.30480
Rod to crankshaft assembled side clearance:		0.010-0.020	0.254-0.508
Service limit:		0.02300	0.58400

91193C13

91193C14

7.5L ENGINE MECHANICAL SPECIFICATIONS

Description	English Specifications	Metric Specifications
Pistons		
Diameter [9]		
Coded red:	4.3577-4.3583	110.686-110.700
Coded blue:	4.3589-4.3595	110.716-110.731
.003 oversize:	4.3601-4.3607	110.747-110.762
Piston to bore clearance selective fit:	0.0022-0.0030	0.056-0.076
Piston pin bore diameter:	1.0401-1.0406	26.419-26.431
Ring groove width with compression:		
Top:	0.0805-0.0815	2.045-2.070
Bottom:	0.0805-0.0815	2.045-2.070
Oil:	0.188-0.189	4.775-4.801
Piston pins		
Length:	3.290-3.320	83.566-84.328
Diameter		
Standard:	1.0398-1.0403	26.411-26.424
.001 oversize:	1.0410-1.0413	26.441-26.449
To piston pin bore clearance (selective fit):	0.0002-0.0004	0.005-0.010
To connecting rod bushing clearance: Interference fit		
Piston rings [10]		
Ring width		
Top Compression:	0.077-0.078	1.956-1.981
Bottom compression:	0.077-0.078	1.956-1.981
Side clearance		
Top compression:	0.0013-0.0033	0.033-0.084
Bottom compression:	0.0013-0.0033	0.0330-0.0840
Oil: snug		
Ring gap		
Top compression:	0.010-0.020	0.2540-0.5080
Bottom compression:	0.010-0.020	0.2540-0.5080
Oil (steel rail):	0.010-0.035	0.2540-0.8890
Camshaft		
Lobe lift [11]		
Intake:	0.25200	6.40080
Exhaust:	0.27800	7.06120
End-play		
Standard:	0.001-0.006	0.0254-0.1524
Maximum:	0.00900	0.22800
Camshaft journal to bearing clearance [12]	0.001-0.003	0.0254-0.076
Camshaft drive [13]		
Journal diameter (standard)		
No. 1:	2.1238-2.1248	53.9445-53.9699
No. 2:	2.1238-2.1248	53.9445-53.9699
No. 3:	2.1238-2.1248	53.9445-53.9699
No. 4:	2.1238-2.1248	53.9445-53.9699
No. 5:	2.1238-2.1248	53.9445-53.9699
Bearing inside diameter		
No. 1:	2.1258-2.1268	53.9953-54.0207
No. 2:	2.1258-2.1268	53.9953-54.0207
No. 3:	2.1258-2.1268	53.9953-54.0207
No. 4:	2.1258-2.1268	53.9953-54.0207
No. 5:	2.1258-2.1268	53.9953-54.0207
Camshaft front bearing location (max.): [14]	0.040-0.060	1.0160-1.5240
Timing chain deflection (max.):	0.50000	12.70000
Oil pump and oil capacity		
Relief valve spring pressure @ specified length:	20.6 lbs.-22.6 @ 2.49 in.	9.35-10.26 kg @ 6.32mm
Driveshaft to housing clearance:	0.0015-0.0030	0.0381-0.076
Relief valve to housing clearance:	0.0015-0.0030	0.0381-0.076
Rotor assembly end clearance:	0.0040 maximum	0.100 maximum
Outer race to housing clearance:	0.0010-0.0130	0.0254-0.3300
Engine oil capacity		
U.S. quarts: 5		
Imperial quarts: 4.2		
Litres: 4.7		

1 Unless otherwise specified with a different measurement (for example, psi, kPa, lbs., N, etc.)
2 Compression pressure (PSI) of the lowest cylinder must be at least 75 percent of the highest to be within specification
3 Valve seat angle: 45 degrees
4 Service limit: 0.005 in. (0.127mm)
5 Time required for plunger to leak down 0.625 in. (15.87mm) under load of 50 lbs. (22.5 kg) using leak down fluid in tappet
6 Service limit: 10 percent loss pressure
7 Service limit: 0.005 in. (0.127mm)

9193C15

7.5L ENGINE MECHANICAL SPECIFICATIONS

Description	English Specifications	Metric Specifications

8 Pin bushing and crankshaft bore must be parallel and in the same vertical plane with specified total difference when measured at the ends of an
8-inch long bar, 4 inches on each side of the pin centerline
9 Measured at the piston pin bore centerline at 90 degrees to the pin
10 Service limit: 0.002 in. (0.0508mm) maximum increase in clearance
11 Maximum allowable lift loss: 0.005 in. (0.127mm)
12 Service limit: 0.006 in. (0.1524mm)
13 Camshaft journal runout: 0.005 in. (0.127mm) TIR maximum
14 Distance in inches/millimeters that the front edge of the bearing is installed below the front face of the cylinder block

9193C16

Engine

REMOVAL & INSTALLATION

In the process of removing the engine, you will come across a number of steps which call for the removal of a separate component or system, such as "disconnect the exhaust system" or "remove the radiator." In most instances, a detailed removal procedure can be found elsewhere in this manual.

It is virtually impossible to list each individual wire and hose which must be disconnected, simply because so many different model and engine combinations have been manufactured. Careful observation and common sense are the best possible approaches to any repair procedure.

Removal and installation of the engine can be made easier if you follow these basic points:

• If you have to drain any of the fluids, use a suitable container.

• Always tag any wires or hoses and, if possible, the components they came from before disconnecting them.

• Because there are so many bolts and fasteners involved, store and label the retainers from components separately in muffin pans, jars or coffee cans. This will prevent confusion during installation.

• After unbolting the transmission, always make sure it is properly supported.

• If it is necessary to disconnect the air conditioning system, have this service performed by a qualified technician using a recovery/recycling station. If the system does not have to be disconnected, unbolt the compressor and set it aside.

• When unbolting the engine mounts, always make sure the engine is properly supported. When removing the engine, make sure that any lifting devices are properly attached to the engine. It is recommended that if your engine is supplied with lifting hooks, your lifting apparatus be attached to them.

• Lift the engine from its compartment slowly, checking that no hoses, wires or other components are still connected.

• After the engine is clear of the compartment, place it on an engine stand or workbench.

• After the engine has been removed, you can perform a partial or full teardown of the engine using the procedures outlined in this manual.

4.2L Engine

✳✳ CAUTION

Fuel injection systems remain under pressure, even after the engine has been turned OFF. The fuel system pressure must be relieved before disconnecting any fuel lines. Failure to do so may result in fire and/or personal injury.

1. Disconnect the negative battery cable.
2. Mark the position of the hood on the hinges and remove the hood.
3. Drain the engine cooling system into a suitable container.
4. Have the A/C system discharged by an EPA-certified technician.
5. Properly relieve the fuel system pressure.
6. Remove the engine cooling fan, shroud and radiator.
7. Remove the engine air cleaner outlet tube.
8. Disconnect the accelerator and cruise control cables at the throttle body.
9. Disconnect the Vapor Management Valve (VMV) hose.
10. Detach the manifold vacuum connection.
11. Detach the Intake Manifold Runner Control (IMRC) vacuum connectors, fuel pressure regulator vacuum connector, IMRC solenoid vacuum connector and vacuum reservoir connector.
12. Detach the EGR valve vacuum connector.
13. Remove the three power steering reservoir retaining bolts and position aside.
14. If equipped with air conditioning, remove the A/C compressor manifold bolt and disconnect, then position the A/C lines aside.
15. Remove the four power steering pump retaining bolts and position the pump aside.
16. Detach the alternator electrical harness connectors. Remove the positive battery cable nut and disconnect the battery cable.
17. Detach the electrical harness connectors to the fuel injectors.
18. Tag and disconnect the ignition wires at the spark plugs.

19. Disconnect both heater hoses.
20. Disconnect the brake booster vacuum hose.
21. Disconnect the EGR Differential Pressure Feedback (DPFE) transducer hose.
22. Remove the breather tube from the cylinder head cover.
23. Remove the upper intake manifold.
24. Disconnect and plug the fuel supply and return lines and remove the fuel injection supply manifold.
25. Raise and safely support the vehicle.
26. If equipped, disconnect the block heater cable.
27. Disconnect the exhaust system from the exhaust manifolds and support with wire hung from the crossmember.
28. Remove the starter motor.
29. Remove the transmission from the vehicle. If equipped with a manual transmission, remove the clutch assembly.
30. Remove the right-hand and left-hand engine support insulator throughbolts.
31. Lower the vehicle.
32. Install a suitable engine lifting bracket and connect suitable engine lifting equipment to the lifting brackets.
33. Carefully raise the engine out of the engine compartment and position on a work stand. Remove the engine lifting equipment.

To install:

34. Install the engine lifting brackets. Support the engine using a suitable floor crane installed to the lifting equipment and remove the engine from the work stand.
35. Carefully lower the engine into the engine compartment aligning the engine support insulators.
36. Remove the engine lifting equipment and brackets.
37. Raise and safely support the vehicle.
38. Install the left-hand and right-hand engine support insulator throughbolts and tighten them to 51–67 ft. lbs. (68–92 Nm).
39. If equipped with a manual transmission, install the clutch assembly.
40. Install the transmission.
41. The balance of the installation is the reverse of the removal.

4.6L, 5.4L and 6.8L Engines

✳✳ CAUTION

Fuel injection systems remain under pressure, even after the engine has been turned OFF. The fuel system pressure must be relieved before disconnecting any fuel lines. Failure to do so may result in fire and/or personal injury.

1. Disconnect the negative battery cable.
2. Mark the position of the hood on the hinges and remove the hood.
3. Drain the engine cooling system into a suitable container.
4. Have the A/C system discharged by an EPA-certified technician.
5. Properly relieve the fuel system pressure.
6. Remove the engine cooling fan, shroud and radiator.
7. Remove the accessory drive belt.
8. Remove the engine air cleaner outlet tube.
9. Remove the intake manifold assembly.
10. Remove the bulkhead connector cover and detach the bulkhead connector.
11. Remove the three power steering reservoir bracket retaining bolts and move the reservoir aside.
12. Disconnect two DPFE transducer hoses.
13. Disconnect the upper and lower EGR valve to exhaust manifold tube fittings and remove the tube.
14. Slide the heater water hose clamp back and remove the hose.
15. Remove the ignition coil, radio capacitor and Camshaft Position (CMP) sensor electrical harness connectors.
16. Remove both ignition coils and mounting bracket bolts and remove the coil and bracket assemblies.
17. Raise and safely support the vehicle.
18. Remove the starter motor.
19. Remove the three lower radiator air deflector screws. Remove the five clips and remove the air deflector.
20. Detach the A/C compressor electrical harness connector.

21. Remove the A/C manifold-to-compressor bolt and remove the manifold and tube assembly.
22. Remove the three A/C compressor retaining bolts and remove the A/C compressor.
23. Remove the fluid cooler hoses from the block mounted clip.
24. On vehicles with automatic transmissions, remove the inspection cover, torque converter bolts and transmission-to-engine retaining bolts.
25. On vehicles with manual transmission, remove the transmission and the clutch assembly.
26. Remove the upper and lower power steering pump bolts and move the power steering pump aside.
27. Disconnect the exhaust system from the exhaust manifolds and support with wire hung from the crossmember.
28. Remove the right-hand and left-hand engine support insulator (mount) through-bolts.
29. Lower the vehicle.
30. Install a suitable engine lifting bracket and connect suitable engine lifting equipment to the lifting brackets.
31. Carefully raise the engine out of the engine compartment and place on a work stand. Remove the engine lifting equipment.

To install:
32. Install the engine lifting brackets. Support the engine using a suitable floor crane installed to the lifting equipment and remove the engine from the work stand.
33. Carefully lower the engine into the engine compartment. Start the converter pilot into the flywheel and align the paint marks on the flywheel and torque converter. Be sure the studs on the torque converter align with the holes in the flywheel.
34. Fully engage the engine to the transmission and lower onto the engine support insulators.
35. Remove the engine lifting equipment and brackets.
36. Raise and safely support the vehicle.
37. If equipped with a manual transmission, install the clutch and transmission assemblies.
38. Install the six engine-to-transmission retaining bolts and tighten to 30–44 ft. lbs. (40–60 Nm).
39. Install the engine support insulator through-bolts and tighten to 15–22 ft. lbs. (20–30 Nm).
40. Install the four torque converter retaining nuts and tighten to 22–25 ft. lbs. (20–30 Nm).
41. Install the transmission housing cover to the cylinder block.
42. The balance of the installation is the reverse of the removal.

5.8L and 7.5L Engines

1. Remove the hood.
2. Drain the cooling system and crankcase.
3. Disconnect the negative battery cable.
4. Remove the air intake hoses, PCV tube and carbon canister hose.
5. Disconnect the upper and lower radiator hoses.
6. Have the A/C system discharged by an EPA-certified technician.
7. Disconnect the refrigerant lines at the compressor. Cap all openings immediately.
8. If so equipped, disconnect the automatic transmission oil cooler lines.
9. Remove the fan shroud and lay it over the fan.
10. Remove the radiator and fan, shroud, fan, spacer, pulley and belt.
11. Remove the alternator pivot and adjusting bolts. Remove the alternator.
12. Detach the oil pressure sending unit lead from the sending unit.
13. Disconnect the fuel tank-to-pump fuel line at the fuel pump and plug the line.
14. Disconnect the chassis fuel line at the fuel rails.
15. Disconnect the accelerator linkage and speed control linkage at the throttle body.
16. Disconnect the automatic transmission kick-down rod and remove the return spring, if so equipped.
17. Disconnect the power brake booster vacuum hose.
18. Disconnect the throttle bracket from the upper intake manifold and swing it out of the way with the cables still attached.
19. Disconnect the heater hoses from the water pump and intake manifold or tee.
20. Disconnect the temperature sending unit wire from the sending unit.
21. Remove the upper bell housing-to-engine attaching bolts.

22. Remove the wiring harness from the left rocker arm cover and position the wires out of the way.
23. Disconnect the ground strap from the cylinder block.
24. Disconnect the air conditioning compressor clutch wire.
25. Raise and safely support the front of the vehicle and disconnect the starter cable from the starter.
26. Remove the starter.
27. Disconnect the exhaust pipe from the exhaust manifolds.
28. Disconnect the engine mounts from the brackets on the frame.
29. On vehicles with automatic transmissions, remove the converter inspection plate and remove the torque converter-to-flywheel attaching bolts.
30. Remove the remaining bell housing-to-engine attaching bolts.
31. Lower the vehicle and support the transmission with a jack.
32. Install an engine lifting device.
33. Raise the engine slightly and carefully pull it out of the transmission. Lift the engine out of the engine compartment.

To install:
34. Remove the engine mount brackets from the frame and attach them to the engine mounts. Tighten the mount-to-bracket nuts just enough to hold them securely.
35. Lower the engine carefully into the transmission. Be sure that the dowel in the engine block engage the holes in the bell housing through the rear cover plate. If the engine hangs up after the transmission input shaft enters the clutch disc (manual transmission only), turn the crankshaft with the transmission in gear until the input shaft splines mesh with the clutch disc splines.
36. Install the engine mount nuts and washers. Tighten the nuts to 80 ft. lbs. (108 Nm). Tighten the bracket-to-frame bolts to 70 ft. lbs. (95 Nm).
37. Remove the engine lifting device.
38. Install the lower bell housing-to-engine attaching bolts. Tighten the bolts to 50 ft. lbs. (68 Nm).
39. Remove the transmission support jack.
40. On vehicles with automatic transmissions, install the torque converter-to-flywheel attaching bolts. Tighten the bolts to 30 ft. lbs. (41 Nm).
41. Install the converter inspection plate. Tighten the bolts to 60 inch lbs. (7 Nm).
42. The balance of the installation is the reverse of the removal.

7.3L Diesel Engine

1. Disconnect the negative battery cable(s).
2. Remove the hood.
3. Drain and recycle the engine coolant.
4. Properly relieve the fuel system pressure.
5. If equipped with air conditioning, have the A/C system discharged by an EPA-certified technician.
6. On automatic transmission equipped vehicles, remove the turbocharger. Refer to the procedure in this section.
7. Remove the air cleaner and intake duct assembly and cover the air intake opening with a clean rag to keep out the dirt.
8. Remove the engine fan and the fan shroud.
9. Remove the radiator.
10. Remove the alternator.
11. Detach the A/C compressor electrical connector.
12. Disconnect the lines from the A/C compressor.
13. Disconnect the vacuum pump hose from the vacuum pump.
14. Disconnect the power steering pump lines from the power steering pump.
15. Disconnect the A/C lines at the condenser and position the lines aside.
16. Disconnect the heater hoses at the water pump and the right cylinder head.
17. Disconnect the radiator hose from the water pump.
18. Detach the MAP sensor vacuum hose from the engine.
19. Detach the driver's side engine compartment components and lay the wiring harness to the side.
20. Remove the jack handle.
21. Remove the engine charge exhaust pipe-to-turbocharger clamp.
22. Disconnect the wiring harness from the starter relay.
23. Raise and support the vehicle.
24. On manual transmission equipped vehicles, remove the transmission.
25. Remove the right and left turbocharger inlet pipe bolts and nuts.
26. Disconnect the engine block heater.
27. Remove the starter.

28. Remove the oil filter.
29. Remove the right and left side engine mount nuts.
30. On automatic transmission equipped vehicles:
    a. Remove the transmission housing cover.
    b. Remove the four converter-to-flywheel attaching nuts.
    c. Remove the four lower transmission attaching bolts.
31. Lower the vehicle.
32. On automatic transmission equipped vehicles:
    a. Remove the ground strap bolt at the rear of the engine.
    b. Remove the two upper transmission retaining bolts.
33. Support the transmission using a suitable jack.
34. Remove the front lamp harness plastic fasteners and lay the harness aside.
35. Make sure no other component interferes with the engine removal.
36. Attach an engine lifting device and remove the engine from the truck.

To install:
37. Lower the engine into vehicle.
38. Align the converter to the flexplate and the engine dowels to the transmission.
39. Install the engine mount bolts and tighten them to 71–94 ft. lbs. (96–127 Nm).
40. Remove the engine lifting sling.
41. Install the four lower transmission attaching bolts. Tighten the bolts to 65 ft. lbs. (88 Nm).
42. Remove transmission jack.
43. Raise and support the front end.
44. If equipped with an automatic transmission, install the four converter-to-flywheel attaching nuts. Tighten the nuts to 89 ft. lbs. (121 Nm).
45. Install the flywheel inspection plate. Tighten the bolts to 13–17 ft. lbs. (17–23 Nm).
46. The balance of the installation is the reverse of the removal.

Rocker Arm (Valve) Cover

REMOVAL & INSTALLATION

4.2L Engine

▶ See Figure 1

DRIVER'S SIDE VALVE COVER

1. Disconnect the negative battery cable.
2. Remove the positive crankcase ventilation valve.
3. Loosen the valve cover retaining bolts and studs.
4. Remove the valve cover.
5. Remove and discard the valve cover gasket.

To install:
6. Install the valve cover onto the cylinder head.
7. Tighten the two bolts and the three stud bolts retaining the valve cover to 6–8 ft. lbs. (8–11 Nm).
8. Install the positive crankcase ventilation valve.
9. Connect the negative battery cable.
10. Check the oil level and add as necessary.

PASSENGER SIDE VALVE COVER

1. Disconnect the negative battery cable.
2. Remove the bolts and position the EGR bracket aside.
3. Remove the crankcase ventilation hose.
4. Loosen the valve cover retaining bolts and studs.
5. Remove the valve cover.
6. Remove and discard the valve cover gasket.

To install:
7. Install a new valve cover gasket.
8. Install the valve cover onto the cylinder head.
9. Tighten the two bolts and the three stud bolts retaining the valve cover to 6–8 ft. lbs. (8–11 Nm).
10. Install the crankcase ventilation hose.
11. Install the EGR bracket.
12. Connect the negative battery cable.
13. Check the oil level and add as necessary.

4.6L, 5.4L and 6.8L Engines

DRIVER'S SIDE VALVE COVER

▶ See Figures 2, 3, 4 and 5

1. Disconnect the negative battery cable.
2. Remove the engine air cleaner and the air cleaner outlet tube.
3. On the 5.4L DOHC engine, remove the upper intake manifold. Refer to the procedure outlined in this section.
4. Remove the bolts and position the power steering fluid reservoir and bracket aside.
5. Remove the crankcase ventilation tube from the valve cover.
6. Disconnect the EGR valve-to-exhaust manifold tube fittings and the two DPFE hoses and remove the EGR valve-to-exhaust manifold tube.
7. Detach the fuel injector electrical connections on the driver's side.
8. On 5.4L and 6.8L engines, detach the ignition coil electrical connections on the driver's side.
9. Detach the camshaft position (CMP) sensor connector.
10. Remove the engine sensor control wiring harness from the valve cover studs.

➡ The bolts are part of the valve cover and should not be removed.

11. Loosen the valve cover retaining bolts and remove the valve cover.
12. Inspect the valve cover gasket and clean the mating surface of the cylinder head.

➡ The valve cover gasket can be reused, however if the gasket appears to be cracked, dry-rotted, or signs of leakage appeared before the teardown, replace the gasket.

To install:

➡ If not secured within four minutes, the sealant must be removed and the sealing area cleaned with Metal Surface Cleaner F4AZ-19A536-A or equivalent meeting Ford specification WSE-M5B392-RA. Allow to dry until there is no sign of wetness, or four minutes, whichever is longer. Failure to follow this procedure can cause future oil leakage.

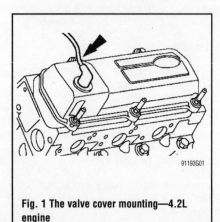

Fig. 1 The valve cover mounting—4.2L engine

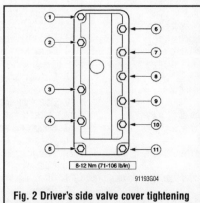

Fig. 2 Driver's side valve cover tightening sequence—4.6L Romeo engine

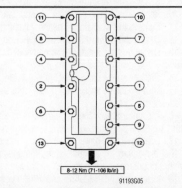

Fig. 3 Driver's side valve cover tightening sequence—4.6L Windsor engine

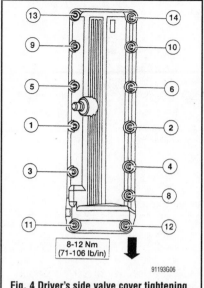

Fig. 4 Driver's side valve cover tightening sequence—5.4L engine

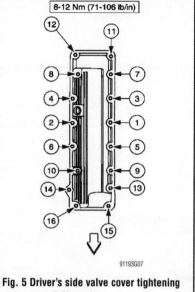

Fig. 5 Driver's side valve cover tightening sequence—6.8L engine

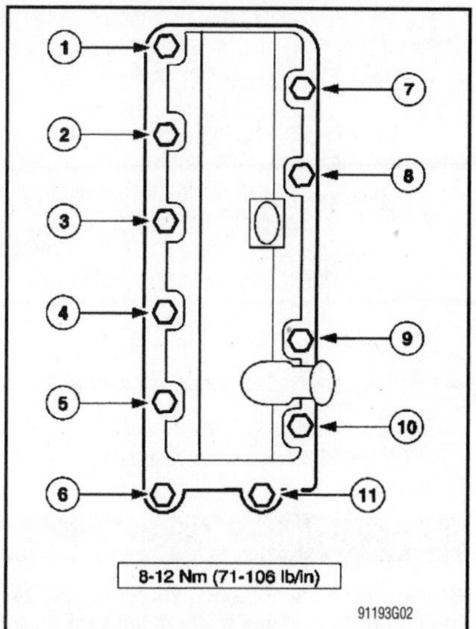

Fig. 6 Passenger side valve cover tightening sequence—4.6L Romeo engine

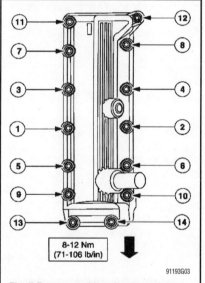

Fig. 7 Passenger side valve cover tightening sequence—4.6L Windsor engine

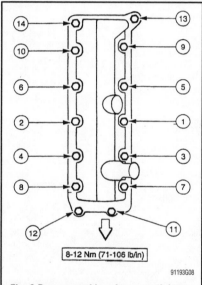

Fig. 8 Passenger side valve cover tightening sequence—5.4L engine

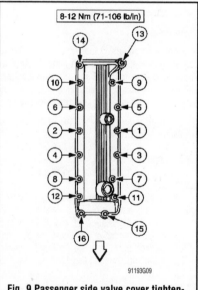

Fig. 9 Passenger side valve cover tightening sequence—6.8L engine

13. Apply a bead of silicone in two places where the engine front cover meets the cylinder head.

Use Silicone Gasket and Sealer F6AZ-19562-AA or equivalent meeting Ford specification WSE-M4G323-A6.

14. Position the valve cover and the valve cover gasket on the cylinder head, and loosely install the bolts.

15. Tighten the valve cover retaining bolts in sequence, referring to the graphics in this section, to 71–106 inch lbs. (8–12 Nm).

16. Position the engine sensor control wiring harness onto the valve cover studs.

17. Attach the CMP electrical connector.

18. On 5.4L and 6.8L engines, attach the ignition coil electrical connectors.

19. Connect the fuel injector electrical connectors.

20. On the 5.4L DOHC engine, install the upper intake manifold.

21. Connect the EGR valve to exhaust manifold tube upper fitting.

22. Connect the crankcase ventilation tube to the valve cover.

23. Install the power steering fluid reservoir and bracket.

24. Install the engine air cleaner and air cleaner outlet tube.

25. Connect the negative battery cable.

26. Check the oil level and add as necessary.

PASSENGER SIDE VALVE COVER

▶ See Figures 6, 7, 8 and 9

1. Disconnect the negative battery cable.

2. Remove the engine air cleaner.

3. On the 5.4L DOHC engine, remove the upper intake manifold. Refer to the procedure outlined in this section.

4. Remove the bolts and remove the accelerator control splash shield.

5. Disconnect the crankcase ventilation hose from the valve cover.

6. Disconnect the two fuse block cable ends from the starter relay.

7. Detach the two 42-pin bulkhead electrical connections and remove them from the junction block bracket.

8. Detach the 16-pin electrical connection and the single pin electrical connection.

9. Remove the bolts and the junction block bracket.

10. Disconnect the heater water hose.

11. Disconnect the heater water hose from the heater core and remove the heater water hose.

12. Detach the fuel injector electrical connections on the passenger side.

13. On 5.4L and 6.8L engines, detach the ignition coil electrical connections on the passenger side.

14. Detach the climate control vacuum connection.

15. Raise and support the vehicle.

16. Detach the A/C compressor electrical connection.

17. Detach the crankshaft position (CKP) sensor electrical connection.

18. Position the wiring harness aside.

19. Lower the vehicle.

➡The bolts are part of the valve cover and should not be removed.

20. Loosen the valve cover retaining bolts and remove the valve cover.

21. Inspect the valve cover gasket and clean the mating surface of the cylinder head.

✳✳ CAUTION

Do not use metal scrapers, wire brushes, power abrasive discs or other abrasive means to clean the sealing surfaces. These tools cause scratches and gouges which make cause leak paths to develop. Use a plastic scraping tool to remove all traces of old sealant.

➡**The valve cover gasket can be reused, however if the gasket appears to be cracked, dry-rotted, or signs of leakage appeared before the teardown, replace the gasket.**

To install:

➡**If not secured within four minutes, the sealant must be removed and the sealing area cleaned with Metal Surface Cleaner F4AZ-19A536-A or equivalent meeting Ford specification WSE-M5B392-RA. Allow to dry until there is no sign of wetness, or four minutes, whichever is longer. Failure to follow this procedure can cause future oil leakage.**

22. Apply a bead of silicone in two places where the engine front cover meets the cylinder head.

Use Silicone Gasket and Sealer F6AZ-19562-AA or equivalent meeting Ford specification WSE-M4G323-A6.

23. Position the valve cover and the valve cover gasket on the cylinder head, and loosely install the bolts.

24. Tighten the valve cover retaining bolts in sequence, referring to the graphics in this section, to 71–106 inch lbs. (8–12 Nm).

25. Connect the heater water hose to the heater core.

26. Connect the heater water hose and position the clamp.

27. Connect the heater water hose and position the clamp.

28. Install the junction block bracket and the bolts.

29. Attach the 16-pin electrical connection and the single pin electrical connection.

30. Attach the two 42-pin bulkhead electrical connections.

31. Connect the two fuse cable leads to the starter relay.

32. Raise and support the vehicle.

33. Attach the crankshaft position sensor electrical connection.

34. Connect the A/C compressor electrical connection.

35. Lower the vehicle.

36. On the 5.4L DOHC engine, install the upper intake manifold.

37. Install the positive crankcase ventilation valve and crankcase ventilation hose into the valve cover.

38. Install the accelerator control splash shield.

39. Install the engine air cleaner.

40. Connect the negative battery cable.

41. Check the oil level and add as necessary.

5.8L Engine

▶ See Figure 10

1. Disconnect the negative battery cable.
2. Remove the air cleaner and inlet duct.
3. Remove the coil.
4. For the right cover, remove the lifting eye; for the left cover, remove the oil filler pipe attaching bolt and the lifting eye.

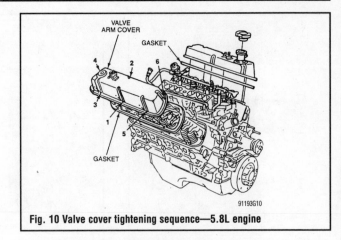

Fig. 10 Valve cover tightening sequence—5.8L engine

5. Mark and remove the spark plug wires.

6. Remove any vacuum lines, wires or pipes in the way. Make sure that you tag them for identification.

7. Remove the cover bolts and lift off the cover. It may be necessary to break the cover loose by rapping on it with a rubber mallet. NEVER pry the cover off!

To install:

8. Thoroughly clean the mating surfaces of both the cover and head.

9. Place the new gasket(s) in the cover(s) with the locating tabs engaging the slots.

10. Place the cover on the head making sure the gasket is evenly seated. Tighten the bolts in sequence to 12–15 ft. lbs. (16–20 Nm). After 2 minutes, retighten the bolts to the same specifications.

11. Install the vacuum lines, wires and pipes.

12. Install the spark plug wires.

13. For the right cover, install the lifting eye; for the left cover, install the oil filler pipe attaching bolt.

14. Install the coil.

15. Install the air cleaner and inlet duct.

16. Connect the negative battery cable.

17. Check the oil level and add as necessary.

7.5L Engine

1. Disconnect the negative battery cable(s).
2. Remove the air cleaner and inlet duct.
3. Remove the coil.
4. Mark and remove the spark plug wires.
5. Remove any vacuum lines, wires or pipes in the way. Make sure that you tag them for identification.
6. Remove the cover bolts and lift off the cover. It may be necessary to break the cover loose by rapping on it with a rubber mallet. NEVER pry the cover off!

To install:

7. Thoroughly clean the mating surfaces of both the cover and head.

8. Place the new cover seal(s) in the cover(s) with the locating tab engaging the slot.

9. Place the cover on the head. Tighten the bolts to 6–9 ft. lbs. (8–12 Nm) from right to left.

10. Install the vacuum lines, wires and pipes.

11. Install the spark plug wires.

12. Install the coil.

13. Install the air cleaner and inlet duct.

14. Connect the negative battery cable(s).

15. Check the oil level and add as necessary.

7.3L Diesel Engine

PASSENGER SIDE COVER

1. Disconnect the negative battery cables.
2. Remove the alternator bolt and move the heater hose out of the way.
3. Remove the drive belt.
4. Remove the alternator.

5. Remove the oil level indicator bracket and dipstick.

6. Remove the fuel injector harness clip and disengage the engine harness connectors from the valve covers.

7. Remove the valve cover bolts and lift off the covers. It may be necessary to break the covers loose by rapping on them with a rubber mallet. NEVER pry a cover off!

8. Disconnect the fuel injectors and glow plugs.

9. Remove the valve cover gasket.

To install:

10. Clean the mating surfaces of the cover and head thoroughly. Install a new gasket.

11. Connect the fuel injectors and glow plugs.

12. Install the valve cover. Tighten the bolts to 8 ft. lbs. (11 Nm).

13. Install the oil tube and dipstick.

14. Install the alternator.

15. Install the drive belt.

16. Position the heater hose as specified and install the alternator bolt. Tighten the bolt to 30–40 ft. lbs. (40–54 Nm).

17. Connect both negative battery cables.

18. Check the oil level and add as necessary.

DRIVER'S SIDE COVER

1. Disconnect both negative battery cables.

2. Remove the air inlet duct assembly between the turbocharger and air cleaner.

3. Remove the crankcase breather assembly.

4. Remove the intake duct and retaining nuts.

5. Remove the vacuum pump hose at the pump.

6. Remove the cover bolts and lift off the covers. It may be necessary to break the covers loose by rapping on them with a rubber mallet. NEVER pry a cover off!

7. Disconnect the fuel injectors and glow plugs.

8. Remove the valve cover gasket.

To install:

9. Clean the mating surfaces of the cover and head thoroughly. Install a new gasket.

10. Connect the fuel injectors and glow plugs.

11. Install the valve cover. Tighten the bolts to 8 ft. lbs. (11 Nm).

12. Connect the vacuum pump hose to the pump.

13. Install the intake duct bracket.

14. Install the crankcase breather assembly.

15. Install the intake duct tube assembly.

16. Connect both negative battery cables.

17. Check the oil level and add as necessary.

Rocker Arm/Shafts

REMOVAL & INSTALLATION

4.2L Engine

➡ **If removing more than one rocker arm, mark the components for proper location.**

1. Disconnect the negative battery cable.

2. Remove the lower intake manifold.

3. Remove the rocker arm cover.

4. Remove the rocker arm hold-down bolt, then remove the rocker arm from the cylinder head.

To install:

5. Position the rocker arms in place, then install the hold-down bolts. Tighten the bolts to 23–29 ft. lbs. (30–40 Nm).

6. Install the rocker arm cover and the lower intake manifold.

7. Connect the negative battery cable.

4.6L and 5.4L Engines

▶ **See Figure 11**

1. Disconnect the negative battery cable.

2. Remove the camshaft covers.

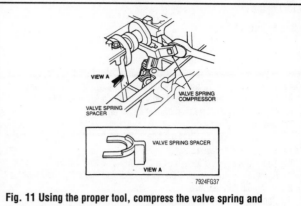

Fig. 11 Using the proper tool, compress the valve spring and remove the rocker arm—4.6L and 5.4L engine

3. Position the cylinder being serviced at the bottom of it's travel.

➡ **Two different valve spring compressor tools are used for this procedure. Valve Spring Compressor (T91P-6565-A) is used on the exhaust camshaft and Valve Spring Compressor (T93P-6565-A) is used on the intake camshaft.**

4. Compress the valve spring using the appropriate spring compressor and remove the rocker arm.

To install:

5. Position the cylinder being serviced at the bottom of it's travel.

6. Apply clean engine oil to the rocker arm, valve stem tip and tappet bore.

➡ **Valve tappet should have no more than 1/16 inch (1.5mm) of travel before installing the rocker arm.**

7. Compress the valve spring using the correct tool and install the rocker arm.

8. Install the valve covers.

9. Connect the negative battery cable.

5.8L Engine

▶ **See Figure 12**

1. Remove the upper intake manifold. Refer to the procedure in this section.

2. Remove the rocker arm covers.

3. Loosen the rocker arm fulcrum bolts, fulcrum seats and rocker arms; keep all parts in order for installation.

To install:

4. Apply multipurpose grease to the valve stem tips, the fulcrum seats and sockets.

5. Install the fulcrum guides, rocker arms, seats and bolts. Tighten the bolts to 18–25 ft. lbs. (25–34 Nm).

6. Install the rocker arm covers.

7. Install the intake manifold. Refer to the procedure in this section.

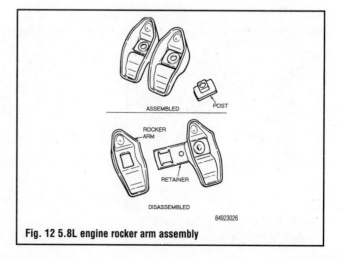

Fig. 12 5.8L engine rocker arm assembly

6.8L Engine

▶ See Figure 13

1. Disconnect the negative battery cable.
2. Remove the valve covers.
3. Position the base circle of the camshaft lobe on the rocker arm to be serviced. Also, be sure the piston is not at the top of it's travel near the valve.
4. Compress the valve spring using Valve Spring Compressor 303–381(TJ91P-6565-A) and remove the rocker arm.

To install:

5. Position the base circle of the camshaft lobe over the place where the rocker arm is to be installed.
6. Apply clean engine oil to the rocker arm, valve stem tip and tappet bore.
7. Compress the valve using the special tool and install the rocker arm.
8. Install the valve covers.
9. Connect the negative battery cable.

7.5L Engine

▶ See Figure 14

1. Remove the intake manifold.
2. Remove the rocker arm covers.
3. Loosen the rocker arm fulcrum bolts, fulcrum, oil deflector, seat and rocker arms; keep everything in order for installation.

To install:

4. Coat each end of each pushrod with multipurpose grease.
5. Coat the top of the valve stems, the rocker arms and the fulcrum seats with multipurpose grease.
6. Rotate the crankshaft by hand until No. 1 piston is at TDC of compression. The firing order marks on the damper will be aligned at TDC with the timing pointer.
7. Install the rocker arms, seats, deflectors and bolts on the following valves:
- No. 1 intake and exhaust
- No. 3 intake
- No. 8 exhaust
- No. 7 intake
- No. 5 exhaust
- No. 8 intake
- No. 4 exhaust

8. Engage the rocker arms with the pushrods and tighten the rocker arm fulcrum bolts to 18–25 ft. lbs. (25–34 Nm).
9. Rotate the crankshaft one full turn—360 degrees—and realign the TDC mark and pointer. Install the parts and tighten the bolts on the following valves:
- No. 2 intake and exhaust
- No. 4 intake
- No. 3 exhaust
- No. 5 intake
- No. 6 intake and exhaust
- No. 7 exhaust

10. Install the rocker arm covers.
11. Install the intake manifold.
12. Check the valve clearance as outlined in Section 1.

7.3L Diesel Engine

▶ See Figure 15

1. Disconnect the ground cables from both batteries.
2. Remove the valve covers.
3. Remove the valve rocker arm mounting bolts.
4. Remove the rocker arms assembly in order and mark them with tape so they can be installed in their original positions.
5. Remove the pushrods. Make a holder for the pushrods out of a piece of wood or cardboard and remove the pushrods in order. It is very important that the pushrods be reinstalled in their original order. The pushrods can remain in position if no further disassembly is required.

✷✷ WARNING

Be careful when removing the rocker arm retaining clip. Do not lose the steel ball.

6. Remove the rocker arm retaining clip.
7. Remove the rocker arm and steel ball from the rocker arm pedestal.

To install:

8. Assemble the rocker arms as follows:
a. Place the steel ball in the rocker arm cup and lubricate with clean engine oil.
b. Place the rocker arm pedestal on the steel ball.
c. Snap the retaining clip over the pedestal groove.
9. If the pushrods were removed, install them in their original locations. be sure they are fully seated in the tappet seats.

➡ **The copper colored end of the pushrod goes toward the rocker arm.**

10. Apply a polyethylene grease to the valve stem tips. Install the rocker arms and posts in their original positions.
11. Turn the engine over by hand until the valve timing mark is at the 11:00 o'clock position, as viewed from the front of the engine. Install all of the rocker arm post attaching bolts and tighten to 20 ft. lbs. (27 Nm).
12. Install new valve cover gaskets and install the valve cover.
13. Install the battery cables.
14. Start the engine and check for leaks.

Thermostat

REMOVAL & INSTALLATION

4.2L Engine

▶ See Figure 16

1. Disconnect the negative battery cable.
2. Allow the engine to cool, then drain the engine cooling system to a level below the water outlet housing.
3. Remove 2 water outlet housing retaining bolts and slide the housing with the hose attached to one side.

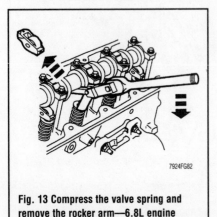

Fig. 13 Compress the valve spring and remove the rocker arm—6.8L engine

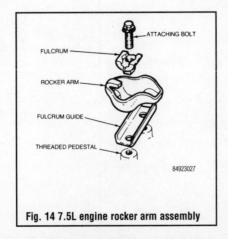

Fig. 14 7.5L engine rocker arm assembly

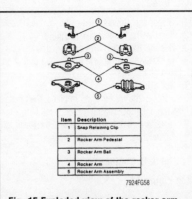

Item	Description
1	Snap Retaining Clip
2	Rocker Arm Pedestal
3	Rocker Arm Ball
4	Rocker Arm
5	Rocker Arm Assembly

Fig. 15 Exploded view of the rocker arm assembly—7.3L diesel engine

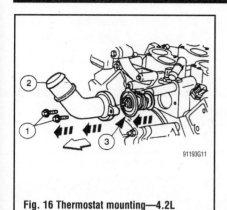

Fig. 16 Thermostat mounting—4.2L engine

Fig. 17 Remove the thermostat housing bolts and remove the housing from the intake manifold

Fig. 18 Remove the thermostat from the intake manifold

Fig. 19 Make sure that the air valve is positioned in the 3 o'clock position after the thermostat is installed

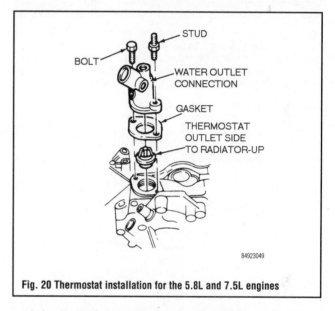

Fig. 20 Thermostat installation for the 5.8L and 7.5L engines

4. Remove the thermostat and gasket.

To install:

5. Clean the gasket sealing surfaces.

6. Install the thermostat with the bridge (opposite end of the spring) inside the elbow connection. Ensure that the notch is properly positioned.

7. Coat a new housing gasket with water resistant sealer and position it on the water outlet connection. Ensure that the notch is properly positioned.

8. Place the water outlet connection on the lower intake manifold and install 2 retaining bolts. Tighten the bolts to 103 inch lbs. (12 Nm).

9. Fill the engine cooling system.

10. Connect the negative battery cable.

11. Start the engine and allow it to reach normal operating temperature while checking for coolant leaks.

12. Road test the vehicle and check for proper engine operation.

13. Check the coolant level and adjust if necessary.

4.6L, 5.4L And 6.8L Engines

▶ See Figures 17, 18, and 19

1. Disconnect the negative battery cable.

2. Drain and recycle the engine coolant.

3. Remove the power steering reservoir support bracket.

4. Remove the upper radiator hose at the thermostat housing.

5. Remove 2 thermostat housing retaining bolts and remove the housing.

6. Remove the thermostat and O-ring from the lower intake manifold. Discard the O-ring.

To install:

7. Clean the O-ring sealing surfaces.

8. Install a new O-ring, on the thermostat and position the thermostat in the lower intake manifold.

9. Place the thermostat housing on the lower intake manifold and install 2 retaining bolts. Tighten the bolts to 15–22 ft. lbs. (20–30 Nm).

10. Install the power steering reservoir support bracket.

11. Fill the engine cooling system.

12. Connect the negative battery cable.

13. Start the engine and allow it to reach normal operating temperature while checking for coolant leaks.

14. Road test the vehicle and check for proper engine operation.

15. Check the coolant level and add if necessary.

5.8L and 7.5L Engines

▶ See Figure 20

1. Disconnect the negative battery cable.

2. Drain the engine cooling system below the level of the thermostat housing.

3. Disconnect the bypass hose at the thermostat housing and the intake manifold. Remove the bypass hose.

4. Remove the upper radiator hose at the thermostat housing.

5. Remove 2 thermostat housing retaining bolts.

6. Remove the thermostat housing from the intake manifold.

7. Remove the thermostat and gasket.

8. Clean the thermostat housing and intake manifold gasket sealing surfaces.

To install:

9. Coat a new thermostat housing gasket with a suitable sealing compound and place the gasket on the intake manifold. The gasket must be in place before the thermostat is installed.

10. Install the thermostat to the intake manifold opening with the copper pellet or opening towards the engine and the thermostat flange positioned in the recess.

11. Place the thermostat housing in position and install 2 retaining bolts. Tighten the bolts to 12–18 ft. lbs. (16–24 Nm) on the 5.8L engine, and 22–38 ft. lbs. (32–37 Nm) for the 7.5L engine.

12. Install the bypass and upper radiator hoses.

13. Connect the negative battery cable.

14. Fill and bleed the engine cooling system.

15. Start the engine and allow to reach normal operating temperature while checking for leaks.

16. Road test the vehicle and check for proper engine operation.

17. Check the coolant level and add if needed.

7.3L Diesel Engine

▶ See Figure 21

✳✳ CAUTION

The factory specified thermostat does not contain an internal bypass. On these engines, an internal bypass is located in the block. The use of any replacement thermostat other than that meeting the manufacturer's specifications will result in engine overheating. Use only thermostats meeting the specifications of Ford or Navistar International.

1. Disconnect both battery ground cables.
2. Drain the coolant to a point below the thermostat housing.

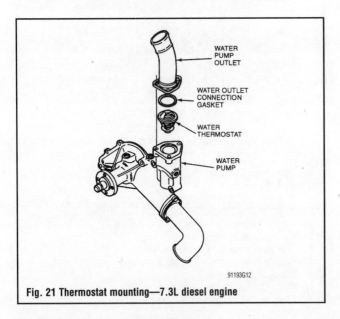

WATER PUMP OUTLET

WATER OUTLET CONNECTION GASKET

WATER THERMOSTAT

WATER PUMP

91193G12

Fig. 21 Thermostat mounting—7.3L diesel engine

3. Remove the upper radiator hose from the thermostat housing.
4. Remove the thermostat housing attaching bolts.
5. Remove the thermostat and gasket.
6. Clean the thermostat housing and block surfaces thoroughly.

To install:

7. Coat a new gasket with sealer and position the gasket on the manifold outlet opening.

8. Install the thermostat in the manifold opening with the spring downward and the flange positioned in the recess in the manifold.

9. Place the outlet housing into position and install the bolts. Torque the bolts to 15 ft. lbs. (20 Nm).

10. Install the upper radiator hose onto the thermostat housing and tighten the hose clamp.

11. Fill and bleed the cooling system.

12. Connect both battery cables.

13. Run the engine and check for leaks.

Intake Manifold

REMOVAL & INSTALLATION

➡When the battery is disconnected and reconnected, some abnormal drive symptoms may occur while the vehicle relearns its adaptive strategy. The vehicle may need to be driven 10 miles (16 km) or more to relearn the strategy.

4.2L Engine

▶ See Figures 22, 23 and 24

1. Remove the engine air cleaner outlet tube.
2. Detach the following ignition coil electrical connections:
   a. Ignition coil electrical connector.
   b. Radio ignition interference capacitor electrical connector.
3. Label, then detach the six spark plug wires.
4. Remove the accelerator control splash shield.
5. Disconnect the accelerator cable end, if equipped, the speed control actuator cable end.
6. Remove the accelerator cable and actuator cable aside, after removing the hold-down bolts.
7. Disconnect the Vapor Management Valve (VMV) hose.
8. Disconnect the brake booster vacuum hose.
9. Disengage the manifold vacuum connection.
10. Remove the PCV valve from the rocker arm cover.
11. Position the Engine Vacuum Regulator (EVR) bracket aside.
12. Detach the throttle position sensor and idle air control valve electrical connectors.
13. Remove the breather from the rocker arm cover.
14. Remove the 12 upper intake manifold retaining bolts, then lift the manifold off of the engine. Discard the intake manifold upper gasket.
15. Detach the six fuel injector electrical connectors.
16. Detach the engine coolant temperature sensor and the water temperature indicator sending unit electrical connectors.

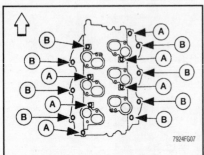

7924FG07

Fig. 22 Make certain to install the long bolts (A) and the short bolts (B) in the correct lower intake manifold holes—4.2L engine

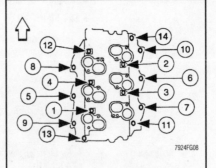

7924FG08

Fig. 23 Tighten the lower manifold bolts in the sequence shown—4.2L engine

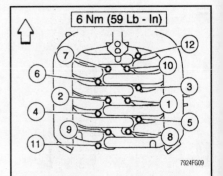

6 Nm (59 Lb - In)

7924FG09

Fig. 24 Tighten the upper intake manifold mounting bolts in the sequence shown—4.2L engine

17. Disconnect the EGR valve vacuum hose.
18. Remove the EGR valve tube upper fitting.
19. Remove the radiator hose from the lower intake manifold.
20. Position the Intake Manifold Runner Control (IMRC) actuator brackets aside.
21. Disconnect the fuel pressure regulator vacuum line.
22. Disconnect the fuel lines.
23. Disconnect the water pump bypass hose.

➡**Remove the lower intake manifold with the fuel injection supply manifold and fuel injectors as one unit.**

24. Remove the six long bolts and the eight short bolts, then lift the lower intake manifold off of the engine.
25. Remove and discard the lower intake manifold sealing components.
To install:
26. Clean all components of dirt, grease and old gasket material.
27. Install the lower intake manifold front and rear end seals as follows:
    a. Apply a bead of sealant (Silicone Gasket and Sealant F6AZ-19562-A or equivalent) to the intake manifold front and rear end seal mounting points.
    b. Install the lower intake manifold front and rear end seals.
28. Install new lower intake manifold gaskets onto the cylinder heads.

➡**The lower intake manifold must be installed within 15 minutes of applying sealant.**

29. Apply a bead of the same sealant to the end of the lower intake manifold end seals, where they stop on the cylinder head surface. Position the intake manifold onto the engine block and cylinder heads.
30. Install the lower intake manifold mounting bolts in the correct positions. Refer to the illustration for the correct placement of the long (A) and the short (B) mounting bolts.

➡**Be sure to tighten the intake manifold bolts in two steps.**

31. Tighten the lower intake manifold mounting bolts in the sequence shown, first to 44 inch lbs. (5 Nm), then to 71–101 inch lbs. (8–12 Nm).
32. Connect the water bypass hose.
33. Attach the fuel lines.
34. Connect the fuel pressure regulator vacuum line.
35. Install the IMRC actuators. Tighten the bolts on the brackets to 71–102 inch lbs. (8–12 Nm).
36. Install the upper radiator hose to the lower intake manifold.
37. Connect the EGR valve vacuum hose.
38. Install the EGR tube upper fitting to 25–34 ft. lbs. (37–47 Nm).
39. Attach the engine coolant temperature sensor and water temperature indicator sending unit electrical connectors.
40. Install the six fuel injector electrical connectors.
41. Install a new intake manifold upper gasket.

➡**Be sure to tighten the upper intake manifold bolts in the sequence shown.**

42. Position the upper intake manifold onto the lower intake manifold, then tighten the upper intake manifold bolts in the sequence shown to 59 inch lbs. (6 Nm). Tighten the upper intake manifold bolts to 6–8 ft. lbs. (8–12 Nm) in the sequence shown.

43. Install the breather into the rocker arm cover.
44. Attach the throttle position sensor and idle air control valve electrical connectors.
45. Install the Engine Vacuum Regulator (EVR) bracket.
46. Attach the manifold vacuum connection.
47. Install the PCV valve.
48. Connect the brake booster vacuum hose.
49. Connect the Vapor Management Valve (VMV) hose.
50. Install the accelerator and speed actuator cables.
51. Install the accelerator control splash shield.
52. Install the spark plug wires.
53. Attach the ignition coil and the radio ignition interference capacitor electrical connectors.
54. Install the engine air cleaner outlet tube.

4.6L, 5.4L and 6.8L Engines, Except 5.4L Lightning and 5.4L DOHC

▶ **See Figures 25 thru 42**

1. Disconnect the negative battery cable.
2. Relieve the fuel system pressure.
3. Drain the cooling system.
4. Disconnect the upper radiator hose from the intake manifold.
5. Remove the engine air cleaner outlet tube.
6. Disconnect the accelerator cable from the bracket and the throttle body cam.
7. If equipped, remove the speed control actuator cable from the throttle body.
8. Disconnect all vacuum hoses, fuel lines and electrical wires from the throttle body and intake manifold.
9. Remove the brake booster vacuum hose bracket.
10. Remove the EGR valve-to-exhaust manifold tube.
11. Detach the fuel injector electrical connectors.
12. On the 6.8L engine, remove the radio interference capacitors from the left side of the intake manifold.
13. Label, then remove the spark plug wires, if necessary.
14. Remove the accessory drive belt.
15. Remove the alternator.
16. Remove the power steering oil reservoir bracket and set aside.
17. Disconnect the heater water hose from the intake manifold.
18. Remove the intake manifold bolts.
19. Lift the intake manifold off of the engine, then detach the Intake Manifold Tuning Valve (IMTV) electrical connector. Remove and discard the upper intake manifold gaskets.
20. Remove the upper-to-lower intake manifold bolts, then separate the upper intake manifold from the lower intake manifold. Discard the old gasket.
To install:
21. Position the lower intake manifold gasket and the upper intake manifold onto the lower intake manifold, then loosely install the upper-to-lower intake manifold bolts.

➡**Be sure to tighten the lower-to-upper manifold bolts in two steps.**

22. Tighten the eight lower-to-upper intake manifold bolts in two steps following the tightening sequence shown. The first step should be to 18 inch lbs. (2 Nm) and the second step to 6–8 ft. lbs. (8–12 Nm).
23. Position the two upper intake manifold gaskets on the cylinder heads.

Fig. 25 Remove the accelerator cable bracket retaining bolt and remove the bracket

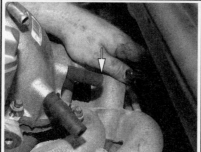

Fig. 26 Disconnect the PCV hose from the nipple on the back of the intake manifold

Fig. 27 Disconnect the fuel feed and return line quick connect fittings

Fig. 28 Disconnect the heater hose to facilitate intake manifold removal

Fig. 29 After the bolts are removed and all necessary components are disconnected, lift the intake manifold from the engine

Fig. 30 Remove the throttle body adapter retaining bolts and . . .

Fig. 31 . . . remove the assembly from the intake manifold

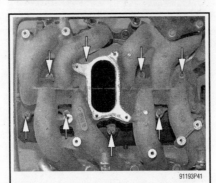

Fig. 32 Remove the eight upper manifold-to-lower manifold retaining bolts and . . .

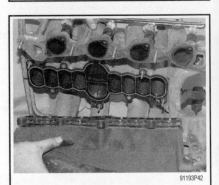

Fig. 33 . . . separate the upper intake manifold from the lower manifold

Fig. 34 Remove the intake manifold gaskets from the cylinder head

Fig. 35 Thoroughly clean the mating surfaces of the cylinder head and the intake manifold

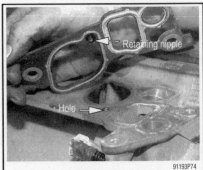

Fig. 36 Install new gaskets on the cylinder heads aligning the retaining nipple with the holes in the cylinder head

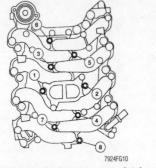

Fig. 37 Tighten the lower-to-upper intake manifold bolts in two steps following the sequence shown—4.6L engine

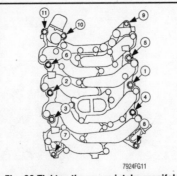

Fig. 38 Tighten the upper intake manifold-to-cylinder head mounting bolts in the sequence shown—4.6L engine

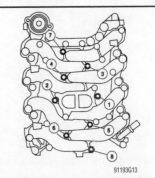

Fig. 39 Tighten the lower-to-upper intake manifold bolts in two steps following the sequence shown—5.4L engine

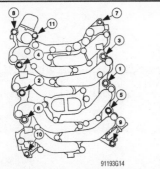

Fig. 40 Tighten the upper intake manifold-to-cylinder head mounting bolts in the sequence shown—5.4L engine

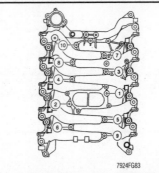

Fig. 41 Tighten the upper-to-lower intake manifold bolts in the sequence shown—6.8L engine

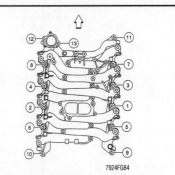

Fig. 42 Tighten the upper intake manifold-to-cylinder head bolts using the sequence shown—6.8L engine

Set the upper intake manifold in place on the engine, then loosely install the nine intake manifold-to-cylinder head bolts.

24. Attach the IMTV electrical connector.

➡**Check that the thermostat housing is in the correct position before the thermostat housing is installed.**

25. Install the thermostat housing and start the two housing bolts.

➡**Make certain to tighten the intake manifold in two steps.**

26. Tighten the thermostat housing bolts in the sequence shown, first to 18 inch lbs. (2 Nm), then to 15–22 ft. lbs. (20–30 Nm).

27. Install the heater water hose.

28. Position the power steering bracket and install the power steering pump bracket bolts to 71–107 inch lbs. (8–12 Nm).

29. Attach all electrical connections, fuel lines, vacuum tubes and coolant hoses to the intake manifold, fuel injectors and throttle body assembly.

30. Install the alternator and the accessory drive belt.

31. Install the spark plug wires.

32. Install the EGR valve-to-exhaust manifold tube. The tube fittings should be tightened to 26–33 ft. lbs. (35–45 Nm).

33. Install the speed actuator cable, if equipped, and the accelerator cable to the throttle body.

34. Install the engine air cleaner outlet tube.

35. Install the heater water hose.

36. Fill the cooling system with the correct amount and type of coolant.

37. Connect the negative battery cable.

38. Start the engine and check for fuel, vacuum or coolant leaks.

5.4L DOHC

UPPER INTAKE MANIFOLD

▸ **See Figures 43, 44, 45, 46 and 47**

1. Remove the air cleaner outlet tube.
2. Remove the three bolts and the engine appearance cover.

3. Disconnect the accelerator cable, speed control cable, and the return spring.

4. Remove the bolts and position the cables and bracket out of the way.

5. Disconnect the evaporative emission return line.

6. Disconnect the positive crankcase ventilation tube from the upper intake manifold.

7. Remove the PCV valve from the valve cover.

8. Disconnect the PCV valve tube from the water heated fitting and remove the tube assembly.

9. Disconnect the coolant lines and plug the lines.

10. Detach the electrical connector from the communication valve.

11. Remove the bolts and the communication valve.

12. Remove the wiring harness shield bolts and five clips and remove the shield.

13. Remove the balance tube from the engine.

14. Detach the throttle position (TP) sensor and the idle air control (IAC) motor.

15. Disconnect the vacuum lines and detach the electrical connector from the EGR vacuum regulator (EVR).

16. Detach the two hoses and detach the electrical connector from the differential pressure feedback EGR.

17. Remove the bolts from the power steering reservoir bracket and position it aside.

18. Remove the stud and position the oil fill tube aside.

19. Disconnect the brake booster vacuum line.

20. Disconnect the vacuum line from the exhaust gas recirculation (EGR) valve.

21. Remove the bolts from the EGR adapter.

22. Remove the retaining bolts and remove the upper intake manifold.

To install:

23. Clean and inspect the sealing surfaces.

24. Install the upper intake manifold:

25. Install the bolts.

26. Tighten the bolts to 89 inch lbs. (10 Nm) and then an additional 90 degrees in the sequence shown.

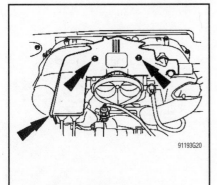

Fig. 43 Remove the three bolts and the engine appearance cover

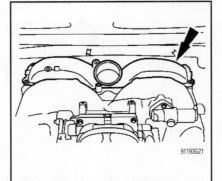

Fig. 44 Remove the balance tube from the engine and . . .

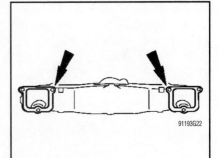

Fig. 45 . . . discard and replace the balance tube gaskets

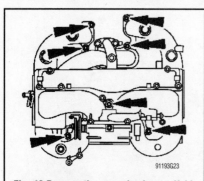

Fig. 46 Remove the upper intake manifold retaining bolts and remove the manifold from the engine

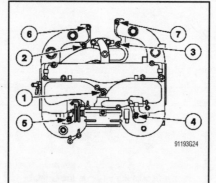

Fig. 47 Upper intake manifold tightening sequence—5.4L DOHC engine

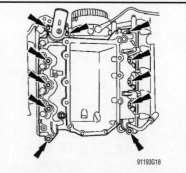

Fig. 48 Remove the lower intake manifold retaining bolts and remove the intake manifold from the engine

27. Install the EGR adapter with a new gasket.
28. Connect the vacuum line to the EGR valve.
29. Connect the brake booster vacuum line.
30. Position the oil fill tube and install the stud.
31. Position the power steering reservoir bracket and install the bolts.
32. Tighten the EGR valve at the exhaust manifold.
33. Attach the two hoses and the electrical connector to the differential pressure feedback EGR.
34. Attach the vacuum lines and the electrical connector to the EVR.
35. Connect the IAC valve and the TP sensor.
36. Install the balance tube on the engine.
37. Install the communication valve and the bolts.
38. Install the wiring harness shield, the bolts and five clips.
39. Attach the electrical connector to the communication valve.
40. Install the tube assembly and connect the PCV valve tube to the water heated fitting.
41. Connect the coolant hoses.
42. Install the PCV valve in the valve cover.
43. Connect the EVAP return line.
44. Position the cables and bracket and install the bolts.
45. Connect the accelerator cable, speed control cable, and the return spring.
46. Install the engine appearance cover and the three bolts.
47. Install the engine air cleaner and outlet tube.

LOWER INTAKE MANIFOLD

▶ See Figures 48 and 49

1. Drain and recycle the engine coolant.
2. Remove the upper intake manifold.
3. Disconnect the fuel lines.
4. Disconnect the engine water bypass hose.
5. Detach the electrical connector from the water temperature indicator sender.
6. Disconnect the upper radiator hose, the heater water inlet hose and the heated positive crankcase ventilation (PCV) water fitting inlet hose.

7. Remove the four bolts and the upper generator support bracket.
8. Disconnect the eight fuel injectors.
9. Disconnect the vacuum line from the fuel injector pressure regulator and position out of the way.
10. Remove the bolts and the lower intake manifold.
11. Remove the bolts and the radio ignition interference capacitors.

To install:
12. Remove and inspect the gaskets, install new gaskets if necessary.
13. Clean the sealing surfaces.
14. Install the radio ignition interference capacitors.

➡**Bolts should be hand-started, positions 7–12 first then 1–6.**

15. Install the lower intake manifold:
16. Position the gaskets.
17. Install the intake manifold and the retaining bolts.
18. Tighten the bolts to 89 inch lbs. (10 Nm) and then an additional 90 degrees in the sequence shown.
19. Connect the water temperature indicator sensor.
20. Position the vacuum harness and connect the vacuum line to the fuel injector pressure regulator.
21. Connect the eight fuel injectors.
22. Install the upper generator support bracket and the four bolts.
23. Connect the heater water inlet hose, the upper radiator hose and the water heated fitting inlet hose.
24. Connect the engine water bypass return hose.
25. Connect the fuel lines.
26. Install the upper intake manifold.
27. Fill the cooling system.

5.4L Lightning

▶ See Figures 50, 51 and 52

1. Remove the charge air cooler.
2. Properly relieve the fuel system pressure.
3. Disconnect the fuel lines.

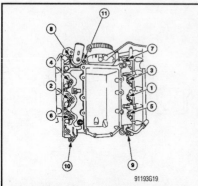

Fig. 49 Lower intake manifold tightening sequence—5.4L DOHC engine

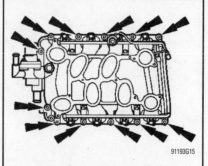

Fig. 50 Remove the retaining bolts for the intake manifold and remove the manifold from the engine

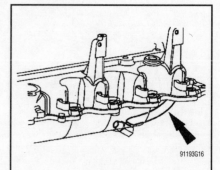

Fig. 51 Make sure that the PCV system hose is securely connected

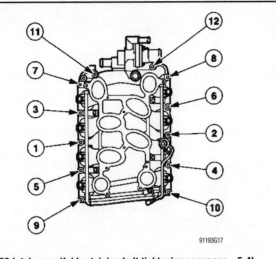

Fig. 52 Intake manifold retaining bolt tightening sequence—5.4L Lightning

4. Drain and recycle the engine coolant.

5. Remove the accelerator cable bracket retaining bolts and remove the bracket.

6. Disconnect the upper radiator hose from the thermostat housing.

✳✳ CAUTION

Do not disconnect the PCV hose system from the intake. Installation can not be carried out with the intake in place.

7. Disconnect the positive crankcase ventilation (PCV) system.

8. Disconnect the ground strap and both radio ignition interference capacitors.

9. Disconnect the vacuum line.

10. Detach the charge air cooler temperature sensor connector.

11. Disconnect the heater hose.

12. Detach the eight fuel injector electrical connectors.

13. Disconnect the vapor management valve vacuum line.

14. Disconnect the vacuum line near the brake vacuum booster.

15. Remove the fuel injection supply manifold.

16. Detach the eight ignition coil connectors.

17. Remove the eight ignition coils.

18. Release the tension from the accessory drive belt.

19. Remove the generator bracket.

20. Remove the retaining bolts and remove the intake manifold.

21. Remove the gaskets.

✳✳ CAUTION

Do not use metal scrapers, wire brushes, power abrasive discs or other abrasive means to clean the sealing surfaces. These tools cause scratches and gouges which make leak paths. Use a plastic scraping tool to clean the sealing surfaces.

22. Clean the sealing surfaces.

To install:

23. Position the gaskets.

✳✳ CAUTION

If the PCV system hose becomes disconnected, the intake manifold will have to be removed to reattach the hose.

24. Make sure that the PCV system hose is securely connected.

25. Install the intake manifold.

26. Position the manifold.

27. Position the thermostat outlet.

28. Install the intake manifold bolts. Tighten the bolts in two stages in the sequence shown.

a. Stage 1: tighten to 18 inch lbs. (2 Nm).

b. Stage 2: tighten to 19 ft. lbs. (25 Nm).

29. Install the generator bracket.

30. Install the accessory drive belt.

31. Install the eight ignition coils.

32. Attach the eight ignition coil connectors.

33. Position the fuel injection supply manifold and install the bolts.

34. Connect the vacuum line near the brake vacuum booster.

35. Connect the vapor management valve vacuum line.

36. Connect the fuel injector electrical connectors.

37. Connect the heater hose.

38. Attach the charge air cooler temperature sensor.

39. Connect the vacuum line.

40. Connect the ground strap and both radio ignition interference capacitors.

41. Connect the positive crankcase ventilation (PCV) system.

42. Connect the upper radiator hose.

43. Position the accelerator cable bracket and tighten the bolts.

44. Connect the fuel lines.

45. Install the charge air cooler.

46. Fill and bleed the engine cooling system.

5.8L and 7.5L Engines

➡**Relieve the fuel system pressure before starting any work that involves disconnecting fuel system lines.**

UPPER INTAKE MANIFOLD

▶ **See Figure 53**

1. Disconnect the negative battery cable.

2. Remove the air cleaner.

3. Disengage the electrical connectors at the air bypass valve, throttle position sensor and EGR position sensor.

4. Disconnect the throttle linkage at the throttle ball and the AOD transmission linkage from the throttle body. Remove the bolts that secure the bracket to the intake and position the bracket and cables out of the way.

5. Disengage the upper manifold vacuum fitting connections by removing all the vacuum lines at the vacuum tree (label lines for position identification). Remove the vacuum lines to the EGR valve and fuel pressure regulator.

6. Disengage the PCV system by disconnecting the hose from the fitting at the rear of the upper manifold.

7. Remove the two canister purge lines from the fittings at the throttle body.

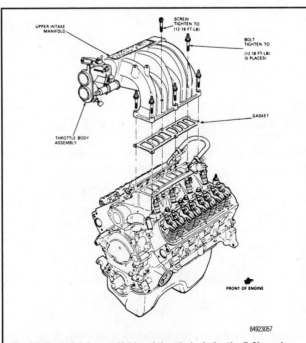

Fig. 53 Upper intake manifold and throttle body for the 5.8L engine

8. Disconnect the EGR tube from the EGR valve by loosening the flange nut.

9. Remove the bolt from the upper intake support bracket to upper manifold.

10. Remove the upper manifold retaining bolts and remove the upper intake manifold and throttle body as an assembly.

11. Clean and inspect all mounting surfaces of the upper and lower intake manifolds.

To install:

12. Position a new mounting gasket on the lower intake manifold.

13. Install the upper intake manifold and throttle body as an assembly.

14. Install the upper manifold retaining bolts and install the bolt at the upper intake support bracket. Mounting bolts are tightened to 12–18 ft. lbs. (16–25 Nm).

15. Connect the EGR tube at the EGR valve.

16. Install the two canister purge lines at the fittings at the throttle body.

17. Connect the PCV system hose at the fitting at the rear of the upper manifold.

18. Connect the upper manifold vacuum lines at the vacuum tree. Install the vacuum lines at the EGR valve and fuel pressure regulator.

19. Install the throttle bracket on the intake manifold. Attach the throttle linkage at the throttle ball and the transmission linkage at the throttle body.

20. Attach the electrical connectors at the air bypass valve, throttle position sensor and EGR position sensor.

21. Install the air cleaner.

LOWER INTAKE MANIFOLD

▶ See Figures 54, 55, 56 and 57

1. Upper manifold and throttle body must be removed first.

2. Drain the cooling system.

3. Remove the distributor assembly, cap and wires.

4. Disengage the electrical connectors at the engine, coolant temperature sensor and sending unit, at the air charge temperature sensor and at the knock sensor.

5. Disconnect the injector wiring harness from the main harness assembly.

6. Remove the ground wire from the intake manifold stud. The ground wire must be installed at the same position it was removed from.

7. Disconnect the fuel supply and return lines from the fuel rails.

8. Remove the upper radiator hose from the thermostat housing. Remove the bypass hose. Remove the heater outlet hose at the intake manifold.

9. Remove the air cleaner mounting bracket.

10. Remove the intake manifold mounting bolts and studs. Pay attention to the location of the bolts and studs for reinstallation.

11. Remove the lower intake manifold assembly.

To install:

12. Clean and inspect the mounting surfaces of the heads and manifold.

13. Apply a 1/16 in. (1.5mm) bead of RTV sealer to the ends of the manifold seal (the junction point of the seals and gaskets).

14. Install the end seals and intake gaskets on the cylinder heads. The gaskets must interlock with the seal tabs.

15. Install locator bolts at opposite ends of each head and carefully lower the intake manifold into position.

16. Install and tighten the mounting bolts and studs in sequence to 23–25 ft. lbs. (31–34 Nm).

17. Install the air cleaner mounting bracket.

18. Install the heater outlet hose at the intake manifold.

19. Install the bypass hose.

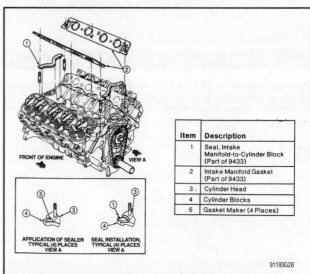

Fig. 56 7.5L engine lower intake manifold gasket installation

Item	Description
1	Seal, Intake Manifold-to-Cylinder Block (Part of 9433)
2	Intake Manifold Gasket (Part of 9433)
3	Cylinder Head
4	Cylinder Blocks
5	Gasket Maker (4 Places)

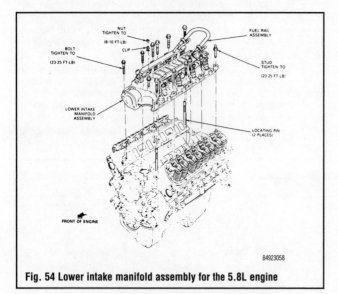

Fig. 54 Lower intake manifold assembly for the 5.8L engine

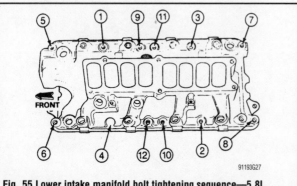

Fig. 55 Lower intake manifold bolt tightening sequence—5.8L engine

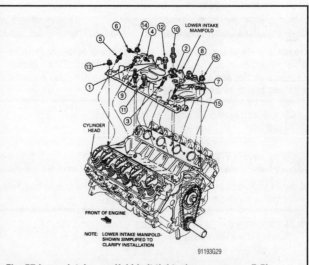

Fig. 57 Lower intake manifold bolt tightening sequence—7.5L engine

20. Install the upper radiator hose.
21. Connect the fuel supply and return lines at the fuel rails.
22. Connect the injector wiring harness from the main harness assembly.
23. Install the ground wire onto the intake manifold stud.
24. Attach the electrical connectors at the engine, coolant temperature sensor and sending unit, at the air charge temperature sensor and at the knock sensor.
25. Install the distributor assembly, cap and wires.
26. Fill the cooling system.

7.3L Diesel Engine

The intake manifold on the 7.3L DIT engine is integral to the cylinder heads. Refer to cylinder head removal and installation in this section.

Exhaust Manifold

REMOVAL & INSTALLATION

4.2L Engine

♦ See Figures 58 and 59

1. Disconnect the negative battery cable.
2. For the right-hand manifold, remove the EGR valve-to-exhaust manifold tube.
3. For the left-hand manifold, remove the oil level indicator tube bracket nut, then remove the oil level indicator tube. Remove and discard the oil level indicator tube O-ring.
4. Raise and safely support the front of the vehicle.
5. Detach the heated oxygen sensor electrical connector.
6. Remove the two catalytic converter-to-exhaust manifold nuts, then disconnect the Y-pipe from the left-hand exhaust manifold.
7. Remove the exhaust manifold stud bolts, then remove the manifold mounting bolts.

8. Remove the exhaust manifold. Remove and discard the exhaust manifold gasket.

To install:

9. Position the new exhaust manifold gasket onto the engine, then install the exhaust manifold.
10. Tighten the bolts and stud bolts in the sequence shown to 15–22 ft. lbs. (20–30 Nm).
11. Connect the Y-pipe to the exhaust manifold, then install and tighten the catalytic converter nuts to 25–34 ft. lbs. (34–46 Nm).
12. Attach the oxygen sensor connector, then lower the vehicle.
13. For the left-hand exhaust manifold, install a new oil level indicator tube O-ring onto the tube. Insert the tube into the engine block and tighten the bracket retaining nut to 15–22 ft. lbs. (20–30 Nm).
14. For the right-hand exhaust manifold, Install the EGR valve-to-exhaust manifold tube. Tighten the upper and lower fittings to 25–34 ft. lbs. (34–47 Nm).
15. Connect the negative battery cable.

4.6L, 5.4L and 6.8L Engines

♦ See Figures 60 thru 68

1. Raise and safely support the vehicle.
2. Remove the front fender splash shield.
3. For the left-hand exhaust manifold, remove the EGR valve-to-exhaust manifold tube and disconnect the Differential Pressure Feedback Exhaust (DPFE) gas recirculation transducer hoses.
4. Remove the oil dipstick from the engine.
5. On the 4.6L and 5.4L engines, remove the catalytic converter-to-exhaust manifold bolts. On the 6.8L engine, remove the front exhaust pipe from the manifold.
6. Remove the exhaust manifold mounting nuts, then remove the exhaust manifold itself.
7. Remove and discard the old gasket.
8. Clean and inspect the exhaust manifold for damage.

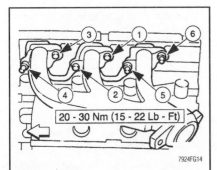

Fig. 58 Tighten the driver's side exhaust manifold bolts in the order shown—4.2L engine

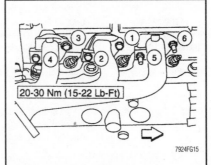

Fig. 59 Tighten the passenger side exhaust manifold bolts in the order shown—4.2L engine

Fig. 60 Remove the catalytic converter-to-exhaust manifold flange bolts

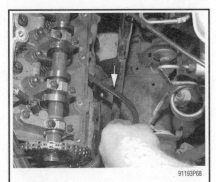

Fig. 61 Remove the oil dipstick tube from the engine

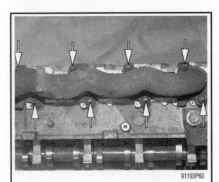

Fig. 62 Remove the exhaust manifold-to-cylinder head retaining nuts/studs and . .

Fig. 63 . . . remove the manifold from the cylinder head

Fig. 64 Remove the exhaust manifold gaskets and . . .

Fig. 65 . . . thoroughly clean the cylinder head and exhaust manifold gasket mating surfaces

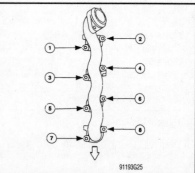

Fig. 66 Tighten the driver's side exhaust manifold bolts in the order shown—4.6L and 5.4L engines

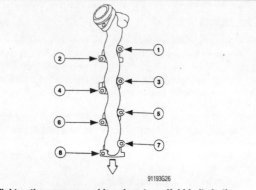

Fig. 67 Tighten the passenger side exhaust manifold bolts in the order shown—4.6L and 5.4L engines

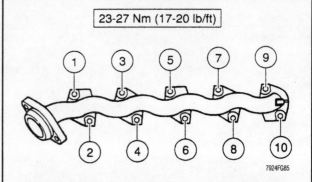

Fig. 68 Tighten the exhaust manifold bolts in the sequence shown—right side of 6.8L engine shown

To install:

9. Position a new gasket and the exhaust manifold onto the engine block.

10. Install the mounting nuts and tighten, in the sequence shown, to 13–16 ft. lbs. (18–22 Nm) on the 4.6L and 5.4L engines. Tighten the nuts to 17–20 ft. lbs. (23–27 Nm) on the 6.8L engine.

11. On the 6.8L engine, tighten the exhaust manifold-to-front pipe fasteners to 27–34 ft. lbs. (34–46 Nm).

12. On the 4.6L and 5.4L engines, attach the catalytic converter to the exhaust manifold, then install the catalytic converter-to-exhaust manifold bolts and tighten to 25–34 ft. lbs. (34–46 Nm).

13. Install the oil dipstick tube.

14. For the left-hand exhaust manifold, install the DPFE transducer hoses if equipped, and the EGR valve-to-exhaust manifold tube. Tighten the upper and lower fittings to 26–33 ft. lbs. (35–45 Nm).

15. Install the front fender splash shield.

16. Lower the vehicle to the ground.

5.8L and 7.5L Engines

▶ See Figure 69

1. Raise and safely support the vehicle securely on jackstands.

2. Disconnect the exhaust pipe or catalytic converter from the exhaust manifold. Remove and discard the doughnut gasket.

3. Lower the vehicle.

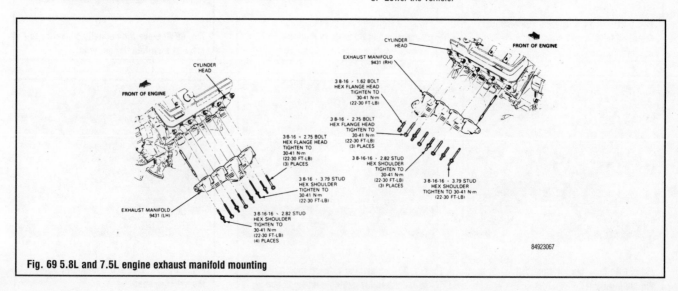

Fig. 69 5.8L and 7.5L engine exhaust manifold mounting

4. Disconnect any necessary emission components to access the exhaust manifolds.

5. Remove the exhaust manifold attaching screws and remove the manifold from the cylinder head.

To install:

6. Apply a light coat of graphite grease to the mating surface of the manifold. Install and tighten the attaching bolts, starting from the center and working to both ends alternately. Tighten to 25–35 ft. lbs. (34–47 Nm).

7. Connect any necessary emission components removed to access the exhaust manifolds.

8. Raise and safely support the vehicle securely on jackstands.

9. Install the exhaust pipe or catalytic converter to the exhaust manifold using a new doughnut gasket. Tighten the retaining bolts to 25–35 ft. lbs. (34–47 Nm).

10. Lower the vehicle.

7.3L Diesel Engine

1. Disconnect the ground cables from both batteries.

2. If removing the passenger side manifold and the vehicle is equipped with an automatic, remove the transmission fill tube bracket bolt and rotate the bracket to the side.

3. Raise the vehicle and safely support it.

4. Disconnect the turbocharger inlet pipe-to-exhaust manifold retaining bolts.

5. Remove the manifold retaining bolts and remove the manifold.

To install:

6. Before installing, clean all mounting surfaces on the cylinder heads and the manifold. Apply an anti-seize compound on the manifold bolt threads and install the manifold, using a new gasket and new locking tabs.

7. Tighten the bolts to 45 ft. lbs. (61 Nm).

8. Install the turbocharger inlet pipe onto the exhaust manifold and tighten the retaining bolts to 28 ft. lbs. (38 Nm).

9. Lower the vehicle.

10. On the passenger side manifold, install the transmission fill tube bracket if equipped.

11. Connect the negative battery cables.

Turbocharger

REMOVAL & INSTALLATION

7.3L Diesel Engine

♦ **See Figure 70**

1. Disconnect the negative battery cable.

2. Remove the two air intake tube assembly bolts, clamps at the turbocharger, crankcase breather assembly, engine air cleaner and air intake tube and hoses.

3. Remove the exhaust outlet clamp from the turbocharger.

4. Raise and safely support the vehicle.

5. Remove the engine charge exhaust pipe bolt from the transmission, if so equipped.

6. Remove the bolts and nuts from the catalytic converter-to-engine charge exhaust pipe, if so equipped.

7. Loosen two bolts retaining the turbocharger exhaust inlet pipe to the left exhaust manifold.

8. For automatic transmissions, remove the bolts retaining the left turbocharger exhaust inlet pipe to the turbocharger exhaust inlet adapter.

9. Loosen the two bolts retaining the turbocharger exhaust inlet pipe to the right exhaust manifold.

10. Remove the lower bolt retaining the right turbocharger exhaust inlet pipe to the turbocharger exhaust inlet adapter.

11. Lower the vehicle.

12. For automatic transmissions, remove the upper bolts retaining the right and left turbocharger exhaust inlet pipes to the turbocharger exhaust inlet adapter.

13. Remove the right engine lift hook and bolt.

14. Loosen the air inlet hose clamp at the turbocharger. Disconnect the hose and lay aside.

15. For automatic transmissions, loosen the four intake manifold hose clamps, and one clamp retaining the compressor manifold to the turbocharger. Remove the compressor manifold.

16. Remove the four bolts retaining the turbocharger pedestal assembly to the cylinder block.

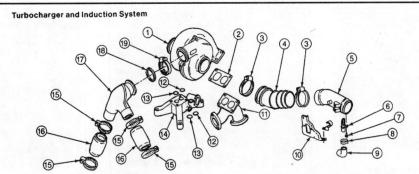

Turbocharger and Induction System

Item	Part Number	Description
1	—	Turbocharger and EBPV Assembly (Part of 6K682)
2	6N640	Exhaust Turbo Inlet Adapter Gasket
3	–·—	Compressor Duct Elbow Clamp (2 Req'd) (Part of 6K682)
4	—	Compressor Duct Elbow (Part of 6K682)
5	6K854	Turbocharger Compressor Inlet Pipe
6	—	Compressor Inlet Duct (Pitot) Tube (Part of 6K854)
7	—	Compressor Inlet Duct (Pitot) Tube Screw (Part of 6K854)
8	—	Breather Hose Elbow Clamp (Part of 6K854)
9	—	Breather Hose Elbow (Part of 6K854)
10	6K864	Air Inlet Bracket

Item	Part Number	Description
11	6K854	Turbocharger Exhaust Inlet Adapter
12	—	Turbocharger Oil Supply O-Ring (2 Req'd) (Part of 6K682)
13	—	Turbocharger Oil Drain O-Ring (2 Req'd) (Part of 6K682)
14	—	Turbocharger Pedestal Assembly (Part of 6K682)
15	—	Turbocharger Manifold Hose Clamp (4 Req'd) (Part of 6K682)
16	—	Turbocharger Manifold Hose (2 Req'd) (Part of 6K682)
17	—	Compressor Manifold (Crossover Pipe) (Part of 6K682)
18	—	Turbocharger Compressor Outlet Seal (Part of 6K682)
19	—	Turbocharger Compressor Outlet Clamp (Part of 6K682)

88283G03

Fig. 70 Turbocharger and induction system components—7.3L diesel engine

17. Remove the turbocharger assembly and detach all electrical connectors from it.

➡️**If the turbocharger is not being removed for service, install the Fuel/Oil turbo Protector Cap Set T94T-9395-AH or equivalent.**

18. Remove the oil gallery O-rings.

To install:

19. Install new oil gallery O-rings.

20. Attach the turbocharger electrical connectors and install the turbocharger assembly.

21. Install the four bolts retaining the turbocharger pedestal assembly to the engine block. Tighten the bolts to 18 ft. lbs. (25 Nm).

22. Loosely install the four bolts retaining the right and left turbocharger exhaust inlet pipes to the turbocharger exhaust inlet adapter.

23. Install the compressor manifold, intake manifold hoses and clamps. Be sure the compressor outlet seal is in position.

24. Install the right engine lift hook and bolt.

25. Raise and safely support the front of the vehicle.

26. Tighten the two right and left lower bolts (retaining the turbocharger exhaust inlet pipes to the turbocharger exhaust inlet adapter) to 36 ft. lbs. (49 Nm).

27. Tighten the four right and left bolts and nuts (retaining the turbocharger exhaust inlet pipes to the exhaust manifolds) to 36 ft. lbs. (49 Nm).

28. Install the catalytic converter to the engine charge exhaust pipe bolts and nuts.

29. Lower the vehicle.

30. Tighten the two right and left upper bolts (retaining the turbocharger exhaust inlet pipes to the turbocharger exhaust inlet adapter) to 36 ft. lbs. (49 Nm).

31. Install the exhaust outlet clamp to the turbocharger.

32. Install the air intake tube and hose assembly.

33. Connect the negative battery cable.

Radiator

REMOVAL & INSTALLATION

◆ **See Figures 71 thru 86**

All gasoline-engine equipped trucks use a cross-flow radiator. In this type, the coolant flows horizontally from a radiator inlet tank to a radiator outlet tank.

Fig. 71 Remove the retaining clips for the radiator support brace trim cover and . . .

Fig. 72 . . . remove the trim panel from the vehicle

Fig. 73 Remove the fan shroud-to-radiator retaining bolts

Fig. 74 Place the special fan removal tools over the water pump pulley bolts and onto the fan clutch hub and loosen the fan clutch assembly

Fig. 75 Remove the fan clutch from the water pump and . . .

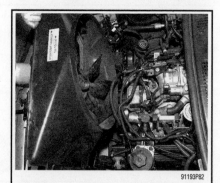

Fig. 76 . . . remove the fan clutch and the shroud assembly from the vehicle

Fig. 77 Slide the hose clamps back and . . .

Fig. 78 . . . remove the upper and . . .

Fig. 79 . . . the lower hoses from the radiator

Fig. 80 Remove the recovery tank hose from the radiator

Fig. 81 Using a back-up wrench to support the radiator fitting, loosen the transmission cooler lines from the radiator and . .

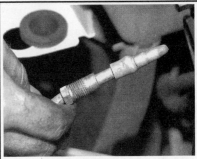

Fig. 82 . . . plug the lines to prevent contamination from entering the transmission

Fig. 83 The radiator is retained by two upper support mounts

Fig. 84 Remove the radiator upper support mount bolts and . . .

Fig. 85 . . . remove the support mount brackets from the radiator

Fig. 86 Remove the radiator by lifting it straight out of the engine compartment

The 7.3L diesel engine is equipped with an aluminum downflow radiator.

1. Drain the cooling system.

✳✳ CAUTION

When draining the coolant, keep in mind that cats and dogs are attracted by ethylene glycol antifreeze and are quite likely to drink any that is left in an uncovered container or in puddles on the ground. This will prove fatal in sufficient quantity. Always drain the coolant into a sealable container. Coolant should be reused unless it is contaminated or several years old.

2. If applicable, use a suitable prytool (see photo) to remove the push-in fasteners that retain the air intake duct, then remove the duct from its mounting on the radiator support.

3. On 1999–00 Super Duty trucks, remove the expansion tank from the top of the radiator.

4. Remove the radiator support brace trim cover.

5. Remove the fan and fan shroud from the vehicle.

6. Disconnect the upper and lower hoses from the radiator.

7. Disconnect the recovery tank hose from the radiator.

8. On automatic transmission equipped trucks only, disconnect the transmission cooling lines from the bottom of the radiator and plug the lines.

9. Remove the radiator retaining bolts or the upper supports and lift the radiator from the vehicle.

To install:

10. Lower the radiator into the vehicle.

11. Install the radiator retaining bolts or the upper supports.

12. Connect the transmission cooling lines at the bottom of the radiator.

13. Connect the upper and lower hoses at the radiator.

14. Connect the recovery tank hose to the radiator.

15. Install the fan and shroud.

16. If applicable, install the air intake duct.

17. Fill and bleed the cooling system.

Engine Fan

REMOVAL & INSTALLATION

4.2L, 4.6L, 5.4L and 6.8L Engines

▸ See Figures 87, 88, 89 and 90

1. Disconnect the negative battery cable.
2. Remove the engine air cleaner outlet tube.
3. Remove the fan shroud-to-radiator retaining bolts

Fig. 87 Remove the fan shroud-to-radiator retaining bolts

Fig. 88 Place the special fan removal tools over the water pump pulley bolts and onto the fan clutch hub and loosen the fan clutch assembly

Fig. 89 Remove the fan clutch from the water pump and . . .

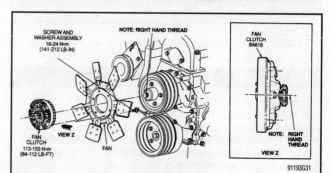

Fig. 90 . . . remove the fan clutch and the shroud assembly from the vehicle

❉❉❉ WARNING

The large nut on the fan clutch has a left-hand thread and must be removed by turning the nut clockwise.

4. Remove the fan clutch using Fan Clutch Holding Tool T84T-6312-C and Fan Clutch Wrench T93T-6312-B, or equivalents.
5. Lift the fan and the shroud assembly from the engine compartment.
6. If the fan or clutch are to be replaced, remove 4 retaining bolts and separate the fan from the clutch assembly.
To install:
7. Assemble the fan and clutch, if separated. Install 4 retaining bolts and tighten to 12–15 ft. lbs. (16–20 Nm).
8. Place the fan assembly and shroud in place at the same time and thread the fan clutch nut onto the water pump shaft. Tighten the fan clutch nut using Fan Clutch Holding Tool T84T-6312-C and Fan Clutch Wrench T93T-6312-B, or equivalents to 45 ft. lbs. (61 Nm).

❉❉❉ WARNING

The large nut on the fan clutch has a left-hand thread and must be tightened by turning the nut counterclockwise.

9. Install the fan shroud and tighten the shroud retaining bolts.
10. Install the engine air cleaner outlet tube.
11. Connect the negative battery cable.
12. Start the engine and check for proper operation.

5.8L and 7.5L Engines

❉❉❉ CAUTION

The large nut on the fan clutch has a right-hand thread and must be removed by turning the nut counterclockwise.

1. Remove the clutch by turning the large nut on the back of the clutch assembly. (The nut is part of the clutch assembly). Use fan clutch holding tool T84T-6312-C and fan clutch wrench T93T-6312-B or equivalents.
2. Remove the 2 fan shroud retaining screws.
3. Remove the fan and clutch along with the shroud.
4. If the fan and clutch need to be separated, remove the 4 retaining bolts.
To Install:
5. Assemble the fan and clutch. Tighten to bolts to 12–18 ft. lbs. (16–24 Nm).
6. Position the fan assembly and shroud in place. Tighten the fan clutch nut to the water pump shaft with fan clutch holding tool T84T-6312-C and fan clutch wrench T93T-6312-B or equivalents.

❉❉❉ CAUTION

The large nut on the fan clutch has a right-hand thread and must be tightened by turning the nut clockwise.

7. Tighten the 2 fan shroud retaining screws.

7.3L Diesel Engine

♦ See Figure 91

1. Disconnect the negative battery cable.
2. Remove the engine air cleaner outlet tube.
3. Remove the fan shroud-to-radiator retaining bolts

❉❉❉ WARNING

The large nut on the fan clutch has a right-hand thread and must be removed by turning the nut counter-clockwise.

Fig. 91 Fan assembly—7.3L diesel engine

4. Remove the fan clutch using Fan Clutch Holding Tool T94T-6312-AH and Fan Clutch Wrench T93T-6312-B, or equivalents.

5. Lift the fan and the shroud assembly from the engine compartment.

6. If the fan or clutch are to be replaced, remove 4 retaining bolts and separate the fan from the clutch assembly.

To install:

7. Assemble the fan and clutch, if separated. Install 4 retaining bolts and tighten to 12–18 ft. lbs. (16–24 Nm).

8. Place the fan assembly and shroud in place at the same time and thread the fan clutch nut onto the water pump shaft. Tighten the fan clutch nut using Fan Clutch Holding Tool T94T-6312-AH and Fan Clutch Wrench T93T-6312-B, or equivalents to 84–112 ft. lbs. (113–153 Nm).

∗∗∗ WARNING

The large nut on the fan clutch has a left-hand thread and must be tightened by turning the nut counterclockwise.

9. Install the fan shroud and tighten the shroud retaining bolts.
10. Install the engine air cleaner outlet tube.
11. Connect the negative battery cable.
12. Start the engine and check for proper operation.

Water Pump

REMOVAL & INSTALLATION

4.2L, 4.6L, 5.4L and 6.8L Engines

▶ See Figures 92 thru 99

1. Disconnect the negative battery cable.
2. Drain the engine cooling system.
3. Remove the engine cooling fan and fan shroud.

Fig. 92 Remove the fan shroud-to-radiator retaining bolts

Fig. 93 Place the special fan removal tools over the water pump pulley bolts and onto the fan clutch hub and loosen the fan clutch assembly

Fig. 94 Remove the fan clutch from the water pump and . . .

Fig. 95 . . . remove the fan clutch and the shroud assembly from the vehicle

Fig. 96 Remove the four water pump retaining bolts and . . .

Fig. 97 . . . remove the water pump from the engine

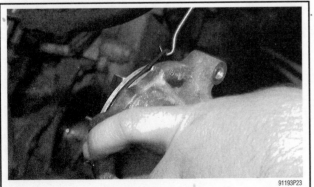

Fig. 98 Remove the water pump O-ring using a pick or other suitable tool

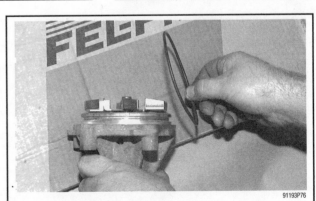

Fig. 99 Always replace the water pump O-ring with a quality replacement such as a Fel-Pro®

4. Release the belt tensioner and remove the accessory drive belt.

5. Remove 4 bolts retaining the water pump pulley to the water pump and remove the pulley.

6. Remove 4 bolts retaining the water pump to the cylinder block and remove the water pump.

To install:

7. Clean the sealing surfaces of the water pump and cylinder block.

8. Lubricate a new O-ring seal with clean antifreeze and install on the water pump.

9. Install the water pump and 4 retaining bolts. Tighten the retaining bolts to 15–22 ft. lbs. (20–30 Nm).

10. Install the water pump pulley and 4 retaining bolts. Tighten the retaining bolts to 15–22 ft. lbs. (20–30 Nm).

11. Release the belt tensioner and install the accessory drive belt.

12. Install the engine cooling fan and fan shroud.

13. Fill the engine cooling system.

14. Connect the negative battery cable.

15. Start the engine and allow to reach normal operating temperature while checking for coolant leaks.

16. Road test the vehicle and check for proper operation.

5.8L and 7.5L Engines

1. Drain the cooling system.

2. Remove the engine fan and fan shroud.

3. Disconnect the lower radiator hose, heater hose and by-pass hose at the water pump.

4. Remove the water pump pulley.

5. Loosen the alternator pivot bolt and the bolt attaching the alternator adjusting arm to the water pump. Remove the power steering pump, and air conditioning compressor bracket from the water pump and position it out of the way.

6. Remove the bolts securing the water pump to the timing chain cover and remove the water pump.

To install:

7. Coat a new gasket with sealer and install the water pump. Tighten the bolts to 18 ft. lbs. (25 Nm).

8. Install the power steering pump bracket.

9. Connect the lower radiator hose, heater hose and by-pass hose at the water pump.

10. Install the water pump pulley, fan, fan shroud and drive belt.

11. Fill the cooling system.

7.3L Diesel Engine

▶ **See Figures 100 and 101**

1. Disconnect both battery ground cables.

2. Drain the cooling system.

3. Remove the radiator shroud and the fan clutch and fan.

➥**The fan clutch bolts are right-hand thread. Remove them by turning counter-clockwise.**

4. Loosen, but do not remove, the water pump pulley bolts.

5. Remove the drive belt.

6. Remove the water pump pulley bolts and remove the pulley from the pump.

7. Detach the ECT sensor connector.

8. Remove the heater hose from the water pump.

9. Remove the bolts attaching the water pump to the front cover and lift off the pump.

To install:

10. Thoroughly clean the mating surfaces of the pump and front cover.

11. Using a new gasket, position the water pump over the dowel pins and into place on the front cover.

12. Install the attaching bolts. Tighten the bolts to 15 ft. lbs. (20 Nm).

13. Connect the heater hose to the pump.

14. Attach the ECT sensor connector.

15. Install the water pump pulley and start the water pump pulley bolts.

16. Install the drive belt.

17. Install and tighten the pulley retaining bolts to 12–18 ft. lbs. (16–24 Nm).

18. Install the fan and fan shroud assembly.

19. Fill and bleed the cooling system.

20. Connect the battery ground cables.

21. Start the engine and check for leaks.

Cylinder Head

REMOVAL & INSTALLATION

4.2L Engine

▶ **See Figure 102**

1. The A/C system, should be discharged by a qualified mechanic using an approved refrigerant recovery/recycling machine.

2. Disconnect the negative battery cable.

3. Drain the cooling system.

4. Remove the upper and lower intake manifolds and related components.

5. Remove the valve covers.

6. Remove the exhaust manifold (s).

7. If removing the left-hand cylinder head, perform the following:

    a. Position the power steering pump reservoir aside and remove the A/C compressor.

    b. Remove and support the A/C compressor bracket and power steering pump aside.

8. If removing the right-hand cylinder head, perform the following:

    a. Remove the alternator.

    b. Remove the idler pulley.

    c. Remove the alternator bracket.

➥**If the cylinder head components, such as rocker arms, valve springs, etc., are to be reinstalled, they must be installed in the same position. Mark the components for original location.**

9. Remove the six rocker arms by removing the retaining bolts.

10. Pull the pushrods out of the engine. Once again, be sure to label or mark the components removed for reinstallation in their original location.

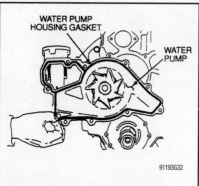

Fig. 100 Water pump mounting—7.3L diesel engine

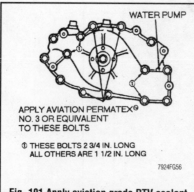

Fig. 101 Apply aviation grade RTV sealant to the bolts indicated—7.3L diesel engine

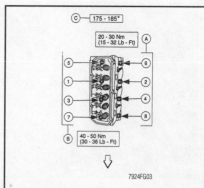

Fig. 102 Cylinder head torque sequence— 4.2L engines

11. Remove and discard the eight cylinder head mounting bolts. New bolts are a must for installation.

12. Lift the cylinder head off of the engine block. Remove the cylinder head gasket and discard.

To install:

13. Clean and inspect the cylinder head for flatness.

14. Install a new cylinder head gasket on the cylinder block with the small hole to the front of the engine, then install the cylinder head.

✳✳ WARNING

Always use new cylinder head bolts for installation.

15. Lubricate the cylinder head bolts with clean engine oil prior to installation.

➡**Be sure to tighten the cylinder head bolts in three (3) steps.**

16. Install the new cylinder head bolts. Tighten the cylinder head bolts in the sequence shown and in three steps to the following values:
- Step 1—14 ft. lbs. (20 Nm)
- Step 2—29 ft. lbs. (40 Nm)
- Step 3—36 ft. lbs. (50 Nm)

✳✳ WARNING

Do not loosen all of the cylinder head bolts at one time. Each cylinder head bolt must be loosened and the final tightening performed prior to loosening the next bolt in the sequence.

17. In the same sequence as used previously, loosen the cylinder head bolt three turns, then tighten the cylinder head bolt to the specific value according to its length. The short bolts (A) should be tightened to 15–32 ft. lbs. (20–30 Nm) and the long bolts (B) to 30–36 ft. lbs. (40–50 Nm). Finally, tighten each cylinder head bolt, in sequence, an additional 175–185 degrees (C). It would be very helpful to utilize a degree socket wrench for this last step.

18. Lubricate the pushrods with clean engine oil prior to installation, then install them into their original positions.

19. Install the rocker arms. Tighten the rocker arm mounting bolts to 23–29 ft. lbs. (30–40 Nm).

20. If the valvetrain components were replaced with new components, inspect the valve clearance.

21. If installing the right-hand cylinder head, perform the following:

a. Position the alternator bracket in place, then install the two long bolts to 31–39 ft. lbs. (41–54 Nm). Install the short bolt and tighten to 18–22 ft. lbs. (24–31 Nm).

b. Install the idler pulley. Tighten the center retaining bolt to 35–46 ft. lbs. (47–63 Nm).

c. Install the alternator.

22. If installing the left-hand cylinder head, complete the following steps:

a. Position the A/C compressor bracket and power steering pump in place, then start the A/C compressor bracket bolt. Install the three compressor bracket bolts to 30–40 ft. lbs. (40–55 Nm). Then, install the two compressor bracket nuts to 16–21 ft. lbs. (21–29 Nm).

b. Install the A/C compressor.

c. Install the power steering pump reservoir. Tighten the hold-down bolts to 80–107 inch lbs. (9–12 Nm).

23. Install the exhaust manifold.

24. Install the two rocker arm covers. Inspect the rocker arm cover gaskets for damage prior to installation; replace them if necessary.

25. Install the lower intake manifold and related components.

26. Install the upper intake manifold and related components.

27. Fill the cooling system and connect the negative battery cable.

28. Change the engine oil.

29. Start the engine and check for any fuel, coolant and vacuum leaks.

4.6L, 5.4L and 6.8L Engines

▶ **See Figures 103, 104, 105 and 106**

1. The A/C system, should be discharged by an EPA certified mechanic utilizing the appropriate refrigerant recovery/recycling machine.

2. Disconnect the negative battery cable.

3. Remove the valve covers.

4. Remove the intake manifold(s).

5. Remove the timing chains from the engine.

6. Remove the exhaust manifolds.

7. Remove the two heater hose retaining bolts, then compress and slide the hose clamp back to remove the heater water hose.

8. Remove the cylinder head bolts, then lift the cylinder head from the engine block.

9. Discard the cylinder head gasket and clean the engine block surface.

To install:

✳✳ WARNING

Cylinder head bolts must be replaced with new ones. They are torque-to-yield designed and cannot be reused.

10. Turn the crankshaft to position the key-way at the 12 o'clock position.

11. Clean and inspect the cylinder head for damage or warpage. Install the cylinder head gasket over the dowel pins. Then, install the cylinder head onto the engine block. Loosely install NEW cylinder head bolts.

➡**Be sure to tighten the head bolts in three steps.**

12. Tighten the cylinder head bolts in the sequence shown in three steps, as follows:
a. Step 1—27–31 ft. lbs. (37–43 Nm).
b. Step 2—tighten an additional 85–95 degrees.
c. Step 3—tighten another 85–95 degrees.

13. Install the heater water hose and slide the hose clamp back into position. Install the two heater water hose bolts.

14. Install the exhaust manifolds.

15. Install the timing chains.

16. Install the intake manifold.

17. Install the valve covers.

18. Connect the negative battery cable, then start the engine and check for leaks.

19. If the vehicle is equipped with A/C, have the system evacuated and

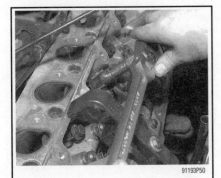

Fig. 103 Remove the cylinder head bolts and . . .

Fig. 104 . . . carefully lift the cylinder head off of the engine block and place it in a safe location

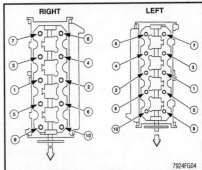

Fig. 105 Tighten the cylinder head bolts in three steps using the sequence shown— 4.6L and 5.4L engines

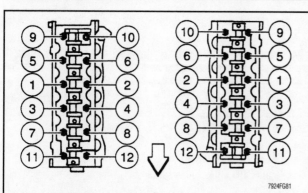

Fig. 106 Be sure to tighten the cylinder head bolts in three steps using the sequence shown—6.8L engine

recharged by an EPA certified mechanic utilizing the appropriate refrigerant recovery/recycling machine.
20. Change the engine oil.
21. Connect the negative battery cable.

5.8L Engine

▶ See Figure 107

1. Disconnect the negative battery cable.
2. Drain the cooling system.
3. Remove the intake manifolds.
4. Remove the valve cover(s).
5. If the right cylinder head is to be removed:
• Lift the tensioner and remove the drive belt
• Loosen the alternator adjusting arm bolt and remove the alternator mounting bracket bolt and spacer
• Swing the alternator down and out of the way.
6. Remove the air cleaner inlet duct.
7. If the left cylinder head is being removed:
• Remove the air conditioning compressor
• Remove the oil dipstick and tube
• Remove the cruise control bracket
8. Disconnect the exhaust manifold(s) from the muffler inlet pipe(s).
9. Loosen the rocker arm stud nuts so the rocker arms can be rotated to the side. Remove the pushrods and identify them so they can be reinstalled in their original positions.
10. Remove the cylinder head bolts and lift the cylinder head from the block. Remove the discard the gasket.

To install:

11. Clean the cylinder head, intake manifold, the valve cover and the head gasket surfaces.

❊❊ WARNING

A specially treated composition head gasket is used. Do not apply sealer to a composition gasket.

12. Position the new gasket over the locating dowels on the cylinder block.
13. Position the cylinder head on the block and install the attaching bolts.
14. The cylinder head bolts are tightened in progressive steps. Tighten all the bolts in the proper sequence to:

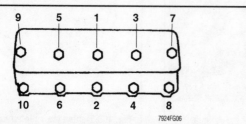

Fig. 107 Cylinder head bolt torque sequence—5.8L and 7.5L engines

• Step 1—85 ft. lbs.(115 Nm)
• Step 2—95 ft. lbs. (129 Nm)
• Step 3—105–112 ft. lbs. (143–152 Nm)
15. Clean the pushrods. Blow out the oil passage in the rods with compressed air. Check the pushrods for straightness by rolling them on a piece of glass. Never try to straighten a pushrod; always replace it.
16. Apply Lubriplate® to the ends of the pushrods and install them in their original positions.
17. Apply Lubriplate® to the rocker arms and their fulcrum seats and install the rocker arms. Adjust the valves.
18. Position a new gasket(s) on the muffler inlet pipe(s) as necessary. Connect the exhaust manifold(s) at the muffler inlet pipe(s).
19. If the right cylinder head was removed, install the alternator, air cleaner duct, and the drive belt. If the left cylinder head was removed, install the compressor, the dipstick and cruise control bracket.
20. Clean the valve rocker arm cover and the cylinder head gasket surfaces. Place the new gaskets in the covers, making sure the tabs of the gasket engage the notches provided in the cover. Evacuate, charge and leak test the air conditioning system.
21. Install the intake manifold and related parts.
22. Fill and bleed the cooling system.
23. Change the engine oil.
24. Connect the negative battery cable.

7.5L Engine

▶ See Figure 107

1. Disconnect the negative battery cable.
2. Drain the cooling system.
3. Remove the upper and lower intake manifolds..
4. Disconnect the exhaust pipe from the exhaust manifold.
5. Remove the drive belts.
6. Loosen the alternator attaching bolts and remove the bolt attaching the alternator bracket to the right cylinder head.
7. Disconnect the air conditioning compressor from the engine and move it aside, out of the way. Do not discharge the air conditioning system.
8. Remove the bolts securing the power steering reservoir bracket to the left cylinder head. Position the reservoir and bracket out of the way. On motor home chassis, remove the oil filler tube.
9. Remove the valve covers.
10. Remove the rocker arm bolts, rocker arms, oil deflectors, fulcrums and pushrods in sequence so they can be reinstalled in their original positions.
11. Remove the cylinder head bolts and lift the head and exhaust manifold off the engine. If necessary, pry at the forward corners of the cylinder head against the casting bosses provided on the cylinder block. Do not damage the gasket mating surfaces of the cylinder head and block by prying against them.

To install:

12. Remove all gasket material from the cylinder head and block. Clean all gasket material from the mating surfaces of the intake manifold. If the exhaust manifold was removed, clean the mating surfaces of the cylinder head and exhaust manifold. Apply a thin coat of graphite grease to the cylinder head exhaust port areas and install the exhaust manifold.
13. Position the two long cylinder head bolts in the two rear lower bolt holes of the left cylinder head. Place a long cylinder head bolt in the rear lower bolt hole of the right cylinder head. Use rubber bands to keep the bolts in position until the cylinder heads are installed on the cylinder block.
14. Position new cylinder head gaskets on the cylinder block dowels. Do not apply sealer to the gaskets, heads, or block.
15. Place the cylinder heads on the block, guiding the exhaust manifold studs into the exhaust pipe connections. Install the remaining cylinder head bolts. The longer bolts go in the lower row of holes.
16. Tighten all the cylinder head attaching bolts in the proper sequence in three stages: 80–90 ft. lbs. (109–122 Nm), 100–110 ft. lbs. (136–149 Nm), and finally to 130–140 ft. lbs. (176–190 Nm). When this procedure is used, it is not necessary to retighten the heads after extended use.
17. Be sure the oil holes in the pushrods are open and install the pushrods in their original positions. Place a dab of Lubriplate® to the ends of the pushrods before installing them.
18. Lubricate and install the valve rockers. Be sure the pushrods remain seated in their lifters.
19. Connect the exhaust pipes to the exhaust manifolds.

20. Install the upper and lower intake manifolds.
21. Install the air conditioning compressor.
22. Install the power steering reservoir.
23. Install the valve covers.
24. Install the alternator and adjust the drive belts.
25. On motor home chassis, install the oil filler tube.
26. Fill and bleed the cooling system.
27. Change the engine oil.
28. Connect the negative battery cable.
29. Start the engine and check for leaks.

7.3L Diesel Engine

RIGHT CYLINDER HEAD

♦ **See Figures 108 thru 114**

1. Disconnect both negative battery cables.
2. Drain the cooling system.
3. Remove the radiator.
4. Remove the turbocharger assembly.
5. Disconnect the fuel lines by disconnecting them from the rear of both cylinder heads and the fuel pump.
6. Label and disconnect the wiring from the alternator.
7. Remove the adjusting bolts and pivot bolts from the alternator and the vacuum pump and remove both units.
8. Remove the alternator and its bracket.
9. Remove the engine oil dipstick tube.
10. Remove the MAP sensor and position it aside.
11. Remove the valve cover
12. Remove the connectors from the injectors and glow plugs.
13. Remove the valve cover gasket.
14. Remove the high pressure oil pump supply line to the right cylinder head.
15. Remove the exhaust back pressure line.
16. Remove the three glow plug relay bracket nuts and the ground wire.
17. Disconnect the heater hose from the cylinder head.

18. Remove the outer half of the heater distribution box.
19. Remove the four outboard fuel injector hold-down bolts, retaining screws and four oil deflectors.

❊❊ WARNING

Remove the oil drain plugs prior to removing the injectors or oil could enter the combustion chamber which could result in hydrostatic lock and severe engine damage.

20. Remove the oil rail drain plugs.
21. Remove the fuel injectors using Injector Remover No. T94T–9000–AH1, or equivalent. Position the tool's fulcrum beneath the fuel injector hold-down plate and over the edge of the cylinder head. Install the remover screw in the threaded hole of the fuel injector plate (see illustration). Tighten the screw to lift out the injector from its bore. Place the injector in a suitable protective sleeve such as Rotunda Injector Protective Sleeve, No. 014–00933–2, and set the injector in a suitable holding rack.
22. Use a suitable vacuum tool, such as Rotunda Vacuum Pump, No. 021–00037, or equivalent to remove the oil and fuel left over in the injector bores.
23. Remove the rocker arms and pushrods, KEEP EVERYTHING IN ORDER.
24. Remove the four glow plugs.
25. Remove the right turbo exhaust inlet pipe.
26. Remove the ground strap from the rear of the cylinder head.
27. Disconnect the fuel return line at the front of the cylinder head.
28. Remove the four inboard fuel injector shoulder bolts.
29. Remove the cylinder head bolts and attach a Rotunda Cylinder Head Lifting Bracket, 014–00932–2, or equivalent.
30. Carefully lift the cylinder head out of the engine compartment and remove the head gaskets.

To install:

➡To prepare a good seat for the fuel injector O-rings, use a suitable injector sleeve brush to clean any debris from the bore.

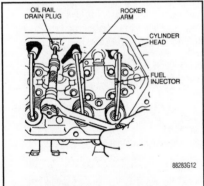

Fig. 108 Remove the oil rail drain plug as shown—7.3L DI turbo diesel engine

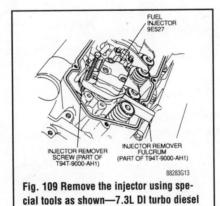

Fig. 109 Remove the injector using special tools as shown—7.3L DI turbo diesel engine

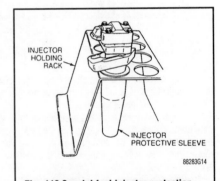

Fig. 110 Special fuel injector protection sleeve and holding rack—7.3L DI turbo diesel engine

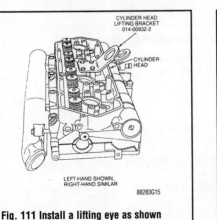

Fig. 111 Install a lifting eye as shown

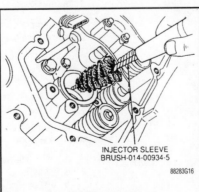

Fig. 112 Use a suitable bore brush to clean out the injector bores

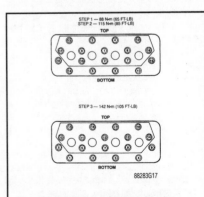

Fig. 113 Cylinder head bolt tightening sequence—7.3L DI turbo diesel engine

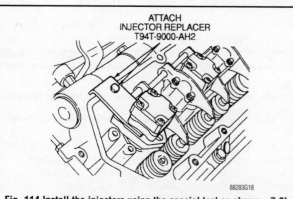

ATTACH
INJECTOR REPLACER
T94T-9000-AH2

88283G18

Fig. 114 Install the injectors using the special tool as shown—7.3L DI turbo diesel engine

31. Carefully clean the cylinder block and head mating surfaces.
32. Position the cylinder head gasket on the engine block and carefully lower the cylinder head in place.
33. Install the cylinder head bolt and torque in 3 steps using the sequence shown in the illustration.

➡**Lubricate the threads and the mating surfaces of the bolt heads and washers with engine oil.**

34. Connect the fuel return line to the cylinder head.
35. Install the four inboard injector shoulder bolts. Tighten them to 9 ft. lbs. (12 Nm).
36. Install the fuel injectors using special tools as follows:
    a. Lubricate the injectors with clean engine oil. Using new copper washers, carefully push the injectors square into the bore using hand pressure only to seat the O-rings.
    b. Position the open end of Injector Replacer, No. T94T–9000–AH2, or equivalent between the fuel injector body and injector hold-down plate, while positioning the opposite end of the tool over the edge of the cylinder head.
    c. Align the hole in the tool with the threaded hole in the cylinder head and install the bolt from the tool kit. Tighten the bolt to fully seat the injector, then remove the bolt and tool.
37. Install the four outboard fuel injector hold-down bolts, the four oil deflectors and retaining screws. Tighten them to 9 ft. lbs. (12 Nm).
38. Dip the pushrod ends in clean engine oil and install the pushrods with the copper colored ends toward the rocker arms, making sure the pushrods are fully seated in the tappet pushrod seats.
39. Install the rocker arms and posts in their original positions. Apply Lubriplate® grease to the valve stem tips. Turn the engine over by hand until the timing mark is at the 11 o'clock position as viewed from the front. Install the rocker arm posts, bolts and tighten to 27 ft. lbs. (37 Nm). Install the valve covers.
40. Install the fuel rail drain plugs, tightening them to 8 ft. lbs. (11 Nm).
41. Install the oil rail drain plugs, tightening them to 53 inch lbs. (6 Nm).
42. Install the heater distribution box.
43. Install the heater hose to the cylinder head.
44. Install the glow plug relay bracket and ground wire.
45. Install the exhaust back pressure line.
46. Install the oil supply line to the cylinder head, tightening it to 19 ft. lbs. (26 Nm).
47. Install the dipstick tube.
48. Install the MAP sensor and screws.
49. Install the valve cover gasket.
50. Connect the wiring to the fuel injectors and glow plugs.
51. Install the valve cover, tightening the bolts to 8 ft. lbs. (11 Nm).
52. Connect the injector wiring harness to the valve cover gasket.
53. Install the alternator, tightening the bracket bolts to 40–55 ft. lbs. (54–75 Nm).
54. Connect the alternator wiring and install the drive belt.
55. The remainder of the installation is the reverse of the removal. Tighten the fuel pump-to-fuel line banjo bolt to 40 ft. lbs. (54 Nm).
56. Connect both negative battery cables.
57. Refill and bleed the cooling system.
58. Run the engine and check for fuel, coolant and exhaust leaks.

LEFT CYLINDER HEAD

◆ **See Figures 108 thru 114**

1. Disconnect both negative battery cables.
2. Drain the cooling system.
3. Remove the radiator.
4. Remove the turbocharger assembly.
5. Remove the two crankcase breather screws and the breather.
6. Disconnect the wiring from the air conditioning compressor.
7. Remove the four left accessory bracket bolts.
8. Disconnect the vacuum hose at the brake vacuum pump.
9. Disconnect the A/C lines from the compressor.
10. Remove the power steering lines from the pump.
11. Remove the left accessory bracket and accessories as an assembly.
12. Remove the valve cover.
13. Disconnect the fuel line assembly between the cylinder heads and fuel pump.
14. Remove the fuel line nut from the intake manifold stud.
15. Disconnect the fuel return line from the cylinder head.
16. Remove the high pressure oil pump supply line from the cylinder head.
17. Raise the vehicle and support it safely on jackstands.
18. Remove the left turbo exhaust pipe from the manifold.
19. Lower the vehicle.
20. Remove the oil rail drain plugs.
21. Remove the four outboard fuel injector hold-down bolts, retaining screws and four oil deflectors.

※※ **WARNING**

Remove the oil drain plugs prior to removing the injectors or oil could enter the combustion chamber which could result in hydrostatic lock and severe engine damage.

22. Remove the oil rail drain plugs.
23. Remove the fuel injectors using Injector Remover No. T94T–9000–AH1, or equivalent. Position the tool's fulcrum beneath the fuel injector hold-down plate and over the edge of the cylinder head. Install the remover screw in the threaded hole of the fuel injector plate (see illustration). Tighten the screw to lift out the injector from its bore. Place the injector in a suitable protective sleeve such as Rotunda Injector Protective Sleeve, No. 014–00933–2, and set the injector in a suitable holding rack.
24. Use a suitable vacuum tool, such as Rotunda Vacuum Pump, No. 021–00037, or equivalent to remove the oil and fuel left over in the injector bores.
25. Remove the rocker arms and pushrods, KEEP EVERYTHING IN ORDER.
26. Remove the four glow plugs.
27. Remove the left turbo exhaust inlet pipe.
28. Remove the main engine harness connectors in the left fender well and position the harness aside.
29. Remove the four inboard fuel injector shoulder bolts.
30. Remove the cylinder head bolts and attach a Rotunda Cylinder Head Lifting Bracket, 014–00932–2, or equivalent.
31. Carefully lift the cylinder head out of the engine compartment and remove the head gaskets.
To install:

➡**To prepare a good seat for the fuel injector O-rings, use a suitable injector sleeve brush to clean any debris from the bore.**

32. Carefully clean the cylinder block and head mating surfaces.
33. Position the cylinder head gasket on the engine block and carefully lower the cylinder head in place.
34. Install the cylinder head bolt and torque in 3 steps using the sequence shown in the illustration.

➡**Lubricate the threads and the mating surfaces of the bolt heads and washers with engine oil.**

35. Apply anti-seize paste and install the glow plugs, tightening them to 14 ft. lbs. (19 Nm).
36. Install the four outboard fuel injector hold-down bolts, the four oil deflectors and retaining screws. Tighten them to 9 ft. lbs. (12 Nm).
37. Dip the pushrod ends in clean engine oil and install the pushrods with

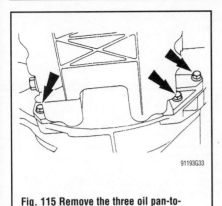

Fig. 115 Remove the three oil pan-to-transmission bolts

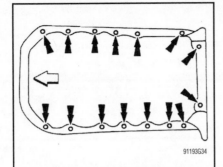

Fig. 116 Remove the 15 oil pan-to-cylinder block mounting bolts, then lower the oil pan

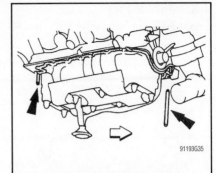

Fig. 117 Temporarily install two locator dowels in two of the oil pan-to-engine block corner mounting bolt holes

the copper colored ends toward the rocker arms, making sure the pushrods are fully seated in the tappet pushrod seats.

38. Install the rocker arms and posts in their original positions. Apply Lubriplate® grease to the valve stem tips. Turn the engine over by hand until the timing mark is at the 11 o'clock position as viewed from the front. Install the rocker arm posts, bolts and tighten to 27 ft. lbs. (37 Nm). Install the valve covers.

39. Install the four inboard injector shoulder bolts. Tighten them to 9 ft. lbs. (12 Nm).

40. Install the fuel injectors using special tools as follows:

   a. Lubricate the injectors with clean engine oil. Using new copper washers, carefully push the injectors square into the bore using hand pressure only to seat the O-rings.

   b. Position the open end of Injector Replacer, No. T94T–9000–AH2, or equivalent between the fuel injector body and injector hold-down plate, while positioning the opposite end of the tool over the edge of the cylinder head.

   c. Align the hole in the tool with the threaded hole in the cylinder head and install the bolt from the tool kit. Tighten the bolt to fully seat the injector, then remove the bolt and tool.

41. Install the fuel rail drain plugs, tightening them to 8 ft. lbs. (11 Nm).

42. Install the oil rail drain plugs, tightening them to 53 inch lbs. (6 Nm).

43. Install the heater distribution box.

44. Install the valve cover gasket.

45. Connect the wiring to the fuel injectors and glow plugs.

46. Install the valve cover, tightening the bolts to 8 ft. lbs. (11 Nm).

47. Connect the engine wiring harness.

48. Raise and safely support the vehicle on jackstands.

49. Loosely install the turbo exhaust pipe to the manifold.

50. Lower the vehicle.

51. The remainder of the installation is the reverse of the removal. Tighten the fuel pump-to-fuel line banjo bolt to 40 ft. lbs. (54 Nm).

52. Connect both negative battery cables.

53. Refill and bleed the cooling system.

54. Run the engine and check for fuel, coolant and exhaust leaks.

Oil Pan

REMOVAL & INSTALLATION

4.2L Engine

♦ **See Figures 115, 116, 117 and 118**

1. Raise and safely support the front of the vehicle.
2. Remove the oil pan plug and drain the engine oil.
3. If equipped with 4 wheel drive:
   a. Remove the two front wheel driveshafts and joints, if so equipped.
   b. Remove the front differential from the vehicle.
   c. Remove the front differential support.
4. Remove the three oil pan-to-transmission bolts.

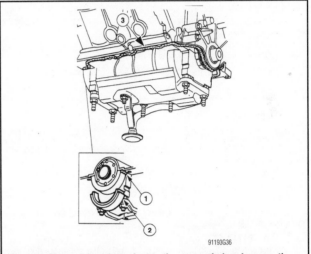

Fig. 118 Clean and apply sealant to the rear main bearing cap, the oil pan mating surface, the front cover mounting area, the front cover-to-engine block joints

5. Remove the 15 oil pan-to-cylinder block mounting bolts, then lower the oil pan.

To install:

➡**If the oil pan is not installed within 15 minutes, remove the sealer and reapply.**

6. Temporarily install two locator dowels in two of the oil pan-to-engine block corner mounting bolt holes.

7. Clean and apply sealant to the rear main bearing cap, the oil pan mating surface, the front cover mounting area, the front cover-to-engine block joints, then install the oil pan rear seal. Make certain to use Silicone Gasket and Sealant F6AZ-19562-A or equivalent for the sealant.

8. Position the oil pan, then install 13 of the oil pan mounting bolts loosely.

9. Remove the two locator dowels and install the remaining two oil pan-to-engine block bolts.

10. Starting from the rear and alternating from the right to left, tighten the 15 oil pan mounting bolts to 36–44 inch lbs. (4–5 Nm), then retighten the bolts to 80–106 inch lbs. (9–12 Nm).

11. Install the oil pan-to-transmission bolts to 28–38 ft. lbs. (38–51 Nm).

12. Install the oil pan drain plug to 16–22 ft. lbs. (22–30 Nm).

13. Install the front differential and front differential support.

14. Install the front driveshafts and joints.

15. Lower the vehicle to the ground.

16. Fill the engine with the correct type and amount of engine oil.

4.6L and 5.4L Engines

▶ See Figure 119

1. Raise and safely support the vehicle.
2. On 4 X 4 equipped models, remove the front axle housing from the vehicle.
3. Drain the engine oil.
4. Remove the 16 oil pan-to-engine block bolts.
5. Remove the oil pan and the oil pan gasket.

To install:

6. Clean the oil pan and engine block mating surfaces of oil and old gasket material.
7. Install the new oil pan gasket and the oil pan, then install the 16 oil pan-to-engine block bolts loosely.

➡ **Be sure to tighten the oil pan bolts in three steps.**

8. Tighten the oil pan-to-engine bolts in the sequence shown, in the following three steps:
   a. Step 1—18 inch lbs. (2 Nm).
   b. Step 2—15 ft. lbs. (20 Nm).
   c. Step 3—tighten an additional 60 degrees (one hex head flat of a bolt).
9. Install the oil drain plug.
10. If removed, install the front axle housing.
11. Lower the vehicle.
12. Fill the engine with the correct amount and type of engine oil.

5.8L Engine

▶ See Figure 120

1. Drain the cooling system.
2. Remove the bolts attaching the fan shroud to the radiator and position the shroud over the fan.
3. Remove the upper intake manifold and throttle body.
4. Remove the nuts and lockwashers attaching the engine support insulators to the chassis bracket.
5. If equipped with an automatic transmission, disconnect the oil cooler line at the left side of the radiator.
6. Remove the exhaust system.
7. Raise the engine and place wood blocks under the engine supports.
8. Drain the engine oil.
9. Support the transmission with a floor jack and remove the transmission crossmember.
10. Remove the oil pan attaching bolts and lower the oil pan onto the crossmember.
11. Remove the two bolts attaching the oil pump pick-up tube to the oil

pump. Remove the nut attaching the oil pump pick-up tube to the No. 3 main bearing cap stud. Lower the pick-up tube and screen into the oil pan.

12. Remove the oil pan from the vehicle.

To install:

13. Clean the oil pan, inlet tube and gasket surfaces. Inspect the gasket sealing surface for damages and distortion due to over tightening of the bolts. Repair and straighten as required.
14. Position a new oil pan gasket and seal to the cylinder block.
15. Position the oil pick-up tube and screen to the oil pump, and install the lower attaching bolt and gasket loosely. Install the nut on the No. 3 main bearing cap stud.
16. Place the oil pan on the crossmember. Install the upper pick-up tube bolt. Tighten the pick-up tube bolts.
17. Position the oil pan to the cylinder block and install the attaching bolts. Tighten to 10–12 ft. lbs. (14–16 Nm).
18. Install the transmission crossmember.
19. Raise the engine and remove the blocks under the engine supports. Bolt the engine to the supports.
20. Install the exhaust system.
21. If equipped with an automatic transmission, connect the oil cooler line at the left side of the radiator.
22. Install the nuts and lockwashers attaching the engine support insulators to the chassis bracket.
23. Install the upper intake manifold and throttle body.
24. Install the fan shroud.
25. Fill the engine with the proper type and amount of oil.
26. Fill and bleed the cooling system.

6.8L Engine

▶ See Figures 121 and 122

1. Disconnect the negative battery cable.
2. Relieve the fuel system pressure.
3. Drain the cooling system.
4. Disconnect the upper radiator hose from the intake manifold.
5. Remove the engine air cleaner outlet tube.
6. Disconnect the accelerator cable from the bracket and the throttle body cam.
7. If equipped, remove the speed control actuator cable from the throttle body.
8. Disconnect all vacuum hoses, fuel lines and electrical wires from the throttle body and intake manifold.
9. Remove the brake booster vacuum hose bracket.
10. Remove the EGR valve-to-exhaust manifold tube and disconnect the vacuum line.
11. Remove the connector and vacuum line from the Engine Vacuum Regulator (EVR) solenoid.

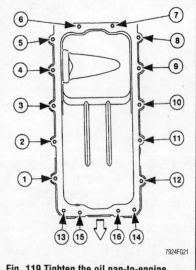

Fig. 119 Tighten the oil pan-to-engine block bolts in three steps following the sequence shown—4.6L and 5.4L engines

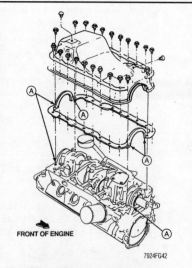

Fig. 120 Exploded view of the oil pan mounting. apply RTV sealant to the areas marked "A"—5.8L engine

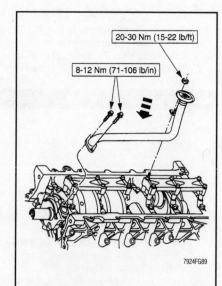

Fig. 121 Oil pump pick-up tube and screen assembly—6.8L engine

12. Remove the four bolts and the throttle body adapter.

13. Remove the upper fan shroud mounting screws and position the shroud toward the engine.

14. Remove the generator and install the Modular Engine Support Bracket on the engine using the generator mounting holes.

15. Raise and safely support the vehicle.

16. Remove the lower engine mount-to-frame nuts.

17. Clean the area around the Turbine Shaft Speed (TSS) and Output Shaft Speed (OSS) sensors and remove them from the transmission. Plug the openings.

18. Lower the vehicle to the floor and raise the engine using a hoist attached to the support bracket.

19. Install an engine support fixture with a J hook to keep the engine raised, then remove the hoist.

20. Raise and safely support the vehicle.

21. Drain the engine oil and remove the bypass filter.

22. Remove the dual converter Y-pipe and the flywheel inspection cover.

23. Remove the driveshaft and the two transmission mounting nuts.

24. Raise the transmission assembly with a transmission jack. Be sure to support the transmission along the rails of the pan to avoid damage.

25. Remove the oil pan mounting bolts and partially lower the pan.

26. Remove the oil pump pick-up tube and screen assembly and allow it to drop into the pan.

27. Remove the oil pan towards the rear of the vehicle.

To install:

✳✳ WARNING

To prevent possible oil leaks, use only a plastic scraper to clean the oil pan mounting surface.

28. Clean the oil pan-to-engine mounting surface.

29. Place the oil pump pick-up tube and screen assembly in the oil pan, then position the pan and gasket near the engine.

30. Install the oil pump pick-up tube and screen assembly. Tighten the nut to 15–22 ft. lbs. (20–30 Nm) and the two bolts to 71–106 in lbs. (8–12 Nm).

31. Apply a bead of silicone sealant to the areas where the front cover and rear bearing cap meet the engine block.

32. Install the oil pan. Tighten the bolts in sequence using three steps as follows:

- Step one—18 inch lbs. (2 Nm)
- Step two—15 ft. lbs. (20 Nm)
- Step three—tighten an additional 60°

33. Lower the transmission and install the two mounting nuts. Tighten the nuts to 60–80 ft. lbs. (81–108 Nm).

34. Install the driveshaft and the TSS and OSS sensors.

35. Install the flywheel cover and dual converter Y-pipe.

36. Install the oil bypass filter.

37. Lower the vehicle and remove the engine support fixture.

38. Install the engine mounting nuts. Tighten the nuts to 66 ft. lbs. (90 Nm).

39. Remove the modular engine support bracket and install the generator.

40. Install the fan shroud.

41. Use a new gasket and install the throttle body adapter. Tighten the bolts in two steps first to 71–88 in lbs. (8–10 Nm), then tighten them an additional 85–95°.

42. Connect the EVR solenoid harness and vacuum line.

43. Attach the vacuum line to the EGR valve.

44. Install the EGR valve-to-exhaust manifold tube. Tighten the fittings to 55 ft. lbs. (41 Nm).

45. Install the EGR transducer.

46. Install all remaining components in the reverse of the removal.

✳✳ WARNING

Operating the engine without the proper amount and type of engine oil will result in severe engine damage.

47. Fill the engine with the proper amount and type of engine oil

48. Fill and bleed the cooling system.

7.5L Engine

▶ **See Figure 123**

1. Remove the hood.

2. Disconnect the battery ground cable.

3. Drain the cooling system.

4. Remove the air intake tube and air cleaner assembly.

5. Disconnect the throttle linkage at the throttle body.

6. Disconnect the power brake vacuum line at the manifold.

7. Disconnect the fuel lines at the fuel rail.

8. Disconnect the air tubes at the throttle body.

9. Remove the radiator.

10. Remove the power steering pump and position it out of the way without disconnecting the lines.

11. Remove the oil dipstick tube. On motor home chassis, remove the oil filler tube.

12. Remove the front engine mount through-bolts.

13. Position the air conditioner refrigerant hoses so they are clear of the firewall. If necessary, discharge the system and remove the compressor.

14. Remove the upper intake manifold and throttle body.

15. Drain the crankcase. Remove the oil filter.

16. Disconnect the exhaust pipe at the manifolds.

17. Disconnect the transmission linkage at the transmission.

18. Remove the driveshaft(s).

19. Remove the transmission fill tube.

20. Raise the engine with a jack placed under the crankshaft damper and a block of wood to act as a cushion. Raise the engine until the transmission contacts the underside of the floor. Place wood blocks under the engine supports. The engine **must** remain centralized at a point at least 4 in. (102mm) above the mounts, to remove the oil pan!

21. Remove the oil pan attaching screws and lower the oil pan onto the crossmember. Remove the two bolts attaching the oil pump pick-up tube to the oil pump. Lower the assembly from the oil pump. Leave it on the bottom of the

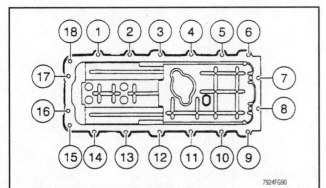

Fig. 122 To prevent leaks, tighten the oil pan bolts in the order shown—6.8L engine

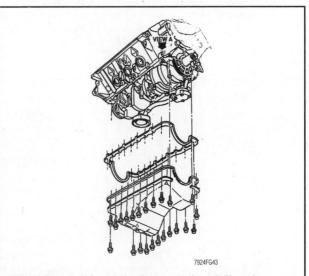

Fig. 123 Exploded view of the oil pan mounting—7.5L engine

oil pan. Remove the oil pan and gaskets. Remove the inlet tube and screen from the oil pan.

To install:

22. Clean the gasket surfaces of the oil pan and cylinder block.
23. Apply a coating of gasket adhesive on the block mating surface and stick the one-piece silicone gasket on the block.
24. Clean the inlet tube and screen assembly and place on the pump.
25. Position the oil pan against the cylinder block and install the retaining bolts. Tighten all bolts to 10 ft. lbs. (14 Nm).
26. Lower the engine and bolt it in place.
27. Install the transmission fill tube.
28. Install the driveshaft(s).
29. Attach the transmission linkage at the transmission.
30. Connect the exhaust pipe at the manifolds.
31. Install the oil filter.
32. Install the upper intake manifold and throttle body.
33. Install the compressor or reposition the hoses.
34. Install the oil dipstick tube. On motor home chassis, install the oil filler tube.
35. Install the power steering pump.
36. Install the radiator.
37. Connect the air tubes at the throttle body.
38. Connect the fuel lines at the fuel rail.
39. Connect the power brake vacuum line at the manifold.
40. Connect the throttle linkage at the throttle body.
41. Install the air intake tube and air cleaner assembly.
42. Fill and bleed the cooling system.
43. Fill the crankcase.
44. Connect the battery ground cable.
45. Install the hood.

7.3L Diesel Engine

▶ See Figures 124 and 125

1. Remove the engine.
2. Remove the oil pan bolts.
3. Lower the oil pan.

➡ **The oil pan is sealed to the crankcase with RTV silicone sealant in place of a gasket. It may be necessary to separate the pan from the crankcase with a utility knife. Also, the crankshaft may have to be turned to allow the pan to clear the crankshaft throws.**

4. Clean the pan and crankcase mating surfaces thoroughly.

To install:

5. Apply a ⅛ in. (3mm) bead of RTV silicone sealant to the pan mating surfaces, and a ¼ in. (6mm) bead on the front and rear covers and in the corners; you have 15 minutes within which to install the pan!
6. Install the locating dowels into position.
7. Position the pan on the engine and install the pan bolts loosely.
8. Remove the dowels.
9. Tighten the pan bolts to 7 ft. lbs. (10 Nm) for ¼ in.-20 bolts; 14 ft. lbs. (19 Nm) for 5/16 in.-18 bolts; 24 ft. lbs. (33 Nm) for ⅜ in.-16 bolts.
10. Install the engine.

Oil Pump

REMOVAL & INSTALLATION

4.2L Engine

▶ See Figure 126

1. Raise and support the front of the vehicle.
2. Drain the engine oil and dispose.
3. Remove the oil filter.
4. Remove the six oil pump bolts, then remove the oil pump drive gear, the oil pump driven gear, the oil pump O-ring and the oil pump itself. Discard the used oil pump O-ring.
5. Inspect the oil pump components for damage or excessive wear.
6. Check the oil pump face for warpage with a flat edge ruler. The face cannot exhibit more than 0.00157 in. (0.04mm) of distortion.
7. Remove the plug over the oil pressure relief; valve.
8. Remove the oil pressure relief valve ball and spring, then clean the parts.

To install:

➡ **Lubricate the parts with clean engine oil before assembly.**

9. Assemble the oil pressure relief valve ball and spring with a new plug.
10. Install the oil pump, along with a new O-ring, the oil pump driven gear and the drive gear. Install and tighten the six oil pump mounting bolts to the torque value specifications indicated in the illustration.
11. Apply a film of clean engine oil to the rubber O-ring on the new filter, then install the filter onto the filter mount.
12. Install the oil pan drain plug.
13. Lower the vehicle.
14. Fill the engine with the correct amount and type of new engine oil.
15. Start the engine and make certain that the oil light on the instrument panel extinguishes within 6–8 seconds after the engine starts.

4.6L and 5.4L Engines

▶ See Figure 127

1. Remove the timing chain.
2. Remove the oil pan.
3. Remove the three oil pump screen and cover bolts, then remove the screen and cover.
4. Remove the oil pump screen and cover spacer.
5. Remove the four oil pump mounting bolts, then remove the oil pump from the engine.

To install:

6. Clean and inspect the mating surfaces.
7. Install the oil pump and loosely install the four oil pump mounting bolts. Tighten the four oil pump bolts in the sequence shown to 71–106 inch lbs. (8–12 Nm).
8. Install the oil pump screen and cover spacer to 15–22 ft. lbs. (20–30 Nm).
9. Install the oil pump screen and cover, then install the three oil pump screen and cover bolts. Tighten the bolts near the oil pick-up screen to 15–22

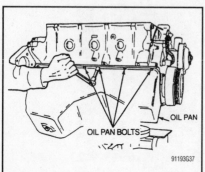
Fig. 124 Remove the twelve oil pan retaining bolts and remove the oil pan from the engine

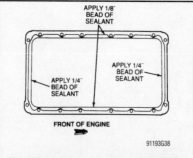
Fig. 125 Apply a ⅛ in. (3mm) bead of RTV silicone sealant to the pan mating surfaces, and a ¼ in. (6mm) bead on the front and rear covers and in the corners

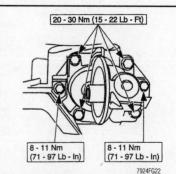
Fig. 126 Tighten the oil pump mounting bolts to the specifications shown—4.2L engines

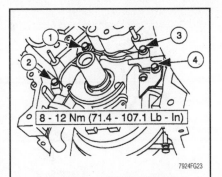

Fig. 127 Tighten the oil pump mounting bolts in the sequence shown—4.6L and 5.4L engines

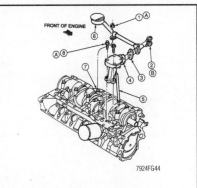

Fig. 128 Exploded view of the oil pump mounting—5.8L and 7.5L engines

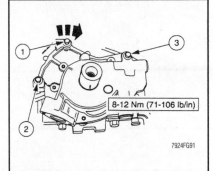

Fig. 129 Be sure to tighten the oil pump mounting bolts in the sequence shown—6.8L engine

ft. lbs. (20–30 Nm) and the bolts at the opposite end of the pick-up to 70–106 inch lbs. (8–12 Nm).

10. Install the timing chains, then install the oil pan.

5.8L and 7.5L Engines

▶ See Figure 128

1. Remove the oil pan.
2. Remove the oil pump inlet tube and screen assembly.
3. Remove the oil pump attaching bolts and remove the oil pump gasket and intermediate driveshaft.

To install:

4. Before installing the oil pump, prime it by filling the inlet and outlet port with oil and rotating the shaft of the pump to distribute it.
5. Position the intermediate driveshaft into the distributor socket.
6. Position the new gasket on the pump body and insert the intermediate driveshaft into the pump body.
7. Install the pump and intermediate driveshaft as an assembly. Do not force the pump if it does not seal readily. The driveshaft may be misaligned with the distributor shaft. To align it, rotate the intermediate driveshaft into a new position.
8. Install the oil pump attaching bolts and tighten them to 20–25 ft. lbs. (27–34 Nm) on the 5.8L and 7.5L engines.

6.8L Engine

▶ See Figure 129

1. Disconnect the negative battery cable.
2. Remove the engine front cover and crankshaft sprocket.
3. Remove the oil pan.
4. Remove the three oil pump mounting bolts, then remove the oil pump from the engine.

To install:

5. Clean and inspect the mating surfaces.
6. Install the oil pump and loosely install the oil pump mounting bolts. Tighten the bolts in the sequence shown to 71–106 inch lbs. (8–12 Nm).

7. Install the oil pan.
8. Install the crankshaft sprocket and timing chains.
9. Install the front cover.

7.3L Diesel Engine

▶ See Figure 130

1. Disconnect the negative battery cable.
2. Remove the radiator.
3. Remove the drive belt.
4. Remove the crankshaft damper.
5. Remove the oil pump retaining bolts.
6. Remove the oil pump housing and square cut O-ring.

To install:

7. Install the oil pump housing and tighten the bolts to 14 ft. lbs. (19 Nm).
8. Install the crankshaft damper.
9. Install the drive belt.
10. Install the radiator.
11. Connect the negative battery cable.

Crankshaft Damper

REMOVAL & INSTALLATION

Gasoline Engines Except Lightning

▶ See Figures 131, 132 and 133

1. Disconnect the negative battery cable.
2. Remove the fan shroud and engine fan.
3. Remove the drive belt(s).
4. On the 4.2L, 5.8L and 7.5L engines, the crankshaft pulley is removable from the damper. Remove the crankshaft pulley retaining bolts.

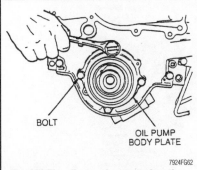

Fig. 130 The oil pump is mounted on the cylinder block with four bolts—diesel engine

Fig. 131 Remove the crankshaft damper retaining bolt and . . .

Fig. 132 . . . install a suitable puller onto the damper assembly

Fig. 133 Tighten the puller forcing screw until the damper assembly releases from the crankshaft

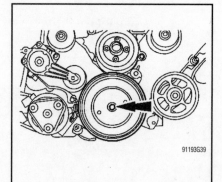

Fig. 134 Remove the supercharger pulley and brace assembly

Fig. 135 Remove the supercharger pulley adapter

5. Remove the vibration damper/pulley retaining bolt from the center of the damper/pulley.

6. Using a suitable puller, remove the damper/pulley from the crankshaft.

To install:

7. Align the key slot of the pulley hub to the crankshaft key, then install the damper, tightening the retaining hardware to the following torque:

- On the 4.2L engine tighten to 103–117 ft. lbs. (140–160 Nm)
- On the 4.6L, 5.4L and 6.8L engines tighten to 66 ft. lbs. (90 Nm), then back off the bolt 90°, tighten to 35–39 ft. lbs. (47–53 Nm), then tighten an additional 85–95°.
- On the 5.8L and 7.5L engines tighten to 70–90 ft. lbs. (95–122 Nm)

8. If the pulley is separate, install the pulley and tighten the pulley retaining bolts to the following torque:

- On the 4.2L engine tighten to 20–28 ft. lbs. (26–38 Nm)
- On the 5.8L and 7.5L engines tighten to 40–52 ft. lbs. (54–71 Nm)

9. Install the drive belt.

10. Install the fan and fan shroud.

11. Connect the negative battery cable.

5.4L Lightning

♦ **See Figures 134 and 135**

1. Disconnect the negative battery cable.
2. Remove the drive belt.
3. Raise and safely support the vehicle securely on jackstands.
4. Remove the nuts and position the under vehicle shield aside.
5. Remove the two nuts and one bolt.
6. Remove the starter motor.
7. Install Crankshaft Damper Remover T58P-6316-D or equivalent onto the crankshaft pulley.

➡**The auxiliary supercharger pulley has left-hand threads.**

8. Remove the pulley and brace assembly.
9. Remove the supercharger pulley adapter.
10. Remove the bolt.
11. Using the special tool, remove the crankshaft pulley.

To install:

➡**The crankshaft pulley must be installed within four minutes after applying the silicone.**

12. Apply silicone sealant to the woodruff key slot on the crankshaft pulley.
13. Using the special tool, install the crankshaft pulley.
14. Install the bolt and washer. Tighten the bolt in four stages.
    a. Stage 1: tighten to 66 ft. lbs. (90 Nm).
    b. Stage 2: loosen the bolt.
    c. Stage 3: tighten to 34–39 ft. lbs. (47–53 Nm).
    d. Stage 4: tighten an additional 85–90 degrees.
15. Install the supercharger pulley adapter.

➡**Coat the threads of the supercharger pulley with High Temperature Nickel Anti-Seize Lubricant F6AZ-9L494–AA or equivalent meeting Ford specification ESE-M12A4–A.**

➡**The auxiliary supercharger pulley has left-hand threads.**

16. Install the pulley and brace assembly.
17. Remove the special tool.
18. Install the starter motor.
19. Position the transmission cooler line clip and install the two nuts and one bolt.
20. Position the shield and install the nut.
21. Lower the vehicle.
22. Install the drive belt.
23. Connect the negative battery cable.

7.3L Diesel Engine

♦ **See Figures 136, 137 and 138**

1. Disconnect the negative battery cable.
2. Drain the cooling system.
3. Remove the radiator as outlined in this Section.
4. Raise the vehicle and safely support it with jackstands.
5. Remove the flywheel housing cover.
6. Install a suitable flywheel holding tool onto the flywheel.
7. Remove the crankshaft pulley bolt and washer.
8. Remove the crankshaft vibration damper using a suitable puller.
9. Remove the crankshaft damper wear ring by assembling Step Plate Adapter D80L-630-A, Damper Wear Ring Remover T94T-6379-AH1, Bearing Collet Sleeve T77F-7025-C, Remover Tube T77J-7025-B and Forcing Screw T84T-7025-B, or their equivalents to the crankshaft damper. Tighten the forcing screw until the damper wear ring is pulled free from the hub (see illustration).

To install:

10. Assemble Driver Handle T80T–4000–W to Damper Wear Ring Replacer T94T–6379–AH2. Insert the crankshaft damper wear ring into the Damper Wear Ring Replacer T94T–6379–AH2 and position the tool assembly onto the vibration damper.

11. Use a ball peen hammer to seat the wear ring into the hub. Use Loctite® 271, or equivalent to the inside diameter of the wear sleeve to prevent oil from travelling through.

12. Install a new crankshaft front seal.

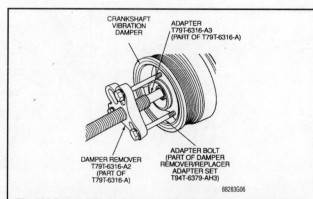

Fig. 136 Remove the diesel engine vibration damper as illustrated (Ford Special tools shown)

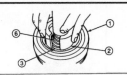
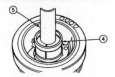
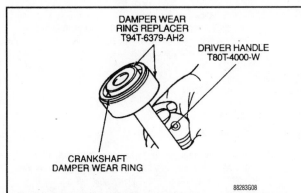

Item	Part Number	Description
1	6316	Crankshaft Vibration Damper
2	T94T-6379-AH1	Damper Wear Ring Remover
3	6310	Crankshaft Damper Wear Ring
4	T77F-7025-C	Bearing Collet Sleeve
5	T77J-7025-B	Remover Tube
6	—	Step Plate Adapter (Part of D80L-630-A)

88283G07

Fig. 137 Special tools used in the removal of the crankshaft damper wear ring—7.3L diesel engine

DAMPER WEAR RING REPLACER T94T-6379-AH2

DRIVER HANDLE T80T-4000-W

CRANKSHAFT DAMPER WEAR RING

88283G08

Fig. 138 Special tools used in the installation of the crankshaft damper wear ring—7.3L diesel engine

13. Apply RTV sealant to the damper key-way, then drive on the damper using a suitable installation tool set.
14. Install the crankshaft pulley bolt and washer.
15. tighten the crankshaft pulley bolt to 212 ft. lbs. (287 Nm).
16. Remove the flywheel holding tool and install the flywheel housing cover.
17. Lower the vehicle.
18. Install the radiator, the fan and clutch and fan shroud assembly.
19. Refill and bleed the cooling system.
20. Connect the negative battery cable.

Front Cover Seal

REMOVAL & INSTALLATION

4.2L Engine

▶ See Figure 139

1. Disconnect the negative battery cable.
2. Remove the accessory drive belt.
3. Remove the fan blade assembly.

➡Match mark the crankshaft pulley to damper positioning for installation reference.

4. Remove 4 crankshaft pulley retaining bolts from the crankshaft damper and remove the pulley.
5. Remove the crankshaft damper retaining bolt and washer and remove the damper with Damper Remover T58P-6316-D and Adapter T82L-6316-B, or equivalents.
6. Remove the front cover oil seal using special tool T92C-6700-CH or equivalent.

To install:

7. Clean and inspect the front cover seal recess and damper.
8. Apply clean engine oil to the front cover oil seal lip.
9. Install the front cover oil seal using Seal Replacer T94P-6701-AH, Aligner T88T-6701-A (aligner) and Adapter T82L-6316-B or equivalents.
10. Apply a bead of silicone sealer to the crankshaft key-way. Line up the damper key-way with the key on the crankshaft and push the damper onto the crankshaft. Install the bolt and washer and tighten to 103–117 ft. lbs. (140–160 Nm).
11. Install the crankshaft pulley, aligning the match marks made during removal. Install 4 retaining bolts and tighten to 20–28 ft. lbs. (26–38 Nm).
12. Install the fan blade assembly.
13. Install the accessory drive belt.
14. Connect the negative battery cable.
15. Start the engine and check for oil leaks.
16. Road test the vehicle and check for proper engine operation.

4.6L, 5.4L and 6.8L Engines Except 5.4L Lightning

▶ See Figures 140, 141 and 142

1. Disconnect the negative battery cable.
2. Remove the engine cooling fan and fan shroud.
3. Release the drive belt tensioner and remove the accessory drive belt.
4. Remove the crankshaft pulley retaining bolt.
5. Remove the crankshaft pulley using Crankshaft Damper Remover T58P-6316-D, or equivalent.
6. Remove the front cover oil seal using a suitable seal remover.

To install:

7. Clean the engine front cover seal bore, then lubricate the seal bore and the seal lip with clean engine oil.
8. Install the new front cover oil seal using Seal Installer T88T-6701-A, or equivalent. Make sure the seal is installed evenly and straight.

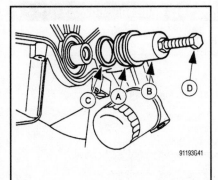

91193G41

Fig. 139 Install the seal into the engine using the necessary tools

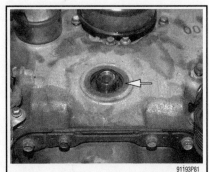

91193P81

Fig. 140 The front crankshaft seal is located in the cover—4.6L, 5.4L and 6.8L engines

91193P83

Fig. 141 Remove the seal from the cover using a suitable seal puller by carefully prying on the seal to . . .

Fig. 142 . . . remove the seal from the cover

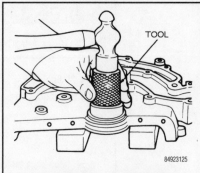

Fig. 143 Installing the oil seal into the 7.5L engine front cover. The tool makes it easier to drive in the seal evenly

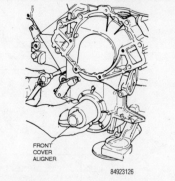

Fig. 144 Aligning the front cover on the 7.5L engine

9. Install the crankshaft pulley using Crankshaft Damper Replacer T74P-6316-B, or equivalent.

10. Apply a suitable silicone sealer to the outer end of the crankshaft damper key-way.

11. Install the crankshaft pulley retaining bolt.

12. Tighten the bolt in 4 steps as follows:
- Tighten the bolt to 66 ft. lbs. (120 Nm)
- Loosen the bolt 1 full turn
- Tighten the bolt to 34–39 ft. lbs. (47–53 Nm)
- Rotate the bolt an additional 85–95 degrees

13. Release the drive belt tensioner and install the accessory drive belt.

14. Install the engine cooling fan and shroud assembly.

15. Check the engine oil level.

16. Connect the negative battery cable.

17. Start the engine and check for leaks.

18. Road test the vehicle and check for proper engine operation.

5.4L Lightning

1. Disconnect the negative battery cable.

2. Remove the drive belt.

3. Raise and safely support the vehicle securely on jackstands.

4. Remove the nuts and position the under vehicle shield aside.

5. Remove the two nuts and one bolt.

6. Remove the starter motor.

7. Install Crankshaft Damper Remover T58P-6316-D or equivalent onto the crankshaft pulley.

➤The auxiliary supercharger pulley has left-hand threads.

8. Remove the pulley and brace assembly.

9. Remove the supercharger pulley adapter.

10. Remove the bolt.

11. Using the special tool, remove the crankshaft pulley.

12. Remove the front cover oil seal using Front Cover Seal Remover T74P-6700-A, or equivalent.

To install:

13. Clean the engine front cover seal bore, then lubricate the seal bore and the seal lip with clean engine oil.

14. Install the new front cover oil seal using Seal Installer T88T-6701-A, or equivalent. Make sure the seal is installed evenly and straight.

➤The crankshaft pulley must be installed within four minutes after applying the silicone.

15. Apply silicone sealant to the woodruff key slot on the crankshaft pulley.

16. Using the special tool, install the crankshaft pulley.

17. Install the bolt and washer. Tighten the bolt in four stages.
   a. Stage 1: tighten to 66 ft. lbs. (90 Nm).
   b. Stage 2: loosen the bolt.
   c. Stage 3: tighten to 34–39 ft. lbs. (47–53 Nm).
   d. Stage 4: tighten an additional 85–90 degrees.

18. Install the supercharger pulley adapter.

➤Coat the threads of the supercharger pulley with High Temperature

Nickel Anti-Seize Lubricant F6AZ-9L494–AA or equivalent meeting Ford specification ESE-M12A4–A.

➤The auxiliary supercharger pulley has left-hand threads.

19. Install the pulley and brace assembly.

20. Remove the special tool.

21. Install the starter motor.

22. Position the transmission cooler line clip and install the two nuts and one bolt.

23. Position the shield and install the nut.

24. Lower the vehicle.

25. Install the drive belt.

26. Connect the negative battery cable.

5.8L and 7.5L Engines

▶ See Figures 143 and 144

1. Remove the fan shroud, radiator fan, spacer, pulley and drive belts.

2. Remove the crankshaft pulley from the crankshaft damper. Remove the damper attaching bolt and washer and remove the damper with a puller.

3. Remove the front cover seal using special tool T70P-6B070-B or equivalent. Tighten the two long bolts to force the tool under the seal flange, then tighten the four corner bolts to force the tool away from the cover.

To install:

4. Apply Lubriplate® or equivalent to the oil seal lip and fit the seal into place. Install special tool T70P-6B070-A or an equivalent seal installation tool and carefully press the new seal into place.

5. Apply Lubriplate® or equivalent to the crankshaft vibration damper to the to prevent damage to the seal. Coat the front of the crankshaft with engine oil for damper installation.

6. Line up the damper key-way with the key on the crankshaft and push the damper onto the crankshaft. Install the bolt and washer and tighten to 80 ft. lbs. Install the crankshaft pulley.

7. Install the fan, spacer, pulley and drive belts.

8. Install the fan shroud to the radiator.

Timing Chain, Sprockets and Front Cover

REMOVAL & INSTALLATION

4.2L Engine

▶ See Figures 145, 146, 147, 148 and 149

1. Disconnect the negative battery cable.

2. Remove the accessory drive belt.

3. Drain the coolant into a suitable clean container.

4. Remove the radiator, fan blade assembly and fan shroud.

5. Remove the water pump.

6. Remove the EGR valve vacuum hose.

7. Remove the EGR tube upper fitting.

8. Remove the EGR valve and adapter assembly.

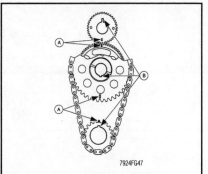

Fig. 145 After removing the CMP drive gear, be sure the timing marks (A) and key-ways (B) are aligned—4.2L engine

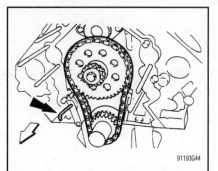

Fig. 146 Compress the tensioner assembly and install a pin into the hole in the tensioner body

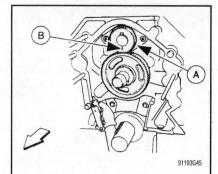

Fig. 147 Turn the balance shaft so that the timing mark (B) on the gear (A) is in alignment

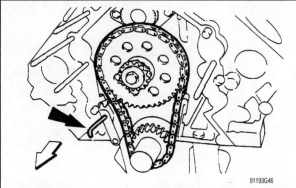

Fig. 148 After the timing chains are installed, remove the retaining pin from the tensioner

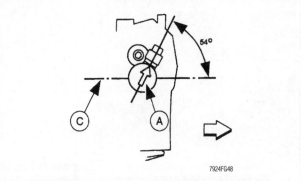

Fig. 149 Install the camshaft synchronizer (A) in the orientation shown (white arrow points to front of engine)—4.2L engines

9. Detach the wiring harness from the heater water outlet tube.
10. Remove the heater water outlet bolt and position the outlet tube aside.
11. Remove the Camshaft Position (CMP) sensor electrical harness connector and mark the position of the connector for proper installation.
12. Rotate the crankshaft until the TDC timing mark lines up with the timing mark.
13. Remove the two bolts retaining the CMP and remove the CMP from the camshaft synchronizer.
14. Remove the camshaft synchronizer adjustment bolt and remove the camshaft synchronizer.

➡The oil pump drive shaft may come out with the camshaft synchronizer.

15. Raise and safely support the vehicle.
16. Remove the oil pan drain plug and drain the engine oil in a suitable container.
17. Remove the crankshaft pulley and damper using appropriate tools.
18. Remove the engine oil pan.
19. Remove the two engine front cover stud bolts, front cover bolt and cap screw.
20. Slide the engine front cover and gasket off the dowels and discard the gasket.
21. Remove the CMP sensor drive gear bolt and remove the drive gear.
22. Be sure the timing marks and key-ways align.
23. Compress and install a retaining pin to hold the timing chain tensioner.
24. Slide both sprockets and timing chain forward and remove as an assembly.
25. Remove the three bolts retaining the timing chain tensioner and remove the tensioner.
26. Check the timing chain and sprockets for excessive wear. Replace if necessary.

To install:
27. Before installation, clean and inspect all parts. Clean the gasket material from the engine oil pan, cylinder block and engine front cover.
28. Place the timing chain tensioner in position and install the three retaining bolts. Tighten the bolts to 6–10 ft. lbs. (8–14 Nm).

29. Verify that the balance shaft timing gears are in correct alignment.
30. Slide both sprockets and the timing chain onto the camshaft and crankshaft with the timing marks aligned. Install the CMP sensor drive gear and bolt. Tighten the bolt to 30–36 ft. lbs. (40–50 Nm).
31. Remove the retaining pin.
32. Inspect the engine front cover seal for wear or damage and replace if necessary.
33. Install the engine front cover gasket and front cover onto the guide studs.
34. Install the two engine front cover stud bolts, front cover bolt and cap screw. Tighten the bolts to 15–22 ft. lbs. (20–30 Nm).
35. Install the engine oil pan.
36. Install the crankshaft damper and pulley.

✺✺ WARNING

A Synchro Positioning Tool must be used prior to installation. Failure to using this procedure will result in the fuel system being out of time, possibly causing engine damage.

37. Install Synchro Positioning Tool T89P-12200-A or equivalent, on the camshaft synchronizer by rotating the tool until it engages the notch in the housing.
38. Install the camshaft synchronizer housing assembly so that the arrow on the tool is 54 degrees from the centerline of the engine.
39. Install the adjustment bolt and tighten to 15–22 ft. lbs. (21–30 Nm).
40. Remove the tool and position the CMP sensor. Install the 2 bolts and 40–70 inch lbs. (5–8 Nm) and install the CMP electrical harness connector.
41. Install the water pump.
42. Install the fan shroud, fan blade assembly and radiator.
43. Install the accessory drive belt.
44. Fill the crankcase with the correct amount and type of engine oil.
45. Fill and bleed the engine cooling system.
46. Connect the negative battery cable.
47. Start the engine and check for coolant and oil leaks.
48. Road test the vehicle and check for proper engine operation.

Fig. 150 Remove the driver's side ignition coil bracket bolts

Fig. 151 Remove the passenger side ignition coil bracket bolts along with the belt tensioner retaining bolts and the idler pulley retaining bolt

Fig. 152 Remove the power steering pump mounting bolts and position the pump to the side

Fig. 153 Remove the four front oil pan-to-timing cover retaining bolts

Fig. 154 Once the necessary components are removed, the timing cover bolts are accessible, remove the bolts and . . .

Fig. 155 . . . remove the cover from the engine

Fig. 156 Install the camshaft holding tool

Fig. 157 Remove the crankshaft position sensor trigger wheel from the crankshaft

Fig. 158 Remove the timing chain tensioner retaining bolts and . . .

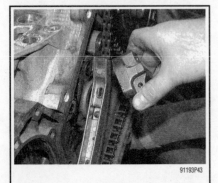

Fig. 159 . . . remove the tensioner from the engine

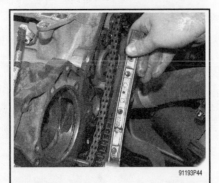

Fig. 160 Remove the tensioner arm from the engine

Fig. 161 Remove the timing chain from around the camshaft pulley

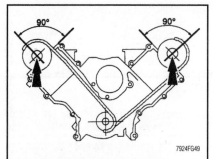

Fig. 162 When removing the timing chains, rotate the crankshaft so that the camshaft key-ways are positioned as shown—4.6L engines

Fig. 163 Remove the timing chain guide retaining bolts and remove the guides from the engine

Fig. 164 Place the tensioner into a bench vise or other suitable device and retract the plunger

Fig. 165 Using a small screwdriver or other suitable tool, push back and hold the ratchet mechanism

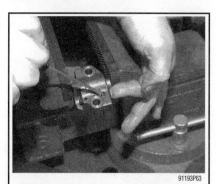

Fig. 166 While holding the ratchet mechanism, push the ratchet arm back into the tensioner assembly

Fig. 167 After the ratchet mechanism is retracted, place a paper clip or other suitable tool into the hole in the tensioner body to hold the ratchet arm and plunger during installation

Fig. 168 Place the tensioner assembly onto the engine and tighten the retaining bolts

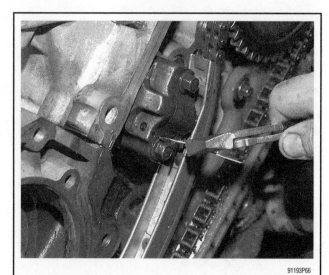

Fig. 169 Remove the paper clip from the tensioner assembly

4.6L Engine

▶ See Figures 150 thru 172

1. Disconnect the negative battery cable.
2. Remove the radiator, fan blade and fan shroud assembly.
3. Remove the accessory drive belt.
4. Remove the water pump pulley.
5. Detach the electrical harness connectors from both ignition coils.
6. Remove both ignition coils with their brackets attached.
7. Remove the left-hand and right-hand cylinder head covers.
8. Raise and safely support the vehicle.

9. Remove the two upper power steering pump retaining bolts.
10. Remove the two lower power steering pump retaining bolts and move the pump aside.
11. Detach the Crankshaft Position (CKP) sensor electrical harness connector. Remove the retaining bolt and remove the CKP sensor.
12. Drain the engine oil into a suitable container.
13. Remove the four oil pan-to-engine front cover retaining bolts.
14. Lower the vehicle.
15. Remove the crankshaft damper retaining bolt and washer from the crankshaft.
16. Install Crankshaft Damper Remover T58P-6316-D or equivalent and pull the damper from the crankshaft.

17. Remove the Camshaft Position (CMP) sensor retaining bolt and remove the CMP sensor.

18. Remove the idler pulley bolt and remove the pulley.

19. Remove the three belt tensioner retaining bolts and remove the tensioner.

20. Remove the eight engine front cover retaining bolts and the seven nuts. Swing the top of the cover out off the dowel pins and remove the cover.

21. Remove the sensor ring from the crankshaft.

22. Use Camshaft Positioning Tool T91P-6256-A and Camshaft Positioning Adapters T92P-6256-A or equivalents, to position the camshaft.

23. Rotate the crankshaft until both camshaft key-ways are 90 degrees from the cam cover surface. Be sure the copper links line up with the dots on the camshaft sprockets.

❊❊ WARNING

At no time, when the timing chains are removed and the cylinder heads are installed may the crankshaft or the camshaft be rotated. Severe piston and valve damage will occur.

24. Remove the two left-hand and right-hand tensioner bolts and remove the timing chain tensioners.

25. Slide the left-hand and right-hand tensioner guides off the dowel pins.

26. Remove the right-hand timing chain from the camshaft sprocket.

27. Remove the left-hand timing chain from the camshaft sprocket.

28. Remove the left-hand and right-hand timing chain guide bolts and remove the timing chain guides.

29. If necessary, remove the camshaft gear bolt and remove the camshaft gear.

To install:

30. Examine the timing chains, looking for the copper links. If the copper links are not visible, lay the chain on a flat surface and pull the chain taught until the opposite sides of the chain contact one another. Mark the links at each end of the chain and use these marks in place of the copper links.

➡ **If the engine jumped time, damage has been done to valves and possibly pistons and/or connecting rods. Any damage must be corrected before installing the timing chains.**

31. If removed, install the camshaft gears and tighten the retaining bolt to 81–95 ft. lbs. (110–130 Nm).

32. Install the left-hand and right-hand timing chain guides and retaining bolts. Tighten the retaining bolts to 71–106 inch lbs. (8–12 Nm).

33. If removed, install the left-hand crankshaft sprocket with the tapered part of the sprocket facing away from the engine block.

➡ **The crankshaft sprockets are identical. They may only be installed one way, with the tapered part of the sprockets facing each other. Ensure that the key-way and timing marks on the crankshaft sprockets are aligned.**

34. Install the left-hand timing chain on the camshaft and crankshaft sprockets. Be sure the copper links of the timing chain line up with the timing marks on both sprockets.

35. If removed, install the right-hand crankshaft sprocket with the tapered part of the sprocket facing the left-hand crankshaft sprocket.

36. Install the right-hand timing chain on the camshaft and crankshaft sprockets. Be sure the copper links of the timing chain line up with the timing marks on both sprockets.

37. It is necessary to bleed the timing chain tensioners before installation. Proceed as follows:

a. Place the timing chain tensioner in a soft-jawed vise.

b. Using a small pick or similar tool, hold the ratchet lock mechanism away from the ratchet stem and slowly compress the tensioner plunger by rotating the vise handle.

❊❊ WARNING

The tensioner must be compressed slowly or damage to the internal seals will result.

c. Once the tensioner plunger bottoms in the tensioner bore, continue to hold the ratchet lock mechanism and push down on the ratchet stem until flush with the tensioner face.

d. While holding the ratchet stem flush to the tensioner face, release the ratchet lock mechanism and install a paper clip or similar tool in the tensioner body to lock the tensioner in the collapsed position.

e. The paper clip must not be removed until the timing chain, tensioner, tensioner arm and timing chain guide are completely installed on the engine.

38. Install the left-hand and right-hand timing chain tensioner guides on the dowel pins.

39. Place the left-hand and right-hand timing chain tensioners in position and install the retaining bolts. Tighten the bolts to 15–22 ft. lbs. (20–30 Nm).

40. Remove the retaining pins from the timing chain tensioners.

41. Remove Camshaft Positioning Tool T91P-6256-A and Camshaft Positioning Adapters T92P-6256-A or equivalents. from the camshaft.

42. Install the crankshaft sensor ring on the crankshaft.

43. Apply a bead of silicone sealer along the cylinder head-to-cylinder block and the oil pan-to-cylinder block sealing surfaces.

44. Install the engine front cover carefully onto the dowel pins.

45. Tighten the engine front cover bolts, in sequence, to 15–22 ft. lbs. (20–30 Nm).

46. Place the idler pulley in position and install the retaining bolt. Tighten the bolt to 15–22 ft. lbs. (20–30 Nm).

47. Install the drive belt tensioner and the three retaining bolts. Tighten the bolts to 15–22 ft. lbs. (20–30 Nm).

48. Install the CMP sensor and the retaining bolt. Tighten the bolt to 106 inch lbs. (12 Nm).

49. Place the damper on the crankshaft. Ensure the crankshaft key and key-way are aligned.

50. Using Crankshaft Damper Replacer T74P-6316-B or equivalent, install the crankshaft damper.

51. Raise and safely support the vehicle.

52. Install the four oil pan-to-engine front cover bolts and tighten, in sequence, in 2 steps:

a. Tighten the bolts to 15 ft. lbs. (20 Nm).

b. Rotate the bolts an additional 60 degrees.

53. Install the CKP sensor and the retaining bolt. Tighten the bolt to 106 inch lbs. (12 Nm). Connect the CKP sensor electrical harness connector.

54. Install the power steering pump and the two upper and two lower retaining bolts. Tighten the bolts to 15–20 ft. lbs. (20–30 Nm).

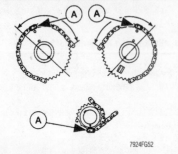

Fig. 170 When installing the timing chains, make certain that the copper colored links (A) are aligned with the timing marks—4.6L engine

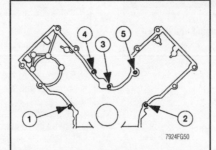

Fig. 171 Tighten the first five front cover fasteners in the sequence shown—4.6L engine

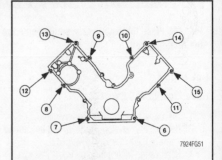

Fig. 172 Continue tightening the remaining fasteners in the sequence shown here—4.6L engine

55. Lower the vehicle.
56. Place the ignition coil and brackets on the engine front cover and install the bracket bolts. Tighten the bolts to 15–22 ft. lbs. (20–30 Nm).
57. Connect the ignition coil and capacitor electrical harness connectors.
58. Connect the CMP electrical harness connector.
59. Install the water pump pulley and tighten the bolts to 15–22 ft. lbs. (20–30 Nm).
60. Install the radiator, fan blade and fan shroud assembly.
61. Install the accessory drive belt.
62. Connect the negative battery cable.
63. Start the engine and check for leaks.
64. Road test the vehicle and check for proper engine operation.

5.4L and 6.8L Engines

▶ See Figures 173 and 174

1. Disconnect the negative battery cable.
2. Remove the radiator, fan blade and fan shroud assembly.
3. Remove the accessory drive belt.
4. Remove the water pump pulley.
5. Detach the electrical harness connectors from both ignition coils.
6. Remove both ignition coils with their brackets attached.
7. Raise and safely support the vehicle.
8. Remove the two upper power steering pump retaining bolts.
9. Remove the two lower power steering pump retaining bolts and move the pump aside.
10. Detach the Crankshaft Position (CKP) sensor electrical harness connector. Remove the retaining bolt and remove the CKP sensor.
11. Drain the engine oil into a suitable container.
12. Remove the four oil pan-to-engine front cover retaining bolts.
13. Lower the vehicle.
14. Remove the crankshaft damper retaining bolt and washer from the crankshaft.
15. Install Crankshaft Damper Remover T58P-6316-D or equivalent and pull the damper from the crankshaft.
16. Remove the Camshaft Position (CMP) sensor retaining bolt and remove the CMP sensor.
17. Remove the idler pulley bolt and remove the pulley.
18. Remove the three belt tensioner bolts and remove the tensioner.
19. Remove the eight engine front cover retaining bolts and the seven nuts. Swing the top of the cover out off the dowel pins and remove the cover.
20. Remove the sensor ring from the crankshaft.
21. Use Camshaft Positioning Tool T96T-6256-A or equivalent, to position the camshaft.
22. Rotate the crankshaft until both camshaft key-ways are 90 degrees from the cam cover surface. Be sure the copper links line up with the dots on the camshaft sprockets.

❊❊ WARNING

At no time, when the timing chains are removed and the cylinder

heads are installed may the crankshaft or the camshaft be rotated. Severe piston and valve damage will occur.

23. Install Camshaft Holding Tool T96T-6256-B or equivalent, on the camshaft.
24. Remove 2 left-hand and right-hand tensioner bolts and remove the timing chain tensioners.
25. Slide the left-hand and right-hand tensioner guides off the dowel pins.
26. Remove the right-hand timing chain from the camshaft sprocket.
27. Remove the left-hand timing chain from the camshaft sprocket.
28. Remove the left-hand and right-hand timing chain guide bolts and remove the timing chain guides.

To install:

29. Examine the timing chains, looking for the copper links. If the copper links are not visible, lay the chain on a flat surface and pull the chain taught until the opposite sides of the chain contact one another. Mark the links at each end of the chain and use these marks in place of the copper links.

➡ **If the engine jumped time, damage has been done to valves and possibly pistons and/or connecting rods. Any damage must be corrected before installing the timing chains.**

30. Install the left-hand and right-hand timing chain guides and retaining bolts. Tighten the retaining bolts to 71–106 inch lbs. (8–12 Nm).
31. If removed, install the left-hand crankshaft sprocket with the tapered part of the sprocket facing away from the engine block.

➡ **The crankshaft sprockets are identical. They may only be installed one way, with the tapered part of the sprockets facing each other. Ensure that the key-way and timing marks on the crankshaft sprockets are aligned.**

32. Install the left-hand timing chain on the camshaft and crankshaft sprockets. Be sure the one copper link aligns with the mark on the crankshaft sprocket and the two copper links align with the mark on the camshaft sprocket.
33. Install the right-hand crankshaft sprocket with the tapered part of the sprocket facing the left-hand crankshaft sprocket.
34. Install the right-hand timing chain on the camshaft and crankshaft sprockets. Be sure the copper links of the timing chain line up with the timing marks on both sprockets.
35. It is necessary to bleed the timing chain tensioners before installation. Proceed as follows:
   a. Place the timing chain tensioner in a soft-jawed vise.
   b. Using a small pick or similar tool, hold the ratchet lock mechanism away from the ratchet stem and slowly compress the tensioner plunger by rotating the vise handle.

❊❊ WARNING

The tensioner must be compressed slowly or damage to the internal seals will result.

   c. Once the tensioner plunger bottoms in the tensioner bore, continue to hold the ratchet lock mechanism and push down on the ratchet stem until flush with the tensioner face.
   d. While holding the ratchet stem flush to the tensioner face, release the

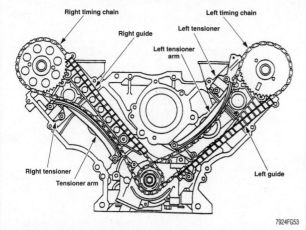

Fig. 173 Timing chains and related components—5.4L and 6.8L engines

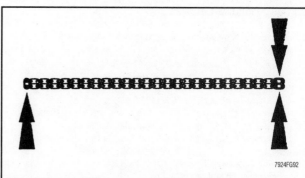

Fig. 174 If the copper links are not visible, mark one link on one end of the chain and two links on the opposite end of the chain—5.4L and 6.8L engines

ratchet lock mechanism and install a paper clip or similar tool in the tensioner body to lock the tensioner in the collapsed position.

  e. The paper clip must not be removed until the timing chain, tensioner, tensioner arm and timing chain guide are completely installed on the engine.

36. Install the left-hand and right-hand timing chain tensioner guides on the dowel pins.

37. Place the left-hand and right-hand timing chain tensioners in position and install the retaining bolts. Tighten the bolts to 15–22 ft. lbs. (20–30 Nm).

38. Remove the retaining pins from the timing chain tensioners.

39. Remove Cam Holding Tool T96T-6256-B or equivalent, from the camshaft.

40. Install the crankshaft sensor ring on the crankshaft.

41. Apply silicone gasket along the cylinder head-to-cylinder block and engine oil pan-to-cylinder block sealing surfaces.

42. Install the engine front cover carefully onto the dowel pins.

43. Tighten the engine front cover bolts, in sequence, in the following manner:
  a. Tighten bolts 1 through 5 to 15–22 ft. lbs. (20–30 Nm).
  b. Tighten bolts 6 through 15 to 29–40 ft. lbs. (40–55 Nm).

44. Place the idler pulley in position and install the retaining bolt. Tighten the bolt to 15–22 ft. lbs. (20–30 Nm).

45. Place the drive belt tensioner in position and install 3 retaining bolts. Tighten the bolts to 15–22 ft. lbs. (20–30 Nm).

46. Place the CMP sensor in position and install the retaining bolt. Tighten the bolt to 106 inch lbs. (12 Nm).

47. Install the damper on the crankshaft. Ensure the crankshaft key and keyway are aligned.

48. Using Crankshaft Damper Replacer T74P-6316-B or equivalent, install the crankshaft damper.

49. Raise and safely support the vehicle.

50. Install 4 front oil pan-to-engine front cover retaining bolts and tighten in sequence in 2 steps:
  a. Tighten the bolts to 15 ft. lbs. (20 Nm).
  b. Rotate the bolts an additional 60 degrees.

51. Place the CKP sensor in position and install the retaining bolt. Tighten the bolt to 106 inch lbs. (12 Nm).

52. Connect the CKP sensor electrical harness connector.

53. Install the power steering pump with 2 upper and 2 lower retaining bolts. Tighten the bolts to 15–20 ft. lbs. (20–30 Nm).

54. Lower the vehicle.

55. Place the ignition coil and brackets on the engine front cover and install the bracket bolts. Tighten the bolts to 15–22 ft. lbs. (20–30 Nm).

56. Connect the ignition coil and capacitor electrical harness connectors.

57. Connect the CMP electrical harness connector.

58. Install the water pump pulley and tighten the bolts to 15–22 ft. lbs. (20–30 Nm).

59. Install the radiator.

60. Connect the negative battery cable.

61. Start the engine and check for leaks.

62. Road test the vehicle and check for proper engine operation.

5.8L Engine

♦ **See Figure 175**

1. Drain the cooling system and the crankcase.

2. Disconnect the upper and lower radiator hoses and the transmission oil cooler lines and remove the radiator.

3. Disconnect the heater hose from the water pump. Slide the water pump bypass hose clamp toward the water pump.

4. Loosen the alternator pivot bolt and the bolt which secures the alternator adjusting arm to the water pump. Position the alternator out of the way.

5. Remove the power steering pump and air conditioning compressor from their mounting brackets, if so equipped.

6. Remove the fan, spacer, pulley and drive belts.

7. Remove the crankshaft pulley from the crankshaft damper. Remove the damper attaching bolt and washer and remove the damper with a puller.

8. If equipped with a manual fuel pump, disconnect the fuel pump outlet line at the fuel pump. Disconnect the vacuum inlet and outlet lines from the fuel pump. Remove the fuel pump attaching bolts and lay the pump to one side with the fuel inlet line still attached.

9. If necessary, remove the oil level dipstick and the bolt holding the dipstick tube to the exhaust manifold.

10. Remove the oil pan-to-cylinder front cover attaching bolts. Use a sharp,

thin cutting blade to cut the oil pan gasket flush with the cylinder block. Remove the front cover and water pump as an assembly.

11. Discard the front cover gasket. If necessary, properly support the cover and carefully drive the oil seal out towards the front of the cover.

12. Rotate the crankshaft counterclockwise to take up the slack on the left side of the chain.

13. Establish a reference point on the cylinder block and measure from this point to the chain.

14. Rotate the crankshaft in the opposite direction to take up the slack on the right side of the chain.

15. Force the left side of the chain out with your fingers and measure the distance between the reference point and the chain. The timing chain deflection is the difference between the two measurements. If the deflection exceeds ½ in. (13mm), replace the timing chain and sprockets.

16. Turn the crankshaft until the timing marks on the sprockets are aligned vertically.

17. Remove the camshaft sprocket retaining screw, if equipped, remove the fuel pump eccentric and washers.

18. Alternately slide both of the sprockets and timing chain off the crankshaft and camshaft until free of the engine.

To install:

19. Clean the front cover mating surfaces of all gasket material and/or sealer. If the front cover seal is being replaced, support the cover to prevent damage and drive out the seal. Coat the new seal with heavy SJ engine oil and install it in the cover, making sure it is not cocked.

20. Position the timing chain on the sprockets so that the timing marks on the sprockets are aligned vertically. Alternately slide the sprockets and chain onto the crankshaft and camshaft sprockets.

21. Cut the new oil pan gasket as needed for a correct fit. Apply sealing compound to the oil pan and fit the gasket into place.

22. Apply sealing compound to the gasket surfaces on the cylinder block and back side of the front cover. Position the gasket onto the cylinder block and fit the front cover onto the engine.

23. Coat the screw threads with sealing compound and start all the screws. Center the cover by inserting an alignment tool (T74P-6019-a or equivalent) in the oil seal.

24. Tighten the oil pan screws first to 12–18 ft. lbs. (17–24 Nm), then tighten the front cover screws to the same torque.

25. Apply Lubriplate® or equivalent to the oil seal lip and to the vibration damper to prevent damage to the seal. Coat the front of the crankshaft with engine oil for damper installation.

26. Line up the damper key-way with the key on the crankshaft and push the damper onto the crankshaft. Install the bolt and washer and tighten to 80 ft. lbs. Install the crankshaft pulley.

27. Install the fan, spacer, pulley and drive belts.

28. Install the bolts holding the fan shroud to the radiator, if so equipped.

29. Install the power steering pump and air conditioning compressor.

30. Install the alternator and adjust the belt tension.

31. Connect the heater hose at the water pump.

32. Install the radiator.

33. Connect the upper and lower radiator hoses, and transmission oil cooler lines.

34. Fill the cooling system and the crankcase.

7924FG55

Fig. 175 Align the marks when installing the timing chain—5.8L and 7.5L engines

7.5L Engine

▶ See Figures 176 and 177

1. Drain the cooling system and crankcase.
2. Remove the radiator shroud and fan.
3. Disconnect the upper and lower radiator hoses and the automatic transmission oil cooler lines from the radiator.
4. Remove the radiator upper support and remove the radiator.
5. Loosen the alternator attaching bolts and air conditioning compressor idler pulley and remove the drive belts with the water pump pulley. Remove the bolts attaching the compressor support to the water pump and remove the bracket (support), if equipped.
6. Remove the crankshaft pulley from the vibration damper. Remove the bolt and washer attaching the crankshaft damper and remove the damper with a puller. Remove the woodruff key from the crankshaft.
7. Loosen the bypass hose at the water pump and disconnect the heater return tube at the water pump.
8. Disconnect and plug the fuel inlet and outlet lines at the fuel pump and remove the fuel pump.
9. Remove the bolts attaching the front cover to the cylinder block. Cut the oil pan seal flush with the cylinder block face with a thin knife blade prior to separating the cover from the cylinder block. Remove the cover and water pump as an assembly. Discard the front cover gasket and oil pan seal.
10. Rotate the crankshaft counterclockwise to take up the slack on the left side of the chain.
11. Establish a reference point on the cylinder block and measure from this point to the chain.
12. Rotate the crankshaft in the opposite direction to take up the slack on the right side of the chain.
13. Force the left side of the chain out and measure the distance between the reference point and the chain. The timing chain deflection is the difference between the two measurements. If the deflection exceeds ½ in. (13mm), replace the timing chain and sprockets.
14. Turn the crankshaft until the timing marks on the sprockets are aligned vertically.
15. Remove the camshaft sprocket retaining screw and remove the fuel pump eccentric and washers.
16. Alternately slide both of the sprockets and timing chain off the crankshaft and camshaft until free of the engine.

To install:

17. Position the timing chain on the sprockets so the timing marks on the sprockets are aligned vertically. Alternately slide the sprockets and chain onto the crankshaft and camshaft sprockets.
18. Transfer the water pump if a new cover is going to be installed. Clean all of the gasket sealing surfaces on both the front cover and the cylinder block.
19. Coat the gasket surface of the oil pan with sealer. Cut and position the required sections of a new seal on the oil pan. Apply sealer to the corners.
20. Drive out the old front cover oil seal with a pin punch. Clean out the seal recess in the cover. coat a new seal with Lubriplate® or equivalent grease. Install the seal, making sure the seal spring remains in the proper position. A front cover seal tool, Ford part no. T72J-117 or equivalent, makes installation easier.
21. Coat the gasket surfaces of the cylinder block and cover with sealer and position the new gasket on the block.

22. Position the front cover on the cylinder block. Use care not to damage the seal and gasket or misplace them.
23. Coat the front cover attaching screws with sealer and install them.

➡ It may be necessary to force the front cover downward to compress the oil pan seal in order to install the front cover attaching bolts. Use a prybar or drift to engage the cover screw holes through the cover and pry downward.

24. Install the fuel pump.
25. Connect the fuel inlet and outlet lines at the fuel pump.
26. Tighten the bypass hose at the water pump.
27. Connect the heater return tube at the water pump.
28. Install the woodruff key from the crankshaft.
29. Install the damper.
30. Install the crankshaft pulley on the vibration damper.
31. Install the compressor support on the water pump and install the bracket (support), if equipped.
32. Install the drive belts with the water pump pulley.
33. Install the radiator and upper support.
34. Connect the upper and lower radiator hoses and the automatic transmission oil cooler lines.
35. Install the radiator shroud and fan.
36. Fill the cooling system and crankcase.

Tighten the fasteners to the following specifications:
- Front cover bolts: 15–20 ft. lbs. (20–27 Nm)
- Water pump attaching screws: 12–15 ft. lbs. (16–20 Nm)
- Crankshaft damper: 70–90 ft. lbs. (95–122 Nm)
- Crankshaft pulley: 35–50 ft. lbs. (47–68 Nm)
- Oil pan bolts: 9–11 ft. lbs. (12.2–15.0 Nm) for the ⁵⁄₁₆ in. (7.9mm) screws and to 7–9 ft. lbs. (9.5–12.2 Nm) for the ¼ in. (6.3mm) screws
- Alternator pivot bolt: 45–57 ft. lbs. (61–77 Nm)

Timing Gears and Front Cover

REMOVAL & INSTALLATION

7.3L Diesel Engine

▶ See Figures 178 and 179

1. Disconnect the negative battery cable.
2. Remove the engine.
3. Remove the water pump.
4. Remove the crankshaft damper.
5. Remove the oil pan.
6. Remove the four front cover retaining bolts.
7. Remove the front cover from the engine.

➡ The crankshaft gear sprocket is not serviced separately from the crankshaft. Do not try to remove the sprocket or you will damage the crankshaft. To replace the crankshaft sprocket crankshaft replacement is necessary.

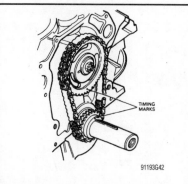

Fig. 176 Align the timing marks on the pulleys

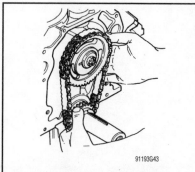

Fig. 177 Alternately slide both of the sprockets and timing chain off the crankshaft and camshaft until free of the engine

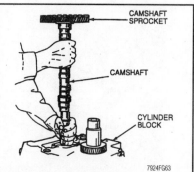

Fig. 178 The camshaft gear is removed with the camshaft, then pressed off—7.3L diesel engine

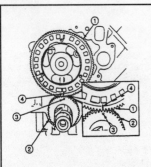

Fig. 179 Be sure the timing marks are aligned as illustrated—Diesel engines

Remove the camshaft sprocket as follows:
8. Remove the camshaft.
9. Use a press to remove the sprocket from the camshaft.
10. Remove the thrust plate and sprocket key.
11. Inspect the camshaft and related parts for wear and damage.

To install:
12. Clean the nose of the camshaft and install the thrust plate.
13. Place the key in the key-way on the camshaft.
14. Heat the sprocket in an oven to 500° F (260° C).
15. Remove the sprocket from the oven, align the sprocket key-way with the camshaft key and install the sprocket on the camshaft until it is fully seated. Allow the camshaft assembly to cool before installation
16. Install the camshaft in the engine and align the timing marks on the gears.
17. Install new gaskets onto the engine front cover and apply silicone sealant into the sealing grooves on the front cover.
18. Install the front cover onto the engine.
19. Install the four front cover retaining bolts and tighten the bolts to 15 ft. lbs. (20 Nm).
20. Install the oil pan.
21. Install the crankshaft damper.
22. Install the water pump.
23. Install the engine.
24. Connect the negative battery cable.

Camshaft and Lifters

REMOVAL & INSTALLATION

4.2L Engine

▶ **See Figure 180**

1. Disconnect the negative battery cable.
2. Remove the lower intake manifold.

3. Remove the rocker arm cover.
4. Remove the rocker arm hold-down bolt, then remove the rocker arm from the cylinder head.
5. Remove the pushrods.
6. Remove the valve lifters by pulling them up out of their bores.
7. Remove the timing chain and sprockets.
8. Remove the camshaft key from the end of the camshaft, then slide the engine dynamic balance shaft drive gear off of the camshaft.
9. Remove the two camshaft thrust plate retaining bolts (1), then remove the thrust plate (2). Remove the camshaft spacer (3), then slide the camshaft (4) out of the front of the engine block. Be cautious not to gouge or scratch the camshaft bearing journals.

To install:
10. Lubricate the camshaft with engine oil prior to installation.
11. Carefully slide the camshaft into the camshaft bore. Do not scratch the bearing surfaces.
12. Install the camshaft thrust plat with the spacer. Tighten the thrust plate mounting bolts to 6–10 ft. lbs. (8–14 Nm).
13. Slide the engine dynamic balance shaft drive gear onto the camshaft. Install the camshaft key to the camshaft groove.
14. Install the timing chain and sprockets.
15. Install the valve lifters, pushrods, intake manifolds and rocker arm covers.

4.6L, 5.4L, and 6.8L Engines

▶ **See Figures 181, 182, 183 and 184**

1. Remove the cylinder head covers from the engine.
2. Remove the timing chain.

❊❊ CAUTION

At no time, when the timing chains are removed and the cylinder heads are installed may the crankshaft or camshaft be rotated. Severe piston and valve damage will occur.

3. On the 6.8L engine, remove the six bolts securing the balance shaft to the cylinder head and remove the shaft.
4. Remove the camshaft roller lifters.
5. On VIN W engines, remove the timing chain camshaft gear by removing the gear retaining bolt.

➡**Keep the bearing caps in order so they can be installed in the same position.**

6. Remove the camshaft bearing cap bolts, then lift the camshaft bearing caps off of the cylinder head.
7. Lift the camshaft from the cylinder head.
8. Remove the rocker arms and pull the lash adjusters out of their bores. Keep all the parts in order. They must be installed in their original positions.

To install:
9. Install the lash adjusters and rocker arms in their original positions.
10. Lubricate the camshaft journals and bearing caps with super premium SAE 5W30 engine oil which meets Ford specifications WSS-M2C153-G. On the

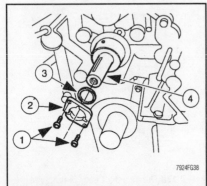

Fig. 180 Exploded view of the camshaft retaining hardware—4.2L engine

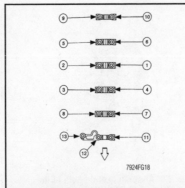

Fig. 181 Tighten the bearing caps in the sequence shown—4.6L and 5.4L engines

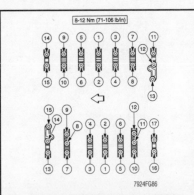

Fig. 182 Camshaft bearing cap bolt tightening sequence—6.8L engine

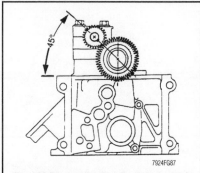

Fig. 183 Be sure to align the balance shaft timing mark with the mark on the camshaft gear—6.8L engine

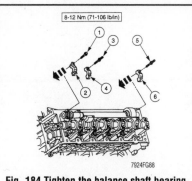

Fig. 184 Tighten the balance shaft bearing cap bolts in the sequence shown—6.8L engine

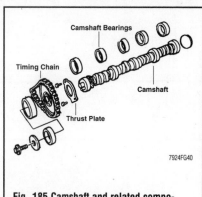

Fig. 185 Camshaft and related components—5.8L and 7.5L engines

6.8L engine, lubricate the balance shaft journals and bearing caps with the same lubricant.

11. Lower the camshaft onto the camshaft bearing journals.

12. Install the camshaft bearing caps, then loosely install the bearing cap bolts.

13. Tighten the camshaft bearing cap mounting bolts, in the sequence shown for the particular engine, to 71–107 inch lbs. (8–12 Nm).

14. On the 6.8L engine, align the timing marks and position the balance shaft on the journals, then install the bearing caps. Tighten the bolts in sequence to 71–106 in lbs. (8–12 Nm).

15. On VIN W engines, install the camshaft timing chain gear by tightening the retaining bolt to 81–95 ft. lbs. (110–130 Nm).

16. Install the valve lifters.

17. Install the timing chain and sprockets, if applicable.

18. Install the cylinder head covers.

5.8L and 7.5L Engines

▶ See Figure 185

1. Remove the intake manifold and valley pan, if equipped.

2. Remove the rocker covers, and loosen the rockers on their pivots and remove the pushrods. The pushrods must be reinstalled in their original positions.

3. Remove the valve lifters in sequence with a magnet. They must be replaced in their original positions.

4. Remove the timing gear cover, timing chain and sprockets.

5. In addition to the radiator and air conditioning condenser, if equipped, it may be necessary to remove the front grille assembly and the hook lock assembly to gain the necessary clearance to code the camshaft out of the front of the engine.

➡A camshaft removal tool, Ford part no. T65L-6250-a and adapter 14-0314 are needed to remove the Diesel camshaft.

To install:

6. Coat the camshaft liberally with clean engine oil before installing it. Slide the camshaft into the engine very carefully so as not to scratch the bearing bores with the camshaft lobes. Install the camshaft thrust plate and tighten the attaching screws to 9–12 ft. lbs. (12–16 Nm). Measure the camshaft end-play. If the end-play is more than 0.009 in. (0.228mm), replace the thrust plate. Assemble the remaining components in the reverse order of removal.

7. Install the radiator, front grille, hood lock assembly and air conditioning condenser, if removed.

8. Install the timing chain and front cover.

9. Install the valve lifters. They must be replaced in their original positions.

10. Install the pushrods, the rocker arms and the rocker arm covers.

11. Install the intake manifold and valley pan, if equipped.

7.3L Diesel Engine

▶ See Figures 178 and 179

➡Ford recommends removing the Diesel engine from the vehicle for camshaft removal.

1. Remove the valve covers, and either remove the rocker arm shafts or loosen the rockers on their pivots and remove the pushrods. The pushrods must be reinstalled in their original positions.

2. Remove the timing gear cover.

3. Remove the valve lifters in sequence with a magnet. They must be replaced in their original positions.

4. Rotate the crankshaft to align the camshaft sprocket timing marks.

5. Remove the camshaft thrust plate retaining bolts.

6. Remove the camshaft sprocket, thrust plate and camshaft as an assembly from the engine.

To install:

7. Inspect the camshaft as described in this section.

8. liberally coat the camshaft with oil before installing it. Slide the camshaft with the thrust plate and sprocket attached into the engine very carefully so as not to scratch the bearing bores with the camshaft lobes.

9. Tighten the camshaft thrust plate retaining bolts to 9–12 ft. lbs. (12–16 Nm). Measure the camshaft end-play. If the end-play is more than 0.009 in. (0.228mm), replace the thrust plate.

10. Install the valve lifters. They must be replaced in their original positions.

11. Install the timing gear cover.

12. Install the pushrods, the rocker arms and the rocker arm covers.

13. Install the engine.

INSPECTION

▶ See Figures 186, 187 and 188

Using solvent, degrease the camshaft and clean out all of the oil holes. Visually inspect the cam lobes and bearing journals for excessive wear. If a lobe is questionable, check all of the lobes as indicated. If a journal or lobe is worn, the camshaft MUST BE or replaced.

➡If a journal is worn, there is a good chance that the bearings or journals are worn and need replacement.

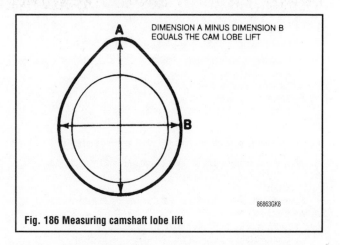

Fig. 186 Measuring camshaft lobe lift

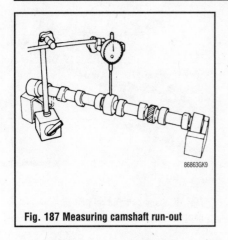

Fig. 187 Measuring camshaft run-out

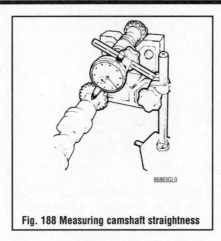

Fig. 188 Measuring camshaft straightness

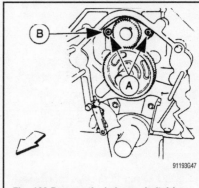

Fig. 189 Remove the balance shaft drive gear and spacer

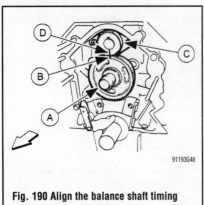

Fig. 190 Align the balance shaft timing marks

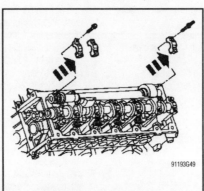

Fig. 191 Remove the bolts and the balance shaft bearing caps

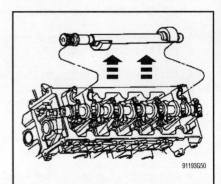

Fig. 192 Remove the balance shafts from the cylinder head

If the lobes and journals appear intact, place the front and rear journals in V-blocks and rest a dial indicator on the center journal. Rotate the camshaft to check the straightness. If deviation exceeds 0.001 in. (0.0254mm), replace the camshaft.

Check the camshaft lobes with a micrometer, by measuring the lobes from the nose to the base and again at 90° (see illustration). The lobe lift is determined by subtracting the second measurement from the first. If all of the exhaust and intake lobes are not identical, the camshaft must be reground or replace.

Balance Shaft

REMOVAL & INSTALLATION

4.2L Engine

▶ See Figures 189 and 190

1. Disconnect the negative battery cable.
2. Drain and recycle the engine coolant.
3. Drain and recycle the engine oil.
4. Remove the engine oil pan.
5. Remove the engine front cover.
6. Remove the timing chain and sprockets.
7. Remove 2 bolts retaining the balance shaft thrust plate.

➡Use care not to damage the balance shaft bearing surfaces.

8. Carefully slide the balance shaft, driven gear and thrust plate out the front of the cylinder block.

To install:

9. Inspect the balance shaft rear bearing cover. If damaged or leaking, replace the balance shaft rear bearing cover. Inspect the balance shaft and bearings for signs of wear or damage and replace as necessary.
10. Lubricate the balance shaft journals with engine assembly lubricant.

11. Install the balance shaft, driven gear and thrust plate, being careful not to damage the bearing surfaces while sliding it into position. Install 2 thrust plate retaining bolts and tighten to 70–124 inch lbs. (8–14 Nm).
12. Install the balance shaft drive gear and spacer.
13. Align the balance shaft timing marks.
14. Install the timing chain and sprockets.
15. Install the engine front cover.
16. Install the engine oil pan.
17. Fill the crankcase with the proper grade and quantity of engine oil.
18. Fill and bleed the engine cooling system.
19. Connect the negative battery cable.
20. Start the engine and check for leaks.
21. Road test the vehicle and check for proper engine operation.

6.8L Engine

▶ See Figures 191, 192, 193 and 194

1. Disconnect the negative battery cable.
2. Remove the engine air cleaner assembly.
3. Remove the radiator.
4. Remove the engine front cover.
5. Remove the crankshaft sensor ring from the crankshaft.
6. Remove the 6 bolts retaining the balance shaft bearing caps. Remove the bearing caps.
7. Remove the balance shaft.

To install:

8. Lubricate the balance shaft journals with clean engine oil.
9. Install the balance shaft onto the journals. Align the balance shaft timing marks.
10. Install the bearing caps and tighten the bolts in the proper sequence. Torque the bolts to 71–106 inch lbs. (8–12 Nm).
11. Clean the front engine cover sealant off the engine. Allow to dry and apply a bead of silicone along the head-to-block surface. Apply a bead of silicone along the oil pan-to-block surface.
12. Install a new gasket and install the engine front cover.

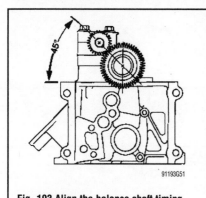

Fig. 193 Align the balance shaft timing marks as shown

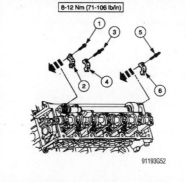

Fig. 194 Tighten the balance shaft bearing caps in the sequence shown

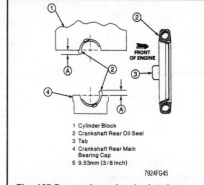

1 Cylinder Block
2 Crankshaft Rear Oil Seal
3 Tab
4 Crankshaft Rear Main
  Bearing Cap
5 9.53mm (3 / 8 Inch)

Fig. 195 Rear main seal and related components—7.5L engines

13. Install the radiator.
14. Fill and bleed the cooling system.
15. Install the engine air cleaner.
16. Connect the negative battery cable.

Rear Main Seal

REMOVAL & INSTALLATION

7.5L Engine

▶ **See Figure 195**

1. Raise and safely support the vehicle.
2. Remove the oil pan.
3. Loosen all the crankshaft main bearing cap bolts and lower the crankshaft no more than ¹⁄₃₂ in. (0.7938mm).

> **✳✳ CAUTION**
>
> **Be careful that the crankshaft sealing surfaces are not damaged in this process**

4. Remove the rear main bearing cap and remove the seal. On the cylinder block half of the seal, use a seal removal tool, or install a small metal screw in one end of the seal and pull on the screw to remove the seal.
   To install:
5. Clean the seal groove in the crankshaft main bearing cap and the block using a brush and a solvent such as metal surface cleaner F4AZ-19A536-RA or its equivalent.
6. Clean the areas where the sealer is to be applied later and dry the area thoroughly so that no solvent contacts the rear main seal.
7. Dip the seal halves in engine oil.

> **✳✳ CAUTION**
>
> **Be sure no rubber has been removed from the outside diameter of the seal by the bottom edge of the groove. Do not allow oil to get on the sealer.**

8. Install the upper half of the seal (cylinder block side) into its groove with the undercut side of the seal towards the front of the engine (with the tab side of the seal towards the rear face of the block), by rotating it on the seal journal until approximately ³⁄₈ in. (9.525mm) protrudes below the parting surface.
9. Tighten all the crankshaft main bearing cap bolts, EXCEPT THE REAR MAIN BEARING, to 95–105 ft. lbs. (129–142 Nm).
10. Install the lower half of the seal in the rear crankshaft main bearing cap with the undercut side of the seal towards the front of the engine (with the tab side of the seal towards the rear face of the block), Allow the seal to protrude ³⁄₈ in. (9.525mm) above the parting surface to mate with the upper half of the seal.
11. Apply a ¹⁄₁₆ in. (1.588mm) bead of gasket maker E2AZ-19562-B or its equivalent to the rear oil seal area of the block starting from the forward face of the return groove and overlaying the end of the wire seal retainer.

➡ **Do not allow the sealer to contact the inside diameter of the seal.**

12. Install the rear main cap and tighten the bolts to 95–105 ft. lbs. (129–142 Nm).
13. Install the oil pan.

Gasoline Engines Except 7.5L Engine

▶ **See Figure 196**

If the crankshaft rear oil seal replacement is the only operation being performed, it can be done in the vehicle as detailed in the following procedure. If the oil seal is being replaced in conjunction with a rear main bearing replacement, the engine must be removed from the vehicle and installed on a work stand.

1. Remove the transmission from the vehicle. Refer to Section 7.
2. Remove the flywheel/flexplate. If equipped, remove the crankshaft oil slinger from the crankshaft.
3. Use an awl to punch two holes in the crankshaft rear oil seal. Punch the holes on opposite sides of the crankshaft and just above the bearing cap-to-cylinder block split line.
4. Install a sheet metal screw in each hole. Use two small prybars to pry against both screws at the same time to remove the crankshaft rear oil seal. It may be necessary to place small blocks of wood against the cylinder block to provide a fulcrum point for the prybars. Use caution throughout this procedure to avoid scratching or otherwise damaging the crankshaft oil seal surface.
5. Clean the oil seal recess in the cylinder block and main bearing cap.
   To install:
6. Clean, inspect and polish the rear oil seal rubbing surface on the crankshaft.
7. Coat the new oil seal and the crankshaft with a light film of engine oil.
8. Start the seal in the recess with the seal lip facing forward and install it with a seal driver. Keep the tool straight with the centerline of the crankshaft and install the seal until the tool contacts the cylinder block surface. Remove the tool and inspect the seal to be sure it was not damaged during installation.

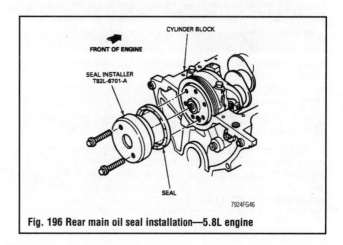

Fig. 196 Rear main oil seal installation—5.8L engine

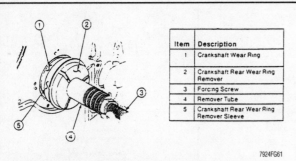

Item	Description
1	Crankshaft Wear Ring
2	Crankshaft Rear Wear Ring Remover
3	Forcing Screw
4	Remover Tube
5	Crankshaft Rear Wear Ring Remover Sleeve

7924FG61

Fig. 197 Assemble the seal and wear ring removal tools, then remove the wear ring—7.3L diesel engine

9. If equipped, install the crankshaft oil slinger.
10. Install the flywheel.
11. Install the transmission. Refer to Section 7.

7.3L Diesel Engine

♦ See Figure 197

1. Remove the transmission. Refer to Section 7.
2. Remove the flywheel.
3. Loosen the crankshaft rear oil seal bolts and remove the seal.
4. Clean the seal mating surfaces.
5. If installing the old seal, inspect it for damage.
6. Using crankshaft wear ring removal tool T94T-6701-AH1, forcing screw T84T-7025-B, remover tube T77J-7025-B and wear ring remover sleeve T94T-6701-AH2 (refer to the illustration), or their equivalents, remove the wear ring.

To install:

7. Apply silicone sealant D6AZ-19562-BA, or equivalent, to the seal retaining ring and the seal retaining bolts.
8. using seal replacers T94T-6701-AH3 and T94T-AH4, driver sleeve T79T-6316-A4 (part of T79T-6316-A) and guide pins T94P-7000-P or their equivalents, install the wear ring and oil seal.
9. Install and tighten the seal retaining bolts.
10. Remove the installation tools and install the flywheel.
11. Install the transmission. Refer to Section 7.

Flywheel/Flexplate

REMOVAL & INSTALLATION

♦ See Figure 198

➡The ring gear is replaceable only on engines mated with a manual transmission. Engines with automatic transmissions have ring gears which are welded to the flexplate.

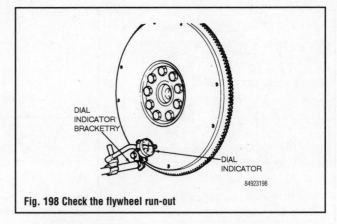

84923198

Fig. 198 Check the flywheel run-out

1. Remove the transmission assembly. Refer to Section 7.
2. If equipped with a manual transmission, remove the clutch and pressure plate assembly. Refer to Section 7.
3. Loosen the flywheel bolts a little at a time in a cross pattern to avoid warping the flywheel.
4. Remove the flywheel from the engine.
5. On trucks with manual transmissions, replace the pilot bearing in the end of the crankshaft.
6. The flywheel should be checked for cracks and glazing. It can be resurfaced by a machine shop.
7. If the ring gear is to be replaced, drill a hole in the gear between two teeth, being careful not to contact the flywheel surface. Using a cold chisel at this point, crack the ring gear and remove it.
8. Polish the inner surface of the new ring gear and heat it in an oven to about 600°F (316°C). Quickly place the ring gear on the flywheel and tap it into place, making sure that it is fully seated.

❊❊ WARNING

Never heat the ring gear past 800°F (426°C), or the tempering will be destroyed.

To install:

9. Position the flywheel on the end of the crankshaft. Tighten the bolts a little at a time, in a cross pattern, to the following torque:
   - 4.2L Engine 54–64 ft. lbs. (73–87 Nm)
   - 4.6L Engine 54–64 ft. lbs. (73–87 Nm)
   - 5.4L Engine 54–64 ft. lbs. (73–87 Nm)
   - 5.8L Engine 75–85 ft. lbs. (103–115 Nm)
   - 6.8L Engine 54–64 ft. lbs. (73–87 Nm)
   - 7.3L Engine 89 ft. lbs. (121 Nm)
   - 7.5L Engine 75–85 ft. lbs. (103–115 Nm)
10. Install the clutch and pressure plate assembly. Refer to Section 7.
11. Install the transmission assembly. Refer to Section 7.

EXHAUST SYSTEM

Inspection

➡Safety glasses should be worn at all times when working on or near the exhaust system. Older exhaust systems will almost always be covered with loose rust particles which will shower you when disturbed. These particles are more than a nuisance and could injure your eye.

❊❊ CAUTION

DO NOT perform exhaust repairs or inspection with the engine or exhaust hot. Allow the system to cool completely before attempting any work. Exhaust systems are noted for sharp edges, flaking metal and rusted bolts. Gloves and eye protection are required. A healthy supply of penetrating oil and rags is highly recommended.

Your vehicle must be raised and supported safely to inspect the exhaust system properly. By placing 4 safety stands under the vehicle for support should provide enough room for you to slide under the vehicle and inspect the system completely. Start the inspection at the exhaust manifold or turbocharger pipe where the header pipe is attached and work your way to the back of the vehicle. On dual exhaust systems, remember to inspect both sides of the vehicle. Check the complete exhaust system for open seams, holes loose connections, or other deterioration which could permit exhaust fumes to seep into the passenger compartment. Inspect all mounting brackets and hangers for deterioration, some models may have rubber O-rings that can be overstretched and non-supportive. These components will need to be replaced if found. It has always been a practice to use a pointed tool to poke up into the exhaust system where the deterioration spots are to see whether or not they crumble. Some models may have heat shield covering certain parts of the exhaust system , it will be necessary to remove these shields to have the exhaust visible for inspection also.

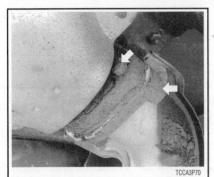

Fig. 199 Nuts and bolts will be extremely difficult to remove when deteriorated with rust

Fig. 200 Example of a flange type exhaust system joint

Fig. 201 Example of a common slip joint type system

REPLACEMENT

♦ See Figure 199

There are basically two types of exhaust systems. One is the flange type where the component ends are attached with bolts and a gasket in-between. The other exhaust system is the slip joint type. These components slip into one another using clamps to retain them together.

✳✳ CAUTION

Allow the exhaust system to cool sufficiently before spraying a solvent exhaust fasteners. Some solvents are highly flammable and could ignite when sprayed on hot exhaust components.

Before removing any component of the exhaust system, ALWAYS squirt a liquid rust dissolving agent onto the fasteners for ease of removal. A lot of knuckle skin will be saved by following this rule. It may even be wise to spray the fasteners and allow them to sit overnight.

Flange Type

♦ See Figure 200

✳✳ CAUTION

Do NOT perform exhaust repairs or inspection with the engine or exhaust hot. Allow the system to cool completely before attempting any work. Exhaust systems are noted for sharp edges, flaking metal and rusted bolts. Gloves and eye protection are required. A healthy

supply of penetrating oil and rags is highly recommended. Never spray liquid rust dissolving agent onto a hot exhaust component.

Before removing any component on a flange type system, ALWAYS squirt a liquid rust dissolving agent onto the fasteners for ease of removal. Start by unbolting the exhaust piece at both ends (if required). When unbolting the headpipe from the manifold, make sure that the bolts are free before trying to remove them. if you snap a stud in the exhaust manifold, the stud will have to be removed with a bolt extractor, which often means removal of the manifold itself. Next, disconnect the component from the mounting; slight twisting and turning may be required to remove the component completely from the vehicle. You may need to tap on the component with a rubber mallet to loosen the component. If all else fails, use a hacksaw to separate the parts. An oxy-acetylene cutting torch may be faster but the sparks are DANGEROUS near the fuel tank, and at the very least, accidents could happen, resulting in damage to the under-car parts, not to mention yourself.

Slip Joint Type

♦ See Figure 201

Before removing any component on the slip joint type exhaust system, ALWAYS squirt a liquid rust dissolving agent onto the fasteners for ease of removal. Start by unbolting the exhaust piece at both ends (if required). When unbolting the headpipe from the manifold, make sure that the bolts are free before trying to remove them. if you snap a stud in the exhaust manifold, the stud will have to be removed with a bolt extractor, which often means removal of the manifold itself. Next, remove the mounting U-bolts from around the exhaust pipe you are extracting from the vehicle. Don't be surprised if the U-bolts break while removing the nuts. Loosen the exhaust pipe from any mounting brackets retaining it to the floor pan and separate the components.

ENGINE RECONDITIONING

Determining Engine Condition

Anything that generates heat and/or friction will eventually burn or wear out (for example, a light bulb generates heat, therefore its life span is limited). With this in mind, a running engine generates tremendous amounts of both; friction is encountered by the moving and rotating parts inside the engine and heat is created by friction and combustion of the fuel. However, the engine has systems designed to help reduce the effects of heat and friction and provide added longevity. The oiling system reduces the amount of friction encountered by the moving parts inside the engine, while the cooling system reduces heat created by friction and combustion. If either system is not maintained, a break-down will be inevitable. Therefore, you can see how regular maintenance can affect the service life of your vehicle. If you do not drain, flush and refill your cooling system at the proper intervals, deposits will begin to accumulate in the radiator, thereby reducing the amount of heat it can extract from the coolant. The same applies to your oil and filter; if it is not changed often enough it becomes laden with contaminates and is unable to properly lubricate the engine. This increases friction and wear.

There are a number of methods for evaluating the condition of your engine. A

compression test can reveal the condition of your pistons, piston rings, cylinder bores, head gasket(s), valves and valve seats. An oil pressure test can warn you of possible engine bearing, or oil pump failures. Excessive oil consumption, evidence of oil in the engine air intake area and/or bluish smoke from the tailpipe may indicate worn piston rings, worn valve guides and/or valve seals. As a general rule, an engine that uses no more than one quart of oil every 1000 miles is in good condition. Engines that use one quart of oil or more in less than 1000 miles should first be checked for oil leaks. If any oil leaks are present, have them fixed before determining how much oil is consumed by the engine, especially if blue smoke is not visible at the tailpipe.

COMPRESSION TEST

A noticeable lack of engine power, excessive oil consumption and/or poor fuel mileage measured over an extended period are all indicators of internal engine wear. Worn piston rings, scored or worn cylinder bores, blown head gaskets, sticking or burnt valves, and worn valve seats are all possible culprits. A check of each cylinder's compression will help locate the problem.

Gasoline Engines

▸ **See Figure 202**

➡ **A screw-in type compression gauge is more accurate than the type you simply hold against the spark plug hole. Although it takes slightly longer to use, it's worth the effort to obtain a more accurate reading.**

1. Make sure that the proper amount and viscosity of engine oil is in the crankcase, then ensure the battery is fully charged.
2. Warm-up the engine to normal operating temperature, then shut the engine **OFF**.
3. Disable the ignition system.
4. Label and disconnect all of the spark plug wires from the plugs.
5. Thoroughly clean the cylinder head area around the spark plug ports, then remove the spark plugs.
6. Set the throttle plate to the fully open (wide-open throttle) position. You can block the accelerator linkage open for this, or you can have an assistant fully depress the accelerator pedal.
7. Install a screw-in type compression gauge into the No. 1 spark plug hole until the fitting is snug.

✳✳ WARNING

Be careful not to crossthread the spark plug hole.

8. According to the tool manufacturer's instructions, connect a remote starting switch to the starting circuit.
9. With the ignition switch in the **OFF** position, use the remote starting switch to crank the engine through at least five compression strokes (approximately 5 seconds of cranking) and record the highest reading on the gauge.
10. Repeat the test on each cylinder, cranking the engine approximately the same number of compression strokes and/or time as the first.
11. Compare the highest readings from each cylinder to that of the others. The indicated compression pressures are considered within specifications if the lowest reading cylinder is within 75 percent of the pressure recorded for the highest reading cylinder. For example, if your highest reading cylinder pressure was 150 psi (1034 kPa), then 75 percent of that would be 113 psi (779 kPa). So the lowest reading cylinder should be no less than 113 psi (779 kPa).
12. If a cylinder exhibits an unusually low compression reading, pour a tablespoon of clean engine oil into the cylinder through the spark plug hole and repeat the compression test. If the compression rises after adding oil, it means that the cylinder's piston rings and/or cylinder bore are damaged or worn. If the pressure remains low, the valves may not be seating properly (a valve job is needed), or the head gasket may be blown near that cylinder. If compression in any two adjacent cylinders is low, and if the addition of oil doesn't help raise compression, there is leakage past the head gasket. Oil and coolant in the combustion chamber, combined with blue or constant white smoke from the tailpipe, are symptoms of this problem. However, don't be alarmed by the normal white smoke emitted from the tailpipe during engine warm-up or from cold weather driving. There may be evidence of water droplets on the engine dipstick and/or oil droplets in the cooling system if a head gasket is blown.

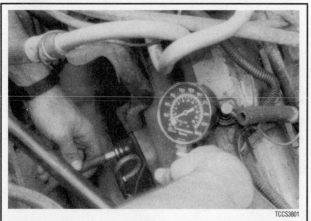

TCCS3801

Fig. 202 A screw-in type compression gauge is more accurate and easier to use without an assistant

Diesel Engines

Checking cylinder compression on diesel engines is basically the same procedure as on gasoline engines except for the following:
1. A special compression gauge adapter suitable for diesel engines (because these engines have much greater compression pressures) must be used.
2. Remove the injector tubes and remove the injectors from each cylinder.

✳✳ WARNING

Do not forget to remove the washer underneath each injector. Otherwise, it may get lost when the engine is cranked.

3. When fitting the compression gauge adapter to the cylinder head, make sure the bleeder of the gauge (if equipped) is closed.
4. When reinstalling the injector assemblies, install new washers underneath each injector.

OIL PRESSURE TEST

Check for proper oil pressure at the sending unit passage with an externally mounted mechanical oil pressure gauge (as opposed to relying on a factory installed dash-mounted gauge). A tachometer may also be needed, as some specifications may require running the engine at a specific rpm.
1. With the engine cold, locate and remove the oil pressure sending unit.
2. Following the manufacturer's instructions, connect a mechanical oil pressure gauge and, if necessary, a tachometer to the engine.
3. Start the engine and allow it to idle.
4. Check the oil pressure reading when cold and record the number. You may need to run the engine at a specified rpm, so check the specifications.
5. Run the engine until normal operating temperature is reached (upper radiator hose will feel warm).
6. Check the oil pressure reading again with the engine hot and record the number. Turn the engine **OFF**.
7. Compare your hot oil pressure reading to that given in the chart. If the reading is low, check the cold pressure reading against the chart. If the cold pressure is well above the specification, and the hot reading was lower than the specification, you may have the wrong viscosity oil in the engine. Change the oil, making sure to use the proper grade and quantity, then repeat the test.

Low oil pressure readings could be attributed to internal component wear, pump related problems, a low oil level, or oil viscosity that is too low. High oil pressure readings could be caused by an overfilled crankcase, too high of an oil viscosity or a faulty pressure relief valve.

Buy or Rebuild?

Now that you have determined that your engine is worn out, you must make some decisions. The question of whether or not an engine is worth rebuilding is largely a subjective matter and one of personal worth. Is the engine a popular one, or is it an obsolete model? Are parts available? Will it get acceptable gas mileage once it is rebuilt? Is the car it's being put into worth keeping? Would it be less expensive to buy a new engine, have your engine rebuilt by a pro, rebuild it yourself or buy a used engine from a salvage yard? Or would it be simpler and less expensive to buy another car? If you have considered all these matters and more, and have still decided to rebuild the engine, then it is time to decide how you will rebuild it.

➡ **The editors at Chilton feel that most engine machining should be performed by a professional machine shop. Don't think of it as wasting money, rather, as an assurance that the job has been done right the first time. There are many expensive and specialized tools required to perform such tasks as boring and honing an engine block or having a valve job done on a cylinder head. Even inspecting the parts requires expensive micrometers and gauges to properly measure wear and clearances. Also, a machine shop can deliver to you clean, and ready to assemble parts, saving you time and aggravation. Your maximum savings will come from performing the removal, disassembly, assembly and installation of the engine and purchasing or renting only the tools required to perform the above tasks. Depending on the particular circumstances, you may save 40 to 60 percent of the cost doing these yourself.**

A complete rebuild or overhaul of an engine involves replacing all of the moving parts (pistons, rods, crankshaft, camshaft, etc.) with new ones and machining the non-moving wearing surfaces of the block and heads. Unfortunately, this may not be cost effective. For instance, your crankshaft may have been damaged or worn, but it can be machined undersize for a minimal fee.

So, as you can see, you can replace everything inside the engine, but, it is wiser to replace only those parts which are really needed, and, if possible, repair the more expensive ones. Later in this section, we will break the engine down into its two main components: the cylinder head and the engine block. We will discuss each component, and the recommended parts to replace during a rebuild on each.

Engine Overhaul Tips

Most engine overhaul procedures are fairly standard. In addition to specific parts replacement procedures and specifications for your individual engine, this section is also a guide to acceptable rebuilding procedures. Examples of standard rebuilding practice are given and should be used along with specific details concerning your particular engine.

Competent and accurate machine shop services will ensure maximum performance, reliability and engine life. In most instances it is more profitable for the do-it-yourself mechanic to remove, clean and inspect the component, buy the necessary parts and deliver these to a shop for actual machine work.

Much of the assembly work (crankshaft, bearings, piston rods, and other components) is well within the scope of the do-it-yourself mechanic's tools and abilities. You will have to decide for yourself the depth of involvement you desire in an engine repair or rebuild.

TOOLS

The tools required for an engine overhaul or parts replacement will depend on the depth of your involvement. With a few exceptions, they will be the tools found in a mechanic's tool kit (see Section 1 of this manual). More in-depth work will require some or all of the following:

- A dial indicator (reading in thousandths) mounted on a universal base
- Micrometers and telescope gauges
- Jaw and screw-type pullers
- Scraper
- Valve spring compressor
- Ring groove cleaner
- Piston ring expander and compressor
- Ridge reamer
- Cylinder hone or glaze breaker
- Plastigage®
- Engine stand

The use of most of these tools is illustrated in this section. Many can be rented for a one-time use from a local parts jobber or tool supply house specializing in automotive work.

Occasionally, the use of special tools is called for. See the information on Special Tools and the Safety Notice in the front of this book before substituting another tool.

OVERHAUL TIPS

Aluminum has become extremely popular for use in engines, due to its low weight. Observe the following precautions when handling aluminum parts:
- Never hot tank aluminum parts (the caustic hot tank solution will eat the aluminum.
- Remove all aluminum parts (identification tag, etc.) from engine parts prior to the tanking.
- Always coat threads lightly with engine oil or anti-seize compounds before installation, to prevent seizure.
- Never overtighten bolts or spark plugs especially in aluminum threads.

When assembling the engine, any parts that will be exposed to frictional contact must be prelubed to provide lubrication at initial start-up. Any product specifically formulated for this purpose can be used, but engine oil is not recommended as a prelube in most cases.

When semi-permanent (locked, but removable) installation of bolts or nuts is desired, threads should be cleaned and coated with Loctite® or another similar, commercial non-hardening sealant.

CLEANING

▶ See Figures 203, 204, 205

Before the engine and its components are inspected, they must be thoroughly cleaned. You will need to remove any engine varnish, oil sludge and/or carbon deposits from all of the components to insure an accurate inspection. A crack in the engine block or cylinder head can easily become overlooked if hidden by a layer of sludge or carbon.

Most of the cleaning process can be carried out with common hand tools and readily available solvents or solutions. Carbon deposits can be chipped away using a hammer and a hard wooden chisel. Old gasket material and varnish or sludge can usually be removed using a scraper and/or cleaning solvent. Extremely stubborn deposits may require the use of a power drill with a wire brush. If using a wire brush, use extreme care around any critical machined surfaces (such as the gasket surfaces, bearing saddles, cylinder bores, etc.). Use of a wire brush is NOT RECOMMENDED on any aluminum components. Always follow any safety recommendations given by the manufacturer of the tool and/or solvent. You should always wear eye protection during any cleaning process involving scraping, chipping or spraying of solvents.

An alternative to the mess and hassle of cleaning the parts yourself is to drop them off at a local garage or machine shop. They will, more than likely, have the necessary equipment to properly clean all of the parts for a nominal fee.

✳✳ CAUTION

Always wear eye protection during any cleaning process involving scraping, chipping or spraying of solvents.

Remove any oil galley plugs, freeze plugs and/or pressed-in bearings and carefully wash and degrease all of the engine components including the fasteners and bolts. Small parts such as the valves, springs, etc., should be placed in

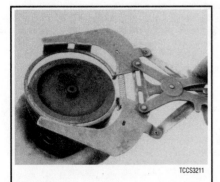

TCCS3211

Fig. 203 Use a ring expander tool to remove the piston rings

TCCS3208

Fig. 204 Clean the piston ring grooves using a ring groove cleaner tool, or . . .

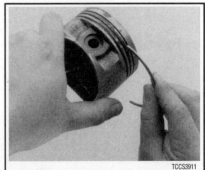

TCCS3911

Fig. 205 . . . use a piece of an old ring to clean the grooves. Be careful, the ring can be quite sharp

a metal basket and allowed to soak. Use pipe cleaner type brushes, and clean all passageways in the components. Use a ring expander and remove the rings from the pistons. Clean the piston ring grooves with a special tool or a piece of broken ring. Scrape the carbon off of the top of the piston. You should never use a wire brush on the pistons. After preparing all of the piston assemblies in this manner, wash and degrease them again.

✳✳ WARNING

Use extreme care when cleaning around the cylinder head valve seats. A mistake or slip may cost you a new seat.

When cleaning the cylinder head, remove carbon from the combustion chamber with the valves installed. This will avoid damaging the valve seats.

REPAIRING DAMAGED THREADS

Several methods of repairing damaged threads are available. Heli-Coil® (shown here), Keenserts® and Microdot® are among the most widely used. All involve basically the same principle—drilling out stripped threads, tapping the hole and installing a prewound insert—making welding, plugging and oversize fasteners unnecessary.

Two types of thread repair inserts are usually supplied: a standard type for most inch coarse, inch fine, metric course and metric fine thread sizes and a spark lug type to fit most spark plug port sizes. Consult the individual tool manufacturer's catalog to determine exact applications. Typical thread repair kits will contain a selection of prewound threaded inserts, a tap (corresponding to the outside diameter threads of the insert) and an installation tool. Spark plug inserts usually differ because they require a tap equipped with pilot threads and a combined reamer/tap section. Most manufacturers also supply blister-packed thread repair inserts separately in addition to a master kit containing a variety of taps and inserts plus installation tools.

Before attempting to repair a threaded hole, remove any snapped, broken or damaged bolts or studs. Penetrating oil can be used to free frozen threads. The offending item can usually be removed with locking pliers or using a screw/stud extractor. After the hole is clear, the thread can be repaired.

Engine Preparation

To properly rebuild an engine, you must first remove it from the vehicle, then disassemble and diagnose it. Ideally you should place your engine on an engine stand. This affords you the best access to the engine components. Follow the manufacturer's directions for using the stand with your particular engine. Remove the flywheel or flexplate before installing the engine to the stand.

Now that you have the engine on a stand, and assuming that you have drained the oil and coolant from the engine, it's time to strip it of all but the necessary components. Before you start disassembling the engine, you may want to take a moment to draw some pictures, or fabricate some labels or containers to mark the locations of various components and the bolts and/or studs which fasten them. Modern day engines use a lot of little brackets and clips which hold wiring harnesses and such, and these holders are often mounted on studs and/or bolts that can be easily mixed up. The manufacturer spent a lot of time and money designing your vehicle, and they wouldn't have wasted any of it by haphazardly placing brackets, clips or fasteners on the vehicle. If it's present when you disassemble it, put it back when you assemble, you will regret not remembering that little bracket which holds a wire harness out of the path of a rotating part.

You should begin by unbolting any accessories still attached to the engine, such as the water pump, power steering pump, alternator, etc. Then, unfasten any manifolds (intake or exhaust) which were not removed during the engine removal procedure. Finally, remove any covers remaining on the engine such as the rocker arm, front or timing cover and oil pan. Some front covers may require the vibration damper and/or crank pulley to be removed beforehand. The idea is to reduce the engine to the bare necessities (cylinder head(s), valve train, engine block, crankshaft, pistons and connecting rods), plus any other 'in block' components such as oil pumps, balance shafts and auxiliary shafts.

Finally, remove the cylinder head(s) from the engine block and carefully place on a bench. Disassembly instructions for each component follow later in this section.

Cylinder Head

There are two basic types of cylinder heads used on today's automobiles: the Overhead Valve (OHV) and the Overhead Camshaft (OHC). The latter can also be broken down into two subgroups: the Single Overhead Camshaft (SOHC) and the Dual Overhead Camshaft (DOHC). Generally, if there is only a single camshaft on a head, it is just referred to as an OHC head. Also, an engine with an OHV cylinder head is also known as a pushrod engine.

Most cylinder heads these days are made of an aluminum alloy due to its light weight, durability and heat transfer qualities. However, cast iron was the material of choice in the past, and is still used on many vehicles today. Whether made from aluminum or iron, all cylinder heads have valves and seats. Some use two valves per cylinder, while the more hi-tech engines will utilize a multivalve configuration using 3, 4 and even 5 valves per cylinder. When the valve contacts the seat, it does so on precision machined surfaces, which seals the combustion chamber. All cylinder heads have a valve guide for each valve. The guide centers the valve to the seat and allows it to move up and down within it. The clearance between the valve and guide can be critical. Too much clearance and the engine may consume oil, lose vacuum and/or damage the seat. Too little, and the valve can stick in the guide causing the engine to run poorly if at all, and possibly causing severe damage. The last component all cylinder heads have are valve springs. The spring holds the valve against its seat. It also returns the valve to this position when the valve has been opened by the valve train or camshaft. The spring is fastened to the valve by a retainer and valve locks (sometimes called keepers). Aluminum heads will also have a valve spring shim to keep the spring from wearing away the aluminum.

An ideal method of rebuilding the cylinder head would involve replacing all of the valves, guides, seats, springs, etc. with new ones. However, depending on how the engine was maintained, often this is not necessary. A major cause of valve, guide and seat wear is an improperly tuned engine. An engine that is running too rich, will often wash the lubricating oil out of the guide with gasoline, causing it to wear rapidly. Conversely, an engine which is running too lean will place higher combustion temperatures on the valves and seats allowing them to wear or even burn. Springs fall victim to the driving habits of the individual. A driver who often runs the engine rpm to the redline will wear out or break the springs faster then one that stays well below it. Unfortunately, mileage takes it toll on all of the parts. Generally, the valves, guides, springs and seats in a cylinder head can be machined and re-used, saving you money. However, if a valve is burnt, it may be wise to replace all of the valves, since they were all operating in the same environment. The same goes for any other component on the cylinder head. Think of it as an insurance policy against future problems related to that component.

Unfortunately, the only way to find out which components need replacing, is to disassemble and carefully check each piece. After the cylinder head(s) are disassembled, thoroughly clean all of the components.

DISASSEMBLY

4.2L, 5.8L, and 7.5L Gas Engines and 7.3L Diesel Engine

▶ See Figures 206 thru 211

Before disassembling the cylinder head, you may want to fabricate some containers to hold the various parts, as some of them can be quite small (such as keepers) and easily lost. Also keeping yourself and the components organized will aid in assembly and reduce confusion. Where possible, try to maintain a components original location; this is especially important if there is not going to be any machine work performed on the components.

1. If you haven't already removed the rocker arms and/or shafts, do so now.
2. Position the head so that the springs are easily accessed.
3. Use a valve spring compressor tool, and relieve spring tension from the retainer.

➡**Due to engine varnish, the retainer may stick to the valve locks. A gentle tap with a hammer may help to break it loose.**

4. Remove the valve locks from the valve tip and/or retainer. A small magnet may help in removing the locks.
5. Lift the valve spring, tool and all, off of the valve stem.
6. If equipped, remove the valve seal. If the seal is difficult to remove with

Fig. 206 When removing an OHV valve spring, use a compressor tool to relieve the tension from the retainer

Fig. 207 A small magnet will help in removal of the valve locks

Fig. 208 Be careful not to lose the small valve locks (keepers)

Fig. 209 Remove the valve seal from the valve stem—O-ring type seal shown

Fig. 210 Removing an umbrella/positive type seal

Fig. 211 Invert the cylinder head and withdraw the valve from the valve guide bore

the valve in place, try removing the valve first, then the seal. Follow the steps below for valve removal.

7. Position the head to allow access for withdrawing the valve.

➡Cylinder heads that have seen a lot of miles and/or abuse may have mushroomed the valve lock grove and/or tip, causing difficulty in removal of the valve. If this has happened, use a metal file to carefully remove the high spots around the lock grooves and/or tip. Only file it enough to allow removal.

8. Remove the valve from the cylinder head.
9. If equipped, remove the valve spring shim. A small magnetic tool or screwdriver will aid in removal.
10. Repeat Steps 3 though 9 until all of the valves have been removed.

4.6L, 5.4L and 6.8L Engines

▶ See Figures 212 and 213

Whether it is a single or dual overhead camshaft cylinder head, the disassembly procedure is relatively unchanged. One aspect to pay attention to is careful labeling of the parts on the dual camshaft cylinder head. There will be an intake camshaft and followers as well as an exhaust camshaft and followers and they must be labeled as such. In some cases, the components are identical and could easily be installed incorrectly. DO NOT MIX THEM UP! Determining which is which is very simple; the intake camshaft and components are on the same side of the head as was the intake manifold. Conversely, the exhaust camshaft and components are on the same side of the head as was the exhaust manifold.

ROCKER ARM TYPE CAMSHAFT FOLLOWERS

▶ See Figures 214 thru 222

Most cylinder heads with rocker arm-type camshaft followers are easily disassembled using a standard valve spring compressor. However, certain models may not have enough open space around the spring for the standard tool and may require you to use a C-clamp style compressor tool instead.

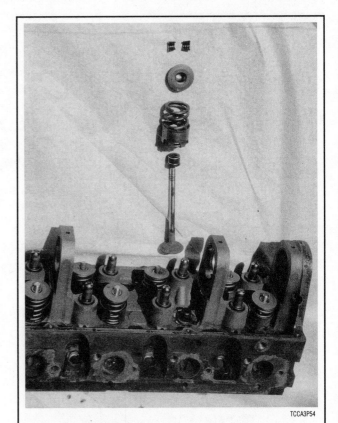

Fig. 212 Exploded view of a valve, seal, spring, retainer and locks from an OHC cylinder head

Fig. 213 Example of a multi-valve cylinder head. Note how it has 2 intake and 2 exhaust valve ports

1. If not already removed, remove the rocker arms and/or shafts and the camshaft. If applicable, also remove the hydraulic lash adjusters. Mark their positions for assembly.
2. Position the cylinder head to allow access to the valve spring.
3. Use a valve spring compressor tool to relieve the spring tension from the retainer.

➡ Due to engine varnish, the retainer may stick to the valve locks. A gentle tap with a hammer may help to break it loose.

4. Remove the valve locks from the valve tip and/or retainer. A small magnet may help in removing the small locks.
5. Lift the valve spring, tool and all, off of the valve stem.
6. If equipped, remove the valve seal. If the seal is difficult to remove with the valve in place, try removing the valve first, then the seal. Follow the steps below for valve removal.
7. Position the head to allow access for withdrawing the valve.

➡ Cylinder heads that have seen a lot of miles and/or abuse may have mushroomed the valve lock grove and/or tip, causing difficulty in removal of the valve. If this has happened, use a metal file to carefully remove the high spots around the lock grooves and/or tip. Only file it enough to allow removal.

8. Remove the valve from the cylinder head.
9. If equipped, remove the valve spring shim. A small magnetic tool or screwdriver will aid in removal.
10. Repeat Steps 3 though 9 until all of the valves have been removed.

INSPECTION

Now that all of the cylinder head components are clean, it's time to inspect them for wear and/or damage. To accurately inspect them, you will need some specialized tools:
- A 0–1 in. micrometer for the valves
- A dial indicator or inside diameter gauge for the valve guides

Fig. 214 Example of the shaft mounted rocker arms on some OHC heads

Fig. 215 Another example of the rocker arm type OHC head. This model uses a follower under the camshaft

Fig. 216 Before the camshaft can be removed, all of the followers must first be removed . . .

Fig. 217 . . . then the camshaft can be removed by sliding it out (shown), or unbolting a bearing cap (not shown)

Fig. 218 Compress the valve spring . . .

Fig. 219 . . . then remove the valve locks from the valve stem and spring retainer

Fig. 220 Remove the valve spring and retainer from the cylinder head

Fig. 221 Remove the valve seal from the guide. Some gentle prying or pliers may help to remove stubborn ones

Fig. 222 All aluminum and some cast iron heads will have these valve spring shims. Remove all of them as well

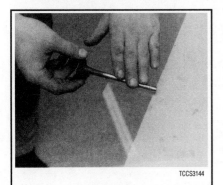

Fig. 223 Valve stems may be rolled on a flat surface to check for bends

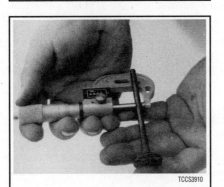

Fig. 224 Use a micrometer to check the valve stem diameter

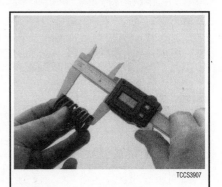

Fig. 225 Use a caliper to check the valve spring free-length

- A spring pressure test gauge

If you do not have access to the proper tools, you may want to bring the components to a shop that does.

Valves

▶ **See Figures 223 and 224**

The first thing to inspect are the valve heads. Look closely at the head, margin and face for any cracks, excessive wear or burning. The margin is the best place to look for burning. It should have a squared edge with an even width all around the diameter. When a valve burns, the margin will look melted and the edges rounded. Also inspect the valve head for any signs of tulipping. This will show as a lifting of the edges or dishing in the center of the head and will usually not occur to all of the valves. All of the heads should look the same, any that seem dished more than others are probably bad. Next, inspect the valve lock grooves and valve tips. Check for any burrs around the lock grooves, especially if you had to file them to remove the valve. Valve tips should appear flat, although slight rounding with high mileage engines is normal. Slightly worn valve tips will need to be machined flat. Last, measure the valve stem diameter with the micrometer. Measure the area that rides within the guide, especially towards the tip where most of the wear occurs. Take several measurements along its length and compare them to each other. Wear should be even along the length with little to no taper. If no minimum diameter is given in the specifications, then the stem should not read more than 0.001 in. (0.025mm) below the unworn area of the valve stem. Any valves that fail these inspections should be replaced.

Springs, Retainers and Valve Locks

▶ **See Figures 225 and 226**

The first thing to check is the most obvious, broken springs. Next check the free length and squareness of each spring. If applicable, insure to distinguish between intake and exhaust springs. Use a ruler and/or carpenter's square to measure the length. A carpenter's square should be used to check the springs

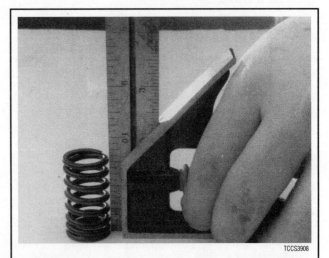

Fig. 226 Check the valve spring for squareness on a flat surface; a carpenter's square can be used

for squareness. If a spring pressure test gauge is available, check each springs rating and compare to the specifications chart. Check the readings against the specifications given. Any springs that fail these inspections should be replaced.

The spring retainers rarely need replacing, however they should still be checked as a precaution. Inspect the spring mating surface and the valve lock retention area for any signs of excessive wear. Also check for any signs of cracking. Replace any retainers that are questionable.

Valve locks should be inspected for excessive wear on the outside contact area as well as on the inner notched surface. Any locks which appear worn or broken and its respective valve should be replaced.

Cylinder Head

There are several things to check on the cylinder head: valve guides, seats, cylinder head surface flatness, cracks and physical damage.

VALVE GUIDES

▶ See Figure 227

Now that you know the valves are good, you can use them to check the guides, although a new valve, if available, is preferred. Before you measure anything, look at the guides carefully and inspect them for any cracks, chips or breakage. Also if the guide is a removable style (as in most aluminum heads), check them for any looseness or evidence of movement. All of the guides should appear to be at the same height from the spring seat. If any seem lower (or higher) from another, the guide has moved. Mount a dial indicator onto the spring side of the cylinder head. Lightly oil the valve stem and insert it into the cylinder head. Position the dial indicator against the valve stem near the tip and zero the gauge. Grasp the valve stem and wiggle towards and away from the dial indicator and observe the readings. Mount the dial indicator 90 degrees from the initial point and zero the gauge and again take a reading. Compare the two readings for a out of round condition. Check the readings against the specifications given. An Inside Diameter (I.D.) gauge designed for valve guides will give you an accurate valve guide bore measurement. If the I.D. gauge is used, compare the readings with the specifications given. Any guides that fail these inspections should be replaced or machined.

VALVE SEATS

A visual inspection of the valve seats should show a slightly worn and pitted surface where the valve face contacts the seat. Inspect the seat carefully for severe pitting or cracks. Also, a seat that is badly worn will be recessed into the cylinder head. A severely worn or recessed seat may need to be replaced. All cracked seats must be replaced. A seat concentricity gauge, if available, should be used to check the seat run-out. If run-out exceeds specifications the seat must be machined (if no specification is given use 0.002 in. or 0.051mm).

CYLINDER HEAD SURFACE FLATNESS

▶ See Figures 228 and 229

After you have cleaned the gasket surface of the cylinder head of any old gasket material, check the head for flatness.

Place a straightedge across the gasket surface. Using feeler gauges, determine the clearance at the center of the straightedge and across the cylinder head at several points. Check along the centerline and diagonally on the head surface. If the warpage exceeds 0.003 in. (0.076mm) within a 6.0 in. (15.2cm) span, or 0.006 in. (0.152mm) over the total length of the head, the cylinder head must be resurfaced. After resurfacing the heads of a V-type engine, the intake manifold flange surface should be checked, and if necessary, milled proportionally to allow for the change in its mounting position.

CRACKS AND PHYSICAL DAMAGE

Generally, cracks are limited to the combustion chamber, however, it is not uncommon for the head to crack in a spark plug hole, port, outside of the head or in the valve spring/rocker arm area. The first area to inspect is always the hottest: the exhaust seat/port area.

A visual inspection should be performed, but just because you don't see a crack does not mean it is not there. Some more reliable methods for inspecting for cracks include Magnaflux®, a magnetic process or Zyglo®, a dye penetrant. Magnaflux® is used only on ferrous metal (cast iron) heads. Zyglo® uses a spray on fluorescent mixture along with a black light to reveal the cracks. It is strongly recommended to have your cylinder head checked professionally for cracks, especially if the engine was known to have overheated and/or leaked or consumed coolant. Contact a local shop for availability and pricing of these services.

Physical damage is usually very evident. For example, a broken mounting ear from dropping the head or a bent or broken stud and/or bolt. All of these defects should be fixed or, if unrepairable, the head should be replaced.

Camshaft and Followers

Inspect the camshaft(s) and followers as described earlier in this section.

REFINISHING & REPAIRING

Many of the procedures given for refinishing and repairing the cylinder head components must be performed by a machine shop. Certain steps, if the inspected part is not worn, can be performed yourself inexpensively. However, you spent a lot of time and effort so far, why risk trying to save a couple bucks if you might have to do it all over again?

Valves

Any valves that were not replaced should be refaced and the tips ground flat. Unless you have access to a valve grinding machine, this should be done by a machine shop. If the valves are in extremely good condition, as well as the valve seats and guides, they may be lapped in without performing machine work.

It is a recommended practice to lap the valves even after machine work has been performed and/or new valves have been purchased. This insures a positive seal between the valve and seat.

LAPPING THE VALVES

➡Before lapping the valves to the seats, read the rest of the cylinder head section to insure that any related parts are in acceptable enough condition to continue.

➡Before any valve seat machining and/or lapping can be performed, the guides must be within factory recommended specifications.

1. Invert the cylinder head.
2. Lightly lubricate the valve stems and insert them into the cylinder head in their numbered order.
3. Raise the valve from the seat and apply a small amount of fine lapping compound to the seat.
4. Moisten the suction head of a hand-lapping tool and attach it to the head of the valve.
5. Rotate the tool between the palms of both hands, changing the position of the valve on the valve seat and lifting the tool often to prevent grooving.
6. Lap the valve until a smooth, polished circle is evident on the valve and seat.

TCCS3142

Fig. 227 A dial gauge may be used to check valve stem-to-guide clearance; read the gauge while moving the valve stem

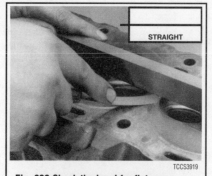

TCCS3919

Fig. 228 Check the head for flatness across the center of the head surface using a straightedge and feeler gauge

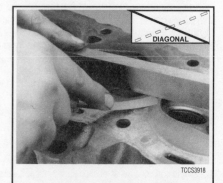

TCCS3918

Fig. 229 Checks should also be made along both diagonals of the head surface

7. Remove the tool and the valve. Wipe away all traces of the grinding compound and store the valve to maintain its lapped location.

❊❊ WARNING

Do not get the valves out of order after they have been lapped. They must be put back with the same valve seat with which they were lapped.

Springs, Retainers and Valve Locks

There is no repair or refinishing possible with the springs, retainers and valve locks. If they are found to be worn or defective, they must be replaced with new (or known good) parts.

Cylinder Head

Most refinishing procedures dealing with the cylinder head must be performed by a machine shop. Read the sections below and review your inspection data to determine whether or not machining is necessary.

VALVE GUIDE

➡**If any machining or replacements are made to the valve guides, the seats must be machined.**

Unless the valve guides need machining or replacing, the only service to perform is to thoroughly clean them of any dirt or oil residue.

There are only two types of valve guides used on automobile engines: the replaceable-type (all aluminum heads) and the cast-in integral-type (most cast iron heads). There are four recommended methods for repairing worn guides.

* Knurling
* Inserts
* Reaming oversize
* Replacing

Knurling is a process in which metal is displaced and raised, thereby reducing clearance, giving a true center, and providing oil control. It is the least expensive way of repairing the valve guides. However, it is not necessarily the best, and in some cases, a knurled valve guide will not stand up for more than a short time. It requires a special knurlizer and precision reaming tools to obtain proper clearances. It would not be cost effective to purchase these tools, unless you plan on rebuilding several of the same cylinder head.

Installing a guide insert involves machining the guide to accept a bronze insert. One style is the coil-type which is installed into a threaded guide. Another is the thin-walled insert where the guide is reamed oversize to accept a split-sleeve insert. After the insert is installed, a special tool is then run through the guide to expand the insert, locking it to the guide. The insert is then reamed to the standard size for proper valve clearance.

Reaming for oversize valves restores normal clearances and provides a true valve seat. Most cast-in type guides can be reamed to accept an valve with an oversize stem. The cost factor for this can become quite high as you will need to purchase the reamer and new, oversize stem valves for all guides which were reamed. Oversizes are generally 0.003 to 0.030 in. (0.076 to 0.762mm), with 0.015 in. (0.381mm) being the most common.

To replace cast-in type valve guides, they must be drilled out, then reamed to accept replacement guides. This must be done on a fixture which will allow centering and leveling off of the original valve seat or guide, otherwise a serious guide-to-seat misalignment may occur making it impossible to properly machine the seat.

Replaceable-type guides are pressed into the cylinder head. A hammer and a stepped drift or punch may be used to install and remove the guides. Before removing the guides, measure the protrusion on the spring side of the head and record it for installation. Use the stepped drift to hammer out the old guide from the combustion chamber side of the head. When installing, determine whether or not the guide also seals a water jacket in the head, and if it does, use the recommended sealing agent. If there is no water jacket, grease the valve guide and its bore. Use the stepped drift, and hammer the new guide into the cylinder head from the spring side of the cylinder head. A stack of washers the same thickness as the measured protrusion may help the installation process.

VALVE SEATS

➡**Before any valve seat machining can be performed, the guides must be within factory recommended specifications.**

➡**If any machining or replacements were made to the valve guides, the seats must be machined.**

If the seats are in good condition, the valves can be lapped to the seats, and the cylinder head assembled. See the valves section for instructions on lapping.

If the valve seats are worn, cracked or damaged, they must be serviced by a machine shop. The valve seat must be perfectly centered to the valve guide, which requires very accurate machining.

CYLINDER HEAD SURFACE

If the cylinder head is warped, it must be machined flat. If the warpage is extremely severe, the head may need to be replaced. In some instances, it may be possible to straighten a warped head enough to allow machining. In either case, contact a professional machine shop for service.

➡**Any OHC cylinder head that shows excessive warpage should have the camshaft bearing journals align bored after the cylinder head has been resurfaced.**

❊❊ WARNING

Failure to align bore the camshaft bearing journals could result in severe engine damage including but not limited to: valve and piston damage, connecting rod damage, camshaft and/or crankshaft breakage.

CRACKS AND PHYSICAL DAMAGE

Certain cracks can be repaired in both cast iron and aluminum heads. For cast iron, a tapered threaded insert is installed along the length of the crack. Aluminum can also use the tapered inserts, however welding is the preferred method. Some physical damage can be repaired through brazing or welding. Contact a machine shop to get expert advice for your particular dilemma.

ASSEMBLY

The first step for any assembly job is to have a clean area in which to work. Next, thoroughly clean all of the parts and components that are to be assembled. Finally, place all of the components onto a suitable work space and, if necessary, arrange the parts to their respective positions.

4.2L, 5.8L, And 7.5L Gas Engines and 7.3L Diesel Engine

1. Lightly lubricate the valve stems and insert all of the valves into the cylinder head. If possible, maintain their original locations.
2. If equipped, install any valve spring shims which were removed.
3. If equipped, install the new valve seals, keeping the following in mind:
* If the valve seal presses over the guide, lightly lubricate the outer guide surfaces.
* If the seal is an O-ring type, it is installed just after compressing the spring but before the valve locks.
4. Place the valve spring and retainer over the stem.
5. Position the spring compressor tool and compress the spring.
6. Assemble the valve locks to the stem.
7. Relieve the spring pressure slowly and insure that neither valve lock becomes dislodged by the retainer.
8. Remove the spring compressor tool.
9. Repeat Steps 2 through 8 until all of the springs have been installed.

4.6L, 5.4L and 6.8L Engines

▶ See Figure 230

1. Lightly lubricate the valve stems and insert all of the valves into the cylinder head. If possible, maintain their original locations.
2. If equipped, install any valve spring shims which were removed.
3. If equipped, install the new valve seals, keeping the following in mind:
* If the valve seal presses over the guide, lightly lubricate the outer guide surfaces.
* If the seal is an O-ring type, it is installed just after compressing the spring but before the valve locks.
4. Place the valve spring and retainer over the stem.
5. Position the spring compressor tool and compress the spring.

Fig. 230 Once assembled, check the valve clearance and correct as needed

6. Assemble the valve locks to the stem.
7. Relieve the spring pressure slowly and insure that neither valve lock becomes dislodged by the retainer.
8. Remove the spring compressor tool.
9. Repeat Steps 2 through 8 until all of the springs have been installed.
10. Install the camshaft(s), rockers, shafts and any other components that were removed for disassembly.

Engine Block

GENERAL INFORMATION

A thorough overhaul or rebuild of an engine block would include replacing the pistons, rings, bearings, timing belt/chain assembly and oil pump. For OHV engines also include a new camshaft and lifters. The block would then have the cylinders bored and honed oversize (or if using removable cylinder sleeves, new sleeves installed) and the crankshaft would be cut undersize to provide new wearing surfaces and perfect clearances. However, your particular engine may not have everything worn out. What if only the piston rings have worn out and the clearances on everything else are still within factory specifications? Well, you could just replace the rings and put it back together, but this would be a very rare example. Chances are, if one component in your engine is worn, other components are sure to follow, and soon. At the very least, you should always replace the rings, bearings and oil pump. This is what is commonly called a "freshen up".

Cylinder Ridge Removal

Because the top piston ring does not travel to the very top of the cylinder, a ridge is built up between the end of the travel and the top of the cylinder bore.

Pushing the piston and connecting rod assembly past the ridge can be difficult, and damage to the piston ring lands could occur. If the ridge is not removed before installing a new piston or not removed at all, piston ring breakage and piston damage may occur.

➡It is always recommended that you remove any cylinder ridges before removing the piston and connecting rod assemblies. If you know that new pistons are going to be installed and the engine block will be bored oversize, you may be able to forego this step. However, some ridges may actually prevent the assemblies from being removed, necessitating its removal.

There are several different types of ridge reamers on the market, none of which are inexpensive. Unless a great deal of engine rebuilding is anticipated, borrow or rent a reamer.

1. Turn the crankshaft until the piston is at the bottom of its travel.
2. Cover the head of the piston with a rag.
3. Follow the tool manufacturers instructions and cut away the ridge, exercising extreme care to avoid cutting too deeply.
4. Remove the ridge reamer, the rag and as many of the cuttings as possible. Continue until all of the cylinder ridges have been removed.

DISASSEMBLY

▶ **See Figures 231 and 232**

The engine disassembly instructions following assume that you have the engine mounted on an engine stand. If not, it is easiest to disassemble the engine on a bench or the floor with it resting on the bell housing or transmission mounting surface. You must be able to access the connecting rod fasteners and turn the crankshaft during disassembly. Also, all engine covers (timing, front, side, oil pan, whatever) should have already been removed. Engines which are seized or locked up may not be able to be completely disassembled, and a core (salvage yard) engine should be purchased.

4.2L, 5.8L, 7.5L and 7.3L Diesel Engines

If not done during the cylinder head removal, remove the pushrods and lifters, keeping them in order for assembly. Remove the timing gears and/or timing chain assembly, then remove the oil pump drive assembly and withdraw the camshaft from the engine block. Remove the oil pick-up and pump assembly. If equipped, remove any balance or auxiliary shafts. If necessary, remove the cylinder ridge from the top of the bore. See the cylinder ridge removal procedure earlier in this section.

4.6L, 5.4L and 6.8L Engines

If not done during the cylinder head removal, remove the timing chain/belt and/or gear/sprocket assembly. Remove the oil pick-up and pump assembly and, if necessary, the pump drive. If equipped, remove any balance or auxiliary shafts. If necessary, remove the cylinder ridge from the top of the bore. See the cylinder ridge removal procedure earlier in this section.

All Engines

Rotate the engine over so that the crankshaft is exposed. Use a number punch or scribe and mark each connecting rod with its respective cylinder number. The cylinder closest to the front of the engine is always number 1. However, depending on the engine placement, the front of the engine could either be the flywheel or damper/pulley end. Generally the front of the engine faces the front

Fig. 231 Place rubber hose over the connecting rod studs to protect the crankshaft and cylinder bores from damage

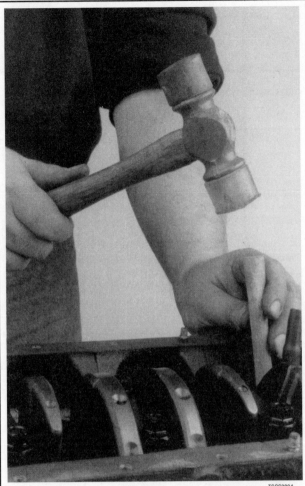

Fig. 232 Carefully tap the piston out of the bore using a wooden dowel

of the vehicle. Use a number punch or scribe and also mark the main bearing caps from front to rear with the front most cap being number 1 (if there are five caps, mark them 1 through 5, front to rear).

⁂ WARNING

Take special care when pushing the connecting rod up from the crankshaft because the sharp threads of the rod bolts/studs will score the crankshaft journal. Insure that special plastic caps are installed over them, or cut two pieces of rubber hose to do the same.

Again, rotate the engine, this time to position the number one cylinder bore (head surface) up. Turn the crankshaft until the number one piston is at the bottom of its travel, this should allow the maximum access to its connecting rod. Remove the number one connecting rods fasteners and cap and place two lengths of rubber hose over the rod bolts/studs to protect the crankshaft from damage. Using a sturdy wooden dowel and a hammer, push the connecting rod up about 1 in. (25mm) from the crankshaft and remove the upper bearing insert. Continue pushing or tapping the connecting rod up until the piston rings are out of the cylinder bore. Remove the piston and rod by hand, put the upper half of the bearing insert back into the rod, install the cap with its bearing insert installed, and hand-tighten the cap fasteners. If the parts are kept in order in this manner, they will not get lost and you will be able to tell which bearings came form what cylinder if any problems are discovered and diagnosis is necessary. Remove all the other piston assemblies in the same manner. On V-style engines, remove all of the pistons from one bank, then reposition the engine with the other cylinder bank head surface up, and remove that banks piston assemblies.

The only remaining component in the engine block should now be the crankshaft. Loosen the main bearing caps evenly until the fasteners can be turned by hand, then remove them and the caps. Remove the crankshaft from the engine block. Thoroughly clean all of the components.

INSPECTION

Now that the engine block and all of its components are clean, it's time to inspect them for wear and/or damage. To accurately inspect them, you will need some specialized tools:
- Two or three separate micrometers to measure the pistons and crankshaft journals
- A dial indicator
- Telescoping gauges for the cylinder bores
- A rod alignment fixture to check for bent connecting rods

If you do not have access to the proper tools, you may want to bring the components to a shop that does.

Generally, you shouldn't expect cracks in the engine block or its components unless it was known to leak, consume or mix engine fluids, it was severely overheated, or there was evidence of bad bearings and/or crankshaft damage. A visual inspection should be performed on all of the components, but just because you don't see a crack does not mean it is not there. Some more reliable methods for inspecting for cracks include Magnaflux®, a magnetic process or Zyglo®, a dye penetrant. Magnaflux® is used only on ferrous metal (cast iron). Zyglo® uses a spray on fluorescent mixture along with a black light to reveal the cracks. It is strongly recommended to have your engine block checked professionally for cracks, especially if the engine was known to have overheated and/or leaked or consumed coolant. Contact a local shop for availability and pricing of these services.

Engine Block

ENGINE BLOCK BEARING ALIGNMENT

Remove the main bearing caps and, if still installed, the main bearing inserts. Inspect all of the main bearing saddles and caps for damage, burrs or high spots. If damage is found, and it is caused from a spun main bearing, the block will need to be align-bored or, if severe enough, replacement. Any burrs or high spots should be carefully removed with a metal file.

Place a straightedge on the bearing saddles, in the engine block, along the centerline of the crankshaft. If any clearance exists between the straightedge and the saddles, the block must be align-bored.

Align-boring consists of machining the main bearing saddles and caps by means of a flycutter that runs through the bearing saddles.

DECK FLATNESS

The top of the engine block where the cylinder head mounts is called the deck. Insure that the deck surface is clean of dirt, carbon deposits and old gasket material. Place a straightedge across the surface of the deck along its centerline and, using feeler gauges, check the clearance along several points. Repeat the checking procedure with the straightedge placed along both diagonals of the deck surface. If the reading exceeds 0.003 in. (0.076mm) within a 6.0 in. (15.2cm) span, or 0.006 in. (0.152mm) over the total length of the deck, it must be machined.

CYLINDER BORES

◆ See Figure 233

The cylinder bores house the pistons and are slightly larger than the pistons themselves. A common piston-to-bore clearance is 0.0015–0.0025 in. (0.0381mm–0.0635mm). Inspect and measure the cylinder bores. The bore should be checked for out-of-roundness, taper and size. The results of this inspection will determine whether the cylinder can be used in its existing size and condition, or a rebore to the next oversize is required (or in the case of removable sleeves, have replacements installed).

The amount of cylinder wall wear is always greater at the top of the cylinder than at the bottom. This wear is known as taper. Any cylinder that has a taper of 0.0012 in. (0.305mm) or more, must be rebored. Measurements are taken at a number of positions in each cylinder: at the top, middle and bottom and at two points at each position; that is, at a point 90 degrees from the crankshaft centerline, as well as a point parallel to the crankshaft centerline. The measurements

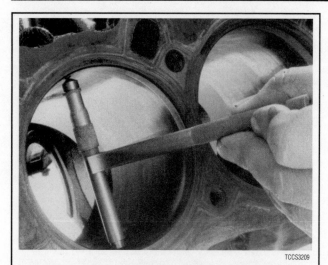

TCCS3209

Fig. 233 Use a telescoping gauge to measure the cylinder bore diameter—take several readings within the same bore

are made with either a special dial indicator or a telescopic gauge and micrometer. If the necessary precision tools to check the bore are not available, take the block to a machine shop and have them mike it. Also if you don't have the tools to check the cylinder bores, chances are you will not have the necessary devices to check the pistons, connecting rods and crankshaft. Take these components with you and save yourself an extra trip.

For our procedures, we will use a telescopic gauge and a micrometer. You will need one of each, with a measuring range which covers your cylinder bore size.

1. Position the telescopic gauge in the cylinder bore, loosen the gauges lock and allow it to expand.

➡ **Your first two readings will be at the top of the cylinder bore, then proceed to the middle and finally the bottom, making a total of six measurements.**

2. Hold the gauge square in the bore, 90 degrees from the crankshaft centerline, and gently tighten the lock. Tilt the gauge back to remove it from the bore.

3. Measure the gauge with the micrometer and record the reading.

4. Again, hold the gauge square in the bore, this time parallel to the crankshaft centerline, and gently tighten the lock. Again, you will tilt the gauge back to remove it from the bore.

5. Measure the gauge with the micrometer and record this reading. The difference between these two readings is the out-of-round measurement of the cylinder.

6. Repeat steps 1 through 5, each time going to the next lower position, until you reach the bottom of the cylinder. Then go to the next cylinder, and continue until all of the cylinders have been measured.

The difference between these measurements will tell you all about the wear in your cylinders. The measurements which were taken 90 degrees from the crankshaft centerline will always reflect the most wear. That is because at this position is where the engine power presses the piston against the cylinder bore the hardest. This is known as thrust wear. Take your top, 90 degree measurement and compare it to your bottom, 90 degree measurement. The difference between them is the taper. When you measure your pistons, you will compare these readings to your piston sizes and determine piston-to-wall clearance.

Crankshaft

Inspect the crankshaft for visible signs of wear or damage. All of the journals should be perfectly round and smooth. Slight scores are normal for a used crankshaft, but you should hardly feel them with your fingernail. When measuring the crankshaft with a micrometer, you will take readings at the front and rear of each journal, then turn the micrometer 90 degrees and take two more readings, front and rear. The difference between the front-to-rear readings is the journal taper and the first-to-90 degree reading is the out-of-round measurement. Generally, there should be no taper or out-of-roundness found, however,

up to 0.0005 in. (0.0127mm) for either can be overlooked. Also, the readings should fall within the factory specifications for journal diameters.

If the crankshaft journals fall within specifications, it is recommended that it be polished before being returned to service. Polishing the crankshaft insures that any minor burrs or high spots are smoothed, thereby reducing the chance of scoring the new bearings.

Pistons and Connecting Rods

PISTONS

▶ **See Figure 234**

The piston should be visually inspected for any signs of cracking or burning (caused by hot spots or detonation), and scuffing or excessive wear on the skirts. The wrist pin attaches the piston to the connecting rod. The piston should move freely on the wrist pin, both sliding and pivoting. Grasp the connecting rod securely, or mount it in a vise, and try to rock the piston back and forth along the centerline of the wrist pin. There should not be any excessive play evident between the piston and the pin. If there are C-clips retaining the pin in the piston then you have wrist pin bushings in the rods. There should not be any excessive play between the wrist pin and the rod bushing. Normal clearance for the wrist pin is approx. 0.001–0.002 in. (0.025mm–0.051mm).

Use a micrometer and measure the diameter of the piston, perpendicular to the wrist pin, on the skirt. Compare the reading to its original cylinder measurement obtained earlier. The difference between the two readings is the piston-to-wall clearance. If the clearance is within specifications, the piston may be used as is. If the piston is out of specification, but the bore is not, you will need a new piston. If both are out of specification, you will need the cylinder rebored and oversize pistons installed. Generally if two or more pistons/bores are out of specification, it is best to rebore the entire block and purchase a complete set of oversize pistons.

TCCS3210

Fig. 234 Measure the piston's outer diameter, perpendicular to the wrist pin, with a micrometer

CONNECTING ROD

You should have the connecting rod checked for straightness at a machine shop. If the connecting rod is bent, it will unevenly wear the bearing and piston, as well as place greater stress on these components. Any bent or twisted connecting rods must be replaced. If the rods are straight and the wrist pin clearance is within specifications, then only the bearing end of the rod need be checked. Place the connecting rod into a vice, with the bearing inserts in place, install the cap to the rod and torque the fasteners to specifications. Use a telescoping gauge and carefully measure the inside diameter of the bearings. Compare this reading to the rods original crankshaft journal diameter measurement. The difference is the oil clearance. If the oil clearance is not within specifications, install new bearings in the rod and take another measurement. If the clearance is still out of specifications, and the crankshaft is not, the rod will need to be reconditioned by a machine shop.

➡You can also use Plastigage® to check the bearing clearances. The assembling section has complete instructions on its use.

Camshaft

Inspect the camshaft and lifters/followers as described earlier in this section.

Bearings

All of the engine bearings should be visually inspected for wear and/or damage. The bearing should look evenly worn all around with no deep scores or pits. If the bearing is severely worn, scored, pitted or heat blued, then the bearing, and the components that use it, should be brought to a machine shop for inspection. Full-circle bearings (used on most camshafts, auxiliary shafts, balance shafts, etc.) require specialized tools for removal and installation, and should be brought to a machine shop for service.

Oil Pump

➡**The oil pump is responsible for providing constant lubrication to the whole engine and so it is recommended that a new oil pump be installed when rebuilding the engine.**

Completely disassemble the oil pump and thoroughly clean all of the components. Inspect the oil pump gears and housing for wear and/or damage. Insure that the pressure relief valve operates properly and there is no binding or sticking due to varnish or debris. If all of the parts are in proper working condition, lubricate the gears and relief valve, and assemble the pump.

REFINISHING

♦ **See Figure 235**

Almost all engine block refinishing must be performed by a machine shop. If the cylinders are not to be rebored, then the cylinder glaze can be removed with a ball hone. When removing cylinder glaze with a ball hone, use a light or penetrating type oil to lubricate the hone. Do not allow the hone to run dry as this may cause excessive scoring of the cylinder bores and wear on the hone. If new pistons are required, they will need to be installed to the connecting rods. This should be performed by a machine shop as the pistons must be installed in the correct relationship to the rod or engine damage can occur.

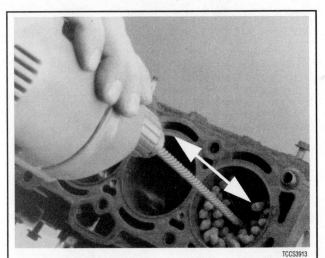

Fig. 235 Use a ball type cylinder hone to remove any glaze and provide a new surface for seating the piston rings

Pistons and Connecting Rods

♦ **See Figure 236**

Only pistons with the wrist pin retained by C-clips are serviceable by the home-mechanic. Press fit pistons require special presses and/or heaters to remove/install the connecting rod and should only be performed by a machine shop.

Fig. 236 Most pistons are marked to indicate positioning in the engine (usually a mark means the side facing the front)

All pistons will have a mark indicating the direction to the front of the engine and the must be installed into the engine in that manner. Usually it is a notch or arrow on the top of the piston, or it may be the letter F cast or stamped into the piston.

C-CLIP TYPE PISTONS

1. Note the location of the forward mark on the piston and mark the connecting rod in relation.
2. Remove the C-clips from the piston and withdraw the wrist pin.

➡**Varnish build-up or C-clip groove burrs may increase the difficulty of removing the wrist pin. If necessary, use a punch or drift to carefully tap the wrist pin out.**

3. Insure that the wrist pin bushing in the connecting rod is usable, and lubricate it with assembly lube.
4. Remove the wrist pin from the new piston and lubricate the pin bores on the piston.
5. Align the forward marks on the piston and the connecting rod and install the wrist pin.
6. The new C-clips will have a flat and a rounded side to them. Install both C-clips with the flat side facing out.
7. Repeat all of the steps for each piston being replaced.

ASSEMBLY

Before you begin assembling the engine, first give yourself a clean, dirt free work area. Next, clean every engine component again. The key to a good assembly is cleanliness.

Mount the engine block into the engine stand and wash it one last time using water and detergent (dishwashing detergent works well). While washing it, scrub the cylinder bores with a soft bristle brush and thoroughly clean all of the oil passages. Completely dry the engine and spray the entire assembly down with an anti-rust solution such as WD-40® or similar product. Take a clean lint-free rag and wipe up any excess anti-rust solution from the bores, bearing saddles, etc. Repeat the final cleaning process on the crankshaft. Replace any freeze or oil galley plugs which were removed during disassembly.

Crankshaft

♦ **See Figures 237, 238, 239 and 240**

1. Remove the main bearing inserts from the block and bearing caps.
2. If the crankshaft main bearing journals have been refinished to a definite undersize, install the correct undersize bearing. Be sure that the bearing inserts and bearing bores are clean. Foreign material under inserts will distort bearing and cause failure.
3. Place the upper main bearing inserts in bores with tang in slot.

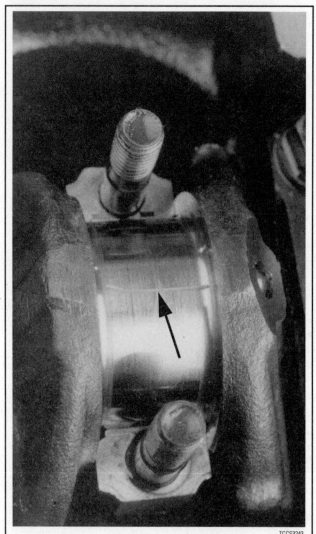

Fig. 237 Apply a strip of gauging material to the bearing journal, then install and torque the cap

➡ The oil holes in the bearing inserts must be aligned with the oil holes in the cylinder block.

4. Install the lower main bearing inserts in bearing caps.
5. Clean the mating surfaces of block and rear main bearing cap.
6. Carefully lower the crankshaft into place. Be careful not to damage bearing surfaces.

7. Check the clearance of each main bearing by using the following procedure:
    a. Place a piece of Plastigage® or its equivalent, on bearing surface across full width of bearing cap and about ¼ in. off center.
    b. Install cap and tighten bolts to specifications. Do not turn crankshaft while Plastigage® is in place.
    c. Remove the cap. Using the supplied Plastigage® scale, check width of Plastigage® at widest point to get maximum clearance. Difference between readings is taper of journal.
    d. If clearance exceeds specified limits, try a 0.001 in. or 0.002 in. undersize bearing in combination with the standard bearing. Bearing clearance must be within specified limits. If standard and 0.002 in. undersize bearing does not bring clearance within desired limits, refinish crankshaft journal, then install undersize bearings.
8. Install the rear main seal.
9. After the bearings have been fitted, apply a light coat of engine oil to the journals and bearings. Install the rear main bearing cap. Install all bearing caps except the thrust bearing cap. Be sure that main bearing caps are installed in original locations. Tighten the bearing cap bolts to specifications.
10. Install the thrust bearing cap with bolts finger-tight.
11. Pry the crankshaft forward against the thrust surface of upper half of bearing.
12. Hold the crankshaft forward and pry the thrust bearing cap to the rear. This aligns the thrust surfaces of both halves of the bearing.
13. Retain the forward pressure on the crankshaft. Tighten the cap bolts to specifications.
14. Measure the crankshaft end-play as follows:
    a. Mount a dial gauge to the engine block and position the tip of the gauge to read from the crankshaft end.
    b. Carefully pry the crankshaft toward the rear of the engine and hold it there while you zero the gauge.
    c. Carefully pry the crankshaft toward the front of the engine and read the gauge.
    d. Confirm that the reading is within specifications. If not, install a new thrust bearing and repeat the procedure. If the reading is still out of specifications with a new bearing, have a machine shop inspect the thrust surfaces of the crankshaft, and if possible, repair it.
15. Rotate the crankshaft so as to position the first rod journal to the bottom of its stroke.

Pistons and Connecting Rods

▶ See Figures 241, 242, 243 and 244

1. Before installing the piston/connecting rod assembly, oil the pistons, piston rings and the cylinder walls with light engine oil. Install connecting rod bolt protectors or rubber hose onto the connecting rod bolts/studs. Also perform the following:
    a. Select the proper ring set for the size cylinder bore.
    b. Position the ring in the bore in which it is going to be used.
    c. Push the ring down into the bore area where normal ring wear is not encountered.
    d. Use the head of the piston to position the ring in the bore so that the

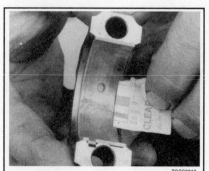

Fig. 238 After the cap is removed again, use the scale supplied with the gauging material to check the clearance

Fig. 239 A dial gauge may be used to check crankshaft end-play

Fig. 240 Carefully pry the crankshaft back and forth while reading the dial gauge for end-play

Fig. 241 Checking the piston ring-to-ring groove side clearance using the ring and a feeler gauge

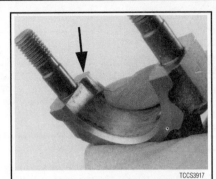

Fig. 242 The notch on the side of the bearing cap matches the tang on the bearing insert

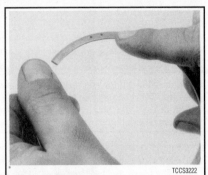

Fig. 243 Most rings are marked to show which side of the ring should face up when installed to the piston

Fig. 244 Install the piston and rod assembly into the block using a ring compressor and the handle of a hammer

ring is square with the cylinder wall. Use caution to avoid damage to the ring or cylinder bore.

  e. Measure the gap between the ends of the ring with a feeler gauge. Ring gap in a worn cylinder is normally greater than specification. If the ring gap is greater than the specified limits, try an oversize ring set.

  f. Check the ring side clearance of the compression rings with a feeler gauge inserted between the ring and its lower land according to specification. The gauge should slide freely around the entire ring circumference without binding. Any wear that occurs will form a step at the inner portion of the lower land. If the lower lands have high steps, the piston should be replaced.

2. Unless new pistons are installed, be sure to install the pistons in the cylinders from which they were removed. The numbers on the connecting rod and bearing cap must be on the same side when installed in the cylinder bore. If a connecting rod is ever transposed from one engine or cylinder to another, new bearings should be fitted and the connecting rod should be numbered to correspond with the new cylinder number. The notch on the piston head goes toward the front of the engine.

3. Install all of the rod bearing inserts into the rods and caps.

4. Install the rings to the pistons. Install the oil control ring first, then the second compression ring and finally the top compression ring. Use a piston ring expander tool to aid in installation and to help reduce the chance of breakage.

5. Make sure the ring gaps are properly spaced around the circumference of the piston. Fit a piston ring compressor around the piston and slide the piston and connecting rod assembly down into the cylinder bore, pushing it in with the wooden hammer handle. Push the piston down until it is only slightly below the top of the cylinder bore. Guide the connecting rod onto the crankshaft bear-

ing journal carefully, to avoid damaging the crankshaft.

6. Check the bearing clearance of all the rod bearings, fitting them to the crankshaft bearing journals. Follow the procedure in the crankshaft installation above.

7. After the bearings have been fitted, apply a light coating of assembly oil to the journals and bearings.

8. Turn the crankshaft until the appropriate bearing journal is at the bottom of its stroke, then push the piston assembly all the way down until the connecting rod bearing seats on the crankshaft journal. Be careful not to allow the bearing cap screws to strike the crankshaft bearing journals and damage them.

9. After the piston and connecting rod assemblies have been installed, check the connecting rod side clearance on each crankshaft journal.

10. Prime and install the oil pump and the oil pump intake tube.

11. On the 4.2L and 6.8L engines install the balance shaft assembly.

4.2L, 5.8L, 7.5L Gas Engines and 7.3L Diesel Engine

CAMSHAFT, LIFTERS AND TIMING ASSEMBLY

1. Install the camshaft.
2. Install the lifters/followers into their bores.
3. Install the timing gears/chain assembly.

CYLINDER HEAD(S)

1. Install the cylinder head(s) using new gaskets.
2. Assemble the rest of the valve train (pushrods and rocker arms and/or shafts).

4.6L, 5.4L and 6.8L Engines

CYLINDER HEAD(S)

1. Install the cylinder head(s) using new gaskets.
2. Install the timing sprockets/gears and the belt/chain assemblies.

Engine Covers and Components

Install the timing cover(s) and oil pan. Refer to your notes and drawings made prior to disassembly and install all of the components that were removed. Install the engine into the vehicle.

Engine Start-up and Break-In

STARTING THE ENGINE

Now that the engine is installed and every wire and hose is properly connected, go back and double check that all coolant and vacuum hoses are connected. Check that your oil drain plug is installed and properly tightened. If not already done, install a new oil filter onto the engine. Fill the crankcase with the proper amount and grade of engine oil. Fill the cooling system with a 50/50 mixture of coolant/water.

1. Connect the vehicle battery.
2. Start the engine. Keep your eye on your oil pressure indicator; if it does not indicate oil pressure within 10 seconds of starting, turn the vehicle off.

❋❋ WARNING

Damage to the engine can result if it is allowed to run with no oil pressure. Check the engine oil level to make sure that it is full. Check for any leaks and if found, repair the leaks before continuing. If there is still no indication of oil pressure, you may need to prime the system.

3. Confirm that there are no fluid leaks (oil or other).
4. Allow the engine to reach normal operating temperature (the upper radiator hose will be hot to the touch).
5. At this point you can perform any necessary checks or adjustments, such as checking the ignition timing.
6. Install any remaining components or body panels which were removed.

BREAKING IT IN

Make the first miles on the new engine, easy ones. Vary the speed but do not accelerate hard. Most importantly, do not lug the engine, and avoid sustained high speeds until at least 100 miles. Check the engine oil and coolant levels frequently. Expect the engine to use a little oil until the rings seat. Change the oil and filter at 500 miles, 1500 miles, then every 3000 miles past that.

KEEP IT MAINTAINED

Now that you have just gone through all of that hard work, keep yourself from doing it all over again by thoroughly maintaining it. Not that you may not have maintained it before, heck you could have had one to two hundred thousand miles on it before doing this. However, you may have bought the vehicle used, and the previous owner did not keep up on maintenance. Which is why you just went through all of that hard work. See?

TORQUE SPECIFICATIONS

Components	English	Metric
Balance shaft		
Thrust plate bolts		
4.2L engine	70-124 inch lbs.	8-14 Nm
6.8L engine		
Bearing caps	①	①
Camshaft		
4.2L engine		
Thrust plate bolts	6-10 ft. lbs.	8-14 Nm
4.6L, 5.4L and 6.8L engines		
Timing gear retaining bolt	81-95 ft. lbs.	110-130 Nm
Bearing caps	①	①
5.8L and 7.5L engines		
Thrust plate bolts	9-12 ft. lbs.	12-16 Nm
7.3L diesel engine		
Thrust plate bolts	9-12 ft. lbs.	12-16 Nm
Crankshaft damper retaining bolt		
4.2L engine	103-117 ft. lbs.	140-160 Nm
4.6L, 5.4L and 6.8L engines	②	②
5.8L and 7.5L engines	70-90 ft. lbs.	95-122 Nm
7.3L diesel engine	212 ft. lbs.	287 Nm
Crankshaft main bearing caps		
7.5L engine	95-105 ft. lbs.	129-142 Nm
Cylinder head bolts		
All engines	①	①
EGR tube-to-valve/manifold nut		
4.2L engine	25-34 ft. lbs.	34-46 Nm
4.6L, 5.4L and 6.8L engines	26-33 ft. lbs.	35-45 Nm
Engine fan clutch-to-water pump nut/bolts		
4.2L, 4.6L, 5.4L and 6.8L engines	45 ft. lbs.	61 Nm
5.8L and 7.5L engines	12-18 ft. lbs.	16-25 Nm
7.3L diesel engine	84-112 ft. lbs.	113-153 Nm
Engine mounts		
4.2L engine	51-67 ft. lbs.	68-92 Nm
4.6L, 5.4L and 6.8L engines	15-22 ft. lbs.	20-30 Nm
5.8L and 7.5L engines		
Through-bolts	80 ft. lbs.	108 Nm
Nuts	70 ft. lbs.	95 Nm
7.3L diesel engine	71-94 ft. lbs.	96-127 Nm
Engine-to-transmission retaining bolts		
4.6L, 5.4L and 6.8L engines	30-44 ft. lbs.	40-60 Nm
5.8L and 7.5L engines	50 ft. lbs.	68 Nm
7.3L diesel engine	65 ft. lbs.	88 Nm
Exhaust manifold retaining bolts		
4.2L engine	15-22 ft. lbs.	20-30 Nm
4.6L and 5.4L engines	13-16 ft. lbs.	18-22 Nm
5.8L and 7.5L engines	25-35 ft. lbs.	34-47 Nm
6.8L engine	17-20 ft. lbs.	23-27 Nm
7.3L diesel engine	45 ft. lbs.	61 Nm
Exhaust manifold-to-exhaust pipe/catalytic converter bolts		
4.2L, 4.6L, 5.4L and 6.8L engines	25-34 ft. lbs.	34-46 Nm
5.8L and 7.5L engines	25-35 ft. lbs.	34-47 Nm

91193C17

TORQUE SPECIFICATIONS

Components	English	Metric
Flywheel/flexplate retaining bolts		
4.2L, 4.6L, 5.4L and 6.8L engines	54-64 ft. lbs.	73-87 Nm
5.8L and 7.5L engines	75-85 ft. lbs.	103-115 Nm
7.3L diesel engine	89 ft. lbs.	121 Nm
Intake manifold retaining bolts		
4.2L engine		
Lower intake	①	①
Upper intake	①	①
4.6L engine		
Lower intake-to-upper intake	①	①
Upper intake-to-engine	①	①
5.4L SOHC engine		
Lower intake-to-upper intake	①	①
Upper intake-to-engine	①	①
5.4L DOHC engine		
Lower intake	89 inch lbs. + 90 degrees	10 Nm + 90 degrees
Upper intake	89 inch lbs. + 90 degrees	10 Nm + 90 degrees
5.4L Lightning engine	①	①
5.8L engine		
Lower intake	23-25 ft. lbs.	31-34 Nm
Upper Intake	12-18 ft. lbs.	16-25 Nm
6.8L engine		
Lower intake-to-upper intake	6-8 ft. lbs. ①	8-11 Nm ①
Upper intake-to-engine	15-22 ft. lbs.	20-30 Nm
7.5L engine		
Lower intake	23-25 ft. lbs.	31-34 Nm
Upper Intake	12-18 ft. lbs.	16-25 Nm
Oil pan retaining bolts		
4.2L engine		
Oil pan retaining bolts	①	①
Oil pan-to-transmission bolts	28-38 ft. lbs.	38-51 Nm
4.6L, 5.4L and 6.8L engines	10-12 ft. lbs.	14-16 Nm
5.8L engine		
7.3L diesel engine		
7.5L engine	10 ft. lbs.	14 Nm
Oil pump retaining bolts		
4.2L engine	71-106 inch lbs.	8-12 Nm
4.6L and 5.4L engines	15-22 ft. lbs.	20-30 Nm
Oil pump screen and cover spacer bolts	②	②
Oil pump screen and cover bolts	20-25 ft. lbs.	27-34 Nm
5.8L engine		
6.8L engine	71-106 inch lbs. ①	8-12 Nm ①
7.3L diesel engine	14 ft. lbs.	19 Nm
7.5L engine	20-25 ft. lbs.	27-34 Nm
Rocker arm retaining bolts		
4.2L engine	23-29 ft. lbs.	30-40 Nm
5.8L engine	18-25 ft. lbs.	25-34 Nm
6.8L engine		
7.3L diesel engine	20 ft. lbs.	27 Nm
7.5L engine	18-25 ft. lbs.	25-34 Nm

91193C18

TORQUE SPECIFICATIONS

Components	English	Metric
Thermostat housing retaining bolts		
4.2L engine	103 inch lbs.	12 Nm
4.6L, 5.4L and 6.8L engines	15-22 ft. lbs.	20-30 Nm
5.8L engine	12-18 ft. lbs.	16-24 Nm
7.3L diesel engine	15 ft. lbs.	20 Nm
7.5L engine	22-38 ft. lbs.	32-37 Nm
Timing chain guide retaining bolts		
4.6L, 5.4L and 6.8L engines	71-106 inch lbs.	8-12 Nm
Timing chain tensioner retaining bolts		
4.2L engine	6-10 ft. lbs.	8-14 Nm
4.6L, 5.4L and 6.8L engines	15-22 ft. lbs.	20-30 Nm
7.3L diesel engine	15 ft. lbs.	20 Nm
Timing cover retaining bolts		
4.2L engine	15-22 ft. lbs.	20-30 Nm
4.6L and 5.4L engines	①	①
5.8L engine	12-18 ft. lbs.	16-24 Nm
6.8L engine	①	①
7.3L diesel engine	15 ft. lbs.	20 Nm
7.5L engine	15-20 ft. lbs.	20-27 Nm
Torque converter retaining nuts		
4.6L, 5.4L and 6.8L engines	22-25 ft. lbs.	20-30 Nm
5.8L and 7.5L engines	30 ft. lbs.	41 Nm
7.3L diesel engine	89 ft. lbs.	121 Nm
Turbocharger (7.3L diesel only)		
Turbocharger-to-engine bolts	18 ft. lbs.	25 Nm
Turbocharger exhaust inlet pipe-to-exhaust inlet pipe adapter bolts	36 ft. lbs.	49 Nm
Turbocharger inlet pipe-to-exhaust manifold bolts	28 ft. lbs.	38 Nm
Valve cover retaining bolts		
4.2L engine	6-8 ft. lbs.	8-11 Nm
4.6L, 5.4L and 6.8L engines	71-106 inch lbs.	8-12 Nm
5.8L engine	12-15 ft. lbs.	16-20 Nm
7.3L diesel engine	8 ft. lbs.	11 Nm
7.5L engine	6-9 ft. lbs.	8-12 Nm
Water pump bolts		
4.2L, 4.6L, 5.4L and 6.8L engines	15-22 ft. lbs.	20-30 Nm
5.8L and 7.5L engines	18 ft. lbs.	25 Nm
7.3L diesel engine	15 ft. lbs.	20 Nm
Water pump pulley-to-water pump bolts		
4.2L, 4.6L, 5.4L and 6.8L engines	15-22 ft. lbs.	20-30 Nm
5.8L and 7.5L engines	12-18 ft. lbs.	16-25 Nm
7.3L diesel engine	12-18 ft. lbs.	16-25 Nm

① Refer to procedure for specific directions on tightening torque/sequence
② Tighten the bolts near the screen to 15-22 ft. lbs.(20-30 Nm), tighten the bolts away from the screen to 71-106 inch lbs (8-12 Nm)
③ Tighten the bolt to 66 ft. lbs. (90 Nm), then back off the bolt 90 degrees, tighten it to 35-39 ft. lbs. (47-53 Nm), then an additional 85-95 degrees

91193C19

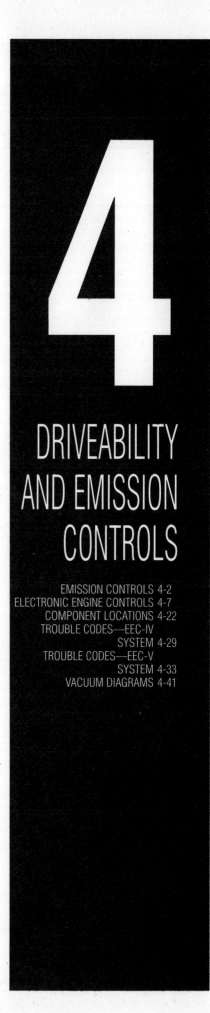

4
DRIVEABILITY AND EMISSION CONTROLS

EMISSION CONTROLS

Crankcase Ventilation System

OPERATION

▶ See Figure 1

When the engine is running, a small portion of the gases which are formed in the combustion chamber leak by the piston rings and enter the crankcase. Since these gases are under pressure they tend to escape from the crankcase and enter into the atmosphere. If these gases are allowed to remain in the crankcase for any length of time, they would contaminate the engine oil and cause sludge to build up. If the gases are allowed to escape into the atmosphere, they would pollute the air, as they contain unburned hydrocarbons. The crankcase ventilation system recycles these gases back into the engine combustion chamber, where they are burned.

Crankcase gases are recycled in the following manner. While the engine is running, clean filtered air is drawn into the crankcase through the intake air filter and then through a hose leading to the oil filler cap or the valve cover. As the air passes through the crankcase it picks up the combustion gases and carries them out of the crankcase, up through the PCV valve, and into the intake manifold. After they enter the intake manifold they are drawn into the combustion chamber and are burned.

The most critical component of the system is the PCV valve. This vacuum-controlled valve regulates the amount of gases which are recycled into the combustion chamber. At low engine speeds the valve is partially closed, limiting the flow of gases into the intake manifold. As engine speed increases, the valve opens to admit greater quantities of the gases into the intake manifold. If the valve should become blocked or plugged, the gases will be prevented from escaping the crankcase by the normal route. Since these gases are under pressure, they will find their own way out of the crankcase. This alternate route is usually a weak oil seal or gasket in the engine. As the gas escapes by the gasket, it also creates an oil leak. Besides causing oil leaks, a clogged PCV valve also allows these gases to remain in the crankcase for an extended period of time, promoting the formation of sludge in the engine.

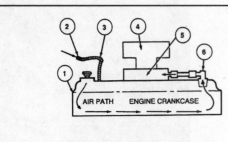

Item	Description
1	Valve Cover
2	To Fresh Air Source
3	Crankcase Ventilation Tube
4	Throttle Body
5	Intake Manifold
6	Positive Crankcase Ventilation Valve (PCV Valve)

91054G01

Fig. 1 Typical PCV air flow diagram

COMPONENT TESTING

▶ See Figure 2

1. Remove the PCV valve from the valve cover grommet.
2. Shake the PCV valve.
   a. If the valve rattles when shaken, reinstall it and proceed to Step 3.
   b. If the valve does not rattle, it is sticking and must be replaced.
3. Start the engine and allow it to reach normal operating temperature.

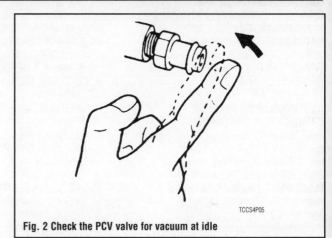

TCCS4P05

Fig. 2 Check the PCV valve for vacuum at idle

4. Check the PCV valve for vacuum by placing your finger over the end of the valve.
   a. If vacuum exists, proceed to Step 5.
   b. If vacuum does not exist, check for loose hose connections, vacuum leaks or blockage. Correct as necessary.
5. Disconnect the fresh air intake hose from the air inlet tube (connects the air cleaner housing to the throttle body).
6. Place a stiff piece of paper over the hose end and wait 1 minute.
   a. If vacuum holds the paper in place, the system is OK; reconnect the hose.
   b. If the paper is not held in place, check for loose hose connections, vacuum leaks or blockage. Correct as necessary.

REMOVAL & INSTALLATION

Refer to Section 1 for removal and installation of the PCV valve.

Evaporative Emission Controls

OPERATION

Changes in atmospheric temperature cause fuel tanks to breathe, that is, the air within the tank expands and contracts with outside temperature changes. If an unsealed system was used, when the temperature rises, air would escape through the tank vent tube or the vent in the tank cap. The air which escapes contains gasoline vapors.

The Evaporative Emission Control System provides a sealed fuel system with the capability to store and condense fuel vapors. When the fuel evaporates in the fuel tank, the vapor passes through the EVAP emission valve, through vent hoses or tubes to a carbon filled evaporative canister. When the engine is operating the vapors are drawn into the intake manifold and burned during combustion.

A sealed, maintenance free evaporative canister is used. The canister is filled with granules of an activated carbon mixture. Fuel vapors entering the canister are absorbed by the charcoal granules. A vent cap is located on the top of the canister to provide fresh air to the canister when it is being purged. The vent cap opens to provide fresh air into the canister, which circulates through the charcoal, releasing trapped vapors and carrying them to the engine to be burned.

Fuel tank pressure vents fuel vapors into the canister. They are held in the canister until they can be drawn into the intake manifold. The canister purge valve allows the canister to be purged at a pre-determined time and engine operating conditions.

Vacuum to the canister is controlled by the canister purge valve. The valve is operated by the PCM. The PCM regulates the valve by switching the ground circuit on and off based on engine operating conditions. When energized, the valve prevents vacuum from reaching the canister. When not energized the valve allows vacuum to purge the vapors from the canister.

During warm up and for a specified time after hot starts, the PCM energizes (grounds) the valve preventing vacuum from reaching the canister. When the engine temperature reaches the operating level of about 120°F (49°C), the PCM removes the ground from the valve allowing vacuum to flow through the canister and purges vapors through the throttle body. During certain idle conditions, the purge valve may be grounded to control fuel mixture calibrations.

The fuel tank is sealed with a pressure-vacuum relief filler cap. The relief valve in the cap is a safety feature, preventing excessive pressure or vacuum in the fuel tank. If the cap is malfunctioning, and needs to be replaced, ensure that the replacement is the identical cap to ensure correct system operation.

OBD-II EVAP System Monitor

Some of the models covered in this manual have added system components due to the EVAP system monitor incorporated in the OBD-II engine control system. A pressure sensor is mounted on the fuel tank which measures pressure inside the tank, and a purge flow sensor measures the flow of the gases from the canister into the engine. The purge valve is now called the Vapor Management Valve (VMV). It performs the same functions as the purge valve, however it looks slightly different. A canister vent solenoid is mounted on the canister, taking the place of the vent cap, providing a source of fresh air to the canister.

The PCM can store trouble codes for EVAP system performance, a list of the codes is provided later in this section. Normal testing procedure can be used, see EVAP System Component Testing in this Section.

TESTING

Evaporative Emissions Canister

Generally, the only testing done to the canister is a visual inspection. Look the canister over and replace it with a new one if there is any evidence of cracks or other damage.

Evaporative Hoses and Tubes

Inspect all system hoses and tubes for signs of damage or cracks. Any damage or leakage must be repaired.

Evaporative Emissions Valve

▶ See Figure 3

Inspect the valve for open air passage through the orifice. The valve is molded directly to the fuel tank and is not serviceable separately. If the orifice is blocked, replace the fuel tank.

Canister Purge Valve/Vapor Management Valve

▶ See Figure 4

1. Remove the canister purge valve.
2. Measure the resistance between the two valve terminals.
   a. If the resistance is between 30–36 ohms, proceed to the Step 3.
   b. If the resistance is not between 30–36 ohms, replace the valve.
3. Attach a hand-held vacuum pump to the intake manifold vacuum side of

the valve, then apply 16 in. Hg (53 kPa) of vacuum to the valve.
   a. If the valve will not hold vacuum for at least 20 seconds replace it with a new one.
   b. If the valve holds vacuum, proceed to Step 4. Keep the vacuum applied to the valve.
4. Using an external voltage source, apply 9–14 DC volts to the valve electrical terminals.
   a. If the valve opens and the vacuum drops, the valve is working properly. Check power and ground circuits.
   b. If the valve does not open and the vacuum remains, replace the valve is faulty.

REMOVAL & INSTALLATION

Evaporative Emissions Valve

1. Raise and support the vehicle.
2. Remove the fuel tank. See Section 5.
3. Disconnect the vapor hose from the valve.
4. Twist and remove the valve.
5. Installation is the reverse of removal.

Pressure Sensor

1. Raise and support the vehicle.
2. Remove the fuel tank. See Section 5.
3. Detach the connector from the sensor.
4. Twist and remove the sensor.
5. Installation is the reverse of removal.

Evaporative Emissions Canister

F-150, F-250, EXPEDITION, NAVIGATOR AND 1999–00 SUPER DUTY MODELS

▶ See Figure 5

1. Raise and safely support the vehicle securely on jackstands.
2. Detach the canister vent solenoid electrical connector.
3. Remove the canister retaining bolts.
4. Disconnect the canister vent solenoid hose assembly.
5. Lower the canister and bracket.
6. Loosen the evaporative emissions (EVAP) canister purge outlet tube clamp and disconnect the tube.
7. Remove the canister vent solenoid from the canister.
8. Remove the evaporative emissions canister.
To install:

➡Lubricate all O-rings with Merpol Æ or equivalent meeting Ford specification ESE-M99B144-B before installation.

9. Installation is the reverse of removal.

1997–98 F-250HD, F-350 AND F-SUPER DUTY

1. Label and disconnect the vapor hoses from the canister.

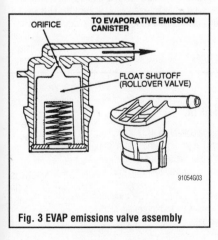

Fig. 3 EVAP emissions valve assembly

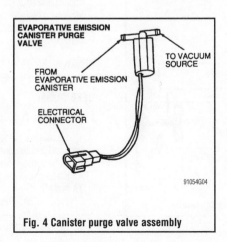

Fig. 4 Canister purge valve assembly

Fig. 5 The EVAP canister is located under the vehicle near the spare tire—F-150, F-250, Expedition, Navigator and 1999–00 super duty models

2. Remove the retaining screw for the canister bracket.

3. Lift the canister to disengage the retaining tab on the back of the canister and remove the canister.

To install:

4. Installation is the reverse of removal.

Canister Purge Valve/Vapor Management Valve

F-150, F-250, EXPEDITION, NAVIGATOR AND 1999–00 SUPER DUTY MODELS

1. Detach the electrical connector from the evaporative emission (EVAP) canister purge valve.

2. Label and disconnect the evaporative emissions vacuum control hose.

3. Label and disconnect the two fuel vapor tubes.

4. Remove the two retaining bolts and remove the evaporative emission canister purge valve.

To install:

5. Installation is the reverse of removal.

1997–98 F-250HD, F-350 AND F-SUPER DUTY

1. Detach the purge valve electrical connector.

2. Label and remove the EVAP hoses from the purge valve and remove the valve.

To install:

3. Installation is the reverse of removal.

Exhaust Gas Recirculation System

OPERATION

▶ **See Figure 6**

The Exhaust Gas Recirculation (EGR) system is designed to reintroduce exhaust gas into the combustion chambers, thereby lowering combustion temperatures and reducing the formation of Oxides of Nitrogen (NO_x).

The amount of exhaust gas that is reintroduced into the combustion cycle is determined by several factors, such as: engine speed, engine vacuum, exhaust system backpressure, coolant temperature, throttle position. All EGR valves are vacuum operated. The EGR vacuum diagram for your particular vehicle is displayed on the Vehicle Emission Control Information (VECI) label.

The EGR system is Differential Pressure Feedback EGR (DPFE) system, controlled by the Powertrain Control Module (PCM) and composed of the following components: DPFE sensor (also referred to as the backpressure transducer), EGR Vacuum Regulator (EVR) solenoid, EGR valve, and assorted hoses.

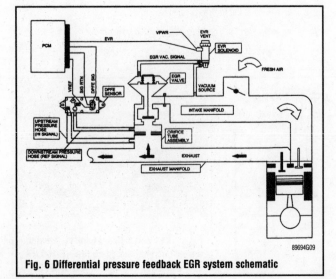

Fig. 6 Differential pressure feedback EGR system schematic

89694G09

COMPONENT TESTING

DPFE Sensor

1. Disconnect the pressure hoses at the DPFE sensor.

2. Connect a hand vacuum pump to the downstream pickup marked **REF** on the sensor.

3. Using a multimeter, backprobe the SIG RTN circuit at the DPFE connector.

4. With the ignition **ON**, signal voltage should be 0.20–0.70 volts.

5. Apply 8–9 in. Hg of vacuum to the sensor. Voltage should be greater than 4 volts.

6. Quickly release the vacuum from the sensor. Voltage should drop to less than 1 volt in 3 seconds.

7. If the sensor does not respond as specified, check the power and ground circuits.

8. If power and ground circuits are functional, the sensor is faulty.

EGR Valve Control Solenoid

1. Remove the EVR solenoid.

2. Attempt to lightly blow air into the EVR solenoid.

   a. If air blows through the solenoid, replace the solenoid with a new one.

   b. If air does not pass freely through the solenoid, continue with the test.

3. Apply battery voltage (approximately 12 volts) and a ground to the EVR solenoid electrical terminals. Attempt to lightly blow air, once again, through the solenoid.

   a. If air does not pass through the solenoid, replace the solenoid with a new one.

   b. If air does not flow through the solenoid, the solenoid is OK.

4. If the solenoid is functional but the problem still exists, check the power and ground circuits.

EGR Valve

1. Install a tachometer on the engine, following the manufacturer's instructions.

2. Detach the engine wiring harness connector from the Idle Air Control (IAC) solenoid.

3. Disconnect and plug the vacuum supply hose from the EGR valve.

4. Start the engine, then apply the parking brake, block the rear wheels and position the transmission in Neutral.

5. Observe and note the idle speed.

➡ **If the engine will not idle with the IAC solenoid disconnected, provide an air bypass to the engine by slightly opening the throttle plate or by creating an intake vacuum leak. Do not allow the idle speed to exceed typical idle rpm.**

6. Using a hand-held vacuum pump, slowly apply 5–10 in. Hg (17–34 kPa) of vacuum to the EGR valve nipple.

   a. If the idle speed drops more than 100 rpm with the vacuum applied and returns to normal after the vacuum is removed, the EGR valve is OK.

   b. If the idle speed does not drop more than 100 rpm with the vacuum applied and return to normal after the vacuum is removed, inspect the EGR valve for a blockage; clean it if a blockage is found. Replace the EGR valve if no blockage is found, or if cleaning the valve does not remedy the malfunction.

REMOVAL & INSTALLATION

DPFE Sensor

▶ **See Figures 7, 8, 9 and 10**

1. Disconnect the negative battery cable.

2. Label and disconnect the wiring harness from the DPFE sensor.

3. Label and disconnect the vacuum hoses.

4. Remove the mounting screws and remove the DPFE sensor.

To install:

5. Position the DPFE sensor and tighten the mounting screws.

6. Attach all necessary hoses and wiring to the sensor.

7. Connect the negative battery cable.

Fig. 7 Detach the connector for the DPFE sensor

Fig. 8 Matchmark and remove the vacuum hoses for the DPFE sensor and . . .

Fig. 9 . . . remove the retaining nuts from the DPFE sensor and . . .

Fig. 10 . . . remove the DPFE sensor from the intake manifold

Fig. 11 Detach the connector for the EVR solenoid

Fig. 12 Matchmark and remove the vacuum hoses from the EVR solenoid

Fig. 13 Remove the retaining nut and solenoid from the intake manifold

EGR Valve Control Solenoid

▶ See Figures 11, 12 and 13

1. Disconnect the negative battery cable.
2. Label and detach the vacuum hoses from the EVR solenoid.
3. Detach the electrical connector from the solenoid.
4. Remove the retaining hardware, and remove the solenoid.

To install:

5. Position the solenoid and install the retaining hardware.
6. Attach the main emission vacuum control connector and the wiring harness connector to the EVR solenoid.
7. Connect the negative battery cable.

EGR Valve

5.8L AND 7.5L ENGINES

1. Disconnect the negative battery cable.
2. Remove the air cleaner outlet tube.
3. Detach the EVP sensor connector.
4. Disconnect the EGR valve-to-exhaust manifold tube from the EGR valve.
5. Remove the vacuum hose from the EGR valve.
6. Remove the EGR valve mounting bolts, then separate the valve from the intake manifold.
7. Remove and discard the old EGR valve gasket, and clean the gasket mating surfaces on the valve and the intake manifold.

To install:

➡If replacing the EGR valve, transfer the EVP sensor onto the new valve.

8. Install the EGR valve, along with a new gasket, on the upper intake manifold, then install and tighten the mounting bolts.
9. Connect the EGR valve-to-exhaust manifold tube to the valve, then tighten the tube nut to 25–35 ft. lbs. (34–47 Nm).
10. Connect the vacuum hose to the EGR valve.
11. Attach the EVP sensor connector.
12. Install the air cleaner outlet tube.
13. Connect the negative battery cable.

4.2L, 4.6L, 5.4L AND 6.8L ENGINES

▶ See Figures 14 thru 21

1. Disconnect the negative battery cable.
2. Remove the vacuum hose from the EGR valve.
3. On the 4.6L engine, remove the nut and the brake booster bracket.
4. On the 5.4L engine, remove the DPFE sensor retaining nuts and place the sensor to the side to allow access to the EGR tube.
5. Disconnect the EGR valve-to-exhaust manifold tube from the EGR valve.

Fig. 14 Remove the vacuum hose from the EGR valve

Fig. 15 On the 4.6L engine, remove the nut and the brake booster bracket from the

Fig. 16 Using a suitable size wrench, loosen the EGR valve-to-exhaust manifold

Fig. 17 . . . remove the tube from the EGR valve

Fig. 18 Remove the EGR valve mounting bolts and . . .

Fig. 19 . . . remove the EGR valve from the intake manifold

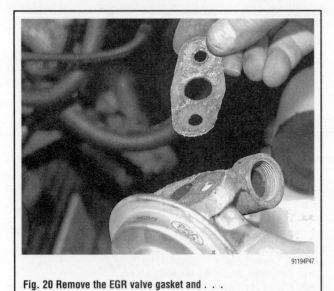

Fig. 20 Remove the EGR valve gasket and . . .

Fig. 21 . . . thoroughly clean the EGR valve mounting surface

6. Remove the EGR valve mounting bolts, then separate the valve from the intake manifold.

7. Remove and discard the old EGR valve gasket, and clean the gasket mating surfaces on the valve and the intake manifold.

To install:

8. Install the EGR valve, along with a new gasket, on the intake manifold, then install and tighten the mounting bolts.

9. Connect the EGR valve-to-exhaust manifold tube to the valve, then tighten the tube nut to 25–35 ft. lbs. (34–47 Nm).

10. Connect the vacuum hose to the EGR valve.

11. On the 5.4L engine, install the DPFE sensor.

12. On the 4.6L engine install the brake booster bracket and the retaining nut.

13. Connect the negative battery cable.

ELECTRONIC ENGINE CONTROLS

Powertrain Control Module (PCM)

OPERATION

The Powertrain Control Module (PCM) performs many functions on your vehicle. The module accepts information from various engine sensors and computes the required fuel flow rate necessary to maintain the correct amount of air/fuel ratio throughout the entire engine operational range.

Based on the information that is received and programmed into the PCM's memory, the PCM generates output signals to control relays, actuators and solenoids. The PCM also sends out a command to the fuel injectors that meters the appropriate quantity of fuel. The module automatically senses and compensates for any changes in altitude when driving your vehicle.

REMOVAL & INSTALLATION

▶ See Figure 22

1997–00 F-150, F-250, Expedition and Navigator

▶ See Figures 23, 24, 25, and 26

1. Remove the battery and the battery tray.
2. Loosen the connector retaining bolt and remove the PCM connector.
3. Remove the passenger side front door scuff plate.
4. Remove the passenger side kick panel.
5. Remove the PCM bracket clip.
6. Remove the PCM.

To install:
7. Installation is the reverse of removal.
8. Tighten the PCM connector retaining bolt to 36–44 inch lbs. (4–5 Nm).

1997–98 F-250HD, F-350 and F-Super Duty

▶ See Figure 27

1. Disconnect the negative battery cable.
2. Loosen the connector retaining bolt and remove the PCM connector.
3. Remove the two PCM seal nuts and loosen the driver's side fender liner screws and remove the liner or bend it down to allow the necessary clearance for the PCM.
4. Remove the PCM.

To install:
5. Installation is the reverse of removal.
6. Tighten the PCM seal nuts to 27–35 inch lbs. (3–4 Nm).
7. Tighten the PCM connector retaining bolt to 36–44 inch lbs. (4–5 Nm).

1999–00 F-Super Duty Models

▶ See Figures 28, 29, 30, and 31

1. Disconnect the negative battery cable.
2. Remove the bolt, screws, and pushpins from the fenderwell trim. Remove the fenderwell trim.
3. Loosen the connector retaining bolt and remove the PCM connector.
4. Remove the PCM bracket retaining screws and remove the PCM and bracket assembly.
5. Remove the PCM from the bracket.

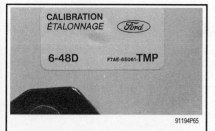

Fig. 22 The calibration number will be needed to order such parts as a replacement PCM, various sensors, and almost any emission control component. Typically this number is attached to a label found on the driver's door or the door pillar

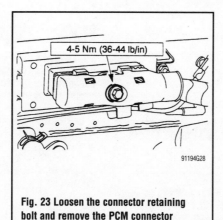

Fig. 23 Loosen the connector retaining bolt and remove the PCM connector

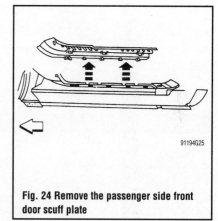

Fig. 24 Remove the passenger side front door scuff plate

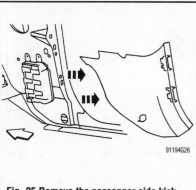

Fig. 25 Remove the passenger side kick panel

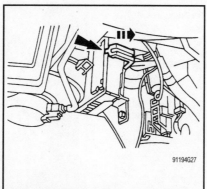

Fig. 26 Remove the PCM bracket clip and remove the PCM

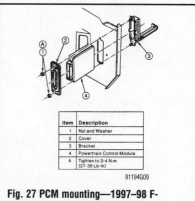

Fig. 27 PCM mounting—1997–98 F-250HD, F-350 and F-Super Duty

Fig. 28 Remove the fenderwell trim

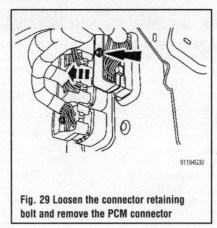

Fig. 29 Loosen the connector retaining bolt and remove the PCM connector

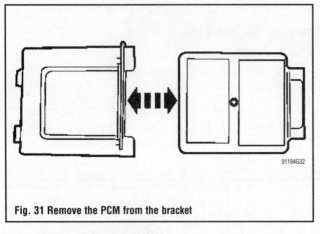

Fig. 30 Remove the PCM bracket retaining screws and remove the PCM and bracket assembly

Fig. 31 Remove the PCM from the bracket

To install:
6. Installation is the reverse of removal.
7. Tighten the PCM connector retaining bolt to 36–44 inch lbs. (4–5 Nm).

Heated Oxygen Sensor

OPERATION

The oxygen (O2) sensor is a device which produces an electrical voltage when exposed to the oxygen present in the exhaust gases. The sensor is mounted in the exhaust system, usually in the manifold or a boss located on the down pipe before the catalyst.. The oxygen sensors used on the Ford F-series, Expedition and the Lincoln Navigator are electrically heated internally for faster switching when the engine is started cold. The oxygen sensor produces a voltage within 0 and 1 volt. When there is a large amount of oxygen present (lean mixture), the sensor produces a low voltage (less than 0.4v). When there is a lesser amount present (rich mixture) it produces a higher voltage (0.6–1.0v).The stoichiometric or correct fuel to air ratio will read between 0.4 and 0.6v. By monitoring the oxygen content and converting it to electrical voltage, the sensor acts as a rich-lean switch. The voltage is transmitted to the PCM.

Some models have two sensors, one before the catalyst and one after. This is done for a catalyst efficiency monitor that is a part of the OBD-II engine controls that are on all models covered by this manual except for those with the 5.8L or 7.5L engines. The sensor before the catalyst measures the exhaust emissions right out of the engine, and sends the signal to the PCM about the state of the mixture as previously talked about. The second sensor reports the difference in the emissions after the exhaust gases have gone through the catalyst. This sensor reports to the PCM the amount of emissions reduction the catalyst is performing.

The oxygen sensor will not work until a predetermined temperature is reached, until this time the PCM is running in what as known as OPEN LOOP operation. OPEN LOOP means that the PCM has not yet begun to correct the air-to-fuel ratio by reading the oxygen sensor. After the engine comes to operating temperature, the PCM will monitor the oxygen sensor and correct the air/fuel ratio from the sensor's readings. This is what is known as CLOSED LOOP operation.

A heated oxygen sensor (HO2S) has a heating element that keeps the sensor at proper operating temperature during all operating modes. Maintaining correct sensor temperature at all times allows the system to enter into CLOSED LOOP operation sooner.

In CLOSED LOOP operation the PCM monitors the sensor input (along with other inputs) and adjusts the injector pulse width accordingly. During OPEN LOOP operation the PCM ignores the sensor input and adjusts the injector pulse to a preprogrammed value based on other inputs.

TESTING

▶ See Figure 32

❊❊ WARNING

Do not pierce the wires when testing this sensor; this can lead to wiring harness damage. Backprobe the connector to properly read the voltage of the HO2S.

1. Disconnect the HO2S.
2. Measure the resistance between PWR and GND terminals of the sensor. Resistance should be approximately 6 ohms at 68°F (20°C). If resistance is not within specification, the sensor's heater element is faulty.
3. With the HO2S connected and engine running, measure the voltage with a Digital Volt-Ohmmeter (DVOM) between terminals **HO2S** and **SIG RTN** (GND) of the oxygen sensor connector. Voltage should fluctuate between 0.01–1.0 volts. If voltage fluctuation is slow or voltage is not within specification, the sensor may be faulty.

Fig. 32 The HO2S can be monitored with an appropriate and Datastream capable scan tool

REMOVAL & INSTALLATION

▶ See Figures 33 thru 39

➠An oxygen sensor socket/wrench is available from Ford or aftermarket manufacturers to ease the removal and installation of the oxygen sensor(s). If one is not available, an open end wrench can be used.

✳✳ WARNING

The sensor uses a permanently attached pigtail and connector. This pigtail should not be removed from the sensor. Damage or removal of

the pigtail or connector will affect the proper operation of the sensor. Keep the electrical connector and louvered end of the sensor clean and free of grease. NEVER use cleaning solvents of any type on the sensor! The oxygen sensor may be difficult to remove when the temperature of the engine is below 120°F (49°C). Excessive force may damage the threads in the exhaust manifold or exhaust pipe.

1. Disconnect the negative battery cable.
2. Raise and support the vehicle.
3. Unplug the electrical connector and any attaching hardware.

➠Lubricate the sensor with penetrating oil prior to removal.

4. Remove the sensor using an appropriate tool. Special oxygen sensor sockets are available to remove the sensor and can be purchased at many parts stores or where automotive tools are sold. The proper size wrench can be used, most sensors are 7/8 inch or 22mm sizes.

To install:

5. Coat the threads of the sensor with a suitable anti-seize compound before installation. New sensors are precoated with this compound.
6. Install the sensor and tighten it. Use care in making sure the silicone boot is in the correct position to avoid melting it during operation.
7. Attach the electrical connector.
8. Lower the vehicle.
9. Connect the negative battery cable.

Idle Air Control Valve

OPERATION

The Idle Air Control (IAC) valve adjusts the engine idle speed. The valve is located on the side of the throttle body. The valve is controlled by a duty cycle signal from the PCM and allows air to bypass the throttle plate in order to maintain the proper idle speed.

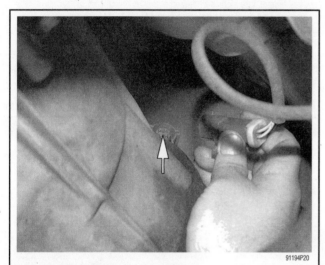

91194P20

Fig. 33 Detach the connector for the H2O sensor

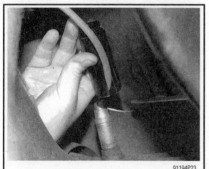

91194P23

Fig. 34 A special socket is available to remove the H2O sensor that contains a slot for the wire harness to slide out of

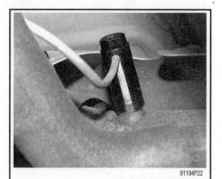

91194P22

Fig. 35 Place the socket onto the sensor and . . .

91194P21

Fig. 36 . . . loosen the sensor using a suitable drive tool

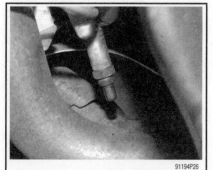

91194P26

Fig. 37 After the sensor is sufficiently loose using the drive tool, remove the sensor from the exhaust pipe by hand

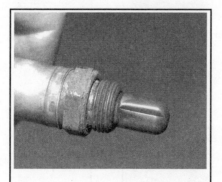

91194P25

Fig. 38 Inspect the sensor tip for any signs of build-up or damage

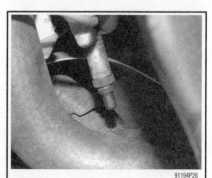

91194P26

Fig. 39 Coat the threads of the sensor with a suitable anti-seize compound before installation

➡Do not attempt to clean the IAC valve. Carburetor tune-up cleaners or any type of solvent cleaners will damage the internal components of the valve.

TESTING

▶ **See Figure 40**

1. Turn the ignition switch to the **OFF** position.
2. Disconnect the wiring harness from the IAC valve.
3. Measure the resistance between the terminals of the valve.

➡Due to the diode in the solenoid, place the ohmmeter positive lead on the VPWR terminal and the negative lead on the ISC terminal.

4. Resistance should be 6–13 ohms.
5. If resistance is not within specification, the valve may be faulty.

REMOVAL & INSTALLATION

▶ **See Figures 41, 42 and 43**

1. Disconnect the negative battery cable.
2. Remove the air cleaner inlet tube and the throttle cover, if necessary.
3. Disconnnect the wiring harness from the IAC valve.
4. Remove the two retaining bolts.
5. Remove the IAC valve and discard the old gasket.

To install:

6. Clean the gasket mating surfaces thoroughly.
7. Using a new gasket, position the IAC valve on the throttle body.

8. Install and tighten the retaining bolts to 71–106 inch lbs. (8–12 Nm).
9. Connect the wiring harness to the IAC valve.
10. If removed, install the air cleaner tube and throttle cover.
11. Connect the negative battery cable.

Engine Coolant Temperature Sensor

OPERATION

The Engine Coolant Temperature (ECT) sensor resistance changes in response to engine coolant temperature. The sensor resistance decreases as the coolant temperature increases, and increases as the coolant temperature decreases. This provides a reference signal to the PCM, which indicates engine coolant temperature. The signal sent to the PCM by the ECT sensor helps the PCM to determine spark advance, EGR flow rate, air/fuel ratio, and engine temperature. The ECT is a two wire sensor, a 5-volt reference signal is sent to the sensor and the signal return is based upon the change in the measured resistance due to temperature.

TESTING

▶ **See Figures 44 and 45**

1. Disconnect the engine wiring harness from the ECT sensor.
2. Connect an ohmmeter between the ECT sensor terminals.
3. With the engine cold and the ignition switch in the **OFF** position, measure and note the ECT sensor resistance.
4. Connect the engine wiring harness to the sensor.

Fig. 40 The IAC can be monitored with an appropriate and Data-stream capable scan tool

Fig. 41 Detach the connector for the IAT valve and . . .

Fig. 42 . . . remove the retaining bolts for the IAC

Fig. 43 Now lift the IAC valve off of the engine

Temperature		Engine Coolant/Intake Air Temperature Sensor Values
°F	°C	Resistance (K ohms)
248	120	1.18
230	110	1.55
212	100	2.07
194	90	2.80
176	80	3.84
158	70	5.37
140	60	7.70
122	50	10.97
104	40	16.15
86	30	24.27
68	20	37.30
50	10	58.75

89694G23

Fig. 44 ECT resistance-to-temperature specifications

Fig. 45 Test the ECT resistance across the two sensor terminals

5. Start the engine and allow the engine to reach normal operating temperature.

6. Once the engine has reached normal operating temperature, turn the engine **OFF**.

7. Once again, disconnect the engine wiring harness from the ECT sensor.

8. Measure and note the ECT sensor resistance with the engine hot.

9. Compare the cold and hot ECT sensor resistance measurements with the accompanying chart.

10. If readings do not approximate those in the chart, the sensor may be faulty.

REMOVAL & INSTALLATION

▶ **See Figures 46, 47 and 48**

1. Disconnect the negative battery cable.
2. Drain and recycle the engine coolant.

✳✳ CAUTION

Never open, service or drain the radiator or cooling system when hot; serious burns can occur from the steam and hot coolant. Also, when draining engine coolant, keep in mind that cats and dogs are attracted to ethylene glycol antifreeze and could drink any that is left in an uncovered container or in puddles on the ground. This will prove fatal in sufficient quantities. Always drain coolant into a sealable container. Coolant should be reused unless it is contaminated or is several years old.

3. Remove the air cleaner outlet tube.

4. Disconnect the ECT sensor connector.
5. Remove the ECT sensor from the intake manifold.

To install:

6. Coat the sensor threads with Teflon® sealant.
7. Thread the sensor into position and tighten to:
- 10–15 ft. lbs. (13–20 Nm) on the 5.8L and 7.5L engine
- 71–106 inch lbs. (8–13 Nm) on the 4.2L engine
- 12–17 ft. lbs. (16–24 Nm) on the 4.6L engine
8. Attach the ECT sensor connector.
9. Install the air cleaner outlet tube.
10. Connect the negative battery cable.
11. Refill the engine cooling system.
12. Start the engine and check for coolant leaks.
13. Bleed the cooling system.

Intake Air Temperature Sensor

OPERATION

▶ **See Figure 49**

The Intake Air Temperature (IAT) sensor determines the air temperature inside the intake manifold. Resistance changes in response to the ambient air temperature. The sensor has a negative temperature coefficient. As the temperature of the sensor rises the resistance across the sensor decreases. This provides a signal to the PCM indicating the temperature of the incoming air charge. This sensor helps the PCM to determine spark timing and air/fuel ratio. Information

Fig. 49 The tip of the IAT sensor has an exposed thermistor that changes the resistance of the sensor based upon the force of the air rushing past it

Fig. 46 Detach the connector for the ECT sensor . . .

Fig. 47 . . . and loosen the sensor using a suitable socket or other drive tool

Fig. 48 Once the sensor is sufficiently loose, remove the sensor from the intake

from this sensor is added to the pressure sensor information to calculate the air mass being sent to the cylinders. The IAT is a two wire sensor, a 5-volt reference signal is sent to the sensor and the signal return is based upon the change in the measured resistance due to temperature.

TESTING

▸ See Figures 50, 51 and 52

1. Turn the ignition switch **OFF**.
2. Disconnect the wiring harness from the IAT sensor.

Fig. 50 The IAT sensor can be monitored with an appropriate and data-stream capable scan tool

Temperature		Engine Coolant/Intake Air Temperature Sensor Values
°F	°C	Resistance (K ohms)
248	120	1.18
230	110	1.55
212	100	2.07
194	90	2.80
176	80	3.84
158	70	5.37
140	60	7.70
122	50	10.97
104	40	16.15
86	30	24.27
68	20	37.30
50	10	58.75

Fig. 51 IAT resistance-to-temperature specifications

Fig. 52 Measure the resistance of the IAT sensor across the two sensor pins

3. Measure the resistance between the sensor terminals.
4. Compare the resistance reading with the accompanying chart.
5. If the resistance is not within specification, the IAT may be faulty.
6. Connect the wiring harness to the sensor.

REMOVAL & INSTALLATION

5.8L and 7.5L Engines

▸ See Figure 53

1. Disconnect the negative battery cable.
2. Detach the electrical connector from the IAT sensor.
3. Remove the IAT sensor from the intake manifold.

➡ On California emissions equipped models, the IAT sensor is located in the air cleaner-to-throttle body tube.

4. Installation is the reverse of removal. Tighten the IAT sensor to 12–17 ft. lbs. (16–24 Nm).

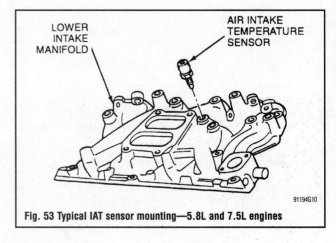

Fig. 53 Typical IAT sensor mounting—5.8L and 7.5L engines

7.3L Diesel Engine

▸ See Figure 54

1. Disconnect the negative battery cable.
2. Detach the electrical connector from the IAT sensor.
3. Remove the IAT sensor from the air cleaner housing.
4. Installation is the reverse of removal. Tighten the IAT sensor to 12–17 ft. lbs. (16–24 Nm).

4.2L, 4.6L, 5.4L and 6.8L Engines Except 5.4L Lightning

▸ See Figures 55 and 56

1. Disconnect the negative battery cable.
2. Detach the electrical connector from the IAT sensor.

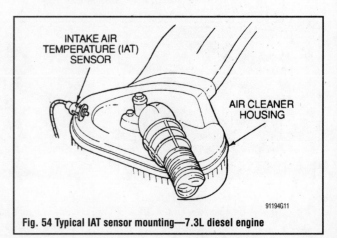

Fig. 54 Typical IAT sensor mounting—7.3L diesel engine

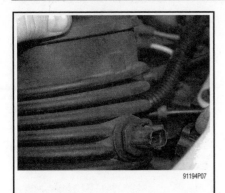

Fig. 55 Detach the connector for the IAT sensor and . . .

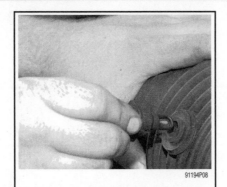

Fig. 56 . . . carefully twist the sensor from the air cleaner outlet tube

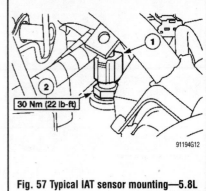

Fig. 57 Typical IAT sensor mounting—5.8L Lightning

3. Remove the IAT sensor from the air cleaner outlet tube by carefully twisting it out.

To install:

4. Lubricate the IAT sensor opening in the air cleaner outlet tube with a suitable lubricant such as a penetrating oil.
5. Carefully twist the sensor into the tube.
6. Attach the electrical connector to the IAT sensor.
7. Connect the negative battery cable.

5.4L Lightning

♦ **See Figure 57**

1. Disconnect the negative battery cable.
2. Remove the front EGR vacuum regulator bracket assembly nut.
3. Remove the EGR vacuum regulator bracket assembly bolts.
4. Remove the rear EGR vacuum regulator bracket assembly nut.
5. Detach the barometric pressure sensor electrical connector.
6. Disconnect the vacuum lines and detach the electrical connector from the EGR vacuum regulator and remove the regulator and bracket assembly.
7. Disconnect the supercharger bypass vacuum solenoid vacuum lines and detach the electrical connector.
8. Remove the solenoid.
9. Disconnect the differential pressure feedback EGR (DPFE) exhaust pressure lines.
10. Detach the DPFE electrical connector and remove the DPFE sensor.
11. Detach the intake air temperature (IAT) sensor electrical connector.
12. Remove the sensor.
13. Installation is the reverse of removal.

Mass Airflow Sensor

OPERATION

The Mass Air Flow (MAF) sensor directly measures the mass of air being drawn into the engine. The sensor output is used to calculate injector pulse width. The MAF sensor is what is referred to as a "hot-wire sensor". The sensor uses a thin platinum wire filament, wound on a ceramic bobbin and coated with glass, that is heated to 200°C (417°F) above the ambient air temperature and subjected to the intake airflow stream. A "cold-wire" is used inside the MAF sensor to determine the ambient air temperature.

Battery voltage from the EEC power relay, and a reference signal and a ground signal from the PCM are supplied to the MAF sensor. The sensor returns a signal proportionate to the current flow required to keep the "hot-wire" at the required temperature. The increased airflow across the "hot-wire" acts as a cooling fan, lowering the resistance and requiring more current to maintain the temperature of the wire. The increased current is measured by the voltage in the circuit, as current increases, voltage increases. As the airflow increases the signal return voltage of a normally operating MAF sensor will increase.

TESTING

1. Using a multimeter, check for voltage by backprobing the MAF sensor connector.
2. With the key **ON**, and the engine **OFF**, verify that there is at least 10.5 volts between the VPWR and GND terminals of the MAF sensor connector. If voltage is not within specification, check power and ground circuits and repair as necessary.
3. With the key **ON**, and the engine **ON**, verify that there is at least 4.5 volts between the SIG and GND terminals of the MAF sensor connector. If voltage is not within specification, check power and ground circuits and repair as necessary.
4. With the key **ON**, and the engine **ON**, check voltage between GND and SIG RTN terminals. Voltage should be approximately 0.34–1.96 volts. If voltage is not within specification, the sensor may be faulty.

REMOVAL & INSTALLATION

5.8L and 7.5L Engines

See Figure 58

1. Disconnect the negative battery cable.
2. Remove the air intake tube from the MAF sensor and the throttle body.
3. Detach the connector from the MAF sensor.
4. Remove the four sensor retaining screws and remove the sensor.

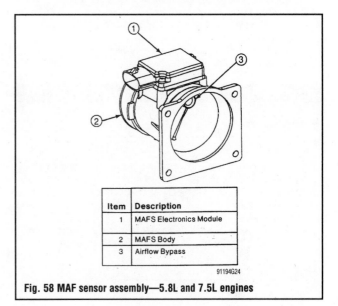

Item	Description
1	MAFS Electronics Module
2	MAFS Body
3	Airflow Bypass

Fig. 58 MAF sensor assembly—5.8L and 7.5L engines

Fig. 59 Remove the wire harness grommet from the air cleaner assembly

Fig. 60 After the air cleaner lid is separated, carefully push the MAF sensor and plate up to . . .

Fig. 61 . . . access the MAF sensor connector, unplug the sensor and remove the sensor from the air cleaner assembly

Fig. 62 Remove the two MAF-to-plate retaining nuts and remove the MAF sensor from the plate

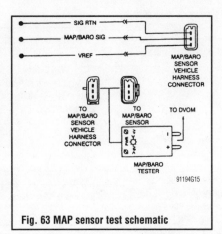

Fig. 63 MAP sensor test schematic

Approximate Altitude (Feet)	Signal Voltage (±0.04V)
0	1.59
1000	1.56
2000	1.53
3000	1.50
4000	1.47
5000	1.44
6000	1.41
7000	1.39

Fig. 64 MAP sensor altitude/voltage output relationship

5. Remove the sensor gasket.
6. Installation is the reverse of removal.

4.2L, 4.6L, 5.4L and 6.8L Engines

♦ See Figures 59, 60, 61 and 62

1. Disconnect the negative battery cable.
2. Release the air cleaner clamp and separate the air cleaner halves.
3. Remove the grommet from the air cleaner housing and slide the grommet down the harness.
4. Remove the MAF sensor plate and MAF sensor from the air cleaner.
5. Detach the MAF sensor from the harness.
6. Remove the retaining nuts and remove the MAF sensor.
7. Installation is the reverse of removal.

Manifold Air Pressure Sensor

OPERATION

The most important information for measuring engine fuel requirements comes from the pressure sensor. Using the pressure and temperature data, the PCM calculates the intake air mass. It is connected to the engine intake manifold through a hose and takes readings of the absolute pressure. A piezoelectric crystal changes a voltage input to a frequency output which reflects the pressure in the intake manifold.

Atmospheric pressure is measured both when the engine is started and when driving fully loaded, then the pressure sensor information is adjusted accordingly.

TESTING

♦ See Figures 63 and 64

1. Connect MAP/BARO tester to the sensor connector and sensor harness connector. With ignition **ON** and engine **OFF**, use DVOM to measure voltage

across tester terminals. If the tester's 4-6V indicator is ON, the reference voltage input to the sensor is okay.
2. Measure the reference signal of the MAP sensor. If the DVOM voltage reading is as indicated in the table, the sensor is okay.

REMOVAL & INSTALLATION

1. Disconnect the negative battery cable.
2. Disengage the electrical connector and the vacuum line from the sensor.
3. Unfasten the sensor mounting bolts and remove the sensor.
To install:
4. Installation is the reverse of removal.

Barometric Pressure Sensor

OPERATION

The barometric pressure sensor (BARO sensor) is a variable capacitance sensor that when supplied with a %-volt reference signal from the PCM, produces an analog voltage that indicates barometric pressure. The sensor signal is used to determine altitude to adjust the ignition timing and quantity of fuel to optimize engine operation. The output of the barometric sensor is one of the variables used to calculate glow plug on time on diesel engines.

TESTING

♦ See Figures 65 and 66

1. Connect MAP/BARO tester to the sensor connector and sensor harness connector. With ignition **ON** and engine **OFF**, use DVOM to measure voltage across tester terminals. If the tester's 4-6V indicator is ON, the reference voltage input to the sensor is okay.

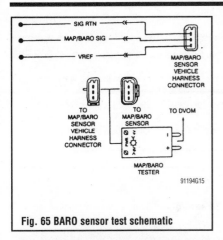

Fig. 65 BARO sensor test schematic

Approximate Altitude (Feet)	Signal Voltage (±0.04V)
0	1.59
1000	1.56
2000	1.53
3000	1.50
4000	1.47
5000	1.44
6000	1.41
7000	1.39

Fig. 66 BARO sensor altitude/voltage output relationship

Fig. 67 Testing the TP sensor signal return voltage at idle

Fig. 68 Test the operation of the TP sensor by gently opening the throttle while observing the signal return voltage. The voltage should move smoothly according to the amount the throttle is opened

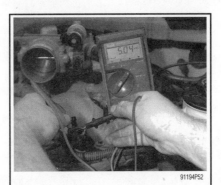

Fig. 69 Testing the supply voltage at the TP sensor connector

Fig. 70 The TP sensor can be monitored with an appropriate and Data-stream capable scan tool

2. Measure the reference signal of the BARO sensor. If the DVOM voltage reading is as indicated in the table, the sensor is okay.

REMOVAL & INSTALLATION

1. Disconnect the negative battery cable.
2. Detach the electrical connector from the BARO sensor.
3. Slide the sensor out of the retaining clip and remove the sensor.

To install:

4. Installation is the reverse of removal.
5. Installation is the reverse of removal.

Throttle Position Sensor

OPERATION

The Throttle Position (TP) sensor is a potentiometer that provides a signal to the PCM that is directly proportional to the throttle plate position. The TP sensor is mounted on the side of the throttle body and is connected to the throttle plate shaft. The TP sensor monitors throttle plate movement and position, and transmits an appropriate electrical signal to the PCM. These signals are used by the PCM to adjust the air/fuel mixture, spark timing and EGR operation according to engine load at idle, part throttle, or full throttle. The TP sensor is not adjustable.

The TP sensor receives a 5 volt reference signal and a ground circuit from the PCM. A return signal circuit is connected to a wiper that runs on a resistor internally on the sensor. The further the throttle is opened, the wiper moves along the resistor, at wide open throttle, the wiper essentially creates a loop between the reference signal and the signal return returning the full or nearly full 5 volt signal back to the PCM. At idle the signal return should be approximately 0.9 volts.

TESTING

▶ See Figures 67, 68, 69 and 70

1. With the engine **OFF** and the ignition **ON**, check the voltage at the signal return circuit of the TP sensor by carefully backprobing the connector using a DVOM.
2. Voltage should be between 0.2 and 1.4 volts at idle.
3. Slowly move the throttle pulley to the wide open throttle (WOT) position and watch the voltage on the DVOM. The voltage should slowly rise to slightly less than 4.8v at Wide Open Throttle (WOT).
4. If no voltage is present, check the wiring harness for supply voltage (5.0v) and ground (0.3v or less), by referring to your corresponding wiring guide. If supply voltage and ground are present, but no output voltage from TP, replace the TP sensor. If supply voltage and ground do not meet specifications, make necessary repairs to the harness or PCM.

REMOVAL & INSTALLATION

▶ See Figure 71

1. Disconnect the negative battery cable.
2. If necessary, remove the throttle cover from the engine.
3. Disconnect the wiring harness from the TP sensor.
4. Remove the two sensor mounting screws, then pull the TP sensor off of the throttle shaft.

To install:

5. Carefully slide the rotary tangs on the sensor into position over the throttle shaft, then rotate the sensor clockwise to the installed position..

✳ CAUTION

Failure to install the TP sensor in this manner may result in sensor damage or high idle speeds.

→**The TP sensor is not adjustable.**

6. Install and tighten the sensor mounting screws to 27 inch lbs. (3 Nm).
7. Connect the wiring harness to the sensor.
8. If removed, install the throttle cover.
9. Connect the negative battery cable.

Camshaft Position Sensor

OPERATION

4.2L Engine

The camshaft position sensor (CMP) is a single hall-effect magnetic switch that is triggered by a single vane which is driven by the camshaft. The CMP sends a signal relating camshaft position back to the PCM which is used by the PCM to control engine timing.

4.6L, 5.4L and 6.8L Engines

The camshaft position sensor (CMP) is a variable reluctance sensor that is triggered by a high point on the left-hand exhaust camshaft sprocket. The CMP sends a signal relating camshaft position back to the PCM which is used by the PCM to control engine timing.

Diesel Engine

The Camshaft Position Sensor, is a Hall-effect sensor that generates a digital frequency while windows in a target wheel pass through its magnetic field. The frequency of the windows passing by the sensor, as well as the width of selected windows, allows the PCM to detect engine speed and position.

TESTING

1. Check voltage between the camshaft position sensor terminals PWR GND and CID.
2. With engine running, voltage should be greater than 0.1 volt AC and vary with engine speed.
3. If voltage is not within specification, check for proper voltage at the VPWR terminal.
4. If VPWR voltage is greater than 10.5 volts, sensor may be faulty.

REMOVAL & INSTALLATION

4.2L Engine

▶ **See Figures 72, 73, 74 and 75**

1. Disconnect the negative battery cable.
2. Drain and recycle the engine coolant.
3. Remove the air cleaner assembly.
4. Detach the electrical connector from the heater water outlet tube.
5. Remove the retaining bolt and position the heater water outlet tube aside.
6. Detach the electrical connector for the CMP sensor.
7. Remove the CMP sensor retaining bolts and remove the CMP sensor from the engine.
8. Installation is the reverse of removal.

Except 4.2L Engine

▶ **See Figures 76, 77 and 78**

1. Disconnect the negative battery cable.
2. Detach the electrical connector for the CMP sensor.

Fig. 71 Remove the two retaining screws for the TP sensor and remove the sensor from the throttle body

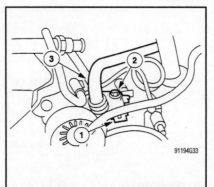

Fig. 72 Remove the retaining bolt and position the heater water outlet tube aside

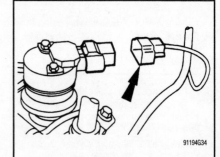

Fig. 73 Detach the electrical connector for the CMP sensor

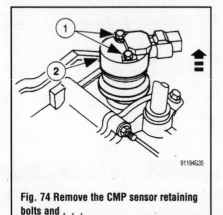

Fig. 74 Remove the CMP sensor retaining bolts and . . .

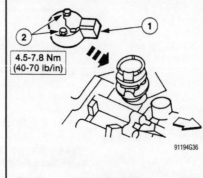

Fig. 75 . . . remove the CMP sensor from the engine

Fig. 76 Detach the connector for the CMP sensor and . . .

Fig. 77 . . . remove the bolt retaining the CMP sensor to the front cover and . . .

Fig. 78 . . . remove the sensor

Fig. 79 The CKP sensor trigger wheel rides on the front of the crankshaft. The missing tooth creates a fluctuation of voltage in the sensor

3. Remove the CMP sensor retaining bolt(s) and remove the CMP sensor from the front cover.
4. Installation is the reverse of removal.

Crankshaft Position Sensor

OPERATION

▶ See Figure 79

The Crankshaft Position (CKP) sensor is a variable reluctance sensor that uses a trigger wheel to induce voltage. The CKP sensor is a fixed magnetic sensor mounted to the engine block and monitors the trigger or "pulse" wheel which is attached to the crank pulley/damper. As the pulse wheel rotates by the CKP sensor, teeth on the pulse wheel induce voltage inside the sensor through magnetism. The pulse wheel has a missing tooth that changes the reading of the sensor. This is used for the Cylinder Identification (CID) function to properly monitor and adjust engine timing by locating the number 1 cylinder. The voltage created by the CKP sensor is alternating current (A/C). This voltage reading is sent to the PCM and is used to determine engine RPM, engine timing, and is used to fire the ignition coils.

TESTING

1. Measure the voltage between the sensor CKP sensor terminals by back-probing the sensor connector.

➡If the connector cannot be backprobed, fabricate or purchase a test harness.

2. Sensor voltage should be more than 0.1 volt AC with the engine running and should vary with engine RPM.
3. If voltage is not within specification, the sensor may be faulty.

REMOVAL & INSTALLATION

4.2L Engine

1. Disconnect the negative battery cable.
2. Raise and safely support the vehicle.
3. Detach the electrical connector for the CKP sensor.
4. Remove the CKP sensor shield retaining nuts and remove the sensor shield.
5. Remove the CKP sensor retaining bolts and remove the CKP sensor.
6. Installation is the reverse of removal.

4.6L, 5.4L and 6.8L Engines

▶ See Figure 80

1. Disconnect the negative battery cable.
2. Remove the accessory drive belt from the engine.

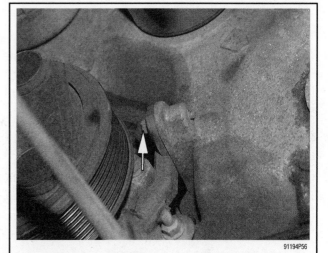
Fig. 80 Remove the retaining bolt for the CKP sensor and remove the sensor from the front cover

3. Raise and safely support the vehicle.
4. Remove the A/C compressor mounting bolts, but do not disconnect the A/C lines. Remove and support the compressor out of the way.
5. Detach the electrical connector for the CKP sensor.
6. Remove the CKP sensor retaining bolts and remove the CKP sensor.
7. Installation is the reverse of removal.

Knock Sensor

OPERATION

The operation of the Knock Sensor (KS) is to monitor preignition or "engine knocks" and send the signal to the PCM. The PCM responds by adjusting ignition timing until the "knocks" stop. The sensor works by generating a signal produced by the frequency of the knock as recorded by the piezoelectric ceramic disc inside the KS. The disc absorbs the shock waves from the knocks and exerts a pressure on the metal diaphragm inside the KS. This compresses the crystals inside the disc and the disc generates a voltage signal proportional to the frequency of the knocks ranging from zero to 1 volt.

TESTING

This sensor produces it's own signal based on information gathered while the engine is running. The sensors also are usually inaccessible without major component removal. The sensors can be monitored with an appropriate scan tool using a data display or other data stream information. Follow the instructions included with the scan tool for information on accessing the data. The only test available is to test the continuity of the harness from the PCM to the sensor.

REMOVAL & INSTALLATION

4.2L Engine

1. Disconnect the negative battery cable.
2. Detach the knock sensor connector.
3. Remove the knock sensor from the engine.
To install:
4. The installation is the reverse of removal.

4.6L, 5.4L and 6.8L Engines

▶ See Figure 81

1. Disconnect the negative battery cable.
2. Remove the upper intake manifold. Refer to Section 3.
3. Detach the knock sensor connector.
4. Remove the knock sensor from the engine.
5. The installation is the reverse of removal.

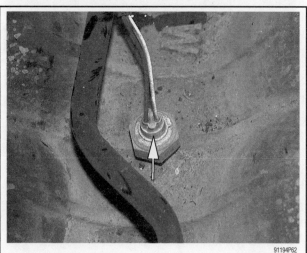

Fig. 81 The knock sensor is located under the intake manifold—4.6L, 5.4L and 6.8L engines

Vehicle Speed Sensor

OPERATION

The Vehicle Speed Sensor (VSS) is a magnetic pick-up sensor that sends a signal to the Powertrain Control Module (PCM) and the speedometer. The sensor measures the rotation of the transmission output shaft or the ring gear on the differential and sends an AC voltage signal to the PCM which determines the corresponding vehicle speed.

TESTING

1. Disconnect the negative battery cable.
2. Disengage the wiring harness connector from the VSS.
3. Using a Digital Volt-Ohmmeter (DVOM), measure the resistance (ohmmeter function) between the sensor terminals. If the resistance is 190–250 ohms, the sensor is okay.

REMOVAL & INSTALLATION

1997–98 F-250HD, F-350 and F-Super Duty

▶ See Figure 82

1. Disconnect the negative battery cable.
2. Raise and safely support the vehicle securely on jackstands.
3. Detach the connector for the VSS.
4. Remove the VSS retaining bolt and remove the VSS from the differential.
5. Remove the driven gear retainer and the drive gear.
To install:
6. Inspect the O-ring on the sensor and replace if necessary.
7. Install the driven gear and the retainer.
8. Place the VSS into the differential.
9. Tighten the retaining bolt to 25–30 ft. lbs. (34–40 Nm).
10. Attach the VSS electrical connector.
11. Lower the vehicle.
12. Connect the negative battery cable.

Except 1997–98 F-250HD, F-350 and F-Super Duty

▶ See Figures 83, 84, 85, 86 and 87

1. Disconnect the negative battery cable.
2. Raise and safely support the vehicle securely on jackstands.
3. Detach the connector for the VSS.
4. Remove the VSS retaining bolt and remove the VSS from the transmission.

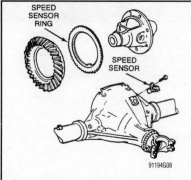

Fig. 82 Differential mounted VSS assembly

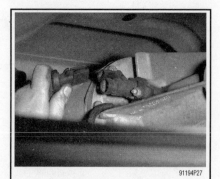

Fig. 83 Detach the connector for the VSS sensor

Fig. 84 Remove the retaining bolt for the VSS sensor and . . .

Fig. 85 . . . remove the VSS sensor from the transmission

Fig. 86 Pry the retainer for the VSS gear off and . . .

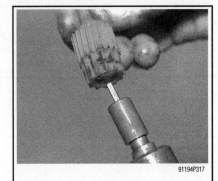

Fig. 87 . . . remove the gear from the VSS

5. Remove the driven gear retainer and the drive gear.

To install:

6. Inspect the O-ring on the sensor and replace if necessary.
7. Install the driven gear and the retainer.
8. Place the VSS into the transmission.
9. Tighten the retaining bolt to 98–115 inch lbs. (11–13 Nm).
10. Attach the VSS electrical connector.
11. Lower the vehicle.
12. Connect the negative battery cable.

Injector Driver Module

OPERATION

The injector driver module (IDM) applies 115volts DC to all of the fuel injectors on the 7.3L DIT diesel engine. The IDM receives signals from the PCM for cylinder identification and fuel delivery command. The PCM controls when the timing of the injectors should start and how long the injector is open. The IDM controls the injector firing sequence through output drivers. The IDM has an output driver for each injector: one low side driver for each injector and one high side injector for each bank of injectors. The injector is fired when the output driver closes the circuit to ground.

REMOVAL & INSTALLATION

1. Disconnect the negative battery cable.
2. Remove the module retaining bolts.
3. Loosen the module wiring harness connector retaining bolt and remove the connector from the module.
4. Remove the module from the vehicle.
5. The installation is the reverse of the removal.

Accelerator Pedal Position Sensor

OPERATION

The accelerator pedal position (APP) sensor is a potentiometer that provides a signal to the PCM proportional to the accelerator pedal position. This sensor is only on models equipped with the 7.3L DIT diesel engine. The 7.3L DIT diesel engine incorporates a "drive by wire" system in which there is no cable to open the throttle plate. The APP sensor sends a signal to the PCM and the PCM control the air/fuel mixture accordingly. The accelerator pedal position sensor acts similar to the TP sensor on a gasoline engine. It provides the input to the PCM directly proportional to the engine load.

TESTING

The accelerator pedal position sensor is tested just like the throttle position sensor. See throttle position sensor for testing.

REMOVAL & INSTALLATION

▶ **See Figure 88**

The accelerator pedal position sensor is not serviced separately. If the accelerator pedal position sensor is bad, replacement of the pedal and shaft assembly is required.

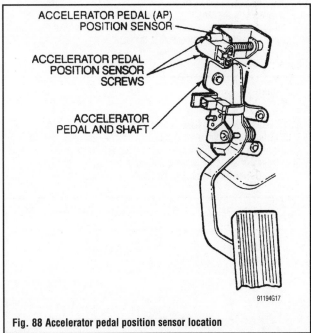

Fig. 88 Accelerator pedal position sensor location

Idle Validation Switch

OPERATION

The idle validation switch (IDS) provides the PCM with a redundant signal to verify when the accelerator pedal is in the idle position. Any detected malfunction of the idle validation switch will illuminate the check engine light and cause the engine to operate at idle only.

REMOVAL & INSTALLATION

▶ **See Figure 89**

The idle validation switch is not serviced separately. If the IDS is bad, replacement of the pedal and shaft assembly is required.

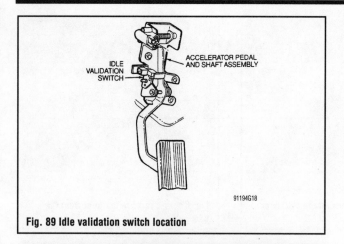

Fig. 89 Idle validation switch location

Engine Oil Temperature Sensor

OPERATION

The engine oil temperature (EOT) sensor changes resistance in response to the changing temperature of the engine oil. This sensor is located on the high pressure oil pump used to fire the fuel injectors on the 7.3L DIT diesel engine. The EOT sensor is a standard thermistor type sensor like an ECT or IAT. The EOT resistance decreases as the oil temperature increases providing the PCM with a signal relevant to the temperature of the engine oil.

TESTING

◆ **See Figure 90**

1. Turn the ignition switch **OFF**.
2. Disconnect the wiring harness from the EOT sensor.
3. Measure the resistance between the sensor terminals.
4. Compare the resistance reading with the accompanying chart.
5. If the resistance is not within specification, the EOT may be faulty.
6. Connect the wiring harness to the sensor.

Temperature		Engine Coolant/Intake Air Temperature Sensor Values
°F	°C	Resistance (K ohms)
248	120	1.18
230	110	1.55
212	100	2.07
194	90	2.80
176	80	3.84
158	70	5.37
140	60	7.70
122	50	10.97
104	40	16.15
86	30	24.27
68	20	37.30
50	10	58.75

Fig. 90 EOT resistance-to-temperature specifications

REMOVAL & INSTALLATION

◆ **See Figure 91**

1. Disconnect the negative battery cable.

➡**Approximately 1 quart of oil needs to be drained before the EOT sensor can be removed.**

2. Drain 1 quart of oil from the oil reservoir. This is easily accomplished using a vacuum hand pump and removing the oil from the high pressure oil pump reservoir.
3. Detach the EOT sensor connector.
4. Using a suitable tool, remove the sensor from the pump reservoir.
To install:
5. The installation is the reverse of the removal.
6. Add 1 quart of oil to the reservoir.

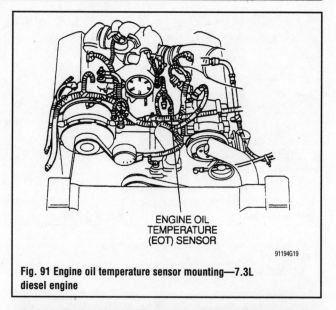

Fig. 91 Engine oil temperature sensor mounting—7.3L diesel engine

Exhaust Back Pressure Sensor

OPERATION

The exhaust back pressure (EBP) sensor is a variable capacitance sensor that when supplied with a 5-volt reference signal from the PCM, produces a linear analog voltage signal that indicates exhaust back pressure. The EBP sensor is the input to the PCM used to control the exhaust back pressure regulator.

REMOVAL & INSTALLATION

◆ **See Figure 92**

1. Disconnect the negative battery cable.
2. Detach the EBP sensor connector.
3. Using a suitable tool, remove the EBP sensor from the engine.
4. The installation is the reverse of the removal.

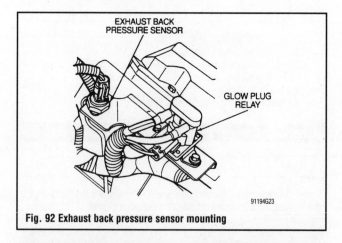

Fig. 92 Exhaust back pressure sensor mounting

Exhaust Back Pressure Regulator

OPERATION

The exhaust back pressure regulator (EPR) is a variable position valve that control the exhaust back pressure during cold ambient temperatures to decrease the amount of time required to bring the engine to normal operating temperature. The PCM measures the exhaust back pressure, ambient air temperature, and the engine oil temperature to determine the desired exhaust back pressure.

REMOVAL & INSTALLATION

▶ **See Figure 93**

1. Disconnect the negative battery cable.
2. Remove the turbocharger from the engine.
3. Remove the four EPR-to-turbocharger retaining screws and remove the EPR from the turbocharger.
4. The installation is the reverse of the removal.

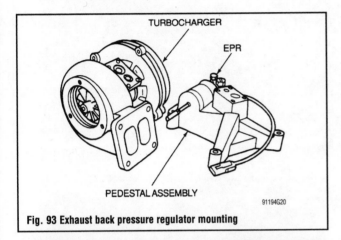

Fig. 93 Exhaust back pressure regulator mounting

Injection Control Pressure Sensor

OPERATION

The injection control pressure sensor (ICP) is a variable capacitance sensor that when supplied with a 5-volt reference signal from the PCM, produces a linear analog voltage signal that indicates oil pressure in the high pressure oil pump on the 7.3L DIT diesel engine. The ICP sensor provides a feedback signal to indicate high oil pressure so that the PCM can command the correct injector timing, pulse width and injection control pressure for proper fuel delivery at all speed and load conditions.

REMOVAL & INSTALLATION

▶ **See Figure 94**

1. Disconnect the negative battery cable.
2. Detach the ICP sensor connector.
3. Using a suitable tool, remove the ICP sensor from the engine.
4. The installation is the reverse of the removal.

Injection Pressure Regulator

OPERATION

The Injection Pressure Regulator (IPR) is a variable position valve that controls injection control pressure on the 7.3L DIT diesel engine. Battery voltage is supplied to the IPR when the ignition switch is in the **ON** position. The valve position is controlled by switching the output signal circuit to ground inside

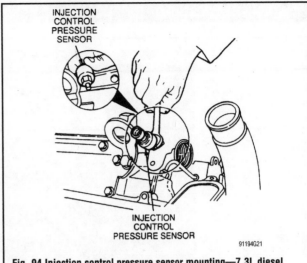

Fig. 94 Injection control pressure sensor mounting—7.3L diesel engine

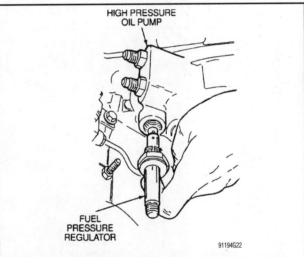

Fig. 95 Injection control pressure regulator mounting—7.3L diesel engine

the PCM. The injection control pressure is controlled by the PCM based on inputs received from the IAT, EOT, MAP/BARO, and accelerator pedal position sensors.

REMOVAL & INSTALLATION

▶ **See Figure 95**

1. Disconnect the negative battery cable.
2. Properly relieve the fuel system pressure.
3. Remove the fuel filter/fuel heater/water separator assembly.
4. Deatch the IPR connector.
5. Remove the solenoid retaining nut and remove the solenoid.
6. Remove the IPR from the high pressure oil pump assembly.
7. The installation is the reverse of the removal.

COMPONENT LOCATIONS

COMMON EMISSIONS AND ELECTRONIC ENGINE CONTROL COMPONENT LOCATIONS—4.2L ENGINE

1) PCV valve
2) Differential Pressure Feedback EGR (DPFE) sensor
3) Exhaust Gas Recirculation (EGR) valve
4) Throttle Position (TP) sensor
5) Idle Air Control (IAC) valve
6) Engine Coolant Temperature (ECT) sensor
7) Vapor management valve

9119AP74

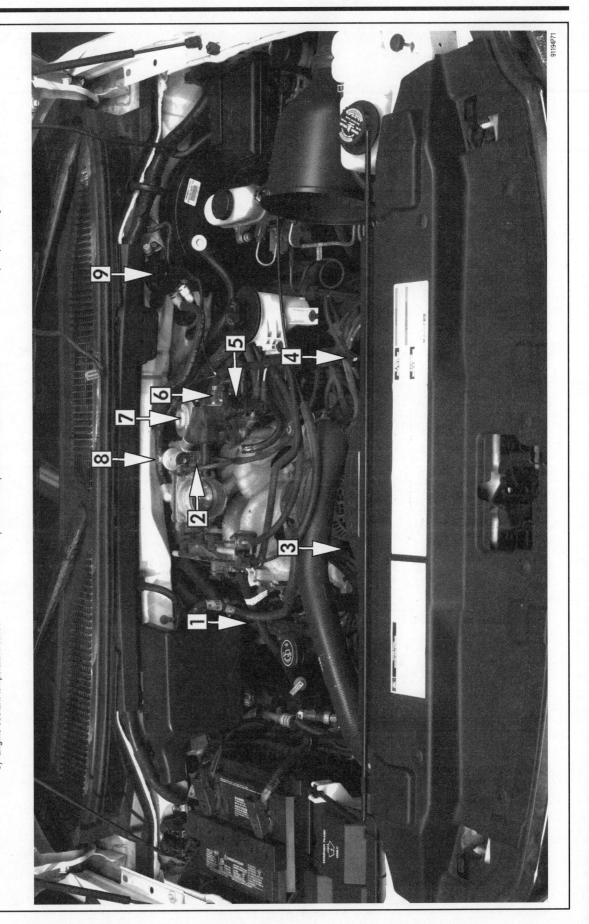

COMMON EMISSIONS AND ELECTRONIC ENGINE CONTROL COMPONENT LOCATIONS—4.6L ENGINE

1) PCV valve
2) Throttle position sensor
3) Engine coolant temperature sensor
4) Intake air temperature sensor connector
5) EGR vacuum control solenoid
6) Differential pressure feedback EGR sensor
7) Exhaust Gas Recirculation (EGR) valve
8) Idle air control valve
9) Vapor management valve

COMMON EMISSIONS AND ELECTRONIC ENGINE CONTROL COMPONENT LOCATIONS—5.4L DOHC ENGINE

1) PCV valve
2) Exhaust Gas Recirculation (EGR) valve (under balance tube)
3) Differential Pressure Feedback EGR (DPFE) sensor (under balance tube)
4) Engine Coolant Temperature (ECT) sensor
5) Throttle Position (TP) sensor
6) Idle Air Control (IAC) sensor
7) EGR vacuum control solenoid
8) Vapor management valve

COMMON EMISSIONS AND ELECTRONIC ENGINE CONTROL COMPONENT LOCATIONS—6.8L ENGINE

1) PCV valve
2) Vapor management valve
3) Idle Air Control (IAC) valve

4) Throttle Position (TP) sensor
5) Engine Coolant Temperature (ECT) sensor
6) Differential Pressure Feedback EGR (DPFE) sensor

7) Exhaust Gas Recirculation (EGR) valve
8) EGR vacuum control solenoid
9) Evaporative emissions canister

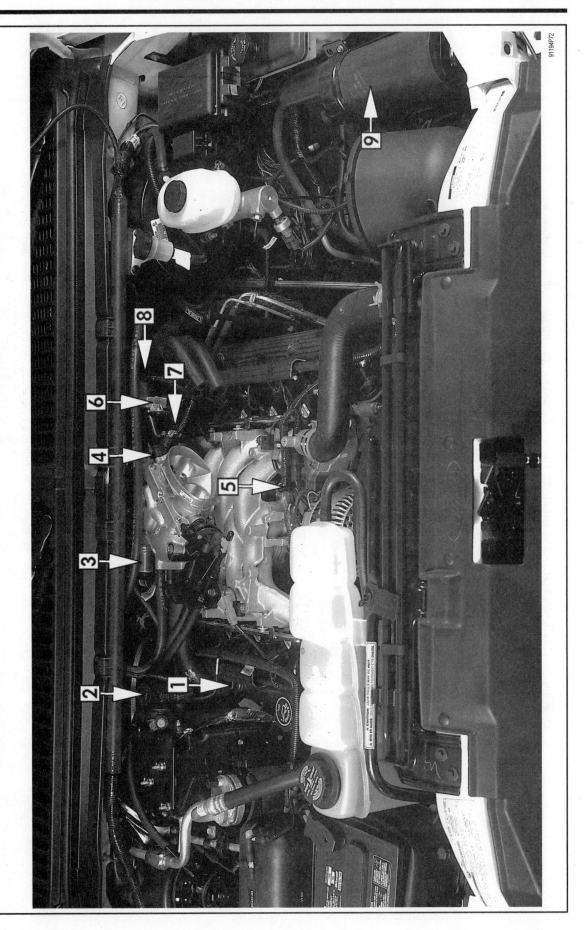

91194P72

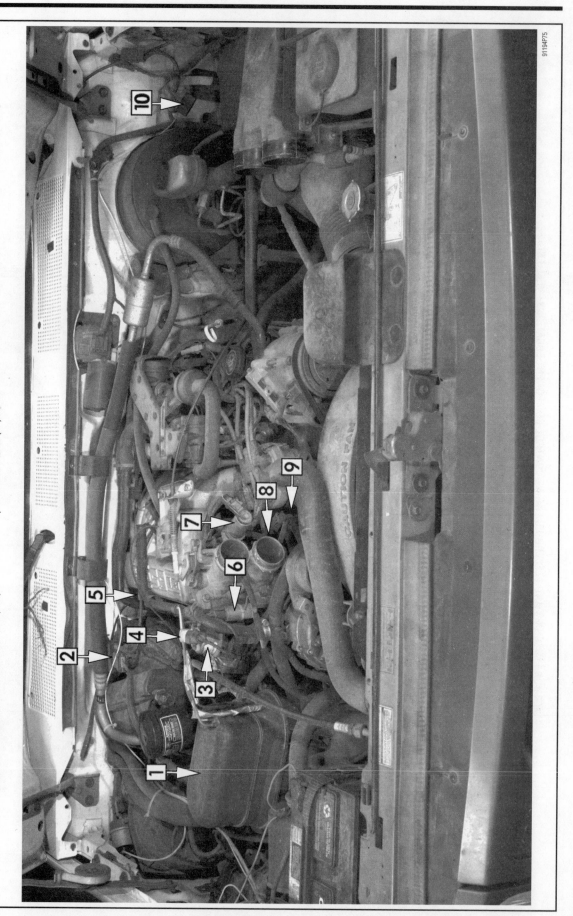

COMMON EMISSIONS AND ELECTRONIC ENGINE CONTROL COMPONENT LOCATIONS—5.8L/7.5L ENGINES

1) Evaporative emissions canister
2) Manifold Absolute Pressure (MAP) sensor
3) Exhaust Gas Recirculation (EGR) valve
4) Exhaust Gas Recirculation Valve Position sensor (EVP)
5) PCV valve (under upper intake manifold)
6) Evaporative emissions purge solenoid
7) Idle Air Control (IAC) sensor
8) Throttle Position (TP) sensor
9) Engine Coolant Temperature (ECT) sensor
   (in the front of lower intake manifold)
10) EEC-IV Data Link Connector (DLC)

COMMON EMISSIONS AND ELECTRONIC ENGINE CONTROL COMPONENT LOCATIONS—7.3L DIESEL ENGINE

1) Manifold Absolute Pressure (MAP) sensor
2) Engine oil temperature sensor (under cover)
3) Turbocharger
4) Exhaust backpressure regulator
5) High-pressure oil pump
6) Air filter restriction gauge

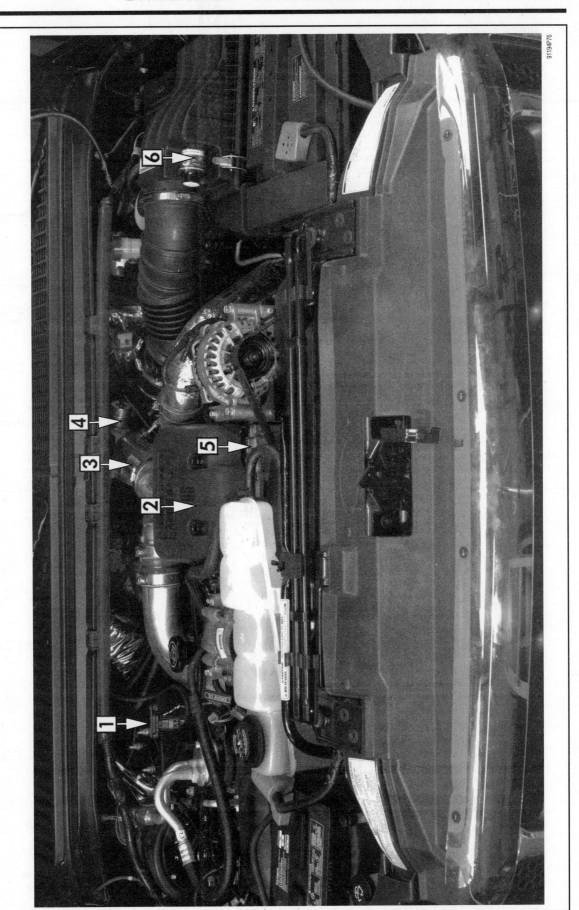

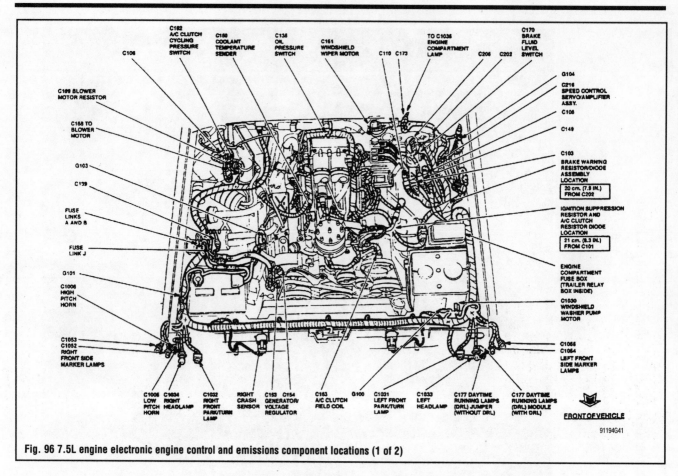

Fig. 96 7.5L engine electronic engine control and emissions component locations (1 of 2)

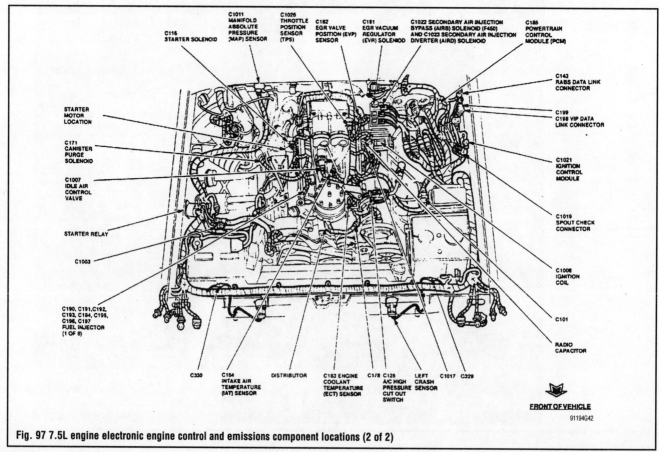

Fig. 97 7.5L engine electronic engine control and emissions component locations (2 of 2)

TROUBLE CODES—EEC-IV SYSTEM

General Information

The only vehicles covered by this manual equipped with the EEC-IV system are the F-250 HD, F-350 and F-Super Duty models equipped with the 5.8L or 7.5L gasoline engines.

One part of the Powertrain Control Module (PCM) is devoted to monitoring both input and output functions within the system. This ability forms the core of the self-diagnostic system. If a problem is detected within a circuit, the controller will recognize the fault, assign it an identification code, and store the code in a memory section. Depending on the year and model, the fault code(s) may be represented by two or three-digit numbers. The stored code(s) may be retrieved during diagnosis.

While the EEC-IV system is capable of recognizing many internal faults, certain faults will not be recognized. Because the computer system sees only electrical signals, it cannot sense or react to mechanical or vacuum faults affecting engine operation. Some of these faults may affect another component which will set a code. For example, the PCM monitors the output signal to the fuel injectors, but cannot detect a partially clogged injector. As long as the output driver responds correctly, the computer will read the system as functioning correctly. However, the improper flow of fuel may result in a lean mixture. This would, in turn, be detected by the oxygen sensor and noticed as a constantly lean signal by the PCM. Once the signal falls outside the pre-programmed limits, the engine control assembly would notice the fault and set an identification code.

FAILURE MODE EFFECTS MANAGEMENT (FMEM)

The PCM contains back-up programs which allow the engine to operate if a sensor signal is lost. If a sensor input is seen to be out of range—either high or low—the FMEM program is used. The processor substitutes a fixed value for the missing sensor signal. The engine will continue to operate, although performance and driveability may be noticeably reduced. This function of the con-troller is sometimes referred to as the limp-in or fail-safe mode. If the missing sensor signal is restored, the FMEM system immediately returns the system to normal operation. The dashboard warning lamp will be lit when FMEM is in effect.

HARDWARE LIMITED OPERATION STRATEGY (HLOS)

This mode is only used if the fault is too extreme for the FMEM circuit to handle. In this mode, the processor has ceased all computation and control; the entire system is run on fixed values. The vehicle may be operated but performance and driveability will be greatly reduced. The fixed or default settings provide minimal calibration, allowing the vehicle to be carefully driven in for service. The dashboard warning lamp will be lit when HLOS is engaged. Codes cannot be read while the system is operating in this mode.

Diagnostic Link Connector

➡Some of the vehicles covered by this manual utilize two Diagnostic Link Connectors (DLCs), both of which are in the same vicinity.

The Diagnostic Link Connector(s) (DLC) may be found in the following location:

• Under the hood near the firewall behind the driver's side strut tower.

The DLC is rectangular in design and capable of allowing access to 16 terminals. The connector has keying features that allow easy connection. The test equipment and the DLC have a latching feature to ensure a good mated connection.

HAND-HELD SCAN TOOLS

⧫ See Figures 98, 99, 100 and 101

Although stored codes may be read through the flashing of the CHECK ENGINE or SERVICE ENGINE SOON lamp, the use of hand-held scan tools such as Ford's Self-Test Automatic Readout (STAR) tester or the second generation SUPER STAR II tester or their equivalent is highly recommended. There are many manufacturers of these tools; the purchaser must be certain that the tool is proper for the intended use.

The scan tool allows any stored faults to be read from the engine controller memory. Use of the scan tool provides additional data during troubleshooting, but does not eliminate the use of the charts. The scan tool makes collecting information easier, but the data must be correctly interpreted by an operator familiar with the system.

ELECTRICAL TOOLS

The most commonly required electrical diagnostic tool is the digital multimeter, also known as a Digital Volt Ohmmeter (DVOM), which permits voltage, resistance (ohms) and amperage to be read by one instrument. Many of the diagnostic charts require the use of a volt or ohmmeter during diagnosis. The multimeter must be a high impedance unit, with 10 megaohms of

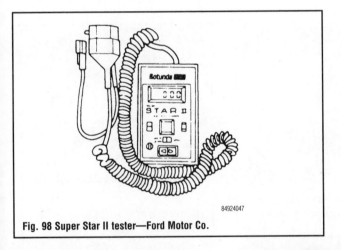

84924047

Fig. 98 Super Star II tester—Ford Motor Co.

TCCS4P11

Fig. 99 Inexpensive scan tools, such as this Auto Xray®, are available to interface with your Ford vehicle

91054P14

Fig. 100 An economically friendly alternative is this Code Scanner® from SunPro. They are purchased according to manufacturer and are available at many parts stores

91054P16

Fig. 101 The Code Scanner® from SunPro has no LCD display, just a LED that will flash out the codes and an audible buzzer to alert that the test is in progress

impedance in the voltmeter. This type of meter will not place an additional load on the circuit it is testing; this is extremely important in low voltage circuits. The multimeter must be of high quality in all respects. It should be handled carefully and protected from impact or damage. Replace the batteries frequently in the unit.

Additionally, an analog (needle type) voltmeter may be used to read stored fault codes if the STAR tester is not available. The codes are transmitted as visible needle sweeps on the face of the instrument.

Almost all diagnostic procedures will require the use of a Breakout Box, a device which connects into the EEC-IV harness and provides testing ports for the 60 wires in the harness. Direct testing of the harness connectors at the terminals or by backprobing is not recommended; damage to the wiring and terminals is almost certain to occur.

Other necessary tools include a quality tachometer with inductive (clip-on) pickup, a fuel pressure gauge with system adapters and a vacuum gauge with an auxiliary source of vacuum.

Reading Codes

Diagnosis of a driveability problem requires attention to detail and following the diagnostic procedures in the correct order. Resist the temptation to begin extensive testing before completing the preliminary diagnostic steps. The preliminary or visual inspection must be completed in detail before diagnosis begins. In many cases this will shorten diagnostic time and often cure the problem without electronic testing.

VISUAL INSPECTION

This is possibly the most critical step of diagnosis. A detailed examination of all connectors, wiring and vacuum hoses can often lead to a repair without further diagnosis. Performance of this step relies on the skill of the technician performing it; a careful inspector will check the undersides of hoses as well as the integrity of hard-to-reach hoses blocked by the air cleaner or other components. Wiring should be checked carefully for any sign of strain, burning, crimping or

terminal pull-out from a connector.

Checking connectors at components or in harnesses is required; usually, pushing them together will reveal a loose fit. Pay particular attention to ground circuits, making sure they are not loose or corroded. Remember to inspect connectors and hose fittings at components not mounted on the engine, such as the evaporative canister or relays mounted on the fender aprons. Any component or wiring in the vicinity of a fluid leak or spillage should be given extra attention during inspection.

Additionally, inspect maintenance items such as belt condition and tension, battery charge and condition and the radiator cap carefully. Any of these very simple items may affect the system enough to set a fault.

ELECTRONIC TESTING

If a code was set before a problem self-corrected (such as a momentarily loose connector), the code will be erased if the problem does not reoccur within 80 warm-up cycles. Codes will be output and displayed as numbers on the hand-held scan tool, such as 23. If the codes are being read on an analog voltmeter, the needle sweeps indicate the code digits. code 23 will appear as two needle pulses (sweeps) then, after a 1.6 second pause, the needle will pulse (sweep) three times.

Key On Engine Off (KOEO) Test

▶ See Figures 102 thru 108

1. Connect the scan tool to the self-test connectors. Make certain the test button is unlatched or up.
2. Start the engine and run it until normal operating temperature is reached.
3. Turn the engine **OFF** for 10 seconds.
4. Activate the test button on the STAR tester.
5. Turn the ignition switch **ON** but do not start the engine.
6. The KOEO codes will be transmitted. Six to nine seconds after the last KOEO code, a single separator pulse will be transmitted. Six to nine seconds after this pulse, the codes from the Continuous Memory will be transmitted.

Fig. 102 Connect the scan tool to the DLC connector

Fig. 103 The scan tool menu will be displayed, follow the instructions included with the scan tool

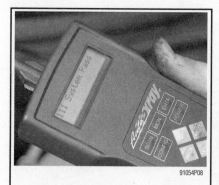

Fig. 104 This PCM had no DTC's stored and passed the KOEO

Fig. 105 This PCM had a DTC 113 stored. Most scan tools will give a code definition on-screen as the Auto X-ray shown here informs what code 113 is for the IAT sensor

Fig. 106 If the A/C or Blower motor is left on, a code 539 will be tripped. Turn the A/C or blower motor off and retest

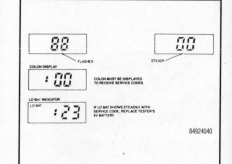

Fig. 107 STAR tester displays; note that the colon must be present before codes can be received

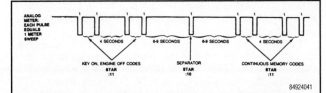

Fig. 108 Code transmission during KOEO test. Note that the continuous memory codes are transmitted after a pause and a separator pulse

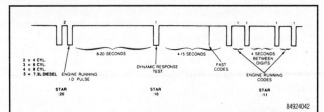

Fig. 109 Code transmission during KOER testing begins with the engine identification pulse and may include a dynamic response prompt

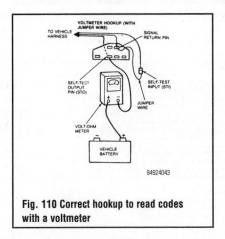

Fig. 110 Correct hookup to read codes with a voltmeter

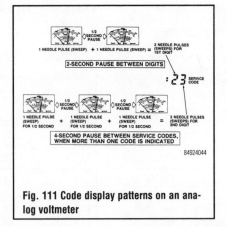

Fig. 111 Code display patterns on an analog voltmeter

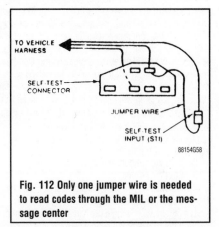

Fig. 112 Only one jumper wire is needed to read codes through the MIL or the message center

7. Record all service codes displayed. Do not depress the throttle on gasoline engines during the test.

Key On Engine Running (KOER) Test

▶ See Figures 98, 107 and 109

1. Make certain the self-test button is released or de-activated on the STAR tester.

2. Start the engine and run it at 2000 rpm for two minutes. This action warms up the oxygen sensor.

3. Turn the ignition switch **OFF** for 10 seconds.

4. Activate or latch the self-test button on the scan tool.

5. Start the engine. The engine identification code will be transmitted. This is a single digit number representing ½ the number of cylinders in a gasoline engine. On the STAR tester, this number may appear with a zero, such as 20 = 2. The code is used to confirm that the correct processor is installed and that the self-test has begun.

6. If the vehicle is equipped with a Brake On/Off (BOO) switch, the brake pedal must be depressed and released after the ID code is transmitted.

7. If the vehicle is equipped with a Power Steering Pressure Switch (PSPS), the steering wheel must be turned at least ½ turn and released within 2 seconds after the engine ID code is transmitted.

8. Certain Ford vehicles will display a Dynamic Response code 6–20 seconds after the engine ID code. This will appear as one pulse on a meter or as a 10 on the STAR tester. When this code appears, briefly take the engine to wide open throttle. This allows the system to test the throttle position, MAF and MAP sensors.

9. All relevant codes will be displayed and should be recorded. Remember that the codes refer only to faults present during this test cycle. Codes stored in Continuous Memory are not displayed in this test mode.

10. Do not depress the throttle during testing unless a dynamic response code is displayed.

Reading Codes With Analog Voltmeter

▶ See Figures 110 and 111

In the absence of a scan tool, an analog voltmeter may be used to retrieve stored fault codes. Set the meter range to read DC 0–15 volts. Connect the + lead of the meter to the battery positive terminal and connect the -; lead of the meter to the self-test output pin of the diagnostic connector.

Follow the directions given previously for performing the KOEO and KOER tests. To activate the tests, use a jumper wire to connect the signal return pin on the diagnostic connector to the self-test input connector. The self-test input line is the separate wire and connector with or near the diagnostic connector.

The codes will be transmitted as groups of needle sweeps. This method may be used to read either 2 or 3-digit codes. The Continuous Memory codes are separated from the KOEO codes by 6 seconds, a single sweep and another 6 second delay.

Malfunction Indicator Lamp Method

▶ See Figures 112 and 113

The Malfunction Indicator Lamp (MIL) on the dashboard may also be used to retrieve the stored codes. This method displays only the stored codes and does not allow any system investigation. It should only be used in field conditions where a quick check of stored codes is needed.

Follow the directions given previously for performing the scan tool procedure. To activate the tests, use a jumper wire to connect the signal return pin on the diagnostic connector to the Self-Test Input (STI) connector. The self-test input line is the separate wire and connector with or near the diagnostic connector.

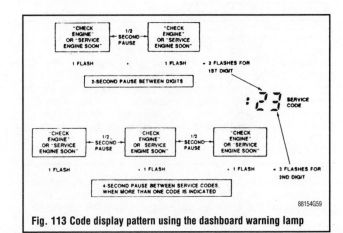

Fig. 113 Code display pattern using the dashboard warning lamp

Codes are transmitted by place value with a pause between the digits; for example, code 32 would be sent as 3 flashes, a pause and 2 flashes. A slightly longer pause divides codes from each other. Be ready to count and record codes; the only way to repeat a code is to recycle the system. This method may be used to read either 2 or 3-digit codes. The Continuous Memory codes are separated from the other codes by 6 seconds, a single flash and another 6 second delay.

Other Test Modes

CONTINUOUS MONITOR OR WIGGLE TEST

Once entered, this mode allows the operator to attempt to recreate intermittent faults by wiggling or tapping components, wiring or connectors. The test may be performed during either KOEO or KOER procedures. The test requires the use of either an analog voltmeter or a hand-held scan tool.

To enter the continuous monitor mode during KOEO testing, turn the ignition switch **ON**. Activate the test, wait 10 seconds, then deactivate and reactivate the test; the system will enter the continuous monitor mode. Tap, move or wiggle the harness, component or connector suspected of causing the problem; if a fault is detected, the code will store in the memory. When the fault occurs, the dash warning lamp will illuminate, the STAR tester will light a red indicator (and possibly beep) and the analog meter needle will sweep once.

To enter this mode in the KOER test:
1. Start the engine and run it at 2000 rpm for two minutes. This action warms up the oxygen sensor.
2. Turn the ignition switch **OFF** for 10 seconds.
3. Start the engine.
4. Activate the test, wait 10 seconds, then deactivate and reactivate the test; the system will enter the continuous monitor mode.
5. Tap, move or wiggle the harness, component or connector suspected of causing the problem; if a fault is detected, the code will store in the memory.
6. When the fault occurs, the dash warning lamp will illuminate, the STAR tester will light a red indicator (and possibly beep) and the analog meter needle will sweep once.

OUTPUT STATE CHECK

This testing mode allows the operator to energize and de-energize most of the outputs controlled by the EEC-IV system. Many of the outputs may be checked at the component by listening for a click or feeling the item move or engage by a hand placed on the case. To enter this check:
1. Enter the KOEO test mode.
2. When all codes have been transmitted, depress the accelerator all the way to the floor and release it.
3. The output actuators are now all ON. Depressing the throttle pedal to the floor again switches the all the actuator outputs OFF.
4. This test may be performed as often as necessary, switching between ON and OFF by depressing the throttle.
5. Exit the test by turning the ignition switch **OFF**, disconnecting the jumper at the diagnostic connector or releasing the test button on the scan tool.

Clearing Codes

CONTINUOUS MEMORY CODES

These codes are retained in memory for 40 warm-up cycles. To clear the codes for purposes of testing or confirming repair, perform the code reading procedure. When the fault codes begin to be displayed, de-activate the test either by disconnecting the jumper wire (if using a meter, MIL or message center) or by releasing the test button on the hand scanner. Stopping the test during code transmission will erase the Continuous Memory. Do not disconnect the negative battery cable to clear these codes; the Keep Alive memory will be cleared and a new code, 19, will be stored for loss of PCM power.

KEEP ALIVE MEMORY

The Keep Alive Memory (KAM) contains the adaptive factors used by the processor to compensate for component tolerances and wear. It should not be routinely cleared during diagnosis. If an emissions related part is replaced during repair, the KAM must be cleared. Failure to clear the KAM may cause severe driveability problems since the correction factor for the old component will be applied to the new component.

To clear the Keep Alive Memory, disconnect the negative battery cable for at least 5 minutes. After the memory is cleared and the battery reconnected, the vehicle must be driven at least 10 miles (16 km) so that the processor may relearn the needed correction factors. The distance to be driven depends on the engine and vehicle, but all drives should include steady-throttle cruise on open roads. Certain driveability problems may be noted during the drive because the adaptive factors are not yet functioning.

EEC-IV Diagnostic Trouble Codes

▶ **See Figures 114 and 115**

Diagnostic Trouble Code	Definitions
111	System pass
112	Intake Air Temp (IAT) sensor circuit below minimum voltage / 254°F indicated
113	Intake Air Temp (IAT) sensor circuit above maximum voltage / -40°F indicated
114	Intake Air Temp (IAT) sensor circuit voltage higher or lower than expected
116	Engine Coolant Temp (ECT) sensor circuit voltage higher or lower than expected
117	Engine Coolant Temp (ECT) sensor circuit below minimum voltage / 254°F indicated
118	Engine Coolant Temp (ECT) sensor circuit above maximum voltage / -40°F indicated
121	Closed throttle voltage higher or lower than expected
122	Throttle Position (TP) sensor circuit below minimum voltage
123	Throttle Position (TP) sensor circuit above maximum voltage
126	MAP sensor circuit voltage higher or lower than expected
128	MAP sensor vacuum hose damaged / disconnected
129	Insufficient MAP change during dynamic response test KOER
167	Insufficient throttle position change during dynamic response test KOER
171	Fuel system at adaptive limits
172	System indicates lean
173	System indicates rich
179	Fuel system at lean adaptive limit at part throttle, system rich
181	Fuel system at rich adaptive limit at part throttle, system lean
211	Profile Ignition Pickup (PIP) circuit failure
212	Loss of Ignition Diagnostic Monitor (IDM) input to PCM / SPOUT circuit grounded
213	SPOUT circuit open
312	Secondary Air Injection (AIR) misdirected during KOER
313	Secondary Air Injection (AIR) not bypassed during KOER
327	EGR (EVP) circuit below minimum voltage
328	EGR (EVP) closed valve voltage lower than expected
332	Insufficient EGR flow detected
334	EGR (EVP) closed valve voltage higher than expected
337	EGR (EVP) circuit above maximum voltage
411	Cannot control RPM during KOER low RPM check
412	Cannot control RPM during KOER high RPM check
452	Insufficient input from Vehicle Speed Sensor (VSS) to Powertrain Control Module (PCM)
511	PCM Read Only Memory (ROM) test failure KOEO
512	PCM Keep Alive Memory (KAM) test failure
513	PCM internal voltage failure (KOEO)
522	Vehicle not in PARK or NEUTRAL during KOEO (%)
536	Brake On / Off (BOO) circuit failure / not actuated during KOER
538	Insufficient RPM change during KOER dynamic response test
539	A/C or Defrost on during KOEO
542	Fuel pump circuit open—PCM to motor ground
543	Fuel pump circuit open—battery to Powertrain Control Module (PCM)
552	Secondary Air Injection Bypass (AIRB) circuit failure KOEO
553	Secondary Air Injection Diverter (AIRD) circuit failure KOEO
556	Fuel pump relay primary circuit failure

(Continued)

91194G06

Fig. 114 EEC-IV trouble codes for 1997–98 F-250HD, F-350 and F-Super Duty models equipped with the 5.8L or 7.5L engines (1 of 2)

Diagnostic Trouble Code	Definitions
558	EGR Vacuum Regulator (EVR) circuit failure
565	EVAP Canister Purge circuit failure KOEO
569	Auxiliary EVAP Canister Purge circuit failure
617	1-2 shift error
618	2-3 shift error
619	3-4 shift error
621	Shift Solenoid 1 (SS1) circuit failure KOEO
622	Shift Solenoid 2 (SS2) circuit failure KOEO
624	Electronic Pressure Control (EPC) circuit failure
625	Electronic Pressure Control (EPC) driver open in PCM
626	Coast Clutch Solenoid (CCS) circuit failure KOEO
628	Excessive converter clutch slippage
629	Torque Converter Clutch (TCC) solenoid circuit failure
631	Transmission Control Indicator Lamp (TCIL) circuit failure KOEO
632	Transmission Control Switch (TCS) circuit did not change states during KOER
633	4x4L (Low) switch closed during KOEO
634	Transmission Range (TR) voltage higher or lower than expected
636	Transmission Fluid Temp (TFT) higher or lower than expected
637	Transmission Fluid Temp (TFT) sensor circuit above maximum voltage / -40°F indicated
638	Transmission Fluid Temp (TFT) sensor circuit below minimum voltage / 290°F indicated
654	Transmission Range (TR) sensor indicating not in PARK during Self-Test
998	Hard fault present—FMEM MODE

91194G07

Fig. 115 EEC-IV trouble codes for 1997–98 F-250HD, F-350 and F-Super Duty models equipped with the 5.8L or 7.5L engines (2 of 2)

TROUBLE CODES—EEC-V SYSTEM

General Information

The Powertrain Control Module (PCM) is given responsibility for the operation of the emission control devices, cooling fans, ignition and advance and in some cases, automatic transmission functions. Because the EEC-V oversees both the ignition timing and the fuel injection operation, a precise air/fuel ratio will be maintained under all operating conditions. The PCM is a microprocessor or small computer which receives electrical inputs from several sensors, switches and relays on and around the engine.

Based on combinations of these inputs, the PCM controls various output devices concerned with engine operation and emissions. The control module relies on the signals to form a correct picture of current vehicle operation. If any of the input signals is incorrect, the PCM reacts to whatever picture is painted for it. For example, if the coolant temperature sensor is inaccurate and reads too low, the PCM may see a picture of the engine never warming up. Consequently, the engine settings will be maintained as if the engine were cold. Because so many inputs can affect one output, correct diagnostic procedures are essential on these systems.

One part of the PCM is devoted to monitoring both input and output functions within the system. This ability forms the core of the self-diagnostic system. If a problem is detected within a circuit, the control module will recognize the fault, assign it an Diagnostic Trouble Code (DTC), and store the code in memory. The stored code(s) may be retrieved during diagnosis.

While the EEC-V system is capable of recognizing many internal faults, certain faults will not be recognized. Because the control module sees only electrical signals, it cannot sense or react to mechanical or vacuum faults affecting engine operation. Some of these faults may affect another component which will set a code. For example, the PCM monitors the output signal to the fuel injectors, but cannot detect a partially clogged injector. As long as the output driver responds correctly, the computer will read the system as functioning correctly. However, the improper flow of fuel may result in a lean mixture. This would, in turn, be detected by the oxygen sensor and noticed as a constantly lean signal by the PCM. Once the signal falls outside the pre-programmed limits, the control module would notice the fault and set an trouble code.

Additionally, the EEC-V system employs adaptive fuel logic. This process is used to compensate for normal wear and variability within the fuel system. Once the engine enters steady-state operation, the control module watches the oxygen sensor signal for a bias or tendency to run slightly rich or lean. If such a bias is detected, the adaptive logic corrects the fuel delivery to bring the air/fuel mixture towards a centered or 14.7:1 ratio. This compensating shift is stored in a non-volatile memory which is retained by battery power even with the ignition switched **OFF**. The correction factor is then available the next time the vehicle is operated.

Malfunction Indicator Lamp

The Malfunction Indicator Lamp (MIL) is located on the instrument panel. The lamp is connected to the PCM and will alert the driver to certain malfunctions within the EEC-V system. When the lamp is illuminated, the PCM has detected a fault and stored an DTC in memory.

The light will stay illuminated as long as the fault is present. Should the fault self-correct, the MIL will extinguish but the stored code will remain in memory.

Under normal operating conditions, the MIL should illuminate briefly when the ignition key is turned **ON**. This is commonly known as a prove-out. As soon as the PCM receives a signal that the engine is cranking, the lamp should extinguish. The lamp should remain extinguished during the normal operating cycle.

Data Link Connector

♦ See Figure 116

The Data Link Connector (DLC) may be found in the following location:
• Under the driver's side dash , near the steering column.

The DLC is rectangular in design and capable of allowing access to 16 terminals. The connector has keying features that allow easy connection. The test equipment and the DLC have a latching feature to ensure a good mated connection.

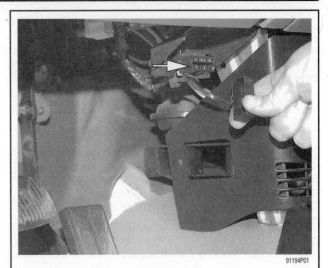

Fig. 116 Remove the cover to access the DLC

ELECTRICAL TOOLS

The most commonly required electrical diagnostic tool is the Digital Multimeter, allowing voltage, resistance, and amperage to be read by one instrument. Many of the diagnostic charts require the use of a volt or ohmmeter during diagnosis.

The multimeter must be a high impedance unit, with 10 megaohms of impedance in the voltmeter. This type of meter will not place an additional load on the circuit it is testing; this is extremely important in low voltage circuits. The multimeter must be of high quality in all respects. It should be handled carefully and protected from impact or damage. Replace the batteries frequently in the unit.

Reading Codes

♦ See Figure 117

The EEC-V equipped engines utilize On Board Diagnostic II (OBD-II) DTC's, which are alpha-numeric (they use letters and numbers). The letters in the OBD-

Fig. 117 When using a scan tool, make sure to follow all of the manufacturer's instructions carefully to ensure proper diagnosis

II DTC's make it highly difficult to convey the codes through the use of anything but a scan tool. Therefore, to read the codes on these vehicles it is necessary to utilize an OBD-II compatible scan tool.

Since each manufacturers scan tool is different, please follow the manufacturer's instructions for connecting the tool and obtaining code information.

Clearing Codes

CONTINUOUS MEMORY CODES

These codes are retained in memory for 40 warm-up cycles. To clear the codes for the purposes of testing or confirming repair, perform the code reading procedure. When the fault codes begin to be displayed, de-activate the test by either disconnecting the jumper wire (meter, MIL or message center) or releasing the test button on the hand scanner. Stopping the test during code transmission will erase the Continuous Memory. Do not disconnect the negative battery cable to clear these codes; the Keep Alive memory will be cleared and a new code, 19, will be stored for loss of PCM power.

KEEP ALIVE MEMORY

The Keep Alive Memory (KAM) contains the adaptive factors used by the processor to compensate for component tolerances and wear. It should not be routinely cleared during diagnosis. If an emissions related part is replaced during repair, the KAM must be cleared. Failure to clear the KAM may cause severe driveability problems since the correction factor for the old component will be applied to the new component.

To clear the Keep Alive Memory, disconnect the negative battery cable for at least 5 minutes. After the memory is cleared and the battery reconnected, the vehicle must be driven at least 10 miles so that the processor may relearn the needed correction factors. The distance to be driven depends on the engine and vehicle, but all drives should include steady-throttle cruise on open roads. Certain driveability problems may be noted during the drive because the adaptive factors are not yet functioning.

EEC-V Diagnostic Trouble Codes (DTC's)

GASOLINE ENGINES

P0000 No Failures
P0100 Mass or Volume Air Flow Circuit Malfunction
P0101 Mass or Volume Air Flow Circuit Range/Performance Problem
P0102 Mass or Volume Air Flow Circuit Low Input
P0103 Mass or Volume Air Flow Circuit High Input
P0104 Mass or Volume Air Flow Circuit Intermittent
P0105 Manifold Absolute Pressure/Barometric Pressure Circuit Malfunction
P0106 Manifold Absolute Pressure/Barometric Pressure Circuit Range/Performance Problem
P0107 Manifold Absolute Pressure/Barometric Pressure Circuit Low Input
P0108 Manifold Absolute Pressure/Barometric Pressure Circuit High Input
P0109 Manifold Absolute Pressure/Barometric Pressure Circuit Intermittent
P0110 Intake Air Temperature Circuit Malfunction
P0111 Intake Air Temperature Circuit Range/Performance Problem
P0112 Intake Air Temperature Circuit Low Input
P0113 Intake Air Temperature Circuit High Input
P0114 Intake Air Temperature Circuit Intermittent
P0115 Engine Coolant Temperature Circuit Malfunction
P0116 Engine Coolant Temperature Circuit Range/Performance Problem
P0117 Engine Coolant Temperature Circuit Low Input
P0118 Engine Coolant Temperature Circuit High Input
P0119 Engine Coolant Temperature Circuit Intermittent
P0120 Throttle/Pedal Position Sensor/Switch "A" Circuit Malfunction
P0121 Throttle/Pedal Position Sensor/Switch "A" Circuit Range/Performance Problem
P0122 Throttle/Pedal Position Sensor/Switch "A" Circuit Low Input
P0123 Throttle/Pedal Position Sensor/Switch "A" Circuit High Input
P0124 Throttle/Pedal Position Sensor/Switch "A" Circuit Intermittent

P0125 Insufficient Coolant Temperature For Closed Loop Fuel Control
P0126 Insufficient Coolant Temperature For Stable Operation
P0130 O2 Circuit Malfunction (Bank no. 1 Sensor no. 1)
P0131 O2 Sensor Circuit Low Voltage (Bank no. 1 Sensor no. 1)
P0132 O2 Sensor Circuit High Voltage (Bank no. 1 Sensor no. 1)
P0133 O2 Sensor Circuit Slow Response (Bank no. 1 Sensor no. 1)
P0134 O2 Sensor Circuit No Activity Detected (Bank no. 1 Sensor no. 1)
P0135 O2 Sensor Heater Circuit Malfunction (Bank no. 1 Sensor no. 1)
P0136 O2 Sensor Circuit Malfunction (Bank no. 1 Sensor no. 2)
P0137 O2 Sensor Circuit Low Voltage (Bank no. 1 Sensor no. 2)
P0138 O2 Sensor Circuit High Voltage (Bank no. 1 Sensor no. 2)
P0139 O2 Sensor Circuit Slow Response (Bank no. 1 Sensor no. 2)
P0140 O2 Sensor Circuit No Activity Detected (Bank no. 1 Sensor no. 2)
P0141 O2 Sensor Heater Circuit Malfunction (Bank no. 1 Sensor no. 2)
P0142 O2 Sensor Circuit Malfunction (Bank no. 1 Sensor no. 3)
P0143 O2 Sensor Circuit Low Voltage (Bank no. 1 Sensor no. 3)
P0144 O2 Sensor Circuit High Voltage (Bank no. 1 Sensor no. 3)
P0145 O2 Sensor Circuit Slow Response (Bank no. 1 Sensor no. 3)
P0146 O2 Sensor Circuit No Activity Detected (Bank no. 1 Sensor no. 3)
P0147 O2 Sensor Heater Circuit Malfunction (Bank no. 1 Sensor no. 3)
P0150 O2 Sensor Circuit Malfunction (Bank no. 2 Sensor no. 1)
P0151 O2 Sensor Circuit Low Voltage (Bank no. 2 Sensor no. 1)
P0152 O2 Sensor Circuit High Voltage (Bank no. 2 Sensor no. 1)
P0153 O2 Sensor Circuit Slow Response (Bank no. 2 Sensor no. 1)
P0154 O2 Sensor Circuit No Activity Detected (Bank no. 2 Sensor no. 1)
P0155 O2 Sensor Heater Circuit Malfunction (Bank no. 2 Sensor no. 1)
P0156 O2 Sensor Circuit Malfunction (Bank no. 2 Sensor no. 2)
P0157 O2 Sensor Circuit Low Voltage (Bank no. 2 Sensor no. 2)
P0158 O2 Sensor Circuit High Voltage (Bank no. 2 Sensor no. 2)
P0159 O2 Sensor Circuit Slow Response (Bank no. 2 Sensor no. 2)
P0160 O2 Sensor Circuit No Activity Detected (Bank no. 2 Sensor no. 2)
P0161 O2 Sensor Heater Circuit Malfunction (Bank no. 2 Sensor no. 2)
P0162 O2 Sensor Circuit Malfunction (Bank no. 2 Sensor no. 3)
P0163 O2 Sensor Circuit Low Voltage (Bank no. 2 Sensor no. 3)
P0164 O2 Sensor Circuit High Voltage (Bank no. 2 Sensor no. 3)
P0165 O2 Sensor Circuit Slow Response (Bank no. 2 Sensor no. 3)
P0166 O2 Sensor Circuit No Activity Detected (Bank no. 2 Sensor no. 3)
P0167 O2 Sensor Heater Circuit Malfunction (Bank no. 2 Sensor no. 3)
P0170 Fuel Trim Malfunction (Bank no. 1)
P0171 System Too Lean (Bank no. 1)
P0172 System Too Rich (Bank no. 1)
P0173 Fuel Trim Malfunction (Bank no. 2)
P0174 System Too Lean (Bank no. 2)
P0175 System Too Rich (Bank no. 2)
P0176 Fuel Composition Sensor Circuit Malfunction
P0177 Fuel Composition Sensor Circuit Range/Performance
P0178 Fuel Composition Sensor Circuit Low Input
P0179 Fuel Composition Sensor Circuit High Input
P0180 Fuel Temperature Sensor "A" Circuit Malfunction
P0181 Fuel Temperature Sensor "A" Circuit Range/Performance
P0182 Fuel Temperature Sensor "A" Circuit Low Input
P0183 Fuel Temperature Sensor "A" Circuit High Input
P0184 Fuel Temperature Sensor "A" Circuit Intermittent
P0185 Fuel Temperature Sensor "B" Circuit Malfunction
P0186 Fuel Temperature Sensor "B" Circuit Range/Performance
P0187 Fuel Temperature Sensor "B" Circuit Low Input
P0188 Fuel Temperature Sensor "B" Circuit High Input
P0189 Fuel Temperature Sensor "B" Circuit Intermittent
P0190 Fuel Rail Pressure Sensor Circuit Malfunction
P0191 Fuel Rail Pressure Sensor Circuit Range/Performance
P0192 Fuel Rail Pressure Sensor Circuit Low Input
P0193 Fuel Rail Pressure Sensor Circuit High Input
P0194 Fuel Rail Pressure Sensor Circuit Intermittent
P0195 Engine Oil Temperature Sensor Malfunction
P0196 Engine Oil Temperature Sensor Range/Performance
P0197 Engine Oil Temperature Sensor Low
P0198 Engine Oil Temperature Sensor High
P0199 Engine Oil Temperature Sensor Intermittent
P0200 Injector Circuit Malfunction
P0201 Injector Circuit Malfunction—Cylinder no. 1

P0202 Injector Circuit Malfunction—Cylinder no. 2
P0203 Injector Circuit Malfunction—Cylinder no. 3
P0204 Injector Circuit Malfunction—Cylinder no. 4
P0205 Injector Circuit Malfunction—Cylinder no. 5
P0206 Injector Circuit Malfunction—Cylinder no. 6
P0207 Injector Circuit Malfunction—Cylinder no. 7
P0208 Injector Circuit Malfunction—Cylinder no. 8
P0209 Injector Circuit Malfunction—Cylinder no. 9
P0210 Injector Circuit Malfunction—Cylinder no. 10
P0211 Injector Circuit Malfunction—Cylinder no. 11
P0212 Injector Circuit Malfunction—Cylinder no. 12
P0213 Cold Start Injector no. 1 Malfunction
P0214 Cold Start Injector no. 2 Malfunction
P0215 Engine Shutoff Solenoid Malfunction
P0216 Injection Timing Control Circuit Malfunction
P0217 Engine Over Temperature Condition
P0218 Transmission Over Temperature Condition
P0219 Engine Over Speed Condition
P0220 Throttle/Pedal Position Sensor/Switch "B" Circuit Malfunction
P0221 Throttle/Pedal Position Sensor/Switch "B" Circuit Range/Performance Problem
P0222 Throttle/Pedal Position Sensor/Switch "B" Circuit Low Input
P0223 Throttle/Pedal Position Sensor/Switch "B" Circuit High Input
P0224 Throttle/Pedal Position Sensor/Switch "B" Circuit Intermittent
P0225 Throttle/Pedal Position Sensor/Switch "C" Circuit Malfunction
P0226 Throttle/Pedal Position Sensor/Switch "C" Circuit Range/Performance Problem
P0227 Throttle/Pedal Position Sensor/Switch "C" Circuit Low Input
P0228 Throttle/Pedal Position Sensor/Switch "C" Circuit High Input
P0229 Throttle/Pedal Position Sensor/Switch "C" Circuit Intermittent
P0230 Fuel Pump Primary Circuit Malfunction
P0231 Fuel Pump Secondary Circuit Low
P0232 Fuel Pump Secondary Circuit High
P0233 Fuel Pump Secondary Circuit Intermittent
P0234 Engine Over Boost Condition
P0261 Cylinder no. 1 Injector Circuit Low
P0262 Cylinder no. 1 Injector Circuit High
P0263 Cylinder no. 1 Contribution/Balance Fault
P0264 Cylinder no. 2 Injector Circuit Low
P0265 Cylinder no. 2 Injector Circuit High
P0266 Cylinder no. 2 Contribution/Balance Fault
P0267 Cylinder no. 3 Injector Circuit Low
P0268 Cylinder no. 3 Injector Circuit High
P0269 Cylinder no. 3 Contribution/Balance Fault
P0270 Cylinder no. 4 Injector Circuit Low
P0271 Cylinder no. 4 Injector Circuit High
P0272 Cylinder no. 4 Contribution/Balance Fault
P0273 Cylinder no. 5 Injector Circuit Low
P0274 Cylinder no. 5 Injector Circuit High
P0275 Cylinder no. 5 Contribution/Balance Fault
P0276 Cylinder no. 6 Injector Circuit Low
P0277 Cylinder no. 6 Injector Circuit High
P0278 Cylinder no. 6 Contribution/Balance Fault
P0279 Cylinder no. 7 Injector Circuit Low
P0280 Cylinder no. 7 Injector Circuit High
P0281 Cylinder no. 7 Contribution/Balance Fault
P0282 Cylinder no. 8 Injector Circuit Low
P0283 Cylinder no. 8 Injector Circuit High
P0284 Cylinder no. 8 Contribution/Balance Fault
P0285 Cylinder no. 9 Injector Circuit Low
P0286 Cylinder no. 9 Injector Circuit High
P0287 Cylinder no. 9 Contribution/Balance Fault
P0288 Cylinder no. 10 Injector Circuit Low
P0289 Cylinder no. 10 Injector Circuit High
P0290 Cylinder no. 10 Contribution/Balance Fault
P0291 Cylinder no. 11 Injector Circuit Low
P0292 Cylinder no. 11 Injector Circuit High
P0293 Cylinder no. 11 Contribution/Balance Fault
P0294 Cylinder no. 12 Injector Circuit Low
P0295 Cylinder no. 12 Injector Circuit High

P0296 Cylinder no. 12 Contribution/Balance Fault
P0300 Random/Multiple Cylinder Misfire Detected
P0301 Cylinder no. 1—Misfire Detected
P0302 Cylinder no. 2—Misfire Detected
P0303 Cylinder no. 3—Misfire Detected
P0304 Cylinder no. 4—Misfire Detected
P0305 Cylinder no. 5—Misfire Detected
P0306 Cylinder no. 6—Misfire Detected
P0307 Cylinder no. 7—Misfire Detected
P0308 Cylinder no. 8—Misfire Detected
P0309 Cylinder no. 9—Misfire Detected
P0310 Cylinder no. 10—Misfire Detected
P0311 Cylinder no. 11—Misfire Detected
P0312 Cylinder no. 12—Misfire Detected
P0320 Ignition/Distributor Engine Speed Input Circuit Malfunction
P0321 Ignition/Distributor Engine Speed Input Circuit Range/Performance
P0322 Ignition/Distributor Engine Speed Input Circuit No Signal
P0323 Ignition/Distributor Engine Speed Input Circuit Intermittent
P0325 Knock Sensor no. 1—Circuit Malfunction (Bank no. 1 or Single Sensor)
P0326 Knock Sensor no. 1—Circuit Range/Performance (Bank no. 1 or Single Sensor)
P0327 Knock Sensor no. 1—Circuit Low Input (Bank no. 1 or Single Sensor)
P0328 Knock Sensor no. 1—Circuit High Input (Bank no. 1 or Single Sensor)
P0329 Knock Sensor no. 1—Circuit Input Intermittent (Bank no. 1 or Single Sensor)
P0330 Knock Sensor no. 2—Circuit Malfunction (Bank no. 2)
P0331 Knock Sensor no. 2—Circuit Range/Performance (Bank no. 2)
P0332 Knock Sensor no. 2—Circuit Low Input (Bank no. 2)
P0333 Knock Sensor no. 2—Circuit High Input (Bank no. 2)
P0334 Knock Sensor no. 2—Circuit Input Intermittent (Bank no. 2)
P0335 Crankshaft Position Sensor "A" Circuit Malfunction
P0336 Crankshaft Position Sensor "A" Circuit Range/Performance
P0337 Crankshaft Position Sensor "A" Circuit Low Input
P0338 Crankshaft Position Sensor "A" Circuit High Input
P0339 Crankshaft Position Sensor "A" Circuit Intermittent
P0340 Camshaft Position Sensor Circuit Malfunction
P0341 Camshaft Position Sensor Circuit Range/Performance
P0342 Camshaft Position Sensor Circuit Low Input
P0343 Camshaft Position Sensor Circuit High Input
P0344 Camshaft Position Sensor Circuit Intermittent
P0350 Ignition Coil Primary/Secondary Circuit Malfunction
P0351 Ignition Coil "A" Primary/Secondary Circuit Malfunction
P0352 Ignition Coil "B" Primary/Secondary Circuit Malfunction
P0353 Ignition Coil "C" Primary/Secondary Circuit Malfunction
P0354 Ignition Coil "D" Primary/Secondary Circuit Malfunction
P0355 Ignition Coil "E" Primary/Secondary Circuit Malfunction
P0356 Ignition Coil "F" Primary/Secondary Circuit Malfunction
P0357 Ignition Coil "G" Primary/Secondary Circuit Malfunction
P0358 Ignition Coil "H" Primary/Secondary Circuit Malfunction
P0359 Ignition Coil "I" Primary/Secondary Circuit Malfunction
P0360 Ignition Coil "J" Primary/Secondary Circuit Malfunction
P0361 Ignition Coil "K" Primary/Secondary Circuit Malfunction
P0362 Ignition Coil "L" Primary/Secondary Circuit Malfunction
P0370 Timing Reference High Resolution Signal "A" Malfunction
P0371 Timing Reference High Resolution Signal "A" Too Many Pulses
P0372 Timing Reference High Resolution Signal "A" Too Few Pulses
P0373 Timing Reference High Resolution Signal "A" Intermittent/Erratic Pulses
P0374 Timing Reference High Resolution Signal "A" No Pulses
P0375 Timing Reference High Resolution Signal "B" Malfunction
P0376 Timing Reference High Resolution Signal "B" Too Many Pulses
P0377 Timing Reference High Resolution Signal "B" Too Few Pulses
P0378 Timing Reference High Resolution Signal "B" Intermittent/Erratic Pulses
P0379 Timing Reference High Resolution Signal "B" No Pulses
P0380 Glow Plug/Heater Circuit "A" Malfunction
P0381 Glow Plug/Heater Indicator Circuit Malfunction

P0382 Glow Plug/Heater Circuit "B" Malfunction
P0385 Crankshaft Position Sensor "B" Circuit Malfunction
P0386 Crankshaft Position Sensor "B" Circuit Range/Performance
P0387 Crankshaft Position Sensor "B" Circuit Low Input
P0388 Crankshaft Position Sensor "B" Circuit High Input
P0389 Crankshaft Position Sensor "B" Circuit Intermittent
P0400 Exhaust Gas Recirculation Flow Malfunction
P0401 Exhaust Gas Recirculation Flow Insufficient Detected
P0402 Exhaust Gas Recirculation Flow Excessive Detected
P0403 Exhaust Gas Recirculation Circuit Malfunction
P0404 Exhaust Gas Recirculation Circuit Range/Performance
P0405 Exhaust Gas Recirculation Sensor "A" Circuit Low
P0406 Exhaust Gas Recirculation Sensor "A" Circuit High
P0407 Exhaust Gas Recirculation Sensor "B" Circuit Low
P0408 Exhaust Gas Recirculation Sensor "B" Circuit High
P0410 Secondary Air Injection System Malfunction
P0411 Secondary Air Injection System Incorrect Flow Detected
P0412 Secondary Air Injection System Switching Valve "A" Circuit Malfunction
P0413 Secondary Air Injection System Switching Valve "A" Circuit Open
P0414 Secondary Air Injection System Switching Valve "A" Circuit Shorted
P0415 Secondary Air Injection System Switching Valve "B" Circuit Malfunction
P0416 Secondary Air Injection System Switching Valve "B" Circuit Open
P0417 Secondary Air Injection System Switching Valve "B" Circuit Shorted
P0418 Secondary Air Injection System Relay "A" Circuit Malfunction
P0419 Secondary Air Injection System Relay "B" Circuit Malfunction
P0420 Catalyst System Efficiency Below Threshold (Bank no. 1)
P0421 Warm Up Catalyst Efficiency Below Threshold (Bank no. 1)
P0422 Main Catalyst Efficiency Below Threshold (Bank no. 1)
P0423 Heated Catalyst Efficiency Below Threshold (Bank no. 1)
P0424 Heated Catalyst Temperature Below Threshold (Bank no. 1)
P0430 Catalyst System Efficiency Below Threshold (Bank no. 2)
P0431 Warm Up Catalyst Efficiency Below Threshold (Bank no. 2)
P0432 Main Catalyst Efficiency Below Threshold (Bank no. 2)
P0433 Heated Catalyst Efficiency Below Threshold (Bank no. 2)
P0434 Heated Catalyst Temperature Below Threshold (Bank no. 2)
P0440 Evaporative Emission Control System Malfunction
P0441 Evaporative Emission Control System Incorrect Purge Flow
P0442 Evaporative Emission Control System Leak Detected (Small Leak)
P0443 Evaporative Emission Control System Purge Control Valve Circuit Malfunction
P0444 Evaporative Emission Control System Purge Control Valve Circuit Open
P0445 Evaporative Emission Control System Purge Control Valve Circuit Shorted
P0446 Evaporative Emission Control System Vent Control Circuit   Malfunction
P0447 Evaporative Emission Control System Vent Control Circuit Open
P0448 Evaporative Emission Control System Vent Control Circuit Shorted
P0449 Evaporative Emission Control System Vent Valve/Solenoid Circuit Malfunction
P0450 Evaporative Emission Control System Pressure Sensor Malfunction
P0451 Evaporative Emission Control System Pressure Sensor Range/Performance
P0452 Evaporative Emission Control System Pressure Sensor Low Input
P0453 Evaporative Emission Control System Pressure Sensor High Input
P0454 Evaporative Emission Control System Pressure Sensor Intermittent
P0455 Evaporative Emission Control System Leak Detected (Gross Leak)
P0460 Fuel Level Sensor Circuit Malfunction
P0461 Fuel Level Sensor Circuit Range/Performance
P0462 Fuel Level Sensor Circuit Low Input
P0463 Fuel Level Sensor Circuit High Input
P0464 Fuel Level Sensor Circuit Intermittent
P0465 Purge Flow Sensor Circuit Malfunction
P0466 Purge Flow Sensor Circuit Range/Performance
P0467 Purge Flow Sensor Circuit Low Input

P0468 Purge Flow Sensor Circuit High Input
P0469 Purge Flow Sensor Circuit Intermittent
P0470 Exhaust Pressure Sensor Malfunction
P0471 Exhaust Pressure Sensor Range/Performance
P0472 Exhaust Pressure Sensor Low
P0473 Exhaust Pressure Sensor High
P0474 Exhaust Pressure Sensor Intermittent
P0475 Exhaust Pressure Control Valve Malfunction
P0476 Exhaust Pressure Control Valve Range/Performance
P0477 Exhaust Pressure Control Valve Low
P0478 Exhaust Pressure Control Valve High
P0479 Exhaust Pressure Control Valve Intermittent
P0480 Cooling Fan no. 1 Control Circuit Malfunction
P0481 Cooling Fan no. 2 Control Circuit Malfunction
P0482 Cooling Fan no. 3 Control Circuit Malfunction
P0483 Cooling Fan Rationality Check Malfunction
P0484 Cooling Fan Circuit Over Current
P0485 Cooling Fan Power/Ground Circuit Malfunction
P0500 Vehicle Speed Sensor Malfunction
P0501 Vehicle Speed Sensor Range/Performance
P0502 Vehicle Speed Sensor Circuit Low Input
P0503 Vehicle Speed Sensor Intermittent/Erratic/High
P0505 Idle Control System Malfunction
P0506 Idle Control System RPM Lower Than Expected
P0507 Idle Control System RPM Higher Than Expected
P0510 Closed Throttle Position Switch Malfunction
P0520 Engine Oil Pressure Sensor/Switch Circuit Malfunction
P0521 Engine Oil Pressure Sensor/Switch Range/Performance
P0522 Engine Oil Pressure Sensor/Switch Low Voltage
P0523 Engine Oil Pressure Sensor/Switch High Voltage
P0530 A/C Refrigerant Pressure Sensor Circuit Malfunction
P0531 A/C Refrigerant Pressure Sensor Circuit Range/Performance
P0532 A/C Refrigerant Pressure Sensor Circuit Low Input
P0533 A/C Refrigerant Pressure Sensor Circuit High Input
P0534 A/C Refrigerant Charge Loss
P0550 Power Steering Pressure Sensor Circuit Malfunction
P0551 Power Steering Pressure Sensor Circuit Range/Performance
P0552 Power Steering Pressure Sensor Circuit Low Input
P0553 Power Steering Pressure Sensor Circuit High Input
P0554 Power Steering Pressure Sensor Circuit Intermittent
P0560 System Voltage Malfunction
P0561 System Voltage Unstable
P0562 System Voltage Low
P0563 System Voltage High
P0565 Cruise Control On Signal Malfunction
P0566 Cruise Control Off Signal Malfunction
P0567 Cruise Control Resume Signal Malfunction
P0568 Cruise Control Set Signal Malfunction
P0569 Cruise Control Coast Signal Malfunction
P0570 Cruise Control Accel Signal Malfunction
P0571 Cruise Control/Brake Switch "A" Circuit Malfunction
P0572 Cruise Control/Brake Switch "A" Circuit Low
P0573 Cruise Control/Brake Switch "A" Circuit High
P0574 **Through P0580** Reserved for Cruise Codes
P0600 Serial Communication Link Malfunction
P0601 Internal Control Module Memory Check Sum Error
P0602 Control Module Programming Error
P0603 Internal Control Module Keep Alive Memory (KAM) Error
P0604 Internal Control Module Random Access Memory (RAM) Error
P0605 Internal Control Module Read Only Memory (ROM) Error
P0606 PCM Processor Fault
P0608 Control Module VSS Output "A" Malfunction
P0609 Control Module VSS Output "B" Malfunction
P0620 Generator Control Circuit Malfunction
P0621 Generator Lamp "L" Control Circuit Malfunction
P0622 Generator Field "F" Control Circuit Malfunction
P0650 Malfunction Indicator Lamp (MIL) Control Circuit Malfunction
P0654 Engine RPM Output Circuit Malfunction
P0655 Engine Hot Lamp Output Control Circuit Malfunction
P0656 Fuel Level Output Circuit Malfunction

P0700 Transmission Control System Malfunction
P0701 Transmission Control System Range/Performance
P0702 Transmission Control System Electrical
P0703 Torque Converter/Brake Switch "B" Circuit Malfunction
P0704 Clutch Switch Input Circuit Malfunction
P0705 Transmission Range Sensor Circuit Malfunction (PRNDL Input)
P0706 Transmission Range Sensor Circuit Range/Performance
P0707 Transmission Range Sensor Circuit Low Input
P0708 Transmission Range Sensor Circuit High Input
P0709 Transmission Range Sensor Circuit Intermittent
P0710 Transmission Fluid Temperature Sensor Circuit Malfunction
P0711 Transmission Fluid Temperature Sensor Circuit Range/Performance
P0712 Transmission Fluid Temperature Sensor Circuit Low Input
P0713 Transmission Fluid Temperature Sensor Circuit High Input
P0714 Transmission Fluid Temperature Sensor Circuit Intermittent
P0715 Input/Turbine Speed Sensor Circuit Malfunction
P0716 Input/Turbine Speed Sensor Circuit Range/Performance
P0717 Input/Turbine Speed Sensor Circuit No Signal
P0718 Input/Turbine Speed Sensor Circuit Intermittent
P0719 Torque Converter/Brake Switch "B" Circuit Low
P0720 Output Speed Sensor Circuit Malfunction
P0721 Output Speed Sensor Circuit Range/Performance
P0722 Output Speed Sensor Circuit No Signal
P0723 Output Speed Sensor Circuit Intermittent
P0724 Torque Converter/Brake Switch "B" Circuit High
P0725 Engine Speed Input Circuit Malfunction
P0726 Engine Speed Input Circuit Range/Performance
P0727 Engine Speed Input Circuit No Signal
P0728 Engine Speed Input Circuit Intermittent
P0730 Incorrect Gear Ratio
P0731 Gear no. 1 Incorrect Ratio
P0732 Gear no. 2 Incorrect Ratio
P0733 Gear no. 3 Incorrect Ratio
P0734 Gear no. 4 Incorrect Ratio
P0735 Gear no. 5 Incorrect Ratio
P0736 Reverse Incorrect Ratio
P0740 Torque Converter Clutch Circuit Malfunction
P0741 Torque Converter Clutch Circuit Performance or Stuck Off
P0742 Torque Converter Clutch Circuit Stuck On
P0743 Torque Converter Clutch Circuit Electrical
P0744 Torque Converter Clutch Circuit Intermittent
P0745 Pressure Control Solenoid Malfunction
P0746 Pressure Control Solenoid Performance or Stuck Off
P0747 Pressure Control Solenoid Stuck On
P0748 Pressure Control Solenoid Electrical
P0749 Pressure Control Solenoid Intermittent
P0750 Shift Solenoid "A" Malfunction
P0751 Shift Solenoid "A" Performance or Stuck Off
P0752 Shift Solenoid "A" Stuck On
P0753 Shift Solenoid "A" Electrical
P0754 Shift Solenoid "A" Intermittent
P0755 Shift Solenoid "B" Malfunction
P0756 Shift Solenoid "B" Performance or Stuck Off
P0757 Shift Solenoid "B" Stuck On
P0758 Shift Solenoid "B" Electrical
P0759 Shift Solenoid "B" Intermittent
P0760 Shift Solenoid "C" Malfunction
P0761 Shift Solenoid "C" Performance Or Stuck Off
P0762 Shift Solenoid "C" Stuck On
P0763 Shift Solenoid "C" Electrical
P0764 Shift Solenoid "C" Intermittent
P0765 Shift Solenoid "D" Malfunction
P0766 Shift Solenoid "D" Performance Or Stuck Off
P0767 Shift Solenoid "D" Stuck On
P0768 Shift Solenoid "D" Electrical
P0769 Shift Solenoid "D" Intermittent
P0770 Shift Solenoid "E" Malfunction
P0771 Shift Solenoid "E" Performance Or Stuck Off
P0772 Shift Solenoid "E" Stuck On
P0773 Shift Solenoid "E" Electrical

P0774 Shift Solenoid "E" Intermittent
P0780 Shift Malfunction
P0781 1–2 Shift Malfunction
P0782 2–3 Shift Malfunction
P0783 3–4 Shift Malfunction
P0784 4–5 Shift Malfunction
P0785 Shift/Timing Solenoid Malfunction
P0786 Shift/Timing Solenoid Range/Performance
P0787 Shift/Timing Solenoid Low
P0788 Shift/Timing Solenoid High
P0789 Shift/Timing Solenoid Intermittent
P0790 Normal/Performance Switch Circuit Malfunction
P0801 Reverse Inhibit Control Circuit Malfunction
P0803 1–4 Upshift (Skip Shift) Solenoid Control Circuit Malfunction
P0804 1–4 Upshift (Skip Shift) Lamp Control Circuit Malfunction
P1000 OBD II Monitor Testing Not Complete More Driving Required
P1001 Key On Engine Running (KOER) Self-Test Not Able To Complete, KOER Aborted
P1100 Mass Air Flow (MAF) Sensor Intermittent
P1101 Mass Air Flow (MAF) Sensor Out Of Self-Test Range
P1111 System Pass 49 State Except Econoline
P1112 Intake Air Temperature (IAT) Sensor Intermittent
P1116 Engine Coolant Temperature (ECT) Sensor Out Of Self-Test Range
P1117 Engine Coolant Temperature (ECT) Sensor Intermittent
P1120 Throttle Position (TP) Sensor Out Of Range (Low)
P1121 Throttle Position (TP) Sensor Inconsistent With MAF Sensor
P1124 Throttle Position (TP) Sensor Out Of Self-Test Range
P1125 Throttle Position (TP) Sensor Circuit Intermittent
P1127 Exhaust Not Warm Enough, Downstream Heated Oxygen Sensors (HO$_2$S) Not Tested
P1128 Upstream Heated Oxygen Sensors (HO$_2$S) Swapped From Bank To Bank
P1129 Downstream Heated Oxygen Sensors (HO$_2$S) Swapped From Bank To Bank
P1130 Lack Of Upstream Heated Oxygen Sensor (HO$_2$S 11) Switch, Adaptive Fuel At Limit (Bank #1)
P1131 Lack Of Upstream Heated Oxygen Sensor (HO$_2$S 11) Switch, Sensor Indicates Lean (Bank #1)
P1132 Lack Of Upstream Heated Oxygen Sensor (HO$_2$S 11) Switch, Sensor Indicates Rich (Bank#1)
P1137 Lack Of Downstream Heated Oxygen Sensor (HO$_2$S 12) Switch, Sensor Indicates Lean (Bank#1)
P1138 Lack Of Downstream Heated Oxygen Sensor (HO$_2$S 12) Switch, Sensor Indicates Rich (Bank#1)
P1150 Lack Of Upstream Heated Oxygen Sensor (HO$_2$S 21) Switch, Adaptive Fuel At Limit (Bank #2)
P1151 Lack Of Upstream Heated Oxygen Sensor (HO$_2$S 21) Switch, Sensor Indicates Lean (Bank#2)
P1152 Lack Of Upstream Heated Oxygen Sensor (HO$_2$S 21) Switch, Sensor Indicates Rich (Bank #2)
P1157 Lack Of Downstream Heated Oxygen Sensor (HO$_2$S 22) Switch, Sensor Indicates Lean (Bank #2)
P1158 Lack Of Downstream Heated Oxygen Sensor (HO$_2$S 22) Switch, Sensor Indicates Rich (Bank#2)
P1169 (HO$_2$S 12) Signal Remained Unchanged For More Than 20 Seconds After Closed Loop
P1170 (HO$_2$S 11) Signal Remained Unchanged For More Than 20 Seconds After Closed Loop
P1173 Feedback A/F Mixture Control (HO$_2$S 21) Signal Remained Unchanged For More Than 20 Seconds After Closed Loop
P1184 Engine Oil Temp Sensor Circuit Performance
P1195 Barometric (BARO) Pressure Sensor Circuit Malfunction (Signal Is From EGR Boost Sensor)
P1196 Starter Switch Circuit Malfunction
P1209 Injection Control Pressure (ICP) Peak Fault
P1210 Injection Control Pressure (ICP) Above Expected Level
P1211 Injection Control Pressure (ICP) Not Controllable—Pressure Above/Below Desired
P1212 Injection Control Pressure (ICP) Voltage Not At Expected Level
P1218 Cylinder Identification (CID) Stuck High

P1219 Cylinder Identification (CID) Stuck Low
P1220 Series Throttle Control Malfunction (Traction Control System)
P1224 Throttle Position Sensor "B" (TP-B) Out Of Self-Test Range (Traction Control System)
P1230 Fuel Pump Low Speed Malfunction
P1231 Fuel Pump Secondary Circuit Low With High Speed Pump On
P1232 Low Speed Fuel Pump Primary Circuit Malfunction
P1233 Fuel Pump Driver Module Off-line (MIL DTC)
P1234 Fuel Pump Driver Module Disabled Or Off-line (No MIL)
P1235 Fuel Pump Control Out Of Range (MIL DTC)
P1236 Fuel Pump Control Out Of Range (No MIL)
P1237 Fuel Pump Secondary Circuit Malfunction (MIL DTC)
P1238 Fuel Pump Secondary Circuit Malfunction (No DMIL)
P1250 Fuel Pressure Regulator Control (FPRC) Solenoid Malfunction
P1260 THEFT Detected—Engine Disabled
P1261 High To Low Side Short—Cylinder #1 (Indicates Low side Circuit Is Shorted To B+ Or To The High Side Between The IDM And The Injector)
P1262 High To Low Side Short—Cylinder #2 (Indicates Low side Circuit Is Shorted To B+ Or To The High Side Between The IDM And The Injector)
P1263 High To Low Side Short—Cylinder #3 (Indicates Low side Circuit Is Shorted To B+ Or To The High Side Between The IDM And The Injector)
P1264 High To Low Side Short—Cylinder #4 (Indicates Low side Circuit Is Shorted To B+ Or To The High Side Between The IDM And The Injector)
P1265 High To Low Side Short—Cylinder #5 (Indicates Low side Circuit Is Shorted To B+ Or To The High Side Between The IDM And The Injector)
P1266 High To Low Side Short—Cylinder #6 (Indicates Low side Circuit Is Shorted To B+ Or To The High Side Between The IDM And The Injector)
P1267 High To Low Side Short—Cylinder #7 (Indicates Low side Circuit Is Shorted To B+ Or To The High Side Between The IDM And The Injector)
P1268 High To Low Side Short—Cylinder #8 (Indicates Low side Circuit Is Shorted To B+ Or To The High Side Between The IDM And The Injector)
P1270 Engine RPM Or Vehicle Speed Limiter Reached
P1271 High To Low Side Open—Cylinder #1 (Indicates A High To Low Side Open Between The Injector And The IDM)
P1272 High To Low Side Open—Cylinder #2 (Indicates A High To Low Side Open Between The Injector And The IDM)
P1273 High To Low Side Open—Cylinder #3 (Indicates A High To Low Side Open Between The Injector And The IDM)
P1274 High To Low Side Open—Cylinder #4 (Indicates A High To Low Side Open Between The Injector And The IDM)
P1275 High To Low Side Open—Cylinder #5 (Indicates A High To Low Side Open Between The Injector And The IDM)
P1276 High To Low Side Open—Cylinder #6 (Indicates A High To Low Side Open Between The Injector And The IDM)
P1277 High To Low Side Open—Cylinder #7 (Indicates A High To Low Side Open Between The Injector And The IDM)
P1278 High To Low Side Open—Cylinder #8 (Indicates A High To Low Side Open Between The Injector And The IDM)
P1280 Injection Control Pressure (ICP) Circuit Out Of Range Low
P1281 Injection Control Pressure (ICP) Circuit Out Of Range High
P1282 Injection Control Pressure (ICP) Excessive
P1283 Injection Pressure Regulator (IPR) Circuit Failure
P1284 Injection Control Pressure (ICP) Failure—Aborts KOER Or CCT Test
P1285 Cylinder Head Temperature (CHT) Over Temperature Sensed
P1288 Cylinder Head Temperature (CHT) Sensor Out Of Self-Test Range
P1289 Cylinder Head Temperature (CHT) Sensor Circuit Low Input
P1290 Cylinder Head Temperature (CHT) Sensor Circuit High Input
P1291 IDM To Injector High Side Circuit #1 (Right Bank) Short To GND Or B+
P1292 IDM To Injector High Side Circuit #2 (Right Bank) Short To GND Or B+
P1293 IDM To Injector High Side Circuit Open Bank #1 (Right Bank)
P1294 IDM To Injector High Side Circuit Open Bank #2 (Left Bank)
P1295 Multiple IDM/Injector Circuit Faults On Bank #1 (Right)
P1296 Multiple IDM/Injector Circuit Faults On Bank#2 (Left)
P1297 High Sides Shorted Together
P1298 IDM Failure
P1299 Engine Over Temperature Condition

P1309 Misfire Detection Monitor Is Not Enabled
P1316 Injector Circuit/IDM Codes Detected
P1320 Distributor Signal Interrupt
P1336 Crankshaft Position Sensor (Gear)
P1345 No Camshaft Position Sensor Signal
P1351 Ignition Diagnostic Monitor (IDM) Circuit Input Malfunction
P1351 Indicates Ignition System Malfunction
P1352 Indicates Ignition System Malfunction
P1353 Indicates Ignition System Malfunction
P1354 Indicates Ignition System Malfunction
P1355 Indicates Ignition System Malfunction
P1356 PIPs Occurred While IDM Pulse width Indicates Engine Not Turning
P1357 Ignition Diagnostic Monitor (IDM) Pulse width Not Defined
P1358 Ignition Diagnostic Monitor (IDM) Signal Out Of Self-Test Range
P1359 Spark Output Circuit Malfunction
P1364 Spark Output Circuit Malfunction
P1390 Octane Adjust (OCT ADJ) Out Of Self-Test Range
P1391 Glow Plug Circuit Low Input Bank #1 (Right)
P1392 Glow Plug Circuit High Input Bank #1 (Right)
P1393 Glow Plug Circuit Low Input Bank #2 (Left)
P1394 Glow Plug Circuit High Input Bank #2 (Left)
P1395 Glow Plug Monitor Fault Bank #1
P1396 Glow Plug Monitor Fault Bank #2
P1397 System Voltage Out Of Self Test Range
P1400 Differential Pressure Feedback EGR (DPFE) Sensor Circuit Low Voltage Detected
P1401 Differential Pressure Feedback EGR (DPFE) Sensor Circuit High Voltage Detected/EGR Temperature Sensor
P1402 EGR Valve Position Sensor Open Or Short
P1403 Differential Pressure Feedback EGR (DPFE) Sensor Hoses Reversed
P1405 Differential Pressure Feedback EGR (DPFE) Sensor Upstream Hose Off Or Plugged
P1406 Differential Pressure Feedback EGR (DPFE) Sensor Downstream Hose Off Or Plugged
P1407 Exhaust Gas Recirculation (EGR) No Flow Detected (Valve Stuck Closed Or Inoperative)
P1408 Exhaust Gas Recirculation (EGR) Flow Out Of Self-Test Range
P1409 Electronic Vacuum Regulator (EVR) Control Circuit Malfunction
P1410 Check That Fuel Pressure Regulator Control Solenoid And The EGR Check Solenoid Connectors Are Not Swapped
P1411 Secondary Air Injection System Incorrect Downstream Flow Detected
P1413 Secondary Air Injection System Monitor Circuit Low Voltage
P1414 Secondary Air Injection System Monitor Circuit High Voltage
P1442 Evaporative Emission Control System Small Leak Detected
P1443 Evaporative Emission Control System—Vacuum System, Purge Control Solenoid Or Purge Control Valve Malfunction
P1444 Purge Flow Sensor (PFS) Circuit Low Input
P1445 Purge Flow Sensor (PFS) Circuit High Input
P1449 Evaporative Emission Control System Unable To Hold Vacuum
P1450 Unable To Bleed Up Fuel Tank Vacuum
P1455 Evaporative Emission Control System Control Leak Detected (Gross Leak)
P1460 Wide Open Throttle Air Conditioning Cut-Off Circuit Malfunction
P1461 Air Conditioning Pressure (ACP) Sensor Circuit Low Input
P1462 Air Conditioning Pressure (ACP) Sensor Circuit High Input
P1463 Air Conditioning Pressure (ACP) Sensor Insufficient Pressure Change
P1464 Air Conditioning (A/C) Demand Out Of Self-Test Range/A/C On During KOER Or CCT Test
P1469 Low Air Conditioning Cycling Period
P1473 Fan Secondary High, With Fan(s) Off
P1474 Low Fan Control Primary Circuit Malfunction
P1479 High Fan Control Primary Circuit Malfunction
P1480 Fan Secondary Low, With Low Fan On
P1481 Fan Secondary Low, With High Fan On
P1483 Power To Fan Circuit Over current

P1484 Open Power/Ground To Variable Load Control Module (VLCM)
P1485 EGR Control Solenoid Open Or Short
P1486 EGR Vent Solenoid Open Or Short
P1487 EGR Boost Check Solenoid Open Or Short
P1500 Vehicle Speed Sensor (VSS) Circuit Intermittent
P1501 Vehicle Speed Sensor (VSS) Out Of Self-Test Range/Vehicle Moved During Test
P1502 Invalid Self Test—Auxiliary Powertrain Control Module (APCM) Functioning
P1504 Idle Air Control (IAC) Circuit Malfunction
P1505 Idle Air Control (IAC) System At Adaptive Clip
P1506 Idle Air Control (IAC) Overspeed Error
P1507 Idle Air Control (IAC) Underspeed Error
P1512 Intake Manifold Runner Control (IMRC) Malfunction (Bank#1 Stuck Closed)
P1513 Intake Manifold Runner Control (IMRC) Malfunction (Bank#2 Stuck Closed)
P1516 Intake Manifold Runner Control (IMRC) Input Error (Bank #1)
P1517 Intake Manifold Runner Control (IMRC) Input Error (Bank #2)
P1518 Intake Manifold Runner Control (IMRC) Malfunction (Stuck Open)
P1519 Intake Manifold Runner Control (IMRC) Malfunction (Stuck Closed)
P1520 Intake Manifold Runner Control (IMRC) Circuit Malfunction
P1521 Variable Resonance Induction System (VRIS) Solenoid #1 Open Or Short
P1522 Variable Resonance Induction System (VRIS) Solenoid#2 Open Or Short
P1523 High Speed Inlet Air (HSIA) Solenoid Open Or Short
P1530 Air Condition (A/C) Clutch Circuit Malfunction
P1531 Invalid Test—Accelerator Pedal Movement
P1536 Parking Brake Applied Failure
P1537 Intake Manifold Runner Control (IMRC) Malfunction (Bank#1 Stuck Open)
P1538 Intake Manifold Runner Control (IMRC) Malfunction (Bank#2 Stuck Open)
P1539 Power To Air Condition (A/C) Clutch Circuit Overcurrent
P1549 Problem In Intake Manifold Tuning (IMT) Valve System
P1550 Power Steering Pressure (PSP) Sensor Out Of Self-Test Range
P1601 Serial Communication Error
P1605 Powertrain Control Module (PCM)—Keep Alive Memory (KAM) Test Error
P1608 PCM Internal Circuit Malfunction
P1609 PCM Internal Circuit Malfunction (2.5L Only)
P1625 B+ Supply To Variable Load Control Module (VLCM) Fan Circuit Malfunction
P1626 B+ Supply To Variable Load Control Module (VLCM) Air Conditioning (A/C) Circuit
P1650 Power Steering Pressure (PSP) Switch Out Of Self-Test Range
P1651 Power Steering Pressure (PSP) Switch Input Malfunction
P1660 Output Circuit Check Signal High
P1661 Output Circuit Check Signal Low
P1662 Injection Driver Module Enable (IDM EN) Circuit Failure
P1663 Fuel Delivery Command Signal (FDCS) Circuit Failure
P1667 Cylinder Identification (CID) Circuit Failure
P1668 PCM—IDM Diagnostic Communication Error
P1670 EF Feedback Signal Not Detected
P1701 Reverse Engagement Error
P1701 Fuel Trim Malfunction (Villager)
P1703 Brake On/Off (BOO) Switch Out Of Self-Test Range
P1704 Digital Transmission Range (TR) Sensor Failed To Transition State
P1705 Transmission Range (TR) Sensor Out Of Self-Test Range
P1705 TP Sensor (AT) Villager
P1705 Clutch Pedal Position (CPP) Or Park Neutral Position (PNP) Problem
P1706 High Vehicle Speed In Park
P1709 Park Or Neutral Position (PNP) Or Clutch Pedal Position (CPP) Switch Out Of Self-Test Range

P1709 Throttle Position (TP) Sensor Malfunction (Aspire 1.3L, Escort/Tracer 1.8L, Probe 2.5L)
P1711 Transmission Fluid Temperature (TFT) Sensor Out Of Self-Test Range
P1714 Shift Solenoid "A" Inductive Signature Malfunction
P1715 Shift Solenoid "B" Inductive Signature Malfunction
P1716 Transmission Malfunction
P1717 Transmission Malfunction
P1719 Transmission Malfunction
P1720 Vehicle Speed Sensor (VSS) Circuit Malfunction
P1727 Coast Clutch Solenoid Inductive Signature Malfunction
P1728 Transmission Slip Error—Converter Clutch Failed
P1729 4x4 Low Switch Error
P1731 Improper 1–2 Shift
P1732 Improper 2–3 Shift
P1733 Improper 3–4 Shift
P1734 Improper 4–5 Shift
P1740 Torque Converter Clutch (TCC) Inductive Signature Malfunction
P1741 Torque Converter Clutch (TCC) Control Error
P1742 Torque Converter Clutch (TCC) Solenoid Failed On (Turns On MIL)
P1743 Torque Converter Clutch (TCC) Solenoid Failed On (Turns On TCIL)
P1744 Torque Converter Clutch (TCC) System Mechanically Stuck In Off Position
P1744 Torque Converter Clutch (TCC) Solenoid Malfunction (2.5L Only)
P1746 Electronic Pressure Control (EPC) Solenoid Open Circuit (Low Input)
P1747 Electronic Pressure Control (EPC) Solenoid Short Circuit (High Input)
P1748 Electronic Pressure Control (EPC) Malfunction
P1749 Electronic Pressure Control (EPC) Solenoid Failed Low
P1751 Shift Solenoid#1 (SS1) Performance
P1754 Coast Clutch Solenoid (CCS) Circuit Malfunction
P1756 Shift Solenoid#2 (SS2) Performance
P1760 Overrun Clutch SN
P1761 Shift Solenoid #(SS2) Performance
P1762 Transmission Malfunction
P1765 3–2 Timing Solenoid Malfunction (2.5L Only)
P1779 TCIL Circuit Malfunction
P1780 Transmission Control Switch (TCS) Circuit Out Of Self-Test Range
P1781 4x4 Low Switch, Out Of Self-Test Range
P1783 Transmission Over Temperature Condition
P1784 Transmission Malfunction
P1785 Transmission Malfunction
P1786 Transmission Malfunction
P1787 Transmission Malfunction
P1788 3–2 Timing/Coast Clutch Solenoid (3–2/CCS) Circuit Open
P1789 3–2 Timing/Coast Clutch Solenoid (3–2/CCS) Circuit Shorted
P1792 Idle (IDL) Switch (Closed Throttle Position Switch) Malfunction
P1794 Loss Of Battery Voltage Input
P1795 EGR Boost Sensor Malfunction
P1797 Clutch Pedal Position (CPP) Switch Or Neutral Switch Circuit Malfunction
P1900 Cooling Fan
U1021 SCP Indicating The Lack Of Air Conditioning (A/C) Clutch Status Response
U1039 Vehicle Speed Signal (VSS) Missing Or Incorrect
U1051 Brake Switch Signal Missing Or Incorrect
U1073 SCP Indicating The Lack Of Engine Coolant Fan Status Response
U1131 SCP Indicating The Lack Of Fuel Pump Status Response
U1135 SCP Indicating The Ignition Switch Signal Missing Or Incorrect
U1256 SCP Indicating A Communications Error
U1451 Lack Of Response From Passive Anti-Theft System (PATS) Module—Engine Disabled

DIESEL ENGINES

▶ **See Figures 118 thru 122**

4 Digit	Description
—	System Pass (No DTCs Available) — California and all Econoline
P0107	BARO Circuit Low Input
P0108	BARO Circuit High Input
P0112	IAT Sensor Circuit Low Input
P0113	IAT Sensor Circuit High Input
P0122 *	Accelerator Pedal Sensor Circuit Low Input
P0123 *	Accelerator Pedal Sensor Circuit High Input
P0196	EOT Sensor Circuit Performance
P0197 *	EOT Sensor Circuit Low Input
P0198 *	EOT Sensor Circuit High Input
P0220 *	Throttle Switch B Circuit Malfunction
P0221 *	Throttle Switch B Circuit Malfunction
P0236 *	Turbo Boost Sensor A Circuit Performance
P0237 *	Turbo Boost Sensor A Circuit Low Input
P0238 *	Turbo Boost Sensor A Circuit High Input
P0261 *	Injector Circuit Low — Cylinder 1
P0262	Injector Circuit High — Cylinder 1
P0263	Cylinder 1 Contribution/Balance Fault
P0264 *	Injector Circuit Low — Cylinder 2
P0265	Injector Circuit High — Cylinder 2
P0266	Cylinder 2 Contribution/Balance Fault
P0267 *	Injector Circuit Low — Cylinder 3
P0268	Injector Circuit High — Cylinder 3
P0269	Cylinder 3 Contribution/Balance Fault
P0270 *	Injector Circuit Low — Cylinder 4
P0271	Injector Circuit High — Cylinder 4
P0272	Cylinder 4 Contribution/Balance Fault
P0273 *	Injector Circuit Low — Cylinder 5
P0274	Injector Circuit High — Cylinder 5
P0275	Cylinder 5 Contribution/Balance Fault
P0276 *	Injector Circuit Low — Cylinder 6
P0277	Injector Circuit High — Cylinder 6
P0278	Cylinder 6 Contribution/Balance Fault
P0279 *	Injector Circuit Low — Cylinder 7
P0280	Injector Circuit High — Cylinder 7
P0281	Cylinder 7 Contribution/Balance Fault
P0282 *	Injector Circuit Low — Cylinder 8
P0283	Injector Circuit High — Cylinder 8

(Continued)

91194G01

Fig. 118 7.3L diesel engine OBDII trouble codes (1 of 5)

4 Digit	Description
P0284	Cylinder 8 Contribution/Balance Fault
P0340	CMP Sensor Circuit Malfunction
P0341 *	CMP Sensor Circuit Performance
P0344 *	CMP Sensor Circuit Intermittent
P0380	Glow Plug Circuit Malfunction
P0381	Glow Plug Indicator Circuit Malfunction
P0470	Exhaust Back Pressure Sensor Circuit Malfunction
P0471	Exhaust Back Pressure Sensor Circuit Performance
P0472	Exhaust Back Pressure Sensor Circuit Low Input
P0473	Exhaust Back Pressure Sensor Circuit High Input
P0475	Exhaust Pressure Control Valve Malfunction
P0476	Exhaust Pressure Control Valve Performance
P0478	Exhaust Pressure Control Valve High Input
P0500	Vehicle Speed Sensor Malfunction — KOER Tests
P0560	System Voltage Malfunction
P0562	System Voltage Low
P0563	System Voltage High
P0565	Cruise "On" Signal Malfunction
P0566	Cruise "Off" Signal Malfunction
P0567	Cruise "Resume" Signal Malfunction
P0568	Cruise "Set" Signal Malfunction
P0569	Cruise "Coast" Signal Malfunction
P0571	Brake Switch A Circuit Malfunction
P0603	Internal Control Module KAM Error
P0605	Internal Control Module ROM Error
P0606	PCM Processor Fault
P0703	Brake Switch B Circuit Malfunction
P0704	Clutch Pedal Position Switch Input Circuit Malfunction
P0705 **	TR Sensor Circuit Malfunction
P0707 **	TR Sensor Circuit Low Input
P0708 **	TR Sensor Circuit High Input
P0712	Transmission Fluid Temp. Sensor CKT Low Input
P0713	Transmission Fluid Temp. Sensor CKT High Input
P0741	TCC Circuit Performance
P0743	Torque Converter Clutch System Electrical Failure
P0750	Shift Solenoid 1 Malfunction

(Continued)

91194G02

Fig. 119 7.3L diesel engine OBDII trouble codes (2 of 5)

4 Digit	Description
P0751	Shift Solenoid A Performance
P0755	Shift Solenoid 2 Malfunction
P0756	Shift Solenoid B Performance
P0760	Shift Solenoid C Malfunction
P0781	1-2 Shift Malfunction
P0781**	1-2 Shift Malfunction
P0782**	2-3 Shift Malfunction
P0783**	3-4 Shift Malfunction
P1000	OBD II Monitor Checks Not Complete, More Driving Required
P1111	System Pass — 49-State except Econoline
P1184	Engine Oil Temp Sensor Circuit Performance
P1209	Injection Control System Pressure Peak Fault
P1210	Injection Control Pressure Above Expected Level
P1211*	ICP Not Controllable — Pressure Above/Below Desired
P1212*	ICP Voltage Not at Expected Level
P1218	CID Stuck High
P1219	CID Stuck Low
P1247	Turbo Boost Pressure Low
P1248	Turbo Boost Pressure Not Detected
P1261	High to Low Side Short — Cylinder 1
P1262	High to Low Side Short — Cylinder 2
P1263	High to Low Side Short — Cylinder 3
P1264	High to Low Side Short — Cylinder 4
P1265	High to Low Side Short — Cylinder 5
P1266	High to Low Side Short — Cylinder 6
P1267	High to Low Side Short — Cylinder 7
P1268	High to Low Side Short — Cylinder 8
P1271	High to Low Side Open — Cylinder 1
P1272	High to Low Side Open — Cylinder 2
P1273	High to Low Side Open — Cylinder 3
P1274	High to Low Side Open — Cylinder 4
P1275	High to Low Side Open — Cylinder 5
P1276	High to Low Side Open — Cylinder 6
P1277	High to Low Side Open — Cylinder 7
P1278	High to Low Side Open — Cylinder 8
P1280*	ICP Circuit Out of Range Low
P1281*	ICP Circuit Out of Range High
P1282	Excessive ICP

(Continued)

91194G03

Fig. 120 7.3L diesel engine OBDII trouble codes (3 of 5)

4 Digit	Description
P1283*	IPR Circuit Failure
P1284	ICP Failure — Aborts KOER or CCT Test
P1291	High Side No. 1 (Right) Short to GND or B+
P1292	High Side No. 2 (Left) Short to GND or B+
P1293	High Side Open Bank No. 1 (Right)
P1294	High Side Open Bank No. 2 (Left)
P1295*	Multiple Faults on Bank No. 1 (Right)
P1296*	Multiple Faults on Bank No. 2 (Left)
P1297	High Sides Shorted Together
P1298	IDM Failure
P1316	Injector Circuit/IDM Codes Detected
P1391	Glow Plug Circuit Low Input Bank No. 1 (Right)
P1392	Glow Plug Circuit High Input Bank No. 1 (Right)
P1393	Glow Plug Circuit Low Input Bank No. 2 (Left)
P1394	Glow Plug Circuit High Input Bank No. 2 (Left)
P1395	Glow Plug Monitor Fault Bank No. 1
P1396	Glow Plug Monitor Fault Bank No. 2
P1397	System Voltage out of Self Test Range
P1464	A/C On During KOER or CCT Test
P1501	Vehicle Moved During Testing
P1502	Invalid Self Test — APCM Functioning
P1531	Invalid Test — Accelerator Pedal Movement
P1536	Parking Brake Applied Failure
P1660	Output Circuit Check Signal High
P1661	Output Circuit Check Signal Low
P1662	IDM EN Circuit Failure
P1663	FDCS Circuit Failure
P1667	CID Circuit Failure
P1668	PCM — IDM Diagnostic Communication Error
P1670	EF Feedback Signal Not Detected
P1704	Digital TRS Failed to Transition State
P1705	TR Sensor out of Self Test Range
P1706**	High Vehicle Speed in Park
P1711	TFT Sensor Out of Self Test Range
P1714	Shift Solenoid A Inductive Signature Malfunction
P1715	Shift Solenoid B Inductive Signature Malfunction
P1727	Coast Clutch Solenoid Inductive Signature Malfunction
P1728**	Transmission Slip Error — Converter Clutch Failed

(Continued)

91194G04

Fig. 121 7.3L diesel engine OBDII trouble codes (4 of 5)

4 Digit	Description
P1729	4x4L Switch Error
P1740	Torque Converter Clutch Inductive Signature Malfunction
P1742	Torque Converter Clutch Failed On
P1744	Torque Converter Clutch System Performance
P1746	EPC Solenoid Open Circuit
P1747	EPC Solenoid Short Circuit
P1748**	EPC Malfunction
P1751	Shift Solenoid A Performance
P1754	CCS (Solenoid) Circuit Malfunction
P1756	Shift Solenoid B Performance
P1779	TCIL Circuit Malfunction
P1780	TCS Circuit out of Self Test Range
P1781	4x4L Circuit out of Self Test Range
P1783**	Transmission Overtemperature Condition
No Code	No Communication
No Code	Auxiliary Powertrain Control System
No Code	Tachometer

91194G05

Fig. 122 7.3L diesel engine OBDII trouble codes (5 of 5)

VACUUM DIAGRAMS

Following are vacuum diagrams for most of the engine and emissions package combinations covered by this manual. Because vacuum circuits will vary based on various engine and vehicle options, always refer first to the vehicle emission control information label, if present. Should the label be missing, or should vehicle be equipped with a different engine from the vehicle's original equipment, refer to the diagrams below for the same or similar configuration.

If you wish to obtain a replacement emissions label, most manufacturers make the labels available for purchase. The labels can usually be ordered from a local dealer.

91194P64

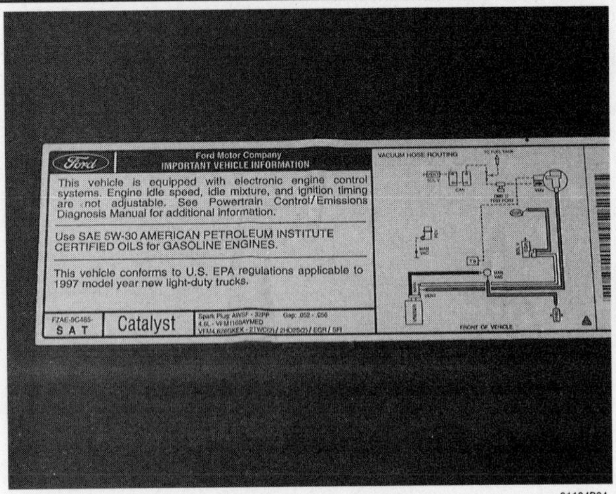

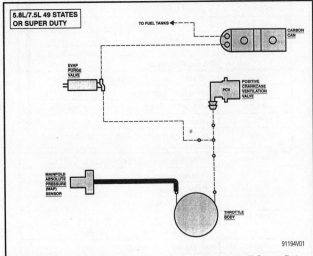

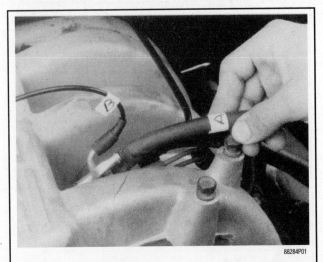

Fig. 123 A vacuum diagram is usually located on the underside of the hood on the emission control label

91194V01

Fig. 125 1997–98 5.8L and 7.5L Federal engines and all Super Duty (1 of 2)

88284P01

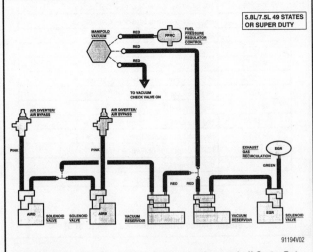

Fig. 124 To avoid a mixup, label vacuum lines prior to removing them

91194V02

Fig. 126 1997–98 5.8L and 7.5L Federal engines and all Super Duty (2 of 2)

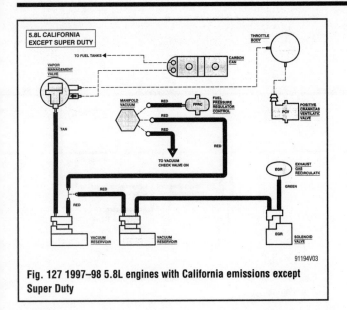

Fig. 127 1997–98 5.8L engines with California emissions except Super Duty

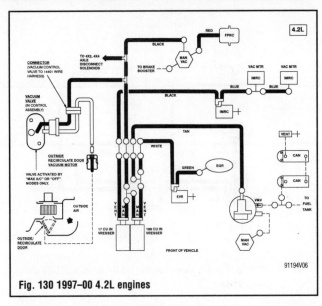

Fig. 130 1997–00 4.2L engines

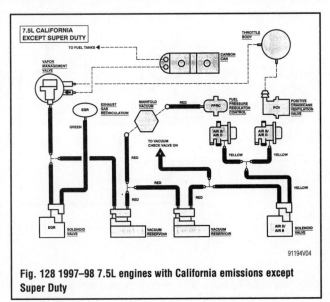

Fig. 128 1997–98 7.5L engines with California emissions except Super Duty

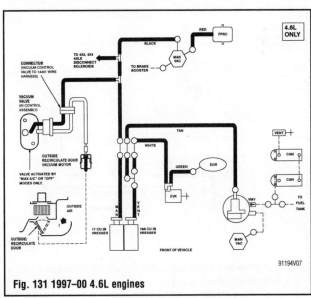

Fig. 131 1997–00 4.6L engines

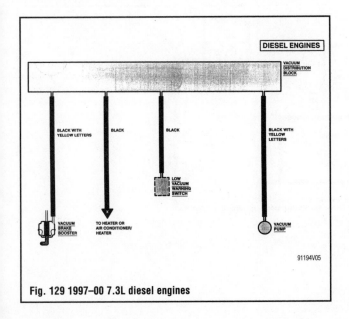

Fig. 129 1997–00 7.3L diesel engines

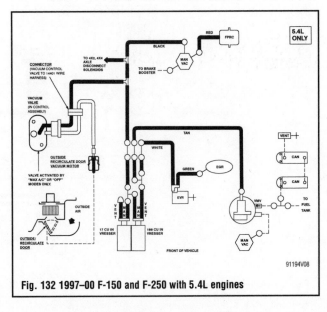

Fig. 132 1997–00 F-150 and F-250 with 5.4L engines

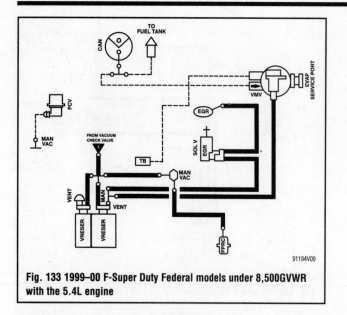

Fig. 133 1999–00 F-Super Duty Federal models under 8,500GVWR with the 5.4L engine

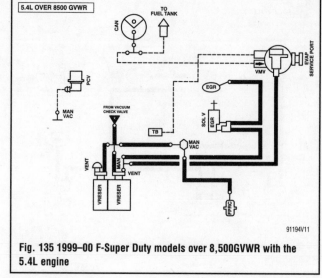

Fig. 135 1999–00 F-Super Duty models over 8,500GVWR with the 5.4L engine

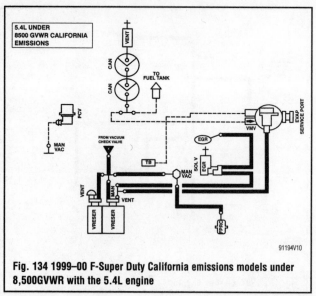

Fig. 134 1999–00 F-Super Duty California emissions models under 8,500GVWR with the 5.4L engine

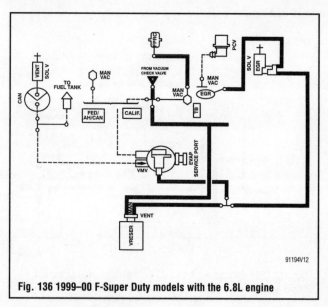

Fig. 136 1999–00 F-Super Duty models with the 6.8L engine

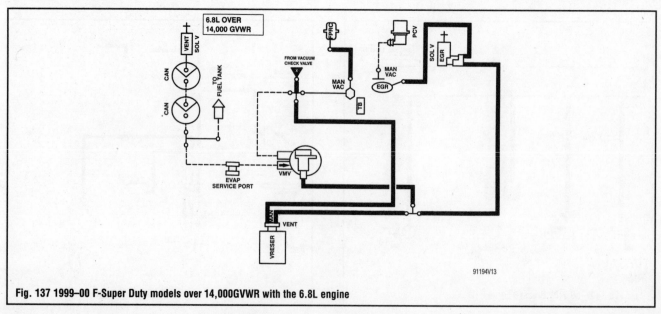

Fig. 137 1999–00 F-Super Duty models over 14,000GVWR with the 6.8L engine

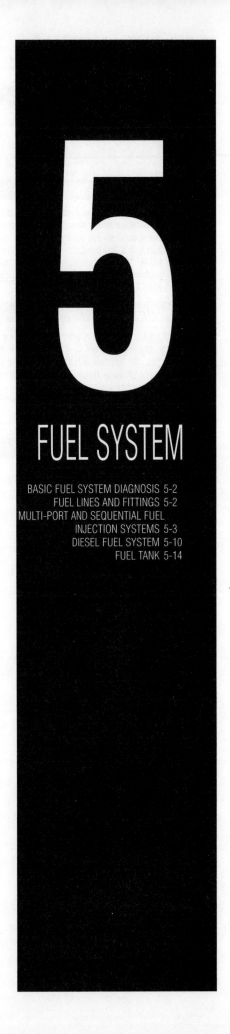

5

FUEL SYSTEM

BASIC FUEL SYSTEM DIAGNOSIS

When there is a problem starting or driving a vehicle, two of the most important checks involve the ignition and the fuel systems. The questions most mechanics attempt to answer first, "is there spark?" and "is there fuel?" will often lead to solving most basic problems. For ignition system diagnosis and testing, please refer to the information on engine electrical components and ignition systems found earlier in this manual. If the ignition system checks out (there is spark), then you must determine if the fuel system is operating properly (is there fuel?).

FUEL LINES AND FITTINGS

➡Quick-connect (push type) fuel line fittings must be disconnected using proper procedure or the fitting may be damaged. There are two types of retainers used on the push connect fittings. Line sizes of ⅜ and ⁵⁄₁₆ in. diameter use a hairpin clip retainer. The ¼ in. diameter line connectors use a duck-bill clip retainer. In addition, some engines use spring-lock connections, secured by a garter spring, which require Ford Tool T81P-19623-G (or equivalent) for removal.

❊❊ CAUTION

Observe all applicable safety precautions when working around fuel. Whenever servicing the fuel system, always work in a well ventilated area. Do not allow fuel spray or vapors to come in contact with a spark or open flame. Keep a dry chemical fire extinguisher near the work area. Always keep fuel in a container specifically designed for fuel storage; also, always properly seal fuel containers to avoid the possibility of fire or explosion.

Hairpin Clip Fitting

REMOVAL & INSTALLATION

1. Clean all dirt and grease from the fitting. Spread the two clip legs about ⅛ in. (3mm) each to disengage from the fitting and pull the clip outward from the fitting. Use finger pressure only; do not use any tools.
2. Grasp the fitting and hose assembly and pull away from the steel line. Twist the fitting and hose assembly slightly while pulling, if the assembly sticks.
3. Inspect the hairpin clip for damage, replacing the clip if necessary. Reinstall the clip in position on the fitting.
4. Inspect the fitting and inside of the connector to ensure freedom from dirt or obstruction. Install the fitting into the connector and push together. A click will be heard when the hairpin snaps into the proper connection. Pull on the line to insure full engagement.

Duckbill Clip Fitting

REMOVAL & INSTALLATION

♦ See Figure 1

1. A special tool is available from Ford and other manufacturers for removing the retaining clips. Use Ford Tool T90T-9550-B or C or equivalent. If the tool is

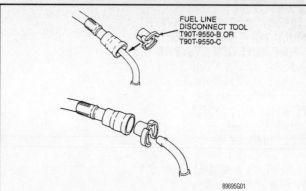

Fig. 1 A fuel line disconnect tool is required to properly separate a duckbill clip fitting

not on hand, go onto step 2. Align the slot on the push connector disconnect tool with either tab on the retaining clip. Pull the line from the connector.

2. If the special clip tool is not available, use a pair of narrow 6-inch slip-jaw pliers with a jaw width of 0.2 in (5mm) or less. Align the jaws of the pliers with the openings of the fitting case and compress the part of the retaining clip that engages the case. Compressing the retaining clip will release the fitting, which may be pulled from the connector. Both sides of the clip must be compressed at the same time to disengage.
3. Inspect the retaining clip, fitting end and connector. Replace the clip if any damage is apparent.
4. Push the line into the steel connector until a click is heard, indicating the clip is in place. Pull on the line to check engagement.

Spring Lock Coupling

REMOVAL & INSTALLATION

♦ See Figures 2 thru 9

The spring lock coupling is held together by a garter spring inside a circular cage. When the coupling is connected together, the flared end of the female fitting slips behind the garter spring inside the cage of the male fitting. The garter spring and cage then prevent the flared end of the female fitting from pulling out of the cage. As an additional locking feature, most vehicles have a horseshoe-shaped retaining clip that improves the retaining reliability of the spring lock coupling.

Fig. 2 This type of removal tool has a hinged center section that allows you to fit it around the fuel line

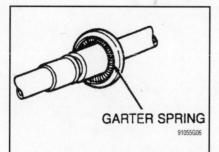

Fig. 3 The garter spring is located inside the fitting and holds the fitting together

Fig. 4 Slide the tool back to unseat the garter spring on the fitting, and pull back on the fuel line to separate them

Fig. 5 This type of removal tool snaps over the line

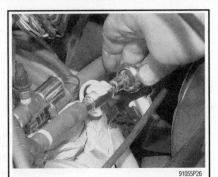

Fig. 6 Slide the tool back to unseat the garter spring on the fitting, and pull back on the fuel line to separate them

Fig. 7 Be sure to check the O-rings for damage; replace them if necessary

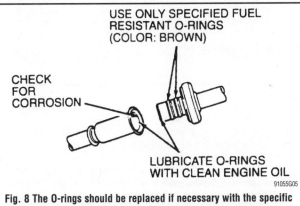

Fig. 8 The O-rings should be replaced if necessary with the specific ones used for the fuel system, a non-specific O-ring could leak

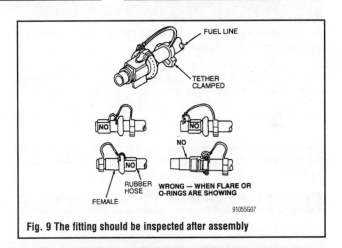

Fig. 9 The fitting should be inspected after assembly

MULTI-PORT AND SEQUENTIAL FUEL INJECTION SYSTEMS

General Information

The Mutli-port Fuel Injection (MFI) and Sequential Fuel Injection (SFI) system includes a high pressure electric fuel pump mounted in the fuel tank, a fuel supply manifold, a throttle body (meters the incoming air charge for the correct mixture with the fuel), a pressure regulator, fuel filters and both solid and flexible fuel lines. The fuel supply manifold includes 6, 8 or 10 electronically-controlled fuel injectors, each mounted directly above an intake port in the intake manifold. Each injector fires once every other crankshaft revolution, in sequence with the engine firing order.

The fuel pressure regulator maintains a constant pressure drop across the injector nozzles. The regulator is referenced to intake manifold vacuum and is connected in parallel to the fuel injectors; it is positioned on the far end of the fuel rail. Any excess fuel supplied by the fuel pump passes through the regulator and is returned to the fuel tank via a return line.

The fuel pressure regulator is a diaphragm-operated relief valve, in which the inside of the diaphragm senses fuel pressure and the other side senses manifold vacuum. Normal fuel pressure is established by a spring preload applied to the diaphragm. Control of the fuel system is maintained through the Powertrain Control Module (PCM), although electrical power is routed through the fuel pump relay and an inertia switch. The fuel pump relay is normally located in the power distribution box, under the hood, and the inertia switch is located in the trunk. The inline fuel pump is mounted in the fuel tank.

The inertia switch opens the power circuit to the fuel pump in the event of a collision or roll over. Once tripped, the switch must be reset manually by pushing the reset button on the assembly.

➡Check that the inertia switch is reset before diagnosing power supply problems to the fuel pump.

The fuel injectors used with MFI and SFI systems are electro-mechanical (solenoid) type, designed to meter and atomize fuel delivered to the intake ports of the engine. The injectors are mounted in the intake manifold and positioned so that their spray nozzles direct the fuel charge in front of the intake valves. The injector body consists of a solenoid-actuated pintle and needle-valve assembly. The control unit sends an electrical impulse that activates the solenoid, causing the pintle to move inward off the seat and allow the fuel to flow. The amount of fuel delivered is controlled by the length of time the injector is energized (pulse width), since the fuel flow orifice is fixed and the fuel pressure drop across the injector tip is constant. Correct atomization is achieved by contouring the pintle at the point where the fuel enters the pintle chamber.

➡Exercise care when handling fuel injectors during service. Be careful not to lose the pintle cap and always replace O-rings to assure a tight seal.

The injectors receive high-pressure fuel from the fuel supply manifold (fuel rail) assembly. The complete assembly includes a single, pre-formed tube with 6, 8 or 10 connectors, the mounting flange for the pressure regulator, and mounting attachments to locate the manifold and provide the fuel injector retainers.

The fuel manifold is normally removed with the fuel injectors and pressure regulator attached. Fuel injector electrical connectors are plastic and have locking tabs that must be released when disconnecting the wiring harness.

FUEL SYSTEM SERVICE PRECAUTIONS

Safety is the most important factor when performing not only fuel system maintenance, but any type of maintenance. Failure to conduct maintenance and repairs in a safe manner may result in serious personal injury or death. Work on a vehicle's fuel system components can be accomplished safely and effectively by adhering to the following rules and guidelines.

• To avoid the possibility of fire and personal injury, always disconnect the negative battery cable unless the repair or test procedure requires that battery voltage by applied.

• Always relieve the fuel system pressure prior to disconnecting any fuel system component (injector, fuel rail, pressure regulator, etc.) fitting or fuel line connection. Exercise extreme caution whenever relieving fuel system pressure to avoid exposing skin, face and eyes to fuel spray. Please be advised that fuel under pressure may penetrate the skin or any part of the body that it contacts.

• Always place a shop towel or cloth around the fitting or connection prior to loosening to absorb any excess fuel due to spillage. Ensure that all fuel spillage is quickly remove from engine surfaces. Ensure that all fuel-soaked cloths or towels are deposited into a flame-proof waste container with a lid.

• Always keep a dry chemical (Class B) fire extinguisher near the work area.

• Do not allow fuel spray or fuel vapors to come into contact with a spark or open flame.

• Always use a second wrench when loosening or tightening fuel line connections fittings. This will prevent unnecessary stress and torsion to fuel piping. Always follow the proper torque specifications.

• Always replace worn fuel fitting O-rings with new ones. Do not substitute fuel hose where rigid pipe is installed.

Relieving Fuel System Pressure

➡A fuel pressure gauge, such as Ford Tool T80L-9974-B, is needed to correctly perform this procedure.

1. Disconnect the negative battery cable and remove the fuel filler cap.
2. Remove the cap from the pressure relief valve on the fuel supply manifold. Install pressure gauge T80L-9974-B or equivalent, to the pressure relief valve.
3. Direct the gauge drain hose into a suitable container and depress the pressure relief button.
4. Remove the gauge and replace the cap on the pressure relief valve.

➡As an alternate method on models except 1997 F-150, F-250, Expedition and Navigator, disconnect the inertia switch and crank the engine for 15–20 seconds until the pressure is relieved.

Fuel Pump

TESTING

※※ CAUTION

Observe all applicable safety precautions when working around fuel. Whenever servicing the fuel system, always work in a well ventilated area. Do not allow fuel spray or vapors to come in contact with a spark or open flame. Keep a dry chemical fire extinguisher near the work area. Always keep fuel in a container specifically designed for fuel storage; also, always properly seal fuel containers to avoid the possibility of fire or explosion.

1. Check all hoses and lines for kinks and leaking. Repair as necessary.
2. Check all electrical connections for looseness and corrosion. Repair as necessary.
3. Turn the ignition key from the **OFF** position to the **RUN** position several times (do not start the engine) and verify that the pump runs briefly each time, (you will here a low humming sound from the fuel tank).

➡Check that the inertia switch is reset before diagnosing power supply problems to the fuel pump.

The use of a scan tool is required to perform these tests.

4. Turn the ignition key **OFF**.
5. Connect a suitable fuel pressure gauge to the fuel test port (Schrader valve) on the fuel rail.
6. Connect the scan tool and turn the ignition key **ON** but do not start the engine.
7. Following the scan tool manufacturer's instructions, enter the output test mode and run the fuel pump to obtain the maximum fuel pressure.
8. The fuel pressure should be between 30–45 psi (210–310 kPa).
9. If the fuel pressure is within specification the pump is working properly. If not, continue with the test.
10. Check the pump ground connection and service as necessary.
11. Turn the ignition key **ON**.

12. Using the scan tool, enter output test mode and turn on the fuel pump circuit.
13. Using a Digital Volt Ohmmeter (DVOM), check for voltage (approximately 10.5 volts) at the fuel pump electrical connector.
14. If the pump is getting a good voltage supply, the ground connection is good and the fuel pressure is not within specification, then replace the pump.

REMOVAL & INSTALLATION

See fuel pump under fuel tank in this section.

Inertia Switch

GENERAL INFORMATION

This switch shuts off the fuel pump in the event of a collision. Once the switch has been tripped, it must be reset manually in order to start the engine.

The inertia switch is located behind the passenger side kick panel on the F-150, F-250, Expedition, Navigator and 1999–00 F-Super Duty models. On 1997–98 F-250HD, F-350 and F-Super Duty models, the switch is located behind the driver's side kick panel.

RESETTING THE SWITCH

▶ See Figure 10

1. Turn the ignition switch **OFF**.
2. Ensure that there is no fuel leaking in the engine compartment, along any of the lines or at the tank. There should be no odor of fuel as well.
3. If no leakage and/or odor is apparent, reset the switch by pushing the reset button on the top of the switch. The reset switch is usually accessible through an opening in the kick panel or by reaching over the top of the panel.
4. Cycle the ignition switch from the **ON** to **OFF** positions several times, allowing five seconds at each position, to build fuel pressure within the system.
5. Again, check the fuel system for leaks. There should be no odor of fuel as well.
6. If there is no leakage and/or odor of fuel, it is safe to operate the vehicle. However, it is recommended that the entire system be checked by a professional, especially if the vehicle was in an accident severe enough to trip the inertia switch.

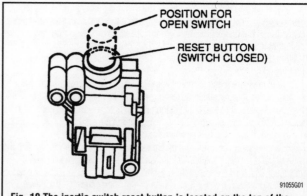

Fig. 10 The inertia switch reset button is located on the top of the switch

REMOVAL & INSTALLATION

1. Disconnect the negative battery cable.
2. Remove the any necessary trim to access the switch.
3. Unplug the connector on the inertia switch.
4. Remove the retaining bolts and remove the switch.
5. Installation is the reverse of removal.

Throttle Body

REMOVAL & INSTALLATION

4.2L Engine

1. Disconnect the negative battery cable.
2. Remove the air cleaner outlet tube.
3. Remove the accelerator cable shield from the throttle body.
4. Unplug the Throttle Position (TP) sensor electrical connection.
5. Remove the two TP sensor retaining screws and remove the sensor from the throttle body. Refer to Section 4 if necessary.
6. Disconnect the accelerator cable from the throttle lever.
7. If equipped with speed control, disconnect the speed control actuator from the throttle lever.
8. Unfasten the throttle body retaining bolts and remove the throttle body.

➡️If scraping is necessary to remove any gasket material, be careful not to damage the gasket mating surfaces or allow any foreign material to enter the intake manifold.

9. Remove the old gasket and clean any gasket residue from both mating surfaces.
   To install:
10. Install a new gasket and the throttle body.
11. Install the throttle body retaining bolts and tighten them to 71–102 inch lbs. (8–12 Nm)
12. Align the throttle shaft onto the TP sensor and install the sensor. Refer to Section 4 if necessary.
13. Attach the TP sensor electrical connection.
14. Connect the accelerator cable to the throttle lever.
15. If equipped with speed control, connect the speed control actuator.
16. Install the accelerator cable shield.
17. Install the air cleaner outlet hose.
18. Connect the negative battery cable.
19. Start the engine and check for vacuum leaks.

4.6L, 5.4L and 6.8L Engines

▶ See Figures 11 thru 18

1. Disconnect the negative battery cable.
2. Remove the air cleaner outlet tube.
3. Remove the accelerator cable shield from the throttle body.
4. Unplug the Throttle Position (TP) sensor electrical connection.
5. Disconnect the accelerator cable from the throttle lever.
6. If equipped with speed control, disconnect the speed control actuator from the throttle lever.
7. Disconnect the accelerator return spring from the throttle body.
8. Unfasten the throttle body retaining bolts and remove the throttle body.

➡️If scraping is necessary to remove any gasket material, be careful not to damage the gasket mating surfaces or allow any foreign material to enter the intake manifold.

9. Remove the old gasket and clean any gasket residue from both mating surfaces.
   To install:
10. Install a new gasket and the throttle body.
11. Install the throttle body retaining bolts and tighten them to 71–89 inch lbs. (8–10 Nm).
12. Attach the Throttle Position (TP) sensor electrical connection.
13. Connect the accelerator cable to the throttle lever.
14. If equipped with speed control, connect the speed control actuator.
15. Connect the accelerator return spring.
16. Install the accelerator cable shield.
17. Install the air cleaner outlet hose.
18. Connect the negative battery cable.
19. Start the engine and check for vacuum leaks.

Fig. 11 Remove the one retaining screw on the passenger side and . . .

Fig. 12 . . . the two retaining screws on the driver's side and . . .

Fig. 13 . . . remove the accelerator cable shield

Fig. 14 Detach the TP sensor connector

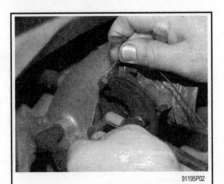

Fig. 15 Disconnect the accelerator cable from the throttle lever

Fig. 16 If equipped with speed control, disconnect the speed control actuator from the throttle lever

Fig. 17 Disconnect the accelerator return spring from the throttle body

Fig. 18 Remove the four retaining bolts and the throttle body from the intake manifold

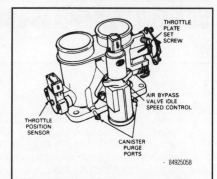

Fig. 19 Throttle body assembly, including throttle position sensor and air bypass valve—5.8L engine

5.8L Engine

▶ See Figure 19

1. Disconnect the negative battery cable.
2. Remove the air cleaner outlet tube.
3. Drain and recycle the engine coolant.
4. Remove the accelerator cable shield from the throttle body.
5. Disconnect the accelerator cable from the throttle lever ball.
6. On automatic transmission equipped models only, disconnect the transmission linkage from the throttle body.
7. If equipped with speed control, disconnect the speed control actuator from the throttle lever.
8. Unplug the Throttle Position (TP) sensor and Idle Air Control (IAC) valve electrical connections.
9. Label and disconnect the coolant hoses and vacuum lines.
10. Remove the bracket to expose the left-hand throttle body mounting bolt.
11. Unfasten the throttle body retaining nuts and remove the throttle body.

➡If scraping is necessary to remove any gasket material, be careful not to damage the gasket mating surfaces or allow any foreign material to enter the intake manifold.

12. Remove the old gasket and clean any gasket residue from both mating surfaces.

To install:

13. Install a new gasket and the throttle body.
14. Install the throttle body retaining nuts and tighten them to 12–18 ft. lbs. (16–24 Nm).
15. Install the bracket onto the throttle body.
16. Connect the coolant and vacuum hoses to the throttle body.
17. Attach the TP sensor and IAC valve electrical connections.
18. Connect the accelerator cable, transmission linkage (automatic transmission only), and speed control actuator (if equipped) to the throttle body.
19. Install the accelerator cable shield.
20. Install the air cleaner outlet hose.
21. Fill the engine with coolant and bleed as necessary.
22. Connect the negative battery cable.
23. Start the engine and check for vacuum leaks.

7.5L Engine

▶ See Figure 20

1. Disconnect the negative battery cable.
2. Remove the air cleaner inlet tubes.
3. Disconnect the accelerator cable from the throttle lever ball.
4. On automatic transmission equipped models only, disconnect the transmission linkage from the throttle body.
5. If equipped with speed control, disconnect the speed control actuator from the throttle lever.
6. Unplug the Throttle Position (TP) sensor electrical connection.
7. Unfasten the throttle body retaining bolts and remove the throttle body.

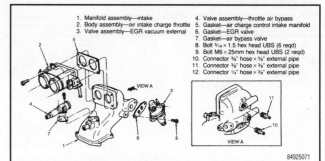

Fig. 20 Throttle body and upper intake manifold—7.5L engine

➡If scraping is necessary to remove any gasket material, be careful not to damage the gasket mating surfaces or allow any foreign material to enter the intake manifold.

8. Remove the old gasket and clean any gasket residue from both mating surfaces.

To install:

9. Install a new gasket and the throttle body.
10. Install the throttle body retaining nuts and tighten them to 14–20 ft. lbs. (19–27 Nm).
11. Connect the accelerator cable, transmission linkage (automatic transmission only), and speed control actuator (if equipped) to the throttle body.
12. Attach the TP sensor connection.
13. Install the air cleaner inlet tubes.
14. Connect the negative battery cable.
15. Start the engine and check for vacuum leaks.

Fuel Injector(s)

REMOVAL & INSTALLATION

4.2L Engine

✳✳ CAUTION

Fuel injection systems remain under pressure, even after the engine has been turned OFF. The fuel system pressure must be relieved before disconnecting any fuel lines. Failure to do so may result in fire and/or personal injury.

1. Disconnect the negative battery cable.
2. Properly relieve the fuel system pressure.
3. Remove the fuel injection supply manifold as described in this section.
4. Remove the fuel injectors from the supply manifold by carefully twisting them out.

To install:

5. Lubricate new O-rings with clean engine oil and install 2 new O-rings on each fuel injector.

6. Make sure the injector cups are clean and undamaged.

7. Install the fuel injectors in the fuel injection supply manifold using a light twisting-pushing motion.

8. Install the fuel injection supply manifold as described in this section.

9. Connect the negative battery cable.

10. Start the engine and let it idle for several minutes while checking for fuel leaks.

11. Turn the engine **OFF** and using a clean paper towel, check each fuel injector for leaks.

12. Road test the vehicle and check for proper engine operation.

4.6L, 5.4L and 6.8L Engines

▶ See Figures 21 and 22

✳✳ CAUTION

Fuel injection systems remain under pressure, even after the engine has been turned OFF. The fuel system pressure must be relieved before disconnecting any fuel lines. Failure to do so may result in fire and/or personal injury.

1. Disconnect the negative battery cable.

2. Partially drain the engine cooling system.

3. Remove the engine air cleaner outlet tube from the throttle body.

4. Properly relieve the fuel system pressure.

5. Remove the fuel injection supply manifold as described in this section.

6. Remove the fuel injectors from the fuel injection supply manifold as follows:

a. Grasp the injector body and pull while gently rocking the injector from side-to-side to remove the injector from the fuel injection supply manifold. Repeat the removal procedure for fuel injectors left in the intake manifold.

7. Inspect the fuel injector end cap, body and washer for signs of dirt and deterioration.

8. Discard the fuel injector O-rings.

To install:

9. Lubricate new O-rings with clean engine oil and install 2 O-rings on each injector. Do not use silicone grease as it will clog the injectors.

10. Install the fuel injectors into the fuel injection supply manifold using a light, twisting, pushing motion.

11. Install the fuel injection supply manifold as described in this section.

12. Install the engine air cleaner outlet tube to the throttle body.

13. Connect the negative battery cable.

14. Start the engine and allow to idle for several minutes while checking for leaks.

15. Turn the engine **OFF** and recheck for leaks.

16. Road test the vehicle and check for proper engine operation.

5.8L and 7.5L Engines

▶ See Figure 23

1. Disconnect the negative battery cable.

2. Relieve the fuel system pressure.

3. Remove the fuel supply manifold as described in this section.

4. Disconnect the wiring at each injector.

5. Pull upward on the injector body while gently rocking it from side-to-side.

To install:

6. Inspect the O-rings on the injector for any sign of leakage or damage. Replace any suspected O-rings.

7. Inspect the plastic cap at the top of each injector and replace it if any sign of deterioration is noticed.

8. Lubricate the O-rings with clean engine oil.

9. Install the injectors by pushing them into the supply manifold with a gentle rocking motion.

10. Install the fuel supply manifold as described in this section.

11. Connect the negative battery cable.

TESTING

The easiest way to test the operation of the fuel injectors is to listen for a clicking sound coming from the injectors while the engine is running. This is accomplished using a mechanic's stethoscope, or a long screwdriver. Place the end of the stethoscope or the screwdriver (tip end, not handle) onto the body of the injector. Place the ear pieces of the stethoscope in your ears, or if using a screwdriver, place your ear on top of the handle. An audible clicking noise should be heard; this is the solenoid operating. If the injector makes this noise, the injector driver circuit and computer are operating as designed. Continue testing all the injectors this way.

✳✳ CAUTION

Be extremely careful while working on an operating engine, make sure you have no dangling jewelry, extremely loose clothes, power tool cords or other items that might get caught in a moving part of the engine.

All Injectors Clicking

If all the injectors are clicking, but you have determined that the fuel system is the cause of your driveability problem, continue diagnostics. Make sure that you have checked fuel pump pressure as outlined earlier in this section. An easy way to determine a weak or unproductive cylinder is a cylinder drop test. This is accomplished by removing one spark plug wire at a time, and seeing which cylinder causes the least difference in the idle. The one that causes the least change is the weak cylinder.

If the injectors were all clicking and the ignition system is functioning prop-

Fig. 21 Replace the injector O-rings before installing the injectors back into the engine

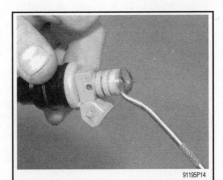

Fig. 22 Remove the O-rings from the injectors using a small pick or other suitable tool

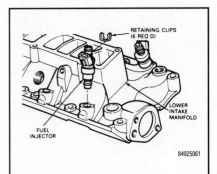

Fig. 23 Fuel injector installation—5.8L engine, 7.5L similar

erly, remove the injector of the suspect cylinder and bench test it. This is accomplished by checking for a spray pattern from the injector itself. Install a fuel supply line to the injector (or rail if the injector is left attached to the rail) and momentarily apply 12 volts DC and a ground to the injector itself; a visible fuel spray should appear. If no spray is achieved, replace the injector and check the running condition of the engine.

One or More Injectors Are Not Clicking

♦ See Figures 24, 25, 26 and 27

If one or more injectors are found to be not operating, testing the injector driver circuit and computer can be accomplished using a "noid" light. First, with the engine not running and the ignition key in the **OFF** position, remove the connector from the injector you plan to test, then plug the "noid" light tool into the injector connector. Start the engine and the "noid" light should flash, signaling that the injector driver circuit is working. If the "noid" light flashes, but the injector does not click when plugged in, test the injector's resistance. resistance should be between 11–18 ohms.

If the "noid" light does not flash, the injector driver circuit is faulty. Disconnect the negative battery cable. Unplug the "noid" light from the injector connector and also unplug the PCM. Check the harness between the appropriate pins on the harness side of the PCM connector and the injector connector. Resistance should be less than 5.0 ohms; if not, repair the circuit. If resistance is within specifications, the injector driver inside the PCM is faulty and replacement of the PCM will be necessary.

Fig. 24 Unplug the fuel injector connector

Fig. 25 Probe the two terminals of a fuel injector to check it's resistance

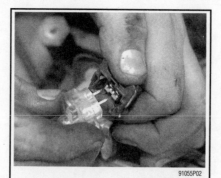

Fig. 26 Plug the correct "noid" light directly into the injector harness connector

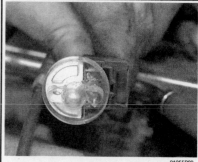

Fig. 27 If the correct "noid" light flashes while the engine is running, the injector driver circuit inside the PCM is working

Fuel Injection Supply Manifold (Fuel Injector Rail)

REMOVAL & INSTALLATION

4.2L Engine

※※ CAUTION

Fuel injection systems remain under pressure, even after the engine has been turned OFF. The fuel system pressure must be relieved before disconnecting any fuel lines. Failure to do so may result in fire and/or personal injury.

1. Disconnect the negative battery cable.
2. Properly relieve the fuel system pressure.
3. Remove the upper intake manifold.
4. Disconnect the fuel supply and return lines at the fuel injection supply manifold.
5. Disconnect the electrical harness connectors from each fuel injector.
6. Remove 4 fuel injection supply manifold retaining bolts.
7. Carefully disengage the fuel injection supply manifold from the lower intake manifold by lifting and gently rocking the manifold.

To install:
8. Replace the O-rings on the fuel injectors. Apply a small amount of engine oil to each O-ring.
9. Carefully install the fuel injection supply manifold and fuel injectors to the lower intake manifold, one side at a time. Make sure the O-rings are seated by pushing down on the fuel manifold.
10. While holding the fuel injection supply manifold in place, install 4 retaining bolts and tighten to 84 inch lbs. (10 Nm).
11. Connect the fuel supply and return lines to the fuel injection supply manifold.
12. Connect the vacuum line to the fuel pressure regulator.
13. Before connecting the fuel injector harness, temporarily connect the negative battery cable and turn the ignition switch to the **ON** position, pressurizing the fuel system.
14. Using a clean paper towel. check for leaks where the fuel injectors attach to the fuel injection supply manifold and the lower intake manifold. Turn the ignition switch **OFF** and disconnect the negative battery cable.
15. Connect the fuel injector electrical harness connectors.
16. Install the upper intake manifold.
17. Connect the negative battery cable.
18. Start the engine and let it idle for several minutes while checking for fuel leaks.
19. Turn the engine **OFF** and using a clean paper towel, check each fuel injector for leaks.
20. Road test the vehicle and check for proper engine operation.

4.6L, 5.4L and 6.8L Engines

♦ See Figures 28, 29, 30 and 31

✸✸ CAUTION

Fuel injection systems remain under pressure, even after the engine has been turned OFF. The fuel system pressure must be relieved before disconnecting any fuel lines. Failure to do so may result in fire and/or personal injury.

1. Disconnect the negative battery cable.
2. Partially drain the engine cooling system.
3. Remove the engine air cleaner outlet tube from the throttle body.
4. Properly relieve the fuel system pressure.
5. Remove 3 power steering reservoir retaining bolts and remove the reservoir bracket.
6. Remove the accelerator splash shield.
7. Disconnect the vacuum line at the fuel pressure regulator.
8. Disconnect the fuel supply and return lines at the fuel injection supply manifold.
9. Carefully disconnect the electrical harness connectors from each fuel injector.
10. Disconnect the heater water inlet tube hose and position aside.
11. Remove the brake booster bracket nut.
12. Remove the brake booster tube.
13. Remove the PCV hose.
14. Disconnect the EGR Differential Pressure Feedback (DPFE) transducer hoses from the EGR tube.

Fig. 28 Disconnect the pressure regulator vacuum hose

15. Remove the upper and lower EGR tube fittings and remove the EGR valve to exhaust manifold tube.
16. Disconnect the vapor management valve hose.
17. Remove 4 fuel injection supply manifold retaining bolts.
18. Carefully disengage the fuel injection supply manifold from the lower intake manifold.
19. Discard the fuel injector O-rings.

To install:

20. Lubricate new O-rings with clean engine oil and install 2 O-rings on each injector. Do not use silicone grease as it will clog the injectors.
21. Install the fuel injection supply manifold, pushing it down to ensure all fuel injector O-rings are fully seated in the fuel rail cups and the intake manifold.
22. Install 4 fuel injection supply manifold retaining bolts while holding the manifold down. Tighten the retaining bolts to 71–106 inch lbs. (8–12 Nm).
23. Connect the fuel supply and return lines to the fuel injection supply manifold.
24. Connect the vacuum line to the fuel pressure regulator.
25. With the fuel injector wiring disconnected, temporarily connect the negative battery cable and turn the ignition switch to the **RUN** position to allow the fuel pump to pressurize the fuel system.
26. Check for fuel leaks.
27. Disconnect the negative battery cable.
28. Connect the electrical harness connectors to each fuel injector.
29. Connect the vapor management valve hose.
30. Install the EGR valve to exhaust manifold tube. Tighten the fittings to 30 ft. lbs (41 Nm).
31. Connect the EGR DPFE hoses to the EGR tube.
32. Install the PCV hose.
33. Install brake booster tube and position 2 clamps. Install the retaining nut and tighten to 108 inch lbs. (12 Nm).
34. Connect the heater water inlet tube hose and properly position clamp.
35. Install the accelerator splash shield and tighten 3 retaining bolts to 3 ft. lbs. (4 Nm).
36. Install 3 power steering reservoir bracket bolts.
37. Install the engine air cleaner outlet tube to the throttle body.
38. Connect the negative battery cable.
39. Start the engine and allow to idle for several minutes while checking for leaks.
40. Turn the engine **OFF** and recheck for leaks.
41. Road test the vehicle and check for proper engine operation.

5.8L and 7.5L Engines

1. Disconnect the negative battery cable.
2. Relieve the fuel system pressure.
3. Remove the upper intake manifold assembly.
4. Disconnect the wiring at each injector.
5. Remove the fuel supply manifold retaining bolts.
6. Pull upward on the supply manifold while gently rocking it from side-to-side.

To install:

7. Inspect the O-rings on the injector for any sign of leakage or damage. Replace any suspected O-rings.

Fig. 29 Detach the fuel injector connectors

Fig. 30 Remove the fuel rail-to-intake manifold retaining bolts and . . .

Fig. 31 . . . carefully lift the injector rail from the intake manifold

8. Lubricate the O-rings with clean engine oil.

9. Install the supply manifold carefully by engaging the injectors into the lower intake manifold by pushing them in with a gentle rocking motion.

10. Install the fuel supply manifold retaining bolts.

11. Connect the electrical wiring.

12. Install the upper intake manifold.

13. Connect the negative battery cable.

Fuel Pressure Regulator

REMOVAL & INSTALLATION

▶ **See Figures 32 and 33**

1. Disconnect the negative battery cable.
2. Properly relieve the fuel system pressure.

Fig. 32 Remove the pressure regulator retaining screws and lift the regulator off of the rail

3. Remove the air cleaner outlet tube(s).

4. Remove any necessary components to access the pressure regulator.

5. Disconnect the vacuum hose from the pressure regulator.

6. Remove the pressure regulator attaching screws.

7. Remove the pressure regulator from the fuel rail.

To install:

8. Discard the O-rings on the pressure regulator and replace them with new ones.

9. Lubricate the O-rings with clean engine oil.

10. Install the regulator into the fuel rail and tighten the retaining screws.

11. Connect the vacuum hose to the regulator.

12. Install any components removed to access the regulator.

13. Install the air cleaner outlet tube(s).

14. Connect the negative battery cable.

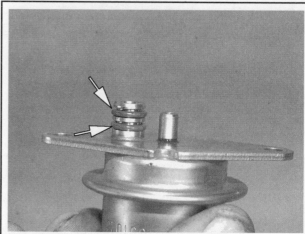

Fig. 33 Replace the O-rings on the bottom of the fuel pressure regulator

DIESEL FUEL SYSTEM

General Information

The 7.3L Direct Injection Turbo (DIT) Engine uses a unique injection system. Absent from a normal diesel injection system are a mechanical injection pump and injection lines. New components include a high pressure oil pump and reservoir, pressure regulator for the oil and passages in the cylinder head for the flow of the fuel to the injectors.

Fuel is drawn from the fuel tank by a tandem fuel pump. The tandem fuel pump circulates fuel at low pressure through the fuel filter/water separator/fuel heater and then fuel is directed back to the fuel pump where fuel is pumped at high pressure into the cylinder head fuel galleries. The injectors are then fired by the PCM, which are controlled by the PCM but hydraulically actuated by the oil pressure from the high pressure oil pump.

The control system for the fuel injection is the PCM, which meets OBD-II compliance. The injectors are fired based on various inputs received by the PCM. Refer to Section 4 for more info on the PCM inputs.

Relieving Fuel System Pressure

❊ CAUTION

Before removing the fuel tank filler cap, turn the fuel tank filler cap ¼ to ¾ turn counterclockwise and wait for the tank pressure to be relieved. Personal injury may result if the fuel tank filler cap is removed without the pressure fully relieved.

1. Remove the fuel tank filler cap to relieve any pressure in the fuel tank.

2. When servicing the fuel lines, loosen the fuel fitting to allow any residual fuel line pressure to be relieved.

Injectors

REMOVAL & INSTALLATION

▶ **See Figures 34, 35, 36 and 37**

❊ CAUTION

Observe all applicable safety precautions when working around fuel. Whenever servicing the fuel system, always work in a well ventilated area. Do not allow fuel spray or vapors to come in contact with a spark or open flame. Keep a dry chemical fire extinguisher near the work area. Always keep fuel in a container specifically designed for fuel storage; also, always properly seal fuel containers to avoid the possibility of fire or explosion.

❊ CAUTION

The red-striped wires on the DI Turbo carry 115 volts DC. A severe electrical shock may be given. Do not pierce the wires.

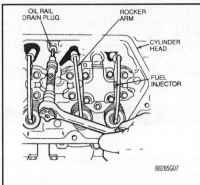

Fig. 34 Don't forget to remove the oil rail drain plug

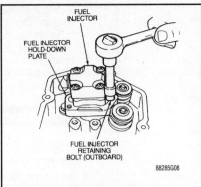

Fig. 35 Remove the outboard fuel injector retaining bolt as shown

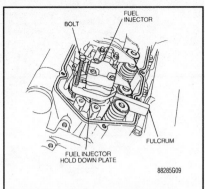

Fig. 36 Install the Injector Remover tool as shown

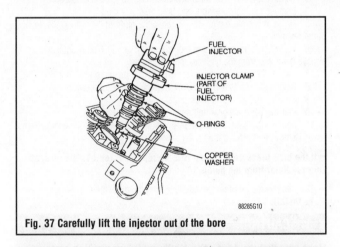

Fig. 37 Carefully lift the injector out of the bore

❊❊ WARNING

Do not pierce the wires or damage to the harness could occur.

Special tools required:
- Slide Hammer, No. T50T–100–A, or equivalent
- Injector Remover, No. T94T–9000–AH1, or equivalent
- Injector Replacer, No. T94T–9000–AH2, or equivalent
1. Remove the valve cover.
2. Disengage the fuel injector electrical connector.

❊❊ WARNING

Remove the oil drain plugs prior to removing the injectors or oil could enter the combustion chamber which could result in hydrostatic lock and severe engine damage.

3. Remove the oil rail drain plugs.
4. Remove the retaining screw and oil deflector. The shoulder bolt on the inboard side of the fuel injector does not require removal.
5. Remove the outboard fuel injector retaining bolt.
6. Remove the heater distribution box screws, nuts and clip. Remove the outer half of the case (to service No. 4 fuel injector only).
7. Remove the fuel injector using Injector Remover No. T94T–9000–AH1, or equivalent. Position the tool's fulcrum beneath the fuel injector hold-down plate and over the edge of the cylinder head. Install the remover screw in the threaded hole of the fuel injector plate (see illustration). Tighten the screw to lift out the injector from its bore. Place the injector in a suitable protective sleeve such as Rotunda Injector Protective Sleeve, No. 014–00933–2, and set the injector in a suitable holding rack.
8. Remove the fuel injector sleeves, if required. Insert the Injector Sleeve Tap Plug, 014–00934–3 into the injector sleeve to prevent debris from entering the combustion chamber. Insert Injector Sleeve Tap Pilot into the fuel injector sleeve and tighten 1–1 ½ turns. Attach Slide Hammer T50T–100–A to the

Injector Sleeve Tap 014–00934–1 and 014–00934–2 Injector Sleeve Tap Pilot and remove the fuel injector sleeve from the bore.
9. Use Rotunda Injector Sleeve Brush 104–00934–A, or equivalent to clean the injector bore of any sealant residue. Make sure to remove any debris.
To install:
10. If removed, install the fuel injector sleeves using Rotunda Sleeve Replacer, No. 014–00934–4, or equivalent. Apply Threadlock, No. 262–E2FZ–19554–B, or equivalent to the fuel injector sleeves as shown (see illustration). Using a rubber mallet, tap on the tool to seat the injector bore. Remove the tool and remove any residue sealant.
11. Clean the fuel injector sleeve using a suitable sleeve brush set. Clean any debris from the sleeve.
12. Clean the injector bore with a lint-free shop towel.
13. Install the fuel injectors using special tools as follows:
    a. Lubricate the injectors with clean engine oil. Using new copper washers, carefully push the injectors square into the bore using hand pressure only to seat the O-rings.
    b. Position the open end of Injector Replacer, No. T94T–9000–AH2, or equivalent between the fuel injector body and injector hold-down plate, while positioning the opposite end of the tool over the edge of the cylinder head.
    c. Align the hole in the tool with the threaded hole in the cylinder head and install the bolt from the tool kit. Tighten the bolt to fully seat the injector, then remove the bolt and tool.
14. Install the outer half of the heater distribution box and retaining hardware (for No. 4 injector only).
15. Install the oil deflector and bolt. Tighten the bolt to 108 inch lbs. (12 Nm).
16. Install the fuel rail drain plug, tightening it to 96 inch lbs. (11 Nm).
17. Install the oil rail drain plug, tightening it to 53 inch lbs. (6 Nm).
18. Install the heater distribution box.
19. Connect the fuel injector wiring harness.
20. Install the valve cover.

TESTING

The procedure for testing the injectors is quite complex, dangerous and requires many special tools that are out of the budget of the average do-it-yourselfer. We at Chilton recommend that you take the vehicle to a professional shop experienced with the complicated injection system on your model.

High Pressure Oil Pump Reservoir

REMOVAL & INSTALLATION

♦ See Figure 38

1. Disconnect the negative battery cable.
2. Remove the plug from the oil reservoir.
3. Using a suitable suction tool, remove the oil from the high-pressure oil pump reservoir.
4. Disconnect the fuel filter assembly from the engine front cover.
5. Detach the electrical connector from the exhaust back pressure sensor.

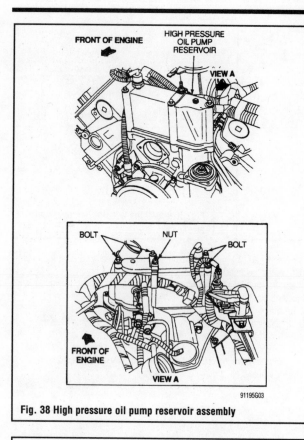

Fig. 38 High pressure oil pump reservoir assembly

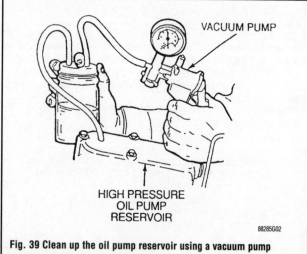

Fig. 39 Clean up the oil pump reservoir using a vacuum pump

6. Remove the fuel filter retaining bolts.
7. Detach the electrical connector from the oil temperature sensor.
8. Detach the electrical connector from the oil pressure switch.
9. Remove the bolts, oil reservoir and seal from the engine front cover.

To install:
10. Replace the reservoir seal.
11. The installation is the reverse of the removal.

High Pressure Oil Pump

REMOVAL & INSTALLATION

▶ **See Figures 39, 40, 41 and 42**

1. Disconnect the negative battery cable.
2. Remove the turbocharger compressor manifold. Refer to Section 3.
3. Remove the fuel filter/water separator assembly. Refer to Section 1.
4. Remove the high-pressure oil pump reservoir plug.
5. Using a suitable suction tool, remove the oil from the high-pressure oil pump reservoir.
6. Using the high-pressure line disconnect tool 303-625 or equivalent, remove the hoses from the high-pressure oil pump.
7. Detach the electrical connector from the oil pressure regulator.
8. Remove the bolts and the cover from the engine front cover.
9. Position the wiring harness aside.
10. Remove the drive gear bolt and washer from the drive gear.
11. Remove the bolts and the high-pressure oil pump from the engine front cover. Remove and discard the gasket.

➡**If the high-pressure oil pump is to be replaced, remove the oil pressure regulator from the pump.**

12. Remove the oil pressure regulator from the oil pump.

To install:

❊❊ CAUTION

Make sure that the drive gear is fully seated on the high-pressure oil pump before installing the bolt and washer. Otherwise, the drive gear may not seat properly, causing binding or slippage resulting in a no oil flow condition.

13. The installation is the reverse of the removal.

High Pressure Oil Pump Drive Gear

REMOVAL & INSTALLATION

1. Remove the high-pressure oil pump reservoir as described in this section.
2. Remove the high-pressure oil pump as described in this section.
3. Remove the drive gear from the crankcase front cover.

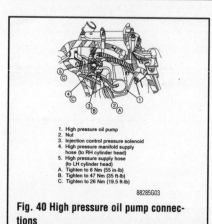

1. High pressure oil pump
2. Nut
3. Injection control pressure solenoid
4. High pressure manifold supply hose (to RH cylinder head)
5. High pressure supply hose (to LH cylinder head)
A. Tighten to 6 Nm (55 in-lb)
B. Tighten to 47 Nm (35 ft-lb)
C. Tighten to 26 Nm (19.5 ft-lb)

Fig. 40 High pressure oil pump connections

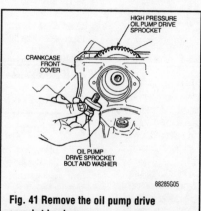

Fig. 41 Remove the oil pump drive sprocket hardware

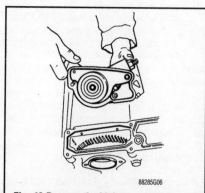

Fig. 42 Remove the high pressure oil pump

4. Remove all gasket residue from the mating surfaces.

To install:

5. Position the drive gear into the crankcase front cover.
6. The balance of the installation is the reverse of the removal.

✷✷ CAUTION

Make sure that the drive gear is fully seated on the high-pressure oil pump before installing the bolt and washer. Otherwise the drive gear may not seat properly, causing binding or slippage resulting in a no oil flow condition.

Fuel Pressure Regulator

REMOVAL & INSTALLATION

▶ See Figure 43

✷✷ WARNING

Clean all fuel residue from the engine compartment. Failure to do so can cause personal injury or damage to the vehicle.

1. Remove the Torx® screws.
2. Remove the cap.
3. Remove O-ring.
4. Remove the spring.
5. Remove the poppet valve and O-ring.
6. Remove the valve seat.
7. Remove O-ring.
8. Thoroughly clean the fuel pressure regulator bore in the fuel filter/water separator.

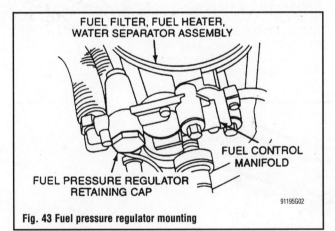

FUEL FILTER, FUEL HEATER, WATER SEPARATOR ASSEMBLY

FUEL CONTROL MANIFOLD

FUEL PRESSURE REGULATOR RETAINING CAP

91195G02

Fig. 43 Fuel pressure regulator mounting

To install:

9. The installation is the reverse of the removal.

Oil Pressure Regulator

REMOVAL & INSTALLATION

▶ See Figure 44

1. Remove the turbocharger compressor manifold. Refer to Section 3.
2. Remove the fuel filter/water separator. Refer to Section 1.
3. Detach the electrical connector from the oil pressure regulator.
4. Remove the pressure regulator from the high-pressure oil pump.
5. The installation is the reverse of the removal.

Fuel Supply Pump

REMOVAL & INSTALLATION

▶ See Figures 45 and 46

1. Disconnect both battery ground cables.
2. Properly relieve the fuel system pressure.
3. Raise and safely support the vehicle securely on jackstands.

➡ **The electrical connector is located behind the fuel pump near the frame rail.**

4. Detach the fuel pump electrical connector.
5. Remove the fuel line retaining clip and discard, then remove the fuel line from the fuel pump.
6. Slide the clip up and off from the quick connect fitting. Insert the fuel line tool and remove the fuel pump delivery line.
7. Unclip the brake lines from the fuel pump bracket.
8. Loosen the pinch bolt and spread the mounting bracket.
9. Remove the fuel pump.
10. The installation is the reverse of the removal.

Glow Plugs

DIAGNOSIS & TESTING

▶ See Figure 47

1. Turn the ignition **OFF**.
2. Detach the connectors from the glow plugs.
3. Connect a test lamp between the battery positive terminal and the glow plug. There should be continuity and the light should go on.
4. If the light does not go on, the glow plug is faulty and must be replaced.

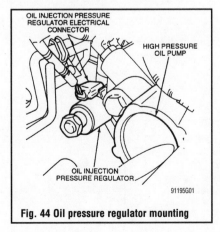

OIL INJECTION PRESSURE REGULATOR ELECTRICAL CONNECTOR

HIGH PRESSURE OIL PUMP

OIL INJECTION PRESSURE REGULATOR

91195G01

Fig. 44 Oil pressure regulator mounting

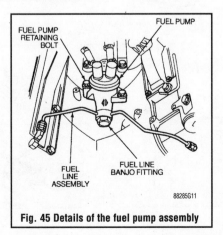

FUEL PUMP RETAINING BOLT

FUEL PUMP

FUEL LINE ASSEMBLY

FUEL LINE BANJO FITTING

88285G11

Fig. 45 Details of the fuel pump assembly

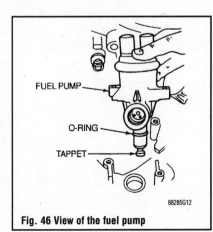

FUEL PUMP

O-RING

TAPPET

88285G12

Fig. 46 View of the fuel pump

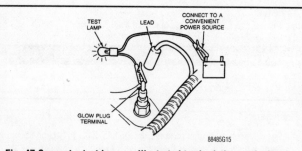

Fig. 47 Connect a test lamp as illustrated to check the continuity of the glow plugs

REMOVAL & INSTALLATION

※ CAUTION

The red-striped wiring harness carries 115v direct current. Severe electrical shock may be received. DO NOT pierce.

FUEL TANK

Tank Assembly

REMOVAL & INSTALLATION

♦ See Figure 48

➡ Some vehicles are equipped with two fuel tanks, one located in the center of the vehicle and one in the rear.

1. Properly relieve the fuel system pressure.
2. Disconnect the negative battery cable.
3. Remove the fuel from the gas tank using a siphon pump or other suitable device.
4. Raise and safely support the vehicle securely on jackstands.

1. Disconnect the negative battery cable.
2. Remove the rocker arm cover.
3. Disconnect the glow plug electrical leads using a pair of pliers.
4. Remove the glow plugs by unscrewing them from the cylinder head with a 10mm socket and wrench.
5. Inspect the tips of the plugs for any evidence of distortion or missing tip ends; replace them if necessary.

To install:

6. Install the glow plug into the cylinder head. Tighten the glow plugs to 14 ft. lbs. (19 Nm).
7. Attach the glow plug electrical connector. Be sure that the glow plug wiring is routed to avoid moving components in the engine bay.
8. Install the rocker arm cover.

➡When the battery is disengaged and reconnected, some abnormal drive symptoms may occur while the vehicle relearns its adaptive strategy. The vehicle may need to be driven 10 miles (16 km) or more to relearn this strategy.

9. Connect the negative battery cable.

5. If the vehicle is equipped with skid plates, remove the skid plates.
6. Place a suitable jack or other support device under the fuel tank.
7. Loosen the fuel tank retaining strap bolts.
8. Carefully lower the fuel tank enough to access the fuel lines, EVAP system hoses and any necessary hoses, lines or electrical wiring that require disconnection before fuel tank removal.
9. Slowly lower the fuel tank from the vehicle.

To install:

10. If the fuel tank is being replaced, transfer any components over to the new fuel tank.
11. Place the fuel tank on a jack or other suitable device and raise the tank, however leave enough room to connect the fuel lines, etc.
12. Connect any fuel lines, EVAP hoses, or any electrical wiring disconnected for removal.

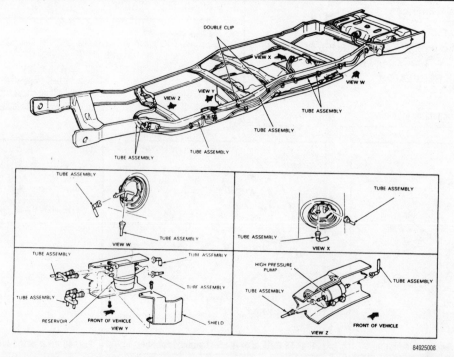

Fig. 48 Typical dual fuel tank mounting

13. Raise the tank into position and position the fuel tank retaining straps.
14. Loosely install the fuel tank retaining strap bolts.
15. Tighten the fuel tank retaining strap bolts.
16. Remove the jack or other device from the fuel tank.
17. If removed, install the skid plates.
18. Lower the vehicle.
19. Fill the fuel tank with gas.
20. Connect the negative battery cable.

Electric Fuel Pump

REMOVAL & INSTALLATION

F-150, F-250, Expedition and Navigator

▶ See Figure 49

1. Disconnect the negative battery cable.
2. Relieve the fuel pressure.
3. Raise and support the vehicle.
4. Remove the fuel tank; refer to the procedure outlined in this section.
5. Remove the fuel pump retaining bolts.
6. Remove the fuel pump.

To install:

7. Thoroughly clean the fuel pump mounting flange.
8. Install a new gasket and place the pump into the tank.
9. Ensure that the fuel tubes face toward the fuel rail and tighten the retaining bolts to 80–107 inch lbs. (9–12 Nm).
10. Install the tank as outlined in this section.
11. Tighten the fuel tank bolts to 66–91 inch lbs. (7.6–10.4 Nm).
12. Tighten the fuel tank strap bolts to 22–30 ft. lbs. (29.7–40.7 Nm).
13. Tighten the skid plate bolts to 9.3–12.7 ft. lbs. (12.7–17.3 Nm).
14. Connect the negative battery.

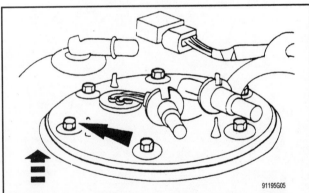

Fig. 49 Fuel pump mounting— F-150, F-250, Expedition and Navigator

1997–98 F-250HD, F-350 and F-Super Duty Models

▶ See Figure 50

1. Release the fuel system pressure.
2. Disconnect the negative battery cable.
3. Raise and safely support the vehicle securely on jackstands.
4. Remove the fuel tank; refer to the procedure outlined in this section.
5. If equipped with a steel fuel tank:
   a. Remove all dirt from the area of the sender.
   b. Turn the locking ring counterclockwise to remove it. There is a wrench designed for this purpose. If the wrench is not available, loosen the locking ring by placing a wood dowel against the tabs on the locking ring and carefully hammer it loose. Never use a metal drift!
   c. Lift out the fuel pump and sending unit. Discard the gasket.

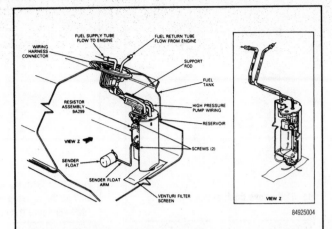

Fig. 50 Electric fuel pump assembly—1997–98 F-250HD, F-350 and F-Super Duty Models

❋❋ CAUTION

Use of a metal drift may result in sparks which could cause an explosion!

6. If equipped with a plastic fuel tank:
   a. Remove all dirt from the area of the sender.
   b. Turn the locking ring counterclockwise to remove it. A band-type oil filter wrench is ideal for this purpose. Lift out the fuel pump and sending unit. Discard the gasket.

To install:

7. Place a new gasket in position in the groove in the tank.
8. Place the sending unit/fuel pump assembly in the tank, indexing the tabs with the slots in the tank. Make sure the gasket stays in place.
9. Hold the assembly in place and position the locking ring.
10. On steel tanks, turn the locking ring clockwise until the stop is against the retainer ring tab.
11. On plastic tanks, turn the retaining ring clockwise until hand-tight, then torque it 40–55 ft. lbs.
12. Make sure the gasket is still in place.
13. Connect the fuel lines and wiring.
14. Install the tank as outlined in this section.

1999–00 F-Super Duty Models

MIDSHIP MOUNTED TANK

▶ See Figures 51 and 52

1. Remove the fuel tank; refer to the procedure outlined in this section.
2. Clean the area around the fuel pump mounting area.

❋❋ WARNING

The fuel pump module must be handled carefully to avoid damage to the pump assembly.

3. Remove the locking retaining ring from the fuel tank mounting flange and lift up on the fuel pump sender flange to gain access to the pump module.
4. Reach into the tank to disconnect the retaining latches by squeezing the latches together while pushing down on the module to release the pump from the mounting bracket in the bottom of the fuel tank.
5. Remove the pump assembly.
6. Remove and discard the fuel pump mounting gasket.

To install:

7. Clean and inspect the fuel pump mounting flange and the fuel tank mounting surface.

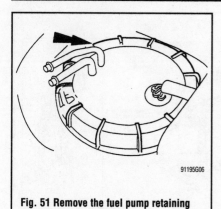

Fig. 51 Remove the fuel pump retaining ring and . . .

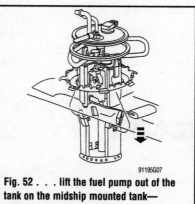
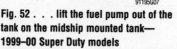

Fig. 52 . . . lift the fuel pump out of the tank on the midship mounted tank—1999–00 Super Duty models

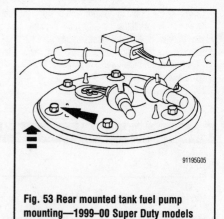

Fig. 53 Rear mounted tank fuel pump mounting—1999–00 Super Duty models

8. Connect the retaining latches of the pump module into the mounting bracket by aligning pump and pushing down until the pump is latched on both sides.

9. Install a new fuel pump mounting gasket and install the fuel pump sender flange.

10. Align the fuel pump tubes so they point toward the frame rail.

11. Tighten the fuel pump retaining cap.

12. Install the tank as outlined in this section.

REAR MOUNTED TANK (AFT AXLE MOUNTED)

▶ See Figure 53

1. Remove the fuel tank; refer to the procedure outlined in this section.
2. Clean the area around the fuel pump mounting flange.

✳✳ WARNING

The fuel pump module must be handled carefully to avoid damage.

3. Remove the bolts and lift up on the fuel pump sender flange.

4. Depress the locking tabs on the pump while applying downward pressure on the pump module to release the pump from the mounting bracket.

5. Remove the pump assembly.

6. Remove and discard the mounting flange gasket.

To install:

7. Clean and inspect the fuel pump mounting flange and the fuel tank mounting surface.

8. Connect the retaining latches of the pump module into the mounting bracket by aligning pump and pushing down until pump is latched on both sides.

9. Install a new fuel pump.

10. Install a new fuel pump mounting gasket and install fuel pump sender flange.

11. Align the fuel pump tubes so they point to the front of the vehicle. Install the bolts.

12. Install the fuel tank as outlined in this section.

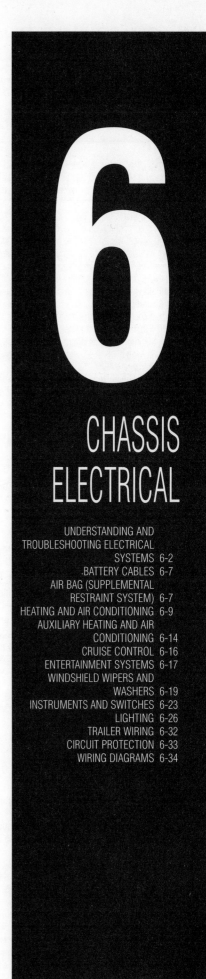

6

CHASSIS ELECTRICAL

UNDERSTANDING AND TROUBLESHOOTING ELECTRICAL SYSTEMS

Basic Electrical Theory

♦ **See Figure 1**

For any 12 volt, negative ground, electrical system to operate, the electricity must travel in a complete circuit. This simply means that current (power) from the positive (+) terminal of the battery must eventually return to the negative (-) terminal of the battery. Along the way, this current will travel through wires, fuses, switches and components. If, for any reason, the flow of current through the circuit is interrupted, the component fed by that circuit will cease to function properly.

Perhaps the easiest way to visualize a circuit is to think of connecting a light bulb (with two wires attached to it) to the battery—one wire attached to the negative (-) terminal of the battery and the other wire to the positive (+) terminal. With the two wires touching the battery terminals, the circuit would be complete and the light bulb would illuminate. Electricity would follow a path from the battery to the bulb and back to the battery. It's easy to see that with longer wires on our light bulb, it could be mounted anywhere. Further, one wire could be fitted with a switch so that the light could be turned on and off.

The normal automotive circuit differs from this simple example in two ways. First, instead of having a return wire from the bulb to the battery, the current travels through the frame of the vehicle. Since the negative (-) battery cable is attached to the frame (made of electrically conductive metal), the frame of the vehicle can serve as a ground wire to complete the circuit. Secondly, most automotive circuits contain multiple components which receive power from a single circuit. This lessens the amount of wire needed to power components on the vehicle.

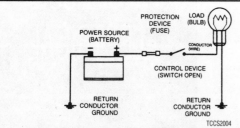

TCCS2004

Fig. 1 This example illustrates a simple circuit. When the switch is closed, power from the positive (+) battery terminal flows through the fuse and the switch, and then to the light bulb. The light illuminates and the circuit is completed through the ground wire back to the negative (-) battery terminal. In reality, the two ground points shown in the illustration are attached to the metal frame of the vehicle, which completes the circuit back to the battery

HOW DOES ELECTRICITY WORK: THE WATER ANALOGY

Electricity is the flow of electrons—the subatomic particles that constitute the outer shell of an atom. Electrons spin in an orbit around the center core of an atom. The center core is comprised of protons (positive charge) and neutrons (neutral charge). Electrons have a negative charge and balance out the positive charge of the protons. When an outside force causes the number of electrons to unbalance the charge of the protons, the electrons will split off the atom and look for another atom to balance out. If this imbalance is kept up, electrons will continue to move and an electrical flow will exist.

Many people have been taught electrical theory using an analogy with water. In a comparison with water flowing through a pipe, the electrons would be the water and the wire is the pipe.

The flow of electricity can be measured much like the flow of water through a pipe. The unit of measurement used is amperes, frequently abbreviated as amps (a). You can compare amperage to the volume of water flowing through a pipe. When connected to a circuit, an ammeter will measure the actual amount of current flowing through the circuit. When relatively few electrons flow through a circuit, the amperage is low. When many electrons flow, the amperage is high.

Water pressure is measured in units such as pounds per square inch (psi); The electrical pressure is measured in units called volts (v). When a voltmeter is connected to a circuit, it is measuring the electrical pressure.

The actual flow of electricity depends not only on voltage and amperage, but also on the resistance of the circuit. The higher the resistance, the higher the force necessary to push the current through the circuit. The standard unit for measuring resistance is an ohm. Resistance in a circuit varies depending on the amount and type of components used in the circuit. The main factors which determine resistance are:

• Material—some materials have more resistance than others. Those with high resistance are said to be insulators. Rubber materials (or rubber-like plastics) are some of the most common insulators used in vehicles as they have a very high resistance to electricity. Very low resistance materials are said to be conductors. Copper wire is among the best conductors. Silver is actually a superior conductor to copper and is used in some relay contacts, but its high cost prohibits its use as common wiring. Most automotive wiring is made of copper.

• Size—the larger the wire size being used, the less resistance the wire will have. This is why components which use large amounts of electricity usually have large wires supplying current to them.

• Length—for a given thickness of wire, the longer the wire, the greater the resistance. The shorter the wire, the less the resistance. When determining the proper wire for a circuit, both size and length must be considered to design a circuit that can handle the current needs of the component.

• Temperature—with many materials, the higher the temperature, the greater the resistance (positive temperature coefficient). Some materials exhibit the opposite trait of lower resistance with higher temperatures (negative temperature coefficient). These principles are used in many of the sensors on the engine.

OHM'S LAW

There is a direct relationship between current, voltage and resistance. The relationship between current, voltage and resistance can be summed up by a statement known as Ohm's law.

Voltage (E) is equal to amperage (I) times resistance ®: $E = I \times R$

Other forms of the formula are $R = E/I$ and $I = E/R$

In each of these formulas, E is the voltage in volts, I is the current in amps and R is the resistance in ohms. The basic point to remember is that as the resistance of a circuit goes up, the amount of current that flows in the circuit will go down, if voltage remains the same.

The amount of work that the electricity can perform is expressed as power. The unit of power is the watt (w). The relationship between power, voltage and current is expressed as:

Power (w) is equal to amperage (I) times voltage (E): $W = I \times E$

This is only true for direct current (DC) circuits; The alternating current formula is a tad different, but since the electrical circuits in most vehicles are DC type, we need not get into AC circuit theory.

Electrical Components

POWER SOURCE

Power is supplied to the vehicle by two devices: The battery and the alternator. The battery supplies electrical power during starting or during periods when the current demand of the vehicle's electrical system exceeds the output capacity of the alternator. The alternator supplies electrical current when the engine is running. Just not does the alternator supply the current needs of the vehicle, but it recharges the battery.

The Battery

In most modern vehicles, the battery is a lead/acid electrochemical device consisting of six 2 volt subsections (cells) connected in series, so that the unit is capable of producing approximately 12 volts of electrical pressure. Each subsection consists of a series of positive and negative plates held a short distance apart in a solution of sulfuric acid and water.

The two types of plates are of dissimilar metals. This sets up a chemical reaction, and it is this reaction which produces current flow from the battery when its positive and negative terminals are connected to an electrical load. The power removed from the battery is replaced by the alternator, restoring the battery to its original chemical state.

The Alternator

On some vehicles there isn't an alternator, but a generator. The difference is that an alternator supplies alternating current which is then changed to direct current for use on the vehicle, while a generator produces direct current. Alternators tend to be more efficient and that is why they are used.

Alternators and generators are devices that consist of coils of wires wound together making big electromagnets. One group of coils spins within another set and the interaction of the magnetic fields causes a current to flow. This current is then drawn off the coils and fed into the vehicles electrical system.

GROUND

Two types of grounds are used in automotive electric circuits. Direct ground components are grounded to the frame through their mounting points. All other components use some sort of ground wire which is attached to the frame or chassis of the vehicle. The electrical current runs through the chassis of the vehicle and returns to the battery through the ground (-) cable; if you look, you'll see that the battery ground cable connects between the battery and the frame or chassis of the vehicle.

➡**It should be noted that a good percentage of electrical problems can be traced to bad grounds.**

PROTECTIVE DEVICES

▶ **See Figure 2**

It is possible for large surges of current to pass through the electrical system of your vehicle. If this surge of current were to reach the load in the circuit, the surge could burn it out or severely damage it. It can also overload the wiring, causing the harness to get hot and melt the insulation. To prevent this, fuses, circuit breakers and/or fusible links are connected into the supply wires of the electrical system. These items are nothing more than a built-in weak spot in the system. When an abnormal amount of current flows through the system, these protective devices work as follows to protect the circuit:

• Fuse—when an excessive electrical current passes through a fuse, the fuse "blows" (the conductor melts) and opens the circuit, preventing the passage of current.

• Circuit Breaker—a circuit breaker is basically a self-repairing fuse. It will open the circuit in the same fashion as a fuse, but when the surge subsides, the circuit breaker can be reset and does not need replacement.

• Fusible Link—a fusible link (fuse link or main link) is a short length of special, high temperature insulated wire that acts as a fuse. When an excessive electrical current passes through a fusible link, the thin gauge wire inside the link melts, creating an intentional open to protect the circuit. To repair the circuit, the link must be replaced. Some newer type fusible links are housed in plug-in modules, which are simply replaced like a fuse, while older type fusible links must be cut and spliced if they melt. Since this link is very early in the electrical path, it's the first place to look if nothing on the vehicle works, yet the battery seems to be charged and is properly connected.

SWITCHES & RELAYS

▶ **See Figures 3 and 4**

Switches are used in electrical circuits to control the passage of current. The most common use is to open and close circuits between the battery and the various electric devices in the system. Switches are rated according to the amount of amperage they can handle. If a sufficient amperage rated switch is not used in a circuit, the switch could overload and cause damage.

Some electrical components which require a large amount of current to operate use a special switch called a relay. Since these circuits carry a large amount of current, the thickness of the wire in the circuit is also greater. If this large wire were connected from the load to the control switch, the switch would have to carry the high amperage load and the fairing or dash would be twice as large to accommodate the increased size of the wiring harness. To prevent these problems, a relay is used.

Relays are composed of a coil and a set of contacts. When the coil has a current passed though it, a magnetic field is formed and this field causes the contacts to move together, completing the circuit. Most relays are normally open, preventing current from passing through the circuit, but they can take any electrical form depending on the job they are intended to do. Relays can be considered "remote control switches." They allow a smaller current to operate devices that require higher amperages. When a small current operates the coil, a larger current is allowed to pass by the contacts. Some common circuits which may use relays are the horn, headlights, starter, electric fuel pump and other high draw circuits.

LOAD

Every electrical circuit must include a "load" (something to use the electricity coming from the source). Without this load, the battery would attempt to deliver its entire power supply from one pole to another. This is called a "short circuit." All this electricity would take a short cut to ground and cause a great amount of damage to other components in the circuit by developing a tremendous amount of heat. This condition could develop sufficient heat to melt the insulation on all the surrounding wires and reduce a multiple wire cable to a lump of plastic and copper.

WIRING & HARNESSES

The average vehicle contains meters and meters of wiring, with hundreds of individual connections. To protect the many wires from damage and to keep them from becoming a confusing tangle, they are organized into bundles, enclosed in plastic or taped together and called wiring harnesses. Different harnesses serve different parts of the vehicle. Individual wires are color coded to help trace them through a harness where sections are hidden from view.

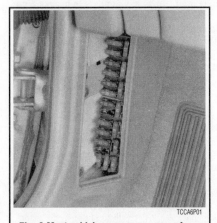

TCCA6P01

Fig. 2 Most vehicles use one or more fuse panels. This one is located on the driver's side kick panel

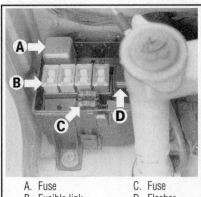

A. Fuse
B. Fusible link
C. Fuse
D. Flasher

TCCA6P02

Fig. 3 The underhood fuse and relay panel usually contains fuses, relays, flashers and fusible links

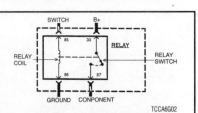

TCCA6G02

Fig. 4 Relays are composed of a coil and a switch. These two components are linked together so that when one operates, the other operates at the same time. The large wires in the circuit are connected from the battery to one side of the relay switch (B+) and from the opposite side of the relay switch to the load (component). Smaller wires are connected from the relay coil to the control switch for the circuit and from the opposite side of the relay coil to ground

Automotive wiring or circuit conductors can be either single strand wire, multi-strand wire or printed circuitry. Single strand wire has a solid metal core and is usually used inside such components as alternators, motors, relays and other devices. Multi-strand wire has a core made of many small strands of wire twisted together into a single conductor. Most of the wiring in an automotive electrical system is made up of multi-strand wire, either as a single conductor or grouped together in a harness. All wiring is color coded on the insulator, either as a solid color or as a colored wire with an identification stripe. A printed circuit is a thin film of copper or other conductor that is printed on an insulator backing. Occasionally, a printed circuit is sandwiched between two sheets of plastic for more protection and flexibility. A complete printed circuit, consisting of conductors, insulating material and connectors for lamps or other components is called a printed circuit board. Printed circuitry is used in place of individual wires or harnesses in places where space is limited, such as behind instrument panels.

Since automotive electrical systems are very sensitive to changes in resistance, the selection of properly sized wires is critical when systems are repaired. A loose or corroded connection or a replacement wire that is too small for the circuit will add extra resistance and an additional voltage drop to the circuit.

The wire gauge number is an expression of the cross-section area of the conductor. Vehicles from countries that use the metric system will typically describe the wire size as its cross-sectional area in square millimeters. In this method, the larger the wire, the greater the number. Another common system for expressing wire size is the American Wire Gauge (AWG) system. As gauge number increases, area decreases and the wire becomes smaller. An 18 gauge wire is smaller than a 4 gauge wire. A wire with a higher gauge number will carry less current than a wire with a lower gauge number. Gauge wire size refers to the size of the strands of the conductor, not the size of the complete wire with insulator. It is possible, therefore, to have two wires of the same gauge with different diameters because one may have thicker insulation than the other.

It is essential to understand how a circuit works before trying to figure out why it doesn't. An electrical schematic shows the electrical current paths when a circuit is operating properly. Schematics break the entire electrical system down into individual circuits. In a schematic, usually no attempt is made to represent wiring and components as they physically appear on the vehicle; switches and other components are shown as simply as possible. Face views of harness connectors show the cavity or terminal locations in all multi-pin connectors to help locate test points.

CONNECTORS

▶ See Figures 5 and 6

Three types of connectors are commonly used in automotive applications—weatherproof, molded and hard shell.

• Weatherproof—these connectors are most commonly used where the connector is exposed to the elements. Terminals are protected against moisture and dirt by sealing rings which provide a weathertight seal. All repairs require the use of a special terminal and the tool required to service it. Unlike standard blade type terminals, these weatherproof terminals cannot be straightened once they are bent. Make certain that the connectors are properly seated and all of the sealing rings are in place when connecting leads.

• Molded—these connectors require complete replacement of the connector if found to be defective. This means splicing a new connector assembly into the harness. All splices should be soldered to insure proper contact. Use care when probing the connections or replacing terminals in them, as it is possible to create a

Fig. 5 Hard shell (left) and weatherproof (right) connectors have replaceable terminals

Fig. 6 Weatherproof connectors are most commonly used in the engine compartment or where the connector is exposed to the elements

short circuit between opposite terminals. If this happens to the wrong terminal pair, it is possible to damage certain components. Always use jumper wires between connectors for circuit checking and NEVER probe through weatherproof seals.

• Hard Shell—unlike molded connectors, the terminal contacts in hard-shell connectors can be replaced. Replacement usually involves the use of a special terminal removal tool that depresses the locking tangs (barbs) on the connector terminal and allows the connector to be removed from the rear of the shell. The connector shell should be replaced if it shows any evidence of burning, melting, cracks, or breaks. Replace individual terminals that are burnt, corroded, distorted or loose.

Test Equipment

Pinpointing the exact cause of trouble in an electrical circuit is most times accomplished by the use of special test equipment. The following describes different types of commonly used test equipment and briefly explains how to use them in diagnosis. In addition to the information covered below, the tool manufacturer's instructions booklet (provided with the tester) should be read and clearly understood before attempting any test procedures.

JUMPER WIRES

✳✳ CAUTION

Never use jumper wires made from a thinner gauge wire than the circuit being tested. If the jumper wire is of too small a gauge, it may overheat and possibly melt. Never use jumpers to bypass high resistance loads in a circuit. Bypassing resistances, in effect, creates a short circuit. This may, in turn, cause damage and fire. Jumper wires should only be used to bypass lengths of wire or to simulate switches.

Jumper wires are simple, yet extremely valuable, pieces of test equipment. They are basically test wires which are used to bypass sections of a circuit. Although jumper wires can be purchased, they are usually fabricated from lengths of standard automotive wire and whatever type of connector (alligator clip, spade connector or pin connector) that is required for the particular application being tested. In cramped, hard-to-reach areas, it is advisable to have insulated boots over the jumper wire terminals in order to prevent accidental grounding. It is also advisable to include a standard automotive fuse in any jumper wire. This is commonly referred to as a "fused jumper". By inserting an in-line fuse holder between a set of test leads, a fused jumper wire can be used for bypassing open circuits. Use a 5 amp fuse to provide protection against voltage spikes.

Jumper wires are used primarily to locate open electrical circuits, on either the ground (-) side of the circuit or on the power (+) side. If an electrical component fails to operate, connect the jumper wire between the component and a good ground. If the component operates only with the jumper installed, the ground circuit is open. If the ground circuit is good, but the component does not operate, the circuit between the power feed and component may be open. By moving the jumper wire successively back from the component toward the power source, you can isolate the area of the circuit where the open is located. When the component stops functioning, or the power is cut off, the open is in the segment of wire between the jumper and the point previously tested.

You can sometimes connect the jumper wire directly from the battery to the "hot" terminal of the component, but first make sure the component uses 12 volts in operation. Some electrical components, such as fuel injectors or sensors, are designed to operate on about 4 to 5 volts, and running 12 volts directly to these components will cause damage.

TEST LIGHTS

▶ **See Figure 7**

The test light is used to check circuits and components while electrical current is flowing through them. It is used for voltage and ground tests. To use a 12 volt test light, connect the ground clip to a good ground and probe wherever necessary with the pick. The test light will illuminate when voltage is detected. This does not necessarily mean that 12 volts (or any particular amount of voltage) is present; it only means that some voltage is present. It is advisable before using the test light to touch its ground clip and probe across the battery posts or terminals to make sure the light is operating properly.

✳✳ WARNING

Do not use a test light to probe electronic ignition, spark plug or coil wires. Never use a pick-type test light to probe wiring on computer controlled systems unless specifically instructed to do so. Any wire insulation that is pierced by the test light probe should be taped and sealed with silicone after testing.

Like the jumper wire, the 12 volt test light is used to isolate opens in circuits. But, whereas the jumper wire is used to bypass the open to operate the load, the 12 volt test light is used to locate the presence of voltage in a circuit. If the test light illuminates, there is power up to that point in the circuit; if the test light does not illuminate, there is an open circuit (no power). Move the test light in successive steps back toward the power source until the light in the handle illuminates. The open is between the probe and a point which was previously probed.

The self-powered test light is similar in design to the 12 volt test light, but contains a 1.5 volt penlight battery in the handle. It is most often used in place of a multimeter to check for open or short circuits when power is isolated from the circuit (continuity test).

The battery in a self-powered test light does not provide much current. A weak battery may not provide enough power to illuminate the test light even when a complete circuit is made (especially if there is high resistance in the circuit). Always make sure that the test battery is strong. To check the battery, briefly touch the ground clip to the probe; if the light glows brightly, the battery is strong enough for testing.

➥**A self-powered test light should not be used on any computer controlled system or component. The small amount of electricity transmit-**

ted by the test light is enough to damage many electronic automotive components.

MULTIMETERS

Multimeters are an extremely useful tool for troubleshooting electrical problems. They can be purchased in either analog or digital form and have a price range to suit any budget. A multimeter is a voltmeter, ammeter and ohmmeter (along with other features) combined into one instrument. It is often used when testing solid state circuits because of its high input impedance (usually 10 megaohms or more). A brief description of the multimeter main test functions follows:

• Voltmeter—the voltmeter is used to measure voltage at any point in a circuit, or to measure the voltage drop across any part of a circuit. Voltmeters usually have various scales and a selector switch to allow the reading of different voltage ranges. The voltmeter has a positive and a negative lead. To avoid damage to the meter, always connect the negative lead to the negative (-) side of the circuit (to ground or nearest the ground side of the circuit) and connect the positive lead to the positive (+) side of the circuit (to the power source or the nearest power source). Note that the negative voltmeter lead will always be black and that the positive voltmeter will always be some color other than black (usually red).

• Ohmmeter—the ohmmeter is designed to read resistance (measured in ohms) in a circuit or component. Most ohmmeters will have a selector switch which permits the measurement of different ranges of resistance (usually the selector switch allows the multiplication of the meter reading by 10, 100, 1,000 and 10,000). Some ohmmeters are "auto-ranging" which means the meter itself will determine which scale to use. Since the meters are powered by an internal battery, the ohmmeter can be used like a self-powered test light. When the ohmmeter is connected, current from the ohmmeter flows through the circuit or component being tested. Since the ohmmeter's internal resistance and voltage are known values, the amount of current flow through the meter depends on the resistance of the circuit or component being tested. The ohmmeter can also be used to perform a continuity test for suspected open circuits. In using the meter for making continuity checks, do not be concerned with the actual resistance readings. Zero resistance, or any ohm reading, indicates continuity in the circuit. Infinite resistance indicates an opening in the circuit. A high resistance reading where there should be none indicates a problem in the circuit. Checks for short circuits are made in the same manner as checks for open circuits, except that the circuit must be isolated from both power and normal ground. Infinite resistance indicates no continuity, while zero resistance indicates a dead short.

✳✳ WARNING

Never use an ohmmeter to check the resistance of a component or wire while there is voltage applied to the circuit.

• Ammeter—an ammeter measures the amount of current flowing through a circuit in units called amperes or amps. At normal operating voltage, most circuits have a characteristic amount of amperes, called "current draw" which can be measured using an ammeter. By referring to a specified current draw rating, then measuring the amperes and comparing the two values, one can determine what is happening within the circuit to aid in diagnosis. An open circuit, for example, will not allow any current to flow, so the ammeter reading will be zero. A damaged component or circuit will have an increased current draw, so the reading will be high. The ammeter is always connected in series with the circuit being tested. All of the current that normally flows through the circuit must also flow through the ammeter; if there is any other path for the current to follow, the ammeter reading will not be accurate. The ammeter itself has very little resistance to current flow and, therefore, will not affect the circuit, but it will measure current draw only when the circuit is closed and electricity is flowing. Excessive current draw can blow fuses and drain the battery, while a reduced current draw can cause motors to run slowly, lights to dim and other components to not operate properly.

Troubleshooting Electrical Systems

When diagnosing a specific problem, organized troubleshooting is a must. The complexity of a modern automotive vehicle demands that you approach any problem in a logical, organized manner. There are certain troubleshooting techniques, however, which are standard:

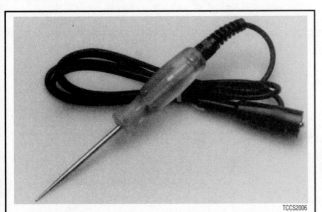

TCCS2006

Fig. 7 A 12 volt test light is used to detect the presence of voltage in a circuit

• Establish when the problem occurs. Does the problem appear only under certain conditions? Were there any noises, odors or other unusual symptoms? Isolate the problem area. To do this, make some simple tests and observations, then eliminate the systems that are working properly. Check for obvious problems, such as broken wires and loose or dirty connections. Always check the obvious before assuming something complicated is the cause.

• Test for problems systematically to determine the cause once the problem area is isolated. Are all the components functioning properly? Is there power going to electrical switches and motors. Performing careful, systematic checks will often turn up most causes on the first inspection, without wasting time checking components that have little or no relationship to the problem.

• Test all repairs after the work is done to make sure that the problem is fixed. Some causes can be traced to more than one component, so a careful verification of repair work is important in order to pick up additional malfunctions that may cause a problem to reappear or a different problem to arise. A blown fuse, for example, is a simple problem that may require more than another fuse to repair. If you don't look for a problem that caused a fuse to blow, a shorted wire (for example) may go undetected.

Experience has shown that most problems tend to be the result of a fairly simple and obvious cause, such as loose or corroded connectors, bad grounds or damaged wire insulation which causes a short. This makes careful visual inspection of components during testing essential to quick and accurate troubleshooting.

Testing

OPEN CIRCUITS

▶ **See Figure 8**

This test already assumes the existence of an open in the circuit and it is used to help locate the open portion.

1. Isolate the circuit from power and ground.
2. Connect the self-powered test light or ohmmeter ground clip to the ground side of the circuit and probe sections of the circuit sequentially.
3. If the light is out or there is infinite resistance, the open is between the probe and the circuit ground.
4. If the light is on or the meter shows continuity, the open is between the probe and the end of the circuit toward the power source.

SHORT CIRCUITS

➡ **Never use a self-powered test light to perform checks for opens or shorts when power is applied to the circuit under test. The test light can be damaged by outside power.**

1. Isolate the circuit from power and ground.
2. Connect the self-powered test light or ohmmeter ground clip to a good ground and probe any easy-to-reach point in the circuit.
3. If the light comes on or there is continuity, there is a short somewhere in the circuit.
4. To isolate the short, probe a test point at either end of the isolated circuit (the light should be on or the meter should indicate continuity).

5. Leave the test light probe engaged and sequentially open connectors or switches, remove parts, etc. until the light goes out or continuity is broken.
6. When the light goes out, the short is between the last two circuit components which were opened.

VOLTAGE

This test determines voltage available from the battery and should be the first step in any electrical troubleshooting procedure after visual inspection. Many electrical problems, especially on computer controlled systems, can be caused by a low state of charge in the battery. Excessive corrosion at the battery cable terminals can cause poor contact that will prevent proper charging and full battery current flow.

1. Set the voltmeter selector switch to the 20V position.
2. Connect the multimeter negative lead to the battery's negative (-) post or terminal and the positive lead to the battery's positive (+) post or terminal.
3. Turn the ignition switch **ON** to provide a load.
4. A well charged battery should register over 12 volts. If the meter reads below 11.5 volts, the battery power may be insufficient to operate the electrical system properly.

VOLTAGE DROP

▶ **See Figure 9**

When current flows through a load, the voltage beyond the load drops. This voltage drop is due to the resistance created by the load and also by small resistances created by corrosion at the connectors and damaged insulation on the wires. The maximum allowable voltage drop under load is critical, especially if there is more than one load in the circuit, since all voltage drops are cumulative.

1. Set the voltmeter selector switch to the 20 volt position.
2. Connect the multimeter negative lead to a good ground.
3. Operate the circuit and check the voltage prior to the first component (load).
4. There should be little or no voltage drop in the circuit prior to the first component. If a voltage drop exists, the wire or connectors in the circuit are suspect.
5. While operating the first component in the circuit, probe the ground side of the component with the positive meter lead and observe the voltage readings. A small voltage drop should be noticed. This voltage drop is caused by the resistance of the component.
6. Repeat the test for each component (load) down the circuit.
7. If a large voltage drop is noticed, the preceding component, wire or connector is suspect.

RESISTANCE

▶ **See Figures 10 and 11**

❉❉ WARNING

Never use an ohmmeter with power applied to the circuit. The ohmmeter is designed to operate on its own power supply. The normal 12 volt electrical system voltage could damage the meter!

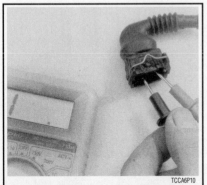

TCCA6P10

Fig. 8 The infinite reading on this multimeter indicates that the circuit is open

TCCA6P07

Fig. 9 This voltage drop test revealed high resistance (low voltage) in the circuit

TCCA6P08

Fig. 10 Checking the resistance of a coolant temperature sensor with an ohmmeter. Reading is 1.04 kilohms

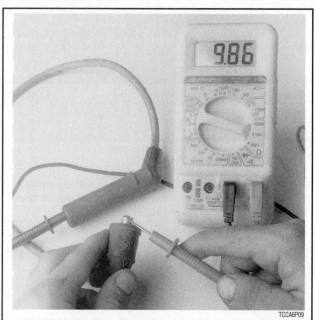

Fig. 11 Spark plug wires can be checked for excessive resistance using an ohmmeter

1. Isolate the circuit from the vehicle's power source.
2. Ensure that the ignition key is **OFF** when disconnecting any components or the battery.
3. Where necessary, also isolate at least one side of the circuit to be checked, in order to avoid reading parallel resistances. Parallel circuit resistances will always give a lower reading than the actual resistance of either of the branches.
4. Connect the meter leads to both sides of the circuit (wire or component) and read the actual measured ohms on the meter scale. Make sure the selector switch is set to the proper ohm scale for the circuit being tested, to avoid misreading the ohmmeter test value.

Wire and Connector Repair

Almost anyone can replace damaged wires, as long as the proper tools and parts are available. Wire and terminals are available to fit almost any need. Even the specialized weatherproof, molded and hard shell connectors are now available from aftermarket suppliers.

Be sure the ends of all the wires are fitted with the proper terminal hardware and connectors. Wrapping a wire around a stud is never a permanent solution and will only cause trouble later. Replace wires one at a time to avoid confusion. Always route wires exactly the same as the factory.

➡**If connector repair is necessary, only attempt it if you have the proper tools. Weatherproof and hard shell connectors require special tools to release the pins inside the connector. Attempting to repair these connectors with conventional hand tools will damage them.**

BATTERY CABLES

Disconnecting the Cables

When working on any electrical component on the vehicle, it is always a good idea to disconnect the negative (-) battery cable. This will prevent potential damage to many sensitive electrical components such as the Powertrain Control Module (PCM), radio, alternator, etc.

➡**Any time you disengage the battery cables, it is recommended that you disconnect the negative (-) battery cable first. This will prevent your accidentally grounding the positive (+) terminal to the body of the vehicle when disconnecting it, thereby preventing damage to the above mentioned components.**

Before you disconnect the cable(s), first turn the ignition to the **OFF** position. This will prevent a draw on the battery which could cause arcing (electricity trying to ground itself to the body of a vehicle, just like a spark plug jumping the gap) and, of course, damaging some components such as the alternator diodes.

When the battery cable(s) are reconnected (negative cable last), be sure to check that your lights, windshield wipers and other electrically operated safety components are all working correctly. If your vehicle contains an Electronically Tuned Radio (ETR), don't forget to also reset your radio stations. Ditto for the clock.

AIR BAG (SUPPLEMENTAL RESTRAINT SYSTEM)

General Information

The Air Bag system or Supplemental Restraint System (SRS) is designed to provide additional protection for front seat occupants when used in conjunction with a seat belt. The system is an electronically controlled, mechanically operated system. The system contains two basic subsytems: the air bag module(s) (the actual air bag(s) themselves), and the electrical system. The system consists of:
- The crash sensors
- The safing sensor
- The air bag module(s)
- The diagnostic monitor
- The instrument cluster indicator
- The sliding contacts (clock spring assembly)

The system is operates as follows: The system remains out of sight until activated in an accident that is determined to be the equivalent of hitting a parked car of the same size and weight at 28 mph (40 km/h) with the vehicle receiving severe front end damage. This determination is made by crash and safing sensors mounted on the vehicle which when an sufficient impact occurs, close their contacts completing the electrical circuit and inflating the air bags. When not activated the system is monitored by the air bag diagnostic monitor and system readiness is indicated by the lamp located on the instrument cluster. Any fault detected by the diagnostic monitor will illuminate the lamp and store a Diagnostic Trouble Code (DTC).

SERVICE PRECAUTIONS

▶ **See Figures 12, 13 and 14**

Whenever working around, or on, the air bag supplemental restraint system, ALWAYS adhere to the following warnings and cautions.
- Always wear safety glasses when servicing an air bag vehicle and when handling an air bag module.
- Carry a live air bag module with the bag and trim cover facing away from your body, so that an accidental deployment of the air bag will have a small chance of personal injury.
- Place an air bag module on a table or other flat surface with the bag and trim cover pointing up.
- Wear gloves, a dust mask and safety glasses whenever handling a deployed air bag module. The air bag surface may contain traces of sodium hydroxide, a by-product of the gas that inflates the air bag and which can cause skin irritation.
- Ensure to wash your hands with mild soap and water after handling a deployed air bag.
- All air bag modules with discolored or damaged cover trim must be replaced, not repainted.
- All component replacement and wiring service must be made with the negative and positive battery cables disconnected from the battery for a minimum of one minute prior to attempting service or replacement.
- NEVER probe the air bag electrical terminals. Doing so could result in air bag deployment, which can cause serious physical injury.

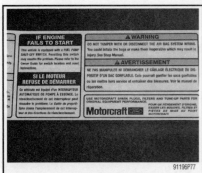

Fig. 12 Typically a warning label will be found on the vehicle regarding the air bag system

Fig. 13 Always carry a live air bag module with the bag and trim cover facing away from your body

Fig. 14 Always place an air bag module on a table or other flat surface with the bag and trim cover pointing up

• If the vehicle is involved in a fender-bender which results in a damaged front bumper or grille, have the air bag sensors inspected by a qualified automotive technician to ensure that they were not damaged.

• If at any time, the air bag light indicates that the computer has noted a problem, have your vehicle's SRS serviced immediately by a qualified automotive technician. A faulty SRS can cause severe physical injury or death.

DISARMING THE SYSTEM

※※ CAUTION

The air bag system must be disarmed before performing service around air bag components or wiring. Failure to do so may cause accidental deployment of the air bag, resulting in unnecessary repairs and/or personal injury.

1. Position the vehicle with the front wheels in a straight ahead position.
2. Disconnect the negative battery cable.

3. Disconnect the positive battery cable.
4. Wait at least one minute for the air bag back-up power supply to drain before continuing.
5. Proceed with the repair.

ARMING THE SYSTEM

1. Connect the positive battery cable.
2. Connect the negative battery cable.
3. Stand outside the vehicle and carefully turn the ignition to the **RUN** position. Be sure that no part of your body is in front of the air bag module on the steering wheel, to prevent injury in case of an accidental air bag deployment.
4. Ensure the air bag indicator light turns off after approximately 6 seconds. If the light does not illuminate at all, does not turn off, or starts to flash, have the system tested by a qualified automotive technician. If the light does turn off after 6 seconds and does not flash, the SRS is working properly.

HEATING AND AIR CONDITIONING

Blower Motor

REMOVAL & INSTALLATION

1997–98 F-250HD, F-350 and F-SuperDuty

WITHOUT AIR CONDITIONING

▶ See Figure 16

1. Disconnect the battery ground.

➡On trucks built for sale in California, remove the emission module located in front of the blower.

2. Disconnect the wiring harness at the blower.
3. Disconnect the blower motor cooling tube at the blower.
4. Remove the 3 blower motor mounting screws.
5. Hold the cooling tube to one side and pull the blower motor from the housing.
   To install:
6. Remove the clamp from the blower cage and remove the blower cage. Mount the cage on the replacement motor.
7. Install the blower motor and tighten the 3 mounting screws.
8. Connect the cooling tube and wiring harness.
9. Connect the negative battery cable. Check the blower motor for proper operation.

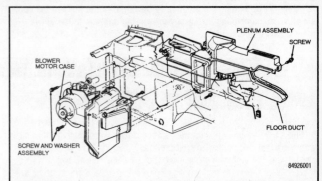

Fig. 16 Heater assembly and plenum removal—without air conditioning

WITH AIR CONDITIONING

1. Disconnect the blower motor wiring at the blower.
2. Disconnect the cooling tube at the blower.
3. Remove the 4 mounting screws and pull the motor from the housing.
   To Install:
4. Remove the clamp from the blower cage and remove the blower cage. Mount the cage on the replacement motor.
5. Install the blower motor and tighten the 4 mounting screws.
6. Connect the cooling tube and wiring harness.

7. Connect the negative battery cable. Check the blower motor for proper operation.

8. Cement the cooling tube on the nipple at the housing using Liquid Butyl Sealer D9AZ–19554—A, or equivalent.

F-150, F-250, Expedition, Navigator and 1999–00 F-Super Duty Models

▶ **See Figures 17 and 18**

1. Disconnect the negative battery cable.
2. Detach the blower motor electrical harness connector.
3. Remove 3 blower motor cover retaining screws.
4. Pry the release tabs and remove the cover.
5. Remove 3 blower motor retaining screws and remove the blower motor assembly.
6. If required, remove the blower cage by removing the retaining clip and sliding the blower cage off of the blower motor shaft.

To install:

7. If removed, slide the blower wheel onto the blower motor shaft and install a new retaining clip.
8. Install the blower motor assembly in the blower housing and secure with 3 retaining screws. Tighten the screws to 30 inch lbs. (3 Nm).
9. Install the blower motor cover ensuring that the tabs are properly positioned. Install and tighten 3 cover screws to 17 inch lbs. (2 Nm).
10. Connect the blower motor electrical harness connector.
11. Connect the negative battery cable.
12. Check the blower motor for proper operation.

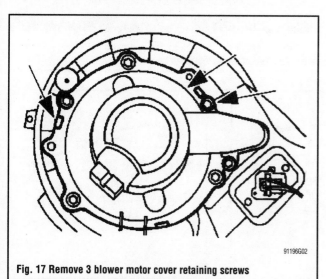

Fig. 17 Remove 3 blower motor cover retaining screws

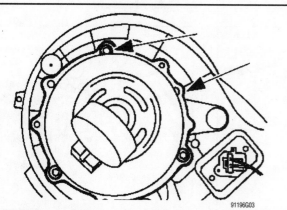

Fig. 18 Remove 3 blower motor retaining screws and remove the blower motor assembly

Heater Core

REMOVAL & INSTALLATION

1997–98 F-250, F-350 and F-Super Duty models

▶ **See Figure 19**

1. Disconnect the negative battery cable.
2. Drain and recycle the engine coolant.

❋❋ CAUTION

When draining the coolant, keep in mind that cats and dogs are attracted by ethylene glycol antifreeze, and are quite likely to drink any that is left in an uncovered container or in puddles on the ground. This will prove fatal in sufficient quantity. Always drain the coolant into a sealable container. Coolant should be reused unless it is contaminated or several years old.

3. Disconnect the coolant hoses at the heater core tubes.
4. Remove the glove compartment.
5. Position the Rear Anti-lock Brake System (RABS) module to the side.
6. From inside the passenger's compartment, remove the 7 screws that secure the heater core access cover to the plenum chamber.
7. Disconnect the vacuum source, but leave the vacuum harness connected to the cover and remove the cover.
8. Remove the heater core.
9. Installation is the reverse of removal. Replace any damaged sealer.

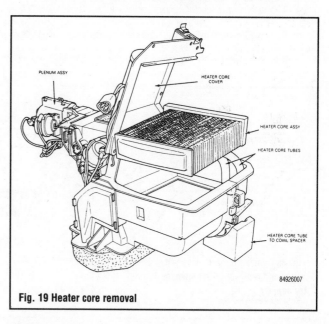

Fig. 19 Heater core removal

F-150 and F-250

▶ **See Figures 20, 21 and 22**

1. Disconnect the battery.
2. Drain and recycle the engine coolant.

❋❋ CAUTION

Never open, service or drain the radiator or cooling system when hot; serious burns can occur from the steam and hot coolant. Also, when draining engine coolant, keep in mind that cats and dogs are attracted to ethylene glycol antifreeze and could drink any that is left in an uncovered container or in puddles on the ground. This will prove fatal in sufficient quantities. Always drain coolant into a sealable container. Coolant should be reused unless it is contaminated or is several years old.

3. Remove the instrument panel. Refer to Section 10.
4. Compress the holding tabs and disconnect the heater water hoses at the heater core.
5. Remove the A/C plenum demister screw and remove the A/C plenum demister adapter.
6. Disconnect the vacuum line.
7. Remove the heater core bracket.
8. Remove the 13 retaining screws and remove the plenum chamber top.
9. Remove the blend door assembly from the case.
10. Remove the heater core.
11. The installation is the reverse of the removal.

Expedition and Navigator

▶ See Figures 20, 21, 22 and 23

1. Disconnect the battery ground cable.
2. Drain and recycle the engine coolant.

✳✳ CAUTION

Never open, service or drain the radiator or cooling system when hot; serious burns can occur from the steam and hot coolant. Also, when draining engine coolant, keep in mind that cats and dogs are attracted to ethylene glycol antifreeze and could drink any that is left in an uncovered container or in puddles on the ground. This will prove fatal in sufficient quantities. Always drain coolant into a sealable container. Coolant should be reused unless it is contaminated or is several years old.

3. Remove the instrument panel. Refer to Section 10.
4. If equipped with the 5.4L 4V engine, remove the junction block splash shield.
5. If equipped with the 5.4L 4V engine, remove the bolts and disconnect the cable ends from the starter relay.
6. If equipped with the 5.4L 4V engine, remove the junction block bracket.

7. Disconnect the heater core hose couplings.
8. Remove the retaining screw and remove the A/C plenum demister adapter.
9. Disconnect the vacuum line from the A/C plenum demister adapter.
10. Remove the heater core bracket.
11. Remove the 13 plenum chamber top retaining screws.
12. Remove the plenum chamber top.
13. Remove the blend door assembly from the case.
14. Remove the heater core.
15. The installation is the reverse of the removal.

1999–00 F-250SD, F-350 and F-Super Duty Models

▶ See Figures 23, 24, 25 and 26

1. Drain and recycle the engine coolant.

✳✳ CAUTION

Never open, service or drain the radiator or cooling system when hot; serious burns can occur from the steam and hot coolant. Also, when draining engine coolant, keep in mind that cats and dogs are attracted to ethylene glycol antifreeze and could drink any that is left in an uncovered container or in puddles on the ground. This will prove fatal in sufficient quantities. Always drain coolant into a sealable container. Coolant should be reused unless it is contaminated or is several years old.

2. Disconnect the heater water hoses from the heater core.
3. Disengage the stops and lower the glove compartment door.
4. Remove the electronic blend door actuator and bracket assembly.

✳✳ WARNING

The heater core cover must be raised vertically before removal to avoid damage to the heater core housing.

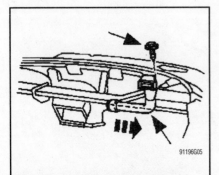

Fig. 20 Remove the A/C plenum demister screw and remove the A/C plenum demister adapter

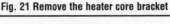

Fig. 21 Remove the heater core bracket

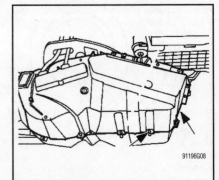

Fig. 22 Remove the 13 retaining screws and remove the plenum chamber top

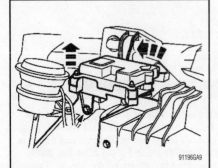

Fig. 23 Remove the electronic blend door actuator and bracket assembly

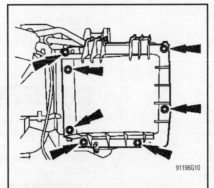

Fig. 24 Remove the heater core cover screws and . . .

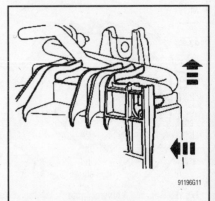

Fig. 25 . . . remove the cover

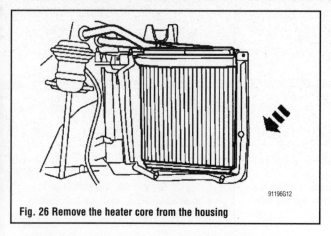

Fig. 26 Remove the heater core from the housing

5. Remove the heater core cover screws and remove the cover.
6. Remove the heater core from the housing.
To install:

☀☀ WARNING

Position the temperature blend door manually to properly align the actuator and the door. Do not power the actuator electrically. If it is not engaged with the temperature blend door, damage to the actuator may occur.

➡Add gasket between housing and cover before installing cover.

7. The installation is the reverse of the removal.

Air Conditioning Components

REMOVAL & INSTALLATION

Repair or service of air conditioning components is not covered by this manual, because of the risk of personal injury or death, and because of the legal ramifications of servicing these components without the proper EPA certification and experience. Cost, personal injury or death, environmental damage, and legal considerations (such as the fact that it is a federal crime to vent refrigerant into the atmosphere), dictate that the A/C components on your vehicle should be serviced only by a Motor Vehicle Air Conditioning (MVAC) trained, and EPA certified automotive technician.

➡If your vehicle's A/C system uses R-12 refrigerant and is in need of recharging, the A/C system can be converted over to R-134a refrigerant (less environmentally harmful and expensive). Refer to Section 1 for additional information on R-12 to R-134a conversions, and for additional considerations dealing with your vehicle's A/C system.

Temperature Control Cable

REMOVAL & INSTALLATION

1997–98 F-250HD, F-350 and F-Super Duty Models

▶ **See Figure 27**

1. Remove the control panel from the instrument panel.
2. Remove the glove compartment.
3. Working through the glove compartment opening, remove the temperature control cable housing from its clip on top of the plenum, by depressing the clip tab and pulling the cable rearward.
4. Using a needle-nosed pliers, at the bottom of the control panel, carefully release the control cable snap-in flag.
5. Rotate the control 90 degrees, so it faces upwards. Disconnect the control cable and move the control panel assembly away from the instrument panel.
6. Disconnect the cable from the cam on top of the plenum.

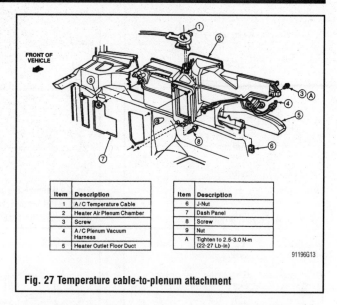

Item	Description	Item	Description
1	A/C Temperature Cable	6	J-Nut
2	Heater Air Plenum Chamber	7	Dash Panel
3	Screw	8	Screw
4	A/C Plenum Vacuum Harness	9	Nut
5	Heater Outlet Floor Duct	A	Tighten to 2.5-3.0 N-m (22-27 Lb-in)

Fig. 27 Temperature cable-to-plenum attachment

7. Pull the cable away from the instrument panel, through the control panel opening.
To install:
8. Feed the wire loop end of the cable through the control panel opening.
9. Attach the loop end to the cam on top of the plenum. Make sure that the wire loop coil is up and the cable is routed under its hold-down on the cam.
10. Hold the control panel with its top towards the steering wheel. Attach the temperature control cable to the control lever. Snap the flag into the top of the control panel bracket.
11. Position the control panel close to the opening in the instrument panel. Route the cable through the opening so that it won't be kinked or have sharp bends.
12. Adjust the cable so that the plenum door functions properly in all modes:
   a. Remove the cable jacket from the clip on top of the plenum. Leave the cable end attached to the lever.
   b. Set the control lever to **COOL** and hold it firmly.
   c. Push gently on the cable bracket to seat the blend door, pushing until resistance is felt.
   d. Install the cable into the clip, until it snaps into place. Operate the controls to make sure they function properly.
13. Install the control panel.
14. Install the glove compartment.

Blend Door Actuator

REMOVAL & INSTALLATION

F-150 and F-250

▶ **See Figures 28 thru 35**

1. Disconnect the negative battery cable.
2. Remove the floor duct panel.
3. Remove the pushpins and release the expander clip.
4. Remove the passenger side instrument panel brace retaining nut and bolt.
5. Remove the brace.
6. Remove the driver's side instrument panel brace lower nut and position the brace aside.
7. Remove the three bolts and position the module aside.
8. Remove the two floor duct screws (one on each side).
9. Remove the floor duct.
10. Rotate the vacuum control motor to disconnect the vacuum control motor rod from the panel/floor door.

Fig. 28 Remove the floor duct panel

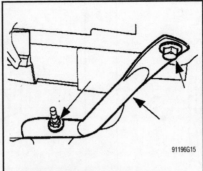

Fig. 29 Remove the passenger side instrument panel brace retaining nut and bolt and remove the brace

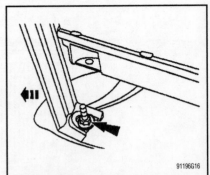

Fig. 30 Remove the driver's side instrument panel brace lower nut and position the brace aside

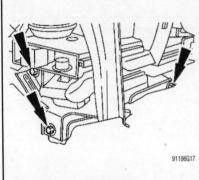

Fig. 31 Remove the three bolts and position the module aside

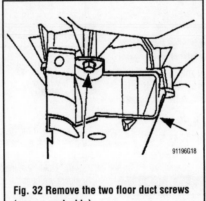

Fig. 32 Remove the two floor duct screws (one on each side).

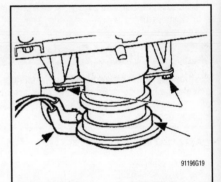

Fig. 33 Remove the panel/floor door vacuum control motor

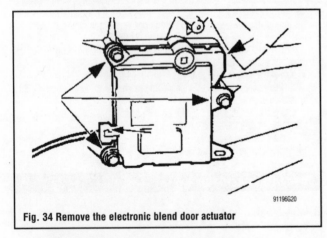

Fig. 34 Remove the electronic blend door actuator

11. Remove the panel/floor door vacuum control motor.
12. Disconnect the vacuum line connector.
13. Remove the screws.
14. Slide the rod out of the door and remove the panel/floor door.
15. Detach the connector.
16. Remove the retaining screws.
17. Pull down to release the actuator shaft and remove the electronic blend door actuator.
18. The installation is the reverse of the removal.

Expedition and Navigator

1. Remove the rear seat floor duct.
2. Detach the connector.
3. Remove the retaining screws.
4. Pull down to release the actuator shaft and remove the electronic actuator.
5. The installation is the reverse of the removal.

1999–00 F-250SD, F-350 and F-Super Duty

♦ See Figures 35, 36 and 37

1. Disconnect the negative battery cable.
2. Release the stops and lower the glove compartment door.
3. Detach the connector.
4. Remove the electronic blend door actuator and bracket assembly.
5. Remove the screw.
6. Rotate the blend door actuator and bracket assembly.
7. Remove the assembly.

✳✳ CAUTION

Position the temperature blend door manually to properly align the actuator and the door. Do not power the actuator electrically. If it is not engaged with the temperature blend door, damage to the actuator may occur.

8. Installation is the reverse of the removal.

Control Panel

REMOVAL & INSTALLATION

1997–98 F-250HD, F-350 and F-Super Duty Models

♦ See Figure 38

WITHOUT AIR CONDITIONING

1. Disconnect the negative battery cable.
2. Pull the center finish panel away from the instrument panel, exposing the control attaching screws.
3. Remove the 4 attaching screws.

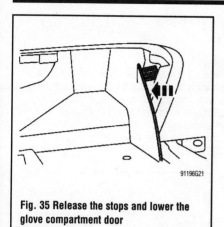

Fig. 35 Release the stops and lower the glove compartment door

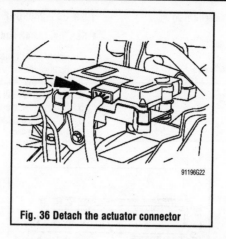

Fig. 36 Detach the actuator connector

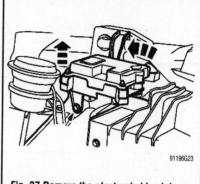

Fig. 37 Remove the electronic blend door actuator and bracket assembly

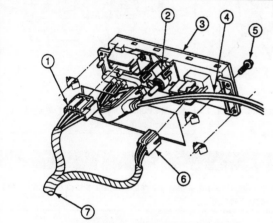

Item	Description
1	Main Wiring (to Function Selector Switch)
2	Temperature Bracket Assy
3	Heater Control
4	A/C Temperature Cable
5	Screw (4 Req'd)
6	Main Wiring (to Blower Switch)
7	Main Wiring

Fig. 38 Control panel connections—1997–98 F-250HD, F-350 and F-Super Duty Models

4. Pull the control towards you just enough to allow disconnection of the wiring and vacuum hoses.

5. Carefully release the function control cable snap-in flag from the underside of the control unit, using a prytool.

6. Pull enough cable through the instrument panel to allow the cable to be held vertical to the control unit.

7. Carefully release the temperature control cable snap-in flag from the topside of the control unit, using a prytool.

8. Rotate the control unit 90° and disconnect the temperature control cable from the temperature control lever.

9. Pull out the control unit.

10. Installation is the reverse of removal. Check the operation of the unit.

WITH AIR CONDITIONING

1. Remove the instrument panel center finish panel.

2. Remove the control unit knobs by prying on the spring retainer while pulling out on the knob.

3. Remove the 4 control unit attaching screws.

4. Disconnect the wiring and vacuum lines from the control unit.

5. Disengage the temperature cable by depressing the locking tabs on the connector.

6. Rotate the control unit 180° and disconnect the function cable from the control assembly. Remove the control assembly by compressing the locking tabs on the connector.

7. Installation is the reverse of removal. Check the operation of the unit.

F-150, F-250, Expedition and Navigator

▶ See Figures 39 thru 44

1. Disconnect the negative battery cable.

2. Carefully pry to release the four clips retaining the center instrument panel finish panel.

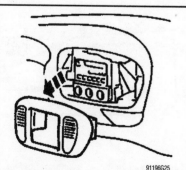

Fig. 39 Carefully pry to release the four clips retaining the center instrument panel finish panel

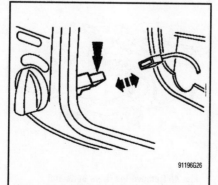

Fig. 40 If equipped, detach the 4WD control switch connector

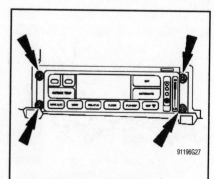

Fig. 41 Remove the four retaining screws—Electronic Automatic Temperature Control (EATC)

3. Detach the two passenger air bag defeat switch electrical connectors.
4. If equipped, detach the 4WD control switch connector.
5. Remove the center instrument panel finish panel.
6. Remove the climate control assembly retaining screws.
7. Pull out the climate control assembly.
8. Detach the electrical connectors.
9. Detach the vacuum line connector.
10. Remove the control panel.
11. The installation is the reverse of the removal.

1999–00 F-250SD, F-350 and F-Super Duty

♦ See Figures 42 and 44

1. Disconnect the negative battery cable.
2. Remove the radio. Refer to the procedure in this section.
3. Remove the cluster opening finish panel.
4. Detach the headlight and dimmer switch wire harness connectors.
5. Remove the screws and remove the climate control assembly.
6. Detach the electrical connectors.
7. Detach the vacuum harness connector.
8. The installation is the reverse of the removal.

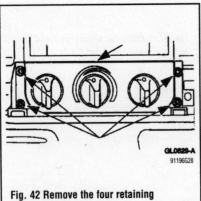
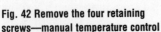

Fig. 42 Remove the four retaining screws—manual temperature control

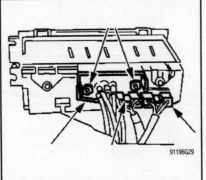

Fig. 43 Panel connections—Electronic Automatic Temperature Control (EATC)

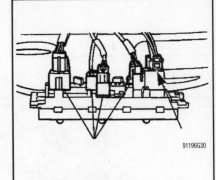

Fig. 44 Panel connections —manual temperature control

AUXILIARY HEATING AND AIR CONDITIONING

Heater Core

REMOVAL & INSTALLATION

♦ See Figures 45, 46 and 47

1. Have a MVAC-trained, EPA-certified, automotive technician recover the air conditioning system refrigerant.
2. Drain and recycle the engine coolant.

❄❄ CAUTION

Never open, service or drain the radiator or cooling system when hot; serious burns can occur from the steam and hot coolant. Also, when draining engine coolant, keep in mind that cats and dogs are attracted to ethylene glycol antifreeze and could drink any that is left in an uncovered container or in puddles on the ground. This will prove fatal in sufficient quantities. Always drain coolant into a seal-

able container. Coolant should be reused unless it is contaminated or is several years old.

3. Remove the driver's side quarter trim panel.
4. Detach the electrical connectors on the auxiliary air conditioning and heater assembly.
5. Disconnect the heater core hose couplings.
6. Remove the evaporator case drain hose.
7. Disconnect the auxiliary A/C evaporator lines.
8. Remove the pin-type retainer.
9. Remove the A/C outlet duct.
10. Remove the three bolts and remove the auxiliary air conditioning and heater assembly.
11. Remove the ten evaporator/heater core access cover retaining bolts and remove the evaporator/heater core access cover.
12. Remove the heater core.
To install:
13. The installation is the reverse of the removal.

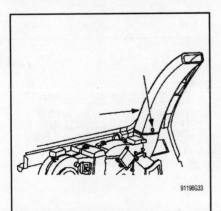

Fig. 45 Remove the pin-type retainer and remove the A/C outlet duct

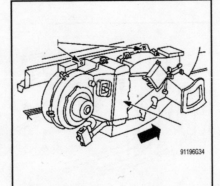

Fig. 46 Remove the three bolts and remove the auxiliary air conditioning and heater assembly

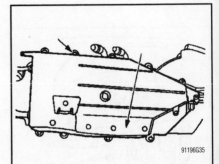

Fig. 47 Remove the ten evaporator/heater core access cover retaining bolts and remove the evaporator/heater core access cover

14. Have a MVAC-trained, EPA-certified, automotive technician recharge the air conditioning system.

Control Panel

REMOVAL & INSTALLATION

Front

▶ **See Figures 48 and 49**

1. Disconnect the negative battery cable.
2. Remove the overhead console retaining screw.
3. Carefully release the three clips and slide the overhead console forward.
4. Detach the panel electrical connectors.
5. Remove the panel retaining screws.
6. Remove the auxiliary climate control panel assembly from the bezel.
7. The installation is the reverse of the removal.

Rear

▶ **See Figure 50**

1. Slide the auxiliary climate control panel assembly forward and downward.
2. Detach the electrical connectors.
3. Remove the auxiliary climate control assembly from the bezel.
4. Detach the electrical connectors.
5. Remove the screws.
6. Remove the climate control panel assembly.
7. The installation is the reverse of the removal.

Blend Door Actuator

REMOVAL & INSTALLATION

▶ **See Figure 51**

1. Remove the LH quarter trim panel.
2. Detach the blend door actuator connector.
3. Remove the actuator retaining screws.
4. Remove the electronic actuator.
5. The installation is the reverse of the removal.

Blower Motor

REMOVAL & INSTALLATION

▶ **See Figure 52**

1. Remove the driver's side quarter trim panel access cover.
2. Detach the motor electrical connector.
3. Remove the three motor cover bolts.
4. Remove the blower motor cover.
5. Remove the blower motor bolts.
6. Remove the blower motor.
7. Remove the push clip.
8. Remove the wheel from the blower motor.
9. The installation is the reverse of the removal.

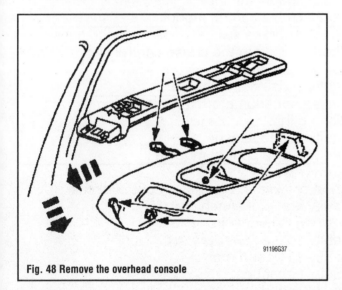

Fig. 48 Remove the overhead console

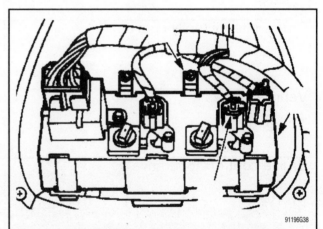

Fig. 49 Detach the panel electrical connectors, remove the panel retaining screws, and remove the auxiliary climate control panel assembly from the bezel

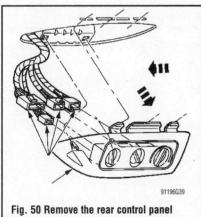

Fig. 50 Remove the rear control panel

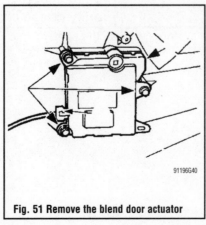

Fig. 51 Remove the blend door actuator

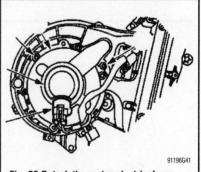

Fig. 52 Detach the motor electrical connector and remove the three motor cover bolts

CRUISE CONTROL

All models covered by this manual were available with an optional speed control system. This system automatically controls the speed of the vehicle when cruising at a stable highway speed. The speed control system consists of the following:

- Speed control amplifier/servo assembly
- Speed control cable
- Vehicle Speed Sensor (VSS)
- Speed control actuator switch
- Stop light switch
- Deactivator switch
- Clutch pedal position switch (manual transmissions only)

The speed control system operates independently of engine vacuum and, therefore, does not utilize any vacuum lines.

The speed control amplifier integrates the system electronics, thereby eliminating any other electronic control modules in the vehicle. The amplifier controls the vehicle's speed via a cable attached to the throttle body lever.

The speed control actuator switch assembly is mounted on the steering wheel and allows the driver to control the system's operation. The switch assembly contains five control buttons for system functioning, namely: ON, OFF, RESUME, SET ACCEL, COAST.

The system will continue to control the vehicle's speed until the OFF button is used, or the brake pedal or clutch pedal (manual transmissions only) is depressed.

CRUISE CONTROL TROUBLESHOOTING

Problem	Possible Cause
Will not hold proper speed	Incorrect cable adjustment
	Binding throttle linkage
	Leaking vacuum servo diaphragm
	Leaking vacuum tank
	Faulty vacuum or vent valve
	Faulty stepper motor
	Faulty transducer
	Faulty speed sensor
	Faulty cruise control module
Cruise intermittently cuts out	Clutch or brake switch adjustment too tight
	Short or open in the cruise control circuit
	Faulty transducer
	Faulty cruise control module
Vehicle surges	Kinked speedometer cable or casing
	Binding throttle linkage
	Faulty speed sensor
	Faulty cruise control module
Cruise control inoperative	Blown fuse
	Short or open in the cruise control circuit
	Faulty brake or clutch switch
	Leaking vacuum circuit
	Faulty cruise control switch
	Faulty stepper motor
	Faulty transducer
	Faulty speed sensor
	Faulty cruise control module

Note: Use this chart as a guide. Not all systems will use the components listed.

TCCA6C01

ENTERTAINMENT SYSTEMS

Radio/Tape Player/CD Player (Dash Mounted)

REMOVAL & INSTALLATION

▶ See Figures 53 thru 59

1. Disconnect the negative battery cable.
2. On the F-150, F-250, Expedition and Navigator models, remove the radio finish panel by carefully prying on the panel to release the retaining clips.

91196P32

Fig. 53 On the F-150, F-250, Expedition and Navigator models, remove the radio finish panel by carefully prying on the panel to release the retaining clips

➡Do not use excessive force when installing the radio removal tool. This will damage the retaining clips, making radio chassis removal difficult and may cause other internal damage.

3. Install Radio Removal Tool (T87P-19061-A) or equivalent into the radio face place. Push the tool in approximately 1 in. (25mm) to release the retaining clips.
4. Apply a slight outward spreading force on both sides and pull the radio chassis out of the instrument panel.
5. Disconnect the radio wiring harness and antenna cable.
6. Remove the radio chassis.
   To install:
7. Position the radio chassis in the vehicle.
8. Connect the radio wiring harness and antenna cable.
9. Push the radio chassis inward until the retaining clips are fully engaged.
10. On the F-150, F-250, Expedition and Navigator models, install the radio finish panel.
11. Connect the negative battery cable.

Amplifier

REMOVAL & INSTALLATION

F-150, F-250, Expedition and Navigator

▶ See Figures 60, 61 and 62

1. Disconnect the negative battery cable.
2. Remove the radio chassis.
3. Remove the climate control panel retaining screws and position the control panel aside.
4. Remove the instrument panel floor duct assembly.

91196P34

Fig. 54 Install Radio Removal Tool (T87P-19061-A) or equivalent into the radio face place

91196P35

Fig. 55 Apply a slight outward spreading force on both sides and . . .

91196P43

Fig. 56 . . . pull the radio chassis out of the instrument panel

91196P36

Fig. 57 Detach the antenna and the . . .

91196P37

Fig. 58 . . . electrical connectors from the back of the radio and remove the radio

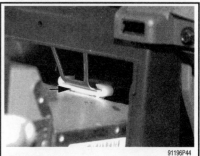

91196P44

Fig. 59 When installing the radio, make sure that the clip is centered on the support bracket before sliding the radio into the instrument panel

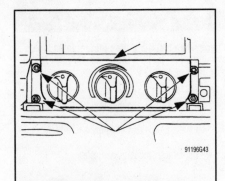

Fig. 60 Remove the four retaining screws and remove the climate control panel assembly

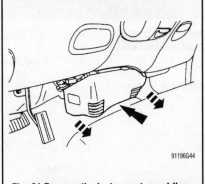

Fig. 61 Remove the instrument panel floor duct assembly

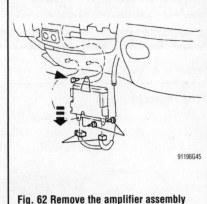

Fig. 62 Remove the amplifier assembly

5. If equipped, remove the center console assembly. Refer to Section 10.
6. Remove the amplifier retaining screws.
7. Lift up on the amplifier assembly and detach the electrical connectors.
8. Remove the amplifier assembly.
9. The installation is the reverse of the removal.

1997–98 F-250HD, F-350 and F-Super Duty Models

➡**The amplifier assembly is located in the instrument panel behind the radio chassis.**

1. Disconnect the negative battery cable.
2. Remove the radio chassis.
3. Detach the electrical connectors for the amplifier.
4. Remove the retaining screws and remove the amplifier from the vehicle.
5. The installation is the reverse of the removal.

CD Changer

REMOVAL & INSTALLATION

F-150 and F-250 Regular Cab

▶ **See Figures 63 and 64**

1. Disconnect the negative battery cable.
2. If not equipped with a rear storage bin, remove the changer cover.
3. If equipped with a rear storage bin, remove the retaining nuts and remove the storage compartment.
4. Remove the CD changer retaining nuts.
5. Lift the changer up and detach the electrical connectors.
6. Remove the CD changer from the vehicle.
7. The installation is the reverse of the removal.

F-150 and F-250 Extended Cab

1. Disconnect the negative battery cable.
2. Remove the driver's side rear cab lower trim panel.
3. Remove the CD changer retaining screws and nuts.
4. Lift the changer up and detach the electrical connectors.
5. Remove the CD changer from the vehicle.
6. The installation is the reverse of the removal.

Expedition and Navigator

▶ **See Figures 65, 66 and 67**

1. Disconnect the negative battery cable.
2. Open the center console lid.

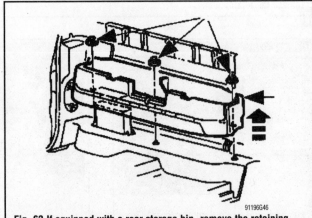

Fig. 63 If equipped with a rear storage bin, remove the retaining nuts and remove the storage compartment

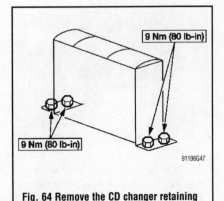

Fig. 64 Remove the CD changer retaining nuts

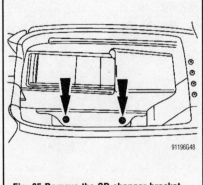

Fig. 65 Remove the CD changer bracket bottom retaining screws

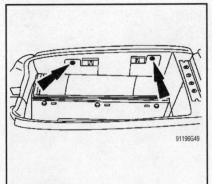

Fig. 66 Remove the upper bracket retaining screws

Fig. 67 Lift the CD changer and bracket assembly up and detach the electrical connector from the changer

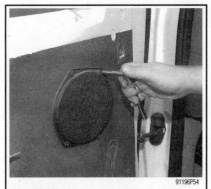

Fig. 68 Remove the speaker retaining screws and pull the speaker out

Fig. 69 Detach the speaker electrical connector and remove the speaker

3. Remove the mat at the bottom of the console bin.
4. Remove the CD changer bracket bottom retaining screws.
5. Remove the upper bracket retaining screws.
6. Lift the CD changer and bracket assembly up and detach the electrical connector from the changer.
7. Remove the changer from the vehicle.
8. If necessary, remove the bracket from the changer and install it on the new changer.
9. The installation is the reverse of the removal.

Speakers

REMOVAL & INSTALLATION

▶ **See Figures 68 and 69**

1. Disconnect the negative battery cable.
2. Remove any necessary trim, speaker grilles, or other components necessary to access the speaker(s).
3. Remove the speaker retaining screws.
4. Pull the speaker out and detach the electrical connector.
5. Remove the speaker from the vehicle.
6. The installation is the reverse of the removal.

WINDSHIELD WIPERS AND WASHERS

Windshield Wiper Blade and Arm

REMOVAL & INSTALLATION

Front

F-150, F-250, EXPEDITION AND NAVIGATOR

▶ **See Figures 70, 71, 72 and 73**

1. Raise the covers over the wiper arm retaining nuts.
2. Remove the retaining nuts on the wiper arm pivots.
3. Matchmark the wiper arms to the pivot for reinstallation.
4. Lift each wiper arm and free it from the pivot shafts.

➡The wiper arms will most likely be stuck, a useful tool for removal of the wiper arms is a battery terminal puller. The battery terminal puller

Fig. 70 Remove the cover over the wiper arm retaining nuts

Fig. 71 Remove the retaining nuts on the wiper arm pivots

Fig. 72 Matchmark the wiper arms to the pivot for reinstallation

Fig. 73 Lift each wiper arm and free it from the pivot shafts

exerts force on the pivot and raises the arm, otherwise prying and other techniques could do damage to the wiper arms, trim, windshield, or painted surfaces of the vehicle.

To install:
5. Place the wiper arm onto the pivot aligning the matchmarks.
6. Tighten the wiper arm retaining nuts.
7. Fasten the retaining nut covers.

EXCEPT F-150, F-250, EXPEDITION AND NAVIGATOR

Raise the blade end of the arm off of the windshield.
1. Move the slide latch away from the pivot shaft.
2. Pull the wiper arm off of the pivot shaft.

To install:
3. Position the wiper arm into place and make sure it is aligned properly with the windshield.
4. Place the wiper arm onto the pivot until the latch engages.
5. Lower the blade to the windshield.

Rear (Expedition And Navigator Only)

♦ See Figure 74

1. Raise the covers over the wiper arm retaining nuts.
2. Remove the retaining nuts on the wiper arm pivots.
3. Matchmark the wiper arms to the pivot for reinstallation.
4. Lift each wiper arm and free it from the pivot shafts.

➡The wiper arms will most likely be stuck, a useful tool for removal of the wiper arms is a battery terminal puller. The battery terminal puller exerts force on the pivot and raises the arm, otherwise prying and other techniques could do damage to the wiper arms, trim, windshield, or painted surfaces of the vehicle.

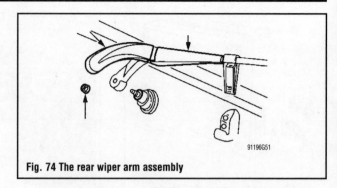

Fig. 74 The rear wiper arm assembly

To install:
5. Place the wiper arm onto the pivot aligning the matchmarks.
6. Tighten the wiper arm retaining nuts.
7. Fasten the retaining nut covers.

Windshield Wiper Motor

REMOVAL & INSTALLATION

Front

1997–98 F-250HD, F-350 AND F-SUPER DUTY

♦ See Figures 75 and 76

1. Disconnect the negative battery cable.
2. Remove the windshield wiper arms.

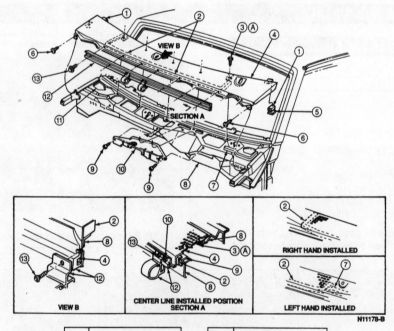

Item	Description
1	Foam Tape
2	Cowl Top Grille Seal Assy
3	Screw (5 Req'd)
4	Cowl Top Vent Panel with Radio Antenna Holes
5	Cowl Top Vent Grille Spacer
6	Screw (2 Req'd)
7	Cowl Top Panel to Hood Seal
8	Cowl Top Outer Panel

Item	Description
9	Screw (4 Req'd)
10	Cowl Top Outer Panel Extension
11	Cowl Top Panel Access Hole (1 Req'd LH Side)
12	Cowl Top Panel to Hood Seal Assy
13	Screw (7 Req'd)
A	Tighten to 1.4-2.0 N·m (12-17 Lb-In)

Fig. 75 Cowl vent panel removal

Item	Description
1	Screw
2	Main Engine Control Wiring Harness
3	Windshield Wiper Motor
A	Tighten to 6.8-9.6 N-m (60-85 Lb-In)

91196G53

Fig. 76 Remove the wiper motor mounting bolts and remove the wiper motor

3. Remove the moulding from the bottom of the windshield.
4. Remove the five screws across the cowl top vent panel. The screws can be accessed through the holes in the vent panel.
5. Remove the ten screws across the vertical surface holding the cowl top vent panel to the cowl top.
6. With the hood partially closed, lift the cowl top vent panel.
7. Disconnect the radio antenna or lead wire, if necessary.
8. Disconnect the washer hose and remove the cowl top vent panel.
9. Remove the metal shield above the windshield wiper motor.
10. Remove the wiper adapter and connecting arm clip where the wiper mounting arm and pivot shaft connect to the wiper motor drive arm.

11. Detach the electrical connectors from the wiper motor.
12. Remove the wiper motor mounting bolts and remove the wiper motor.

To install:

13. Install the wiper motor and torque the mounting bolts 60–85 inch lbs. (6.8–9.6 Nm).
14. Connect the electrical connectors to the wiper motor.
15. Install the wiper adapter and connecting arm clip where the wiper mounting arm and pivot shaft connect to the wiper motor drive arm.
16. Install the metal shield above the windshield wiper motor.
17. Connect the washer hose at the cowl top vent panel.
18. Connect the radio antenna or lead wire, if necessary.
19. Install the cowl top vent panel. Tighten the ten screws across the vertical surface of the cowl top vent panel and the cowl top.
20. Tighten the five screws across the cowl top vent panel.
21. Install the moulding at the bottom of the windshield.
22. Install the wiper pivot arms.
23. Connect the negative battery cable.
24. The vehicle may need to be driven as much as 10 miles for the PCM to relearn its adaptive strategy.

F-150, F-250, EXPEDITION, NAVIGATOR, AND 1999–00 F-SUPER DUTY MODELS

▶ See Figures 77 thru 87

1. Turn the ignition switch to the **ON** position. Turn the ignition switch **ON** until the wiper blades are straight up, then turn the ignition switch **OFF**.
2. Disconnect the negative battery cable.
3. Remove the right-hand and left-hand windshield wiper arm and blade assemblies.
4. Remove the cowl top vent panels.
5. Detach the electrical harness connector at the windshield wiper motor assembly.
6. Remove 3 wiper motor (module assembly) retaining bolts and remove the module assembly from the vehicle.

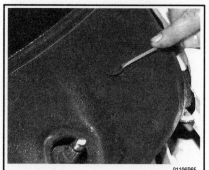

Fig. 77 Pry the covers over the cowl panel retaining screws off and remove the retaining screws

91196P65

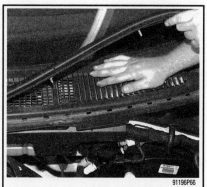

Fig. 78 Lift up to release the clips and remove the hood-to-cowl weather strip

91196P66

Fig. 79 Remove the trim clips from the cowl panels

91196P67

Fig. 80 Remove the cowl panel-to-firewall retaining clips

91196P68

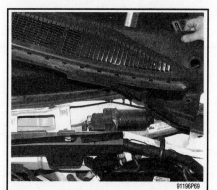

Fig. 81 Remove the driver's side then the . . .

91196P69

Fig. 82 . . . passenger side cowl panel from the vehicle

91196P70

Fig. 83 Detach the electrical connector for the wiper motor

Fig. 84 Remove the three wiper module assembly retaining bolts and . . .

Fig. 85 . . . remove the module from the vehicle

Fig. 86 Remove the wiper linkage retaining bolt and remove the linkage from the wiper motor

Fig. 87 Remove the wiper motor retaining bolts and remove the wiper motor from the vehicle

Fig. 88 Remove the upper liftgate trim panel

7. Remove the wiper linkage retaining bolt and remove the linkage from the wiper motor.

8. Remove 3 retaining nuts and remove the windshield wiper motor.

To install:

9. Place the windshield wiper motor in position and install 3 retaining nuts. Tighten the nuts to 10–12 ft. lbs. (12–17 Nm).

10. Connect the wiper linkage to the windshield wiper motor and install the retaining bolt. Tighten the bolt to 14 ft. lbs. (20 Nm).

11. Place the wiper motor (module assembly) in position and install 3 retaining bolts. Tighten the bolts to 6 ft. lbs (9 Nm).

12. Install the electrical harness connector to the windshield wiper motor.

13. Connect the negative battery cable.

14. Allow the windshield wiper motor to cycle several times while checking for proper wiper motor operation.

15. Turn the windshield wiper motor switch to the **OFF** position to park the wiper motor in the park position.

16. Install the cowl top vent panels.

17. Install the wiper arm and blade assemblies. Install the retaining nuts and tighten to 22–29 ft. lbs. (30–40 Nm). Install the nut covers.

18. Connect the negative battery cable.

19. Check the windshield wiper motor for proper operation and the wiper arms for adjustment.

Rear (Expedition and Navigator Only)

◗ See Figures 88, 89, 90 and 91

1. Remove the rear wiper arm.
2. Remove the upper liftgate trim panel.
3. Remove the liftgate assist strap.
4. Remove the lower liftgate trim panel.
5. Peel back the liftgate watershield.
6. Detach the connector for the wiper motor.
7. Remove the retaining bolts and remove the wiper motor.

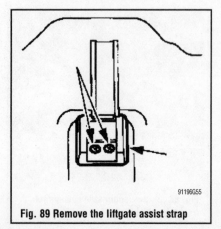
Fig. 89 Remove the liftgate assist strap

Fig. 90 Remove the lower liftgate trim panel

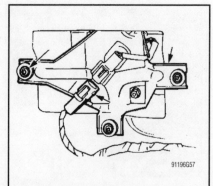
Fig. 91 Remove the retaining bolts and remove the wiper motor

To install:

8. Install the wiper motor and tighten the retaining bolts to 80–107 inch lbs. (9–12 Nm).

9. The balance of the installation is the reverse of the removal.

Windshield Washer Motor

REMOVAL & INSTALLATION

Front

▶ **See Figure 92**

1. Remove the reservoir.
2. Using a small prytool, pry out the motor retaining ring.
3. Using pliers, grip one edge of the electrical connector ring and pull the motor, seal and impeller from the reservoir.

➡️**If the seal and impeller come apart from the motor, it can all be re-assembled.**

To install:

4. Take the time to clean out the reservoir before installing the motor.
5. Coat the seal with a dry lubricant, such as powdered graphite or spray Teflon®. This will aid assembly.
6. Align the small projection on the motor end cap with the slot in the reservoir and install the motor so that the seal seats against the bottom of the motor cavity.

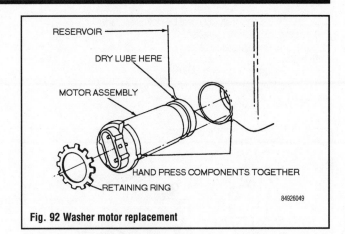

Fig. 92 Washer motor replacement

7. Press the retaining ring into position. A 1 in., 12-point socket or length of 1 in. tubing, will do nicely as an installation tool.
8. Install the reservoir and connect the wiring.

➡️**It's not a good idea to run a new motor without filling the reservoir first. Dry-running will damage a new motor.**

Rear (Expedition And Navigator Only)

The rear washer system on the Expedition and Navigator does contain a separate reservoir, rather uses the washer motor and reservoir from the front.

INSTRUMENTS AND SWITCHES

Instrument Cluster

REMOVAL & INSTALLATION

1997–98 F-250HD, F-350 and F-Super Duty

▶ **See Figures 93, 94 and 95**

1. Disconnect the negative battery cable.
2. Remove the cluster opening trim panel.
3. On vehicles equipped with an automatic transmission, remove the loop on the indicator cable assembly from the retainer pin. Remove the thumbwheel bracket screw from the cable bracket and slide the bracket out of the slot in the steering column tube.
4. Remove the instrument cluster retaining bolts.

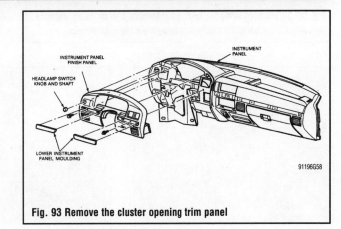

Fig. 93 Remove the cluster opening trim panel

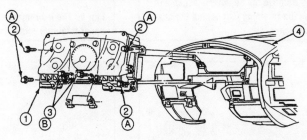
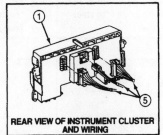

Item	Description
1	Instrument Cluster
2	Screw (4 Req'd)
3	Screw (2 Req'd)
4	Instrument Panel

Item	Description
5	Main Wiring
A	Tighten to 1.9-2.5 N·m (17-22 Lb-In)
B	Tighten to 1.4 N·m (12 Lb-In)

Fig. 94 Instrument cluster mounting

5. Pull the instrument cluster out of the instrument panel.
6. Detach the electrical connectors.
7. Remove the instrument cluster.

To install:

8. The installation is the reverse of the removal.
9. Connect the battery cable, and check the operation of all gauges, lights and signals.

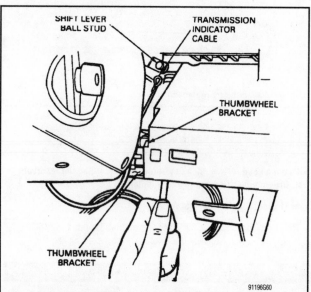

Fig. 95 On vehicles equipped with an automatic transmission, remove the loop on the indicator cable assembly from the retainer pin

F-150, F-250, Expedition and Navigator

◗ See Figures 96 thru 103

> ✳✳ **WARNING**
>
> Prior to removal of module on an electronic instrument cluster, it is necessary to upload module configuration information to New Generation STAR (NGS) Tester. This information needs to be downloaded into the new module once installed.

> ✳✳ **WARNING**
>
> Electronic modules are sensitive to electrical charges. If exposed to these charges, damage may result.

Fig. 96 Carefully release the four clips and remove the steering column opening cover

Fig. 97 Remove the instrument cluster finish panel retaining bolts behind the steering column opening cover

Fig. 98 Remove the headlamp switch and remove the retaining bolt behind the headlamp switch

Fig. 99 The instrument cluster finish panel upper retaining screw locations

Fig. 100 Remove the instrument cluster finish panel upper retaining screws

Fig. 101 The location of the instrument cluster retaining bolts

Fig. 102 Remove the transmission range indicator

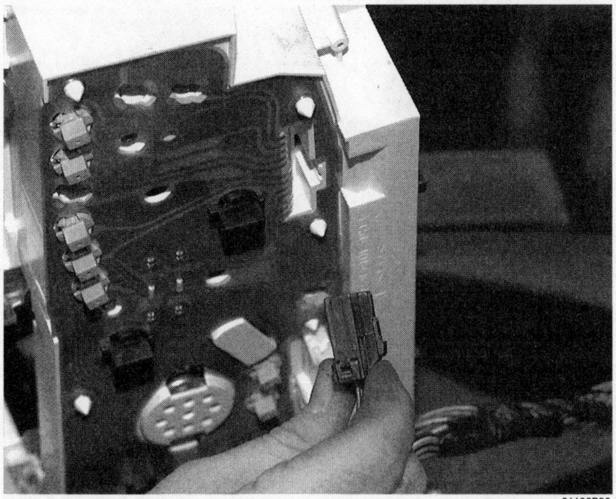

91196P56

Fig. 103 Detach the electrical connectors and remove the cluster from the vehicle

1. Remove the headlamp switch.
2. Carefully release the four clips and remove the steering column opening cover.
3. Remove the instrument panel finish panel retaining bolts.
4. Remove the instrument panel finish panel.
5. Remove the instrument cluster retaining bolts.
6. Pull the instrument cluster out of the instrument panel.
7. Detach the electrical connectors.
8. If equipped, remove the transmission range indicator.
9. On the F-150 Lightning, disconnect the boost gauge vacuum line.
10. Remove the instrument cluster.

To install:

11. The installation is the reverse of the removal.

**** CAUTION**

Once the new module is installed, it is necessary to download the module configuration information from the New Generation STAR (NGS) Tester into the new module.

1999–00 Super Duty Models

1. Remove the radio.
2. If equipped with tilt wheel, lower the steering wheel.
3. Remove the cluster finish panel bolts.
4. Pull the cluster finish panel from the instrument panel.
5. Detach the power point connector.
6. If equipped, detach the passenger air bag deactivation switch connector.
7. Detach the headlight switch electrical connectors.
8. Remove the cluster finish panel.
9. Remove the instrument cluster screws.
10. Pull out the instrument cluster.
11. If equipped, disconnect the transmission range indicator.
12. Push in the two clips and pull out the transmission range indicator. Position it aside.
13. Detach the electrical connectors.
14. Remove the instrument cluster.
15. The installation is the reverse of the removal.

Gauges

REMOVAL & INSTALLATION

1. Disconnect the negative battery cable.
2. Remove the instrument cluster.
3. Remove the retaining screws for the instrument cluster lens and cover assembly. Remove the cover and lens.
4. Remove the retaining screws for the gauge or warning lamp to be replaced and remove the gauge or warning lamp.

To install:

5. Place the gauge or warning lamp into place and tighten the retaining screws.
6. Install the instrument cluster lens and cover assembly.
7. Install the instrument cluster.
8. Connect the negative battery cable.

Headlight Switch

REMOVAL & INSTALLATION

1997–98 F-250HD, F-350 And F-Super Duty

1. Disconnect the negative battery cable.
2. On vehicles equipped with tilt steering column, position the steering wheel in the lowest position.
3. On vehicles equipped with a column shift, lock the parking brake and position the shift lever in the lowest position.
4. Pull the headlight switch **ON**.
5. Insert a small flat bladed tool in the slot behind the headlight switch knob and pull the knob off.
6. Unscrew the headlight switch bezel.
7. Remove the 2 exposed screws from under the right and left lower instrument panel mouldings.
8. Disconnect the 5 retaining clips by pulling the instrument panel finish panel rearward. The 2 lower clips should be pulled first followed by the 3 upper clips.
9. Disconnect the wiring from the instrument panel finish panel.
10. Insert a punch or similar tool into the access hole of the headlight switch and pull on the push rod from the headlight switch to remove the push rod.
11. Remove the mounting nut and remove the headlight switch from the instrument panel. Disconnect the wiring.

To install:

12. Connect the wiring to the headlight switch and install into the instrument panel. Tighten the mounting nut.
13. Install the switch push rod into the headlight switch.
14. Connect the wiring to the instrument panel finish panel.
15. Install the instrument panel finish panel into the instrument panel making sure to engage all 5 clips.
16. Tighten the 2 exposed screws under the right and left lower instrument panel mouldings.
17. Screw the headlight bezel into place.
18. Install the headlight switch knob.
19. On vehicles equipped with a column shift, return the shift lever to the **PARK** position.
20. Connect the negative battery cable.

Except 1997–98 F-250HD, F-350 And F-Super Duty

See Figures 104, 105, 106, 107 and 108

**** WARNING**

The headlamp switch is retained to the instrument panel by a tabs which are located on the switch. This procedure must be followed exactly or damage to the switch and/or instrument panel will occur. This procedure releases (lowers the tabs into the switch body) so that the switch can be puled out.

1. Disconnect the negative battery cable.
2. Rotate the knob on the switch to the headlamp on position.
3. Insert a small thin tool to release the headlamp switch knob and remove the knob from the switch.
4. Turn the knob 180 degrees and install the knob onto the switch.
5. Rotate the knob counterclockwise until the knob points to the **OFF** position.
6. Rotate the knob clockwise one full turn.
7. Grasp the headlamp switch and remove it from the instrument panel.
8. Detach the connectors from the switch and remove the switch from the vehicle.
9. The installation is the reverse of the removal.

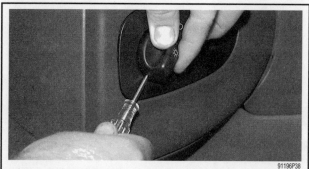

Fig. 104 Rotate the knob on the switch to the headlamp on position and insert a small thin tool to release the headlamp switch knob and remove the knob from the switch

Fig. 105 Turn the knob 180 degrees and install the knob onto the switch

Fig. 106 Rotate the knob counterclockwise until the knob points to the OFF position then rotate the knob clockwise one full turn

Fig. 107 Remove the headlamp switch from the instrument panel and . . .

Fig. 108 . . . detach the electrical connectors from the switch

LIGHTING

Headlights

REMOVAL & INSTALLATION

1997–98 F-250HD, F-350 and F-Super Duty

▶ See Figure 109

1. Raise and support the hood.
2. Detach the headlamp electrical connector.
3. Rotate the headlamp bulb retainer counterclockwise and remove.
4. Remove the headlamp bulb by pulling it straight out with a gentle up-and-down rocking motion.

※※ WARNING

Do not touch the glass bulb with your fingers. Oil from your fingers can severely shorten the life of the bulb. If necessary, wipe off any dirt or oil from the bulb with rubbing alcohol before completing installation.

To install:

5. Install a new bulb into the headlamp assembly.
6. Install the headlamp bulb retainer and turn it clockwise to engage the retaining tabs.
7. Attach the bulb electrical connector.
8. Turn the lights on and check the bulb operation.

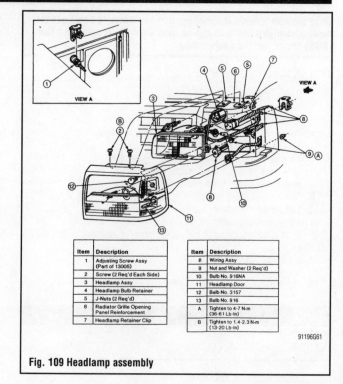

Item	Description
1	Adjusting Screw Assy (Part of 13005)
2	Screw (2 Req'd Each Side)
3	Headlamp Assy
4	Headlamp Bulb Retainer
5	J-Nuts (2 Req'd)
6	Radiator Grille Opening Panel Reinforcement
7	Headlamp Retainer Clip

Item	Description
8	Wiring Assy
9	Nut and Washer (2 Req'd)
10	Bulb No. 916NA
11	Headlamp Door
12	Bulb No. 3157
13	Bulb No. 916
A	Tighten to 4-7 N-m (36-61 Lb-In)
B	Tighten to 1.4-2.3 N-m (13-20 Lb-In)

Fig. 109 Headlamp assembly

F-150, F-250, Expedition and Navigator

▶ **See Figures 110 thru 117**

▶ See Figures 110 thru 117

❊❊ CAUTION

The halogen bulb contains gas under pressure. The bulb may shatter if the glass envelope is scratched or if the bulb is dropped. Handle the bulb carefully. Grasp the bulb only by its base. Avoid touching the glass envelope.

➡ The headlamp bulb should not be removed from the headlamp until just before a replacement bulb is installed. Removing the bulb for an extended period of time may affect headlamp bulb performance. Contaminants may enter the headlamp where they can settle on the lens and reflector. Never turn on the headlamps with the bulb removed from the headlamp.

1. Raise and support the hood.
2. Raise the headlamp retainers by pushing rearward and pulling up.
3. If equipped, rotate the headlamp bulb protective cover counterclockwise and remove.
4. Disconnect the headlamp bulb electrical connector.
5. Remove the headlamp assembly.
6. Rotate the headlamp bulb retainer counterclockwise and remove.
7. Remove the headlamp bulb by pulling it straight out with a gentle up-and-down rocking motion.

❊❊ WARNING

Do not touch the glass bulb with your fingers. Oil from your fingers can severely shorten the life of the bulb. If necessary, wipe off any dirt or oil from the bulb with rubbing alcohol before completing installation.

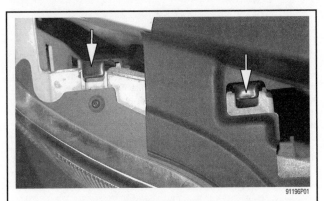

Fig. 110 The headlamp assembly is held by two retainers

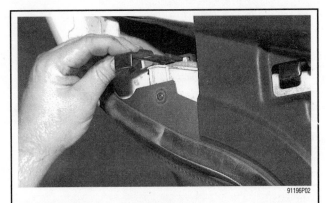

Fig. 111 Lift up on the retainers and . . .

Fig. 112 . . . pull the headlamp assembly out of the front of the vehicle

Fig. 113 Detach the electrical connector for the headlamp bulb

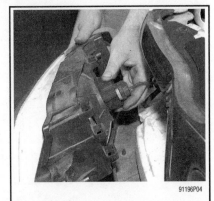

Fig. 114 Rotate the retainer until . . .

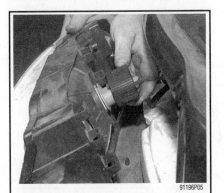

Fig. 115 . . . it is free from the retaining tabs on the headlamp assembly and . . .

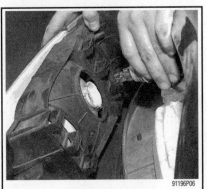

Fig. 116 . . . remove the bulb and retainer from the headlamp

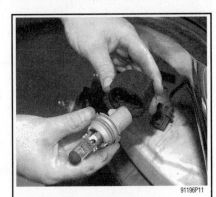

Fig. 117 Remove the bulb from the retainer

To install:

8. Install a new bulb into the headlamp assembly.

9. Install the headlamp bulb retainer and turn it clockwise to engage the retaining tabs.

10. Attach the bulb electrical connector.

11. If equipped, install the headlamp bulb protective cover.

12. Install the headlamp assembly.

➡Be sure the headlamp assembly is positioned correctly with the alignment pins inserted into the proper holes and onto the ribs of the reinforcement.

13. Engage the retainers by gently pushing down.

14. Turn the lights on and check the bulb operation.

1999–00 Super Duty Models

▶ **See Figure 118**

1. Pull up and remove the two upper headlamp clips.
2. Release the lower headlamp clip.
3. Position the headlamp so the connector can be accessed.
4. Detach the headlamp connector.
5. Remove the headlamp assembly from the vehicle.
6. Rotate the headlamp bulb retainer counterclockwise and remove.
7. Remove the headlamp bulb by pulling it straight out with a gentle up-and-down rocking motion.

❊❊ WARNING

Do not touch the glass bulb with your fingers. Oil from your fingers can severely shorten the life of the bulb. If necessary, wipe off any dirt or oil from the bulb with rubbing alcohol before completing installation.

To install:

8. Install a new bulb into the headlamp assembly.

9. Install the headlamp bulb retainer and turn it clockwise to engage the retaining tabs.

10. Attach the bulb electrical connector.

11. Install the headlamp assembly.

12. Turn the lights on and check the bulb operation.

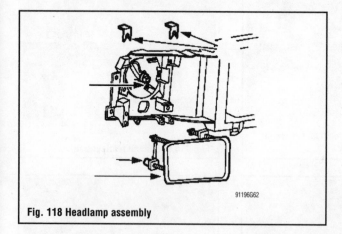

Fig. 118 Headlamp assembly

AIMING THE HEADLIGHTS

▶ **See Figures 119 and 120**

The headlights must be properly aimed to provide the best, safest road illumination. The lights should be checked for proper aim and adjusted as necessary. Certain state and local authorities have requirements for headlight aiming; these should be checked before adjustment is made.

❊❊ CAUTION

About once a year, when the headlights are replaced or any time front end work is performed on your vehicle, the headlight should be accurately aimed by a reputable repair shop using the proper equipment. Headlights not properly aimed can make it virtually impossible to see and may blind other drivers on the road, possibly causing an accident. Note that the following procedure is a temporary fix, until you can take your vehicle to a repair shop for a proper adjustment.

Headlight adjustment may be temporarily made using a wall, as described below, or on the rear of another vehicle. When adjusted, the lights should not glare in oncoming car or truck windshields, nor should they illuminate the passenger compartment of vehicles driving in front of you. These adjustments are rough and should always be fine-tuned by a repair shop which is equipped with headlight aiming tools. Improper adjustments may be both dangerous and illegal.

For most of the vehicles covered by this manual, horizontal and vertical aiming of each sealed beam unit is provided by two adjusting screws which move the retaining ring and adjusting plate against the tension of a coil spring. There is no adjustment for focus; this is done during headlight manufacturing.

➡Because the composite headlight assembly is bolted into position, no adjustment should be necessary or possible. Some applications, however, may be bolted to an adjuster plate or may be retained by adjusting screws. If so, follow this procedure when adjusting the lights, BUT always have the adjustment checked by a reputable shop.

Before removing the headlight bulb or disturbing the headlamp in any way, note the current settings in order to ease headlight adjustment upon reassembly. If the high or low beam setting of the old lamp still works, this can be done using the wall of a garage or a building:

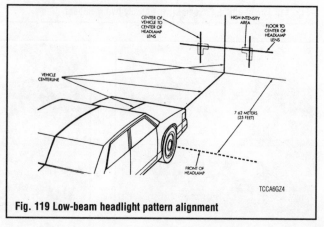

Fig. 119 Low-beam headlight pattern alignment

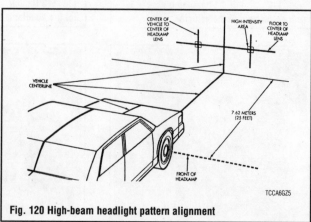

Fig. 120 High-beam headlight pattern alignment

1. Park the vehicle on a level surface, with the fuel tank about ½ full and with the vehicle empty of all extra cargo (unless normally carried). The vehicle should be facing a wall which is no less than 6 feet (1.8m) high and 12 feet (3.7m) wide. The front of the vehicle should be about 25 feet from the wall.

2. If aiming is to be performed outdoors, it is advisable to wait until dusk in order to properly see the headlight beams on the wall. If done in a garage, darken the area around the wall as much as possible by closing shades or hanging cloth over the windows.

3. Turn the headlights **ON** and mark the wall at the center of each light's low beam, then switch on the brights and mark the center of each light's high beam. A short length of masking tape which is visible from the front of the vehicle may be used. Although marking all four positions is advisable, marking one position from each light should be sufficient.

4. If neither beam on one side is working, and if another like-sized vehicle is available, park the second one in the exact spot where the vehicle was and mark the beams using the same-side light. Then switch the vehicles so the one to be aimed is back in the original spot. It must be parked no closer to or farther away from the wall than the second vehicle.

5. Perform any necessary repairs, but make sure the vehicle is not moved, or is returned to the exact spot from which the lights were marked. Turn the headlights **ON** and adjust the beams to match the marks on the wall.

6. Have the headlight adjustment checked as soon as possible by a reputable repair shop.

Signal and Marker Lights

REMOVAL & INSTALLATION

Front Turn Signal and Parking Lights

1997–98 F-250HD, F-350 AND F-SUPER DUTY

♦ **See Figure 121**

1. Remove the headlamp assembly.
2. Unplug the connector for the lamp.
3. Turn the bulb and socket counterclockwise ¼ of a turn to release it from the lens.
4. Pull the bulb straight out to remove it from the socket.
To install:
5. Place a new bulb into the socket and gently push to engage the retaining tabs.
6. Place the bulb and socket assembly into the opening of the lens and turn it ¼ of a turn clockwise to engage it into the lens.
7. Attach the connector for the lamp.
8. Install the headlamp assembly.

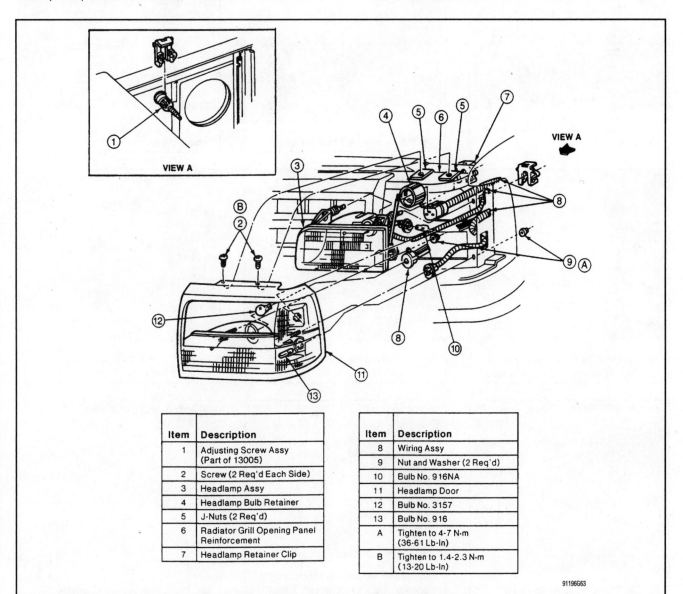

Item	Description
1	Adjusting Screw Assy (Part of 13005)
2	Screw (2 Req'd Each Side)
3	Headlamp Assy
4	Headlamp Bulb Retainer
5	J-Nuts (2 Req'd)
6	Radiator Grill Opening Panel Reinforcement
7	Headlamp Retainer Clip

Item	Description
8	Wiring Assy
9	Nut and Washer (2 Req'd)
10	Bulb No. 916NA
11	Headlamp Door
12	Bulb No. 3157
13	Bulb No. 916
A	Tighten to 4-7 N·m (36-61 Lb-In)
B	Tighten to 1.4-2.3 N·m (13-20 Lb-In)

91196G63

Fig. 121 Parking and turn signal lamp bulb replacement—1997–98 F-250HD, F-350 And F-Super Duty

EXCEPT 1997–98 F-250HD, F-350 AND F-SUPER DUTY

▶ See Figures 122, 123 and 124

1. Open and support the hood.
2. Remove the headlamp assembly.
3. Turn the bulb and socket counterclockwise ¼ of a turn to release it from the lens.
4. Pull the bulb straight out to remove it from the socket.

To install:

5. Place a new bulb into the socket and gently push to engage the retaining tabs.
6. Place the bulb and socket assembly into the opening of the lens and turn it ¼ of a turn clockwise to engage it into the lens.
7. Install the headlamp assembly.
8. Verify the operation of the lamp.
9. Close the hood.

Side Marker Light

1. Carefully pry the lens from the lamp assembly.
2. Remove the bulb from the terminals by gently pulling the bulb upward.

To install:

3. Gently press the bulb into the terminals on the lamp.
4. Snap the lens into the lamp assembly.
5. Verify the operation of the lamp.

Rear Turn Signal, Brake and Parking Lights

▶ See Figures 125 thru 130

1. Remove the lamp retaining screws.
2. Remove the lamp assembly from the vehicle.
3. Unplug the connector for the lamp.
4. Turn the bulb and socket counterclockwise ¼ of a turn to release it from the lens.

Fig. 122 Turn the bulb and socket counterclockwise ¼ of a turn to . . .

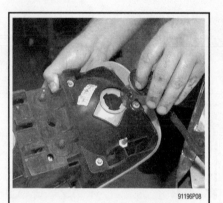

Fig. 123 . . . release it from the lens

Fig. 124 Pull the bulb straight out to remove it from the socket

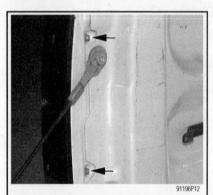

Fig. 125 The taillamp assembly is held by two retaining screws—F-150 model shown

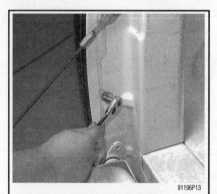

Fig. 126 Remove the two taillamp retaining screws and . . .

Fig. 127 . . . pull the taillamp assembly out of the rear of the vehicle

Fig. 128 Unplug the connector for the lamp

Fig. 129 Turn the bulb and socket counterclockwise ¼ of a turn to release it from the lens

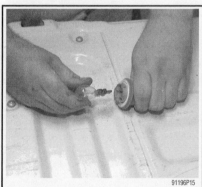

Fig. 130 Pull the bulb straight out to remove it from the socket

5. Pull the bulb straight out to remove it from the socket.

To install:

6. Place a new bulb into the socket and gently push to engage the retaining tabs.

7. Place the bulb and socket assembly into the opening of the lens and turn it ¼ of a turn clockwise to engage it into the lens.

8. Attach the connector for the lamp.

9. Place the lamp assembly into the opening in the vehicle.

10. Tighten the lamp retaining screws.

High-Mount Brake Light

♦ **See Figures 131, 132, and 133**

1. Remove the lamp retaining screws.

2. Remove the lamp assembly from the vehicle.

3. Unplug the connector for the lamp.

4. Turn the bulb and socket counterclockwise ¼ of a turn to release it from the lens.

5. Pull the bulb straight out to remove it from the socket.

To install:

6. Place a new bulb into the socket and gently push to engage the retaining tabs.

7. Place the bulb and socket assembly into the opening of the lens and turn it ¼ of a turn clockwise to engage it into the lens.

8. Attach the connector for the lamp.

9. Place the lamp assembly into the opening in the vehicle.

10. Tighten the lamp retaining screws.

Dome Light

♦ **See Figures 134 and 135**

1. Carefully pry the dome lamp lens from the lamp assembly.

2. Remove the bulb from the terminals by gently pulling the bulb downward.

To install:

3. Gently press the bulb into the terminals on the lamp.

4. Snap the lens into the lamp assembly.

5. Verify the operation of the lamp.

Map Lights

♦ **See Figures 134, 136, 137 and 138**

1. Carefully pry the dome lamp lens from the lamp assembly.

2. Remove the three retaining screws for the map/dome lamp assembly and remove it from the headliner.

3. Remove the bulb(s) from the terminals by gently pulling the bulb upward and out of the lamp assembly.

To install:

4. Slide the bulbs into place and gently press the bulb into the terminals on the lamp.

5. Place the lamp assembly into place and tighten the retaining screws.

6. Snap the lens into the lamp assembly.

7. Verify the operation of the lamp.

License Plate Lights

F-150, F-250, EXPEDITION AND NAVIGATOR

♦ **See Figures 139 and 140**

1. Reach under the bumper and rotate the bulb socket to remove it from the lamp lens.

2. Pull the bulb straight out to remove it from the socket.

3. The installation is the reverse of the removal.

EXCEPT F-150, F-250, EXPEDITION AND NAVIGATOR

♦ **See Figure 141**

1. Remove the retaining screws for the lamp lens.

2. Remove the lens from the lamp assembly.

3. Pull the bulb straight out to remove it from the socket.

4. The installation is the reverse of the removal.

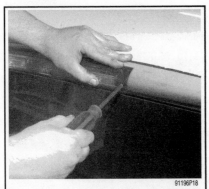

91196P18

Fig. 131 Remove the two retaining screws and . . .

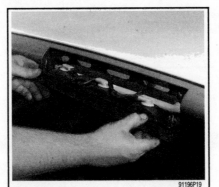

91196P19

Fig. 132 . . . remove the lamp assembly from the body

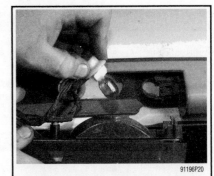

91196P20

Fig. 133 Turn the bulb and socket counterclockwise ¼ of a turn to release it from the lens

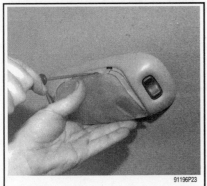

91196P23

Fig. 134 Carefully pry the dome lamp lens from the lamp assembly

91196P24

Fig. 135 Remove the bulb from the terminals by gently pulling the bulb upward

91196P25

Fig. 136 Remove the three lamp assembly retaining screws and . . .

Fig. 137 . . . lower the lamp assembly from the headliner

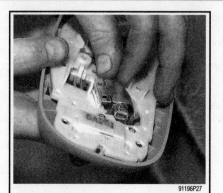

Fig. 138 Grasp the bulb and carefully remove it

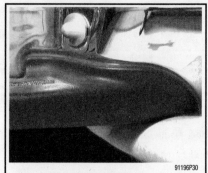

Fig. 139 Reach up and under the bumper to access the license plate bulb socket, rotate the socket and remove it from the lamp

Fig. 140 Pull the bulb straight out to remove it from the socket

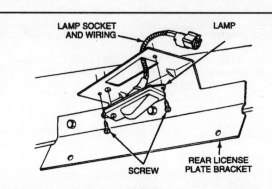

Fig. 141 Remove the lamp cover retaining screws to access the license plate bulb

Instrument Cluster Light Bulbs

REMOVAL & INSTALLATION

1. Remove the instrument cluster as outlined in this section.
2. Turn the desired bulb socket counter clockwise to remove it from the cluster.

3. Grasp the bulb and pull it straight out to remove it from the socket.
To install:
4. Place a new bulb into the socket and lightly press it into place.
5. Place the socket into the cluster and turn the socket clockwise to engage it into the cluster.
6. Install the instrument cluster.

TRAILER WIRING

Wiring the vehicle for towing is fairly easy. There are a number of good wiring kits available and these should be used, rather than trying to design your own.

All trailers will need brake lights and turn signals as well as tail lights and side marker lights. Most areas require extra marker lights for overwide trailers. Also, most areas have recently required back-up lights for trailers, and most trailer manufacturers have been building trailers with back-up lights for several years.

Additionally, some Class I, most Class II and just about all Class III and IV trailers will have electric brakes. Add to this number an accessories wire, to operate trailer internal equipment or to charge the trailer's battery, and you can have as many as seven wires in the harness.

Determine the equipment on your trailer and buy the wiring kit necessary. The kit will contain all the wires needed, plus a plug adapter set which includes the female plug, mounted on the bumper or hitch, and the male plug, wired into, or plugged into the trailer harness.

When installing the kit, follow the manufacturer's instructions. The color coding of the wires is usually standard throughout the industry. One point to note: some domestic vehicles, and most imported vehicles, have separate turn signals. On most domestic vehicles, the brake lights and rear turn signals operate with the same bulb. For those vehicles without separate turn signals, you can purchase an isolation unit so that the brake lights won't blink whenever the turn signals are operated.

One, final point, the best kits are those with a spring loaded cover on the vehicle mounted socket. This cover prevents dirt and moisture from corroding the terminals. Never let the vehicle socket hang loosely; always mount it securely to the bumper or hitch.

CIRCUIT PROTECTION

Fuses

REPLACEMENT

▶ **See Figures 142, 143 and 144**

Fuses are located either in the engine compartment or passenger compartment fuse and relay panels. If a fuse blows, a single component or single circuit will not function properly.
1. Remove the fuse or relay box cover.
2. Inspect the fuses to determine which is faulty.
3. Unplug and discard the fuse.
4. Inspect the box terminals and clean if corroded. If any terminals are damaged, replace the terminals.
5. Plug in a new fuse of the same amperage rating.

✳✳ WARNING

Never exceed the amperage rating of a blown fuse. If the replacement fuse also blows, check for a problem in the circuit.

6. Check for proper operation of the affected component or circuit.

Fig. 142 On some models, it is necessary to remove this door to access the interior fuse box

Maxi-Fuses (Fusible Links)

Maxi-fuses are located in the engine compartment relay box. If a maxi-fuse blows, an entire circuit or several circuits will not function properly.

REPLACEMENT

1. Remove the fuse and relay box cover.
2. Inspect the fusible links to determine which is faulty.
3. Unplug and discard the fusible link.
4. Inspect the box terminals and clean if corroded. If any terminals are damaged, replace the terminals.
5. Plug in a new fusible link of the same amperage rating.

✳✳ WARNING

Never exceed the amperage rating of a blown maxi-fuse. If the replacement fuse also blows, check for a problem in the circuit(s).

6. Check for proper operation of the affected circuit(s).

Circuit Breakers

RESETTING AND/OR REPLACEMENT

Circuit breakers are located inside the fuse panel. They are automatically reset when the problem corrects itself, is repaired, or the circuit cools down to allow operation again.

Flashers

REPLACEMENT

▶ **See Figure 145**

The turn signal flasher assembly is located under the driver's side of the instrument panel, on the front of the fuse panel for the 1997–98 F-250HD, F-350 and F-Super Duty models and under the center section of the instrument panel in the relay/flasher block on all other models.

Fig. 143 Remove the fuse panel cover

Fig. 144 To remove a fuse, grasp the fuse and pull it straight out carefully

Fig. 145 Location of the flasher assembly—F-150 models

WIRING DIAGRAMS

INDEX OF WIRING DIAGRAMS

91196W01

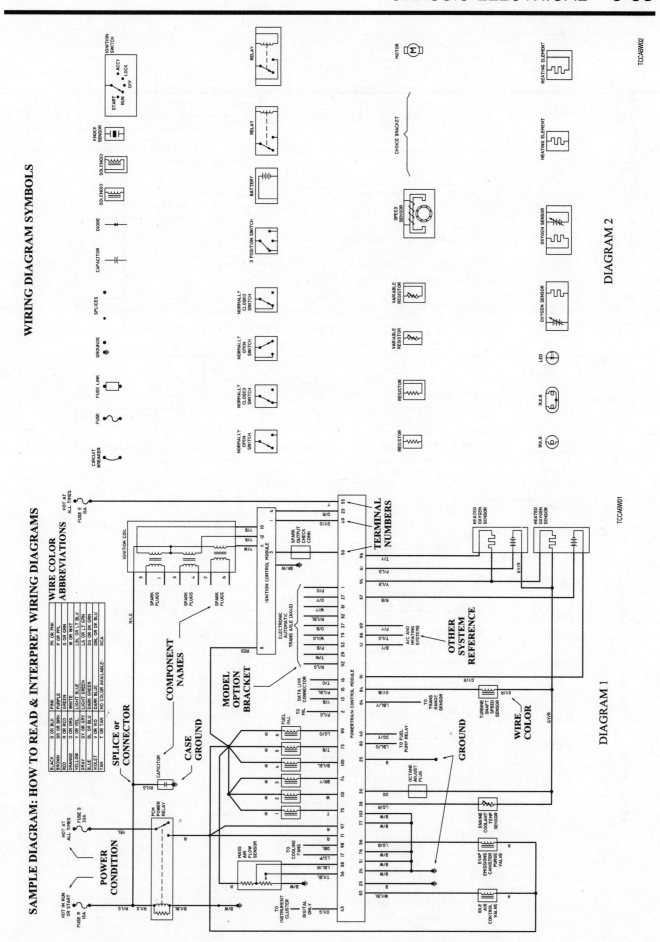

WIRING DIAGRAM SYMBOLS

DIAGRAM 2

SAMPLE DIAGRAM: HOW TO READ & INTERPRET WIRING DIAGRAMS

DIAGRAM 1

1997-00 EXPEDITION/F-150/250 4.6L ENGINE SCHEMATIC

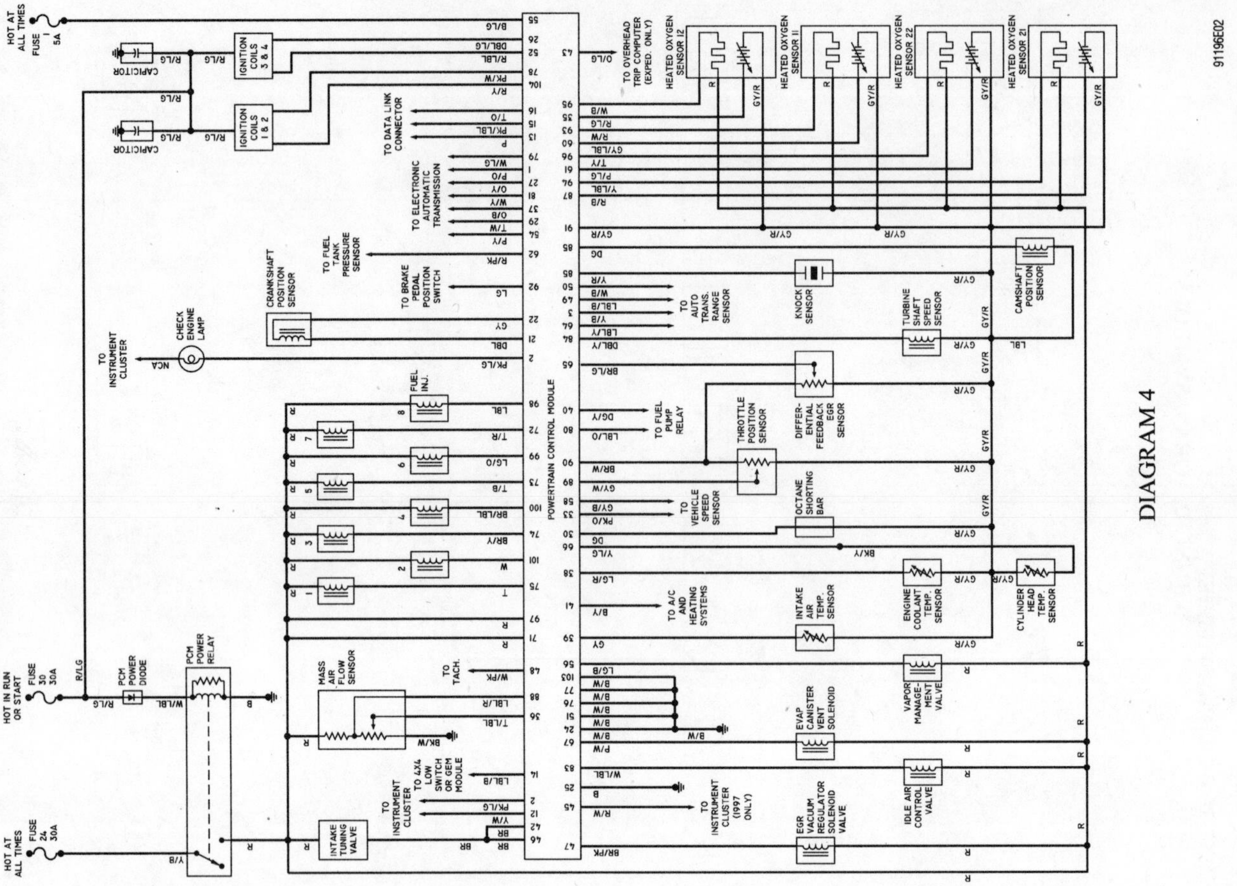

DIAGRAM 4

1997-00 F-150/250 4.2L ENGINE SCHEMATIC

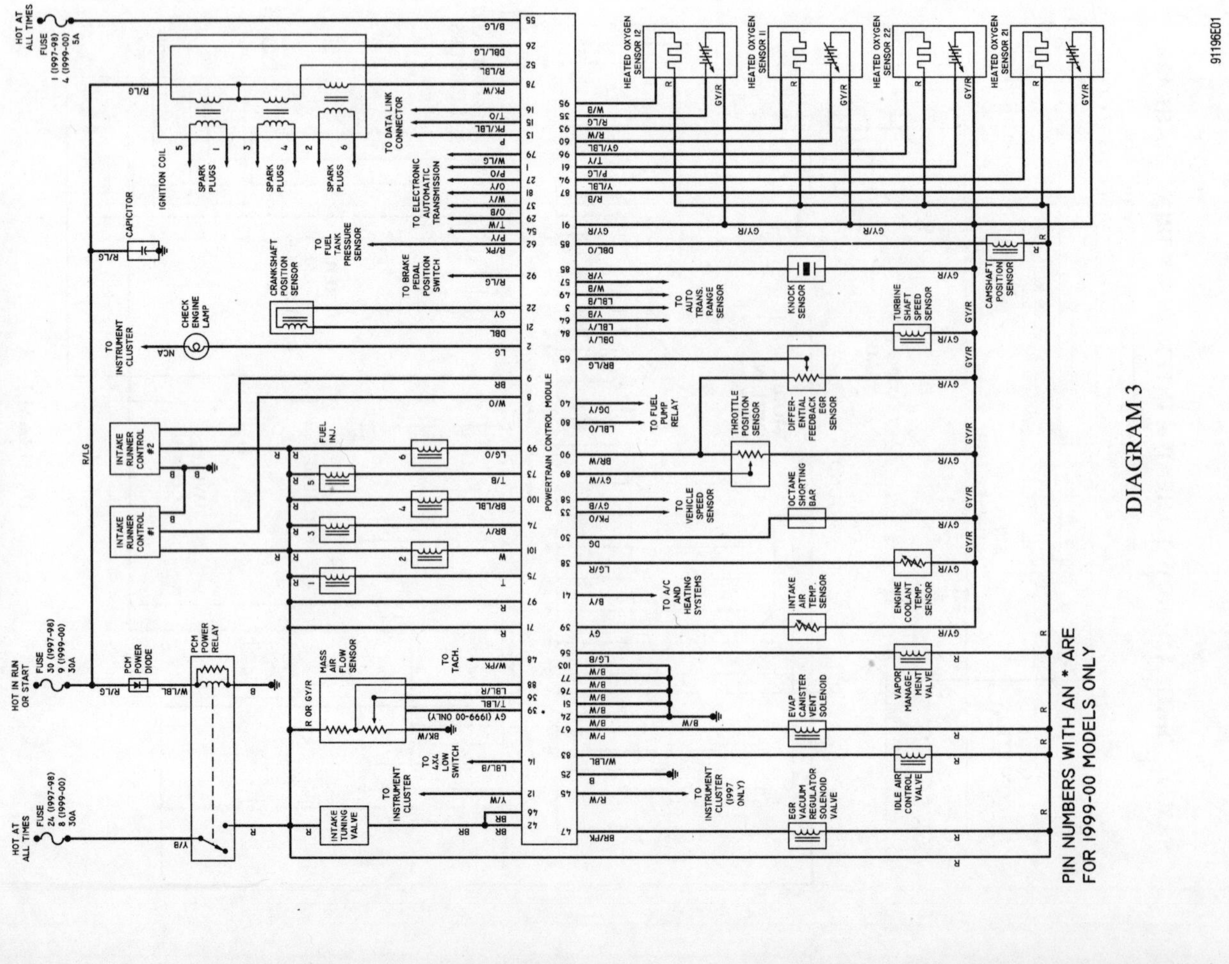

DIAGRAM 3

PIN NUMBERS WITH AN * ARE FOR 1999-00 MODELS ONLY

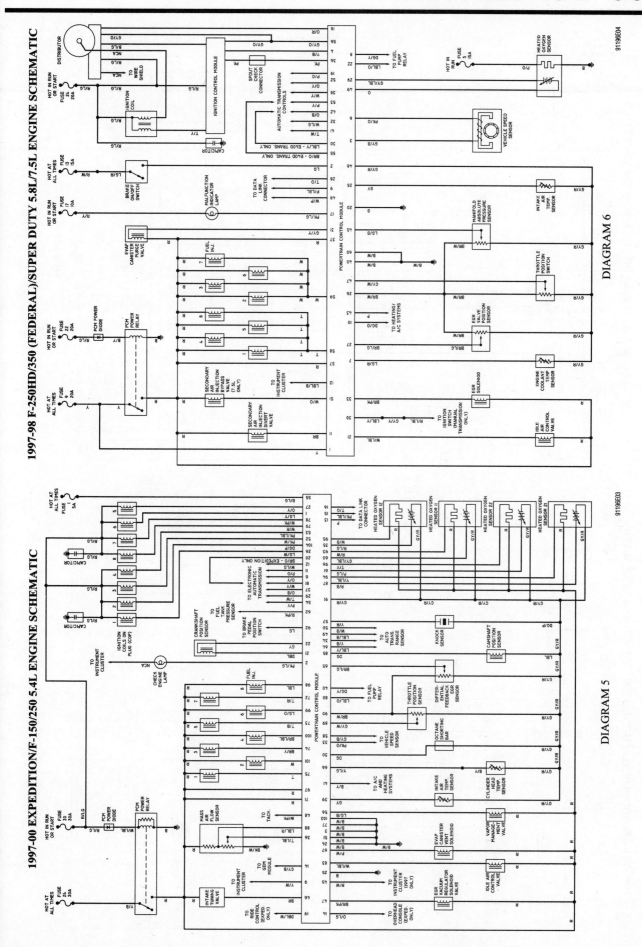

1997-98 F-250HD/350 (FEDERAL)/SUPER DUTY 5.8L/7.5L ENGINE SCHEMATIC

DIAGRAM 6

91196E04

1997-00 EXPEDITION/F-150/250 5.4L ENGINE SCHEMATIC

DIAGRAM 5

91196E03

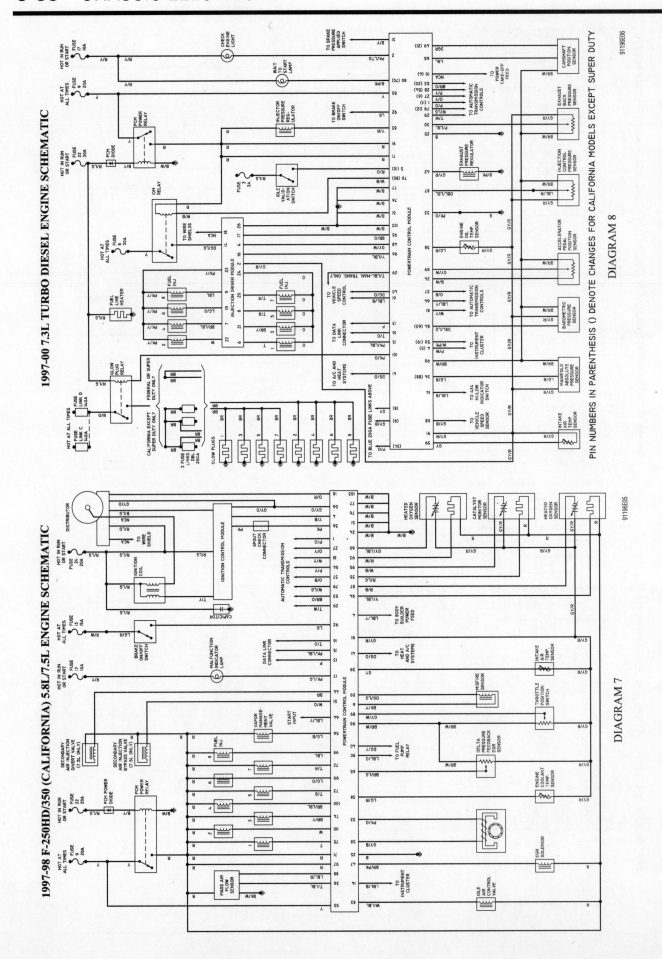

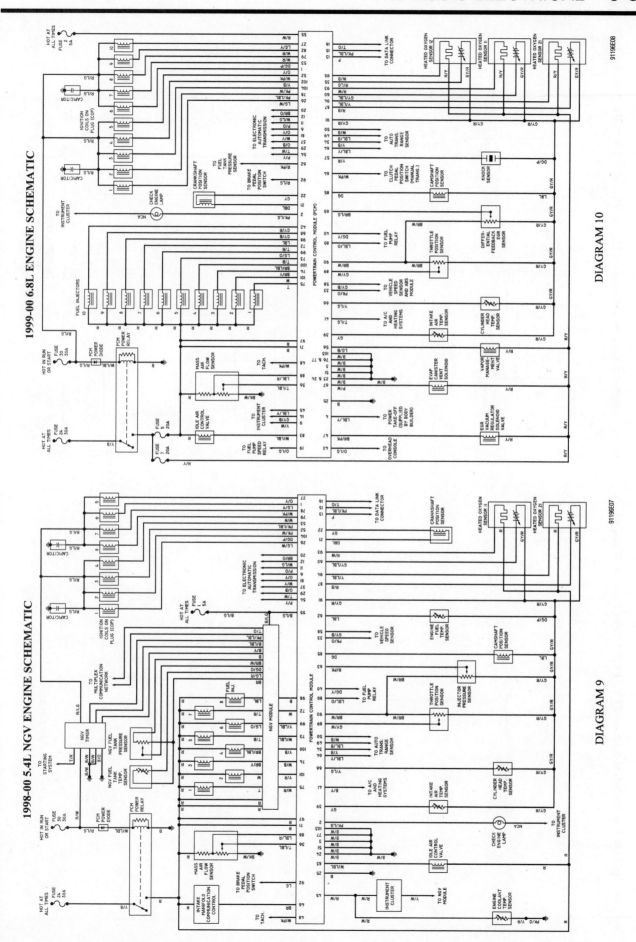

1999-00 6.8L ENGINE SCHEMATIC

1998-00 5.4L NGV ENGINE SCHEMATIC

DIAGRAM 10

DIAGRAM 9

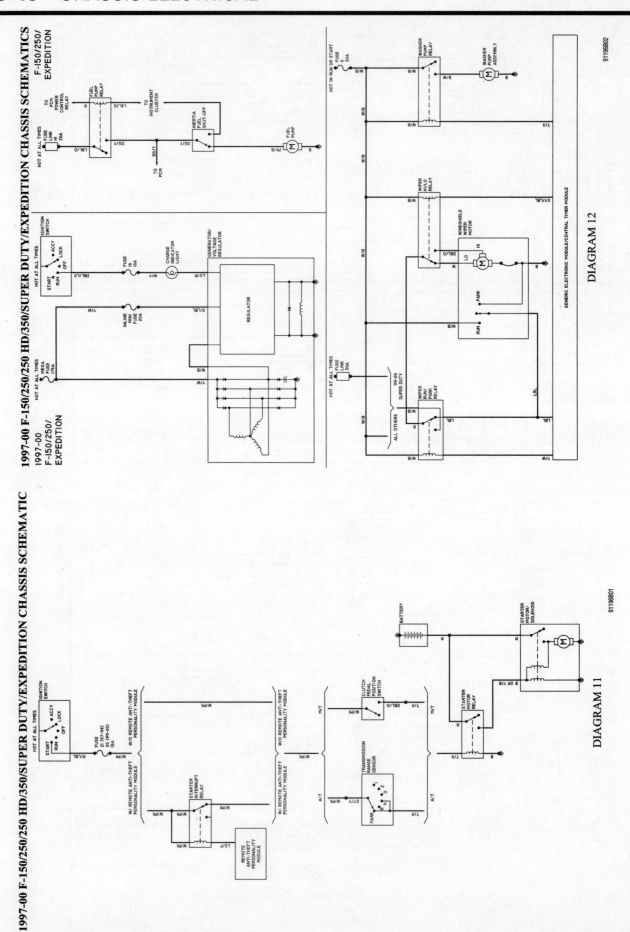

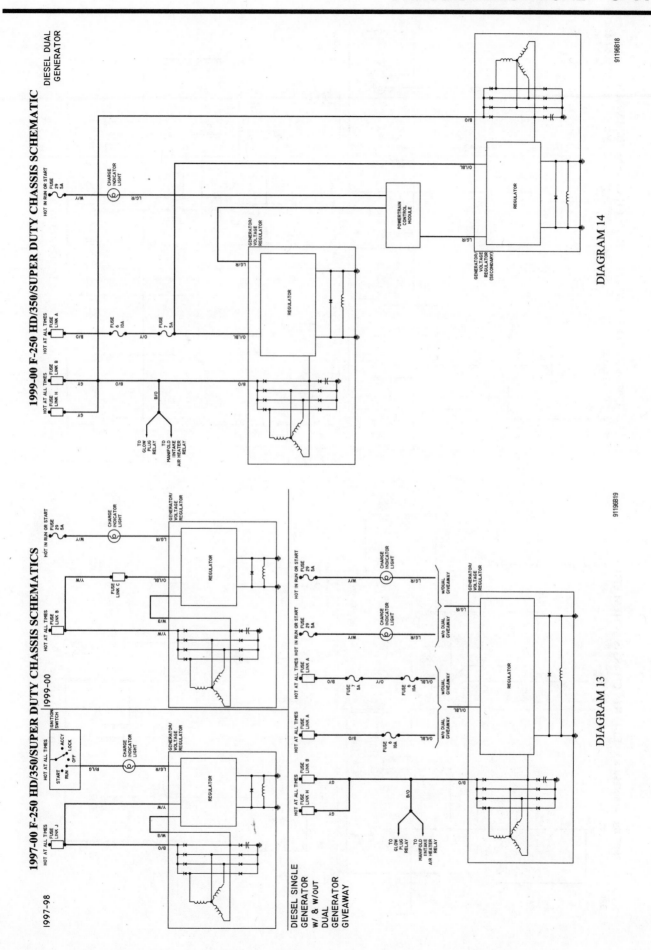

1999-00 F-250 HD/350/SUPER DUTY CHASSIS SCHEMATIC

DIESEL DUAL GENERATOR

DIAGRAM 14

1997-00 F-250 HD/350/SUPER DUTY CHASSIS SCHEMATICS

1997-98

1999-00

DIESEL SINGLE GENERATOR W/ & W/OUT DUAL GENERATOR GIVEAWAY

DIAGRAM 13

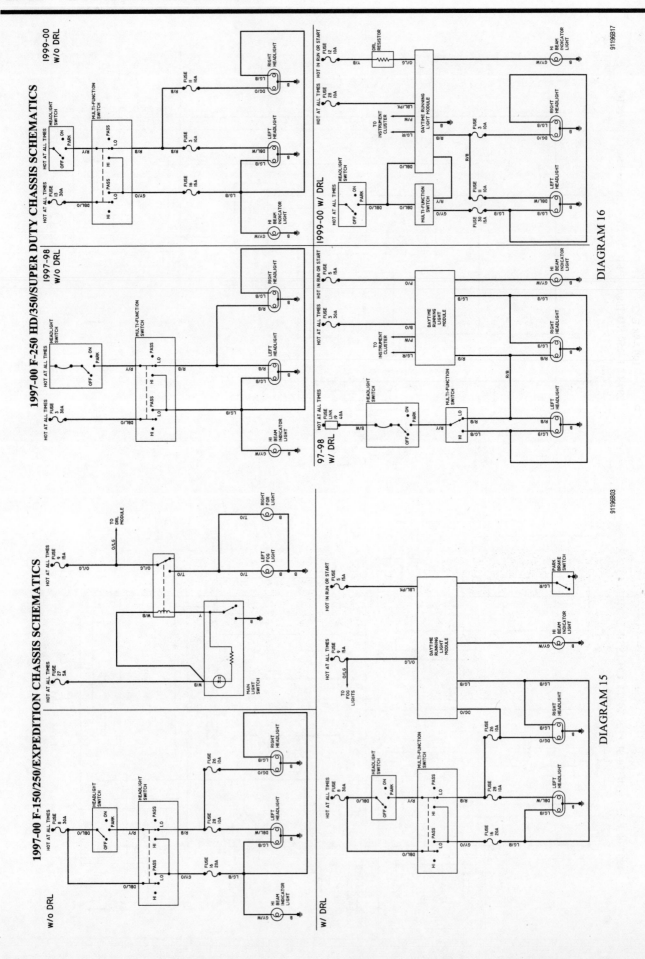

1997-00 F-250 HD/350/SUPER DUTY CHASSIS SCHEMATICS

1997-00 F-150/250/EXPEDITION CHASSIS SCHEMATICS

DIAGRAM 16

DIAGRAM 15

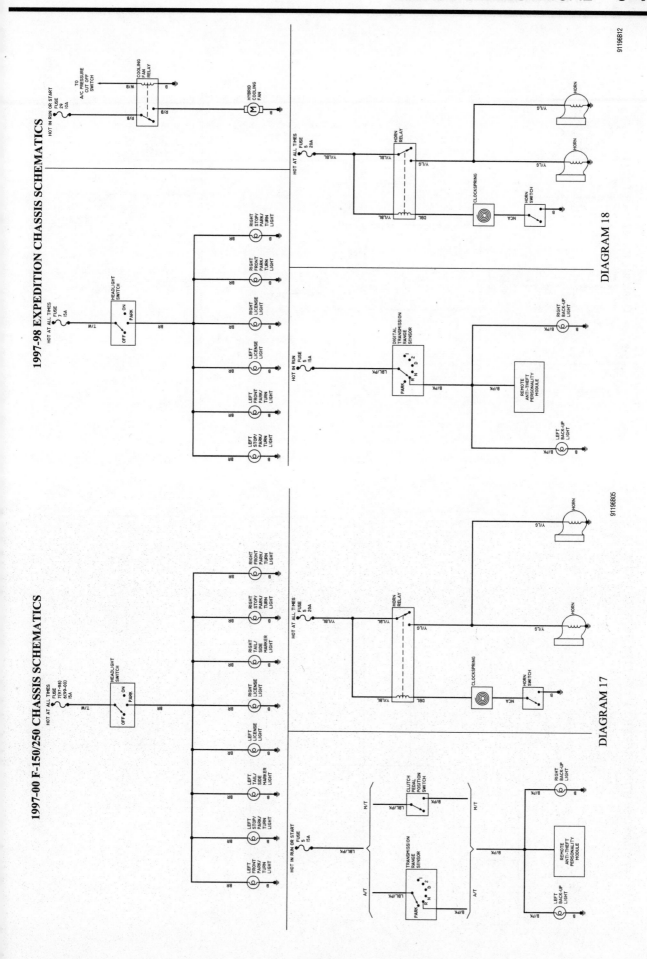

1997-98 EXPEDITION CHASSIS SCHEMATICS

DIAGRAM 18

1997-00 F-150/250 CHASSIS SCHEMATICS

DIAGRAM 17

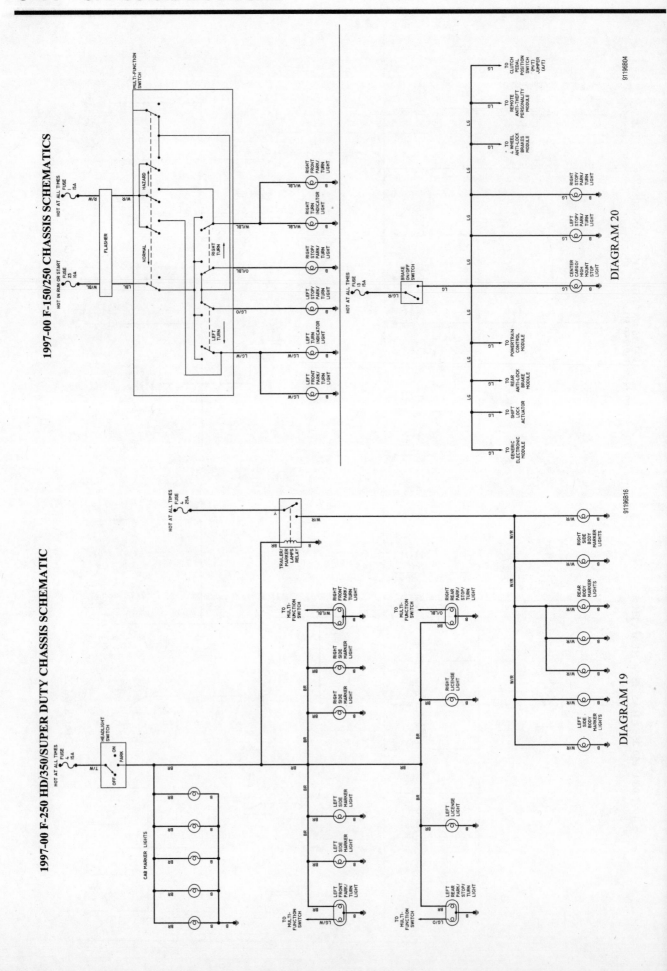

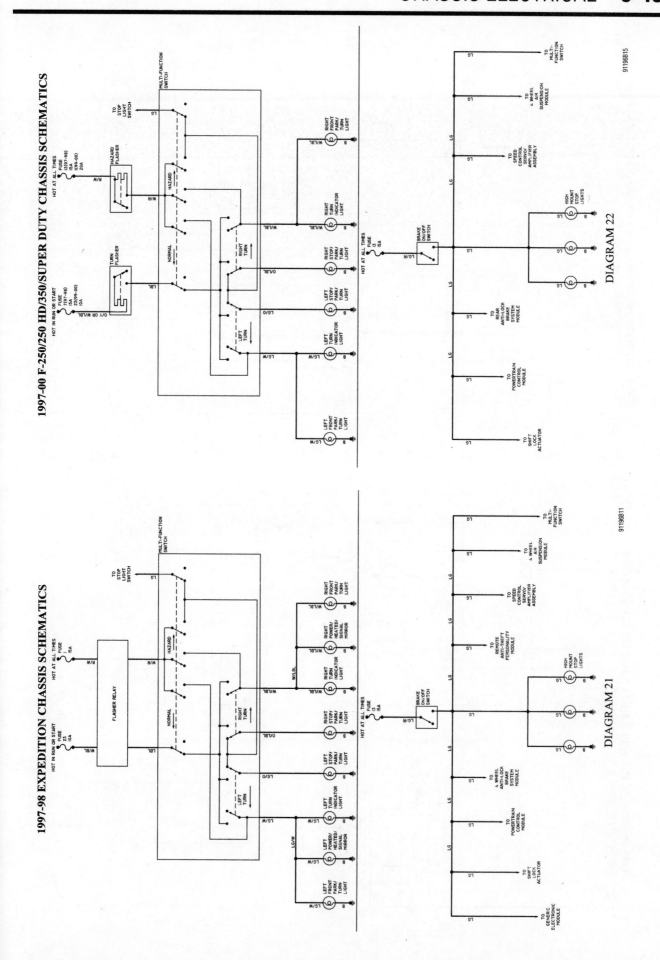

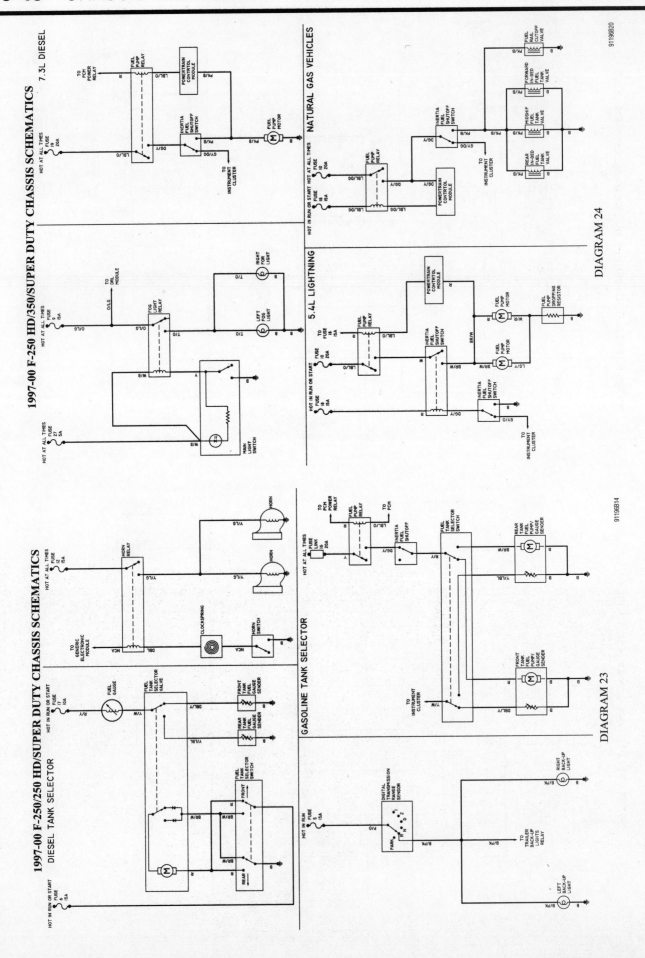

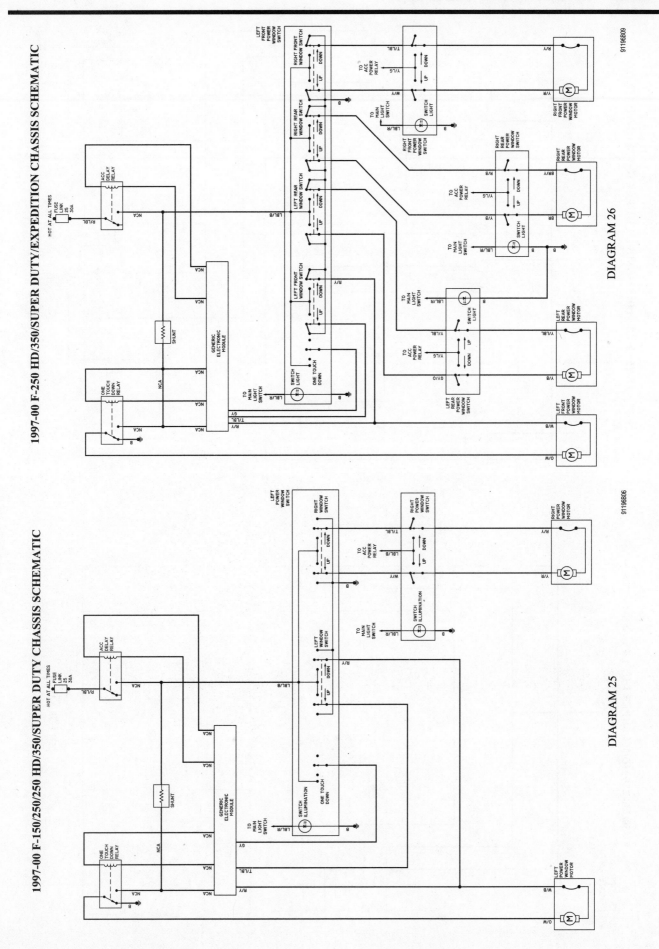

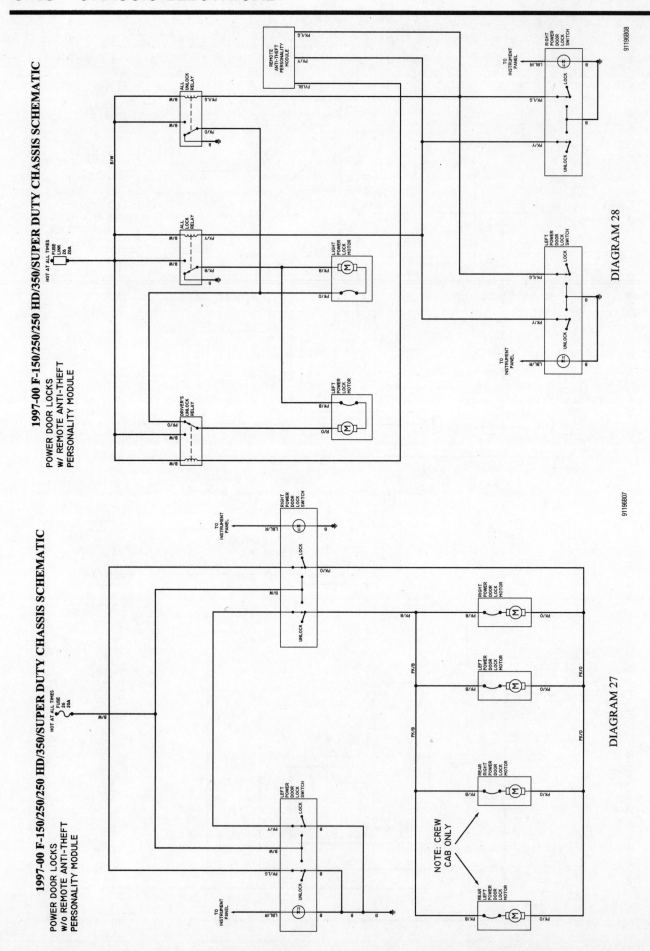

1997-00 F-150/250/250 HD/350/SUPER DUTY CHASSIS SCHEMATIC

POWER DOOR LOCKS
W/ REMOTE ANTI-THEFT
PERSONALITY MODULE

DIAGRAM 28

1997-00 F-150/250/250 HD/350/SUPER DUTY CHASSIS SCHEMATIC

POWER DOOR LOCKS
W/O REMOTE ANTI-THEFT
PERSONALITY MODULE

DIAGRAM 27

1997-98 EXPEDITION CHASSIS SCHEMATIC

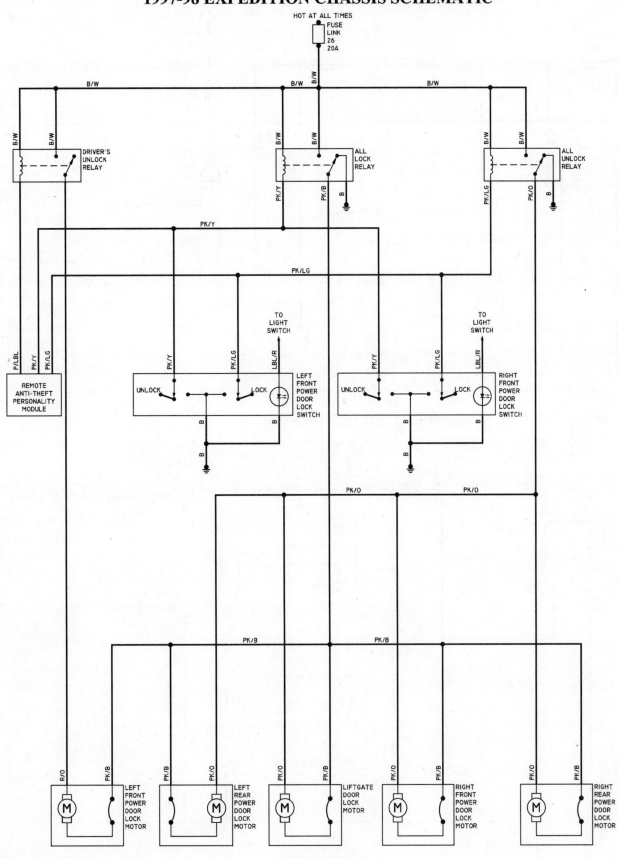

DIAGRAM 29

91196B13

1997-98 EXPEDITION CHASSIS SCHEMATICS

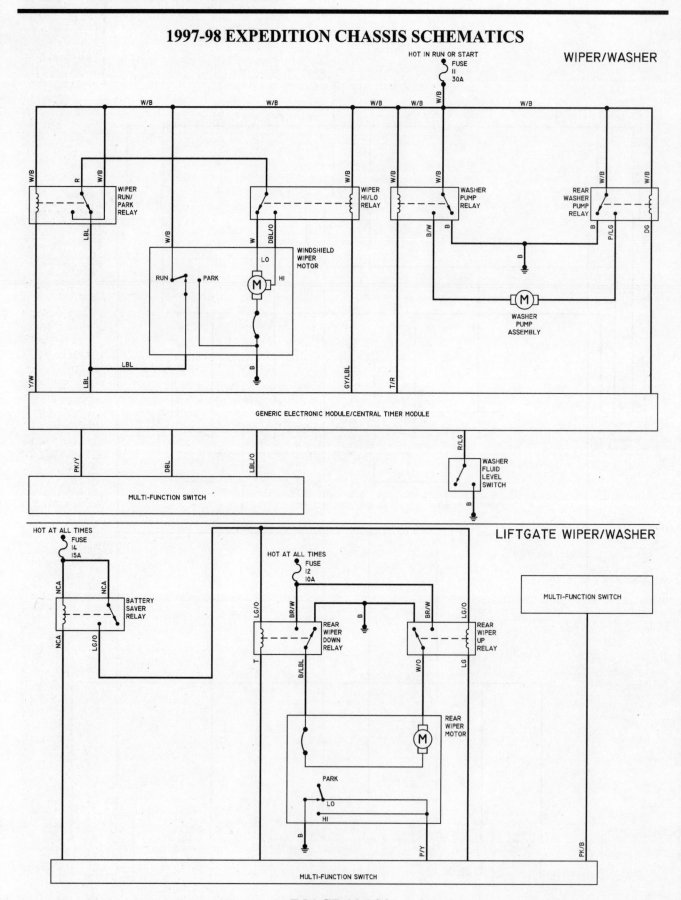

DIAGRAM 30

91196B10

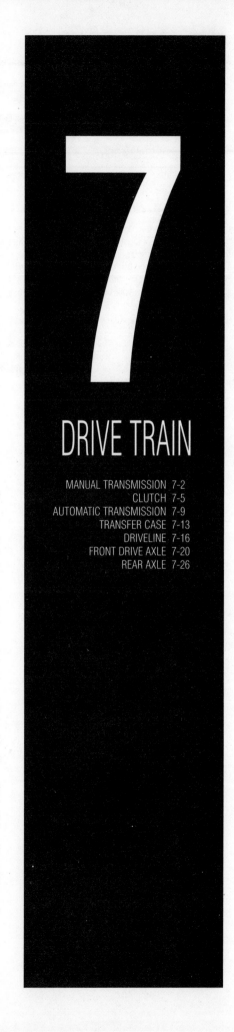

7
DRIVE TRAIN

MANUAL TRANSMISSION

Shift Handle

REMOVAL & INSTALLATION

M5OD

▶ **See Figures 1, 2 and 3**

1. Disconnect the negative battery cable.
2. Remove the shifter boot retaining screws and lift the boot (1) from the transmission opening cover.
3. Remove the bolt (2) retaining the upper shift lever to the lower shift lever (3) and remove the upper shift lever.
4. Unfasten the transmission opening cover retaining screws and remove the cover.
5. Remove the lower shift lever boot.

To install:

6. Install lower shifter boot and transmission opening cover. Tighten the cover retaining bolts.
7. Install the upper shift lever to the lower lever and install the retaining bolt. Tighten 20–29 ft. lbs. (27–40 Nm).
8. Place the shifter boot into position and tighten the retaining screws.
9. Connect the negative battery cable.

ZF

▶ **See Figures 4, 5 and 6**

1. Disconnect the negative battery cable.
2. Remove the carpet or floor mats.
3. Remove the shifter boot retaining screws and slide the boot up the shift lever shaft.
4. Remove the shift lever retaining bolts.
5. Remove the shift lever and shifter boot from the stub shaft.
6. Remove the shifter stub shaft from the transmission by unfastening the six retaining bolts and removing the stub shaft and shifter cover. Detach the electrical connector from the shifter cover and remove the assembly.
7. Installation is the reverse of the removal procedure.

Back-up Light Switch

REMOVAL & INSTALLATION

▶ **See Figure 7**

1. Disconnect the negative battery cable.
2. Raise and safely support the vehicle securely on jackstands.
3. Detach the connector for the back-up light switch.
4. Using a suitable size wrench or socket, remove the back-up light switch.

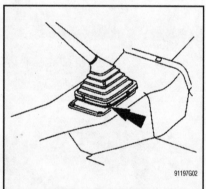

91197G02

Fig. 1 Remove the shifter boot retaining screws and . . .

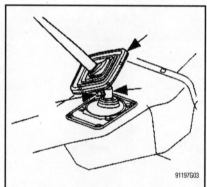

91197G03

Fig. 2 . . . lift the boot (1) from the transmission opening cover

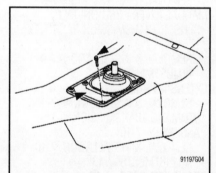

91197G04

Fig. 3 Remove the transmission opening cover retaining screws and remove the cover

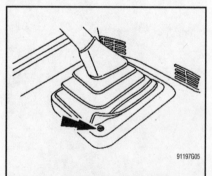

91197G05

Fig. 4 Remove the shifter boot retaining screws and slide the boot up the shift lever shaft

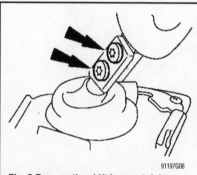

91197G06

Fig. 5 Remove the shift lever retaining bolts and remove the shift lever and shifter boot from the stub shaft

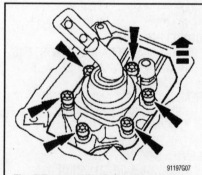

91197G07

Fig. 6 Remove the shifter stub shaft from the transmission by removing the six retaining bolts

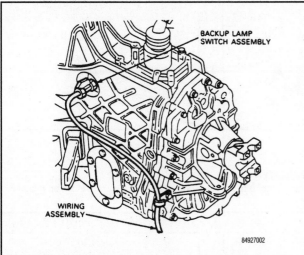

Fig. 7 Typical back-up lamp switch location—mounted on the transmission

To install:

5. Installation is the reverse of the removal procedure.
6. Tighten the switch to 18–26 ft. lbs. (25–35 Nm) on the M5OD and 15 ft. lbs. (20 Nm) on ZF models.

Extension Housing Seal (in-Vehicle)

REMOVAL & INSTALLATION

2WD Models

♦ See Figures 8, 9 and 10

The extension seal on 2WD drive vehicles is located at the rear of the transmission case.

1. Raise and support the vehicle safely.
2. Drain the transmission of lubricant.
3. Matchmark the driveshaft to the yoke for reassembly and remove the driveshaft.
4. Remove the old seal using a seal puller or appropriate prytool.

To install:

5. Install a new seal, coated with sealing compound, using an appropriate seal installation tool.
6. Install the driveshaft, making certain to align the matchmark.
7. Fill the transmission to the level of the fill plug hole.
8. Install the plug and lower the vehicle.

4WD Models

The extension seal on 4WD drive vehicles is located at the rear of the transfer case.

Manual Transmission Assembly

REMOVAL & INSTALLATION

M5OD

♦ See Figures 11 thru 18

➡This type of transmission is found on F-150, F-250 and Expedition models.

1. Disconnect the negative battery cable.
2. Remove the retaining bolt from the transmission electrical harness connector and separate the harness.
3. Place the transmission in **NEUTRAL**.
4. Remove the shift lever assembly.
5. Raise and safely support the vehicle.
6. Support the vehicle with jack stands.
7. Remove the driveshaft.
8. Disconnect the clutch hydraulic line from the slave cylinder using Clutch Coupling Tool T88T-70522-A, or equivalent. Cap the end of the tube and slave cylinder to prevent the entry of dirt, moisture or other contaminants into the hydraulic clutch system.
9. Disconnect the starter motor electrical connectors. Remove 2 starter motor retaining bolts and remove the starter motor.
10. On 4x4 vehicles, remove the transfer case assembly.
11. Disconnect heated oxygen sensor (HO2S) electrical harness connectors.
12. Place a suitable transmission jack under transmission and secure with a strap or chain.
13. Remove the nuts retaining the transmission support insulator (mount) to the crossmember.
14. Remove the 2 heat shield retaining bolts.
15. Remove the nuts and bolts retaining the crossmember to the frame side rails and remove the crossmember.
16. Remove the 2 nuts retaining the exhaust pipe bracket and remove the bracket.
17. Remove the nut retaining the fuel line bracket to the transmission housing.
18. Remove the exhaust system bolts and lower the exhaust for transmission removal.
19. On 4.2L equipped models, remove the oil pan-to-transmission bolts.

➡If the transmission is to be removed from the vehicle for an extended period, support the rear of the engine with a safety stand and wood block, or equivalent.

20. Remove the transmission retaining bolts and bring the transmission

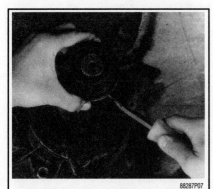

Fig. 8 Removing the extension housing seal

Fig. 9 Always replace the old seal with a new one

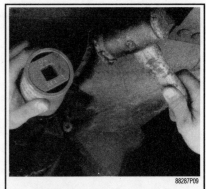

Fig. 10 Using a special tool and mallet, install the new seal

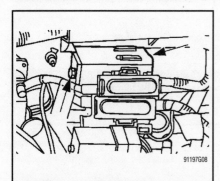

Fig. 11 Remove the retaining bolt from the transmission electrical harness connector and separate the harness

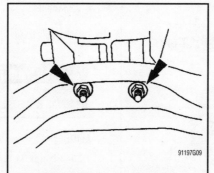

Fig. 12 Remove the nuts retaining the transmission support insulator (mount) to the crossmember

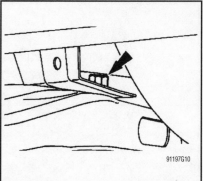

Fig. 13 Remove the 2 heat shield retaining bolts

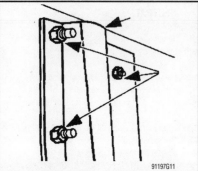

Fig. 14 Remove the nuts and bolts retaining the crossmember to the frame side rails and remove the crossmember

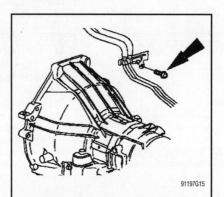

Fig. 15 Remove the nut retaining the fuel line bracket to the transmission housing

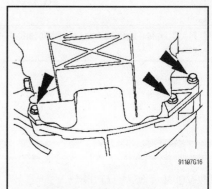

Fig. 16 On 4.2L equipped models, remove the oil pan-to-transmission bolts

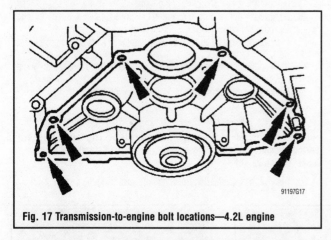

Fig. 17 Transmission-to-engine bolt locations—4.2L engine

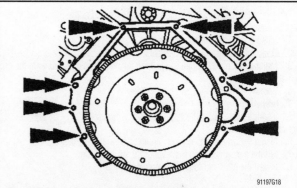

Fig. 18 Transmission-to-engine bolt locations—4.6L and 5.4L engines

rearward to separate the clutch housing from the dowel pins on the rear of the cylinder block. Slowly lower the transmission from the vehicle.

To install:

21. The extension housing seal should be replaced before installing the transmission. Remove the extension housing seal using Removal Tool T74P-77248-A, or equivalent.

22. Lubricate the inside diameter of the oil seal and install the seal into the extension housing using Installer Tool T61L-7657-A, or equivalent. Ensure that the extension housing seal drain hole faces downward.

23. Install 2 dowel pins into the lower clutch housing bolt holes. The dowel pins can be made by cutting the heads from 2 bolts but they must be long enough to be removed after the transmission is in place.

24. Place the transmission on a suitable transmission jack and secure with a strap or chain.

25. Slowly lift the transmission into place. Ensure that the input shaft engages the clutch disc spline and the pilot bearing in the flywheel.

26. Install the bolts retaining the clutch housing to the cylinder block. Tighten the bolts to 38 ft. lbs. (50 Nm). To avoid galvanic corrosion, only aluminum washers can be used to attach the housing to the engine.

27. On 4.2L equipped models, install the oil pan-to-transmission bolts. Tighten the bolts to 38 ft. lbs. (50 Nm).

28. Place the exhaust system in position and install the retaining bolts.

29. Place the fuel line bracket in position and install the retaining nut.

30. Place the exhaust bracket in position and install the retaining nuts.

31. Install the rear crossmember and install 6 crossmember-to-frame bolts. Tighten the bolts to 39–53 ft. lbs. (53–72 Nm).

32. Install the 2 heat shield retaining bolts.

33. Lower the transmission ensuring the rear transmission insulator studs are properly positioned. Install 2 retaining nuts and tighten to 64–81 ft. lbs. (87–110 Nm).

34. Remove the jack and connect the 2 heated oxygen sensors (HO_2S).

35. Install the starter motor and tighten the attaching bolts.

36. On 4x4 vehicles, install the transfer case.
37. Install the driveshaft to the rear axle flange and tighten the bolts.
38. Remove the cap from the hydraulic clutch tube. Install the tube and fitting in the slave cylinder, then install the clip retaining the tube and fitting to the slave cylinder.
39. Check the transmission and transfer case fluid level and fill with specified lubricate.
40. Remove the jack stands.
41. Lower the vehicle.
42. Install the shift lever and retaining bolt.
43. Place the rubber shift boot on the floor and install the retaining bolts.
44. Connect the negative battery cable.
45. Bleed the hydraulic clutch system.
46. Road test the vehicle and check for proper transmission operation.

ZF Series

➡This type of transmission is found on F-250HD/SD, F-350 and F-Super Duty models.

1. Place the transmission in neutral.
2. Remove the shifter from the vehicle. Refer to the procedure in this section.
3. On 7.3L diesel engine equipped models only, loosen the clamp on the turbocharger wastegate exhaust outlet.
4. Raise and support the vehicle safely.
5. Remove the starter.
6. On 7.3L diesel engine equipped models only:
   a. Remove the nuts retaining the exhaust extension pipe to the muffler assembly.
   b. Remove the engine charge exhaust pipe and extension pipe.
7. Place a drain pan under the case and drain the case through the drain plug.
8. Remove the driveshaft(s).
9. Disconnect the back-up lamp switch.
10. Remove the clutch slave cylinder.
11. On 4 wheel drive models, remove the skid plate from under the transfer case.

12. On 4-wheel drive models, remove the transfer case.
13. Remove the transmission rear insulator and lower retainer.
14. Unbolt and remove the crossmember.
15. On the 6-speed ZF transmission, disconnect the transmission cooling tubes
16. Remove the transmission-to-engine block bolts.
17. Roll the transmission rearward until the input shaft clears, lower the jack and remove the transmission.

To install:
18. Install 2 guide studs into the lower bolt holes.
19. Raise the transmission until the input shaft splines are aligned with the clutch disc splines. The clutch release bearing and hub must be properly positioned in the release lever fork.
20. Roll the transmission forward and into position on the front case.
21. Install the bolts and torque them to 39–53 ft. lbs. (53–72 Nm). Remove the guide studs and install and tighten the 2 remaining bolts.
22. On the 6-speed ZF transmission, connect the transmission cooling tubes
23. Install the crossmember and torque the bolts to 55 ft. lbs. (75 Nm).
24. Install the transmission rear insulator and lower retainer. Tighten the bolts to 60 ft. lbs. (81 Nm).
25. On 4-wheel drive models, install the transfer case and skid plate.
26. Install the slave cylinder.
27. Connect the back-up lamp switch.
28. Install the driveshaft(s).
29. Remove the transmission jack.
30. On 7.3L diesel engine equipped models only install the exhaust extension pipe to the muffler assembly.
31. Install the starter.
32. Fill the transmission.
33. Lower the vehicle.
34. Install the shifter.
35. On 7.3L diesel engine equipped models only, tighten the clamp on the turbocharger wastegate exhaust outlet.
36. Connect the negative battery cable.

CLUTCH

Driven Disc and Pressure Plate

REMOVAL & INSTALLATION

◆ **See Figures 19 thru 31**

1. Raise and safely support the vehicle.
2. Remove the transmission.
3. If the clutch and pressure plate are going to be reused, mark the pressure plate and cover assembly and the flywheel so that they can be reinstalled in the same relative position.
4. Loosen the pressure plate and cover attaching bolts evenly in a staggered sequence a turn at time until the pressure plate springs are relieved of their tension. Remove the attaching bolts.
5. Remove the pressure plate and cover assembly and the clutch disc from the flywheel.
6. Remove the pilot bearing in the crankshaft by removing using a suitable puller.

To install:

➡The self-adjusting pressure plate on the F-150, F-250 and Expedition models should always be adjusted before installation.

7. Before installing the self-adjusting pressure plate, adjust as follows:
   a. Place the flywheel and pressure plate in a suitable press.
   b. Using a suitable adapter, press down on the clutch diaphragm fingers until the adjusting ring moves freely.
   c. Rotate the adjusting ring counterclockwise until the tension springs are compressed.
   d. Hold the adjusting ring while releasing the pressure on the clutch fingers.

8. Inspect the flywheel for wear, damage and flatness. Replace or resurface as necessary.
9. Install a new pilot bearing into the crankshaft using a suitable pilot bearing installer.
10. Position the clutch disc on the flywheel so that an aligning tool or spare transmission mainshaft can enter the clutch pilot bearing and align the disc.
11. When reinstalling the original pressure plate and cover assembly, align the assembly and flywheel according to the marks made during removal. Position the pressure plate and cover assembly on the flywheel, align the pressure plate and disc, and install the retaining bolts. Tighten the bolts in an alternating sequence a few turns at a time until the proper torque is reached:

TCCS7116

Fig. 19 Loosen and remove the clutch and pressure plate bolts evenly, a little at a time . . .

Fig. 20 . . . then carefully remove the clutch and pressure plate assembly from the flywheel

Fig. 21 Check across the flywheel surface, it should be flat

Fig. 22 If necessary, lock the flywheel in place and remove the retaining bolts . . .

Fig. 23 . . . then remove the flywheel from the crankshaft in order to replace it or have it machined

Fig. 24 Upon installation, it is usually a good idea to apply a threadlocking compound to the flywheel bolts

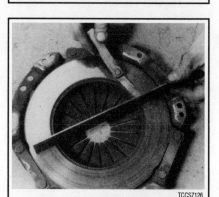

Fig. 25 Check the pressure plate for excessive wear

Fig. 26 Be sure that the flywheel surface is clean, before installing the clutch

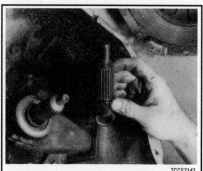

Fig. 27 Typical clutch alignment tool, note how the splines match the transmission's input shaft

Fig. 28 Use the clutch alignment tool to align the clutch disc during assembly

Fig. 29 The pressure plate-to-flywheel bolt holes should align

Fig. 30 You may want to use a threadlocking compound on the clutch assembly bolts

Fig. 31 Be sure to use a torque wrench to tighten all bolts

- 35–46 ft. lbs. (47–63 Nm) on the 4.2L, 4.6L and 5.4L engines (except Super Duty models)
- 30–36 ft. lbs. (41–49 Nm) on the 5.4L and 6.8L engines on Super Duty models
- 22–30 ft. lbs. (30–40 Nm) on the 5.8L engine
- 19–26 ft. lbs. (26–35 Nm) on the 7.3L diesel engine
- 14–19 ft. lbs. (19–26 Nm) on the 7.5L engine

12. Remove the tool used to align the clutch disc.
13. Install the transmission.
14. Install the slave cylinder and bleed the system.

ADJUSTMENTS

Because the clutch system is hydraulic, the clutch pedal free-play is self-adjusting and requires no additional maintenance.

Master Cylinder

REMOVAL & INSTALLATION

1997–98 F-250HD, F-350 and F-Super Duty

☀ WARNING

Prior to any service on models with the externally mounted slave cylinder, that requires removal of the slave cylinder, such as transmission and/or clutch housing removal, the clutch master cylinder pushrod must be disconnected from the clutch pedal. Failure to do this may damage the slave cylinder if the clutch pedal is depressed while the slave cylinder is disconnected.

1. Disconnect the negative battery cable.
2. Disconnect the clutch master cylinder pushrod from the clutch pedal by prying the retainer bushing and pushrod off the pedal pin.
3. Detach the connector for the Clutch Pedal Position (CPP) switch.
4. Remove the retaining nuts and the support bracket retaining the clutch master cylinder reservoir and reservoir to the bulkhead.
5. Thoroughly clean the area around the hydraulic tube and disconnect it from the master cylinder.
6. Remove the clutch master cylinder from the firewall carefully. It will be necessary to rotate the master cylinder 105 degrees counterclockwise to allow the CPP switch to clear the dash panel.
To install:
7. Install the pushrod through the hole in the engine compartment. Make sure it is located on the correct side of the clutch pedal. Install the master cylinder and tighten the nuts.
8. Install the hydraulic tube to the master cylinder.
9. Attach the CPP switch connector.
10. Replace the retainer bushing in the clutch master cylinder pushrod if worn or damaged. Install the retainer and pushrod on the clutch pedal pin. Make sure the flange of the bushing is against the pedal blade. Install the switch.
11. Connect the negative battery cable and bleed the clutch hydraulic system, if necessary.

F-150, F-250, Expedition and 1999–00 F-250SD, F-350 and F-Super Duty

▶ See Figure 32

1. Disconnect the negative battery cable.
2. Disconnect the clutch master cylinder pushrod from the clutch pedal by prying the retainer bushing and pushrod off the clutch pedal pin.
3. On the F-150, F-250 and Expedition, detach the Clutch Pedal Position (CPP) switch electrical harness connector.
4. On the F-250SD, F-350 and F-Super Duty models, remove the CPP switch from the clutch master cylinder pushrod.
5. Remove 2 push pins retaining the clutch master cylinder reservoir to the cowl panel.
6. Raise and safely support the vehicle.
7. On the F-150, F-250 and Expedition, disconnect the clutch hydraulic

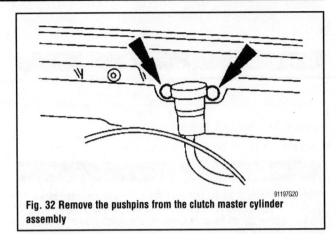

Fig. 32 Remove the pushpins from the clutch master cylinder assembly

line from the transmission using Clutch Coupling Tool T88T-70552-A, or equivalent.
8. On the F-250SD, F-350 and F-Super Duty models, twist and unlock the slave cylinder from the transmission.
9. Lower the vehicle.
10. Rotate the clutch master cylinder 45 degrees clockwise and remove the clutch master cylinder and reservoir.
To install:
11. If replacing the clutch master cylinder, it must be bench bled before it is installed.
12. Install the pushrod through the hole in the engine compartment. Place the clutch master cylinder in position and rotate the body 45 degrees counterclockwise while pushing inward.
13. Place the clutch master cylinder reservoir on the cowl panel and secure with 2 push pins.
14. On the F-150, F-250 and Expedition, connect the clutch hydraulic line to the transmission.
15. On the F-250SD, F-350 and F-Super Duty models, install the slave cylinder onto the transmission.
16. Lower the vehicle.
17. On the F-250SD, F-350 and F-Super Duty models, install the CPP switch to the clutch pedal pushrod. Ensure that the CPP switch is properly positioned on the pushrod.
18. On the F-150, F-250 and Expedition, attach the CPP switch electrical harness connector.
19. Install the retainer and pushrod on the clutch pedal pin with the flange portion of the bushing facing away from the pedal blade of the clutch pedal.
20. Connect the negative battery cable.
21. Verify the starter motor will only crank the engine when the clutch pedal is fully depressed.
22. Bleed the hydraulic clutch system and check for leaks.
23. Road test the vehicle and check the clutch system for proper operation.

BENCH BLEEDING PROCEDURE

➡ **It is recommended to bench bleed a dry clutch master cylinder before installation.**

1. Start with the tube and reservoir attached to the clutch master cylinder, but the system removed from the vehicle. Lightly clamp the reservoir in a vise.
2. Hold the clutch master cylinder vertically with the reservoir feed hose in the highest position on the body.
3. Fill the reservoir and extend above the clutch master cylinder and make sure the quick connect on the clutch line is below the clutch master cylinder.
4. Using a small screwdriver, depress the internal mechanism of the male quick connect coupling to open the valve.
5. Stroke and fully depress and hold the push rod.
6. Release the internal mechanism of the quick end connector and release the push rod.
7. Fill the reservoir and repeat the above steps 4 more times.
8. With the clutch master cylinder still being held with the outlet tube and reservoir feed tube ends high, quick connect closed and the reservoir full,

push the push rod into the body several times quickly to expel any remaining air.

Slave Cylinder

REMOVAL & INSTALLATION

Internally Mounted Slave Cylinder

▶ See Figures 33, 34 and 35

※※ WARNING

Prior to any service on models with the externally mounted slave cylinder, that requires removal of the slave cylinder, such as transmission and/or clutch housing removal, the clutch master cylinder pushrod must be disconnected from the clutch pedal. Failure to do this may damage the slave cylinder if the clutch pedal is depressed while the slave cylinder is disconnected.

1. Disconnect the negative battery cable.
2. Raise and safely support the vehicle.
3. Disconnect the coupling at the transmission, using Clutch Coupling Remover T88T-70522-A, or equivalent. Slide the white plastic sleeve toward the slave cylinder while applying a slight tug on the tube.
4. Remove the transmission assembly.
5. Remove 2 slave cylinder-to-transmission retaining bolts.
6. Remove the slave cylinder from the transmission.

To install:

7. Install the slave cylinder over the transmission input shaft with the bleed screw and coupling facing the left-hand side of the transmission.
8. Install 2 slave cylinder retaining bolts. Tighten the bolts to 13–19 ft. lbs. (18–26 Nm).

8. Replace the hydraulic line retaining pin.
9. Bleed the system.

HYDRAULIC SYSTEM BLEEDING

Externally Mounted Slave Cylinder

▶ See Figure 36

1. Clean the reservoir cap and the slave cylinder connection.
2. Remove the slave cylinder from the housing.
3. Using a ³⁄₃₂ in. punch, drive out the pin that holds the tube in place.
4. Remove the tube from the slave cylinder and place the end of the tube in a container.
5. Hold the slave cylinder so the connector port is at the highest point, by tipping it about 30 degrees from horizontal. Fill the cylinder with DOT 3 brake fluid through the port. It may be necessary to rock the cylinder or slightly depress the pushrod to expel all the air.

※※ WARNING

Pushing too hard on the pushrod will spurt fluid from the port!

6. When all air is expelled—no more bubble are seen—install the slave cylinder.

➡ **Some fluid will be expelled during installation as the pushrod is depressed.**

7. Remove the reservoir cap. Some fluid will run out of the tube end into the container. Pour fluid into the reservoir until a steady stream of fluid runs out of the tube and the reservoir is filled. Quickly install the diaphragm and cap. The flow should stop.
8. Connect the tube and install the pin. Check the fluid level.
9. Check the clutch operation.

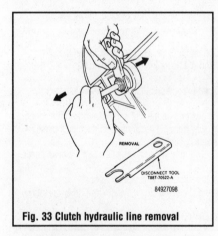

Fig. 33 Clutch hydraulic line removal

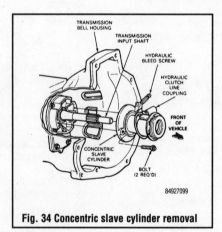

Fig. 34 Concentric slave cylinder removal

Fig. 35 Clutch release bearing removal with the concentric slave cylinder

9. Install the transmission assembly.
10. Connect the clutch tube to the slave cylinder.
11. Lower the vehicle.
12. Bleed the hydraulic clutch system.
13. Connect the negative battery cable.
14. Road test the vehicle and check for proper transmission operation.

Externally Mounted Slave Cylinder

1. Disconnect the negative battery cable.
2. Raise and safely support the vehicle securely on jackstands.
3. Thoroughly clean the area around the hydraulic tube before disconnecting the tube.
4. Remove the retaining pin from the slave cylinder hydraulic line.
5. Remove the retaining clip from the slave cylinder.
6. Remove the slave cylinder from the transmission.

To install:

7. The installation is the reverse of the removal.

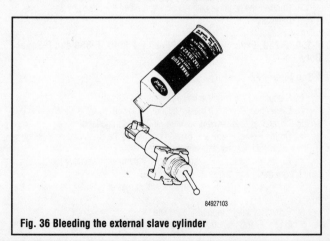

Fig. 36 Bleeding the external slave cylinder

Internally Mounted Slave Cylinder

◗ **See Figure 37**

1. Disconnect the clutch pipe from the transmission using Coupling Tool T88T-70522-A or equivalent, by sliding the clutch white plastic sleeve toward the clutch release cylinder while applying a slight tug on the clutch pipe.
2. Clean dirt and grease from around the reservoir cap.
3. Remove the cap and diaphragm and fill the reservoir to the step with clean DOT 3 or equivalent brake fluid from a closed container.
4. Using a small flat bladed tool, depress the internal mechanism of the male coupling to open the valve. While continuing to hold the valve open, slowly depress the clutch pedal to the floor and hold.
5. Remove the flat bladed tool from the coupling, closing the valve.
6. Release the clutch pedal.
7. Refill the reservoir to the step.

➡**The reservoir must be kept full at all times to ensure that there will be no additional introduction of air into the system.**

8. Repeat the above steps.
9. Install the reservoir cap. Reconnect the clutch pipe to the clutch release cylinder. Check that the connection is secure by applying a slight tug to the clutch tube.
10. Stroke the clutch pedal as rapidly as possible for 5 to 10 strokes.
11. Wait 1 to 3 minutes.
12. Repeat the stroking procedure at least 3 more times.

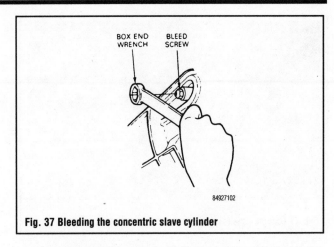

Fig. 37 Bleeding the concentric slave cylinder

13. Loosen the bleed screw (located in the clutch slave cylinder body next to the inlet connection).
14. Depress and hold the clutch pedal while tightening the bleed screw.
15. Refill the reservoir to the step.
16. Check the operation of the clutch system.

AUTOMATIC TRANSMISSION

Fluid Pan

REMOVAL & INSTALLATION

Refer to Section 1 for transmission pan removal and filter service.

Manual Lever Position (MLP) Sensor/Transmission Range (TR) Sensor

REMOVAL & INSTALLATION

◗ **See Figures 38, 39, 40, 41 and 42**

1. Disconnect the negative battery cable.
2. Raise and support the vehicle safely on jackstands.
3. Place the transmission in Neutral.
4. Remove and discard the manual control lever nut, then remove the lever from the transmission.
5. Detach the TR sensor electrical harness connector, remove the TR sensor retaining bolts, then pull the TR sensor off of the transmission case.

To install:

6. Position the TR sensor against the transmission case and loosely install the 2 retaining screws.
7. Attach the TR sensor electrical harness connector.
8. Use an alignment tool, such as the TR Sensor Alignment Tool T93P-70010-A, to align the TR sensor slots.
9. Tighten the TR sensor bolts to 80–100 inch lbs. (9–11 Nm).
10. Position the manual control lever onto the TR sensor, then install the new lever nut to 22–26 ft. lbs. (30–35 Nm).
11. Lower the vehicle.
12. Connect the negative battery cable.

Fig. 38 Unfasten the nut for the manual control lever and . . .

Fig. 39 . . . remove the lever from the sensor

Fig. 40 Detach the connector from the TR sensor

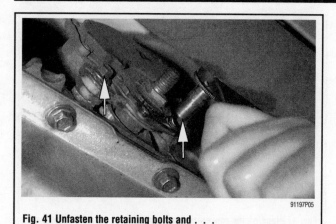

Fig. 41 Unfasten the retaining bolts and . . .

Fig. 42 . . . remove the sensor from the transmission

ADJUSTMENT

♦ See Figure 43

➡Park is the last detent when the manual control lever is full forward. Return 2 detents toward the output shaft for Neutral.

1. Position the manual control lever in **Neutral**.
2. Raise the and safely support the vehicle.
3. Loosen the sensor retaining bolts.
4. Insert Gear Position Sensor Adjuster tool T93P-700 10-A or equivalent, into the slots.
5. Align all 3 slots on the MLP sensor with 3 tabs on the tool.
6. Tighten the attaching screws to 80–100 inch lbs. (9–11 Nm).
7. Lower the vehicle.

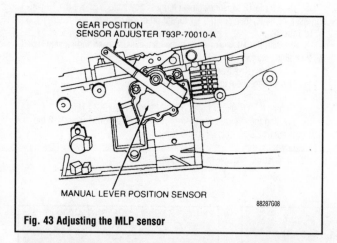

GEAR POSITION
SENSOR ADJUSTER T93P-70010-A

MANUAL LEVER POSITION SENSOR

88287G08

Fig. 43 Adjusting the MLP sensor

Extension Housing Seal

REMOVAL & INSTALLATION

2WD Models

The extension housing seal is located at the rear of the transmission case.
1. Raise and support the vehicle safely.
2. Drain the transmission of lubricant.
3. Matchmark the driveshaft to the yoke for reassembly and remove the driveshaft.
4. Remove the old seal using a seal puller or appropriate prytool.
To install:
5. Install a new seal, coated with sealing compound, using an appropriate seal installation tool.
6. Install the driveshaft, making certain to align the matchmark.

7. Lower the vehicle.
8. Fill the transmission with the proper fluid.

4WD Models

The extension housing seal on 4WD drive vehicles is located at the rear of the transfer case. Refer to the Rear Output Shaft Seal procedure in the Transfer Case portion of this section.

Automatic Transmission Assembly

REMOVAL & INSTALLATION

4R70W

♦ See Figures 44 thru 51

1. Place the shift lever in the **NEUTRAL** position.
2. Disconnect the negative battery cable.
3. Raise the vehicle on hoist or stands.
4. If transmission disassembly is required, drain the fluid.
5. On 4 X 4 vehicles, remove the transfer case. Refer to the procedure in this section.
6. Matchmark and disconnect the driveshaft from the rear axle and slide shaft rearward from the transmission. Install a seal installation tool in the extension housing to prevent fluid leakage.
7. Disconnect the cable from the terminal on the starter motor. Remove the three attaching bolts and remove the starter motor.
8. On 4.2L engine equipped models only, remove the transmission inspection cover.
9. On 4.6L engine equipped models only, remove the rubber access plug.
10. Remove the converter-to-flywheel attaching nuts. Place a wrench on the crankshaft pulley attaching bolt to turn the converter to gain access to the nuts.
11. Disconnect the shift linkage.
12. Disconnect each fluid cooler line from the fittings on the transmission.
13. Place a drain pan under the converter to catch the fluid. With the wrench on the crankshaft pulley attaching bolt, turn the converter to gain access to the converter drain plug and remove the plug. After the fluid has been drained, reinstall the plug.
14. Detach the harness connectors at both the Output Shaft Speed (OSS) sensor, the Transmission Range (TR) sensor and the Vehicle Speed Sensor (VSS).
15. Detach the solenoid body connector.
16. Position a transmission jack under the transmission and raise it slightly.
17. Remove the transmission crossmember.
18. Remove the exhaust Y-pipe.
19. Remove the fuel line bracket retaining bolt.
20. Remove the bolt that secure the transmission fluid filler tube to the cylinder head. Lift the filler tube and the dipstick from the transmission.
21. Secure the transmission to the jack with the chain.
22. Remove the converter housing-to-cylinder block attaching bolts.
23. Carefully move the transmission and converter assembly away from the

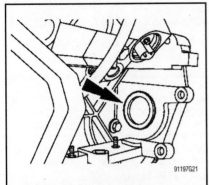

Fig. 44 On 4.6L engine equipped models, remove the rubber access plug to . . .

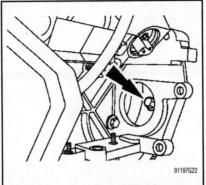

Fig. 45 . . . access and remove the converter-to-flywheel attaching nuts

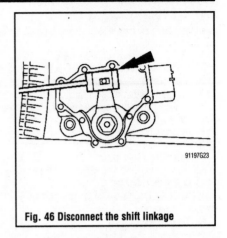

Fig. 46 Disconnect the shift linkage

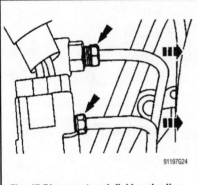

Fig. 47 Disconnect each fluid cooler line from the fittings on the transmission

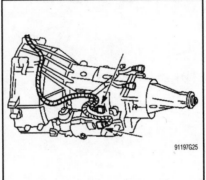

Fig. 48 Detach the harness connectors from the transmission

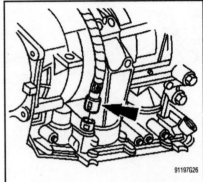

Fig. 49 Detach the solenoid body connector

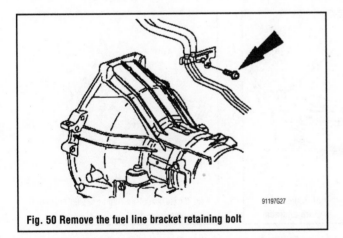

Fig. 50 Remove the fuel line bracket retaining bolt

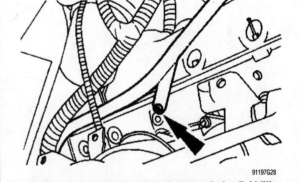

Fig. 51 Remove the bolt that secures the transmission fluid filler tube to the cylinder and remove the dipstick from the transmission

engine and, at the same time, lower the jack to clear the underside of the vehicle.

To install:

24. Position the converter on the transmission, making sure the converter drive flats are fully engaged in the pump gear by rotating the converter.

25. With the converter properly installed, place the transmission on the jack. Secure the transmission to the jack with a chain.

➡**Align the orange balancing marks on the converter stud and flywheel bolt hole if balancing marks are present.**

26. Rotate the converter until the studs and drain plug are in alignment with the holes in the flywheel.

➡**Before torque converter is bolted to the flywheel, a check should be made to ensure that the torque converter is properly seated. The torque converter should move freely with respect to the flywheel. Grasp the**

torque converter stud. Movement back and forth should result in a metallic clank noise if the converter is properly seated. If the torque converter will not move, the transmission must be removed and the torque converter re-position so that the impeller hub is properly engage in the pump gear.

27. Move the converter and transmission assembly forward into position, using care not to damage the flywheel and the converter pilot. The converter must rest squarely against the flywheel. This indicates that the converter pilot is not binding in the engine crankshaft.

28. Install and tighten the converter housing-to-engine attaching bolts to 30–41 ft. lbs. (40–55 Nm).

29. Install the fuel line bracket and tighten the retaining bolt.

30. Install the exhaust Y-pipe.

31. Install the transmission crossmember.

32. Remove the jack from under the transmission.

33. Install a new O-ring on the lower end of the transmission filler tube. Insert the tube in the transmission case and secure the tube to RH cylinder head with the retaining bolt.

34. Attach the solenoid body connector.

35. Attach the connectors for the OSS, TR sensor and the VSS.

36. Connect the oil cooler lines to the right side of transmission case.

37. Connect the transmission shift linkage.

38. Tighten the torque converter nuts and tighten the nuts to 20–34 ft. lbs. (27–46 Nm).

39. On the 4.6L engine, install the rubber access plug.

40. On the 4.2L engine, install the transmission inspection cover.

41. Install the starter motor.

42. Position the drive shaft yoke inside the extension housing.

43. Install the driveshaft.

44. On 4 X 4 models, install the transfer case. Refer to the procedure as outlined in this section.

45. Lower the vehicle.

46. Connect the negative battery cable.

47. Fill the transmission with approved transmission fluid. Road test the vehicle.

E4OD/4R100

▶ See Figures 52 thru 60

1. Disconnect the negative battery cable.

2. Raise and support the truck on jackstands.

3. Place the drain pan under the transmission fluid pan. Starting at the rear of the pan and working toward the front, loosen the attaching bolts and allow the fluid to drain. Finally, remove all of the pan attaching bolts except two at the front, to allow the fluid to further drain. With fluid drained, install two bolts on the rear side of the pan to temporarily hold it in place.

4. Remove the dipstick from the transmission.

5. On 4WD drive models, matchmark and remove the front driveshaft.

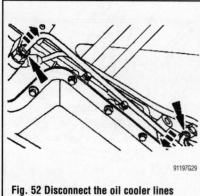

Fig. 52 Disconnect the oil cooler lines from the fittings on the transmission

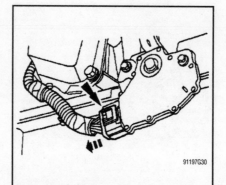

Fig. 53 Detach the manual lever position sensor connector

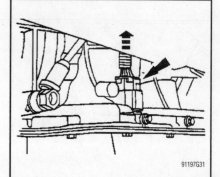

Fig. 54 Detach the solenoid body connector

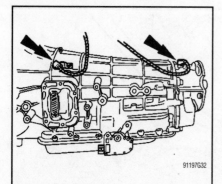

Fig. 55 Detach the turbine shaft and output shaft speed sensors

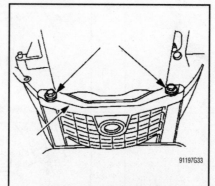

Fig. 56 Remove the flywheel inspection cover retaining bolts—gasoline engines

Fig. 57 Remove the flywheel inspection cover retaining bolts—diesel engines

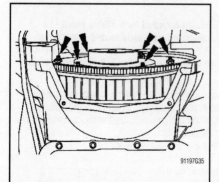

Fig. 58 Remove the flywheel retaining nuts

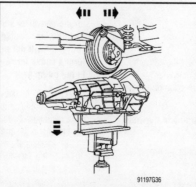

Fig. 59 Lower the transmission from the vehicle using a suitable jack

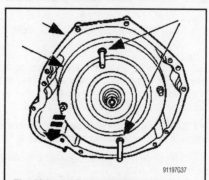

Fig. 60 Install Torque Converter Handles T81P-7902-C, or equivalent, at the 12 o'clock and 6 o'clock positions

6. Matchmark and remove the rear driveshaft. Install a seal installation tool in the extension housing to prevent fluid leakage.

7. Disconnect the linkage from the transmission.

8. On 4WD drive models, disconnect the transfer case linkage.

9. Remove the heat shield and remove the manual lever position sensor connector by squeezing the tabs and pulling on the connector. NEVER ATTEMPT TO PRY THE CONNECTOR APART!

10. Remove the solenoid body heat shield.

11. Remove the solenoid body connector by pushing on the center tab and pulling on the wiring harness. NEVER ATTEMPT TO PRY APART THE CONNECTOR!

12. On 4WD drive models, remove the 4x 4 switch connector from the transfer case. Be careful not to overextend the tabs.

13. Pry the harness connector from the extension housing wire bracket.

14. On 4WD drive models, remove the wiring harness locators from the left side of the connector.

15. On 4WD drive models, remove the transfer case.

16. Detach the turbine shaft and output shaft speed sensors.

17. Remove the converter cover bolts.

18. Remove the rear engine cover plate bolts.

19. Disconnect the cable from the terminal on the starter motor. Remove the three attaching bolts and remove the starter motor. Disconnect the neutral start switch wires at the plug connector.

20. Remove the converter-to-flywheel attaching nuts. Place a wrench on the crankshaft pulley attaching bolt to turn the converter to gain access to the nuts.

21. Secure the transmission to a transmission jack. Use a safety chain.

22. Remove the rear mount-to-crossmember attaching nuts and the two crossmember-to-frame attaching bolts.

23. Disconnect each oil line from the fittings on the transmission. Cap the lines.

24. Remove the 6 converter housing-to-cylinder block attaching bolts.

25. Carefully move the transmission and converter assembly away from the engine and, at the same time, lower the jack to clear the underside of the vehicle.

26. Remove the transmission filler tube.

27. On F-Super Duty, remove the transmission-mounted brake. See Section 9.

28. Install Torque Converter Handles T81P-7902-C, or equivalent, at the 12 o'clock and 6 o'clock positions.

To install:

29. Install the converter with the handles at the 12 o'clock and 6 o'clock positions. Push and rotate the converter until it bottoms out. Check the seating of the converter by placing a straightedge across the converter and bell housing. There must be a gap between the converter and straightedge. Remove the handles.

30. On F-Super Duty, install the transmission-mounted brake. See Section 9.

31. Install the transmission filler tube.

32. Rotate the converter to align the studs with the flywheel mounting holes.

33. Carefully raise the transmission into position at the engine. The converter must rest squarely against the flywheel.

34. Install the 6 converter housing-to-cylinder block attaching bolts. Snug them alternately and evenly, then, tighten them alternately and evenly to 40–50 ft. lbs. (54–68 Nm).

35. Install the converter drain plug cover.

36. Connect each oil line at the fittings on the transmission.

37. Install the rear mount-to-crossmember attaching nuts and the two crossmember-to-frame attaching bolts. Tighten the nuts and bolts to 50 ft. lbs. (68 Nm).

38. Remove the transmission jack.

39. Install the converter-to-flywheel attaching nuts. Place a wrench on the crankshaft pulley attaching bolt to turn the converter to gain access to the nuts. Tighten the nuts to 20–30 ft. lbs. (27–41 Nm).

40. Install the starter motor. Connect the cable at the terminal on the starter motor. Connect the neutral start switch wires at the plug connector.

41. Install the rear engine cover plate bolts.

42. Install the converter cover bolts.

43. On 4WD drive models, install the transfer case.

44. Connect the speedometer cable.

45. On 4WD drive models, install the wiring harness locators at the left side of the connector.

46. Connect the harness connector at the extension housing wire bracket.

47. On 4WD drive models, install the 4x 4 switch connector at the transfer case.

48. Install the solenoid body connector. An audible click indicates connection.

49. Install the solenoid body heat shield.

50. Install the manual lever position sensor connector and the heat shield.

51. On 4WD drive models, connect the transfer case linkage.

52. Connect the linkage at the transmission.

53. Install the rear driveshaft.

54. On 4WD drive models, install the front driveshaft.

55. Install the dipstick.

56. Install the drain pan using a new gasket and sealer.

57. Lower the truck.

58. Refill the transmission and check for leaks.

59. Connect the negative battery cable.

ADJUSTMENTS

The automatic transmissions are electronically controlled, and no adjustments are possible.

TRANSFER CASE

Rear Output Shaft Seal

REMOVAL & INSTALLATION

Borg-Warner 44-07 and New Venture Transfer Case

1. Raise and support the truck on jackstands.
2. Remove the rear driveshaft.
3. Remove the yoke nut and washer.
4. Pull the yoke from the shaft.
5. Center-punch the seal and carefully pry it from its bore. Don't scratch the bore!

To install:

6. Clean the bore thoroughly.
7. Coat the OD of the new seal with sealer and the ID with clean Dexron®II ATF.
8. Position the seal squarely in the bore and drive it into place with a seal driver, or similar tool. Don't hammer directly on the seal.
9. Install the washer and yoke. Coat the threads of the shaft with a thread-locking compound. Install the nut and torque it to 150–180 ft. lbs. (203–244

Nm) on the Borg-Warner 44-07 and 186 ft. lbs. (251 Nm) for the New Venture.

10. Install the driveshaft.
11. Lower the vehicle.

Borg-Warner 13-56, 44-06 and All Wheel Drive Transfer Case on the Expedition and Navigator

♦ See Figures 61 and 62

1. Raise and support the truck on jackstands.
2. Disconnect the driveshaft at the rear axle and slide it from the transfer case.
3. Center-punch the seal and carefully pry it from its bore. Don't scratch the bore!
4. Remove and discard the bushing from the retainer.

To install:

5. Drive a new bushing into place with a seal driver or equivalent tool
6. Position the seal in the retainer so the notch on the seal faces upwards and the drain hole in the rubber boot is downwards. Drive it into place with a seal driver, or similar tool. Don't hammer directly on the seal.
7. Install the driveshaft.
8. Lower the vehicle.

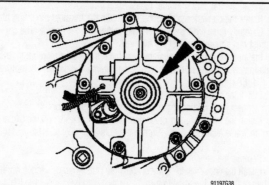

Fig. 61 The rear output shaft seal is accessible after the driveshaft is removed

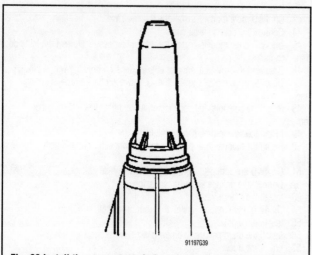

Fig. 62 Install the rear output shaft seal using a suitable seal driver

Front Output Shaft Seal

REMOVAL & INSTALLATION

New Venture Transfer Case (1999–00 Super Duty Models)

1. Raise and support the truck on jackstands.
2. Disconnect the driveshaft at the yoke.
3. Remove the yoke nut and washer.
4. Pull the yoke from the shaft.
5. Center-punch the seal and carefully pry it from its bore. Don't scratch the bore!

To install:

6. Clean the bore thoroughly.
7. Coat the OD of the new seal with sealer and the ID with clean Dexron®II ATF.
8. Position the seal squarely in the bore and drive it into place with a seal driver, or similar tool. Don't hammer directly on the seal.
9. Install the washer and yoke. Coat the threads of the shaft with a thread-locking compound. Install the nut and torque it to 165 ft. lbs. (223 Nm).
10. Install the driveshaft.
11. Lower the vehicle.

Except New Venture Transfer Case

Ford's procedure states that the front output shaft seal is replaceable only on disassembly/overhaul of the transfer case assembly.

Transfer Case Assembly

REMOVAL & INSTALLATION

Borg-Warner Model 13-56

▶ See Figure 63

1. Raise and support the vehicle safely.
2. Drain the fluid from the transfer case.
3. Disconnect the 4WD indicator switch wire connector at the transfer case.

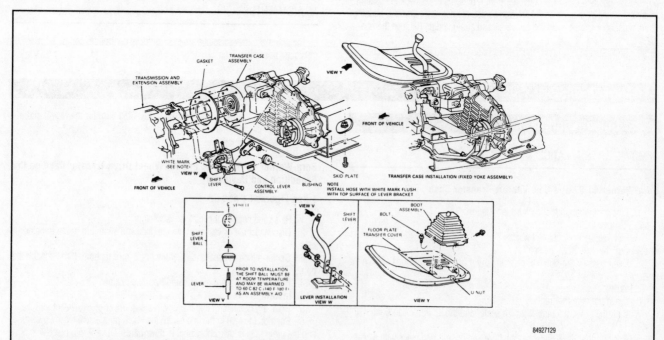

Fig. 63 Borg-Warner 13-56 manual shift transfer case installation

4. Remove the skid plate from the frame, if equipped.

5. Matchmark and disconnect the front driveshaft from the front output yoke.

6. Matchmark and disconnect the rear driveshaft from the rear output shaft yoke.

7. Remove the retaining rings and shift rod from the transfer case shift lever.

8. Disconnect the vent hose from the transfer case.

9. Support the transfer case with a transmission jack.

10. Remove the bolts retaining the transfer case to the extension housing.

11. Lower the transfer case from the vehicle.

To install:

12. When installing place a new gasket between the transfer case and the adapter.

13. Raise the transfer case with the transmission jack so the transmission output shaft aligns with the splined transfer case input shaft.

14. Install the bolts retaining the transfer case to the adapter. Tighten the bolts in sequence to 30–40 ft. lbs. (41–54 Nm).

15. Remove the transmission jack from the transfer case.

16. Connect the rear driveshaft to the rear output shaft yoke.

17. Connect the vent hose to the transfer case.

18. Install the shift lever to the transfer case and install the retaining nut.

19. Connect the 4WD indicator switch wire connector at the transfer case.

20. Connect the front driveshaft to the front output yoke.

21. Install the skid plate to the frame.

22. Install the drain plug.

23. Remove the filler plug and install the proper type and amount of fluid.

24. Lower the vehicle.

Borg-Warner 44-06 and All Wheel Drive Transfer Case on the Expedition and Navigator

▶ See Figures 64, 65, 66, 67 and 68

1. If equipped with air suspension, deactivate the system.

2. Disconnect the negative battery cable.

3. Raise and safely support the vehicle.

4. Mark the rear driveshaft and flange and remove 4 retaining bolts. Remove the driveshaft.

5. Remove 2 front driveshaft shield bolts and remove the shield.

6. Remove the No. 3 and 4 crossmembers.

7. Mark the front driveshaft and flange and remove 4 retaining bolts. Disconnect the driveshaft from the transfer case and secure out of way.

8. Install Torsion Bar Tool T95T-5310-A with Adapter Plates T96T-5310-A, or equivalents.

9. Tighten the tool until it touches the torsion bar adjuster.

10. Remove the adjuster bolt and nut.

11. Remove the tool and the adjuster.

12. Repeat the procedure for the opposite side.

13. Remove 6 torsion bar crossmember support bolts and remove the support.

14. Remove the torsion bars.

15. Remove 4 transfer case skid plate bolts and remove the skid plate.

16. Detach the Vehicle Speed Sensor electrical harness connector.

17. Detach the electric shift motor electrical harness connector.

18. Support the transfer case with a suitable transmission jack. Remove 6 bolts retaining the transfer case to the transmission and extension housing.

19. Slide the transfer case rearward off the transmission output shaft and lower the transfer case from the vehicle. Remove the gasket from between the transfer case and the extension housing.

To install:

20. Clean the transfer case and transmission extension housing gasket sealing surfaces.

21. Install a new gasket on the front mounting face of the transfer case assembly.

22. Raise the transfer case with the transmission jack so the transmission output shaft aligns with the transfer case input shaft. Slide the transfer case forward onto the transmission output shaft and dowel pin. Install 6 retaining bolts and tighten, in sequence, to 29–40 ft. lbs. (40–54 Nm).

23. Remove the transmission jack.

24. Connect the VSS and electric shift motor electrical harness connectors.

25. Place the slid plate in position and install 4 retaining bolts. Tighten the bolts to 10–13 ft. lbs. (13–17 Nm).

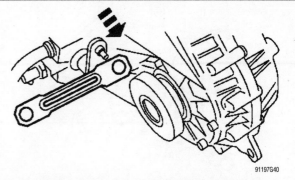

Fig. 64 On manual shift vehicles, use Shift Linkage Insulator Tool T67P-7341-A, or equivalent, to disconnect the shift rod

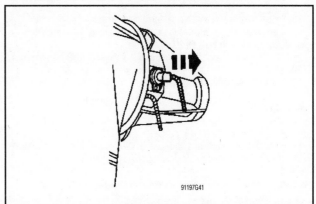

Fig. 65 Detach the Vehicle Speed Sensor (VSS) electrical connector

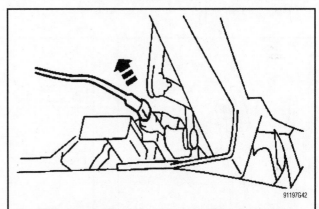

Fig. 66 On manual shift vehicles, detach the 4WD indicator switch

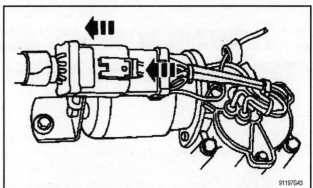

Fig. 67 On electric shift vehicles, detach the electric shift motor wiring harness connector

91197G44

Fig. 68 Remove the 6 transfer case-to-transmission bolts (3 on each side)

26. Install the torsion bars and rear torsion bar support.
27. Place the front driveshaft to the transfer case noting the index marks made during removal. Tighten the retaining bolts.
28. Place the front driveshaft shield in position and tighten the 3 retaining bolts.
29. Install the rear driveshaft noting the index marks made during removal.
30. Install the No. 3 and 4 crossmembers.
31. If drained, fill the transfer case with the proper type and amount of lubricant.
32. Lower the vehicle.
33. Connect the negative battery cable.
34. Road test the vehicle and verify proper 4WD engagement and operation.
35. If equipped with air suspension, reactivate the system.

Borg-Warner 44-07 and New Venture Transfer Case

♦ See Figures 69, 70 and 71

1. Disconnect the negative battery cable.
2. Raise and safely support the vehicle on jackstands.

3. Drain the transfer case fluid into a large pan or container; dispose of the used fluid.
4. Remove the front and rear driveshafts from the transfer case.
5. On manual shift vehicles, disconnect the shift linkage.
6. On manual shift vehicles, detach the 3-position switch harness connector.
7. On electric shift vehicles, detach the electric shift motor wiring harness connector.
8. Support the transfer case with a hydraulic floor transmission jack, or equivalent. Secure the transfer case to the jack with a safety strap.
9. Remove the 6 transfer case-to-transmission bolts (3 on each ide).
10. Lower the transfer case out of the vehicle.
To install:
11. Raise the transfer case into position with the transmission jack.
12. Install the 6 transfer case-to-transmission bolts to 37 ft. lbs. (50 Nm). Remove the transfer case-to-transmission jack securing strap.
13. Remove the jack from under the transfer case.
14. On electric shift models, attach the electric shift motor wiring harness connector.
15. On manual shift vehicles, attach the 3 position switch harness connector.
16. On manual shift vehicles, connect the shift linkage.
17. Install the driveshafts.
18. Fill the transfer case using Motorcraft MERCON Multi-Purpose Automatic Transmission Fluid XT-2-QDX or DDX, or equivalent fluid.
19. Lower the vehicle.
20. Connect the negative battery cable.

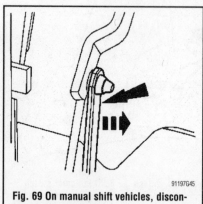

91197G45

Fig. 69 On manual shift vehicles, disconnect the shift linkage

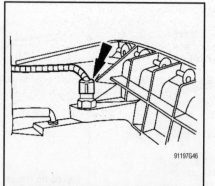

91197G46

Fig. 70 On manual shift vehicles, detach the 3-position switch harness connector

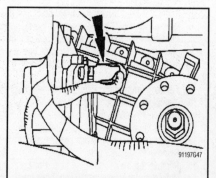

91197G47

Fig. 71 On electric shift vehicles, detach the electric shift motor wiring harness connector

DRIVELINE

Front Driveshaft and U-Joints

REMOVAL & INSTALLATION

♦ See Figure 72

➡ The following procedure applies only to 4 x 4 vehicles.

1. Raise and safely support the vehicle securely on jackstands.
2. If equipped, remove 3 front driveshaft shield retaining nuts and remove the driveshaft shield.
3. Matchmark the driveshaft yoke and axle pinion flange.

4. Matchmark the driveshaft yoke and transfer case flange.
5. Remove the bolts retaining the yoke to the axle flange.
6. Separate the yoke from the flange. It may be necessary to pry it free with a small prybar.
7. Remove the bolts and disconnect the driveshaft from the transfer case. It may be necessary to pry it free with a small prybar.
To install:
8. Place the driveshaft to the transfer case flange and axle pinion flange noting the index marks made during removal. Tighten the bolts to 87 ft. lbs. (119 Nm).
9. If equipped, install the front driveshaft shield and 3 retaining nuts.
10. Road test the vehicle and check for proper operation.

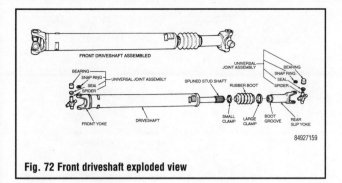

Fig. 72 Front driveshaft exploded view

U-JOINT REPLACEMENT

Single Cardan Universal

◆ See Figures 73, 74 and 75

1. Remove the driveshaft from the vehicle and place it in a vise, being careful not to damage it.

2. Remove the snaprings which retain the bearings in the flange and in the driveshaft.

3. Place U-Joint Tool T74P-4635-C or an equivalent joint press, onto the driveshaft.

4. Slowly tighten the tool to press the spider towards one side. When it will not move any further, remove the tool and pull the bearing cup out of the bore with pliers.

5. Remove the other bearing cup in the same manner and remove the spider assembly from the driveshaft. Discard the spider assemblies.

To install:

6. Clean the yoke bores with light sandpaper being careful not to change the dimension of the bores.

7. Remove the bearing cups from the new universal joint. Make sure all the needle bearings are still in place and held against the sides of the bearing cups with grease.

8. Start a new bearing cup into place with the press. When the cup is firmly held in place but still below the inner edge of the bore, install the spider. Be careful not to push a needle bearing out of place.

9. Fit the bearing cup into the other side of the bore and begin pressing it into place. Press the cup a little at a time and keep checking to make sure the spider turns freely in both cups. When both cups are pressed fully against the spider, install the snaprings.

➡If the bearing cups will not press in far enough to install a snapring or if the spider stops moving freely, a needle bearing has fallen out of place in one of the bearing cups. Stop pressing and disassemble the universal joint to re-position the bearings. If assembly is forced, the needle bearings and cups will be destroyed.

10. Install the remaining joint in the same manner.

11. Install the driveshaft and grease the new universal joints.

Rear Driveshaft and U-Joints

REMOVAL & INSTALLATION

One-Piece Shaft

◆ See Figures 76, 77, 78, 79 and 80

1. Matchmark the driveshaft yoke and axle pinion flange.

2. Remove the bolts retaining the yoke to the axle flange.

3. Separate the yoke from the axle flange. It may be necessary to pry it free with a small prybar.

4. Slip the driveshaft off the transmission output shaft splines.

To install:

5. Lubricate the splines of the yoke with a suitable long life grease (Ford recommends a Teflon® based grease) and install to the transmission output shaft.

6. Connect the driveshaft to the rear axle ensuring the index marks made during removal are lined up.

7. Install the 4 retaining bolts and tighten to 87 ft. lbs. (119 Nm).

8. Road test the vehicle and check for proper operation.

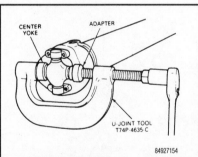

Fig. 73 Partially pressing the bearing from the center yoke

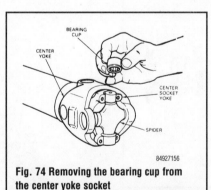

Fig. 74 Removing the bearing cup from the center yoke socket

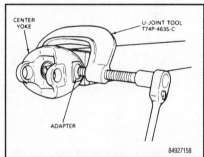

Fig. 75 Removing the bearing from the rear of the center yoke

Fig. 76 The bolts retaining the rear driveshaft yoke-to-differential flange require a 12mm, 12 point wrench or socket to loosen them

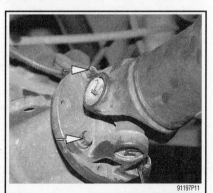

Fig. 77 Remove the bolts retaining the rear driveshaft yoke-to-differential flange

Fig. 78 Separate the driveshaft from the axle flange and . . .

Fig. 79 . . . disengage the driveshaft from the transmission output shaft

Two-Piece Shaft

▶ **See Figure 81**

1. Matchmark the driveshaft yoke and axle pinion flange.
2. Remove the bolts retaining the yoke to the axle flange.
3. Remove 2 center bearing support bolts.
4. Lower the driveshaft and slide the yoke off the transmission output shaft.

To install:

5. Lubricate the splines of the yoke with a suitable long life grease and install to the transmission output shaft.
6. Place the driveshaft in position and start the center bearing support bolts finger-tight.
7. Connect the driveshaft to the rear axle ensuring the index marks made during removal are lined up.
8. Install 4 retaining bolts and tighten to 87 ft. lbs. (119 Nm).
9. Tighten 2 center bearing support bolts to 39–53 ft. lbs. (53–72 Nm).
10. Road test the vehicle and check for proper operation.

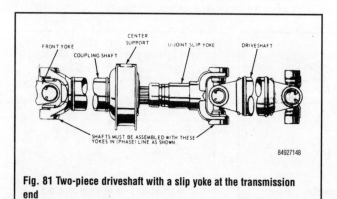

Fig. 81 Two-piece driveshaft with a slip yoke at the transmission end

U-JOINT REPLACEMENT

Single Cardan Universal

Refer to the Single Cardan Universal procedure under the Front Driveshaft portion of this section.

Double Cardan Joint

▶ **See Figure 82**

1. Working at the rear axle end of the shaft, mark the position of the spiders, the center yoke, and the centering socket yoke as related to the companion flange. The spiders must be assembled with the bosses in their original position to provide proper clearances.
2. Remove the snaprings which retain the bearings in the flange and in the driveshaft.

Fig. 80 Insert a plug onto the splines of the transmission output shaft to prevent fluid from leaking out

3. Place U-Joint Tool T74P-4635-C or an equivalent joint press, on the outer universal joint in the center yoke.
4. Slowly tighten the tool to press the spider towards one side. When the bearing cup protrudes about ⅜ inch from the bore, remove the tool, clamp the bearing cup in a vise and tap on the center yoke to drive it away from the cup.
5. Remove the opposite bearing cup in the same manner and remove the spider. Note the position of the lubrication fitting, if equipped.
6. Remove the centering socket yoke and press the other universal joint out in the same manner. Be careful not to distort the slinger ring on the driveshaft yoke.

To install:

7. Clean the yoke bores with light sandpaper, being careful not to change the dimension of the bores.
8. Remove the bearing cups from the new universal joint. Ensure that all needle bearings are still in place and held against the sides of the bearing cups with grease.

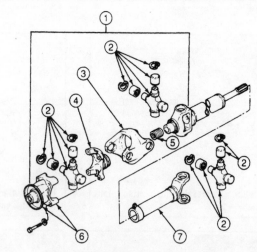

Item	Description
1	Double Cardan Assy
2	Universal-Joint
3	Driveshaft Center Yoke
4	Driveshaft Centering Socket Yoke
5	Centering Spring
6	Transfer Case Yoke (Flange)
7	Driveshaft Slip Yoke

Fig. 82 Exploded view—double cardan universal joint

9. Place the new spider into the driveshaft yoke. Make sure the lubrication fitting is in the original location so that it will be accessible with the driveshaft installed.

10. Fit the new bearing cups into place, then push them in with the press. Be careful not to push a needle bearing out of place. Keep checking to make sure the spider turns freely in both cups. When both cups are pressed fully against the spider, install the snaprings.

➡**If the bearing cups will not press in far enough to install a snapring or if the spider stops moving freely, a needle bearing has fallen out of place in one of the bearing cups. Stop pressing and disassemble the universal joint to re-position the bearings. If assembly is forced, the needle bearings and cups will be destroyed.**

11. Install the centering socket yoke and the remaining joints in the same manner.

12. Install the driveshaft and grease the new universal joints.

DRIVESHAFT BALANCING

◆ **See Figures 83, 84 and 85**

Driveline vibration or shudder, felt mainly on acceleration, coasting or under engine braking, can be caused, among other things, by improper driveshaft installation or imbalance.

If the condition follows driveshaft replacement or installation after disconnection, try disconnecting the driveshaft at the axle and rotating it 180°. Then, reconnect it. If that doesn't work, try the following procedure:

1. Raise and support the truck on jackstands so that all wheels are off the ground and free to rotate. The truck must be as level as possible.

2. Remove the wheels. Install the lug nuts to retain the brake drums or rotors.

3. Start the engine, place the transmission in gear and increase engine speed to the point at which the vibration is most severe. Record this speedometer speed as a reference point.

4. Shift into **Neutral** and shut off the engine.

5. Check all driveshaft attachment fasteners, U-joint bearing caps, U-joint cap retaining rings or cap locating lugs. Tighten any loose fasteners, replace any missing, damaged or shaved retaining rings or lugs. If worn U-joints are suspected, replace them. If everything is normal, or if any corrections made do not solve the problem, continue.

6. Start the engine, place the transmission in gear and increase engine speed to an indicated road speed of 40–50 mph (64–80 km/h). Maintain this speed with some sort of accelerator control, such as a weight on the pedal, or have an assistant hold the pedal.

✳✳ CAUTION

The following procedure can be dangerous! Be careful when approaching the spinning driveline parts!

7. Carefully raise a piece of chalk until it just barely touches the driveshaft at the front, middle and rear. At either end, try touching the shaft about an inch or so from the yokes. Don't touch any existing driveshaft balancing weights. The chalk marks will indicate the heavy points of the driveshaft. Shut off the engine.

➡**It helps greatly to steady your hand on some sort of support.**

8. Check the driveshaft end of the shaft first. If the chalk mark is continuous around the shaft proceed to the opposite end, then the middle. If the chalk mark is not continuous, install 2 screw-type hose clamps on the shaft so that their heads are 180° from the center of the chalk mark.

9. Start the engine and run it to the speed recorded previously. If the vibration persists, stop the engine and move the screw portions of the clamps 45° from each other. Try the run test again.

✳✳ WARNING

Check the engine temperature!

10. If the vibration persists, move the screw portions of the clamps apart in small increments until the vibration disappears. If this doesn't cure the problem, proceed to the other end, then the middle, performing the operation all over again. If the problem persists, investigate other driveline components.

Center Bearing

REMOVAL & INSTALLATION

1. Remove 2 center bearing retaining bolts and remove the center bearing and driveshaft assembly.

2. Check the center bearing for wear or rough action by rotating the inner race while holding the outer race. If wear or roughness is evident, replace the center bearing assembly. Examine the rubber cushion for evidence of hardening, cracking, or deterioration. Replace as required.

To install:

3. Place the bearing in the rubber support and the rubber support in the universal shaped support, if removed.

4. Install the center bearing and drive shaft assembly. While supporting the center bearing in position, install 2 retaining bolts and tighten to 39–53 ft. lbs. (53–72 Nm).

5. Road test the vehicle and check for proper operation.

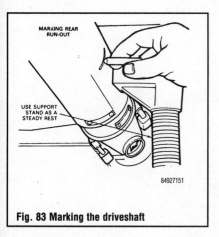

Fig. 83 Marking the driveshaft

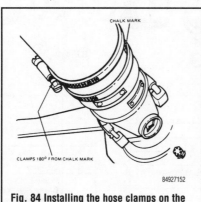

Fig. 84 Installing the hose clamps on the driveshaft

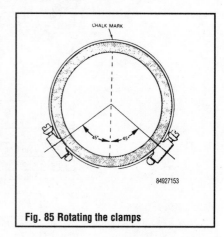

Fig. 85 Rotating the clamps

FRONT DRIVE AXLE

Manual Locking Hubs

DISASSEMBLY AND ASSEMBLY

♦ **See Figures 86, 87 and 88**

1. Raise and safely support the vehicle.
2. Remove the wheel and tire assembly.
3. Remove the three screws retaining the cap and remove the cap from the hub.
4. Remove the lockring seated in the groove of the brake rotor assembly.
5. Remove the hub body assembly from the brake rotor assembly.

To install:

6. The installation is the reverse of the removal.

Automatic Locking Hubs

DISASSEMBLY AND ASSEMBLY

♦ **See Figure 89**

1. Raise and safely support the vehicle.
2. Remove the tire.
3. Remove the three screws and separate the cap from the body.
4. Remove the lock-ring seated in the groove of the hub assembly.
5. Remove the body assembly from the brake rotor/hub.
6. Remove the snapring from the groove in the stub-shaft.
7. Remove the three thrust washers from the stub-shaft.
8. Pull the cam assembly to remove it.

To install:

9. Align the fixed cam retaining key on the cam assembly with the key-way on the spindle. Firmly push the cam assembly on the wheel retaining nut.

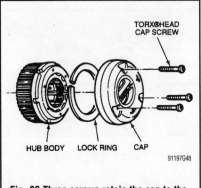

Fig. 86 Three screws retain the cap to the hub body

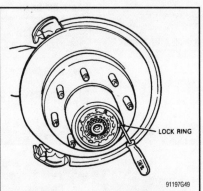

Fig. 87 Remove the lockring seated in the groove of the brake rotor assembly

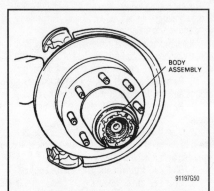

Fig. 88 Remove the hub body assembly from the brake rotor assembly

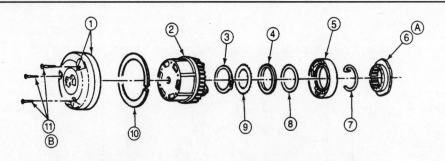

Item	Description
1	Cap
2	Hub Body
3	Snap Ring
4	Plastic Thrust Washer
5	Cam Assy
6	Wheel Retainer (Nut)
7	Wheel Retainer Key
8	Steel Thrust Washer

Item	Description
9	Splined Thrust Washer
10	Lock Ring
11	Capscrews (3)
A	While Rotating Front Disc Brake Hub and Rotor, Tighten Wheel Retainer (Nut) to 68 N·m (50 Lb-Ft) to Seat Wheel Bearings. Back Nut Off 90 Degrees (1/4 Turn). Tighten to 1.8 N·m (16 Lb-In).
B	Tighten to 4-6 N·m (35-53 Lb-In)

Fig. 89 Automatic locking hubs—exploded view

10. Install the metal, plastic, then the splined washers on the stub-shaft.

11. Install the snapring in the groove of the stub-shaft. It may be necessary to push the stub-shaft outward from the back of the knuckle assembly.

✳✳ WARNING

Do not pack the hub assembly with grease. Too much grease will damage the hub assembly.

12. Rotate the moving cam assembly to the one o'clock position in relation to the fixed cam retaining key. Use any one of the three stops.

13. Install the body assembly onto the hub by lining up the three legs with the three pockets in the cam assembly. Be sure the assembly is in far enough to see the groove in the hub.

14. Install the large lock-ring in the groove on the hub. Ensure the lock-ring is seated completely.

15. Install the cap and tighten the three screws.

16. Install the tire and lower the vehicle to the floor.

Axle Shaft, Bearing and Seal

REMOVAL & INSTALLATION

Dana 50 Independent Front Suspension

1. Raise and support the front end on jackstands.
2. Remove the front wheels.
3. Remove the calipers.
4. Remove the hub/rotor assemblies.
5. Remove the nuts retaining the spindle to the steering knuckle. Tap the spindle with a plastic mallet to remove it from the knuckle.
6. Remove the splash shield.
7. On the left side, pull the shaft from the carrier, through the knuckle.
8. On the right side, remove and discard the keystone clamp from the shaft and joint assembly and the stub shaft. Slide the rubber boot onto the shaft and pull the shaft and joint assembly from the splines of the stub shaft.
9. Place the spindle in a soft-jawed vise clamped on the second step of the spindle.
10. Using a slide hammer and bearing puller, remove the needle bearing from the spindle.
11. Inspect all parts. If the spindle is excessively corroded or pitted it must be replaced. If the U-joints are excessively loose or don't move freely, they must be replaced. If any shaft is bent, it must be replaced.

To install:

12. Clean all dirt and grease from the spindle bearing bore. The bore must be free of nicks and burrs.

13. Insert a new spindle bearing in its bore with the printing facing outward. Drive it into place with drive T80T–4000–S for F-150 and F-250, or T80T–4000–R for the F-350, or their equivalents. Install a new bearing seal with the lip facing away from the bearing.

14. Pack the bearing and hub seal with grease. Install the hub seal with a driver.

15. Place the thrust washer on the axle shaft.

16. Place a new slinger on the axle shaft.

17. Install the rubber V-seal on the slinger. The seal lip should face the spindle.

18. Install the plastic spacer on the axle shaft. The chamfered side of the spacer should be inboard against the axle shaft.

19. Pack the thrust face of the seal in the spindle bore and the V-seal on the axle shaft with heavy duty, high temperature, waterproof wheel bearing grease.

20. On the right side, install the rubber boot and new keystone clamps on the stub shaft and slip yoke. The splines permit only one way of meshing so you'll have to properly align the missing spline in the slip yoke with the gapless male spline on the shaft. Slide the right shaft and joint assembly into the slip yoke, making sure that the splines are fully engaged. Slide the boot over the assembly and crimp the keystone clamp.

21. On the left side, slide the shaft and joint assembly through the knuckle and engage the splines in the carrier.

22. Install the splash shield and spindle on the knuckle. Tighten the spindle nuts to 60 ft. lbs. (81 Nm).

23. Install the rotor on the spindle. Install the outer wheel bearing into the cup. Make sure that the grease seal lip totally encircles the spindle.

24. Install the wheel bearing, locknut, thrust bearing, snapring and locking hubs. See Section 1.

25. Install the caliper.

Spindle and Front Axle Shaft

REMOVAL & INSTALLATION

Dana 60 Monobeam

▸ **See Figures 90 thru 96**

1. Raise and support the front end on jackstands.
2. Remove the caliper from the knuckle and wire it out of the way.
3. Remove the free-running hub.
4. Remove the front wheel bearings.
5. Remove the hub and rotor assembly.
6. Remove the spindle-to-knuckle bolts. Tap the spindle from the knuckle using a plastic mallet.
7. Remove the splash shield and caliper support.
8. Pull the axle shaft out through the knuckle.
9. Using a slide hammer and bearing cup puller, remove the needle bearing from the spindle.
10. Clean the spindle bore thoroughly and make sure that it is free of nicks and burrs. If the bore is excessively pitted or scored, the spindle must be replaced.

To install:

11. Insert a new spindle bearing in its bore with the printing facing outward. Drive it into place with driver T80T–4000–R, or its equivalent. Install a new bearing seal with the lip facing away from the bearing.

12. Pack the bearing with waterproof wheel bearing grease.

13. Pack the thrust face of the seal in the spindle bore and the V-seal on the axle shaft with waterproof wheel bearing grease.

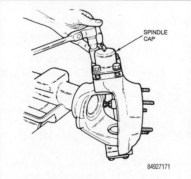

Fig. 90 Spindle cap removal for the Dana 60 Monobeam front drive axle

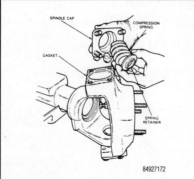

Fig. 91 Compression spring removal for the Dana 60 Monobeam front drive axle

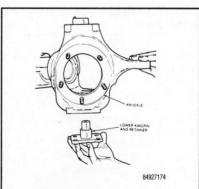

Fig. 92 Lower kingpin removal for the Dana 60 Monobeam front drive axle

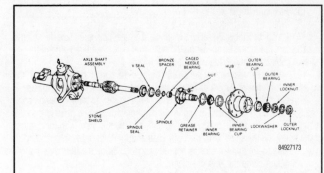

Fig. 93 Axle shift components for the Dana 60 Monobeam front drive axle

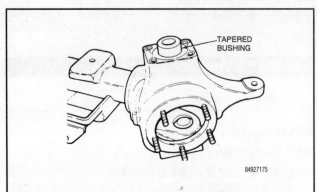

Fig. 94 Tapered bushing removal for the Dana 60 Monobeam front drive axle

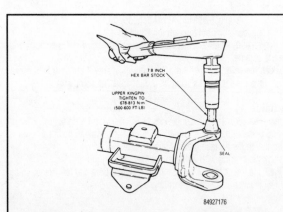

Fig. 95 Installing the upper kingpin on the Dana 60 Monobeam front drive axle

14. Carefully guide the axle shaft through the knuckle and into the housing. Align the splines and fully seat the shaft.

15. Place the bronze spacer on the shaft. The chamfered side of the spacer must be inboard.

16. Install the splash shield and caliper support.

17. Place the spindle on the knuckle and install the bolts. Tighten the bolts to 50–60 ft. lbs. (68–81 Nm).

18. Install the hub/rotor assembly on the spindle.

19. Assemble the wheel bearings.

20. Assemble the free-running hub.

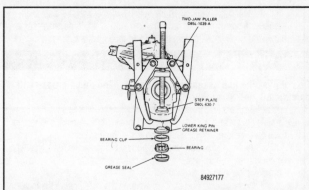

Fig. 96 Removing the lower kingpin on the Dana 60 Monobeam front drive axle

Right Side Slip Yoke and Stub Shaft, Carrier, Carrier Oil Seal and Bearing

REMOVAL & INSTALLATION

Dana 50 Independent Front Axle

▶ See Figure 97

➡ This procedure requires the use of special tools.

1. Raise and support the front end on jackstands.

2. Disconnect the front driveshaft from the carrier and wire it up out of the way.

3. Remove the left and right axle shafts and both spindles.

4. Support the carrier with a floor jack and unbolt the carrier from the support arm.

5. Place a drain pan under the carrier, separate the carrier from the support arm and drain the carrier.

6. Remove the carrier from the truck.

7. Place the carrier in holding fixture T57L–500–B with adapters T80T–4000–B.

8. Rotate the slip yoke and shaft assembly from the carrier.

9. Using a slide hammer/puller remove the caged needle bearing and oil seal as a unit. Discard the oil seal and bearing.

To install:

10. Clean the bearing bore thoroughly and make sure that it is free of nicks and burrs.

11. Insert a new bearing in its bore with the printing facing outward. Drive it into place with driver T83T–1244–A, or its equivalent. Install a new bearing seal with the lip facing away from the bearing. Coat the bearing and seal with waterproof wheel bearing grease.

12. Install the slip yoke and shaft assembly into the carrier so that the groove in the shaft is visible in the differential case.

13. Install the snapring in the groove in the shaft. It may be necessary to force the snapring into place with a small prybar. Don't strike the snapring!

14. Remove the carrier from the holding fixture.

15. Clean all traces of sealant from the carrier and support arm. Make sure the mating surfaces are clean. Apply a ¼ in. (6mm) wide bead of RTV sealant to the mating surface of the carrier. The bead must be continuous and should not pass through or outside of the holes. Install the carrier with 5 minutes of applying the sealer.

16. Position the carrier on the jack and raise it into position using guide pins to align it if you'd like. Install and hand-tighten the bolts. Tighten the bolts in a circular pattern to 30–40 ft. lbs. (41–54 Nm).

17. Install the support arm tab bolts and tighten them to 85–100 ft. lbs. (115–136 Nm).

18. Install all other parts in reverse order of removal.

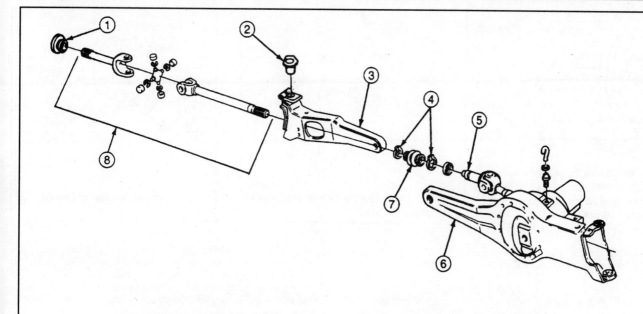

Item	Description	Item	Description
1	Rolling Diaphragm Seal	5	Slip-Yoke and Stub Shaft
2	Camber Adjuster	6	Left Axle Arm
3	Right Support Arm	7	Rubber Boot
4	Keystone Clamp	8	Right Shaft and Joint

Fig. 97 Right side slip yoke and stub shaft, carrier, carrier oil seal and bearing—Dana 50

Halfshaft

REMOVAL & INSTALLATION

F-150, F-250, Expedition and Navigator

♦ See Figures 98, 99, 100, 101 and 102

1. Break the front wheel lug nuts loose while the weight of the vehicle is resting on the front wheels.
2. Raise and safely support the front of the vehicle.
3. Remove the front wheels.
4. Remove the front hub cotter pin, retainer and nut.
5. Using a floor hydraulic jack, support the lower suspension arm.
6. Remove the upper ball joint cotter pin and castle nut.
7. Use a Pitman arm puller, such as Ford Tool T64P-3590-F, to separate the front wheel knuckle from the front suspension upper arm.
8. Lower the lower suspension arm and steering knuckle slightly to facilitate easier halfshaft removal.
9. Remove the two disc caliper mounting bolts, then lift the front disc caliper off of the front disc brake caliper anchor plate and position aside. Do not allow the caliper to hang by the brake hose; suspend it from the vehicle's frame with strong cord or wire.
10. Remove the six front halfshaft-to-differential bolts.

✳ WARNING

Use care to avoid damaging the hub seal when removing the front halfshaft.

11. Remove the inboard end of the halfshaft from the differential case or extension axle case. Separate the front halfshaft and joints from the hub, then remove the halfshaft and joints from the vehicle.

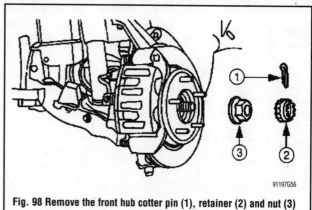
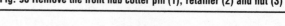

Fig. 98 Remove the front hub cotter pin (1), retainer (2) and nut (3)

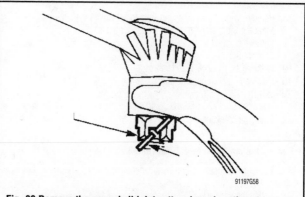

Fig. 99 Remove the upper ball joint cotter pin and castle nut

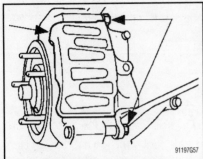

Fig. 100 Remove the two disc caliper mounting bolts, then lift the front disc caliper off of the front disc brake caliper anchor plate and position aside

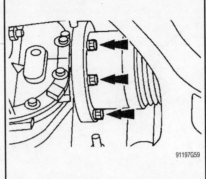

Fig. 101 Remove the six front halfshaft-to-differential bolts

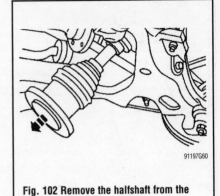

Fig. 102 Remove the halfshaft from the vehicle

To install:

12. Slide the halfshaft outboard end into the hub, making sure that the splines engage.

13. Situate the inboard end of the halfshaft against the front differential flange and install the six halfshaft-to-differential bolts. Tighten the halfshaft bolts to 51–67 ft. lbs. (68–92 Nm).

14. Install the front disc brake caliper onto the rotor and anchor plate, then install and tighten the two caliper mounting bolts.

15. Lift the lower suspension arm and steering knuckle up until the upper ball joint stud is inserted into the steering knuckle. Install and tighten the upper ball joint castle nut. Install a new cotter pin.

16. Install the hub nut onto the halfshaft and tighten the hub nut to 188–254 ft. lbs. (255–345 Nm).

17. Install the hub nut retainer and a new cotter pin.

18. Install the front wheels.

19. Lower the vehicle to the ground.

CV-Joints

REMOVAL & INSTALLATION

F-150, F-250, Expedition and Navigator

➥Before continuing with this procedure, make sure to have available a new CV-joint boot kit, for each CV-joint being serviced. The outer CV-joint cannot be disassembled, only the boot can be replaced.

INNER CV-JOINT AND BOOT

1. Remove the halfshaft assembly from the vehicle.

2. Clamp the halfshaft in a vise equipped with jaw caps to prevent damage to machined surfaces. Do not allow the vise jaws to contact the boot or its clamp.

3. Slide 2 inboard clamp protectors off the boot clamps.

4. Carefully remove 2 boot clamps, and slide the boot off the inner CV-joint and housing.

5. Remove the CV-joint retaining ring and remove the housing.

6. Mark the inner race and the ball cage for assembly.

7. Remove 6 cage balls.

8. Remove the snapring.

9. Remove the inner race and ball cage.

10. Clean all parts in suitable parts cleaning solvent and inspect for wear.

To install:

11. Place the boot and the small boot clamp and protector on the shaft.

12. Place the ball cage on the shaft with the tapered end toward the outer CV-joint.

➥Line up the marks made at disassembly.

13. Position the inner race on the driveshaft in the position marked on disassembly.

14. Install the snapring.

15. Lubricate and position 6 balls with suitable CV-joint grease.

16. Place the boot protector and boot clamp on the CV-joint housing. Fill the housing with 8.29 ounces of suitable CV-joint grease.

17. Place the housing to the cage and bearings and install the retaining ring.

18. Remove any excess grease from the mating surface and position the boot and clamp.

19. Adjust the CV-joint to boot spacing to 16.43 in. (417.25mm).

20. After adjusting the CV-joint to boot spacing, insert a dull bladed screwdriver blade to relieve built up air pressure in the boot.

21. Use CV Boot Clamp Installer T95P-3514-A or equivalent, to install the boot clamps.

22. Place the clamp protectors over the boot clamps.

23. Install the halfshaft into the vehicle.

24. Road test the vehicle and check for proper operation.

OUTER BOOT

1. Remove the inner CV-joint and housing from the halfshaft.

2. Remove the inner boot from the halfshaft.

3. Remove the outer boot clamp protectors and carefully remove the boot clamps.

4. Remove the outer boot from the halfshaft and inspect the grease for contamination.

5. If the grease is contaminated, clean and inspect the joint for wear. Replace the joint and shaft if worn or damaged.

To install:

6. Place the new CV-joint boot on the shaft.

7. Using 5.82 ounces (165 grams) of suitable CV-joint grease, pack the outer CV-joint with grease, then spread the remaining grease inside the boot.

8. Clean the boot mounting surface and position the boot in the joint grooves.

9. Place the clamps in position and use CV Boot Clamp Installer T95P-3514-A or equivalent, to install the boot clamps.

10. Place the clamp protectors over the boot clamps.

11. Install the inner boot on the halfshaft.

12. Install the inner CV-joint and housing on the halfshaft.

13. Install the halfshaft in the vehicle.

14. Road test the vehicle and check for proper operation.

Pinion Seal

REMOVAL & INSTALLATION

Independent Front Axle

♦ See Figures 103 and 104

➥A torque wrench capable of at least 225 ft. lbs. (305 Nm) is required for pinion seal installation.

1. Raise and safely support the vehicle with jackstands under the frame rails. Allow the axle to drop to rebound position for working clearance.

2. Mark the companion flanges and U-joints for correct reinstallation position.

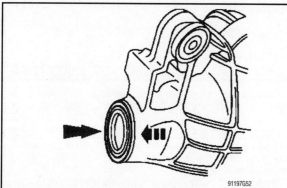

Fig. 103 After the companion flange is removed, the pinion seal is accessible

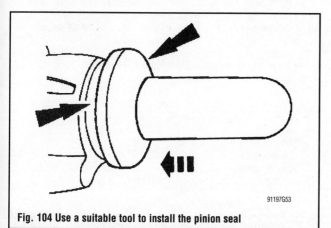

Fig. 104 Use a suitable tool to install the pinion seal

3. Remove the driveshaft. Use a suitable tool to hold the companion flange. Remove the pinion nut and companion flange.

4. Use a slide hammer and hook or sheet metal screw to remove the oil seal.

To install:

5. Install a new pinion seal after lubricating the sealing surfaces. Use a suitable seal driver. Install the companion flange and pinion nut. Tighten the nut to 200–220 ft. lbs. (271–298 Nm).

Monobeam Front Axle

➥A torque wrench capable of at least 300 ft. lbs. (407 Nm) is required for pinion seal installation.

1. Raise and support the truck on jackstands.
2. Allow the axle to hang freely.
3. Matchmark and disconnect the driveshaft from the front axle.
4. Using a tool such as T75T–4851–B, or equivalent, hold the pinion flange while removing the pinion nut.
5. Using a puller, remove the pinion flange.
6. Use a puller to remove the seal, or punch the seal out using a pin punch.

To install:

7. Thoroughly clean the seal bore and make sure that it is not damaged in any way. Coat the sealing edge of the new seal with a small amount of 80W/90 oil and drive the seal into the housing using a seal driver.

8. Coat the inside of the pinion flange with clean 80W/90 oil and install the flange onto the pinion shaft.

9. Install the nut on the pinion shaft and tighten it to 250–300 ft. lbs. (339–407 Nm).

10. Connect the driveshaft.

Axle Housing Assembly

REMOVAL & INSTALLATION

F-150, F-250, Expedition and Navigator

▸ See Figures 105 and 106

✳✳ WARNING

The electrical power to the air suspension system must be shut off prior to hoisting, jacking or towing an air suspension vehicle. This can be accomplished by turning off the air suspension switch. Failure to do so can result in unexpected inflation or deflation of the air springs, which can result in shifting of the vehicle during these operations.

1. With the transmission in Neutral, raise and support the vehicle.
2. Index-mark the front driveshaft to the axle universal joint flange.

✳✳ WARNING

Do not allow the driveshaft to hang unsupported.

3. Disconnect and support the front driveshaft.
4. Remove the six bolts and disconnect the front drive halfshafts on both sides.
5. Disconnect the vacuum lines and the front axle vent tube.
6. Use a high-lift jack to support the axle assembly.

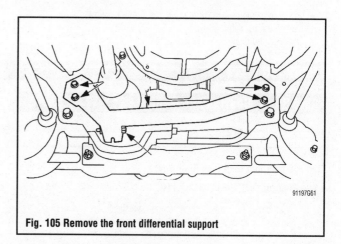

Fig. 105 Remove the front differential support

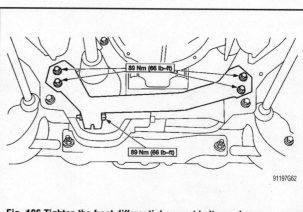

Fig. 106 Tighten the front differential support bolts as shown

7. Remove the front differential supports.
8. Carefully lower the front drive axle assembly.
9. Installation is the reverse of the removal.

Dana 50 Front Axle

1. Raise and support the front end on jackstands placed under the radius arms.
2. Remove the wheels.
3. Remove the calipers and wire them out of the way. Don't disconnect the brake lines.
4. Support the axle arm with a jack and remove the upper coil spring retainers.
5. Lower the jack and remove the coil springs, spring cushions and lower spring seats.
6. Disconnect the shock absorbers at the radius arms and upper mounting brackets.
7. Remove the studs and spring seats at the radius arms and axle arms.
8. Remove the bolts securing the upper attachment to the axle arm and the lower attachment to the axle arm.
9. Disconnect the vent tube at the housing. Remove the vent fitting and install a ⅛ in. pipe plug.
10. Remove the pivot bolt securing the right side axle arm to the crossmember. Remove and discard the boot clamps and remove the boot from the shaft. Remove the right drive axle assembly and pull the axle shaft from the slip shaft.
11. Support the housing with a floor jack. Remove the bolt securing the left side axle assembly to the crossmember. Remove the left side drive axle assembly.
12. Installation is basically a reversal of the removal procedure. Always use new boot clamps. Observe the following torques:
- Left and right drive axles-to-crossmember: 120–150 ft. lbs. (163–203 Nm)
- Axle arm-to-radius arm: 180–240 ft. lbs. (244–325 Nm)
- Coil spring insulator: 30–70 ft. lbs. (41–95 Nm)
- Upper spring retainer: 13–18 ft. lbs. (18–24 Nm)

Dana 60 Front Axle

1. Raise and support the front end on jackstands placed under the frame.
2. Remove the wheels.
3. Remove the calipers and wire them out of the way. Don't disconnect the brake lines.
4. Disconnect the stabilizer links at the stabilizer bar.
5. Remove the U-bolts securing the stabilizer bar and mounting brackets to the axle.
6. Remove the cotter pins and nuts securing the spindle connecting rod to the steering knuckles. Separate the connecting rod to the steering knuckles. Separate the connecting rods from the knuckles with a pitman arm puller. Wire the steering linkage to the spring.
7. Matchmark and disconnect the driveshaft from the front axle.
8. Disconnect the vent tube at the axle and plug the fitting.
9. On the right side, disconnect the track bar from the right spring cap.
10. Raise the front end and position jackstands under front springs at a point about half way between the axle and spring rear hanger. Remove the jackstands from the front of the frame and lower the truck onto the stands under the springs. Make sure that the truck is securely supported.
11. Support the axle with a floor jack.
12. Remove the U-bolts securing the springs to the axle.
13. Lower the axle from the truck.

To install:

14. Installation is the reverse of removal. Observe the following torques:
- Driveshaft-to-flange: 15–20 ft. lbs. (20–27 Nm)
- Track bar nut and bolt: 160–200 ft. lbs. (217–271 Nm)
- Stabilizer link nut: 20–30 ft. lbs. (27–41 Nm)
- Stabilizer bar U-bolt: 50–65 ft. lbs. (68–88 Nm)
- Spindle connecting rod-to-knuckle: 70–100 ft. lbs. (95–136 Nm)
- Front spring U-bolts: 85–100 ft. lbs. (115–136 Nm)

REAR AXLE

Axle Shaft, Bearing and Seal

REMOVAL & INSTALLATION

Ford 8.8 Inch And 9.75 Inch Ring Gear

♦ See Figures 107, 108, 109 and 110

1. Raise and safely support the vehicle on jackstands.
2. Remove the wheels from the brake drums.
3. Place a drain pan under the housing and drain the lubricant by loosening the housing cover.
4. Remove the locks securing the brake drums to the axle shaft flanges and remove the drums.
5. Remove the housing cover and gasket.

6. Remove the side gear pinion shaft lockbolt and the side gear pinion shaft.
7. Push the axle shafts inward and remove the C-locks from the inner end of the axle shafts. Temporarily replace the shaft and lockbolt to retain the differential gears in position.
8. Remove the axle shafts with a slide hammer. Be sure the seal is not damaged by the splines on the axle shaft.
9. Remove the bearing and oil seal from the housing. Both the seal and bearing can be removed with a slide hammer
10. Two types of bearings are used on some axles, one requiring a press fit and the other a loose fit. A loose fitting bearing does not necessarily indicate excessive wear.
11. Inspect the axle shaft housing and axle shafts for burrs or other irregularities. Replace any work or damaged parts. A light yellow color on the bearing journal of the axle shaft is normal, and does not require replacement of the axle shaft. Slight pitting and wear is also normal.

Fig. 107 Remove the side gear pinion shaft lockbolt and . . .

Fig. 108 . . . the side gear pinion shaft

Fig. 109 Push the axles in so that the C-clip groove is accessible, and remove the C-clips from the axle shafts

Fig. 110 Grasp the axle and slide it out of the tube

91197P10

12. Lightly coat the wheel bearing rollers with axle lubricant. Install the bearings in the axle housing until the bearing seats firmly against the shoulder.

13. Wipe all lubricant from the oil seal bore, before installing the seal.

14. Inspect the original seals for wear. If necessary, these may be replaced with new seals, which are prepacked with lubricant and do not require soaking.

To install:

15. Install the oil seal.

16. Remove the lockbolt and pinion shaft. Carefully slide the axle shafts into place. Be careful that you do not damage the seal with the splined end of the axle shaft. Engage the splined end of the shaft with the differential side gears.

17. Install the axle shaft C-locks on the inner end of the axle shafts and seat the C-locks in the counterbore of the differential side gears.

18. Rotate the differential pinion gears until the differential pinion shaft can be installed. Install the differential pinion shaft lockbolt. Tighten to 15–22 ft. lbs. (20–30 Nm).

19. Install the brake drum on the axle shaft flange.

20. Install the wheel and tire on the brake drum and tighten the attaching nuts.

21. Clean the gasket surface of the rear housing and install a new cover gasket and the housing cover. Some covers do not use a gasket. On these models, apply a bead of silicone sealer on the gasket surface. The bead should run inside of the bolt holes.

22. Raise the rear axle so that it is in the running position. Add the amount of specified lubricant to bring the lubricant level to ½ in. (12.7mm) below the filler hole.

Ford 10.25 Inch and 10.50 Inch Ring Gear

▶ **See Figures 111 thru 119**

The wheel bearings on the full floating rear axle are packed with wheel bearing grease. Axle lubricant can also flow into the wheel hubs and bearings, however, wheel bearing grease is the primary lubricant. The wheel bearing grease provides lubrication until the axle lubricant reaches the bearings during normal operation.

1. Set the parking brake and loosen the axle shaft bolts.

2. Raise the rear wheels off the floor and place jackstands under the rear axle housing so that the axle is parallel with the floor.

3. Remove the wheels.

4. Remove the brake drums.

5. Remove the axle shaft bolts.

6. Remove the axle shaft and discard the gaskets.

7. With the axle shaft removed, remove the gasket from the axle shaft flange studs.

8. Install Hub Wrench T85T–4252–AH, or equivalent, so that the drive tangs on the tool engage the slots in the hub nut.

➡ **The hub nuts are right-hand thread on the right hub and left-hand thread on the left hub. The hub nuts should be stamped RH and LH. Never use power or impact tools on these nuts! The nuts will ratchet during removal.**

9. Remove the hub nut.

10. Install step plate adapter tool D80L–630–7, or equivalent, in the hub.

11. Install puller D80L–1002–L, or equivalent and loosen the hub to the point of removal. Remove the puller and step plate.

12. Remove the hub, taking care to catch the outer bearing as the hub comes off.

13. Install the hub in a soft-jawed vise and pry out the hub seal.

14. Lift out the inner bearing.

15. Drive out the inner and outer bearing races with a drift.

16. Wash all the old grease or axle lubricant out of the wheel hub, using a suitable solvent.

17. Wash the bearing races and rollers and inspect them for pitting, galling, and uneven wear patterns. Inspect the roller for end wear. Replace any bearing and race that appears in any way damaged. Always replace the bearings and races as a set.

18. Coat the race bores with a light coat of clean, waterproof wheel bearing grease and drive the races squarely into the bores until they are fully seated. A good indication that the race is seated is when you notice the grease from the bore squashing out under the race when it contact the shoulder. Another indication is a definite change in the metallic tone when you seat the race. Just be very careful to avoid damaging the bearing surface of the race!

19. Pack each bearing cone and roller with a bearing packer or in the manner outlined in Section 1 for the front wheel bearings on 2WD Drive trucks.

To install:

20. Place the inner bearing cone and roller assembly in the wheel hub.

➡ **When installing the new seal, the words OIL SIDE must go inwards towards the bearing!**

21. Place the seal squarely in the hub and drive it into place. The best tool for the job is a seal driver such as T85T–1175–AH, which will stop when the seal is at the proper depth.

➡ **If the seal is misaligned or damaged during installation, a new seal must be installed.**

22. Clean the spindle thoroughly. If the spindle is excessively pitted, damaged or has a predominately bluish tint (from overheating), it must be replaced.

23. Coat the spindle with 80W/90 oil.

24. Pack the hub with clean, waterproof wheel bearing grease.

25. Pack the outer bearing with clean, waterproof wheel bearing grease in the same manner as you packed the inner bearing.

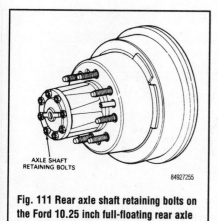

AXLE SHAFT
RETAINING BOLTS

84927255

Fig. 111 Rear axle shaft retaining bolts on the Ford 10.25 inch full-floating rear axle

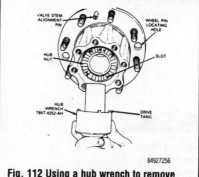

VALVE STEM
ALIGNMENT
PIN

WHEEL PIN
LOCATING
HOLE

HUB
NUT

SLOT

HUB
WRENCH
T85T-4252-AH

DRIVE
TANG

84927256

Fig. 112 Using a hub wrench to remove the hub nuts on the 10.25 inch full-floating axle

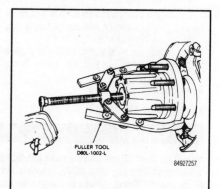

PULLER TOOL
D80L-1002-L

84927257

Fig. 113 Loosening the hub on the 10.25 inch full-floating axle

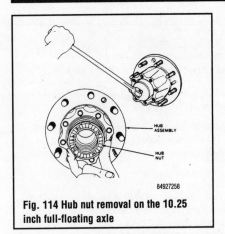

Fig. 114 Hub nut removal on the 10.25 inch full-floating axle

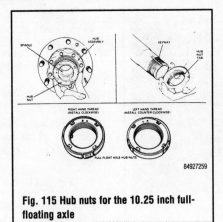

Fig. 115 Hub nuts for the 10.25 inch full-floating axle

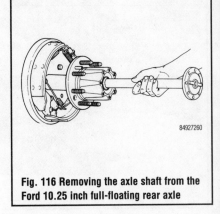

Fig. 116 Removing the axle shaft from the Ford 10.25 inch full-floating rear axle

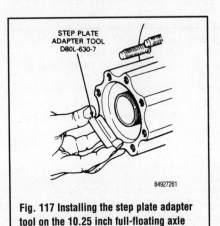

Fig. 117 Installing the step plate adapter tool on the 10.25 inch full-floating axle

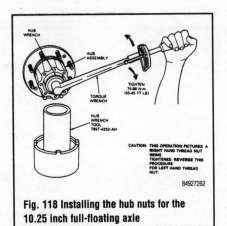

Fig. 118 Installing the hub nuts for the 10.25 inch full-floating axle

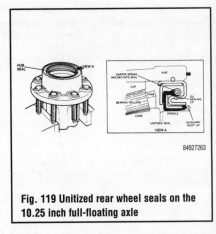

Fig. 119 Unitized rear wheel seals on the 10.25 inch full-floating axle

26. Place the outer bearing in the hub and install the hub and bearing together on the spindle.

27. Install the hub nut on the spindle. Make sure that the nut tab is located in the keyway prior to thread engagement. Turn the hub nut onto the threads as far as you can by hand, noting the thread direction.

28. Install the hub wrench tool and tighten the nut to 55–65 ft. lbs. (75–88 Nm). Rotate the hub occasionally during nut tightening.

29. Ratchet the nut back 5 teeth. Make sure that you hear 5 clicks!

30. Inspect the axle shaft O-ring seal and replace it if it looks at all bad.

31. Install the axle shaft.

32. Coat the axle shaft bolt threads with waterproof seal and install them by hand until they seat. Do not tighten them with a wrench at this time!

33. Check the diameter across the center of the brake shoes. Check the diameter of the brake drum. Adjust the brake shoes so that their diameter is 0.030 in. (0.76mm) less than the drum diameter.

34. Install the brake drum

35. Install the wheel.

36. Loosen the differential filler plug. If lubricant starts to run out, retighten the plug. If not, remove the plug and fill the housing with 80W90 gear oil.

37. Lower the truck to the floor.

38. Tighten the wheel lugs to 140 ft. lbs. (190 Nm).

39. Now tighten the axle shaft bolts. Tighten them to 60–80 ft. lbs. (81–108 Nm).

Dana Axles

▶ See Figures 120 and 121

※ **CAUTION**

New Dual Rear Wheel models have flat-faced lug nut replacing the old cone-shaped lug nuts. NEVER replace these new nuts with the older design! Never replace the newer designed wheels with older design wheels! The newer wheels have lug holes with special shoulders to accommodate the newly designed lug nuts.

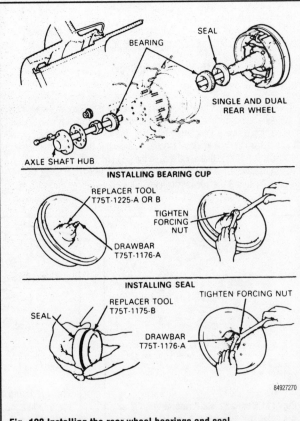

Fig. 120 Installing the rear wheel bearings and seal

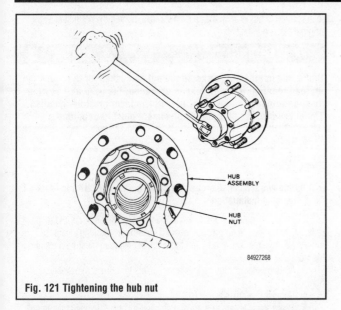

Fig. 121 Tightening the hub nut

The wheel bearings on full floating rear axles are packed with wheel bearing grease. Axle lubricant can also flow into the wheel hubs and bearings, however, wheel bearing grease is the primary lubricant. The wheel bearing grease provides lubrication until the axle lubricant reaches the bearings during normal operation.

1. Set the parking brake and loosen, but do not remove, the axle shaft bolts.
2. Raise the rear wheels off the floor and place jackstands under the rear axle housing so that the axle is parallel with the floor. The axle shafts must turn freely, so release the parking brake.
3. Remove the axle shaft bolts and lockwashers. They should not be re-used.
4. Place a heavy duty wheel dolly under the wheels and raise them so that all weight is off the wheel bearings.
5. Remove the axle shaft and gasket(s).
6. Remove the brake caliper. See Section 9.
7. Using a special hub nut wrench, remove the hub nut.

➡ **The hub nuts for both sides are right-hand thread and marked RH.**

8. Remove the outer bearing cone and pull the wheel straight off the axle.
9. With a piece of hardwood or a brass drift which will just clear the outer bearing cup, drive the inner bearing cone and inner seal out of the wheel hub.
   To install:
10. Wash all the old grease or axle lubricant out of the wheel hub, using a suitable solvent.
11. Wash the bearing cups and rollers and inspect them for pitting, galling, and uneven wear patterns. Inspect the roller for end wear.
12. If the bearing cups are to be replaced, drive them out with a brass drift. Install the new cups with a block of wood and hammer or press them in.
13. If the bearing cups are properly seated, a 0.0015 in. (0.038mm) feeler gauge will not fit between the cup and the wheel hub. The gauge should not fit beneath the cup. Check several places to make sure the cups are squarely seated.
14. Pack each bearing cone and roller with a bearing packer or in the manner outlined for the front wheel bearings on 2WD trucks in Section 1. Use a multi-purpose wheel bearing grease.
15. Place the inner bearing cone and roller assembly in the wheel hub. Install a new inner seal in the hub with a seal installation tool.
16. Wrap the threads of the spindle with tape and carefully slide the hub straight on the spindle. Take care to avoid damaging the seal! Remove the tape.
17. Install the outer bearing. Start the hub nut, making sure that the hub tab is engaged with the keyway prior to threading.
18. Tighten the nut to 65–75 ft. lbs. (88–102 Nm) while rotating the wheel.

➡ **The hub will ratchet at torque is applied. This ratcheting can be avoided by using Ford tool No. T88T-4252-A. Avoiding ratcheting will give more even bearing preloads.**

19. Back off (loosen) the adjusting nut 90° (¼ turn). Then, tighten it to 15–20 ft. lbs. (20–27 Nm).

20. Using a dial indicator, check end-play of the hub. No end-play is permitted.
21. Clean the hub bolt holes thoroughly. Replace the hub if any cracks are found around the holes or if the threads in the holes are in any way damaged.
22. Install the axle shaft, new flange gasket, lock washers and new shaft retaining bolts. Coat the bolt threads with thread adhesive. Tighten them snugly, but not completely.
23. Install the caliper.
24. Install the wheels.
25. Lower the truck to the groups.
26. Tighten the wheel lug nuts.
27. Tighten the axle shaft bolts to 40–55 ft. lbs. (54–75 Nm).

Pinion Seal

REMOVAL & INSTALLATION

Ford 8.8 Inch and 9.75 Inch Ring Gear

▶ **See Figures 122 and 123**

➡ **A torque wrench capable of at least 225 ft. lbs. (305 Nm) is required for pinion seal installation.**

1. Raise and safely support the vehicle with jackstands under the frame rails. Allow the axle to drop to rebound position for working clearance.
2. Remove the rear wheels and brake drums. No drag must be present on the axle.
3. Mark the companion flanges and U-joints for correct reinstallation position.
4. Remove the driveshaft.
5. Using an inch pound torque wrench and socket on the pinion yoke nut measure the amount of torque needed to maintain differential rotation through several clockwise revolutions. Record the measurement.

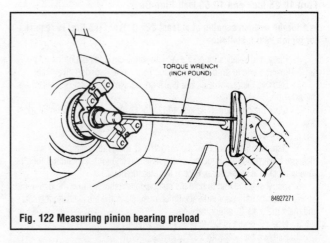

Fig. 122 Measuring pinion bearing preload

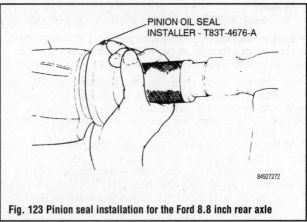

Fig. 123 Pinion seal installation for the Ford 8.8 inch rear axle

6. Use a suitable tool to hold the companion flange. Remove the pinion nut.

7. Place a drain pan under the differential, clean the area around the seal, and mark the yoke-to-pinion relation.

8. Use a 2-jawed puller to remove the pinion.

9. Remove the seal with a small prybar.

To install:

10. Thoroughly clean the oil seal bore.

➡ **If you are not absolutely certain of the proper seal installation depth, the proper seal driver must be used. If the seal is misaligned or damaged during installation, it must be removed and a new seal installed.**

11. Drive the new seal into place with a seal driver such as T83T–4676–A. Coat the seal lip with clean, waterproof wheel bearing grease.

12. Coat the splines with a small amount of wheel bearing grease and install the yoke, aligning the matchmarks. Never hammer the yoke onto the pinion!

13. Install a NEW nut on the pinion.

14. Hold the yoke with a holding tool. Tighten the pinion nut to at least 160 ft. lbs. (217 Nm), taking frequent turning torque readings until the original preload reading is attained. If the original preload reading, that you noted before disassembly, is lower than the specified reading of 8–14 inch lbs. (0.9–1.6 Nm) for used bearings; 16–29 inch lbs. (1.8–3.3 Nm) for new bearings, keep tightening the pinion nut until the specified reading is reached. If the original preload reading is higher than the specified values, tighten the nut just until the original reading is reached.

> ✳✳ **WARNING**
>
> **Under no circumstances should the nut be backed off to reduce the preload reading! If the preload is exceeded, the yoke and bearing must be removed and a new collapsible spacer must be installed. The entire process of preload adjustment must be repeated.**

15. Install the driveshaft using the matchmarks. Tighten the nuts to 15 ft. lbs. (20 Nm).

Ford 10.25 Inch and 10.50 Inch Ring Gear

➡ **A torque wrench capable of at least 225 ft. lbs. (305 Nm) is required for pinion seal installation.**

1. Raise and safely support the vehicle with jackstands under the frame rails. Allow the axle to drop to the rebound position for working clearance.

2. Remove the rear wheels and brake drums. No drag must be present on the axle.

3. Mark the companion flanges and U-joints for correct reinstallation position.

4. Remove the driveshaft.

5. Using an inch pound torque wrench and socket on the pinion yoke nut measure the amount of torque needed to maintain differential rotation through several clockwise revolutions. Record the measurement.

6. Use a suitable tool to hold the companion flange. Remove the pinion nut.

7. Place a drain pan under the differential, clean the area around the seal, and mark the yoke-to-pinion relation.

8. Use a 2-jawed puller to remove the pinion.

9. Remove the seal with a small prybar.

To install:

10. Thoroughly clean the oil seal bore.

➡ **If you are not absolutely certain of the proper seal installation depth, the proper seal driver must be used. If the seal is misaligned or damaged during installation, it must be removed and a new seal installed.**

11. Drive the new seal into place with a seal driver such as T83T–4676–A. Coat the seal lip with clean, waterproof wheel bearing grease.

12. Coat the splines with a small amount of wheel bearing grease and install the yoke, aligning the matchmarks. Never hammer the yoke onto the pinion!

13. Install a NEW nut on the pinion.

14. Hold the yoke with a holding tool. Tighten the pinion nut to at least 160 ft. lbs. (217 Nm), taking frequent turning torque readings until the original preload reading is attained. If the original preload reading, that you noted before disassembly, is lower than the specified reading of 8–14 inch lbs. (0.9–1.6 Nm) for used bearings; 16–29 inch lbs. (1.8–3.3 Nm) for new bearings, keep tightening the pinion nut until the specified reading is reached. If the original pre-

load reading is higher than the specified values, tighten the nut just until the original reading is reached.

> ✳✳ **WARNING**
>
> **Under no circumstances should the nut be backed off to reduce the preload reading! If the preload is exceeded, the yoke and bearing must be removed and a new collapsible spacer must be installed. The entire process of preload adjustment must be repeated.**

15. Install the driveshaft using the matchmarks.

Dana Axles

➡ **A torque wrench capable of at least 500 ft. lbs. (678 Nm) is required for pinion seal installation.**

1. Raise and safely support the vehicle with jackstands under the frame rails. Allow the axle to drop to the rebound position for working clearance.

2. Remove the rear wheels and brake drums. No drag must be present on the axle.

3. Mark the companion flanges and U-joints for correct reinstallation position.

4. Remove the driveshaft.

5. Use a suitable tool to hold the companion flange. Remove the pinion nut.

6. Place a drain pan under the differential, clean the area around the seal, and mark the yoke-to-pinion relation.

7. Use a 2-jawed puller to remove the pinion.

8. Remove the seal with a small prybar.

To install:

9. Thoroughly clean the oil seal bore.

➡ **If you are not absolutely certain of the proper seal installation depth, the proper seal driver must be used. If the seal is misaligned or damaged during installation, it must be removed and a new seal installed.**

10. Coat the new oil seal with wheel bearing grease. Install the seal using oil seal driver T56T–4676–B. After the seal is installed, make sure that the seal garter spring has not become dislodged. If it has, remove and replace the seal.

11. Install the yoke, using flange replacer tool D81T–4858–A if necessary to draw the yoke into place.

12. Install a new pinion nut and washer. Tighten the nut to 440–500 ft. lbs. (597–678 Nm).

13. Connect the driveshaft.

Axle Housing Assembly

REMOVAL & INSTALLATION

Ford 8.8 Inch and 9.75 Inch Ring Gear

EXPEDITION AND NAVIGATOR WITH AIR SUSPENSION

♦ **See Figures 124 thru 135**

> ✳✳ **WARNING**
>
> **Do not remove an air spring under any circumstances when there is pressure in the air spring. Do not remove any components supporting an air spring without either exhausting the air or providing support for the air spring to prevent vehicle damage or personal injury.**

> ✳✳ **WARNING**
>
> **The electrical power to the air suspension system must be shut off prior to hoisting, jacking or towing an air suspension vehicle. This can be accomplished by turning off the air suspension switch located in the RH kick panel area. Failure to do so can result in unexpected inflation or deflation of the air springs, which can result in shifting of the vehicle during these operations.**

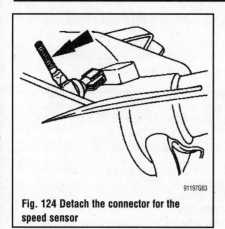

Fig. 124 Detach the connector for the speed sensor

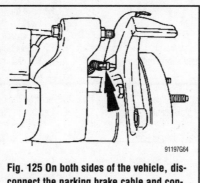

Fig. 125 On both sides of the vehicle, disconnect the parking brake cable and conduit from the rear wheel disc brake adapter

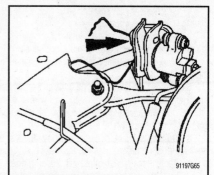

Fig. 126 On both sides of the vehicle, remove the rear disc brake caliper and position it out of the way

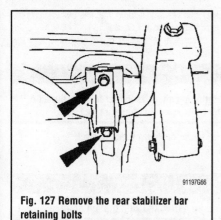

Fig. 127 Remove the rear stabilizer bar retaining bolts

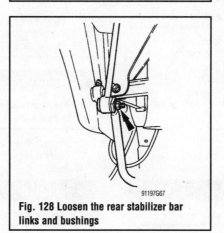

Fig. 128 Loosen the rear stabilizer bar links and bushings

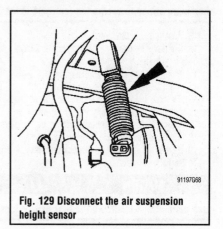

Fig. 129 Disconnect the air suspension height sensor

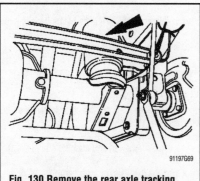
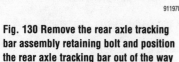

Fig. 130 Remove the rear axle tracking bar assembly retaining bolt and position the rear axle tracking bar out of the way

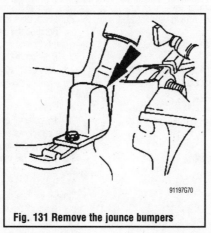

Fig. 131 Remove the jounce bumpers

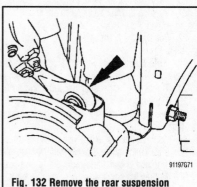

Fig. 132 Remove the rear suspension upper front arm and bushing retaining bolts

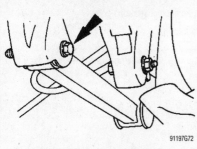

Fig. 133 Remove the rear suspension arms retaining bolts, and position the rear suspension arms and bushings out of the way

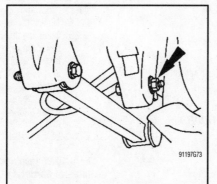

Fig. 134 Remove the lower shock absorber retaining bolts

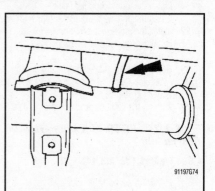

Fig. 135 Remove the rear axle housing vent hose

1. Deactivate the air suspension.
2. Raise and support the vehicle.
3. Remove the rear wheel and tire assembly.
4. Detach the connector for the speed sensor.
5. Mark the driveshaft flange and pinion flange for correct alignment during installation.
6. Remove the four driveshaft bolts and disconnect the driveshaft. Support the driveshaft using a piece of mechanic's wire or other suitable device.
7. On both sides of the vehicle, disconnect the parking brake cable and conduit from the rear wheel disc brake adapter.
8. On both sides of the vehicle, remove the rear disc brake caliper and position it out of the way. Remove the brake discs (rotors).
9. Remove the rear stabilizer bar retaining bolts.
10. Loosen the rear stabilizer bar links and bushings.
11. Disconnect the air suspension height sensor.

❋❋ WARNING

Use extra straps to secure the rear axle to the jack.

12. Install a suitable hydraulic jack under the rear axle housing.
13. Remove the rear axle tracking bar assembly retaining bolt and position the rear axle tracking bar out of the way.
14. Remove the jounce bumpers.
15. Remove the rear suspension upper front arm and bushing retaining bolts.
16. Remove the rear suspension arms retaining bolts and position the rear suspension arms and bushings out of the way.
17. Remove the lower shock absorber retaining bolts.
18. Remove the rear axle housing vent hose.
19. Lower the rear axle on the jack until it is clear of the vehicle.
To install:

❋❋ CAUTION

Use extra straps to secure the rear axle to the jack.

20. Raise the rear axle into place using a suitable hydraulic jack.
21. Position the rear suspension upper front arms and bushings and install the retaining bolts.
22. Position the rear suspension arms and bushings and install the retaining bolts.
23. Raise the rear axle with the jack until the rear suspension arm and bushings are parallel to the ground and install the rear stabilizer bar retaining bolts.
24. Tighten the rear suspension arms and bushings.
25. Tighten the rear suspension upper front arms and bushing retaining bolts.
26. Position the rear axle tracking bars in the bracket and install the retaining bolts.
27. Connect the rear axle housing vent hose.
28. Install and tighten the rear stabilizer bar retaining bolts.
29. Tighten the rear stabilizer bar links and bushings.
30. Tighten the shock absorber retaining bolts.
31. Remove the jack.
32. Install the driveshaft and tighten the retaining capscrews.
33. Lower the vehicle partially.
34. Install the jounce bumper retaining bolts.
35. Install the parking brake rear cables and conduit.
36. Install the brake discs (rotors).
37. Install the rear disc brake calipers.
38. Install the wheels and tires.
39. Connect the air suspension height sensor.
40. Attach the electrical connector at the anti-lock speed sensor.
41. Lower the vehicle.
42. Turn on the air suspension control switch.

F-150, F-250, EXPEDITION AND NAVIGATOR WITHOUT AIR SUSPENSION

♦ See Figures 136 thru 147

1. Raise and support the vehicle.
2. Remove the rear wheel and tire assembly.
3. Mark the driveshaft flange and pinion flange for correct alignment during installation.

4. Remove the four driveshaft bolts and disconnect the driveshaft and wire it out of the way.
5. Wire the driveshaft aside.
6. Disconnect the electrical connector at the anti-lock speed sensor.
7. Disconnect the parking brake cable and conduit from the rear wheel disc brake adapter.
8. Remove the rear disc brake caliper and position it out of the way.
9. Remove the brake disc.
10. Remove the rear stabilizer bar retaining bolts.
11. Loosen the rear stabilizer bar links and bushings.
12. Install jackstands beneath the rear axle and lower the vehicle onto the jack stands.
13. Place a third jackstand under the front of the rear axle housing.
14. Remove the rear axle tracking bar assembly retaining bolts and position the rear axle tracking bars out of the way.
15. Remove the jounce bumpers.
16. Remove the rear suspension upper front arm and bushing retaining bolts.
17. Remove the rear suspension arm and bushing retaining bolt and position the rear suspension arm and bushing out of the way.
18. Remove the lower shock absorber retaining bolts.
19. Remove the rear axle housing vent hose.

❋❋ CAUTION

This step should be performed with an assistant to keep the axle clear of obstructions while the vehicle is being raised.

20. Remove the rear axle from the out from under the vehicle.
21. Remove both rear springs.
To install:

❋❋ CAUTION

The following step should be performed with the aid of an assistant.

22. Position the rear axle on jack stands under the vehicle.
23. Install both rear springs.
24. Position the rear disc brake calipers and brake lines before installing the retaining bolts and nuts.
25. Position the rear suspension upper front arms and bushings and install the retaining bolts and nuts.
26. Position the rear suspension arms and bushings and install the retaining bolts.
27. Install the lower shock absorber retaining bolts.
28. This step should be done with the rear axle resting on jack stands to keep the vehicle as close to ride height as possible.
29. Tighten the rear suspension arm and bushing.
30. Tighten the rear suspension upper front arm and bushing retaining bolts.
31. Raise the vehicle and position the rear axle tracking bar in the bracket and install the retaining bolts.
32. Connect the rear axle housing vent hose.
33. Install and tighten the rear stabilizer bar retaining bolts on both sides.
34. Tighten the rear stabilizer bar links and bushings securely on both sides.
35. Tighten the lower shock absorber retaining bolts.
36. Install the driveshaft and tighten the retaining capscrews.
37. Lower the vehicle partially.
38. Install the jounce bumper retaining bolts.
39. Install the parking brake rear cable and conduit.
40. Install the brake discs (rotors).
41. Install the rear disc brake calipers.
42. Install the wheels and tires.
43. Attach the electrical connector at the anti-lock speed sensor.
44. Lower the vehicle.

Ford 10.25 Inch and 10.50 Inch Ring Gear With Full Floating Integral Carrier

1. Raise and support the rear end on jackstands under the rear frame members, and support the housing with a floor jack.

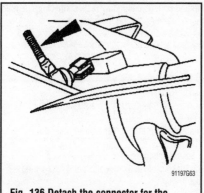

Fig. 136 Detach the connector for the speed sensor

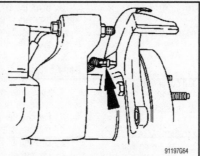

Fig. 137 On both sides of the vehicle, disconnect the parking brake cable and conduit from the rear wheel disc brake adapter

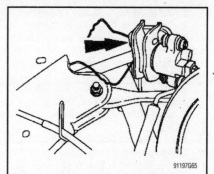

Fig. 138 On both sides of the vehicle, remove the rear disc brake caliper and position it out of the way

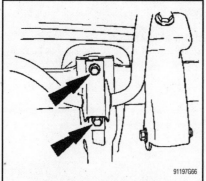

Fig. 139 Remove the rear stabilizer bar retaining bolts

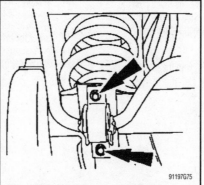

Fig. 140 Loosen the rear stabilizer bar links and bushings

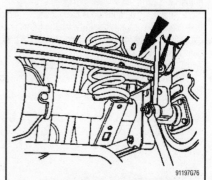

Fig. 141 Remove the rear axle tracking bar assembly retaining bolt and position the rear axle tracking bar out of the way

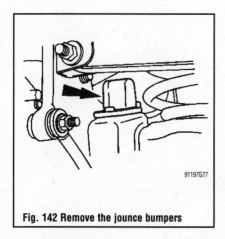

Fig. 142 Remove the jounce bumpers

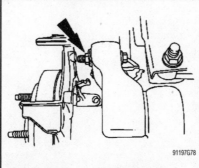

Fig. 143 Remove the rear suspension upper front arm and bushing retaining bolts

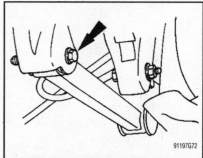

Fig. 144 Remove the rear suspension arms retaining bolts and position the rear suspension arms and bushings out of the way

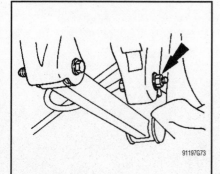

Fig. 145 Remove the lower shock absorber retaining bolts

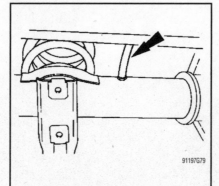

Fig. 146 Remove the rear axle housing vent hose

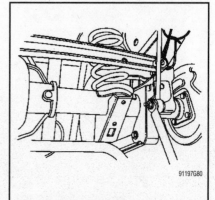

Fig. 147 Remove both coil springs

2. Matchmark and disconnect the driveshaft at the axle.

3. Remove the wheels and brake drums.

4. Disengage the brake line from the clips that retain the line to the housing.

5. Disconnect the vent tube from the housing.

6. Remove the hubs.

7. Remove the brake backing plate from the housing, and support them with wire. Do not disconnect the brake line.

8. Disconnect each rear shock absorber from the mounting bracket stud on the housing.

9. Lower the axle slightly to reduce some of the spring tension. At each rear spring, remove the spring clip (U-bolt) nuts, spring clips, and spring seat caps.

10. Remove the housing from under the vehicle.

To install:

11. Position the axle housing under the rear springs. Install the spring clips (U-bolts), spring seat clamps and nuts. Tighten the spring clamps evenly to 200 ft. lbs. (271 Nm).

12. If a new axle housing is being installed, remove the bolts that attach the brake backing plate and bearing retaining from the old housing flanges. Position the bolts in the new housing flanges to hold the brake backing plates in position. Tighten the bolts.

13. Connect the vent tube to the housing.

14. Position the brake line to the housing, and secure it with the retaining clips.

15. Raise the axle housing and springs enough to allow connecting the rear shock absorbers to the mounting bracket studs on the housing.

16. Connect the driveshaft to the axle.

17. Install the brake drums and wheels.

Dana Axles

1. Loosen the rear axle shaft nuts.

2. Raise and support the rear end on jackstands placed under the frame.

3. Remove the rear wheels.

4. Disconnect the shock absorbers from the rear axle.

5. Disconnect the rear stabilizer bar.

6. Disconnect the brake hose at the frame.

7. Disconnect the parking brake cable at the equalizer and remove the cables from the support brackets.

8. Matchmark the driveshaft-to-axle flange position.

9. Disconnect the driveshaft from the rear axle and move it out of the way.

10. Detach the speed sensor connector.

11. Take up the weight of the axle with a floor jack.

12. Remove the nuts from the spring U-bolts and remove the spring seat caps.

13. Lower the axle and roll it from under the van.

14. Installation is the reverse of removal. Tighten the spring U-bolt nuts to 160 ft. lbs. (217 Nm).

15. Bleed the brake system.

TORQUE SPECIFICATIONS

Components	English	Metric
Automatic transmission		
4R70W-to-engine retaining bolts	30-41 ft. lbs.	40-55 Nm
4R70W torque converter retaining nuts	20-34 ft. lbs.	27-46 Nm
E4OD/4R100-to-engine retaining bolts	40-50 ft. lbs.	54-68 Nm
E4OD/4R100 torque converter retaining nuts	20-30 ft. lbs.	27-40 Nm
E4OD crossmember retaining nuts and bolts	50 ft. lbs.	68 Nm.
Axle hub nuts		
Front		
Dana 50	60 ft. lbs.	81 Nm
Dana 60	50-60 ft. lbs.	68-81 Nm
Ford 8.8 inch	188-254 ft. lbs.	255-345 Nm
Rear		
Ford 10.25 inch	①	
Ford 10.50 inch	①	
Dana Axles	65-75 ft. lbs.	88-102 Nm
Axle shaft retaining bolts (full floating axles)		
Ford 10.25 inch	40-55 ft. lbs.	54-75 Nm
Ford 10.50 inch	40-55 ft. lbs.	54-75 Nm
Dana Axles	60-80 ft. lbs.	81-108 Nm
Back-up lamp switch		
M5OD	18-26 ft. lbs.	25-35 Nm
ZF	15 ft. lbs.	20 Nm
Center bearing retaining bolts	39-53 ft. lbs.	53-72 Nm
Clutch master cylinder retaining nuts	18 ft. lbs.	25 Nm
Driveshaft retaining bolts	87 ft. lbs.	119 Nm
Halfshaft retaining bolts	51-67 ft. lbs.	68-92 Nm
Manual control lever-to-TR/MLP sensor	22-26 ft. lbs.	30-35 Nm
Manual transmission		
M5OD-to-4.2L engine	38 ft. lbs.	50 Nm
M5OD transmission mount nuts	64-81 ft. lbs.	87-110 Nm
ZF-to-engine bolts	39-53 ft. lbs.	53-72 Nm
ZF crossmember retaining bolts	55 ft. lbs.	75 Nm
ZF rear transmission mount bolts	60 ft. lbs.	81 Nm
Pinion nut		
Front		
Dana 50	200-220 ft. lbs.	271-298 Nm
Dana 60	250-300 ft. lbs.	339-407 Nm
Ford 8.8 inch	200-220 ft. lbs.	271-298 Nm
Rear		
Ford 8.8 inch	160 ft. lbs.	217 Nm
Ford 9.75 inch	160 ft. lbs.	217 Nm
Ford 10.25 inch	160 ft. lbs.	217 Nm
Ford 10.50 inch	160 ft. lbs.	217 Nm
Dana Axles	440-500 ft. lbs.	597-678 Nm
Pinion shaft lockbolt		
Ford 8.8 inch	15-22 ft. lbs.	20-30 Nm
Ford 9.75 inch	15-22 ft. lbs.	20-30 Nm

91197C01

TORQUE SPECIFICATIONS

Components	English	Metric
Pressure plate-to-flywheel bolts		
4.2L engine	35-46 ft. lbs.	47-63 Nm
4.6L engine	35-46 ft. lbs.	47-63 Nm
5.4L engine (except Super Duty)	35-46 ft. lbs.	47-63 Nm
5.4L engine (Super Duty)	30-36 ft. lbs.	41-49 Nm
5.8L engine	22-30 ft. lbs.	30-40 Nm
6.8L engine	30-36 ft. lbs.	41-49 Nm
7.3L diesel engine	19-26 ft. lbs.	26-35 Nm
7.5L engine	14-19 ft. lbs.	19-26 Nm
Shift handle		
M5OD	20-29 ft. lbs.	27-42 Nm
Slave cylinder retaining bolts (external)	13-19 ft. lbs.	18-26 Nm
TR/MLP sensor retaining bolts	80-100 inch lbs.	9-11 Nm
Transfer case		
Front output shaft yoke nut		
New Venture	165 ft. lbs.	223 Nm
Rear output shaft yoke nut		
Borg-Warner 44-07	150-180 ft. lbs.	203-244 Nm
New Venture	186 ft. lbs.	251 Nm
Transfer case-to-transmission retaining bolts		
All wheel drive transfer case (Expedition and Navigator)	29-40 ft. lbs.	40-54 Nm
Borg-Warner 13-56	30-40 ft. lbs.	41-54 Nm
Borg-Warner 44-06	29-40 ft. lbs.	40-54 Nm
New Venture	38 ft. lbs.	50 Nm
Borg-Warner 44-07	38 ft. lbs.	50 Nm

① Refer to procedure

91197C02

8

SUSPENSION AND STEERING

WHEELS

Wheel Assembly

REMOVAL & INSTALLATION

♦ See Figure 1

1. Park the vehicle on a level surface.
2. Remove the jack, tire iron and, if necessary, the spare tire from their storage compartments.
3. Check the owner's manual or refer to Section 1 of this manual for the jacking points on your vehicle. Then, place the jack in the proper position.
4. If equipped with lug nut trim caps, remove them by either unscrewing or pulling them off the lug nuts, as appropriate. Consult the owner's manual, if necessary.
5. If equipped with a wheel cover or hub cap, insert the tapered end of the tire iron in the groove and pry off the cover.
6. Apply the parking brake and block the diagonally opposite wheel with a wheel chock or two.

➡**Wheel chocks may be purchased at your local auto parts store, or a block of wood cut into wedges may be used. If possible, keep one or two of the chocks in your tire storage compartment, in case any of the tires has to be removed on the side of the road.**

7. If equipped with an automatic transmission, place the selector lever in P or Park; with a manual transmission, place the shifter in Reverse.
8. With the tires still on the ground, use the tire iron/wrench to break the lug nuts loose.

➡**If a nut is stuck, never use heat to loosen it or damage to the wheel and bearings may occur. If the nuts are seized, one or two heavy hammer blows directly on the end of the bolt usually loosens the rust. Be careful, as continued pounding will likely damage the brake drum or rotor.**

9. Using the jack, raise the vehicle until the tire is clear of the ground. Support the vehicle safely using jackstands.
10. Remove the lug nuts, then remove the tire and wheel assembly.

To install:
11. Make sure the wheel and hub mating surfaces, as well as the wheel lug studs, are clean and free of all foreign material. Always remove rust from the wheel mounting surface and the brake rotor or drum. Failure to do so may cause the lug nuts to loosen in service.
12. Install the tire and wheel assembly and hand-tighten the lug nuts.
13. Using the tire wrench, tighten all the lug nuts, in a crisscross pattern, until they are snug.
14. Raise the vehicle and withdraw the jackstand, then lower the vehicle.
15. Using a torque wrench, tighten the lug nuts in a crisscross pattern to 126–170 ft. lbs. (170–230 Nm) on the 1997–98 F-250HD, F-350 and F-Super Duty; 83–112 ft. lbs. (113–153 Nm) on the F-150, F-250, Expedition and Navigator; and 148 ft. lbs. (200 Nm) on the 1999–00 F-Super Duty models.

✳✳ WARNING

Do not overtighten the lug nuts, as this may cause the wheel studs to stretch or the brake disc (rotor) to warp.

16. If so equipped, install the wheel cover or hub cap. Make sure the valve stem protrudes through the proper opening before tapping the wheel cover into position.
17. If equipped, install the lug nut trim caps by pushing them or screwing them on, as applicable.
18. Remove the jack from under the vehicle, and place the jack and tire iron/wrench in their storage compartments. Remove the wheel chock(s).
19. If you have removed a flat or damaged tire, place it in the storage compartment of the vehicle and take it to your local repair station to have it fixed or replaced as soon as possible.

INSPECTION

Inspect the tires for lacerations, puncture marks, nails and other sharp objects. Repair or replace as necessary. Also check the tires for treadwear and air pressure as outlined in Section 1 of this manual.
Check the wheel assemblies for dents, cracks, rust and metal fatigue. Repair or replace as necessary.

Wheel Lug Studs

REMOVAL & INSTALLATION

With Disc Brakes

♦ See Figures 2 and 3

1. Raise and support the appropriate end of the vehicle safely using jackstands, then remove the wheel.
2. Remove the brake pads and caliper. Support the caliper aside using wire or a coat hanger.
3. Remove the outer wheel bearing and lift off the rotor.
4. Properly support the rotor using press bars, then drive the stud out using an arbor press.

➡**If a press is not available, CAREFULLY drive the old stud out using a blunt drift. MAKE SURE the rotor is properly and evenly supported or it may be damaged.**

To install:
5. Clean the stud hole with a wire brush and start the new stud with a hammer and drift pin. Do not use any lubricant or thread sealer.
6. Finish installing the stud with the press.

➡**If a press is not available, start the lug stud through the bore in the hub, then position about 4 flat washers over the stud and thread the lug**

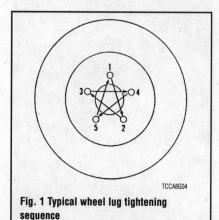

Fig. 1 Typical wheel lug tightening sequence

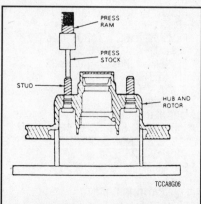
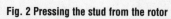

Fig. 2 Pressing the stud from the rotor

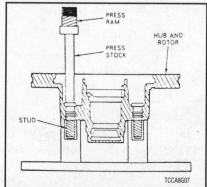

Fig. 3 Use a press to install the stud into the rotor

nut. Hold the hub/rotor while tightening the lug nut, and the stud should be drawn into position. MAKE SURE THE STUD IS FULLY SEATED, then remove the lug nut and washers.

7. Install the rotor and adjust the wheel bearings.
8. Install the brake caliper and pads.
9. Install the wheel, then remove the jackstands and carefully lower the vehicle.
10. Tighten the lug nuts to the proper torque.

With Drum Brakes

◗ **See Figures 4 and 5**

1. Raise the vehicle and safely support it with jackstands, then remove the wheel.
2. Remove the brake drum.

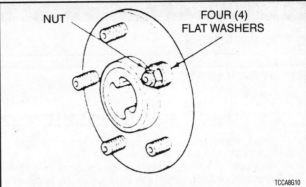

Fig. 5 Force the stud onto the axle flange using washers and a lug nut

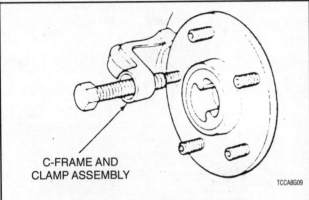

Fig. 4 Use a C-clamp and socket to press out the stud

3. If necessary to provide clearance, remove the brake shoes, as outlined in Section 9 of this manual.
4. Using a large C-clamp and socket, press the stud from the axle flange.
5. Coat the serrated part of the stud with liquid soap and place it into the hole.
To install:
6. Position about 4 flat washers over the stud and thread the lug nut. Hold the flange while tightening the lug nut, and the stud should be drawn into position. MAKE SURE THE STUD IS FULLY SEATED, then remove the lug nut and washers.
7. If applicable, install the brake shoes.
8. Install the brake drum.
9. Install the wheel, then remove the jackstands and carefully lower the vehicle.
10. Tighten the lug nuts to the proper torque.

2-WHEEL DRIVE COIL SPRING FRONT SUSPENSION

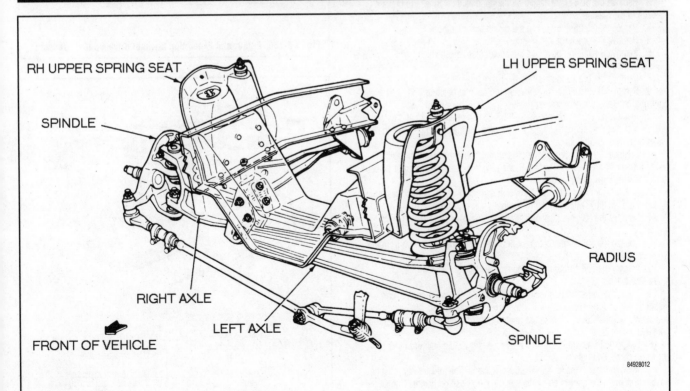

Fig. 6 A common 2-wheel drive Twin I-Beam front suspension

Coil Springs

REMOVAL & INSTALLATION

1997–98 F-250HD and F-350

▶ **See Figure 6**

1. Raise the front of the vehicle and place jackstands under the frame and a jack under the axle.
2. Remove the wheels.
3. Disconnect the shock absorber from the lower bracket.
4. Remove one bolt and nut and remove the rebound bracket.
5. Remove the two spring upper retainer attaching bolts from the top of the spring upper seat and remove the retainer.
6. Remove the nut attaching the spring lower retainer to the lower seat and axle and remove the retainer.
7. Place a safety chain through the spring to prevent it from suddenly coming loose. Slowly lower the axle and remove the spring.

To install:

8. Place the spring in position and raise the front axle.
9. Position the spring lower retainer over the stud and lower seat, and install the two attaching bolts.
10. Position the upper retainer over the spring coil and against the spring upper seat, and install the two attaching bolts.
11. Tighten the upper retaining bolts to 13–18 ft. lbs.; the lower retainer attaching nuts to 70–100 ft. lbs. (95–136 Nm).
12. Connect the shock absorber to the lower bracket. Torque the bolt and nut to 40–60 ft. lbs. (54–81 Nm). Install the rebound bracket.
13. Remove the jack and safety stands.

F-150, F-250 and Expedition

▶ **See Figure 7**

1. Raise and safely support the vehicle.
2. Remove the wheel and tire assembly.
3. Remove the disc brake caliper and support aside with wire to prevent damage to the brake hose.
4. Remove 2 retaining bolts and the disc brake adapter.
5. Remove the brake rotor.
6. Remove 3 retaining bolts and the brake rotor splash shield.
7. Remove the shock absorber.
8. Remove the bracket supporting the brake hose.
9. Remove the stabilizer bar link retaining nut and bushing from the lower control arm. Separate the stabilizer bar link from the lower control arm.
10. Install Coil Spring Compressor D78P-5310A or equivalent and compress the coil spring enough to relieve the tension of the spring between the upper and lower control arms.
11. Remove the cotter pin and castellated nut from the lower ball joint. Using Pitman Arm Puller T64P-3590-F or equivalent, separate the lower ball joint from the wheel spindle.
12. Match mark the lower control arm alignment cams for installation reference.
13. Remove the lower control arm retaining nuts and bolts.
14. Remove the lower control arm and the compressed coil spring as an assembly.
15. Loosen the coil spring compressor and remove the coil spring from the lower control arm.
16. Inspect the coil spring and replace as needed.

To install:

17. Place the coil spring correctly in the saddle of the lower control arm. Install the coil spring compressor and compress the coil spring. The end of the coil spring A, must cover the hole designated B and be visible in the second hole designated as C, for proper installation.
18. Place the lower control arm to the frame. Install the retaining bolts, adjusting cams, and nuts.
19. Align the match marks on the adjusting cams. The forward nut must be tighten first while the control arm is held at the curb position height. Tighten the nuts to 197–241 ft. lbs. (270–330 Nm).
20. Install the lower ball joint stud into the wheel spindle. Install the castellated nut and tighten to 83–113 ft. lbs. (113–153 Nm). Install a new cotter pin.

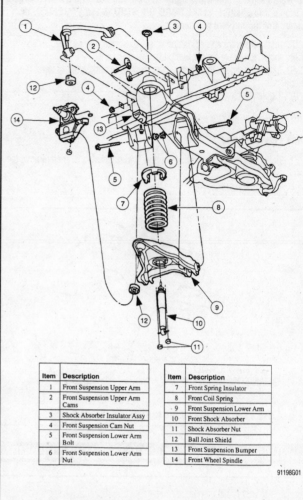

Item	Description	Item	Description
1	Front Suspension Upper Arm	7	Front Spring Insulator
2	Front Suspension Upper Arm Cams	8	Front Coil Spring
3	Shock Absorber Insulator Assy	9	Front Suspension Lower Arm
4	Front Suspension Cam Nut	10	Front Shock Absorber
5	Front Suspension Lower Arm Bolt	11	Shock Absorber Nut
6	Front Suspension Lower Arm Nut	12	Ball Joint Shield
		13	Front Suspension Bumper
		14	Front Wheel Spindle

91198G01

Fig. 7 F-150, F-250, and Expedition 2-wheel drive front suspension

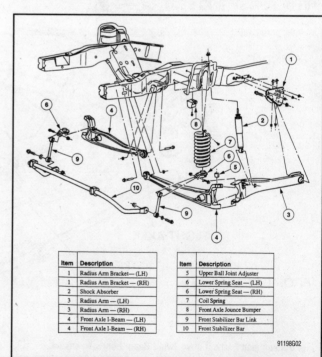

Item	Description	Item	Description
1	Radius Arm Bracket — (LH)	5	Upper Ball Joint Adjuster
1	Radius Arm Bracket — (RH)	6	Lower Spring Seat — (LH)
2	Shock Absorber	6	Lower Spring Seat — (RH)
3	Radius Arm — (LH)	7	Coil Spring
3	Radius Arm — (RH)	8	Front Axle Jounce Bumper
4	Front Axle I-Beam — (LH)	9	Front Stabilizer Bar Link
4	Front Axle I-Beam — (RH)	10	Front Stabilizer Bar

91198G02

Fig. 8 1999–00 F-250SD and F-350 2-wheel drive front suspension

21. Connect the stabilizer bar link to the lower control arm. Install the bushing and retaining nut. Tighten to 15–21 ft. lbs. (21–29 Nm).

22. Remove the coil spring compressor.

23. Install the shock absorber. Tighten the lower bolts to 22 ft. lbs. (32 Nm) and the top nut to 45 ft. lbs. (61 Nm).

24. Connect the brake hose bracket.

25. Install the brake rotor splash shield. Install 3 retaining bolts and tighten to 90–107 inch lbs. (10–14 Nm).

26. Install the disc brake rotor and caliper assemblies.

27. Install the wheel and tire assembly.

28. Lower the vehicle.

29. Pump the brake pedal several times to position the brake pads prior to moving the vehicle.

30. Check the alignment and adjust if out of specification.

31. Road test the vehicle and check for proper operation.

1999–00 F-250SD and F-350

▶ **See Figure 8**

1. Remove the front shock absorber. Refer to the procedure in this section.

2. Remove the wheel and tire assembly.

3. Using a suitable jack, support the front axle assembly.

4. Remove the upper spring retainer.

5. Lower the front axle until the spring is free of the upper spring seat.

6. Using an extension through the top of the spring, remove the lower spring retainer.

7. Remove the front spring.

8. The installation is the reverse of the removal.

Shock Absorbers

TESTING

▶ **See Figure 9**

The purpose of the shock absorber is simply to limit the motion of the spring during compression and rebound cycles. If the vehicle is not equipped with these motion dampers, the up and down motion would multiply until the vehicle was alternately trying to leap off the ground and to pound itself into the pavement.

Contrary to popular rumor, the shocks do not affect the ride height of the vehicle. This is controlled by other suspension components such as springs and tires. Worn shock absorbers can affect handling; if the front of the vehicle is rising or falling excessively, the "footprint" of the tires changes on the pavement and steering is affected.

The simplest test of the shock absorber is simply push down on one corner of the unladen vehicle and release it. Observe the motion of the body as it is released. In most cases, it will come up beyond it original rest position, dip back below it and settle quickly to rest. This shows that the damper is controlling the spring action. Any tendency to excessive pitch (up-and-down) motion or failure to return to rest within 2-3 cycles is a sign of poor function within the shock absorber. Oil-filled shocks may have a light film of oil around the seal, resulting from normal breathing and air exchange. This should NOT be taken as

a sign of failure, but any sign of thick or running oil definitely indicates failure. Gas filled shocks may also show some film at the shaft; if the gas has leaked out, the shock will have almost no resistance to motion.

While each shock absorber can be replaced individually, it is recommended that they be changed as a pair (both front or both rear) to maintain equal response on both sides of the vehicle. Chances are quite good that if one has failed, its mate is weak also.

REMOVAL & INSTALLATION

1997–98 F-250HD and F-350

▶ **See Figure 6**

1. Raise the vehicle and secure on support stands.

2. Remove the self-locking nut, steel washer, and rubber bushings at the upper end of the shock absorber.

3. Remove the bolt and nut at the lower end and remove the shock absorber.

To install:

4. When installing a new shock absorber, use new rubber bushings. Position the shock absorber on the mounting brackets with the stud end at the top. Install the upper bushing, steel washer and self-locking nut at the upper end, and the bolt and nut at the lower end.

5. Torque the upper mounting studs to 18–22 ft. lbs. and the lower mounting nuts to 40–60 ft. lbs.

F-150, F-250 and Expedition

▶ **See Figure 7**

1. Hold the shock absorber stem and remove the nut from the top of the shock.

2. Raise and safely support the vehicle.

3. Remove 2 lower retaining nuts and remove the shock absorber.

To install:

4. Install 1 washer and bushing to the top stem of the shock absorber.

5. Place the shock absorber up through the coil spring.

6. Install 2 lower retaining nuts. Tighten the nuts to 19–25 ft. lbs. (26–34 Nm).

7. Lower the vehicle.

8. Install the bushing, washer and retaining nut to the top of the shock absorber stud. Tighten the nut to 34–46 ft. lbs. (47–63 Nm).

9. Road test the vehicle and check for proper operation.

1999–00 F-250SD and F-350

▶ **See Figure 8**

1. Raise the hood and remove the upper shock absorber retaining nut and upper shock absorber insulator.

2. Raise and support the vehicle.

3. Remove the lower shock absorber retaining nut and remove the shock absorber.

4. The installation is the reverse of the removal.

Upper Ball Joints

INSPECTION

1. Before an inspection of the ball joint, make sure the front wheel bearings are properly packed and adjusted.

2. Jack up the front of the truck and safely support it with jackstands, placing the stands under the I-beam axle, beneath the spring.

3. Have a helper grab the lower edge of the tire and move the wheel assembly in and out.

4. While the wheel is being moved, observe the lower spindle arm and the lower part of the axle jaw (the end of the axle to which the spindle assembly attaches). If there is ⅟₃₂ in. (0.8mm) or greater movement between the lower part of the axle jaw and the lower spindle arm, the lower ball joint must be replaced.

5. To check upper ball joints, grab the upper edge of the tire and move the wheel in and out. If there is ⅟₃₂ in. (0.8mm) or greater movement between the upper spindle arm and the upper part of the jaw, the upper ball joint must be replaced.

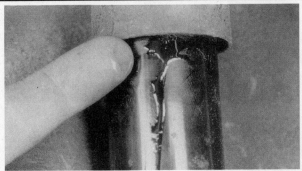

TCCA8P73

Fig. 9 When fluid is seeping out of the shock absorber, it's time to replace it

REMOVAL & INSTALLATION

F-250HD/SD and F-350

▶ See Figures 10 and 11

✳✳ WARNING

Do not use a forked ball joint removal tool to separate the ball joints as this will damage the seal and the ball joint socket. Do not use heat to aid in removal or installation of any suspension parts or components.

1. Raise and safely support the vehicle.
2. Remove the wheel and tire assembly.
3. Remove the front brake caliper assembly and support it from the body way with wire. Do not disconnect the brake line or allow the caliper to hang on the brake line.
4. Remove the brake rotor/hub assembly.
5. Remove the wheel spindle or steering knuckle assembly with the ball joints attached.
6. Place the spindle/knuckle assembly in a suitable vise.
7. Remove the lower ball joint. This is required to access the upper ball joint.
8. Remove the snap-ring from the upper ball joint.
9. Install U-Joint Remover T74P-4635-C and Receiver Cup D81T-3010-A or equivalents, on the upper ball joint. Turn the forcing screw clockwise until the upper ball joint is pressed out of the spindle/knuckle assembly.

To install:

10. Place the new upper ball joint to the spindle/knuckle assembly and install U-Joint Remover T74P-4635-C, Receiver Cup D81T-3010-A5 and Installation Cup D81T-3010-A1, or equivalents. Turn the forcing screw clockwise until the upper ball joint is seated.
11. Install the snap-ring onto the upper ball joint.
12. Install the lower ball joint.
13. Remove the spindle/knuckle assembly from the vise and install to the axle arm.
14. Install the brake rotor/hub assembly.
15. Install the front brake caliper assembly.
16. Install the wheel and tire assembly. Torque the lug nuts to 100 ft. lbs. (135 Nm).
17. Lower the vehicle.
18. Pump the brake pedal several times to position the brake pads before moving the vehicle.
19. Check the alignment and adjust if not within specification.
20. Road test the vehicle and check for proper operation.

F-150, F-250 and Expedition

The upper ball joint is an integral part of the upper control arm and is not a serviceable component. Replacement of the ball joint requires replacing the upper control arm assembly.

Lower Ball Joint

INSPECTION

Refer to Inspection under Upper Ball Joint in this section.

REMOVAL & INSTALLATION

F-250HD/SD and F-350

▶ See Figures 10 and 12

✳✳ WARNING

Do not use a forked ball joint removal tool to separate the ball joints as this will damage the seal and the ball joint socket. Do not use heat to aid in removal or installation of any suspension parts or components.

1. Raise and safely support the vehicle.
2. Remove the wheel and tire assembly.
3. Remove the front brake caliper assembly and support it from the body way with wire. Do not disconnect the brake line or allow the caliper to hang on the brake line.
4. Remove the brake rotor/hub assembly.
5. Remove the wheel spindle or steering knuckle assembly with the ball joints attached.
6. Place the spindle/knuckle assembly in a suitable vise.
7. Remove the lower ball joint. This is required to access the upper ball joint.
8. Remove the snap-ring from the upper ball joint.
9. Install U-Joint Remover T74P-4635-C and Receiver Cup D81T-3010-A or equivalents, on the upper ball joint. Turn the forcing screw clockwise until the upper ball joint is pressed out of the spindle/knuckle assembly.

To install:

10. Place the new upper ball joint to the spindle/knuckle assembly and install U-Joint Remover T74P-4635-C, Receiver Cup D81T-3010-A5 and Installation Cup D81T-3010-A1, or equivalents. Turn the forcing screw clockwise until the upper ball joint is seated.
11. Install the snap-ring onto the upper ball joint.
12. Install the lower ball joint.
13. Remove the spindle/knuckle assembly from the vise and install to the axle arm.
14. Install the brake rotor/hub assembly.
15. Install the front brake caliper assembly.
16. Install the wheel and tire assembly.
17. Lower the vehicle.
18. Pump the brake pedal several times to position the brake pads before moving the vehicle.
19. Check the alignment and adjust if not within specification.
20. Road test the vehicle and check for proper operation.

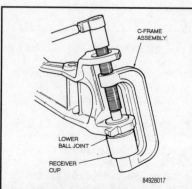

Fig. 10 Remove the ball joint with the special tool

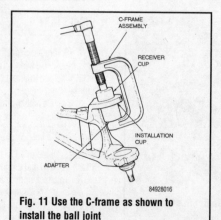

Fig. 11 Use the C-frame as shown to install the ball joint

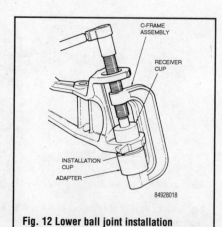

Fig. 12 Lower ball joint installation

F-150, F-250 and Expedition

The lower ball joint is an integral part of the lower control arm and is not a serviceable component. Replacement of the ball joint requires replacing the lower control arm.

Radius Arm

REMOVAL & INSTALLATION

F-250HD/SD and F-350

♦ See Figure 13

➡A torque wrench with a capacity of at least 350 ft. lbs. (475 Nm) is necessary, along with other special tools, for this procedure.

1. Raise the front of the vehicle and place jackstands under the frame and a jack under the wheel or axle. Remove the wheels.
2. Disconnect the shock absorber from the radius arm bracket.
3. Remove the two spring upper retainer attaching bolts from the top of the spring upper seat and remove the retainer.
4. Remove the nut which attached the spring lower retainer to the lower seat and axle and remove the retainer.
5. Lower the axle and remove the spring.
6. Remove the spring lower seat and shim from the radius arm. The, remove the bolt and nut which attach the radius arm to the axle.
7. Remove the cotter pin, nut and washer from the radius arm rear attachment.
8. Remove the bushing from the radius arm and remove the radius arm from the vehicle.
9. Remove the inner bushing from the radius arm.

To install:
10. Position the radius arm to the axle and install the bolt and nut finger-tight.
11. Install the inner bushing on the radius arm and position the arm to the frame bracket.
12. Install the bushing, washer, and attaching nut. Tighten the nut to 120 ft. lbs. (162 Nm) and install the cotter pin.
13. Tighten the radius arm-to-axle bolt to 269–329 ft. lbs. (365–446 Nm).
14. Install the spring seat and insulator on the radius arm so that the hole in the seat fits over the arm-to-axle nut.
15. Install the spring.

16. Connect the shock absorber. Tighten the nut and bolt to 40–60 ft. lbs. (54–81 Nm).
17. Install the wheels.

Stabilizer Bar

REMOVAL & INSTALLATION

1997–98 F-250HD and F-350

1. Raise and support the front end on jackstands.
2. Disconnect the right and left stabilizer bar ends from the link assembly.
3. Disconnect the retainer bolts and remove the stabilizer bar.
4. Disconnect the stabilizer link assemblies by loosening the right and left lock-nuts from their respective brackets on the I-beams.

To install:
5. Loosely install the entire assembly. The links are marked with an R and L for identification.
6. Tighten the link-to-stabilizer bar and axle bracket fasteners to 70 ft. lbs. (95 Nm).
7. Check to make sure that the insulators are properly seated and the stabilizer bar is centered.
8. Tighten the stabilizer bar-to-frame retainer bolts to 35 ft. lbs. (47 Nm). Tighten the frame mounting bracket nuts/bolts to 65 ft. lbs. (88 Nm).

F-150, F-250 and Expedition

1. Raise and safely support the vehicle.
2. Remove both stabilizer bar-to-stabilizer bar link retaining nuts, washers and bushings and separate the stabilizer bar ends from the stabilizer bar links.
3. Remove the stabilizer bar links from the lower control arms, if needed.
4. Remove 4 bolts securing 2 stabilizer bar insulator brackets.
5. Remove the stabilizer bar brackets and the stabilizer bar.

To install:
6. Place the stabilizer bar in position and install 2 stabilizer bar insulator brackets. Install 4 retaining bolts and tighten to 19–26 ft. lbs. (26–35 Nm).
7. Install the stabilizer bar links to the lower control arms, if removed.
8. Connect the stabilizer bar to the stabilizer bar links. Install the bushings, washers and retaining nuts. Tighten the stabilizer bar link retaining nuts to 12–15 ft. lbs. (15–20 Nm).
9. Lower the vehicle.
10. Road test the vehicle and check for proper operation.

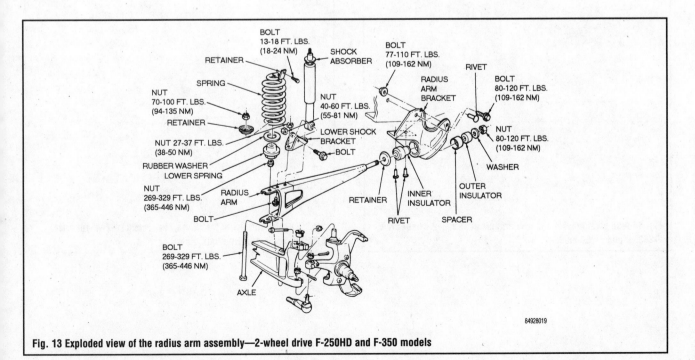

Fig. 13 Exploded view of the radius arm assembly—2-wheel drive F-250HD and F-350 models

1999–00 F-250SD and F-350

1. Raise and support the vehicle.
2. Remove the stabilizer bar retainer brackets retaining bolts and remove the brackets.
3. Remove the lower stabilizer bar link nuts, washers and bolts.
4. Remove the stabilizer bar.
5. Remove the upper stabilizer bar link nuts and bolts, and remove the links.
6. The installation is the reverse of the removal.

Twin I-Beam Axles

REMOVAL & INSTALLATION

F-250HD/SD and F-350

▶ See Figure 14

➡A torque wrench with a capacity of at least 350 ft. lbs. (475 Nm) is necessary, along with other special tools, for this procedure.

1. Raise and support the front end on jackstands.
2. Remove the spindles.
3. Remove the springs.
4. Remove the stabilizer bar.
5. Remove the lower spring seats from the radius arms.
6. Remove the radius arm-to-axle bolts.
7. Remove the axle-to-frame pivot bolts and remove the axles.

To install:

8. Position the axle on the pivot bracket and loosely install the bolt/nut.
9. Position the other end on the radius arm and install the bolt. Tighten the bolt to 269–329 ft. lbs. (365–446 Nm).
10. Install the spring seats.
11. Install the springs.
12. Tighten the axle pivot bolts to 120–150 ft. lbs. (163–203 Nm).
13. Install the spindles.
14. Install the stabilizer bar.

Front Wheel Knuckle and Spindle

REMOVAL & INSTALLATION

F-250HD/SD and F-350

▶ See Figure 15

➡All 2-Wheel Drive pick-ups utilize upper and lower ball joints.

1. Jack up the front of the truck and safely support it with jackstands.
2. Remove the wheels.
3. Remove the front brake caliper assembly and hold it out of the way with a piece of wire. Do not disconnect the brake line.
4. Remove the brake rotor from the spindle.
5. Remove the inner bearing cone and seal. Discard the seal, as you'll be fitting a new one during installation.
6. Remove the brake dust shield.
7. Disconnect the steering linkage from the spindle arm using a tie rod removal tool.
8. Remove the cotter from the upper and lower ball joint stud nuts. Discard the cotter pins, as new ones should be installed during reassembly.
9. Remove the upper ball joint nut and loosen the lower ball joint nut to the end of the threads.
10. Strike the inside area or the spindle as shown in the illustration to pop the ball joints loose from the spindle.

✳✳ WARNING

Do not use a forked ball joint removal tool to separate the ball joints as this will damage the seal and ball joint socket.

11. Remove the nut. Remove the spindle.

To install:

➡Before reassembly, be advised that new cotter pins should be used on the ball joints, and that new bearing seal(s) should also be used. Also, make sure the upper and lower ball joint seals are in place.

12. Place the spindle over the ball joints.
13. Install the nuts on the lower ball joint stud and partially tighten to 35 ft.

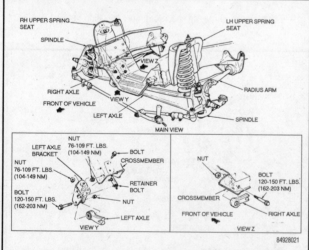

Fig. 14 Axle pivot bracket and axle arm installation—2-wheel drive F-250HD and F-350 models

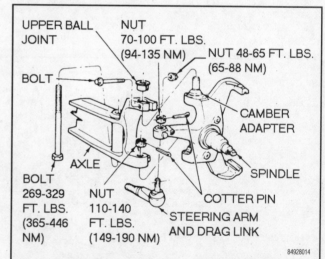

Fig. 15 Exploded view of the front wheel spindle—2-wheel drive F-250HD and F-350 with ball joints

lbs. (47 Nm). Turn the castellated nut until you are able to install the cotter pin.

14. Install the camber adapter in the upper spindle over the upper ball joint stud. Be sure the adapter is aligned properly.

➡**If camber adjustment is necessary special adapters must be installed.**

15. Install the nut on the upper ball joint stud. Hold the camber adapter with a wrench to keep the ball stud from turning. If the ball stud turns, tap the adapter deeper into the spindle. Tighten the nut to 110–140 ft. lbs. (149–190 Nm) and continue tightening the castellated nut until it lines up with the hole in the stud. Install the cotter pin.

16. Tighten the lower nut to 110–140 ft. lbs. (149–190 Nm). Advance the nut to install a new cotter pin.

17. Install the brake dust shield.

18. Pack the inner and outer bearing cone with a quality wheel bearing grease by hand, working the grease through the cage behind the roller.

19. Install the inner bearing cone and seal. Install the hub and rotor on the spindle.

20. Install the outer bearing cone, washer, and nut. Adjust the bearing end-play and install the nut retainer, cotter pin and dust cap.

21. Install the brake caliper. connect the steering linkage to the spindle. Tighten the nut to 70–100 ft. lbs. (95–135 Nm) and advance the nut as far necessary to install the cotter pin.

22. Install the wheels. Lower the truck and adjust toe-in if necessary.

F-150, F-250 and Expedition

> ❋❋ **WARNING**
>
> **The electrical power to the air suspension system must be shut off prior to hoisting, jacking, or towing an air suspension vehicle. This can be accomplished by turning off the air suspension switch located in the PASSENGER SIDE kick panel area. Failure to do so can result in unexpected inflation or deflation of the air springs, which can result in shifting of the vehicle during these operations.**

1. Raise and safely support the vehicle securely on jackstands.
2. Remove the wheel and tire assembly.
3. Remove the brake disc shield.
4. Use a suitable jack to support the front suspension lower arm.
5. Remove the upper ball joint castellated nut.
6. Remove the cotter pin.
7. Remove the ball joint nut.
8. Use the Pitman Arm Puller to separate the ball joint from the front wheel spindle.
9. Remove the upper shock absorber nut.
10. Remove two shock absorber lower nuts.
11. Remove the front shock absorber.
12. Remove the cotter pin.
13. Remove the castellated nut.
14. Use the Pitman Arm Puller to separate the tie rod end from the front wheel spindle.
15. Use the Coil Spring Compressor to compress the coil spring.
16. Remove the lower ball joint cotter pin.
17. Remove lower ball joint castellated nut.
18. Use the Pitman Arm Puller to separate the lower ball joint from the front wheel spindle.
19. Remove the front wheel spindle.

To install:

20. Install the lower ball joint castellated nut.
21. Install a new cotter pin.
22. Install the upper ball joint castellated nut.
23. Install a new cotter pin.
24. Remove the Coil Spring Compressor.
25. Install the tie rod castellated nut.
26. Install a new cotter pin.
27. Install the front shock absorber and the two shock absorber lower nuts.
28. Install the upper shock absorber nut.
29. Install the brake disc shield.

30. If equipped with air suspension, reactivate the system by turning on the air suspension switch.
31. Install the tire and wheel assembly.
32. Inspect and adjust the front end alignment.

Hub and Bearing

REMOVAL & INSTALLATION

F-150, F-250 and Expedition

The hub is part of the disc brake rotor and cannot be serviced separately. The inner and outer wheel bearing and races are serviced individually. Make sure to have a new hub grease seal when servicing the wheel bearings.

1. Raise and safely support the vehicle.
2. Remove the wheel and tire assembly.
3. Remove the disc brake caliper.
4. Remove the disc brake pads and anti-rattle clips.
5. Remove 2 anchor plate retaining bolts and remove the anchor plate.
6. Remove the hub grease cap, cotter pin, retainer washer and the spindle nut.
7. Remove the wheel bearing retainer washer and the outer wheel bearing.
8. Remove the disc brake hub and rotor assembly.
9. Using a suitable seal remover, remove and discard the hub grease seal.
10. Remove the inner wheel bearing.
11. Clean and inspect the wheel bearings and races for unusual wear or damage. Replace parts as necessary.
12. Inspect the hub and brake rotor assembly. If required, the hub and brake rotor assembly must be replaced as a unit.

To install:

13. If needed, pack the wheel bearing with a suitable high temperature wheel bearing grease before assembly.
14. Install the inner wheel bearing in the hub and brake rotor assembly.
15. Install a new grease seal using a suitable installation tool.
16. Place the hub and rotor assembly on the wheel spindle and install the outer wheel bearing.
17. Install the retainer washer and the spindle nut.
18. Adjust the wheel bearings as follows:

a. Torque the spindle nut to 17–24 ft. lbs. (23–34 Nm) while rotating the wheel and tire assembly to seat the wheel bearings.

b. Back off the spindle nut no less than ½ turn.

c. Torque the spindle nut to 17 inch lbs. (2 Nm).

19. Install the retaining washer so the castellations are aligned with the cotter pin hole. Install a new cotter pin.
20. Place the anchor plate and install 2 retaining bolts. Tighten the bolts to 125–168 ft. lbs. (170–230 Nm).
21. Install the brake pad anti-rattle clips and install the disc brake pads.
22. Install the disc brake caliper.
23. Install the wheel and tire assembly. Torque the lug nuts to 83–112 ft. lbs. (113–153 Nm).
24. Check the wheel and tire assembly for proper rotation, then install the grease cap.
25. Lower the vehicle.
26. Road test the vehicle and check for proper operation.

Front Wheel Bearings

Refer to Brake Rotor in Section 9 for removal and installation of the wheel bearings.

Wheel Alignment

If the tires are worn unevenly, if the vehicle is not stable on the highway or if the handling seems poor, the wheel alignment should be checked. If an alignment problem is suspected, first check for improper tire inflation and other possible causes. These can be worn suspension or steering components, accident damage or even unmatched tires. If any worn or damaged components are found, they must be replaced before the wheels can be properly aligned. Wheel alignment requires very expensive equipment and involves minute adjustments which must be accurate; it should only be performed by a trained technician. Take your vehicle to a properly equipped shop.

Following is a description of the alignment angles which are adjustable on most vehicles and how they affect vehicle handling. Although these angles can apply to both the front and rear wheels, usually only the front suspension is adjustable.

CASTER

▶ See Figure 16

Looking at a vehicle from the side, caster angle describes the steering axis rather than a wheel angle. The steering knuckle is attached to the axle yoke through ball joints or king pins. The wheel pivots around the line between these points to steer the vehicle. When the upper point is tilted back, this is described as positive caster. Having a positive caster tends to make the wheels self-centering, increasing directional stability. Excessive positive caster makes the wheels hard to steer, while an uneven caster will cause a pull to one side. Overloading the vehicle or sagging rear springs will affect caster, as will raising the rear of the vehicle. If the rear of the vehicle is lower than normal, the caster becomes more positive.

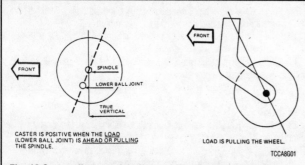

Fig. 16 Caster affects straight-line stability. Caster wheels used on shopping carts, for example, employ positive caster

CAMBER

▶ See Figure 17

Looking from the front of the vehicle, camber is the inward or outward tilt of the top of wheels. When the tops of the wheels are tilted in, this is negative camber; if they are tilted out, it is positive. In a turn, a slight amount of negative camber helps maximize contact of the tire with the road. However, too much negative camber compromises straight-line stability, increases bump steer and torque steer.

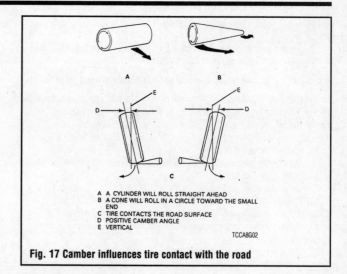

A A CYLINDER WILL ROLL STRAIGHT AHEAD
B A CONE WILL ROLL IN A CIRCLE TOWARD THE SMALL END
C TIRE CONTACTS THE ROAD SURFACE
D POSITIVE CAMBER ANGLE
E VERTICAL

Fig. 17 Camber influences tire contact with the road

TOE

▶ See Figure 18

Looking down at the wheels from above the vehicle, toe angle is the distance between the front of the wheels relative to the distance between the back of the wheels. If the wheels are closer at the front, they are said to be toed-in or to have negative toe. A small amount of negative toe enhances directional stability and provides a smoother ride on the highway.

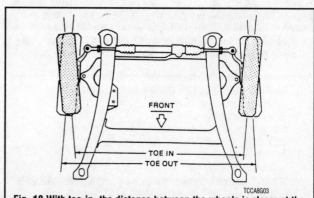

Fig. 18 With toe-in, the distance between the wheels is closer at the front than at the rear

2-WHEEL DRIVE LEAF SPRING FRONT SUSPENSION

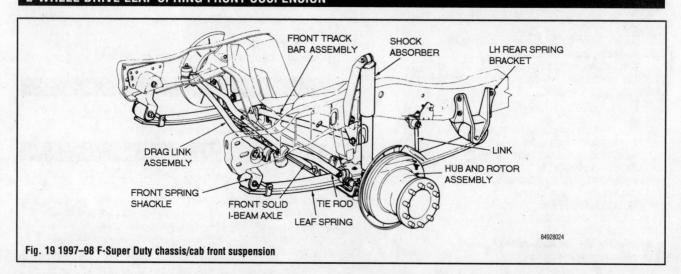

Fig. 19 1997–98 F-Super Duty chassis/cab front suspension

Leaf Springs

REMOVAL & INSTALLATION

1997–98 F-Super Duty

▶ See Figures 20 and 21

1. Raise and support the front end on jackstands with the tires still touching the ground.
2. Using jacks, take up the weight of the axle, off the U-bolts.
3. Disconnect the lower end of each shock absorber.
4. Disconnect the spring from the front bracket or shackle.
5. Disconnect the spring from the rear bracket or shackle.
6. Remove the U-bolt nuts.
7. Remove the U-bolts.
8. Disconnect the jack bracket or stabilizer bar as necessary.
9. Lower the axle slightly and remove the spring. Take note of the position of the spring spacer.

To install

10. Position the spring on its seat on the axle and raise it to align the front of the spring with the bracket or shackle.
11. Coat the bushing with silicone grease.
12. Carefully guide the attaching bolt through the bracket or shackle, and the bushing.
13. Install the nut and, depending on model or which bolts you removed, torque it to:
   - chassis/cab spring-to-shackle: 120–150 ft. lbs. (163–203 Nm)
   - chassis/cab shackle-to-frame: 150–210 ft. lbs. (203–285 Nm)
   - stripped chassis or motor home chassis spring-to-bracket: 148–207 ft. lbs. (200–281 Nm)
14. In a similar fashion, attach the rear of the spring. The torques are:
   - chassis/cab spring-to-bracket: 150–210 ft. lbs. (203–285 Nm)
   - stripped chassis or motor home chassis spring-to-shackle or shackle-to-bracket: 74–110 ft. lbs. (100–149 Nm)
15. Position the spacer on the spring.
16. Install the U-bolts. Install the jack bracket or stabilizer bar bracket on the forward U-bolt. Install the U-bolt nuts. Tighten the nuts, evenly and in gradual increments, in a crisscross fashion, to:
   - chassis/cab: 150–210 ft. lbs. (203–285 Nm)
   - stripped chassis and motor home chassis: 220–300 ft. lbs. (298–407 Nm)
17. Connect the shock absorbers. Tighten them to:
   - chassis/cab models, shock absorber-to-bracket nuts to 52–74 ft. lbs. (71–100 Nm).
   - stripped chassis or motor home chassis models, lower attaching bolt to 220–300 ft. lbs. (298–407 Nm)

Shock Absorbers

▶ See Figures 19, 20 and 21

TESTING

Refer to shock testing under 2 wheel drive coil spring suspension.

REMOVAL & INSTALLATION

1. Remove the nut and bolt which retains the shock to the upper bracket.
2. Remove the nut (chassis/cab) or nut and bolt (stripped chassis and motor home chassis) that retains the lower end of the shock at the spring.
3. Installation is the reverse of removal. It's a good idea to lubricate the bushings with silicone grease prior to installation. Tighten the fasteners as follows:
   - chassis/cab upper and lower: 52–74 ft. lbs. (71–100 Nm)
   - stripped cab and motor home chassis upper and lower: 220–300 ft. lbs. (298–407 Nm)

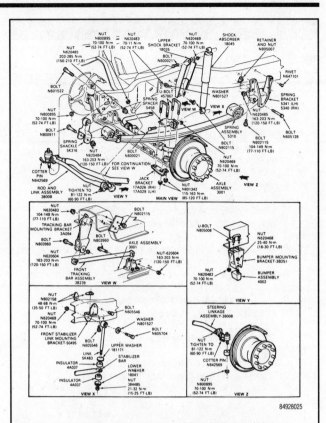

Fig. 20 Front spring and shock absorber installation for F-Super Duty chassis/cab

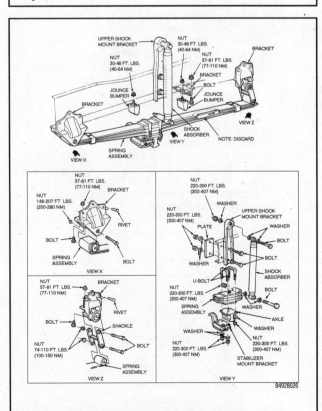

Fig. 21 Front spring and shock absorber installation for F-Super Duty stripped chassis or motor home chassis models

Spindle

REMOVAL & INSTALLATION

1997–98 F-Super Duty

▶ See Figures 22, 23 and 24

1. Raise and support the front end on jackstands.
2. Remove the wheels.
3. Remove the caliper and suspend it out of the way (see Section 9).
4. Remove the hub and rotor assembly (see Section 9).
5. Remove the inner bearing and seal. Discard the seal.
6. Remove the dust shield.
7. Remove the cotter pin and nut, and, using a ball joint separator—the forcing screw type, not the fork type—disconnect the tie rod end from the spindle arm.
8. On stripped chassis and motor home models, disconnect the drag link from the steering arm using a forcing type ball joint separator.
9. Remove the nut and washer from the spindle bolt lock pin and remove the lock pin.
10. Remove the upper and lower spindle pin plugs.
11. Using a brass drift, drive out the spindle pin from the top and remove the spindle and thrust bearing.
12. Remove the thrust bearing and seal.

To install:

13. Clean the spindle pin bore and make sure it is free of corrosion, nicks or burrs. Light corrosion and other irregularities can be removed.
14. Lightly coat the bore with lithium based grease meeting ESA-M1C75-B rating.
15. Install a new spindle pin seal with the metal side facing up into the spindle. Gently press the seal into position being careful to avoid distorting it.
16. Install a new thrust bearing with the lip flange facing downward. Press the bearing in until firmly seated against the surface of the spindle.
17. Lightly coat the bushing surface with lithium based grease and place the spindle on the axle.
18. Hold the spindle, with the thrust bearing in place, tightly against the axle, and measure the space between the axle and spindle at the top of the axle. Determine what thickness of shims is necessary to eliminate all play. Install the shims, available from the dealer.
19. One end of the spindle pin is stamped with a T. Install the spindle pin, from the top, with the T at the top and the notch aligned with the lock pin hole.
20. Install the lock pin with the threads forward and the wedge groove facing the spindle pin notch. Drive the lock pin in all the way and install the nut. Tighten the nut to 40–50 ft. lbs. (54–68 Nm).
21. Install the spindle pin plugs. Tighten them to 35–50 ft. lbs. (47–68 Nm).
22. Lubricate the spindle pin through the fittings until grease seeps past the upper seal and the thrust bearing slip joint at the bottom. If grease can't be forced past these points, the installation was probably done incorrectly and will have to be disassembled and re-assembled.
23. Install the dust shield.
24. Clean, pack and install the bearings. Install a new seal.

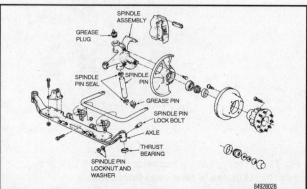

Fig. 22 Front wheel spindle installation for F-Super Duty chassis/cab models

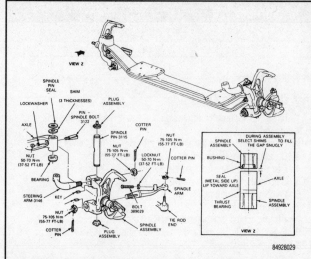

Fig. 23 Front wheel spindle installation for F-Super Duty stripped chassis or motor home chassis models

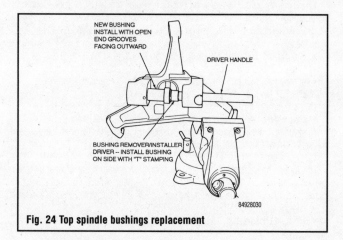

Fig. 24 Top spindle bushings replacement

25. Install the hub and rotor assembly.
26. Install the caliper.
27. Connect the tie rod end and, if necessary, the drag link. Tighten the nuts to 50–70 ft. lbs. (68–95 Nm). Always advance the nut to align the cotter pin holes. NEVER back them off! Always use new cotter pins!
28. Install the wheels.

BRONZE SPINDLE BUSHING REPLACEMENT

▶ See Figures 25, 26, 27 and 28

1. Remove the spindle and secure it in a bench vise.
2. The bushings have an inside diameter of 1.301–1.302 in. (33.05–33.07mm). Use the following tools or their equivalents:
   - Reamer T88T-3110-BH
   - Bushing Remover/Installer T88T-3110-AH
   - Driver Handle T80T-4000-W—One side of the Remover/Installer is marked with a T; the other side with a B. The T side is used on the top bushing; the B side is for the bottom bushing.
3. Remove and discard the seal from the upper bushing bore.
4. Working on the upper bushing first, install the driver handle through the bottom bore. Position a new bushing on the T side of the tool. The bushing must be positioned so that the open end grooves will face outward when installed. Position the bushing and tool over the old bushing, insert the handle and drive out the old bushing while driving in the new bushing. Continue driving until the tool is fully seated. The new bushing should then be seated at the proper depth of 0.08 in. (2.03mm) minimum from the bottom of the upper spindle boss.
5. Working on the bottom bushing, position the driver handle through the top

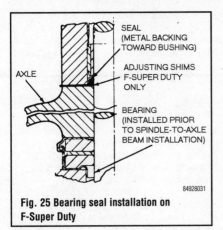

Fig. 25 Bearing seal installation on F-Super Duty

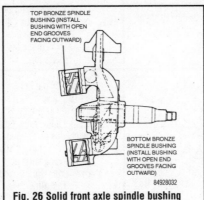

Fig. 26 Solid front axle spindle bushing installation

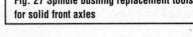

Fig. 27 Spindle bushing replacement tools for solid front axles

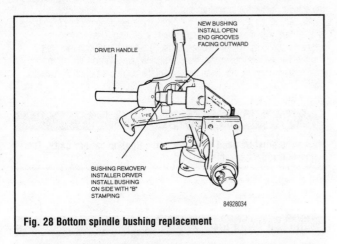

Fig. 28 Bottom spindle bushing replacement

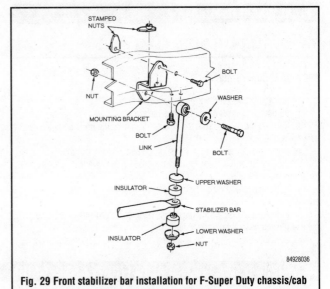

Fig. 29 Front stabilizer bar installation for F-Super Duty chassis/cab

bushing bore. Position a new bushing on the B side of the tool. The bushing must be positioned so that the open end grooves will face outward when installed. Position the bushing and tool over the old bushing, insert the handle and drive out the old bushing while driving in the new bushing. Continue driving until the tool is fully seated. The new bushing should then be seated at the proper depth of 0.13 in. (3.3mm) minimum from the top of the lower spindle boss.

6. Ream the new bushings to 0.001–0.003 in. (0.025–0.076mm) larger than the diameter of the new spindle pin. Ream the top bushing first. Install the smaller diameter of the reamer through the top bore and into the bottom bore until the threads are in position is the top bushing. Ream the bushing until the threads exit the top bushing. Ream the bottom bushing. The larger diameter portion of the tool will act as a pilot in the top bushing to properly ream the bottom bushing.

7. Remove the tool and thoroughly clean all metal shavings from the bushings and surrounding parts. Coat the bushings and spindle pins with grease meeting specification ESA-M1C75-B.

8. Install a new seal on the Remover/Installer on the T side. Using the handle, push the seal into position in the bottom of the top bore.

Stabilizer Bar

REMOVAL & INSTALLATION

1997–98 F-Super Duty Chassis/Cab

▶ See Figure 29

1. Raise and support the front end on jackstands.
2. Disconnect each end of the bar from the links.
3. Disconnect the bar from the axle.
4. Unbolt and remove the links from the frame.
5. Installation is the reverse of removal. Replace any worn or cracked rubber parts. Install the bar loosely and make sure it is centered between the leaf springs. Make sure the insulators are seated in the retainers. When everything is in proper order, tighten the stabilizer bar-to-axle mounting bolts to 35–50 ft.

lbs. (47–68 Nm). Tighten the end link-to-frame bolts to 52–74 ft. lbs. (71–100 Nm). Tighten the bar-to-end link nuts to 15–25 ft. lbs. (20–34 Nm).

1997–98 F-Super Duty Stripped Chassis or Motor Home Chassis

1. Raise and support the front end on jackstands.
2. Disconnect the stabilizer bar ends from the links attached to the axle.
3. Remove the bar-to-frame bolts and remove the bar.
4. Remove the links from the axle brackets.
5. Installation is the reverse of removal. Replace any worn or cracked rubber parts. Assemble all parts loosely and make sure the assembly is centered on the frame. make sure that the insulators are seated in the retainers. When everything is in proper order, tighten the bar-to-frame brackets bolts to 30–47 ft. lbs. (41–64 Nm). Tighten the link-to-axle bracket bolts to 57–81 ft. lbs. (77–110 Nm). Tighten the bar-to-link nuts to 15–25 ft. lbs. (20–34 Nm).

Track Bar

REMOVAL & INSTALLATION

Chassis/Cab Models

▶ See Figure 30

1. Raise and support the front end on jackstands.
2. Unbolt the track bar from the crossmember bracket.
3. Unbolt the track bar from the axle bracket.
4. Installation is the reverse of removal. Tighten the bolts at each end to 120–150 ft. lbs. (163–203 Nm).

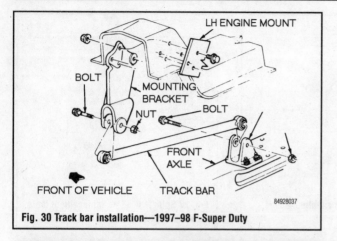

Fig. 30 Track bar installation—1997–98 F-Super Duty

Front Wheel Bearings

REMOVAL & INSTALLATION

1997–98 F-Super Duty

1. Raise and support the front end on jackstands.
2. Remove the wheel cover. Remove the wheel.
3. Remove the caliper from the disc and wire it to the underbody to prevent damage to the brake hose.
4. Remove the grease cap from the hub. Then, remove the cotter pin, nut lock, adjusting nut and flat washer from the spindle. Remove the outer bearing assembly from the hub.
5. Pull the hub and disc assembly off the wheel spindle.
6. Remove and discard the old grease retainer. Remove the inner bearing cone and roller assembly from the hub.
7. Clean all grease from the inner and outer bearing cups with solvent.

4-WHEEL DRIVE LEAF SPRING FRONT SUSPENSION

Leaf Springs

REMOVAL & INSTALLATION

F-250HD/SD and F-350

1. Raise the vehicle frame until the weight is off the front spring with the wheels still touching the floor. Support the axle to prevent rotation.
2. Disconnect the lower end of the shock absorber from the U-bolt spacer. Remove the U-bolts, U-bolt cap and spacer. On F-350 models, remove the 2 bolts retaining the track bar to the spring cap and the track bar bracket.
3. Remove the nut from the hanger bolt retaining the spring at the rear and drive out the hanger bolt.
4. Remove the nut connecting the front shackle and spring eye and drive out the shackle bolt and remove the spring.
   To install:
5. Position the spring on the spring seat. Install the shackle bolt through the shackle and spring. Tighten the nuts to 150 ft. lbs. (203 Nm).
6. Position the rear of the spring and install the hanger bolt. Tighten the nut to 150 ft. lbs. (203 Nm).
7. Position the U-bolt spacer and place the U-bolts in position through the holes in the spring seat cap. Install but do not tighten the U-bolt nut. On the F-350, install the track bar. Tighten the track bar-to-bracket bolts to 200 ft. lbs. (271 Nm).

Inspect the cups for pits, scratches, or excessive wear. If the cups are damaged, remove them with a drift.

8. Clean the inner and outer cone and roller assemblies with solvent and shake them dry. If the cone and roller assemblies show excessive wear or damage, replace them with the bearing cups as a unit.
9. Clean the spindle and the inside of the hub with solvent to thoroughly remove all old grease.
10. Covering the spindle with a clean cloth, brush all loose dirt and dust from the brake assembly. Remove the cloth carefully so as to not get dirt on the spindle.
11. If the inner and/or outer bearing cups were removed, install the replacement cups on the hub. Be sure that the cups seat properly in the hub.
12. It is imperative that all old grease be removed from the bearings and surrounding surfaces before repacking. The new lithium-based grease is not compatible with the sodium base grease used in the past.
    To install:
13. Install the hub and disc on the wheel spindle. To prevent damage to the grease retainer and spindle threads, keep the hub centered on the spindle.
14. Install the outer bearing cone and roller assembly and the flat washer on the spindle. Install the adjusting nut.
15. Adjust the wheel bearings by torquing the adjusting nut to 17–25 ft. lbs. (23–34 Nm) with the wheel rotating to seat the bearing. Then back off the adjusting nut ½ turn. Retighten the adjusting nut to 10–15 inch lbs. (1–1.7 Nm). Install the lock-nut so that the castellations are aligned with the cotter pin hole. Install the cotter pin. Bend the ends of the cotter pin around the castellations of the lock-nut to prevent interference with the radio static collector in the grease cap. Install the grease cap.

❋❋ WARNING

New bolts must be used when servicing floating caliper units. The upper bolt must be tightened first.

16. Install the wheels.
17. Install the wheel cover.

Wheel Alignment

Refer to wheel alignment under 2 wheel drive coil spring suspension.

8. Connect the lower end of the shock absorber to the U-bolt spacer. Tighten the fasteners to 60 ft. lbs. (81 Nm) on the F-250; 70 ft. lbs. (95 Nm) on the F-350.
9. Lower the vehicle and tighten the U-bolt nuts to 120 ft. lbs. (163 Nm).

Shock Absorbers

TESTING

Refer to shock testing under 2 wheel drive coil spring suspension.

REMOVAL & INSTALLATION

F-250HD/SD and F-350

1. Raise and safely support the vehicle securely on jackstands.
2. Remove the nut/bolt retaining the shock to the upper bracket.
3. Remove the lower mounting bolt/nut from the bracket.
4. Compress the shock and remove it.
5. Installation is the reverse of removal. Tighten the upper and lower nut/bolt to 70 ft. lbs. (95 Nm).

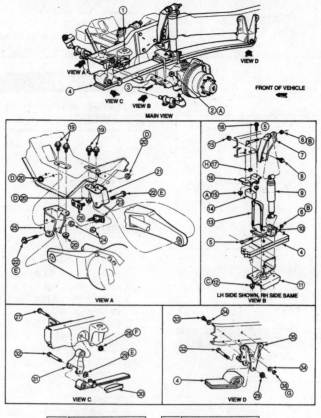

Item	Description
1	Steering Gear Sector Shaft Arm
2	Nut
3	Cotter Pin
4	Front Leaf Spring
5	Bolt
6	Nut
7	Front Shock Absorber Mounting Bracket
8	Bolt
9	Front Shock Absorber
10	Front Spring Plate Spacer
11	U-Bolt Spacer
12	Nut
13	U-Bolt
14	Front Suspension Bumper
15	Nut
16	Front Suspension Bumper Bracket
17	Nut
18	Bolt
19	Bolt
20	Nut
21	Axle Pivot Bracket (RH)
22	Bolt
23	Bolt and Retainer
24	Nut

Item	Description
25	Front Axle Bearing Bracket
26	Bolt and Retainer
27	Bolt
28	Nut
29	Nut
30	Spring Insulator Sleeve
31	Front Spring Front Shackle
32	Bolt
33	Bolt
34	Washer
35	Front Spring Mounting Bracket
36	Nut
A	Tighten to 77-103 N·m (57-76 Lb-Ft)
B	Tighten to 60-80 N·m (44-59 Lb-Ft)
C	Tighten to 113-153 N·m (83-113 Lb-Ft)
D	Tighten to 88-118 N·m (65-87 Lb-Ft)
E	Tighten to 149-201 N·m (110-148 Lb-Ft)
F	Tighten to 170-230 N·m (125-170 Lb-Ft)
G	Tighten to 47-78 N·m (35-58 Lb-Ft)
H	Tighten to 31-40 N·m (23-30 Lb-Ft)

91198G03

Fig. 31 1997-98 F-250HD and F-350 4-wheel drive leaf spring suspension

Stabilizer Bar

REMOVAL & INSTALLATION

1997-98 F-250HD and 1999-00 Super Duty Models

♦ See Figure 32

1. Remove the bolts, washers and nuts securing the links to the spring seat caps. On models with the Monobeam axle, remove the nut, washer and bolt securing the links to the mounting brackets. Remove the nuts, washers and insulators connecting the links to the stabilizer bar. Remove the links.
2. Unbolt and remove the retainers from the mounting brackets.

3. Remove the stabilizer bar.
4. Installation is the reverse of removal. Tighten the connecting links-to-spring seat caps to 70 ft. lbs. (90 Nm). Tighten the nuts securing the connecting links to the stabilizer bar to 25 ft. lbs. (34 Nm). Tighten the retainer-to-mounting bracket nuts to 35 ft. lbs. (47 Nm).

1997-98 F-350

1. Raise and safely support the vehicle securely on jackstands.
2. Remove the bolts, washers and nuts securing the stabilizer bar links to the spring seat caps.
3. Remove the nut, washer and bolt securing the stabilizer bar links to the stabilizer bar brackets.
4. Remove the nuts, washers and insulators attaching the stabilizer bar links to the stabilizer bar and remove the stabilizer bar links.

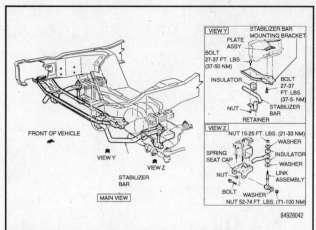

VIEW Y

STABILIZER BAR
MOUNTING BRACKET

PLATE
ASSY

BOLT
27-37 LBS.
(37-50 NM)

INSULATOR

BOLT
27-37
FT. LBS.
(37-5- NM)

NUT
STABILIZER
BAR

RETAINER

VIEW Z

NUT 15-25 FT. LBS. (21-33 NM)

WASHER

SPRING
SEAT CAP

INSULATOR

WASHER

NUT

LINK
ASSEMBLY

BOLT
WASHER

NUT 52-74 FT. LBS. (71-100 NM)

FRONT OF VEHICLE

VIEW Y

VIEW Z

STABILIZER
BAR

MAIN VIEW

84928042

Fig. 32 Front stabilizer bar installation—F-250HD 4-wheel drive models

5. Remove the stabilizer bar retainer bolts and remove the stabilizer bar retainers.
6. Remove the stabilizer bar.
7. The installation is the reverse of the removal.

Knuckle and Spindle

REMOVAL & INSTALLATION

Refer to Section 7 for the knuckle/spindle removal and installation.

Front Wheel Bearings

REMOVAL & INSTALLATION

MANUAL LOCKING HUBS

1. Raise the vehicle and install safety stands.
2. Refer to Manual Locking Hub Removal and Installation and remove the hub assemblies.
3. On F-250 HD (Dana 50 axle) and F-350, use the hub nut tool to unscrew the outer locking nut. Then, remove the lock ring from the bearing adjusting nut. This can be done with your finger tips or a screwdriver. Use the lock-nut socket to remove the bearing adjusting nut.
4. Remove the caliper and suspend it out of the way.
5. Slide the hub and disc assembly off of the spindle. The outer wheel bearing will slide out as the hub is removed, so be prepared to catch it.
6. Lay the hub on a clean work surface. Carefully drive the inner bearing cone and grease seal out of the hub using Tool T69L–1102–A, or equivalent.

To install:

7. Inspect the bearing cups for pits or cracks. If necessary, remove them with a drift. If new cups are installed, install new bearings.
8. Lubricate the bearings with Multi-Purpose Lubricant Ford Specification, ESA–MIC7–B or equivalent. Clean all old grease from the hub. Pack the cones and rollers. If a bearing packer is not available, work as much lubricant as possible between the rollers and the cages.
9. Drive new cups into place with a driver, making sure that they are fully seated.
10. Position the inner bearing cone and roller in the inner cup and install the grease retainer.
11. Carefully position the hub and disc assembly on the spindle.
12. Install the outer bearing cone and roller, and the adjusting nut.
13. On the F-250 HD (Dana 50 axle) and F-350:

➡The adjusting nut has a small dowel on one side. This dowel faces outward to engage the locking ring.

a. Using the hub nut socket and a torque wrench, tighten the bearing adjusting nut to 50 ft. lbs. (68 Nm), while rotating the wheel back and forth to seat the bearings.
b. Back off the adjusting nut approximately 90°.
c. Install the lock ring by turning the nut to the nearest hole and inserting the dowel pin.

❊❊ WARNING

The dowel pin must seat in a lock ring hole for proper bearing adjustment and wheel retention!

d. Install the outer lock nut and tighten to 160–205 ft. lbs. (218–279 Nm). Final end play of the wheel on the spindle should be 0–0.004 in. (0–0.15mm).
14. Assemble the hub parts.
15. Install the caliper.
16. Remove the safety stands and lower the vehicle.

AUTOMATIC LOCKING HUBS

1. Raise the vehicle and install safety stands.
2. Remove the hub assemblies.
3. Using a socket made for that purpose, available at most auto parts stores, use the hub nut tool to unscrew the outer locking nut.
4. Remove the lock ring from the bearing adjusting nut. This can be done with your finger tips or a screwdriver.
5. Use the lock-nut socket to remove the bearing adjusting nut.
6. Remove the caliper and suspend it out of the way.
7. Slide the hub and disc assembly off of the spindle. The outer wheel bearing will slide out as the hub is removed, so be prepared to catch it.
8. Lay the hub on a clean work surface. Carefully drive the inner bearing cone and grease seal out of the hub using Tool T69L–1102–A, or equivalent.

To install:

9. Inspect the bearing cups for pits or cracks. If necessary, remove them with a drift. If new cups are installed, install new bearings.
10. Lubricate the bearings with Multi-Purpose Lubricant Ford Specification, ESA–MIC7–B or equivalent. Clean all old grease from the hub. Pack the cones and rollers. If a bearing packer is not available, work as much lubricant as possible between the rollers and the cages.
11. Drive new cups into place with a driver, making sure that they are fully seated.
12. Position the inner bearing cone and roller in the inner cup and install the grease retainer.
13. Carefully position the hub and disc assembly on the spindle.
14. Install the outer bearing cone and roller, and the adjusting nut.

➡The adjusting nut has a small dowel on one side. This dowel faces outward to engage the locking ring.

15. Using the hub nut socket and a torque wrench, tighten the bearing adjusting nut to 50 ft. lbs. (68 Nm), while rotating the wheel back and forth to seat the bearings.
16. Back off the adjusting nut approximately 90°.
17. Install the lock ring by turning the nut to the nearest hole and inserting the dowel pin.

➡The dowel pin must seat in a lock ring hole for proper bearing adjustment and wheel retention.

18. Install the outer lock nut and tighten to 160–205 ft. lbs. (218–279 Nm). Final end play of the wheel on the spindle should be 0–0.004 in. (0–0.15mm).
19. Assemble the hub parts.
20. Install the caliper.
21. Remove the safety stands and lower the vehicle.

Wheel Alignment

Refer to wheel alignment under 2 wheel drive coil spring suspension.

4-WHEEL DRIVE TORSION BAR FRONT SUSPENSION

FRONT SUSPENSION COMPONENTS

1. Shock absorber
2. Tie rod end
3. Tie rod adjusting sleeve
4. Lower control arm
5. Torsion bars
6. Idler arm
7. Power steering pump
8. Steering gear
9. Pitman arm
10. Stabilizer bar link
11. Stabilizer bar
12. Lower ball joint
13. Hub and bearing assembly
14. Upper ball joint
15. Upper control arm

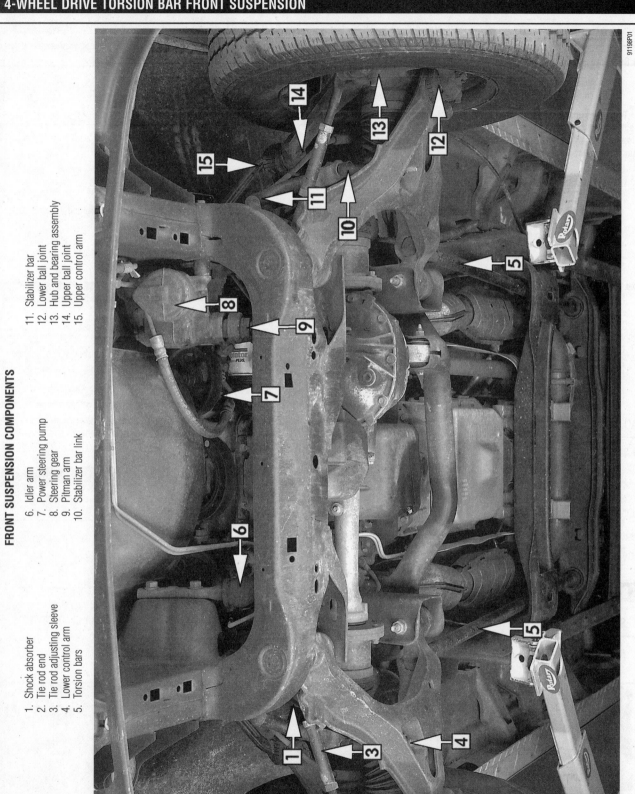

9119BP01

Torsion Bars

REMOVAL & INSTALLATION

▶ **See Figure 33**

1. Raise and safely support the vehicle.
2. Match mark and measure the length of the torsion bar being removed.

➡**Torsion bars are marked for left-hand or right-hand installation. If removing both torsion bars, make sure to reinstall in the correct position. If replacing a torsion bar, make sure that it is the correct torsion bar for the side being replaced.**

3. Install Torsion Bar Adjuster T95T-5310-A and Adapter Plates T96T-5310-A, or equivalents.
4. Tighten the adjuster tool until it touches the torsion bar adjuster.
5. Remove the torsion bar adjuster bolt and nut.
6. Remove 6 torsion bar crossmember retaining bolts.
7. Remove the crossmember support.
8. Remove the torsion bar from the vehicle.

To install:

9. Place the torsion bar in position ensuring that it is the correct torsion bar for the side being installed.
10. Install the crossmember support and 6 retaining bolts. Tighten the retaining bolts to 40–50 ft. lbs. (53–72 Nm).
11. Install the torsion bar adjuster bolt and nut, then remove the torsion bar adjuster tool and adapters.
12. Tighten the adjusting bolt until the match marks are in alignment.
13. Lower the vehicle.
14. Measure the ride height and adjust if necessary.
15. Check the alignment and adjust if not within specification.
16. Road test the vehicle and check for proper operation.

ADJUSTMENT

▶ **See Figure 33**

1. Place the vehicle on a level surface.
2. Bounce the front end to normalize the ride height.
3. Measure the ride height on both sides of the vehicle from the frame to the ground.
4. Loosen the lock nut and add or delete turns until the vehicle is level and at the correct curb height.
5. Tighten the lock nut.
6. Road test the vehicle and recheck the measurements.

Shock Absorbers

TESTING

Refer to shock testing under 2 wheel drive coil spring suspension.

REMOVAL & INSTALLATION

▶ **See Figures 34 and 35**

1. Hold the shock absorber stem and remove the nut, washer and bushing from the top of the shock absorber stud.
2. Raise and support the vehicle.
3. Remove the lower retaining nut and bolt.
4. Remove the shock absorber from the vehicle.

To install:

5. Install 1 washer and bushing to the top stem of the shock absorber.
6. Place the shock absorber up through the coil spring.
7. Install the lower retaining nut and bolt. Tighten to 57–77 ft. lbs. (77–104 Nm).
8. Lower the vehicle.
9. Install the shock absorber upper bushing, washer and retaining nut. Tighten the nut to 22–29 ft. lbs. (30–40 Nm).
10. Lower the vehicle.
11. Road test the vehicle and check for proper operation.

Upper Ball Joint

INSPECTION

Refer to upper ball joint inspection under 2-wheel drive coil spring suspension in this section.

REMOVAL & INSTALLATION

The upper ball joint is an integral part of the upper control arm and is not a serviceable component. Replacement of the ball joint requires replacing the upper control arm assembly.

Lower Ball Joint

INSPECTION

Refer to upper ball joint inspection under 2-wheel drive coil spring suspension in this section.

REMOVAL & INSTALLATION

The lower ball joint is an integral part of the lower control arm and is not a serviceable component. Replacement of the ball joint requires replacing the lower control arm.

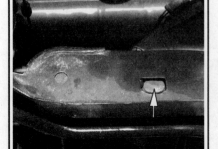

91198P51

Fig. 33 The torsion bar adjusting bolt location

91198P29

Fig. 34 Hold the shock absorber stem and remove the nut, washer and bushing from the top of the shock absorber stud

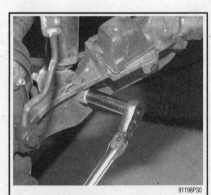

91198P30

Fig. 35 Remove the lower shock retaining nut and bolt

Stabilizer Bar

REMOVAL & INSTALLATION

▶ **See Figures 36 and 37**

1. Raise and safely support the vehicle.
2. Remove the right front wheel and tire assembly.
3. Remove 6 retaining bolts and remove the skid plate.
4. Remove both stabilizer bar-to-stabilizer bar link retaining nuts, washers and bushings and separate the stabilizer bar ends from the stabilizer bar links.
5. Remove the stabilizer bar links from the lower control arms, if needed.
6. Remove 4 bolts securing 2 stabilizer bar insulator brackets.
7. Remove the stabilizer bar brackets and the stabilizer bar.
8. Remove the stabilizer bar by rotating the bar as it is removed through the right-hand side of the vehicle.

To install:

9. Place the stabilizer bar in position, rotating the bar as required for installation.
10. Install 2 stabilizer bar insulator brackets. Install 4 retaining bolts and tighten to 19–25 ft. lbs. (26–34 Nm).
11. Install the stabilizer bar links to the lower control arms, if removed.
12. Connect the stabilizer bar to the stabilizer bar links. Install the bushings, washers and retaining nuts. Tighten the stabilizer bar link retaining nuts to 16–21 ft. lbs. (22–28 Nm).
13. Install the skid plate and 6 retaining bolts. Tighten the bolts to 10–13 ft. lbs. (14–17 Nm).
14. Install the wheel and tire assembly. Torque the lug nuts to 83–112 ft. lbs. (113–153 Nm).
15. Lower the vehicle.
16. Road test the vehicle and check for proper operation.

8. Remove 2 nuts and bolts securing the upper control arm to the body brackets.
9. Remove the upper control arm and ball joint assembly from the vehicle.

To install:

10. Align the match marks on the upper control arm adjusting cams.
11. Place the upper control arm in position to the body brackets and install 2 retaining bolts and nuts. Do not tighten at this time.
12. Install the ball joint stud to the wheel spindle and install the castellated nut. Tighten the nut to 56–77 ft. lbs. (76–104 Nm). Install a new cotter pin.
13. Raise the lower control arm to position the control arms at normal curb height and tighten the front upper control arm retaining nut first, to 84–112 ft. lbs. (113–153 Nm).
14. With the vehicle still at curb height, tighten the rear upper control arm retaining nut to 84–112 ft. lbs. (113–153 Nm).
15. Remove the transmission jack or equivalent from under the lower control arm.
16. If equipped with 4-wheel ABS brake system, position the speed sensor harness and install the bracket bolt. Tighten the speed sensor bracket bolt to 62–80 inch lbs. (7–9 Nm).
17. Install the wheel and tire assembly. Torque the lug nuts to 83–112 ft. lbs. (113–153 Nm).
18. Lower the vehicle.
19. Check the alignment and adjust if not within specification.
20. Road test the vehicle and check for proper operation.

Lower Control Arm

REMOVAL & INSTALLATION

▶ **See Figure 39**

➡ **These vehicles require that the torsion bar tension be relieved before removing the lower control arm. If either the lower control arm or lower ball joint require replacement, the lower control arm and ball joint must be replaced as a unit.**

Fig. 36 Remove both link retaining nuts, washers and bushings and . . .

Fig. 37 . . . separate the stabilizer bar ends from the stabilizer bar links

Fig. 38 The upper control arm-to-body mounts

Upper Control Arm

REMOVAL & INSTALLATION

▶ **See Figure 38**

1. Raise and safely support the vehicle.
2. Remove the wheel and tire assembly.
3. Support the lower control arm with a transmission jack or equivalent adjustable jack.
4. Match mark the upper control arm adjusting cams.
5. If equipped with 4-wheel ABS, remove the speed sensor harness bracket bolt and position the harness aside.
6. Remove the cotter pin and castellated nut from the upper ball joint. Discard the cotter pin.
7. Using Pitman Arm Puller T64P-3590-F or equivalent, separate the ball joint from the wheel spindle.

Fig. 39 The lower control arm-to-body mounts

1. Raise and safely support the vehicle.
2. Match mark and measure the length of the torsion bar being removed.

➡**Torsion bars are marked for left-hand or right-hand installation. If removing both torsion bars, make sure to reinstall in the correct position. If replacing a torsion bar, make sure that it is the correct torsion bar for the side being replaced.**

3. Install Torsion Bar Adjuster T95T-5310-A and Adapter Plates T96T-5310-A, or equivalents.
4. Tighten the adjuster tool until it touches the torsion bar adjuster.
5. Remove the torsion bar adjuster bolt and nut.
6. Remove 6 torsion bar crossmember retaining bolts.
7. Remove the crossmember support.
8. Remove the torsion bar from the vehicle.
9. If equipped with 4 wheel ABS disconnect the sensor wire bracket bolt.
10. Remove the lower shock absorber retaining nut and bolt.
11. Disconnect the lower control arm castle nut and cotter pin and separate the ball joint from the steering knuckle.
12. Disconnect the stabilizer bar link from the lower control arm.
13. Remove the 2 lower control arm nuts and bolts.
14. Remove the lower arm and torsion bar.
To install:
15. Install the lower control arm and torsion bar. Tighten the bolts to 150 ft. lbs. (200 Nm).
16. Connect the lower ball joint and tighten the castle nut to 80–110 ft. lbs. (113–153 Nm).
17. Connect the stabilizer bar link to the lower control arm. tighten the nut to 16–21 ft. lbs. (22–28 Nm).
18. Place the torsion bar in position ensuring that it is the correct torsion bar for the side being installed.
19. Install the lower shock absorber retaining nut and bolt. Tighten to 55–74 ft. lbs. (76–103 Nm).
20. Secure the ABS sensor bracket, if equipped.
21. Install the crossmember support and 6 retaining bolts. Tighten the retaining bolts to 40–50 ft. lbs. (53–72 Nm).
22. Install the torsion bar adjuster bolt and nut, then remove the torsion bar adjuster tool and adapters.
23. Tighten the adjusting bolt until the match marks are in alignment.
24. Lower the vehicle.
25. Measure the ride height and adjust if necessary.
26. Check the alignment and adjust if not within specification.
27. Road test the vehicle and check for proper operation.

Front Hub and Bearing

REMOVAL & INSTALLATION

▶ **See Figure 40**

The wheel bearings are of the cartridge design and are an integral part of the hub assembly. The bearing are permanently lubricated and require no maintenance or adjustments. If required, a new hub assembly must be installed.
1. Raise and safely support the vehicle.
2. Remove the wheel and tire assembly.
3. Remove the disc brake caliper.
4. Remove the disc brake pads and anti-rattle clips.
5. Remove 2 anchor plate retaining bolts and remove the anchor plate.
6. Remove the disc brake rotor.
7. Remove 3 disc brake rotor shield retaining bolts and the shield.
8. If equipped with 4-wheel ABS, remove the speed sensor retaining bolt and move the speed sensor and harness aside.
9. Remove the hub nut cotter pin, retainer and the hub nut. Discard the cotter pin.

91198P43

Fig. 40 The hub-to-knuckle retaining bolts

10. Remove 3 hub assembly retaining bolts from the inside of the steering knuckle.
11. Push the CV-joint inward and remove the hub assembly.

➡**If necessary, use a suitable puller to separate the hub assembly from the CV-joint. Use care not to over extend the CV-joint and boot when removing the hub assembly.**

12. If required, remove the grease seal from the steering knuckle.
To install:
13. If removed, install a new grease seal with Seal Installer T96T-1175-A, Drawbar T77F-1176-A and Cup Replacer T80T-4000-P, or equivalents.
14. Install the hub assembly to the steering knuckle and secure with 3 retaining bolts. Tighten the bolts to 110–145 ft. lbs. (149–201 Nm).
15. Align the splines, then push the CV-joint into the hub assembly.
16. If equipped with 4-wheel ABS, install the speed sensor and secure with 1 retaining bolt. Tighten the bolt to 60–84 inch lbs. (7–9 Nm).
17. Install the disc brake rotor shield and 3 retaining bolts. Tighten the bolts to 80–107 inch lbs. (9–12 Nm).
18. Install the hub nut and tighten to 188–254 ft. lbs. 255–345 Nm).
19. Install the hub nut retainer and a new cotter pin.
20. Install the disc brake rotor.
21. Place the anchor plate in position and install 2 retaining bolts. Tighten the bolts to 125–168 ft. lbs. (170–230 Nm).
22. Install the brake pad anti-rattle clips and install the disc brake pads.
23. Install the disc brake caliper.
24. Install the wheel and tire assembly. Torque the lug nuts to 83–112 ft. lbs. (113–153 Nm).
25. Lower the vehicle.
26. Pump the brake pedal several times to position the brake pads prior to moving the vehicle.
27. Road test the vehicle and check for proper operation.

Wheel Alignment

Refer to wheel alignment under 2 wheel drive coil spring suspension.

STANDARD REAR SUSPENSION

REAR LEAF SPRING SUSPENSION COMPONENTS

1. Rear leaf spring shackle-to-body mounting
2. Leaf spring
3. Front leaf spring shackle-to-body mounting
4. Spring plate and U-bolts
5. Shock absorbers
6. Axle assembly

Coil Springs

REMOVAL & INSTALLATION

Expedition and Navigator

1. Raise and support the vehicle.
2. Remove the wheel and tire assembly.
3. Remove the rear driveshaft. Refer to Section 7.
4. Disconnect the rear brake anti-lock sensor (ABS) electrical connector.

➡Make sure the parking brake control is fully released.

5. Pull the front parking brake cable and conduit.
6. Insert a suitable retainer into the parking brake control.
7. Disconnect the rear parking brake cable and conduit from the rear axle.
8. Remove the rear parking brake cable and conduit from the rear axle bracket assembly.
9. Remove the cable from the caliper.
10. Repeat for the other side.
11. Remove the disc brake caliper bolts.
12. Remove and secure the caliper aside with wire.
13. Repeat for the other side.
14. Disconnect the axle vent tube.
15. Disconnect the stabilizer bar from the rear axle.
16. Remove the bolts from each stabilizer bar retainer.
17. Remove the retainers.
18. Use a suitable jack to support the rear axle.
19. Remove the lower shock absorber nut and bolt.
20. Repeat for the other side.
21. Remove the rear axle-to-trackbar assembly bolt.
22. Remove the rear suspension lower arm assembly-to-axle bolt.
23. Repeat for the other side.
24. Remove the rear suspension upper arm assembly-to-rear axle bolt.
25. Repeat for the other side.
26. Lower the rear axle and remove the coil spring.

To install:

➡Do not tighten any nuts or bolts until the rear suspension is raised so that the rear suspension lower arms are parallel to the ground. Once in position, tighten all the nuts and bolts to specification.

27. Install the rear coil spring.
28. Position the rear suspension upper arm assemblies to the axle and install the bolts.
29. Position the rear suspension lower arm assemblies to the axle and install the bolts.
30. Position the trackbar assembly to the axle and install the bolts.
31. Position the shock absorbers to the axle and install the bolts.
32. Position the stabilizer bar to the axle and install the stabilizer bar retainers and bolts.
33. Position the disc brake caliper and install the bolts.
34. Connect the parking brake cables and conduit to the axle.
35. Install the parking brake cable and conduit to the lever.
36. Install the parking brake cable and conduit to the rear axle bracket assembly.
37. Install the tire and wheel assembly.
38. Position the tire and wheel assembly.
39. Install the lug nuts and lower the vehicle.
40. Tighten the lug nuts in sequence.
41. Install the wheel cover.
42. Remove the pin from the parking brake control assembly.
43. Connect the rear brake anti-lock sensor (ABS) electrical connector.
44. Connect the axle vent tube.
45. Install the driveshaft. Refer to Section 7.
46. Lower the vehicle.

Leaf Springs

REMOVAL & INSTALLATION

1997–98 F-250HD, F-350 and F-SuperDuty

▶ **See Figures 41 and 42**

Semi-elliptic, leaf type springs are used at the rear axle. The front end of the spring is attached to a spring bracket on the frame side member. The rear end of the spring is attached to the bracket on the frame side member with a shackle. Each spring is attached to the axle with two U-bolts. A spacer is located between the spring and the axle on some applications to obtain a level ride position.

1. Raise the vehicle by the frame until the weight is off the rear spring with the tires still on the floor.
2. Remove the nuts from the spring U-bolts and drive the U-bolts from the U-bolt plate. Remove the auxiliary spring and spacer, if so equipped.
3. Remove the spring-to-bracket nut and bolt at the front of the spring.
4. Remove the upper and lower shackle nuts and bolts at the rear of the spring and remove the spring and shackle assembly from the rear shackle bracket.
5. If the bushings in the spring or shackle are worn or damaged, install new bushings.

To install:

➡When installing the components, snug down the fasteners. Don't apply final torque to the fasteners until the vehicle is back on the ground.

6. Position the spring in the shackle and install the upper shackle-to-spring nut and bolt with the bolt head facing outward.
7. Position the front end of the spring in the bracket and install the nut and bolt.
8. Position the shackle in the rear bracket and install the nut and bolt.
9. Position the spring on top of the axle with the spring center bolts centered in the hole provided in the seat. Install the auxiliary spring and spacer, if so equipped.
10. Install the spring U-bolts, plate and nuts.
11. Lower the vehicle to the floor and tighten the attaching hardware as follows:

U-bolts nuts:
- F-250 HD and F-350—150–210 ft. lbs. (204–285 Nm)
- F-Super Duty chassis/cab—200–270 ft. lbs. (272–367 Nm)
- F-Super Duty stripped chassis and motor home chassis—220–300 ft. lbs. (300–408 Nm)

Spring to front spring hanger:
- F-250HD 2WD, F-350 2WD —150–210 ft. lbs. (204–285 Nm)
- F-250HD, 350 4WD—150–175 ft. lbs. (204–285 Nm)
- F-Super Duty—255–345 ft. lbs. (346–469 Nm)

Spring to rear spring hanger:
- All except F-250 and F-350 2WD Chassis Cab—75–115 ft. lbs. (102–156 Nm)
- F-250 and F-350 2WD Chassis Cab; F-Super Duty—150–210 ft. lbs. (204–285 Nm)

F-150 and F-250

▶ **See Figures 43, 44 and 45**

1. Raise and safely support the vehicle.
2. Remove the wheel and tire assembly.
3. Support the axle housing with a transmission jack, or equivalent.
4. Remove 4 retaining nuts from the leaf spring U-bolts.
5. Remove 2 U-bolts and the spring plate. On 4x4 models, remove the spring spacer.
6. Carefully lower the axle housing to allow enough clearance for leaf spring removal.
7. Remove the leaf spring-to-front frame bracket bolt and nut.

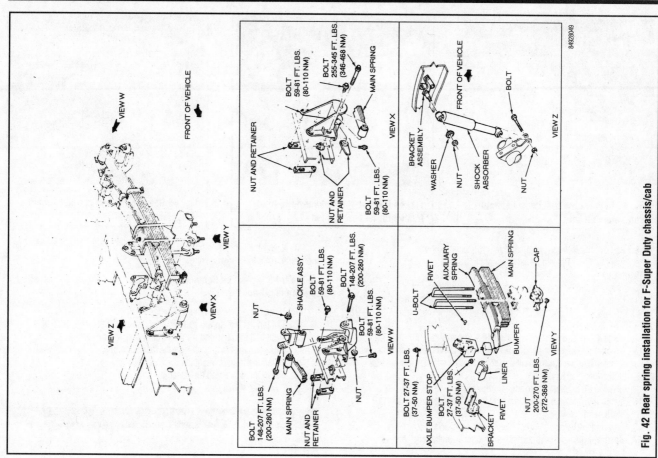

Fig. 42 Rear spring installation for F-Super Duty chassis/cab

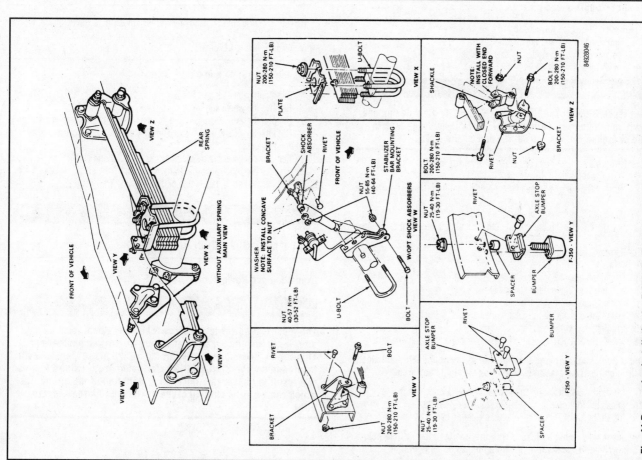

Fig. 41 Rear spring installation for F-250HD, F-350 2-wheel Chassis Cab with Dana axles

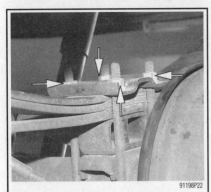

Fig. 43 Remove the U-bolts and spring plate retaining nuts

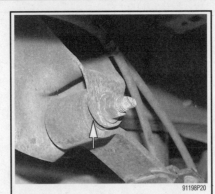

Fig. 44 Remove the leaf spring-to-front frame bracket bolt and nut

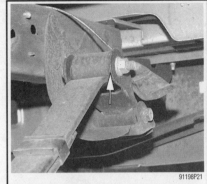

Fig. 45 Remove the leaf spring-to-shackle upper bolt and nut

8. Remove the leaf spring-to-shackle upper bolt and nut.
9. Remove the leaf spring from the vehicle.

To install:

10. Place the leaf spring in position.
11. Install 1 leaf spring-to-shackle upper bolt and nut and 1 leaf spring-to-front frame bracket bolt and nut. Tighten both bolt and nut assemblies to 73–97 ft. lbs. (98–132 Nm).
12. Raise the axle housing to align with the leaf spring.
13. Install the leaf spring plate, 2 U-bolts and 4 U-bolt retaining nuts. On 4x4 vehicles, install the spring spacer. Tighten the U-bolt retaining nuts to 73–97 ft. lbs. (98–132 Nm).
14. Remove the transmission jack, or equivalent.
15. Install the wheel and tire assembly. Torque the lug nuts to 83–112 ft. lbs. (113–153 Nm).
16. Lower the vehicle.
17. Road test the vehicle and check for proper operation.

1999–00 F-250SD, F-350

1. Raise and support the vehicle.
2. Remove the wheel and tire assembly.
3. Position jack stands under the axle housing.
4. Remove the shock absorber.

✳✳ WARNING

Never reuse U-bolts. The U-bolts are a torque-to-yield design and cannot be retightened. Failure to use a new U-bolt can result in loose or broken springs and suspension components.

5. Remove the two U-bolts and the front spring spacer. Discard the U-bolts.
6. Disconnect the front driveshaft.
7. Remove the nut and bolt and position the spring shackle away from the spring.
8. Disconnect the spring hanger nut and bolt.
9. Using a hammer, tap the spring until the spring is free from the hanger bracket.
10. Remove the spring from the vehicle.

To install:

11. Position the spring in the vehicle.
12. Install the spring into the spring hanger.
13. Position the spring in the hanger.
14. Install the bolt and nut. Do not tighten the nut and bolt at this time.
15. Install the spring into the spring shackle.
16. Install the bolt and nut. Do not tighten the nut and bolt at this time.

➡The U-bolts insert through the front spring cap on the left hand side and through the axle assembly bracket on the right hand side.

17. Position the front spring spacer and the new U-bolts.
18. Install the four nuts. Do not tighten the nuts at this time.
19. Install the shock, bolt and nut onto the spring cap.

➡The suspension must be loaded with the weight of the vehicle before the U-bolts and the leaf spring mounting bolts can be tightened.

20. Lower the vehicle onto the jack stands until the front suspension is supporting the weight of the vehicle.

➡The U-bolts must be tightened in a criss-cross sequence. This will tighten the U-bolts evenly.

21. Tighten the U-bolts in a criss-cross sequence.
22. Tighten the leaf spring rear retaining bolt and nut.
23. Tighten the leaf spring front retaining bolt and nut.
24. Raise the vehicle and remove the jack stands.
25. Install the front driveshaft.
26. Install the wheel and tire assembly.
27. Lower the vehicle.

Shock Absorbers

TESTING

Refer to shock testing under 2 wheel drive coil spring suspension.

REMOVAL & INSTALLATION

♦ **See Figures 46, 47 and 48**

1. Raise and safely support the vehicle.
2. Remove the wheel and tire assembly.
3. Support the axle housing with a jackstand, or equivalent.
4. Hold the upper shock absorber shaft and remove the upper retaining nut, washer and bushing.
5. Remove the lower shock absorber retaining nut and bolt.
6. Remove the shock absorber from the vehicle.
7. The installation is the reverse of the removal.

Track Bar

REMOVAL & INSTALLATION

Expedition and Navigator

✳✳ CAUTION

The electrical power to the air suspension system must be shut off prior to hoisting, jacking or towing an air suspension vehicle. This can be accomplished by turning off the air suspension switch located in the PASSENGER SIDE kick panel area. Failure to do so can result in unexpected inflation or deflation of the air springs, which can result in shifting of the vehicle during these operations.

1. Raise and support the vehicle.

Fig. 46 Support the axle housing with a jackstand

Fig. 47 Hold the upper shock absorber shaft and remove the upper retaining nut, washer and bushing

Fig. 48 Remove the lower shock absorber retaining nut and bolt

✹✹ WARNING

The air suspension height sensor has a plastic harness retainer to suspension that must be unclipped prior to removal.

2. Detach the air suspension height sensor electrical connector.
3. Depress the metal retaining tabs and remove the air suspension height sensor from the ball studs.
4. Remove the passenger side trackbar bolt.
5. Remove the driver's side trackbar nut and bolt.
6. Remove the trackbar from the vehicle.
7. The installation is the reverse of the removal.

Stabilizer Bar

REMOVAL & INSTALLATION

1997–98 F-250HD, F-350 and F-SuperDuty

♦ See Figures 49, 50 and 51

1. Remove the nuts from the lower ends of the stabilizer bar link.
2. Remove the outer washers and insulators.
3. Disconnect the bar from the links.

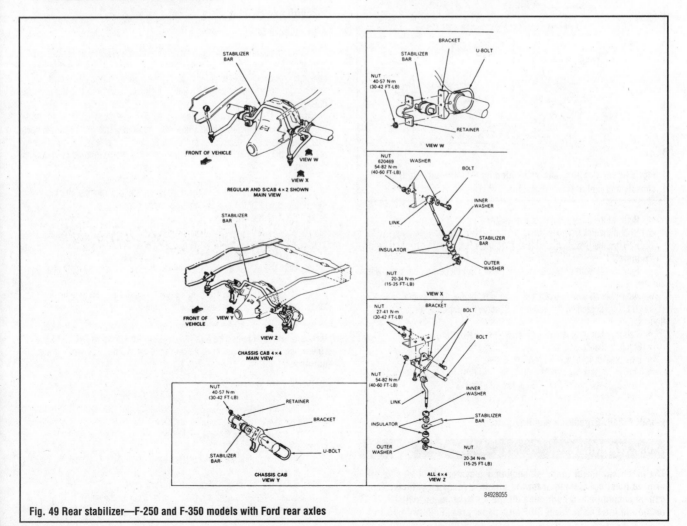

Fig. 49 Rear stabilizer—F-250 and F-350 models with Ford rear axles

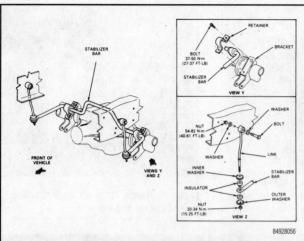

Fig. 50 Rear stabilizer bar installation for F-Super Duty chassis/cab models

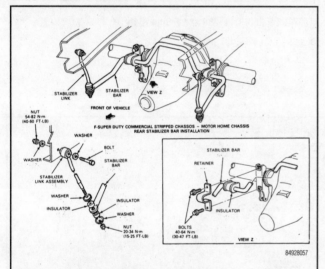

Fig. 51 Rear stabilizer bar installation for F-Super Duty stripped chassis and motor home chassis

4. Remove the inner insulators and washers.
5. Unbolt the link from the frame.
6. Remove the U-bolts, brackets and retainers.

To install:

7. Replace all worn or cracked rubber parts. Coat all new rubber parts with silicone grease.
8. Assemble all parts loosely and make sure the bar assembly is centered before tightening the fasteners. Observe the following torque figures:
- Stabilizer bar-to-axle nut—30–45 ft. lbs. (40–61 Nm)
- Stabilizer bar-to-axle bolt—30–47 ft. lbs. (40–64 Nm)
- Link bracket-to-frame nut (4WD)—30–42 ft. lbs. (40–57 Nm)
- Link-to-bracket nut (4WD)—60 ft. lbs. (80 Nm)
- Link-to-frame nut (2WD)—60 ft. lbs. (80 Nm)
- Stabilizer bar-to-link—15–25 ft. lbs. (20–34 Nm)

F-150, F-250, Expedition and Navigator

✳✳ WARNING

The electrical power to the air suspension system must be shut off prior to hoisting, jacking or towing an air suspension vehicle. This can be accomplished by turning off the air suspension switch located in the PASSENGER SIDE kick panel area. Failure to do so

can result in unexpected inflation or deflation of the air springs, which can result in shifting of the vehicle during these operations.

✳✳ WARNING

Raise and support the vehicle.

1. Remove the stabilizer bar link nut.
2. Remove the stabilizer bar link bolt and the stabilizer bar link.
3. Remove the stabilizer bar retainer bolts.
4. Remove the stabilizer bar retainers and the stabilizer bar.
5. The installation is the reverse of the removal.

1999–00 F-Super Duty Models

1. Raise and support the vehicle.
2. Remove the nuts from both lower ends of the stabilizer bar links and remove the washers.
3. Remove the nuts and washers from both upper ends of the stabilizer bar links-to-frame and remove the links.
4. Remove the nuts from both stabilizer bar retainer-to-axle brackets and remove the stabilizer bar retainers, stabilizer bar mounting brackets, U-bolts and the stabilizer bar.
5. The installation is the reverse of the removal.

Full Floating Rear Axle Bearings

REMOVAL, REPACKING & INSTALLATION

F-250HD and F-350 Models

▶ See Figure 52

The wheel bearings on the Ford 10½ in. full floating rear axle are packed with wheel bearing grease. Axle lubricant can also flow into the wheel hubs and bearings, however, wheel bearing grease is the primary lubricant. The wheel bearing grease provides lubrication until the axle lubricant reaches the bearings during normal operation.

The wheel bearings on the full floating rear axle are packed with wheel bearing grease. Axle lubricant can also flow into the wheel hubs and bearings, however, wheel bearing grease is the primary lubricant. The wheel bearing grease provides lubrication until the axle lubricant reaches the bearings during normal operation.

1. Set the parking brake and loosen the axle shaft bolts.
2. Raise the rear wheels off the floor and place jackstands under the rear axle housing so that the axle is parallel with the floor.
3. Remove the wheels.
4. Remove the brake drums.
5. Remove the axle shaft bolts.
6. Remove the axle shaft and discard the gaskets.
7. With the axle shaft removed, remove the gasket from the axle shaft flange studs.
8. Install Hub Wrench T85T–4252–AH, or equivalent, so that the drive tangs on the tool engage the slots in the hub nut.

➡**The hub nuts are right-hand thread on the right hub and left-hand thread on the left hub. The hub nuts should be stamped RH and LH. Never use power or impact tools on these nuts! The nuts will ratchet during removal.**

9. Remove the hub nut.
10. Install step plate adapter tool D80L–630–7, or equivalent, in the hub.
11. Install puller D80L–1002–L, or equivalent and loosen the hub to the point of removal. Remove the puller and step plate.
12. Remove the hub, taking care to catch the outer bearing as the hub comes off.
13. Install the hub in a soft-jawed vise and pry out the hub seal.
14. Lift out the inner bearing.
15. Drive out the inner and outer bearing races with a drift.
16. Wash all the old grease or axle lubricant out of the wheel hub, using a suitable solvent.

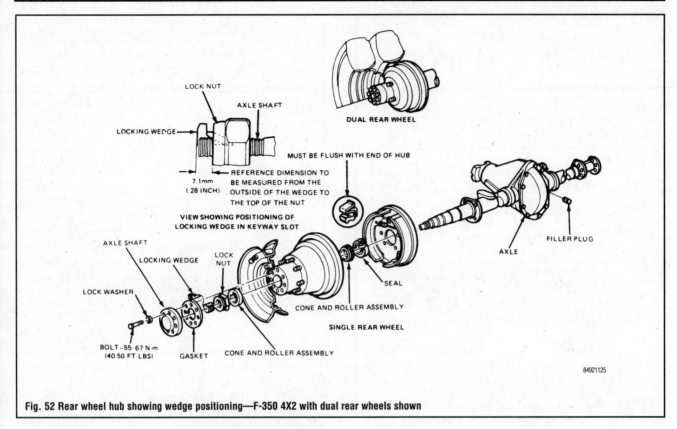

Fig. 52 Rear wheel hub showing wedge positioning—F-350 4X2 with dual rear wheels shown

17. Wash the bearing races and rollers and inspect them for pitting, galling, and uneven wear patterns. Inspect the roller for end wear. Replace any bearing and race that appears in any way damaged. Always replace the bearings and races as a set.

To install:

18. Coat the race bores with a light coat of clean, waterproof wheel bearing grease and drive the races squarely into the bores until they are fully seated. A good indication that the race is seated is when you notice the grease from the bore squashing out under the race when it contact the shoulder. Another indication is a definite change in the metallic tone when you seat the race. Just be very careful to avoid damaging the bearing surface of the race!

19. Pack each bearing cone and roller with a bearing packer or in the manner outlined in Section 1 for the front wheel bearings on 2-Wheel Drive trucks.

20. Place the inner bearing cone and roller assembly in the wheel hub.

➡When installing the new seal, the words OIL SIDE must go inwards towards the bearing!

21. Place the seal squarely in the hub and drive it into place. The best tool for the job is a seal driver such as T85T–1175–AH, which will stop when the seal is at the proper depth.

➡If the seal is misaligned or damaged during installation, a new seal must be installed.

22. Clean the spindle thoroughly. If the spindle is excessively pitted, damaged or has a predominately bluish tint (from overheating), it must be replaced.

23. Coat the spindle with 80W/90 oil.

24. Pack the hub with clean, waterproof wheel bearing grease.

25. Pack the outer bearing with clean, waterproof wheel bearing grease in the same manner as you packed the inner bearing.

26. Place the outer bearing in the hub and install the hub and bearing together on the spindle.

27. Install the hub nut on the spindle. Make sure that the nut tab is located in the keyway prior to thread engagement. Turn the hub nut onto the threads as far as you can by hand, noting the thread direction.

28. Install the hub wrench tool and tighten the nut to 55–65 ft. lbs. (75–88 Nm). Rotate the hub occasionally during nut tightening.

29. Ratchet the nut back 5 teeth. Make sure that you hear 5 clicks!

30. Inspect the axle shaft O-ring seal and replace it if it looks at all bad.

31. Install the axle shaft.

32. Coat the axle shaft bolt threads with waterproof seal and install them by hand until they seat. Do not tighten them with a wrench at this time!

33. Check the diameter across the center of the brake shoes. Check the diameter of the brake drum. Adjust the brake shoes so that their diameter is 0.030 in. (0.76mm) less than the drum diameter.

34. Install the brake drum

35. Install the wheel.

36. Loosen the differential filler plug. If lubricant starts to run out, retighten the plug. If not, remove the plug and fill the housing with 80W/90 gear oil.

37. Lower the truck to the floor.

38. Tighten the wheel lugs to 140 ft. lbs. (190 Nm).

39. Now tighten the axle shaft bolts. Torque them to 60–80 ft. lbs. (81–108 Nm).

F-Super Duty, Stripped Chassis and Motor Home Chassis

◆ **See Figures 53, 54 and 55**

The wheel bearings on full floating rear axles are packed with wheel bearing grease. Axle lubricant can also flow into the wheel hubs and bearings, however, wheel bearing grease is the primary lubricant. The wheel bearing grease provides lubrication until the axle lubricant reaches the bearings during normal operation.

1. Set the parking brake and loosen but DO NOT REMOVE the axle shaft bolts.

2. Raise the rear wheels off the floor and place jackstands under the rear axle housing so that the axle is parallel with the floor. The axle shafts must turn freely, so release the parking brake.

3. Remove the axle shaft bolts and lockwashers. They should not be re-used.

4. Place a heavy duty wheel dolly under the wheels and raise them so that all weight is off the wheel bearings.

5. Remove the axle shaft and gasket(s).

6. Remove the brake caliper (see Section 9).

7. Using a special hub nut wrench, remove the hub nut.

➡The hub nuts for both sides are right-hand thread and marked RH.

8. Remove the outer bearing cone and pull the wheel straight off the axle.

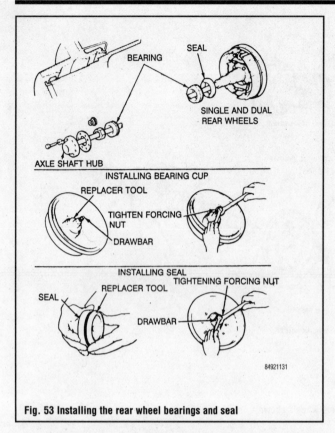

Fig. 53 Installing the rear wheel bearings and seal

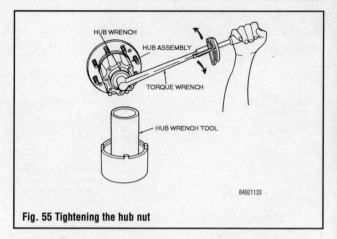

Fig. 55 Tightening the hub nut

9. With a piece of hardwood or a brass drift which will just clear the outer bearing cup, drive the inner bearing cone and inner seal out of the wheel hub.

10. Wash all the old grease or axle lubricant out of the wheel hub, using a suitable solvent.

11. Wash the bearing cups and rollers and inspect them for pitting, galling, and uneven wear patterns. Inspect the roller for end wear.

To install:

12. If the bearing cups are to be replaced, drive them out with a brass drift. Install the new cups with a block of wood and hammer or press them in.

13. If the bearing cups are properly seated, a 0.0015 in. (0.038mm) feeler gauge will not fit between the cup and the wheel hub. The gauge should not fit beneath the cup. Check several places to make sure the cups are squarely seated.

14. Pack each bearing cone and roller with a bearing packer or in the man-ner previously outlined for the front wheel bearings on 2WD trucks. Use a multi-purpose wheel bearing grease.

15. Place the inner bearing cone and roller assembly in the wheel hub. Install a new inner seal in the hub with a seal installation tool.

16. Wrap the threads of the spindle with tape and carefully slide the hub straight on the spindle. Take care to avoid damaging the seal! Remove the tape.

17. Install the outer bearing. Start the hub nut, making sure that the hub tab is engaged with the keyway prior to threading.

18. Tighten the nut to 65–75 ft. lbs. (88–102 Nm) while rotating the wheel.

➡ **The hub will ratchet at torque is applied. This ratcheting can be avoided by using Ford tool No. T88T-4252-A. Avoiding ratcheting will give more even bearing preloads.**

19. Back off (loosen) the adjusting nut 90° (¼ turn). Then, tighten it to 15–20 ft. lbs. (20–27 Nm).

20. Using a dial indicator, check end-play of the hub. No end-play is permit-ted.

21. Clean the hub bolt holes thoroughly. Replace the hub if any cracks are found around the holes or if the threads in the holes are in any way dam-aged.

22. Install the axle shaft, new flange gasket, lock washers and new shaft retaining bolts. Coat the bolt threads with thread adhesive. Tighten them snugly, but not completely.

23. Install the caliper.

24. Install the wheels.

25. Lower the truck to the ground.

26. Tighten the wheel lug nuts.

27. Tighten the axle shaft bolts to 40–55 ft. lbs. (54–75 Nm).

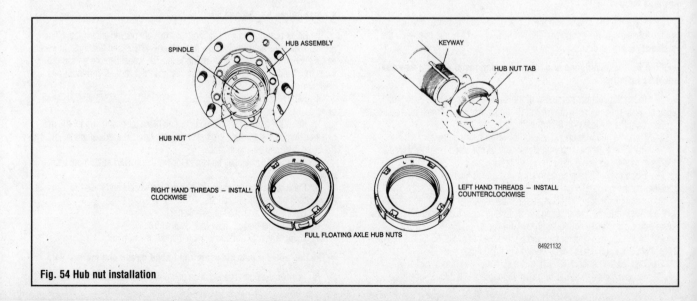

Fig. 54 Hub nut installation

AIR SUSPENSION

REAR AIR SPRING SUSPENSION COMPONENTS

1. Stabilizer bar link
2. Track bar
3. Air spring
4. Stabilizer bar bushing
5. Stabilizer bar
6. Axle assembly
7. Control arm

Air Compressor

REMOVAL & INSTALLATION

1. Remove the windshield washer reservoir.

✳✳ WARNING

Before repairing any air suspension components, disconnect power to the system by turning off the air suspension switch located in the passenger side kick panel area to prevent vehicle damage or personal injury.

2. Turn the air suspension switch to the OFF position.
3. Disconnect the air line tube to the air compressor drier by depressing the red ring. Remove the air line.
4. Detach the air compressor electrical connector.
5. Remove the air compressor bracket bolts.
6. Remove the air compressor.

To install:

➡**When installing the air lines make sure the white air line is fully inserted into the fitting for correct installation.**

7. The installation is the reverse of the removal.

Air Compressor Drier

REMOVAL & INSTALLATION

1. Disconnect the negative battery cable.
2. Remove the air compressor. Refer to the procedure in this section.
3. Remove the air compressor drier retaining screw and rotate 90° to unlock then remove the air compressor drier.

To install:

➡**Inspect the O-ring for damage and replace as necessary. Lubricate the solenoid seal area with Silicone Brake Caliper Grease and Dielectric Compound D7AZ-19A331A or equivalent meeting Ford specification ESE-M1C171-A. When installing the air lines, make sure the white air line is fully inserted into the fitting for correct installation.**

4. The installation is the reverse of the removal. Ride height adjustments must be performed after the air compressor/drier is installed.

Control Module

REMOVAL & INSTALLATION

1. Disconnect the negative battery cable.
2. Remove the instrument cluster panel. Refer to section 6.
3. Remove the front control module mounting bracket screw.
4. Remove the rear control module mounting bracket screw.
5. Lift the control module and mounting bracket from the instrument panel and detach the control module electrical connectors.
6. The installation is the reverse of the removal.

Height Sensor

REMOVAL & INSTALLATION

✳✳ WARNING

The electrical power to the air suspension system must be shut off prior to hoisting, jacking or towing an air suspension vehicle. This can be accomplished by turning off the air suspension switch located in the passenger side kick panel area. Failure to do so may

result in unexpected inflation or deflation of the air springs which may result in shifting of the vehicle during these operations.

1. Raise and support the vehicle.
2. Detach the air suspension height sensor electrical connector.
3. Depress the metal retaining tabs and remove the air suspension height sensor.
4. The installation is the reverse of the removal.

Air Spring

PRECAUTIONS

• The electrical power to the air suspension system must be shut off prior to hoisting, jacking or towing an air suspension vehicle. This can be accomplished by turning off the air suspension switch located in the PASSENGER SIDE kick panel area. Failure to do so may result in unexpected inflation or deflation of the air springs which may result in shifting of the vehicle during these operations.

• Do not attempt to install or inflate any air spring that has become unfolded to prevent vehicle damage or personal injury.

• Do not attempt to inflate any air spring which has collapsed while deflated from the rebound hanging position to the jounce stop.

• When installing a new air spring, care must be taken to not apply a load to the suspension until the air springs have been inflated using the air spring fill procedure.

• After inflating an air spring in the hanging position, it must be inspected for proper shape.

• Do not remove an air spring under any circumstances when there is pressure in the air spring. Do not remove any components supporting an air spring without either exhausting the air or providing support for the air spring to prevent vehicle damage or personal injury.

REMOVAL & INSTALLATION

➡**The vehicle must be positioned on a suitable lifting device prior to deflating the air suspension system.**

1. Access the air suspension diagnostic connector behind the PASSENGER SIDE cowl side trim panel.

➡**New Generation STAR (NGS) Tester can be used to emulate Superstar II Tester.**

2. Turn the air suspension switch to the ON position and the ignition to the key on engine off (KOEO) position. Use Super STAR II Tester plugged into the air suspension diagnostic connector to perform the function test. Set Super STAR II Tester to the EEC-IV/MCU mode; also set it to the FAST mode. Press Super STAR II Tester button to the TEST position; DTC 10 will be displayed. Within two minutes, DTC 12 or 13 will be displayed. After DTC 12 or 13 is displayed, release the Super STAR II Tester button from the HOLD position. Wait at least 20 seconds and then press the Super STAR II Tester button to the TEST position. Within 10 seconds, the following DTCs will be displayed in order:

   23 Vent Right Rear Air Spring
   24 Vent Left Rear Air Spring
   25 Vent Both Rear Air Springs
   26 Compress Right Rear Air Spring
   27 Compress Left Rear Air Spring
   28 Compress Both Rear Air Springs
   31 Cycle Compressor On and Off
   32 Cycle Vent Solenoid Valve Open and Closed
   33 Cycle Spring Solenoid Valves Open and Closed

3. Disconnect Super STAR II Tester after deflation is completed.
4. Within four seconds after DTC 23, 24 or 25 is displayed, depending on which air spring is to be deflated, release the Super STAR II Tester to the HOLD position. After deflation, turn the ignition to the OFF position.
5. Remove the wheel and tire assembly.
6. Remove the air line from the solenoid valve by depressing the red plastic retaining ring and pull the air line out of the solenoid.
7. Detach the solenoid valve electrical connector and position it aside.
8. Remove the retaining clip from the top of the air spring.
9. Compress the deflated air spring and remove it from the vehicle.

To install:

> ✳ **WARNING**
>
> **Any air spring which is unfolded must be refolded prior to being installed in a vehicle.**

10. Position the air spring into place and install the retaining clip at the top of the air spring.
11. Seat bottom of the air spring on the rear axle.
12. Connect the solenoid valve electrical connector.

➡ **When installing the air lines make sure the white air line is fully inserted into the fitting for correct installation.**

13. Connect the air line into the solenoid valve line fitting.
14. Install the rear wheel and tire assembly.
15. Turn the air suspension switch to the ON position.

➡ **Inflation will start after 45 seconds.**

16. Turn the ignition to the key on engine off (KOEO) position until the air springs are inflated to trim height.
17. Visually inspect each air spring to make sure the correct profile has been obtained. There should be no evidence of buckling or folding of the air springs.

Solenoid Valve—Functional

REMOVAL & INSTALLATION

1. Remove the air spring. Refer to the procedure in this section.

> ✳ **WARNING**
>
> **Remove any dirt or other debris from the air spring prior to removing the solenoid valve from the air spring.**

2. Remove the metal retaining clip from the solenoid valve.
3. Inspect the solenoid O-rings and replace as necessary.
4. Twist the solenoid valve and remove.

➡ **Be sure the new air spring solenoid is fully seated into both stages of the air spring. Lightly apply Silicone Brake Caliper Grease and Dielectric Compound D7AZ-19A331-A or equivalent meeting Ford specification ESE-M1C171-A to the O-rings. When installing the air lines, make sure the white air line is fully inserted into the fitting for correct installation.**

5. The installation is the reverse of the removal.

Solenoid Valve—Non-Functional

REMOVAL & INSTALLATION

> ✳ **WARNING**
>
> **Do not remove an air spring under any circumstances when there is pressure in the air spring. Do not remove any components sup-**

porting an air spring without either exhausting the air or providing support for the air spring to prevent vehicle damage or personal injury.

1. Raise and support the vehicle.
2. Remove the air line from the solenoid valve by depressing the red plastic retaining ring and pull the air line out of the solenoid.
3. Detach the solenoid valve electrical connector.

> ✳ **WARNING**
>
> **Remove any dirt or other debris from the air spring prior to removing the solenoid valve from the air spring.**

4. Remove the solenoid valve clip.
5. Hold the solenoid body from the side and rotate the solenoid valve out of the air spring to the first detent to release the air from the assembly.
6. Remove the retaining clip from the top of the air spring.
7. Compress the deflated air spring and remove it from the vehicle.
8. Remove the solenoid valve.

➡ **Be sure the new air spring solenoid is fully seated into both stages of the air spring. Check the solenoid valve O-rings for abrasion or cuts. Replace O-rings as required using air spring connector repair kit. Lightly apply Silicone Brake Caliper Grease and Dielectric Compound D7AZ-19A331-A or equivalent meeting Ford specification ESE-M1C171-A to the O-rings.**

9. The installation is the reverse of the removal.

Air Shocks

REMOVAL & INSTALLATION

> ✳ **WARNING**
>
> **The vehicle must be positioned on a suitable lifting device prior to deflating the air suspension system.**

1. Deflate the air suspension system
2. Raise and support the vehicle.
3. On driver's side air shock removal only, disconnect the top of the front height sensor from the upper frame bracket.
4. Remove the air shock lower nut and bolt.
5. Disconnect the air spring solenoid air line by compressing the quick connect locking ring and pulling out the air line.
6. Remove the air shock upper nut, grommet, and the air shock.
7. The installation is the reverse of the removal.

STEERING

Steering Wheel

REMOVAL & INSTALLATION

▶ See Figures 56 thru 63

✳✳ CAUTION

The Supplemental Inflatable Restraint (SIR) system must be disarmed before performing service around SIR system components or SIR system wiring. Failure to do so may cause accidental deployment of the air bag, resulting in unnecessary SIR system repairs and/or personal injury.

➡Before proceeding, make sure that a new steering wheel retaining bolt is available. Once removed the bolt loses its torque holding ability or retention capability and must not be reused.

1. Make sure that the front wheels are in the straight-ahead position.
2. Disconnect the negative battery cable(s).
3. Wait at least 1 minute before proceeding with the service procedure. This is the time required for the backup power supply to deplete its stored energy.
4. Remove the air bag module retaining bolt covers.
5. Remove air bag module retaining bolts and lift the air bag module from the steering wheel.
6. Detach the air bag sliding contact, horn and if equipped, the speed control electrical harness connectors and remove the air bag module.

✳✳ CAUTION

When carrying a live air bag, make sure the air bag and trim cover are pointed away from the body. In the unlikely event of an accidental deployment, the bag will then deploy with minimal chance if injury. When placing a live air bag on a bench or other surface, always face the bag and trim cover up, away from the surface. This will reduce the motion of the module if it is accidentally deployed.

7. Remove the steering wheel retaining bolt and discard.
8. Install Steering Wheel Puller T67-3600-A or equivalent and loosen the steering wheel from the steering column shaft.
9. Remove the steering wheel while routing the wires from the air bag sliding contact through the steering wheel.

To install:

➡If a new air bag sliding contact is being installed, remove the plastic lock tool after the intermediate shaft is connected to the steering gear.

10. Make sure the vehicle's front wheels are in the straight-ahead position.
11. Route the air bag sliding contact wire harness through the steering wheel opening at the three o'clock position. Position the steering wheel on the steering shaft so that the alignment marks on the wheel and shaft are aligned. Be sure the air bag sliding contact wiring is not pinched.
12. Install a new steering wheel retaining bolt and tighten the bolt to 23–33 ft. lbs. (31–48 Nm) on the 1997–98 F-250HD, F-350 and F-Super Duty and to 23–32 ft. lbs. (31–44 Nm) on all other models.
13. Connect the wire connectors for the horn, speed control and air bag module then position the air bag module on the steering wheel. Install and tighten the 4 air bag module retaining nuts to 35–50 inch lbs. (4.0–5.6 Nm) on 1997–98 F-250HD, F-350 and F-Super Duty models. Tighten the two air bag module retaining screws to 89–115 inch lbs. (10–13 Nm) on all other models.
14. Connect both battery cables, negative cable last.
15. Prove out the air bag system by turning the ignition key to the RUN position and visually monitoring the air bag indicator lamp in the instrument cluster. The indicator lamp should illuminate for approximately 6 seconds and

Fig. 56 Remove the air bag module retaining bolt covers

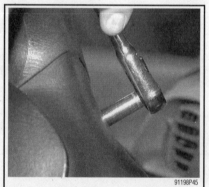
Fig. 57 Remove the air bag module retaining bolts

Fig. 58 Lift the air bag module from the steering wheel and . . .

Fig. 59 . . . detach the connectors on the air bag module and remove the module

Fig. 60 Always carry a live air bag module with the bag and trim cover facing away from your body

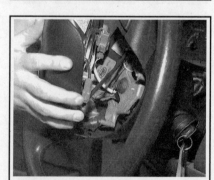
Fig. 61 Always place an air bag module on a table or other flat surface with the bag and trim cover pointing up

Fig. 62 Remove the steering wheel retaining bolt and . . .

Fig. 63 . . . install a suitable puller onto the steering wheel to remove the wheel

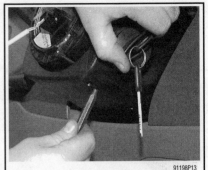

Fig. 64 Turn the ignition switch to the RUN position and push the lock cylinder release pin with a suitable punch while . . .

then turn off. If the indicator lamp does not illuminate, stays on, or flashes at any time, a fault has been detected by the air bag diagnostic monitor.

16. Check the steering wheel, horn and steering column for proper operation.
17. Road test the vehicle and check the speed control for proper operation.

Multi-Function Switch

REMOVAL & INSTALLATION

1997–98 F-250HD, F-350 and F-SuperDuty

1. Disconnect the negative battery cable.
2. Remove the 4 retaining screws from the lower column shroud and remove the upper and lower shrouds.
3. Remove the 2 retaining screws from the multi-function switch and unplug the 2 wiring connectors.
4. Remove the switch.
To install:
5. Install the multi-function switch.
6. Tighten the 2 retaining screws and attach the 2 electrical connectors.
7. Install the upper and lower column shrouds. Tighten the 4 retaining screws.
8. Connect the negative battery cable.

F-150, F-250, Expedition, Navigator and 1999–00 Super Duty Models

▶ See Figures 64 thru 70

1. Disconnect the negative battery cable.
2. Remove the ignition key and tumbler as follows:
   a. Turn the ignition switch to the RUN position.
   b. Push the lock cylinder release pin with a suitable punch while pulling out the lock cylinder.
3. If equipped, twist off the tilt wheel handle and remove.

Fig. 65 . . . pulling out the lock cylinder

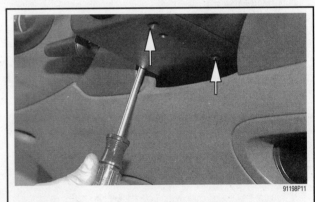

Fig. 66 Remove 3 steering column shroud retaining screws and . . .

Fig. 67 . . . remove the upper and . . .

Fig. 68 . . . lower steering column shrouds

Fig. 69 Remove the switch retaining screws, lift the switch assembly up and . . .

Fig. 70 . . . detach the switch electrical connectors to remove the switch

4. Remove 3 steering column shroud retaining screws and remove the upper and lower shrouds.

5. Remove 2 self-tapping screws that retain the combination switch to the steering column casting. Disengage the switch from the casting.

6. Detach the electrical connectors, being careful not to damage the locking tabs and the shift position indicator cable.

To install:

7. Connect the combination switch electrical harness connectors ensuring that the connectors are fully engaged. The wiring for the switch is to be routed under the shift position indicator cable.

8. Install the combination switch with 2 self-tapping screws. Tighten to 19–25 inch lbs. (2–3 Nm).

9. Install the upper and lower steering column shrouds. Install the retaining screws and tighten to 9 inch lbs. (1 Nm).

10. If equipped, install the tilt wheel handle ad tighten to 44 inch lbs. (5 Nm).

11. Install the ignition key and tumbler assembly.

12. Connect the negative battery cable.

13. Check the steering column and combination switch for proper operation.

Ignition Switch

REMOVAL & INSTALLATION

1. Disconnect the negative battery cable.

2. Remove the steering column shroud and lower the steering column.

3. Detach the ignition switch electrical harness connector.

4. Remove 2 nuts retaining the ignition switch to the steering column housing.

5. Lift the ignition switch upward to disengage the actuator rod from the switch and remove the switch.

To install:

➡**When installing the ignition switch, both the locking mechanism at the top of the column and the switch itself must be in theLOCK position for correct adjustment. To hold the mechanical parts of the column in the LOCK position, move the shift lever into PARK (with automatic transmissions) or REVERSE (with manual transmissions), turn the key to the LOCK position, and remove the key. New replacement switches, when received, are already pinned in the LOCK position by a metal shipping pin inserted in a locking hole on the side of the switch.**

6. Engage the actuator rod in the ignition switch.

7. Place the ignition switch on the steering column housing and loosely install 2 retaining nuts.

8. Move the switch up or down along the column to locate the mid-posi-

tion of the actuator rod lash, then tighten the retaining nuts to 47–64 inch lbs. (5–7 Nm).

9. Raise the steering column into position at instrument panel. Install steering column shroud.

10. Connect the negative battery cable.

11. Remove the locking pin, connect the battery cable, and verify that the engine will only crank in PARK and NEUTRAL.Also check to make certain that the start circuit cannot be actuated in the DRIVE and REVERSE positions.

Ignition Lock Cylinder

REMOVAL & INSTALLATION

With Functional Lock Cylinder

◆ **See Figures 71 and 72**

1. Disconnect the negative battery cable.

2. Detach the key warning chime connector.

3. Turn the key to the RUN position.

4. Place a ⅛ in. wire, pin, or small drift punch into the upper steering column shroud under the lock cylinder. Depress the retaining pin while pulling the lock cylinder out of the column housing.

To install:

5. Install the lock cylinder by turning the key to the RUN position and depressing the retaining clip.

6. Insert the lock cylinder until it is fully seated and aligned with the interlocking washer.

7. Turn the key to the OFF position, allowing the retaining pin to properly seat.

8. Install the 2 shroud halves and retaining screws.

9. Connect the negative battery cable.

10. Check for proper starting in PARK and NEUTRAL.

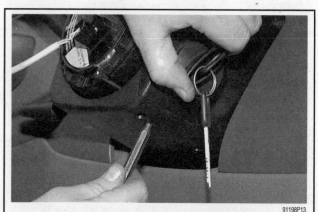

Fig. 71 Turn the ignition switch to the RUN position and push the lock cylinder release pin with a suitable punch while . . .

Fig. 72 . . . pulling out the lock cylinder

Non-Functional Lock Cylinder

◆ See Figures 73 and 74

➡This procedure should be used when the lock cylinder cannot be rotated due to a lost or broken key, or damage to the cylinder prohibiting the insertion of a new key.

1. Disconnect the negative battery cable.

✲✲ CAUTION

Follow the proper procedure to disarm the air bag, if equipped.

2. Remove the horn assembly or air bag.
3. Remove the steering wheel.
4. Remove the air bag clockspring, if equipped with air bag.
5. With a pair of pliers, twist the cap off the lock cylinder.
6. Through the access hole in the lower column shroud, use a small center punch and then with an ⅛ in. drill bit, drill out the retaining clip. Be careful not to drill deeper than ½ in.
7. Using a ⅜ in. drill bit, drill down the middle of the lock cylinder about 1¾ inches until the cylinder breaks away from the housing.
8. Remove the lock cylinder and clean out all metal shavings from the housing. Inspect the housing and replace if damaged.
   To install:
9. Install the lock drive gear, washer and retainer, if necessary.
10. Install the lock cylinder by turning the key to the RUN position and depressing the retaining clip.

11. Insert the lock cylinder until it is fully seated and aligned with the interlocking washer.
12. Turn the key to the OFF position. this allows the retaining pin to properly seat.
13. Connect the key warning chime electrical connector.
14. Install the air bag clockspring if equipped with an air bag. Make sure that the clockspring is properly aligned.
15. Install the steering wheel.
16. Install the air bag or horn assembly, as equipped.
17. Connect the negative battery cable.
18. Check for proper starting in PARK and NEUTRAL.

Steering Linkage

REMOVAL & INSTALLATION

◆ See Figures 75, 76 and 77

Pitman Arm

◆ See Figure 78

EXCEPT F-SUPER DUTY STRIPPED CHASSIS AND MOTOR HOME CHASSIS

1. Place the wheels in a straight-ahead position.
2. Disconnect the drag link at the Pitman arm. You'll need a puller such as a tie rod end remover.

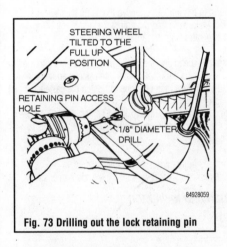

Fig. 73 Drilling out the lock retaining pin

Fig. 74 Breaking the cap away from the lock cylinder

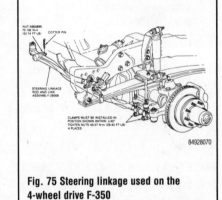

Fig. 75 Steering linkage used on the 4-wheel drive F-350

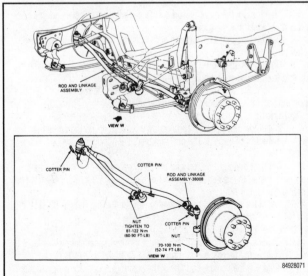

Fig. 76 Steering linkage used on F-Super Duty chassis/cab

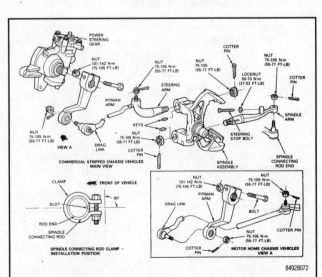

Fig. 77 Steering linkage for F-Super Duty stripped chassis and motor home chassis

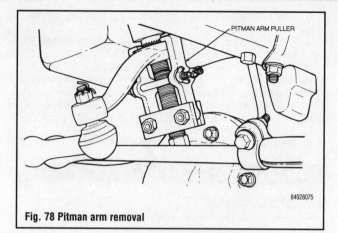

Fig. 78 Pitman arm removal

3. Remove the Pitman arm-to-gear nut and washer.
4. Matchmark the Pitman arm and gear housing for installation purposes.
5. Using a 2-jawed puller, remove the Pitman arm from the gear.
6. Installation is the reverse of removal. Align the matchmarks when installing the Pitman arm. Tighten the Pitman arm nut to 170–230 ft. lbs. (230–312 Nm); torque the drag link ball stud nut to 50–75 ft. lbs. (68–102 Nm), advancing the nut to align the cotter pin hole. Never back off the nut to align the hole.

F-SUPER DUTY STRIPPED CHASSIS MOTOR HOME CHASSIS

1. Matchmark the Pitman arm and sector shaft.
2. Disconnect the drag link from the Pitman arm.
3. Remove the bolt and nut securing the Pitman arm to the sector shaft.
4. Using a 2-jawed gear puller, remove the Pitman arm from the sector shaft.

To install:

5. Aligning the matchmarks, slide the Pitman arm onto the sector shaft. If the arm won't slide on easily, use a cold chisel to spread the separation. NEVER HAMMER THE ARM ONTO THE SHAFT! Hammering on the arm will damage the steering gear!
6. Install the nut and bolt. Tighten the nut to 220–300 ft. lbs. (298–407 Nm).
7. Connect the drag link.

Drag Link

EXCEPT RUBBERIZED BALL SOCKET LINKAGE

1. Place the wheels in a straight-ahead position.
2. Remove the cotter pins and rust from the drag link and tie rod ball studs.
3. Remove the drag link ball studs from the right-hand spindle and Pitman arm.
4. Remove the tie rod ball studs from the left-hand spindle and drag link.
5. Installation is the reverse of removal. Seat the studs in the tapered hole before tightening the nuts. This will avoid wrap-up of the rubber grommets during tightening of the nuts. Tighten the nuts to 70 ft. lbs. (95 Nm). Always use new cotter pins.
6. Have the front end alignment checked.

RUBBERIZED BALL SOCKET LINKAGE

1. Raise and support the front end on jackstands.
2. Place the wheels in the straight-ahead position.
3. Remove the nuts connecting the drag link ball studs to the connecting rod and Pitman arm.
4. Disconnect the drag link using a tie rod end remover.
5. Loosen the bolts on the adjuster clamp. Count the number of turns it take to remove the drag link from the adjuster.

To install:

6. Installation is the reverse of the removal procedure. Install the drag link with the same number of turns it took to remove it. Make certain that the wheels remain in the straight-ahead position during installation. Seat the studs in the tapered hole before tightening the nuts. This will avoid wrap-up of the rubber grommets during tightening of the nuts. Tighten the adjuster clamp nuts to 40 ft. lbs. (54 Nm). Tighten the ball stud nuts to 75 ft. lbs. (102 Nm).
7. Have the front end alignment checked.

Connecting Rod

1. Raise and support the front end on jackstands.
2. Place the wheels in the straight-ahead position.
3. Disconnect the connecting rod from the drag link by removing the nut and separating the two with a tie rod end remover.
4. Loosen the bolts on the adjusting sleeve clamps. Count the number of turns it takes to remove the connecting rod from the connecting rod from the adjuster sleeve and remove the rod.
5. Installation is the reverse of removal. Install the connecting rod the exact number of turns noted during removal. Tighten the tie rod nuts to 40 ft. lbs. (54 Nm); the ball stud nut to 75 ft. lbs. (102 Nm).
6. Have the front end alignment checked.

Tie Rod Ends

F-250HD/SD, F-350 AND F-SUPERDUTY

1. Raise and safely support the vehicle.
2. Place the front wheels in a straight-ahead position.
3. If necessary, remove the wheel and tire assembly.
4. Remove the cotter pin and castellated nut from the tie rod end at the wheel spindle or steering knuckle, as equipped. Discard the cotter pin.
5. Loosen the nuts on the adjusting sleeve clamps.
6. Using Pitman Arm Puller T64P-3590-F, or equivalent, separate the tie rod end
7. Remove the tie rod end from the adjusting sleeve. Count and record the number of turns required to remove the tie rod end from the adjusting sleeve for installation reference.

To install:

8. Install the tie rod end to the adjusting sleeve the same number of turns noted during removal. Make sure that the adjuster clamps are in the correct position and do not to rub or bind against the frame or steering components.
9. Keep the wheels straight ahead and install the tie rod end stud into the wheel spindle or steering knuckle, as equipped. Install the castellated nut and tighten to 51–73 ft. lbs. (70–100 Nm), then continue to tighten the castellated nut as needed to install a new cotter pin.
10. Tighten the adjusting sleeve clamp nuts to 30–42 ft. lbs. (40–57 Nm).
11. If removed, install the wheel and tire assembly. Torque the lug nuts to 100 ft. lbs. (135 Nm).
12. Lower the vehicle.
13. Check the alignment and adjust if not within specification.
14. Road test the vehicle and check for proper steering system operation.

F-150, F-250, EXPEDITION AND NAVIGATOR

▶ See Figures 79 thru 87

1. Raise and safely support the vehicle.
2. Remove the wheel and tire assembly.
3. Match mark the outer tie rod end to the adjusting sleeve and inner tie rod end for assembly reference.
4. Remove the outer tie rod end cotter pin and castellated nut. Discard the cotter pin.
5. Using Pitman Arm Puller T64P-3590-F or equivalent, separate the tie rod end from the wheel spindle or knuckle, as equipped.
6. Loosen the outer tie rod end jam nut. Turn the tie rod end and remove counting the amount of turns for assembly reference.

To install:

7. Install the new outer tie rod end by threading it into the adjusting sleeve the same amount of turns as the one removed. Do not tighten the jam nut at this point.
8. Connect the outer tie rod end to the wheel spindle or knuckle, as equipped. Install the castellated nut and tighten to 55–75 ft. lbs. (77–104 Nm). Install a new cotter pin.
9. Install the wheel and tire assembly. Torque the lug nuts to 83–112 ft. lbs. (113–153 Nm).
10. Lower the vehicle.
11. Check the toe adjustment and adjust if out of specification.
12. Tighten the tie rod end jam nut to 55–75 ft. lbs. (77–104 Nm).
13. Road test the vehicle and check the steering system for proper operation.

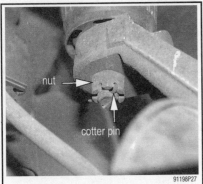

Fig. 79 The tie rod end is attached to the steering knuckle by a nut and cotter pin

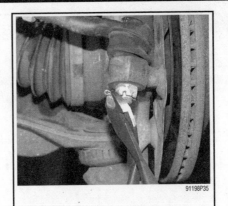

Fig. 80 Remove the cotter pin and the . . .

Fig. 81 . . . castellated nut on the tie rod end

Fig. 82 Attach a suitable puller to the tie rod end and . . .

Fig. 83 . . . tighten down the forcing screw until . . .

Fig. 84 . . . the tie rod end pops up out of the knuckle

Fig. 85 Loosen the outer tie rod end jam nut and . . .

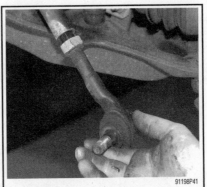

Fig. 86 . . . remove the tie rod end from the adjusting sleeve

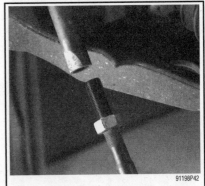

Fig. 87 Count the threads showing on the tie rod end

Inner Tie Rod End

F-150, F-250, EXPEDITION AND NAVIGATOR

1. Raise and safely support the vehicle.
2. Remove the wheel and tire assembly.
3. Match mark the inner tie rod end to the adjusting sleeve for assembly reference.
4. Remove the inner tie rod end cotter pin and castellated nut. Discard the cotter pin.
5. Using Pitman Arm Puller T64P-3590-F or equivalent, separate the inner tie rod end from the drag link.
6. Loosen the jam nut. Turn the inner tie rod end and remove counting the amount of turns for assembly reference.

To install:

7. Install the new inner tie rod end by threading it into the sleeve the same amount of turns as the one removed. Do not tighten the jam nut at this point.
8. Connect the inner tie rod end to the drag link and install the castellated nut. Tighten the nut to 55–75 ft. lbs. (77–104 Nm). Install a new cotter pin.
9. Install the wheel and tire assembly. Torque the lug nuts to 83–112 ft. lbs. (113–153 Nm).
10. Lower the vehicle.
11. Check the toe adjustment and adjust if out of specification.
12. Tighten the inner tie rod end jam nut to 55–75 ft. lbs. (77–104 Nm).
13. Road test the vehicle and check the steering system for proper operation.

Power Steering Gear

REMOVAL & INSTALLATION

1997–98 F-250HD, F-350 and F-Super Duty Except Stripped Chassis and Motorhome

♦ See Figure 88

1. Raise and support the front end on jackstands.
2. Place the wheels in the straight-ahead position.
3. Place a drain pan under the gear and disconnect the pressure and return lines. Cap the openings.
4. Remove the splash shield from the flex coupling.
5. Disconnect the flex coupling at the gear.
6. Matchmark and remove the Pitman arm from the sector shaft.
7. Support the steering gear and remove the mounting bolts.
8. Remove the steering gear. It may be necessary to work it free of the flex coupling.

To install:

9. Place the splash shield on the steering gear lugs.
10. Slide the flex coupling into place on the steering shaft. Make sure the steering wheel spokes are still horizontal.
11. Center the steering gear input shaft with the indexing flat facing downward.
12. Slide the steering gear input shaft into the flex coupling and into place on the frame side rail. Install the flex coupling bolt and torque it to 30–42 ft. lbs. (41–57 Nm).
13. Install the gear mounting bolts and torque them to 65 ft. lbs. (88 Nm).
14. Make sure that the wheels are still straight-ahead and install the Pitman arm. Tighten the nut to 170–288 ft. lbs. (230–390 Nm).
15. Connect the pressure, then, the return lines. Tighten the pressure line to 25 ft. lbs. (34 Nm).
16. Snap the flex coupling shield into place.
17. Fill the steering reservoir.
18. Run the engine and turn the steering wheel lock-to-lock several times to expel air. Check for leaks.

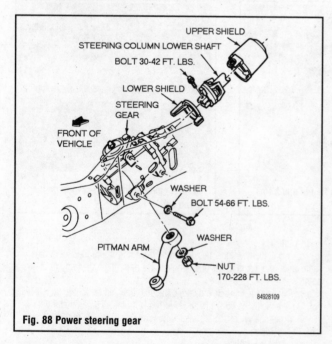

Fig. 88 Power steering gear

1997–98 F-Super Duty Stripped Chassis and Motorhomes

♦ See Figures 89 and 90

1. Raise and support the front end on jackstands.
2. Thoroughly clean all connections.
3. Place a drain pan under the area.

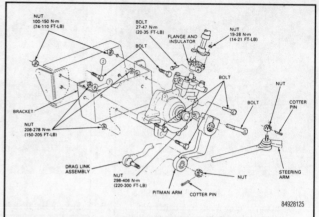

Fig. 89 Steering gear installation on F-Super Duty motor home chassis models

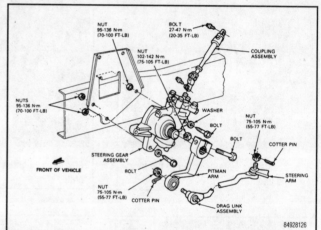

Fig. 90 Steering gear installation on F-Super Duty stripped chassis models

4. Disconnect the hydraulic lines at the gear. Cap all openings at once.
5. Remove the retaining bolt and nut and disconnect the Pitman arm from the sector shaft.
6. Remove the bolt and nut securing the input shaft and U-joint.
7. Support the gear and remove the gear-to-frame bolts and nuts.

To install:

8. Position the gear on the frame and install the bolts and nuts. Tighten the nuts to 150–200 ft. lbs. (203–271 Nm).
9. Install the U-joint bolt and nut. Tighten the nut to 50–70 ft. lbs. (68–95 Nm).
10. Install the Pitman arm.

❊❊❊ CAUTION

Never hammer the Pitman shaft onto the sector shaft! Hammering will damage the gear. Use a cold chisel to separate the Pitman arm opening.

11. Install the bolt and nut. Tighten the nut to 220–300 ft. lbs. (298–407 Nm).
12. Connect the hydraulic lines, fill the reservoir, run the engine and check for leaks.

F-150, F-250, Expedition and Navigator

1. Raise and safely support the vehicle.
2. If equipped, remove 6 retaining bolts securing the skid plate and remove the skid plate.
3. Remove 3 screws and 5 push clips retaining the lower radiator air deflector and remove.
4. Remove the pitman arm (steering sector shaft arm) cotter pin and castellated nut from the drag link.

5. Using Pitman Arm Puller T65P-3590-F or equivalent, separate the pitman arm from the drag link.

6. Remove the dust cover from the steering shaft valve housing.

7. Remove the intermediate shaft pinch bolt and slide the shaft off the steering gear input shaft.

8. Disconnect the power steering pressure hoses at the steering gear.

9. Remove 3 steering gear-to-frame rail retaining bolts and remove the steering gear.

10. If replacing or servicing the steering gear, match mark the sector shaft arm to the sector shaft and remove the steering gear sector shaft arm retaining nut and lock washer. Remove the sector shaft arm using Pitman Arm Puller T65P-3590-F, or equivalent.

To install:

11. If removed, install the steering gear sector shaft arm to the sector shaft aligning the match marks made during removal. Install the retaining nut and lock washer and tighten to 170–228 ft. lbs. (234–316 Nm).

12. Mount the steering gear in position. Install 3 retaining bolts and tighten to 50–68 ft. lbs. (68–92 Nm).

13. Connect the power steering pressure hoses to the steering gear using new seals, if necessary.

14. Slide the intermediate shaft on the steering gear input shaft and install the shaft pinch bolt. Tighten the pinch bolt to 30–42 ft. lbs. (41–57 Nm).

15. Install the dust cover over the steering shaft valve housing.

16. Connect the pitman arm to the drag link. Install the castellated nut and tighten to 57–76 ft. lbs. (77–104 Nm). Install a new cotter pin.

17. Install the radiator air deflector and secure with 3 retaining screws and 5 push clips.

18. Install the skid plate and secure with 6 retaining bolts.

19. Lower the vehicle.

20. Fill and bleed the power steering system.

21. Road test the vehicle and check the steering system for proper operation.

1999–00 F-Super Duty Models Except Motorhome Chassis

1. Remove the air cleaner assembly.

2. Disengage the steering coupling shield from the line fitting and slide upwards on the steering shaft.

3. Make sure the steering column is locked.

4. Remove the intermediate shaft-to-gear pinch bolt. Turn the steering wheel as necessary to access the bolt.

5. Disconnect the power steering lines.

6. Raise and support the vehicle.

7. Remove the drag link cotter pin and nut and disconnect the drag link.

8. Remove the bolts and the steering gear.

9. Remove the steering gear sector shaft arm.

10. The installation is the reverse of the removal.

1999–00 F-Super Duty Motorhome Chassis

1. Drain the power steering reservoir.

2. Remove the steering shaft coupler pinch bolt.

3. Slide the coupler upward and away from the steering gear.

4. Disconnect the two power steering lines.

5. Remove the steering link cotter pin and retaining nut.

6. Remove the steering link from the steering gear sector shaft.

7. Remove the three nuts and bolts and remove the steering gear.

8. The installation is the reverse of the removal.

Power Steering Pump

REMOVAL & INSTALLATION

5.8L, 7.3L, and 7.5L Engines

EXCEPT F-SUPER DUTY STRIPPED CHASSIS AND MOTOR HOME MODELS

1. Disconnect the return line at the pump and drain the fluid into a container.

2. Disconnect the pressure line from the pump.

3. Loosen the pump bracket nuts and remove the drive belt.

4. Remove the nuts and lift out the pump/bracket assembly.

5. If a new pump or bracket is being installed, remove the pulley from the pump; use a press and adapters.

To install:

6. Position the steering pump on the engine and install the mounting fasteners. Tighten the fasteners to the following specifications:
- Pump-to-adjustment bracket—45 ft. lbs. (61 Nm)
- Support bracket-to-engine (5.8L)—65 ft. lbs. (88 Nm)
- Support bracket-to-water pump housing (5.8L)—45 ft. lbs. (61 Nm)
- Pressure line-to-fitting—29 ft. lbs. (39 Nm)
- Adjustment bracket-to-support bracket:
- 5.8L—45 ft. lbs. (61 Nm)
- 7.3L and 7.5L—Long bolt—65 ft. lbs. (88 Nm)
- Short bolt—45 ft. lbs. (61 Nm)

7. Install the accessory drive belt.

8. Attach the fluid lines to the pump, then bleed the hydraulic steering system.

F-SUPER DUTY STRIPPED CHASSIS AND MOTOR HOME MODELS

1. Disconnect the pressure line from the pump and tie up the ends of both hoses in a raised position. Cap the openings.

2. Loosen the pump pivot and adjusting bolts and remove the drive belt.

3. Remove the bolts and lift out the pump.

To install:

4. Install the pump in the vehicle.

5. Install the pivot bolt and nut finger-tight.

6. Install the accessory drive belt, then adjust the belt tension.

7. Tighten the mounting (pivot and adjusting) bolts to 30–45 ft. lbs. (41–61 Nm).

8. Connect the hoses, then refill the reservoir.

9. Bleed the system, then run the engine and check for leaks.

4.2L, 4.6L, 5.4L and 6.8L Engines

1. Remove the engine air cleaner assembly.

2. Remove the accessory drive belt.

3. Disconnect the power steering reservoir pump hose from the power steering pump and drain the fluid into a large catch pan.

4. Disconnect the power steering pressure hose from the steering gear.

5. Remove the 2 top power steering pump bolts.

6. Raise and safely support the front of the vehicle on jackstands.

7. Remove the 2 lower pump bolts and remove the power steering pump from the engine.

8. Lower the vehicle.

9. If necessary, remove the power steering pressure hose fitting from the pump by holding the pump in a vise.

10. If necessary, remove the power steering pump pulley. Hold the Steering Pump Pulley Remover T69L-10300-B, or equivalent and rotate the forcing bolt to remove the pulley from the pump.

To install:

11. If the pulley was removed, thread the forcing bolt into the power steering pump and turn the steering pump pulley replacer tool, or equivalent, to install the pump pulley.

12. Install a new power steering Teflon® seal onto the pressure hose fitting by stretching the Teflon® seal over the Teflon® seal replacer set D90P-3517-A, or equivalent, until it is large enough to slip over the tube nut.

13. Install the power steering pressure hose, then tighten the fitting to 20–30 ft. lbs. (27–41 Nm).

14. Position the steering pump and loosely install the 4 mounting bolts.

15. Tighten the 2 upper mounting bolts to 15–20 ft. lbs. (20–30 Nm).

16. Raise and support the front of the vehicle safely on jackstands.

17. Tighten the 2 lower mounting bolts to 15–20 ft. lbs. (20–30 Nm).

18. Lower the vehicle.

19. Install the other power steering pressure hose to the steering gear, then tighten to 13–17 ft. lbs. (17–23 Nm).

20. Connect the power steering reservoir pump hose to the power steering pump.

21. Fill and bleed the hydraulic power steering system.

BLEEDING

1. Fill the power steering pump reservoir.
2. Raise the front wheel and tire assemblies off the ground and support the vehicle with jack stands.
3. Disable the ignition system.
4. Turn the steering wheel lock to lock while cranking the engine. While cranking, add power steering fluid until the level in the reservoir stays constant.

➡**Do not hold the steering against the lock for more than 5 seconds at a time or damage to the power steering pump may result.**

5. Check the fluid level and add if necessary.
6. Restore the ignition system.
7. Start the engine and allow it to idle for several minutes.
8. Remove the jack stands.
9. Lower the vehicle.
10. Rotate the steering wheel from lock to lock several times.
11. Turn the engine OFF and check the fluid level again.
12. Road test the vehicle and check for proper power steering system operation.

1997-98 F-250HD, F-350 AND F-SUPER DUTY TORQUE SPECIFICATIONS

Components	English	Metric
Air bag retaining screws	90-107 inch lbs.	10-14 Nm
Front Suspension (4 X 2)		
F-250HD and F-350		
Axle pivot bolt retainer nut-to-axle pivot bracket	110-148 ft. lbs.	149-201 Nm
Axle pivot bracket-to-frame bolt	65-87 ft. lbs.	88-118 Nm
Axle-to-radius arm nut and bolt	188-254 ft. lbs.	255-345 Nm
Axle-to-upper ball joint pinch bolt	50-68 ft. lbs.	68-92 Nm
Coil spring-to-lower retainer nut	83-112 ft. lbs.	112-152 Nm
Coil spring upper retainer-to-spring seat nut and bolt	13-17 ft. lbs.	17-23 Nm
Lower ball joint-to-axle nut	83-112 ft. lbs.	112-152 Nm
Lower shock absorber retainer nut	44-59 ft. lbs.	60-80 Nm
Lower spring retainer-to-lower spring seat	99 ft. lbs.	133 Nm
Radius arm retaining bolt-to-radius arm nut	83-112 ft. lbs.	112-152 Nm
Radius arm pivot bolt-to-radius arm bracket	77-110 ft. lbs.	104-149 Nm
Radius arm bracket-to-frame	60 ft. lbs.	80 Nm
Shock absorber-to-shock tower nut	30 ft. lbs.	40 Nm
Stabilizer bar link-to-bracket	52-74 ft. lbs.	71-100 Nm
Stabilizer bar link nut-to-stabilizer bar	53-80 ft. lbs.	72-108 Nm
Stabilizer bar retainer bracket-to-frame	25-34 ft. lbs.	34-46 Nm
Upper shock absorber-to-spring seat nut	25-35 ft. lbs.	34-48 Nm
F-Super Duty		
Axle-to-leaf spring U-bolt bolt	157-211 ft. lbs.	213-287 Nm
Leaf spring-to-frame nut	125-170 ft. lbs.	170-230 Nm
Leaf spring-to-rear hanger bracket	157-211 ft. lbs.	213-287 Nm
Lower shock absorber retainer nut	120-150 ft. lbs.	163-203 Nm
Stabilizer bar link-to-bracket	39-53 ft. lbs.	53-72 Nm
Stabilizer bar link nut-to-stabilizer bar	52-74 ft. lbs.	71-100 Nm
Stabilizer bar retainer bracket-to-frame	15-24 ft. lbs.	21-33 Nm
Track bar retaining nuts and bolts	35-46 ft. lbs.	47-63 Nm
Track bar bracket-to-frame	120-150 ft. lbs.	163-203 Nm
Upper shock absorber-to-spring seat nut	39-53 ft. lbs.	53-72 Nm
Front Suspension (4 X 4)		
F-250HD		
Front spring-to-axle U-bolts	83-113 ft. lbs.	113-153 Nm
Front spring-to-spring hanger nut	109-148 ft. lbs.	149-201 Nm
Front spring-to-shackle nut	109-148 ft. lbs.	149-201 Nm
Front spring shackle-to-frame	125-170 ft. lbs.	170-230 Nm
Shock absorber-to-spring plate spacer nut	44-59 ft. lbs.	60-80 Nm
Shock absorber-to-frame bolts	52-74 ft. lbs.	70-100 Nm
F-350 and F-Super Duty		
Front spring-to-spring bracket	120-150 ft. lbs.	163-203 Nm
Front spring-to-spring shackle	120-150 ft. lbs.	163-203 Nm
Front spring shackle-to-frame nut	126-169 ft. lbs.	170-230 Nm
Shock absorber-to-shock bracket nut	44-59 ft. lbs.	60-80 Nm
Shock absorber-to-spring spacer nut	51-67 ft. lbs.	68-92 Nm
Stabilizer bar-to-link	36-50 ft. lbs.	48-68 Nm
Stabilizer bar link-to-bracket nut	15-24 ft. lbs.	21-33 Nm
Stabilizer bar link-to-bracket	36-50 ft. lbs.	48-68 Nm
Track bar retaining nuts and bolts	120-150 ft. lbs.	163-203 Nm
Power steering pump		
Hose fittings	25-40 ft. lbs.	34-54 Nm
Pump retaining bolts		
CII pump	30-41 ft. lbs.	40-55 Nm
ZF pump	21-30 ft. lbs.	28-41 Nm

91198C01

1997-98 F-250HD, F-350 AND F-SUPER DUTY TORQUE SPECIFICATIONS

Components	English	Metric
Rear suspension		
Leaf spring-to-axle U-bolt nut		
F-250HD, F-350	142-190 ft. lbs.	192-258 Nm
F-Super Duty	189-254 ft. lbs.	255-345 Nm
Leaf spring-to-front bracket nut and bolt		
F-250HD, F-350 (except chassis cab)	142-190 ft. lbs.	192-258 Nm
F-350 chassis cab	157-212 ft. lbs.	213-288 Nm
F-Super Duty	251-339 ft. lbs.	340-460 Nm
Leaf spring-to-rear shackle nut and bolt		
F-250HD, F-350	83-113 ft. lbs.	113-153 Nm
F-Super Duty	157-212 ft. lbs.	213-288 Nm
Rear shackle-to-frame mounted bracket nut and bolt		
F-250HD, F-350 (except chassis cab)	57-75 ft. lbs.	77-103 Nm
F-350 chassis cab and F-Super Duty	157-212 ft. lbs.	213-288 Nm
Shock absorber-to-axle bolt	38-54 ft. lbs.	52-73 Nm
Shock absorber-to-frame bolt	38-54 ft. lbs.	52-73 Nm
Stabilizer bar-to-axle nut	30-40 ft. lbs.	41-54 Nm
Stabilizer bar-to-axle bolt	25-34 ft. lbs.	34-46 Nm
Stabilizer bar bracket-to-axle nut	30-40 ft. lbs.	41-54 Nm
Stabilizer bar-to-axle nut	25-34 ft. lbs.	34-46 Nm
Stabilizer bar link bracket-to-frame nut and bolt	18-23 ft. lbs.	24-31 Nm
Stabilizer bar link-to-bracket nut	41-63 ft. lbs.	55-85 Nm
Stabilizer bar link-to-frame nut	41-63 ft. lbs.	55-85 Nm
Stabilizer bar link-to-stabilizer bar nut	18-23 ft. lbs.	24-31 Nm
Steering gear retaining bolts	54-66 ft. lbs.	73-90 Nm
Steering linkage		
Adjusting sleeve clamp nuts	30-42 ft. lbs.	40-57 Nm
Idler arm-to-sector shaft retaining nut	51-73 ft. lbs.	70-100 Nm
Pitman arm retaining nut	170-228 ft. lbs.	230-310 Nm
Tie-rod end-to-steering knuckle nuts	52-74 ft. lbs.	70-100 Nm
Steering wheel center nut	23-32 ft. lbs.	31-44 Nm
Wheel lug nuts	126-170 ft. lbs.	170-230 Nm

F-150, F-250, EXPEDITION AND NAVIGATOR TORQUE SPECIFICATIONS

Components	English	Metric
Air bag retaining screws	89-115 inch lbs.	10-13 Nm
Front Suspension (4 X 2)		
Lower arm retaining nut	121-148 ft. lbs.	164-200 Nm
Lower ball joint nut	83-112 ft. lbs.	113-153 Nm
Lower shock absorber nut	22-29 ft. lbs.	30-40 Nm
Stabilizer bar link nut-to-stabilizer bar	15-20 ft. lbs.	20-30 Nm
Stabilizer bar retainer bracket-to-frame	19-26 ft. lbs.	26-35 Nm
Upper arm nut	84-112 ft. lbs.	113-153 Nm
Upper ball joint nut	50-67 ft. lbs.	68-92 Nm
Upper shock absorber nut	42-46 ft. lbs.	57-63 Nm
Front Suspension (4 X 4)		
Axle hub nut	188-254 ft. lbs.	255-345 Nm
Lower arm retaining bolts	121-147 ft. lbs.	164-200 Nm
Lower ball joint nut	83-112 ft. lbs.	113-153 Nm
Lower shock absorber nut	57-76 ft. lbs.	77-103 Nm
Stabilizer bar link nut-to-stabilizer bar	15-20 ft. lbs.	20-30 Nm
Stabilizer bar retainer bracket-to-frame	19-26 ft. lbs.	26-35 Nm
Torsion bar crossmember support bolts	29-40 ft. lbs.	40-54 Nm
Torsion bar crossmember support nuts	39-53 ft. lbs.	53-72 Nm
Upper arm nut	84-112 ft. lbs.	113-153 Nm
Upper ball joint nut	57-76 ft. lbs.	77-103 Nm
Upper shock absorber nut	22-29 ft. lbs.	30-40 Nm

91198C02

F-150, F-250, EXPEDITION AND NAVIGATOR TORQUE SPECIFICATIONS

Components	English	Metric
Power steering pump		
Hose fittings	13-17 ft. lbs.	17-23 Nm
Pump retaining bolts	15-20 ft. lbs.	20-30 Nm
Rear suspension		
Leaf spring-to-axle U-bolt nut	73-97 ft. lbs.	98-132 Nm
Leaf spring-to-frame	157-212 ft. lbs.	213-288 Nm
Lower arm-to-axle bolt	94-127 ft. lbs.	128-172 Nm
Lower arm-to-frame bolt	94-127 ft. lbs.	128-172 Nm
Rear shackle-to-frame mounted bracket nut and bolt	73-97 ft. lbs.	98-132 Nm
Shock absorber-to-axle bolt	63-84 ft. lbs.	86-114 Nm
Shock absorber-to-frame bolt	63-84 ft. lbs.	86-114 Nm
Stabilizer bar retainer bracket-to-axle bolt)	43-57 ft. lbs.	55-75 Nm
Stabilizer bar-to-frame nut	63-84 ft. lbs.	86-114 Nm
Stabilizer bar link-to-frame nut	63-84 ft. lbs.	86-114 Nm
Stabilizer bar link-to-stabilizer bar nut	63-84 ft. lbs.	86-114 Nm
Upper arm-to-axle bolt	94-127 ft. lbs.	128-172 Nm
Upper arm-to-frame bolts	94-127 ft. lbs.	128-172 Nm
Steering gear retaining bolts	50-67 ft. lbs.	68-92 Nm
Steering linkage		
Center link retaining nut	57-76 ft. lbs.	77-103 Nm
Drag link-to-inner tie rod retaining nut	57-76 ft. lbs.	77-103 Nm
Drag link-to-steering sector shaft retaining nut	57-76 ft. lbs.	77-103 Nm
Drag link-to-idler arm retaining nut	57-76 ft. lbs.	77-103 Nm
Idler arm-to-frame bolt	126-169 ft. lbs.	170-230 Nm
Steering gear sector shaft arm retaining nut	173-233 ft. lbs.	234-316 Nm
Tie rod jam nut	57-76 ft. lbs.	77-103 Nm
Tie-rod end-to-steering knuckle nuts	57-76 ft. lbs.	77-103 Nm
Steering wheel center nut	23-32 ft. lbs.	31-44 Nm
Wheel lug nuts	83-112 ft. lbs.	113-153 Nm

1999-00 F-SUPER DUTY MODELS TORQUE SPECIFICATIONS

Components	English	Metric
Air bag retaining screws	90-107 inch lbs.	10-14 Nm
Front Suspension (4 X 2)		
Axle pivot bolt retainer nut-to-axle pivot bracket	130 ft. lbs.	170 Nm
Axle pivot bracket nut-to-frame	60 ft. lbs.	80 Nm
Lower shock absorber retainer nut	60 ft. lbs.	80 Nm
Lower spring retainer-to-lower spring seat	99 ft. lbs.	133 Nm
Radius arm retaining bolt-to-radius arm nut	295 ft. lbs.	400 Nm
Radius arm pivot bolt-to-radius arm bracket	185 ft. lbs.	250 Nm
Radius arm bracket-to-frame	60 ft. lbs.	80 Nm
Shock absorber-to-shock tower nut	30 ft. lbs.	40 Nm
Stabilizer bar link nut-to-lower spring seat	60 ft. lbs.	80 Nm
Stabilizer bar link nut-to-stabilizer bar	60 ft. lbs.	80 Nm
Stabilizer bar bracket-to-frame	36 ft. lbs.	43 Nm
Upper spindle pinch bolt nut-to-frame	60 ft. lbs.	80 Nm
Upper spring retainer bolt-to-spring/shock tower	26 ft. lbs.	35 Nm
Front Suspension (4 X 4)		
Front spring-to-axle U-bolts	99 ft. lbs.	133 Nm
Front spring-to-spring hanger nut	259 ft. lbs.	350 Nm
Front spring-to-shackle nut	185 ft. lbs.	250 Nm
Hub and bearing-to-knuckle nuts	55 ft. lbs.	74 Nm
Lower ball joint nut	101 ft. lbs.	136 Nm
Shock absorber-to-shock bracket nut	76 ft. lbs.	103 Nm
Shock absorber-to-shock spacer nut	76 ft. lbs.	103 Nm
Shock absorber-to-frame bolts	76 ft. lbs.	103 Nm
Shackle bracket-to-frame bolts	65 ft. lbs.	87 Nm

1999-00 F-SUPER DUTY MODELS TORQUE SPECIFICATIONS

Components	English	Metric
Front Suspension (4 X 4)-cont'd		
Spring hanger-to-frame bolts	76 ft. lbs.	103 Nm
Spring shackle-to-frame nut	185 ft. lbs.	250 Nm
Stabilizer bar bracket-to-frame bolts	35 ft. lbs.	47 Nm
Stabilizer bar-to-spring spacer bolts	35 ft. lbs.	47 Nm
Stabilizer bar-to-axle assembly bracket bolts	35 ft. lbs.	47 Nm
Stabilizer bar link nut-to-stabilizer bar	60 ft. lbs.	80 Nm
Stabilizer bar link-to-bracket nut	60 ft. lbs.	80 Nm
Trackbar-to-upper mounting bracket nut	129 ft. lbs.	174 Nm
Trackbar-to-lower mounting bracket nut	129 ft. lbs.	174 Nm
Upper ball joint nut	101 ft. lbs.	136 Nm
Power steering pump		
Hose fittings	26 ft. lbs.	35 Nm
Pump retaining bolts		
CII pump	60 ft. lbs.	80 Nm
CIII pump	19 ft. lbs.	26 Nm
Rear suspension		
Leaf spring-to-axle U-bolt nut	185 ft. lbs.	250 Nm
Leaf spring-to-front spring hanger bracket nut and bolt	185 ft. lbs.	250 Nm
Leaf spring-to-rear shackle nut and bolt	185 ft. lbs.	250 Nm
Rear shackle-to-frame mounted bracket nut and bolt	185 ft. lbs.	250 Nm
Shock absorber-to-axle bolt		
Dana axle	46 ft. lbs.	62 Nm
Ford axle	35 ft. lbs.	47 Nm
Shock absorber-to-frame bolt	46 ft. lbs.	62 Nm
Stabilizer bar retainer bracket-to-axle bolt (Dana axle)	30 ft. lbs.	40 Nm
Stabilizer bar retainer bracket-to-axle U-bolt (Ford axle)	35 ft. lbs.	47 Nm
Stabilizer bar link-to-frame nut	52 ft. lbs.	70 Nm
Stabilizer bar link-to-stabilizer bar nut	52 ft. lbs.	70 Nm
Steering gear retaining bolts	45 ft. lbs.	60 Nm
Steering linkage		
Adjusting sleeve clamp nuts	41 ft. lbs.	55 Nm
Drag link retaining nut	67 ft. lbs.	90 Nm
Steering gear sector shaft arm retaining nut	200 ft. lbs.	270 Nm
Tie-rod end-to-steering knuckle nuts	67 ft. lbs.	90 Nm
Steering wheel center nut	23-32 ft. lbs.	31-44 Nm
Wheel lug nuts	148 ft. lbs.	200 Nm

91198C03

91198C04

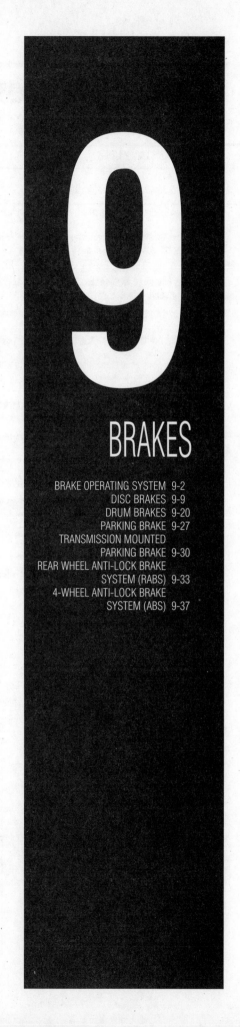

9

BRAKES

BRAKE OPERATING SYSTEM

Brake Light Switch

REMOVAL & INSTALLATION

1997–98 F-250HD, F-350 and F-Super Duty

1. Lift the locking tab on the switch connector and disconnect the wiring.
2. Remove the hairpin retainer, slide the stop lamp switch, pushrod and nylon washer off of the pedal. Remove the washer, then the switch by sliding it up or down.

➡ On trucks equipped with speed control, the spacer washer is replaced by the dump valve adapter washer.

3. To install the switch, position it so that the U-shaped side is nearest the pedal and directly over/under the pin.
4. Slide the switch up or down, trapping the master cylinder pushrod and bushing between the switch side plates.
5. Push the switch and pushrod assembly firmly towards the brake pedal arm. Assemble the outside white plastic washer to the pin and install the hairpin retainer.

✳✳ CAUTION

Don't substitute any other type of retainer. Use only the Ford specified hairpin retainer.

6. Assemble the connector on the switch.
7. Check stop lamp operation.

✳✳ CAUTION

Make sure that the stop lamp switch wiring has sufficient travel during a full pedal stroke!

F-150, F-250, Expedition and Navigator; 1999–00 F-250SD, F-350, and F-Super Duty Models

▶ See Figure 1

1. Disconnect the negative battery cable.
2. Disconnect the brake pedal position switch.
3. Remove the self-locking pin.
4. Remove the brake pedal position switch from the brake master cylinder push rod.
5. Remove the brake master cylinder push rod spacer.
6. Remove the brake master cylinder push rod bushing.
7. The installation is the reverse of the removal.

Master Cylinder

REMOVAL & INSTALLATION

1997–98 F-250HD, F-350 and F-SuperDuty

▶ See Figure 2

1. With the engine OFF, depress the brake pedal several times to expel any vacuum.
2. Disconnect the fluid level warning switch wire.
3. Disconnect the hydraulic system brake lines at the master cylinder.
4. Remove the master cylinder retaining nuts and remove the master cylinder.

To install:
5. Position the master cylinder assembly on the booster and install the retaining nuts. Tighten the nuts to 18–25 ft. lbs. (25–34 Nm).
6. Connect the hydraulic brake system lines to the master cylinder.
7. Connect the wiring.
8. Bleed the master cylinder.

F-150, F-250, Expedition and Navigator

▶ See Figures 3 thru 8

1. Disconnect the negative battery cable.
2. Detach the fluid level electrical harness connector from the master cylinder reservoir.
3. If equipped with speed control, detach the brake pressure switch electrical harness connector.
4. Disconnect and plug 2 brake lines at the brake master cylinder ports.
5. If the vehicle is equipped with rear anti-lock brakes, remove 2 retaining nuts and position the RABS valve out of the way using care not to damage the brake lines.
6. Remove the 2 brake master cylinder retaining nuts and remove the master cylinder.

To install:
7. Bench bleed the brake master cylinder before installation.
8. Place the brake master cylinder to the power brake booster. Install 2 retaining nuts and tighten to 21 ft. lbs. (29 Nm).
9. If equipped, install the RABS valve and 2 retaining nuts. Tighten to 15–21 ft. lbs. (21–29 Nm).
10. Unplug and connect 2 brake lines to the brake master cylinder ports and tighten the fittings to 11–15 ft. lbs. (15–20 Nm).
11. If equipped, connect the brake pressure switch electrical harness connector.
12. Connect the electrical harness connector to the low fluid level warning switch.

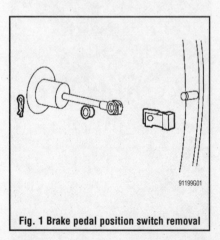

Fig. 1 Brake pedal position switch removal

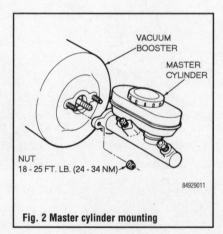

Fig. 2 Master cylinder mounting

Fig. 3 Use a suitable size flare nut wrench to . .

Fig. 4 . . . loosen the brake line fittings at the master cylinder

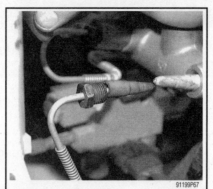

Fig. 5 Plug the brake lines and inlet ports of the master cylinder

Fig. 6 Remove the 2 retaining nuts and position the RABS valve out of the way

Fig. 7 Remove the 2 retaining nuts and . . .

Fig. 8 . . . remove the master cylinder from the brake booster

13. Fill the brake master cylinder with clean DOT 3 or equivalent brake fluid from a closed container.
14. Bleed the entire brake system following the proper procedure.
15. Road test the vehicle and check for proper brake system operation.

1999–00 F-250SD, F-350 and F-Super Duty

EXCEPT HYDRO-MAX

1. Disconnect the negative battery cable.
2. Remove the air cleaner housing.
3. Detach the fluid level sensor connector.
4. Detach the brake pressure switch connector, if so equipped.

5. Disconnect the brake tubes.
6. Remove the bolts retaining the power steering tubes to the bracket.
7. Remove the brake master cylinder nuts.
8. Remove the power steering tube retaining bracket.
9. Remove the brake master cylinder.
10. The installation is the reverse of the removal.

WITH HYDRO-MAX

> ❉❉ **WARNING**
>
> Do not depress the brake pedal while the hydraulic fluid supply line is disconnected. The inlet pressure port check ball may be dislodged which will result in a non-functional backup system.

1. Disconnect the negative battery cable.
2. Remove the support bracket bolt and nut.
3. Disconnect the brake tubes.
4. Remove the ground wire nut and the ground wire.
5. Remove the four master cylinder retaining nuts.
6. Remove the master cylinder.
7. The installation is the reverse of the removal.

BENCH BLEEDING

> ❉❉ **WARNING**
>
> All new master cylinders should be bench bled prior to installation. Bleeding a new master cylinder on the vehicle is not a good idea. With air trapped inside, the master cylinder piston may bottom in the bore and possibly cause internal damage.

1. Secure the master cylinder in a bench vise using soft jaws.
2. Remove the master cylinder reservoir cap.
3. Manufacture or purchase bleeding tubes and install them on the master cylinder as illustrated.
4. Fill the master cylinder reservoir with clean, fresh brake fluid until the level is within 0.25 in. of the reservoir top.

➡Ensure the bleeding tubes are below the level of the brake fluid, otherwise air may get into the system making your bleeding efforts ineffective.

5. Use a blunt tipped rod (a long socket extension works well) to slowly depress the master cylinder piston. Make sure the piston travels full its full stroke.
6. As the piston is depressed, bubbles will come out of the bleeding tubes. Continue depressing and releasing the piston until all bubbles cease.
7. Refill the master cylinder with fluid.
8. Remove the bleeding tubes.
9. Install the master cylinder reservoir cap.
10. Install the master cylinder on the vehicle.

Power Brake Booster

REMOVAL & INSTALLATION

F-150, F-250, Expedition and Navigator

▶ **See Figure 9**

1. Remove the master cylinder.
2. Disconnect the power brake booster hose.
3. Remove the stoplight switch self-locking pin.
4. Slide the stoplight switch and booster push rod off the brake pedal pin.
5. Remove the bulkhead sound insulator.
6. Remove the power brake booster nuts and remove the booster.
7. The installation is the reverse of the removal.

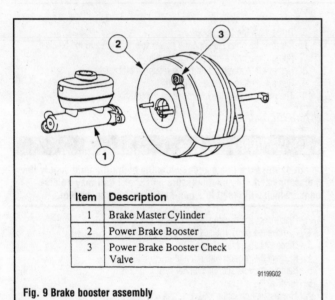

Item	Description
1	Brake Master Cylinder
2	Power Brake Booster
3	Power Brake Booster Check Valve

91199G02

Fig. 9 Brake booster assembly

1997–98 F-250HD, F-350 and F-Super Duty

WITH HYDROBOOST BRAKES
▶ **See Figures 10, 11 and 12**

> ❊❊ **CAUTION**
>
> **Do not depress the brake pedal with the master cylinder removed!**

1. Depress the brake pedal several times with the engine off to exhaust the pressure in the accumulator.
2. Remove the master cylinder from the Hydro-Boost unit. Do not disconnect the brake lines from the master cylinder! Position the master cylinder out of the way.
3. Disconnect the 3 hydraulic lines from the Hydro-Boost unit.
4. Disconnect the pushrod from the brake pedal.
5. Remove the booster mounting nuts and lift the booster from the firewall.

> ❊❊ **CAUTION**
>
> **The booster should never be carried by the accumulator. The accumulator contains high pressure nitrogen and can be dangerous if mishandled! If the accumulator is to be disposed of, do not expose it to fire or other forms of incineration! Gas pressure can be relieved by drilling a ⅟₁₆ in. (1.5mm) hole in the end of the accumulator can. Always wear safety goggles during the drilling!**

6. Installation is the reverse of removal. Tighten the booster mounting nuts to 25 ft. lbs. (34 Nm); the master cylinder nuts to 25 ft. lbs. (34 Nm); connect the hydraulic lines, refill and bleed the booster as follows:
   a. Fill the pump reservoir with Dexron®II ATF.
   b. Disconnect the coil wires and crank the engine for several seconds.
   c. Check the fluid level and refill, if necessary.
   d. Connect the coil wires and start the engine.
   e. With the engine running, turn the steering wheel lock-to-lock twice. Shut off the engine.
   f. Depress the brake pedal several times to discharge the accumulator.
   g. Start the engine and repeat Step 6e.
   h. If foam appears in the reservoir, allow the foam to dissipate.
   i. Repeat Step 6e as often as necessary to expel all air from the system.

➡ **The system is, in effect, self-bleeding and normal vehicle operation will expel any further trapped**

WITH VACUUM ASSISTED BOOSTER

1. Disconnect the brake light switch wires.
2. Support the master cylinder from below, with a prop of some kind.
3. Loosen the clamp and remove the booster check valve hose.
4. Remove the wraparound clip from the booster inboard stud.
5. Remove the master cylinder from the booster. Keep it supported. It will not be necessary to disconnect the brake lines.
6. Working inside the truck below the instrument panel, disconnect the booster valve operating rod from the brake pedal assembly.
7. Remove the 4 bracket-to-dash panel attaching nuts.
8. Remove the booster and bracket assembly from the dash panel, sliding the valve operating rod out from the engine side of the dash panel.

To install:

9. Mount the booster and bracket assembly on the dash panel by sliding the valve operating rod in through the hole in the dash panel, and installing the attaching nuts. Tighten the nuts to 18–25 ft. lbs. (24–34 Nm).
10. Connect the manifold vacuum hose to the booster.
11. Install the master cylinder. Tighten the nuts to 18–25 ft. lbs. (24–34 Nm).
12. Install the wraparound clip.
13. Connect the stop light switch wires.
14. Working inside the truck below the instrument panel, connect the pushrod and stoplight switch.

1999–00 F-250SD, F-350 and F-Super Duty

WITH HYDRO-BOOST BRAKES
▶ **See Figure 13**

> ❊❊ **WARNING**
>
> **The power brake booster should not be carried by the accumulator, nor should it ever be dropped on the accumulator. Check the snap ring on the accumulator for proper seating before the power brake booster is used. The accumulator contains high-pressure nitrogen gas and can be dangerous if mishandled.**

1. With the engine off, depress the brake pedal several times to discharge the accumulator.
2. Disconnect the negative battery cable.
3. Remove the left side battery.
4. Remove the air cleaner housing.
5. Remove the brake pressure switch electrical connector.
6. Disconnect the power steering pressure hoses.
7. Disconnect the power steering return line hose.
8. Remove the three power steering line clamp bolts.
9. Remove the brake master cylinder nuts.
10. Remove the power steering hose mounting bracket and the brake master cylinder, and position aside.
11. Remove the fuse panel cover.
12. Remove the stoplight switch self-locking pin.

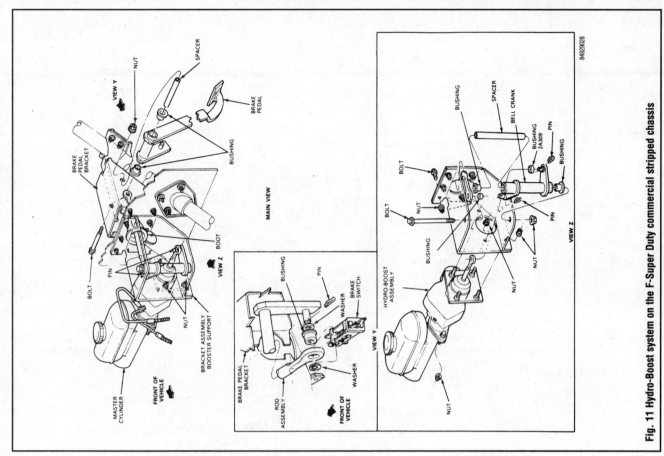

Fig. 11 Hydro-Boost system on the F-Super Duty commercial stripped chassis

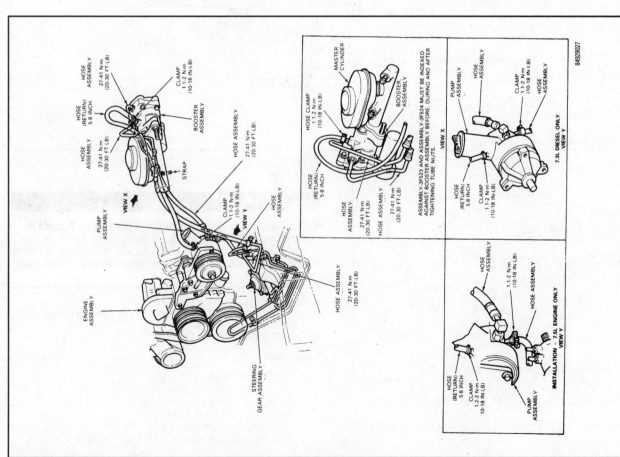

Fig. 10 Hydro-Boost system on the F-Super Duty chassis cab

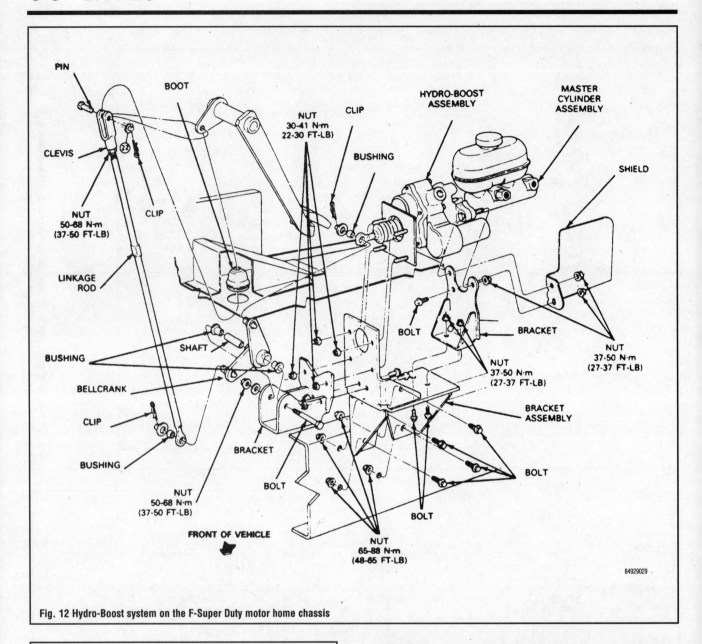

Fig. 12 Hydro-Boost system on the F-Super Duty motor home chassis

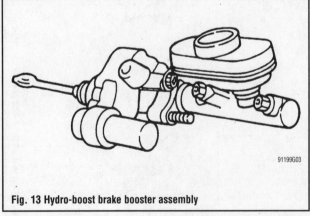

Fig. 13 Hydro-boost brake booster assembly

13. Remove the stoplight switch and the brake booster push rod from the brake pedal pin.

14. Remove the power brake booster nuts, and remove the power brake booster.

To install:

❄ CAUTION

If the accumulator is to be disposed of, it must not be exposed to excessive heat. Before discarding the accumulator, drill a ¹⁄₁₆ inch (1.6-mm) diameter hole in the end of the accumulator can to relieve the gas pressure. Always wear safety glasses when performing this operation.

15. The installation is the reverse of the removal.
16. Install new Teflon® seals on the power steering pressure fittings.

WITH VACUUM ASSISTED BOOSTER

▶ See Figure 9

1. Disconnect the negative battery cable.
2. Remove the air cleaner housing.
3. Remove the brake master cylinder nuts.
4. Position the brake master cylinder aside.
5. Disconnect the booster vacuum hose.
6. Disconnect the power distribution box auxiliary relay and set aside.

7. Remove the fuse panel cover.

8. Remove the stoplight switch self-locking pin.

9. Remove the stoplight switch and the brake booster push rod from the brake pedal pin.

10. Remove the power brake booster nuts.

11. Remove the power brake booster.

To install:

12. The installation is the reverse of the removal.

WITH HYDRO-MAX BRAKES

▶ **See Figure 14**

1. Disconnect the negative battery cable.

2. Remove the support bracket bolt and nut.

3. Remove the ground wire nut and the ground wire.

4. Remove the four master cylinder nuts.

5. Position the master cylinder aside.

6. Remove the electric motor relay bolt.

7. Detach the flow switch electrical connector.

8. Remove the steering column cover.

9. Remove the stoplight switch self-locking pin.

10. Remove the stoplight switch and the brake booster push rod from the brake pedal.

11. Detach the electric pump and motor assembly electric connector.

12. Disconnect the hydraulic fluid return hose.

13. Remove the hydraulic fluid supply line nut.

14. Remove the Hydro-Max booster nuts, and remove the Hydro-Max booster.

15. The installation is the reverse of the removal.

➡ **Start the hydraulic fluid supply line before tightening the Hydro-Max nuts and bolts.**

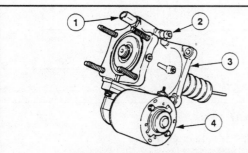

Item	Description
1	Flow Switch Contact Assy
2	Outlet Return Port (Part of 2005)
3	Hydro-Max Booster
4	Electric Pump and Motor Assy

91199G04

Fig. 14 Hydro-max brake booster assembly

Diesel Engine Vacuum Pump

REMOVAL & INSTALLATION

1. Disconnect the negative battery cable.

2. Drain and recycle the engine coolant.

3. Remove the drive belt.

4. Remove the upper radiator hose clamps and upper radiator hose.

5. Disconnect the coolant reservoir hose at the radiator.

6. Remove the fan shroud, fan blade and fan clutch. Refer to Section 3.

7. Remove the vacuum pump pulley using pulley remover T69L-10300-B or equivalent.

8. Remove the vacuum pump retaining bolts.

9. Disconnect the vacuum pump hose and remove the vacuum pump.

To install:

10. The installation is the reverse of the removal.

11. Fill the engine with the proper mixture of coolant and water. Bleed the system.

Proportioning Valve

REMOVAL & INSTALLATION

1997–98 F-Super Duty Only

▶ **See Figures 15 and 16**

➡ **If the linkage is disconnected from the valve, the proper setting of the valve will be lost and a new valve will have to be installed. The new valve will have the shaft preset and secured internally. If the shaft of the new valve turns freely, DO NOT USE IT!—The valve cannot be repaired or disassembled. It is to be replaced as a unit.—If the linkage is damaged or broken and requires replacement, a new sensing valve will also be required.**

1. Raise and support the rear end on jackstands.

2. Raise the frame to obtain a clearance of 6 ⅝ in. (168.3mm) between the bottom edge of the rubber jounce bumper and the top of the axle tube—on BOTH sides of the axle. The is the correct indexing height for the valve.

3. Remove the nut holding the linkage arm to the valve and disconnect the arm.

4. Remove the bolt holding the flexible brake hose to the valve.

5. Disconnect the brake line from the valve.

6. Remove the 2 mounting bolts and remove the valve from its bracket.

To install:

7. Place the new valve on the bracket and tighten the mounting bolts to 12–18 ft. lbs. (16–24 Nm).

8. Install the brake hose, using new copper gaskets and tighten the bolt to 28–34 ft. lbs. (38–46 Nm).

9. Attach the brake line to the lower part of the valve.

10. Connect the linkage arm to the valve and tighten the nut to 8–10 ft. lbs. (11–13 Nm).

11. Bleed the brakes.

➡ **When servicing axle or suspension parts which would require disconnection of the valve, instead, remove the 2 nuts that attach the linkage arm to the axle cover plate. This will avoid disconnecting the valve and avoid having to replace the valve.**

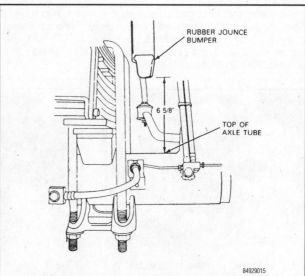

RUBBER JOUNCE BUMPER

6 5/8"

TOP OF AXLE TUBE

84929015

Fig. 15 Setting the correct indexing height for the height sensing proportioning valve

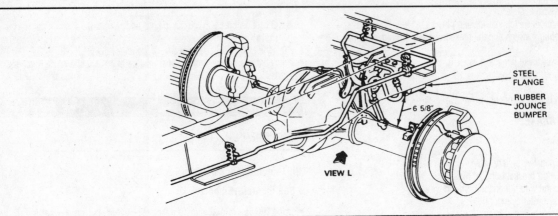

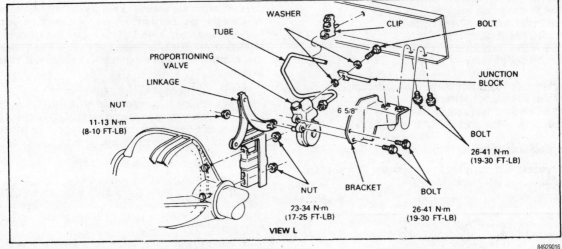

Fig. 16 A common height sensing proportioning valve—F-Super Duty models

Brake Hoses and Lines

Metal lines and rubber brake hoses should be checked frequently for leaks and external damage. Metal lines are particularly prone to crushing and kinking under the vehicle. Any such deformation can restrict the proper flow of fluid and therefore impair braking at the wheels. Rubber hoses should be checked for cracking or scraping; such damage can create a weak spot in the hose and it could fail under pressure.

Any time the lines are removed or disconnected, extreme cleanliness must be observed. Clean all joints and connections before disassembly (use a stiff bristle brush and clean brake fluid); be sure to plug the lines and ports as soon as they are opened. New lines and hoses should be flushed clean with brake fluid before installation to remove any contamination.

REMOVAL & INSTALLATION

▶ **See Figures 17, 18 and 19**

1. Disconnect the negative battery cable.
2. Raise and safely support the vehicle on jackstands.
3. Remove any wheel and tire assemblies necessary for access to the particular line you are removing.
4. Thoroughly clean the surrounding area at the joints to be disconnected.
5. Place a suitable catch pan under the joint to be disconnected.
6. Using two wrenches (one to hold the joint and one to turn the fitting), disconnect the hose or line to be replaced.

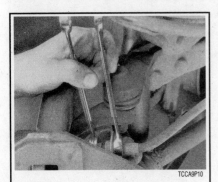

Fig. 17 Use two wrenches to loosen the fitting. If available, use flare nut type wrenches

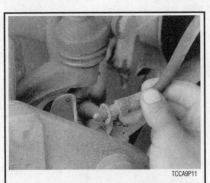

Fig. 18 Any gaskets/crush washers should be replaced with new ones during installation

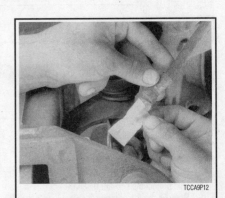

Fig. 19 Tape or plug the line to prevent contamination

7. Disconnect the other end of the line or hose, moving the drain pan if necessary. Always use a back-up wrench to avoid damaging the fitting.

8. Disconnect any retaining clips or brackets holding the line and remove the line from the vehicle.

→If the brake system is to remain open for more time than it takes to swap lines, tape or plug each remaining clip and port to keep contaminants out and fluid in.

To install:

9. Install the new line or hose, starting with the end farthest from the master cylinder. Connect the other end, then confirm that both fittings are correctly threaded and turn smoothly using finger pressure. Make sure the new line will not rub against any other part. Brake lines must be at least 1/2 in. (13mm) from the steering column and other moving parts. Any protective shielding or insulators must be reinstalled in the original location.

✳✳ WARNING

Make sure the hose is NOT kinked or touching any part of the frame or suspension after installation. These conditions may cause the hose to fail prematurely.

10. Using two wrenches as before, tighten each fitting.
11. Install any retaining clips or brackets on the lines.
12. If removed, install the wheel and tire assemblies, then carefully lower the vehicle to the ground.
13. Refill the brake master cylinder reservoir with clean, fresh brake fluid, meeting DOT 3 specifications. Properly bleed the brake system.
14. Connect the negative battery cable.

Bleeding the Brake System

▶ See Figure 20

When any part of the hydraulic system has been disconnected for repair or replacement, air may get into the lines and cause spongy pedal action (because air can be compressed and brake fluid cannot). To correct this condition, it is necessary to bleed the hydraulic system so to be sure all air is purged.

When bleeding the brake system, bleed one brake cylinder at a time, beginning at the cylinder with the longest hydraulic line (farthest from the master cylinder) first. ALWAYS Keep the master cylinder reservoir filled with brake fluid during the bleeding operation. Never use brake fluid that has been drained from the hydraulic system, no matter how clean it is.

The primary and secondary hydraulic brake systems are separate and are bled independently. During the bleeding operation, do not allow the reservoir to run dry. Keep the master cylinder reservoir filled with brake fluid.

Fig. 20 Place a wrench onto the bleeder valve, connect a hose and carefully open the bleeder valve to bleed the brakes

1. Clean all dirt from around the master cylinder fill cap, remove the cap and fill the master cylinder with brake fluid until the level is within ¼ in. (6mm) of the top edge of the reservoir.
2. Clean the bleeder screws at all 4 wheels. The bleeder screws are located on the back of the brake backing plate (drum brakes) and on the top of the brake calipers (disc brakes).
3. Attach a length of rubber hose over the bleeder screw and place the other end of the hose in a glass jar, submerged in brake fluid.
4. Open the bleeder screw ½–¾ turn. Have an assistant slowly depress the brake pedal.
5. Close the bleeder screw and tell your assistant to allow the brake pedal to return slowly. Continue this process to purge all air from the system.
6. When bubbles cease to appear at the end of the bleeder hose, close the bleeder screw and remove the hose. Tighten the bleeder screw to the proper torque:

• Check the master cylinder fluid level and add fluid accordingly. Do this after bleeding each wheel.
• Repeat the bleeding operation at the remaining 3 wheels, ending with the one closet to the master cylinder.
• Fill the master cylinder reservoir to the proper level.

DISC BRAKES

Brake Pads

REMOVAL & INSTALLATION

Front Pads

▶ See Figures 21 thru 34

✳✳ CAUTION

Older brake pads or shoes may contain asbestos, which has been determined to be cancer causing agent. Never clean the brake surfaces with compressed air! Avoid inhaling any dust from any brake surface! When cleaning brake surfaces, use a commercially available brake cleaning fluid.

1. To avoid overflowing of the master cylinder when the caliper pistons are pressed into the caliper cylinder bores, siphon or dip some brake fluid out of the larger reservoir.

Fig. 21 Loosen the caliper mounting bolts

Fig. 22 The pads can be accessed by removing the lower caliper bolt and rotating the caliper up as shown

Fig. 23 Support the caliper with a piece of mechanic's wire or other suitable device

Fig. 24 Remove the outer and . . .

Fig. 25 . . . inner brake pads from the caliper bracket

Fig. 26 A special tool from Lisle®, shown here, is available to compress the caliper piston

Fig. 27 If the special tool is not available, a large C-clamp works well

Fig. 28 Thoroughly clean the caliper brackets before installing the new pads

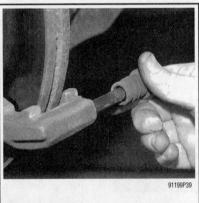

Fig. 29 Remove the caliper slides and . . .

Fig. 30 . . . thoroughly clean the slides

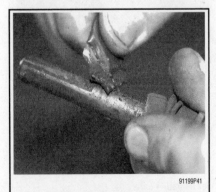

Fig. 31 Lubricate the caliper slides before reinstalling them into the caliper bracket

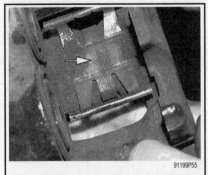

Fig. 32 Make sure that the caliper tension spring is installed into the caliper before installing the caliper

Fig. 33 Before installing the brake pads, it is recommended that you apply a suitable anti-squeal lubricant to the pads and . . .

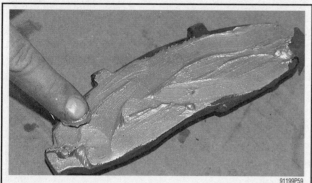
Fig. 34 . . . spread the lubricant evenly over the backing of the brake pads

☼ CAUTION

Brake fluid contains polyglycol ethers and polyglycols. Avoid contact with the eyes and wash your hands thoroughly after handling brake fluid. If you do get brake fluid in your eyes, flush your eyes with clean, running water for 15 minutes. If eye irritation persists, or if you have taken brake fluid internally, IMMEDIATELY seek medical assistance.

2. Raise and support the vehicle on jackstands.
3. Remove the wheels.
4. Place an suitable C-clamp on the caliper and, with the clamp bearing on the outer pad, tighten the clamp to bottom the caliper pistons in the cylinder bores. Remove the C-clamp.
5. Loosen and remove the caliper retaining bolts.
6. Lift the caliper off of the rotor.

➡ Do not allow the caliper to hand by the brake hose.

7. Remove the brake pads and anti-rattle spring.
To install:
8. Thoroughly clean the areas of the caliper and spindle assembly which contact each other during the sliding action of the caliper.
9. Place a new anti-rattle clip on the lower end of the inboard shoe. Make sure that the tabs on the clip are positioned correctly and the loop-type spring is away from the rotor.
10. Place the lower end of the inner brake pad in the spindle assembly pad abutment, against the anti-rattle clip, and slide the upper end of the pad into position. Be sure that the clip is still in position.
11. Check and make sure that the caliper piston is fully bottomed in the cylinder bore. Use a large C-clamp to bottom the piston, if necessary.
12. Position the outer brake pad on the caliper, and press the pad tabs into place with your fingers. If the pad cannot be pressed into place by hand, use a C-clamp. Be careful not to damage the lining with the clamp. Bend the tabs to prevent rattling.
13. Position the caliper on the spindle assembly. Lightly lubricate the caliper sliding pins with a suitable grease.
14. Position the caliper pins into the caliper anchor plate.
15. Tighten the caliper pins to 16–30 ft. lbs. (22–40 Nm) on 19997–98 F-250HD, F-350 and F-Super duty models. Tighten the caliper pins to 21–26 ft. lbs. (28–36 Nm) on the F-150, F-250, Expedition and Navigator. Tighten the caliper pins to 42 ft. lbs. (56 Nm) on the 1999–00 F-250SD, F-350 and F-Super Duty models.
16. Install the wheels.
17. Lower the vehicle.
18. Pump the brake pedal a few times to build adequate pressure in the brake system and check the fluid level in the master cylinder.

Rear Pads

1997–98 F-SUPER DUTY MODELS

▶ See Figure 35

☼ CAUTION

Older brake pads or shoes may contain asbestos, which has been determined to be cancer causing agent. Never clean the brake surfaces with compressed air! Avoid inhaling any dust from any brake surface! When cleaning brake surfaces, use a commercially available brake cleaning fluid.

➡ Never replace the pads on one side only! Always replace pads on both wheels as a set!

1. To avoid overflowing of the master cylinder when the caliper pistons are pressed into the caliper cylinder bores, siphon or dip some brake fluid out of the larger reservoir.
2. Raise and support the rear end on jackstands.
3. Remove the wheels.
4. Place a suitable C-clamp on the caliper and tighten the clamp to bottom the caliper pistons in the cylinder bores. Remove the C-clamp.
5. Clean the excess dirt from around the caliper pin tabs.
6. Drive the upper caliper pin inward until the tabs on the pin touch the caliper support.
7. Insert a small prybar into the slot provided behind the pin tabs on the inboard side of the pin.

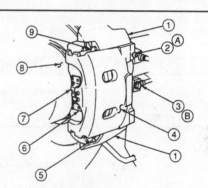

Item	Description
1	Disc Brake Caliper Support Bracket
2	Bleeder Screw
3	Rear Brake Hose-to-Caliper Flow Bolt
4	Disc Brake Caliper
5	Caliper Locking Pin, Lower
6	Brake Shoe and Lining, Outboard
7	Anti-Rattle Clip (Part of 2001)
8	Rear Hub and Rotor Assy
9	Caliper Locking Pin, Upper
A	Tighten to 7-9 N·m (62-79 Lb-In)
B	Tighten to 30-39 N·m (22-29 Lb-Ft)

Fig. 35 Brake caliper assembly—1997–98 F-Super Duty models

8. Using needlenose pliers, compress the outboard end of the pin while, at the same time, prying with the prybar until the tabs slip into the groove in the caliper support.

9. Place the end of a 7/16 in. (11mm) punch against the end of the caliper pin and drive the pin out of the caliper slide groove.

10. Repeat this procedure for the lower pin.

11. Lift the caliper off of the rotor.

12. Remove the brake pads and anti-rattle spring.

➡ **Do not allow the caliper to hand by the brake hose.**

13. Thoroughly clean the areas of the caliper and caliper support assembly which contact each other during the sliding action of the caliper.

To install:

14. Place a new anti-rattle clip on the lower end of the inboard shoe. Make sure that the tabs on the clip are positioned correctly and the loop-type spring is away from the rotor.

15. Place the lower end of the inner brake pad in the caliper support assembly pad abutment, against the anti-rattle clip, and slide the upper end of the pad into position. Be sure that the clip is still in position.

16. Check and make sure that the caliper pistons are fully bottomed in the cylinder bores. Use a large C-clamp to bottom the pistons, if necessary.

17. Position the outer brake pad on the caliper, and press the pad tabs into place with your fingers. If the pad cannot be pressed into place by hand, use a C-clamp. Be careful not to damage the lining with the clamp. Bend the tabs to prevent rattling.

18. Position the caliper on the caliper support. Lightly lubricate the caliper sliding grooves with caliper pin grease.

19. Position the a new upper pin with the retention tabs next to the support groove.

➡ **Don't use the bolt and nut with the new pin.**

20. Carefully drive the pin, at the outboard end, inward until the tabs contact the caliper support face.

21. Repeat the procedure for the lower pin.

❊❊ WARNING

Don't drive the pins in too far, or it will be necessary to drive them back out until the tabs snap into place. The tabs on each end of the pin MUST be free to catch on the support sides!

22. Install the wheels.

23. Lower the vehicle.

24. Pump the brake pedal a few times to build adequate pressure in the brake system and check the fluid level in the master cylinder.

EXCEPT 1997–98 F-SUPER DUTY MODELS

❊❊ CAUTION

Older brake pads or shoes may contain asbestos, which has been determined to be cancer causing agent. Never clean the brake surfaces with compressed air! Avoid inhaling any dust from any brake surface! When cleaning brake surfaces, use a commercially available brake cleaning fluid.

➡ **Never replace the pads on one side only! Always replace pads on both wheels as a set!**

1. Remove the rear brake caliper from the rear hub without disconnecting the brake hose.

❊❊ WARNING

Do not allow the caliper to hand by the brake hose.

2. Remove the brake pads and anti-rattle spring.

3. Thoroughly clean the areas of the caliper and caliper support assembly which contact each other during the sliding action of the caliper.

To install:

4. Retract the caliper piston into the caliper using a suitable tool.

5. Position the brake shoes and anti-rattle clips on the disc brake caliper support bracket.

6. Install the rear disc brake caliper onto the rear support bracket. Tighten the caliper retaining pins on the F-150, F-250, Expedition and Navigator to 20 ft. lbs. (27 Nm). Tighten the caliper retaining bolts on the 1999–00 F-Super Duty models to 27 ft. lbs. (36 Nm.)

7. Bleed the brake system.

8. Clean the wheel hub mounting surface.

9. Install the front wheels and snug the lug nuts to fully seat the wheel against the hub.

10. Lower the vehicle until some of the vehicle's weight rests on the front tires, then tighten the lug nuts to 83–112 ft. lbs. (113–153 Nm).

11. Lower the vehicle completely.

12. Pump the brake pedal a few times to build adequate pressure in the brake system and check the fluid level in the master cylinder.

INSPECTION

▶ **See Figure 36**

❊❊ CAUTION

Older brake pads or shoes may contain asbestos, which has been determined to be cancer causing agent. Never clean the brake surfaces with compressed air! Avoid inhaling any dust from any brake surface! When cleaning brake surfaces, use a commercially available brake cleaning fluid.

Inspect the brake pads for wear using a ruler, Vernier caliper or other suitable device. Compare measurements to the brake specifications chart. If the lining is thinner than specification or there is evidence of the lining being contaminated by brake fluid or oil, make the necessary repairs and replace all brake pad assemblies (a complete axle set).

Brake Caliper

REMOVAL & INSTALLATION

Front Caliper

▶ **See Figures 37, 38, 39, 40 and 41**

1. Raise and safely support the vehicle securely on jackstands.

2. Remove the front wheels.

3. Remove the front brake hose bolt, then remove the copper washers and plug the front brake hose.

4. Remove the 2 front disc brake caliper slide pins, then lift the caliper off of the front caliper anchor plate.

To install:

5. Install the front disc brake caliper onto the caliper anchor plate, then install the 2 slide pins. Tighten the slider pins/bolts to 16–30 ft. lbs. (22–40 Nm) on the 1997–98 F-250HD, F-350 and F-Super Duty models. Tighten the bolts to 21–26 ft. lbs. (28–36 Nm) on the F-150, F-250, Expedition and Navigator. Tighten the bolts to 42 ft. lbs. (56 Nm). On the 1999–00 F-Super Duty models.

6. Using new copper washers, attach the front brake hose to the brake caliper, then install and tighten the retaining bolt to 23–29 ft. lbs. (30–40 Nm).

7. Bleed the brake system.

8. Clean the wheel hub mounting surface.

9. Install the front wheels and snug the lug nuts to fully seat the wheel against the hub.

10. Lower the vehicle until some of the vehicle's weight rests on the front tires, then tighten the lug nuts to 83–112 ft. lbs. (113–153 Nm).

11. Lower the vehicle completely.

12. Make sure that the brakes are operating correctly.

Rear Caliper

1997–98 F-SUPER DUTY

▶ **See Figure 35**

1. Remove sufficient brake fluid from the brake master cylinder reservoir to allow for pressing the caliper pistons into the bores. Discard the used brake fluid.

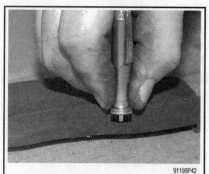

Fig. 36 Make sure to measure the pads in several places since pads can wear unevenly

Fig. 37 Loosen the brake hose bolt and . . .

Fig. 38 . . . remove the brake hose from the caliper

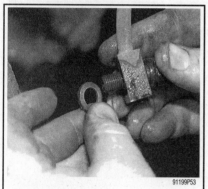

Fig. 39 Discard the copper washers and replace them

Fig. 40 Plug the inlet port on the caliper

Fig. 41 Loosen the caliper mounting bolts

2. Raise and safely support the vehicle.
3. Remove the wheels.
4. Place a suitable C-clamp on the caliper, with he clamp frame on the disc brake caliper and the clamp screw on the outboard brake hoes and lining backing plate, then tighten the clamp to press the caliper pistons in the cylinder bores only enough to give removal clearance. Remove the C-clamp.
5. Remove the rear brake hose-to-caliper flow bolt and discard the used copper washers. Plug the brake hose so that contamination of the brake fluid does not occur.
6. Using the Caliper Pin Remover D89T-2196-A, or equivalent, drive the upper and lower caliper locking pins out.
7. Remove the disc brake caliper from the vehicle.

To install:

8. If necessary, install the brake shoe and anti-rattle clip.
9. Position the disc brake caliper in the support bracket.
10. Lubricate the caliper locking pins with Ford Silicone Dielectric Compound D7AZ-19A331-A or equivalent.
11. Drive the locking pins into the caliper/support bracket assembly until the tabs at each end of the pin snap into place.
12. Using new copper washers, attach the rear brake hose to the disc brake caliper. Tighten the rear brake hose-to-caliper flow bolt to 22–29 ft. lbs. (30–39 Nm).
13. Install the wheel, then lower the vehicle.

➡Check the brake fluid level in the brake master cylinder reservoir and maintain sufficient level to prevent air from entering the system.

14. Pump the brake pedal several times to drive the caliper pistons into contact with the brake shoe and lining.
15. Fill the brake master cylinder reservoir with new DOT 3 brake fluid.
16. Bleed the brake system and test the brakes for proper operation.

F-150, F-250, EXPEDITION, NAVIGATOR AND 1999–00 F-SUPER DUTY MODELS

✳✳ WARNING

The electrical power to the air suspension system must be shut off prior to hoisting, jacking or towing an air suspension vehicle. This can be accomplished by turning off the air suspension switch. Failure to do so can result in unexpected inflation or deflation of the air springs which can result in shifting of the vehicle during these operations.

1. Raise and support the vehicle.
2. Remove the wheel and tire assembly.

✳✳ CAUTION

Brake fluid contains polyglycol ethers and polyglycols. Avoid contact with the eyes and wash your hands thoroughly after handling brake fluid. If you do get brake fluid in your eyes, flush your eyes with clean, running water for 15 minutes. If eye irritation persists, or if you have taken brake fluid internally, IMMEDIATELY seek medical assistance.

3. Remove bolt and disconnect the rear wheel brake hose.
4. Remove the copper washers and plug the brake hose.

✳✳ WARNING

Do not remove the guide pins or guide pin boots unless a problem is suspected. The guide pins are meant to be sealed for life and are not repairable. Use Silicone Brake Caliper Grease and Dielectric Compound D7AZ-19A331-A (Motorcraft WA-10) or an equivalent silicone compound meeting Ford specification ESE-M1C171-A for relubing the caliper slide pins. Other greases can swell the guide pin boots, resulting in contamination and accelerated corrosion or wear of the caliper slide pin mechanism.

5. Remove the brake caliper bolts.
6. Lift the rear disc brake caliper off the rear disc brake caliper anchor plate.
7. Inspect the rear disc brake caliper for leaks.

To install:

➡When installed, the locator notch on the brake pads will be located at the upper end of the rear disc brake caliper.

8. Install the rear disc brake caliper.
9. Install the rear wheel brake hose.
10. Connect the brake hose and install and use new copper washers.
11. Tighten the brake hose bolt.
12. Bleed the disc brake caliper.

➡If equipped with air suspension, reactivate the system by turning on the air suspension switch.

13. Install the wheel and tire assembly.
14. Verify correct brake operation.

OVERHAUL

▶ **See Figures 42 thru 49**

➡Some vehicles may be equipped dual piston calipers. The procedure to overhaul the caliper is essentially the same with the exception of multiple pistons, O-rings and dust boots.

1. Remove the caliper from the vehicle and place on a clean workbench.

Fig. 42 For some types of calipers, use compressed air to drive the piston out of the caliper, but make sure to keep your fingers clear

Fig. 43 Withdraw the piston from the caliper bore

Fig. 44 On some vehicles, you must remove the anti-rattle clip

Fig. 45 Use a prytool to carefully pry around the edge of the boot . . .

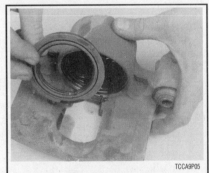

Fig. 46 . . . then remove the boot from the caliper housing, taking care not to score or damage the bore

Fig. 47 Use extreme caution when removing the piston seal; DO NOT scratch the caliper bore

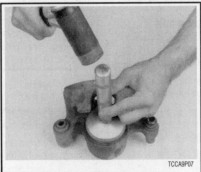

Fig. 48 Use the proper size driving tool and a mallet to properly seal the boots in the caliper housing

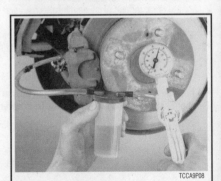

Fig. 49 There are tools, such as this Mighty-Vac, available to assist in proper brake system bleeding

NEVER place your fingers in front of the pistons in an attempt to catch or protect the pistons when applying compressed air. This could result in personal injury!

➡Depending upon the vehicle, there are two different ways to remove the piston from the caliper. Refer to the brake pad replacement procedure to make sure you have the correct procedure for your vehicle.

2. The first method is as follows:
   a. Stuff a shop towel or a block of wood into the caliper to catch the piston.
   b. Remove the caliper piston using compressed air applied into the caliper inlet hole. Inspect the piston for scoring, nicks, corrosion and/or worn or damaged chrome plating. The piston must be replaced if any of these conditions are found.
3. For the second method, you must rotate the piston to retract it from the caliper.
4. If equipped, remove the anti-rattle clip.
5. Use a prytool to remove the caliper boot, being careful not to scratch the housing bore.
6. Remove the piston seals from the groove in the caliper bore.
7. Carefully loosen the brake bleeder valve cap and valve from the caliper housing.
8. Inspect the caliper bores, pistons and mounting threads for scoring or excessive wear.
9. Use crocus cloth to polish out light corrosion from the piston and bore.
10. Clean all parts with denatured alcohol and dry with compressed air.

To assemble:
11. Lubricate and install the bleeder valve and cap.
12. Install the new seals into the caliper bore grooves, making sure they are not twisted.
13. Lubricate the piston bore.
14. Install the pistons and boots into the bores of the calipers and push to the bottom of the bores.
15. Use a suitable driving tool to seat the boots in the housing.
16. Install the caliper in the vehicle.
17. Install the wheel and tire assembly, then carefully lower the vehicle.
18. Properly bleed the brake system.

Brake Disc (Rotor)

REMOVAL & INSTALLATION

1997–98 F-250HD and F-350

4 X 2 MODELS FRONT DISC

▶ See Figure 50

1. Raise and safely support the vehicle.
2. Remove the wheel and tire assembly.
3. Remove the caliper assembly and support it on the frame with a piece of wire without disconnecting the brake fluid hose.
4. Remove the hub grease cap.

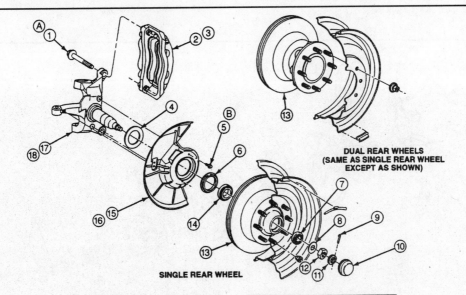

Item	Description
1	Anchor Bracket Bolt, M16-2.0 x 50
2	Disc Brake Caliper (RH)
3	Front Disc Brake Caliper (LH)
4	Front Brake Splash Shield Gasket
5	Screw, M6-1.0 x 10
6	Wheel Hub Grease Seal
7	Front Wheel Bearing
8	Front Wheel Outer Bearing Retainer Washer
9	Cotter Pin
10	Hub Grease Cap
11	Nut Retainer
12	Spindle Nut, 3/4-16

Item	Description
13	Front Disc Brake Hub and Rotor
14	Front Wheel Inner Bearing Cone and Roller Assy
15	Front Disc Brake Rotor Shield (RH)
16	Front Disc Brake Rotor Shield (LH)
17	Front Wheel Spindle Assy (RH)
18	Front Wheel Spindle Assy (LH)
A	Tighten to 191-259 N·m (141-190 Lb-Ft)
B	Tighten to 9-13 N·m (80-115 Lb-In)

Fig. 50 Brake rotor mounting—1997-98 F-250HD and F-350 4 X 2

5. Remove the cotter pin.
6. Remove the retainer nut.
7. Remove the spindle nut.
8. Remove the outer bearing retainer washer and wheel bearing.
9. Remove the disc brake hub and rotor assembly.
10. Remove the bearing grease seal and the inner bearing.

To install:

11. If the brake rotor is being replaced, remove the protective coating from the new rotor. If the original rotor is being installed, ensure that the rotor braking surfaces are clean.
12. Thoroughly clean and inspect the front wheel bearings and the front disc brake hub and rotor.
13. Lubricate the front wheel bearings using premium long-life grease XG-1-C or -K or equivalent meeting Ford specification ESA-M1C75-B.
14. Install the inner front wheel bearing.
15. Install a new wheel hub grease seal.
16. Place the hub and rotor assembly on the wheel spindle and install the outer wheel bearing.
17. Install the washer and spindle nut.
18. Adjust the wheel bearings.
19. Install the retainer nut, cotter pin and dust cap.
20. Install the caliper assembly.
21. Install the wheel and tire assembly.
22. Lower the vehicle.

4 X 4 MODELS FRONT DISC

1. Raise and safely support the vehicle.
2. Remove the wheel and tire assembly.
3. Remove the caliper assembly and support it on the frame with a piece of wire without disconnecting the brake fluid hose.

4. Remove the manual or automatic locking hubs.
5. Remove the front disc brake hub and rotor.
6. Remove the wheel hub grease seal.
7. Remove the inner front wheel bearing.

To install:

8. If the brake rotor is being replaced, remove the protective coating from the new rotor. If the original rotor is being installed, ensure that the rotor braking surfaces are clean.
9. Thoroughly clean and inspect the front wheel bearings and the front disc brake hub and rotor.
10. Lubricate the front wheel bearings using premium long-life grease XG-1-C or -K or equivalent meeting Ford specification ESA-M1C75-B.
11. Install the inner front wheel bearing.
12. Install a new wheel hub grease seal.
13. Place the hub and rotor assembly onto the spindle.
14. Install the hub assembly.
15. Install the caliper assembly.
16. Install the wheel and tire assembly.
17. Lower the vehicle.

1997–98 F-Super Duty

FRONT

▶ **See Figure 51**

1. Raise and safely support the vehicle securely on jackstands.
2. Remove the brake caliper assembly.
3. Remove the front disc brake caliper anchor plate.
4. Remove the hub grease cap.
5. Remove the cotter pin.

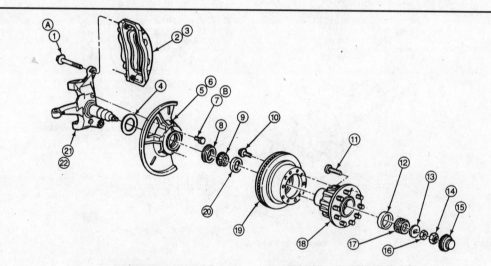

Item	Description
1	Anchor Bracket Bolt, M16-2.0 x 50
2	Disc Brake Caliper (RH)
3	Front Disc Brake Caliper (LH)
4	Front Brake Splash Shield Gasket
5	Front Disc Brake Rotor Shield (RH)
6	Front Disc Brake Rotor Shield (LH)
7	Screw
8	Wheel Hub Grease Seal
9	Front Wheel Inner Bearing Cone and Roller Assy
10	Screw
11	Wheel Lug Nut Stud

Item	Description
12	Bearing Cup
13	Front Wheel Outer Bearing Retainer Washer
14	Nut Retainer
15	Hub Grease Cap
16	Spindle Nut
17	Front Wheel Bearing
18	Wheel Hub
19	Front Disc Brake Rotor
20	Bearing Cup
21	Front Wheel Spindle (RH)
22	Front Wheel Spindle (LH)
A	Tighten to 191-259 N·m (141-190 Lb-Ft)
B	Tighten to 7-16 N·m (62-141 Lb-In)

91199G08

Fig. 51 Brake rotor mounting—1997–98 F-Super-Duty

6. Remove the spindle nut.
7. Remove the front wheel outer bearing retainer washer.
8. Remove the outer front wheel bearing.
9. Remove the hub grease cap gasket.
10. Remove the front disc brake hub and rotor.
11. Remove the wheel hub grease seal.
12. Remove the inner front wheel bearing.

To install:

13. If the brake rotor is being replaced, the hub is removed from the rotor. Remove the hub retaining bolts and remove the hub from the rotor. Install the hub onto the new rotor. Tighten the retaining bolts to 74–89 ft. lbs. (100–120 Nm).

14. Thoroughly clean and inspect the front wheel bearings and the front disc brake hub and rotor.

15. Lubricate the front wheel bearings using premium long-life grease XG-1-C or -K or equivalent meeting Ford specification ESA-M1C75-B.

16. Install the inner front wheel bearing.
17. Install a new wheel hub grease seal.
18. Install the front disc brake hub and rotor.
19. Install the outer front wheel bearing.
20. Install the front wheel outer bearing retainer washer.
21. Install the spindle nut.
22. While rotating the front disc brake hub and rotor, tighten the spindle nut.
23. Loosen the spindle nut two turns.
24. Tighten the spindle nut while rotating the front disc brake hub and rotor.
25. Loosen the spindle nut.
26. Tighten the spindle nut while rotating the front disc brake hub and rotor.
27. Install the cotter pin.
28. Install the hub grease cap gasket and the hub grease cap.
29. Install the front disc brake caliper anchor plate.
30. Install the brake caliper.
31. Install the wheel and tire assembly.
32. Lower the vehicle.

REAR

▶ **See Figure 52**

1. Raise and safely support the vehicle securely on jackstands.
2. Remove the wheel and tire assembly.
3. Remove the axle shaft retaining bolts and remove the axle shaft.
4. Using a suitable hub socket, loosen and remove the hub socket.
5. Remove the outer wheel bearing.
6. Remove the hub and rotor.
7. Remove the rotor-to-hub bolts and separate the hub and rear disc brake rotor.

To install:

8. The installation is the reverse of the removal.

F-150, F-250, Expedition and Navigator

FRONT

▶ **See Figures 53, 54 and 55**

1. Raise and safely support the vehicle.
2. Remove the wheel and tire assembly.
3. Remove 2 caliper slide pins and lift the caliper off the anchor plate.
4. Secure the caliper out of the way without damaging the brake hose.
5. Remove the disc brake pads and anti-rattle clips.
6. Remove 2 anchor plate retaining bolts and remove the anchor plate.
7. On 4x4 vehicles, remove the rotor from the hub assembly by pulling it off the hub studs. If additional force is required to remove the rotor, apply rust penetrating fluid on the front and rear rotor/hub mating surfaces and then strike the rotor between the studs with a plastic hammer. If this does not work, attach a 3-jaw puller and remove the rotor.
8. On 4x2 vehicles:
    a. Remove the hub grease cap.
    b. Remove the cotter pin.
    c. Remove the retainer nut.
    d. Remove the spindle nut.

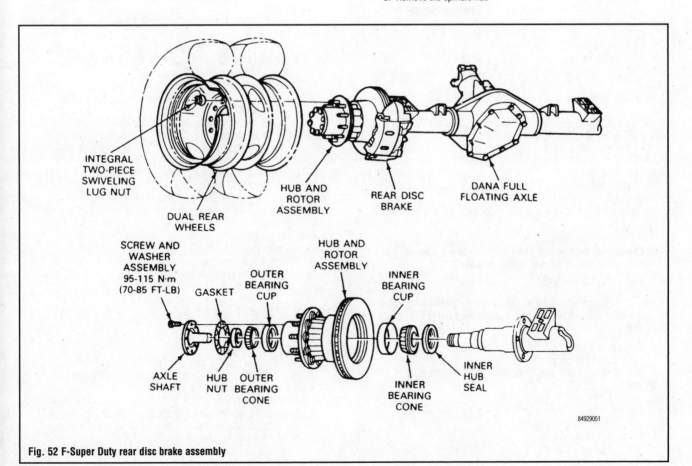

Fig. 52 F-Super Duty rear disc brake assembly

Fig. 53 Remove the two caliper anchor plate retaining bolts and . . .

Fig. 54 . . . remove the caliper anchor plate

Fig. 55 Lift the rotor off of the hub assembly—4 X 4 models only

e. Remove the outer bearing retainer washer and wheel bearing.

f. Remove the disc brake hub and rotor assembly.

➡If excessive force must be used to remove the rotor, it should be checked for lateral run-out before installation.

9. Check the brake rotor for scoring and/or wear. Machine or replace, as necessary. If machining, observe the minimum thickness specification stamped on the rotor.

To install:

10. If the brake rotor is being replaced, remove the protective coating from the new rotor. If the original rotor is being installed, ensure that the rotor braking surfaces are clean.

11. On 4x4 vehicles, apply a small amount of silicone dielectric compound to the pilot diameter of the disc brake rotor and install the rotor on the hub assembly.

12. On 4x2 vehicles:

a. Install the inner wheel bearing with a new grease seal.

b. Place the hub and rotor assembly on the wheel spindle and install the outer wheel bearing.

c. Install the washer and spindle nut.

d. Adjust the wheel bearings.

e. Install the retainer nut, cotter pin and dust cap.

13. Place the anchor plate and install 2 retaining bolts. Tighten the bolts to 125–168 ft. lbs. (170–230 Nm).

14. Install the brake pad anti-rattle clips and install the disc brake pads.

15. Slide the disc brake caliper into position. Install and tighten the caliper sliding pins to 21–26 ft. lbs. (28–36 Nm).

16. Install the wheel and tire assembly. Tighten the lug nuts to 83–112 ft. lbs. (113–153 Nm).

17. Lower the vehicle.

18. Pump the brake pedal several times to position the brake pads prior to moving the vehicle.

19. Road test the vehicle and check for proper brake system operation.

REAR

➡When removing the rear disc brake caliper in this procedure, it is not necessary to disconnect the rear wheel brake hose.

1. Remove the rear disc brake caliper.

➡If the brake disc binds on the parking brake shoe and lining, remove the adjustment hole access plug and contract the parking brake shoe and lining.

2. Remove the press-on keeper nuts, if so equipped.

3. Remove the brake disc.

4. Inspect the brake disc. Replace the brake disc if necessary.

To install:

5. Install the brake disc.

6. Install the rear disc brake caliper.

7. Install the wheel and tire assembly.

8. Lower the vehicle.

1999–00 F-250SD and F-350 4x2

FRONT

▶ See Figure 56

1. Raise and safely support the vehicle securely on jackstands.

2. Remove the wheel and tire assembly.

3. Remove the front disc brake caliper anchor plate.

4. Remove the hub grease cap.

5. Remove the cotter pin.

6. Remove the nut retainer.

7. Remove the spindle nut.

8. Remove the front wheel outer bearing retainer washer.

9. Remove the outer front wheel bearing.

10. Remove the front disc brake hub and rotor.

11. Remove the wheel hub grease seal.

12. Remove the inner front wheel bearing.

To install:

13. Thoroughly clean and inspect the front wheel bearings and the front disc brake hub and rotor.

14. Lubricate the front wheel bearings using premium long-life grease XG-1-C or -K or equivalent meeting Ford specification ESA-M1C75-B.

15. Install the inner front wheel bearing.

16. Install a new wheel hub grease seal.

17. Install the front disc brake hub and rotor.

18. Install the outer front wheel bearing.

19. Install the front wheel outer bearing retainer washer.

20. Install the spindle nut.

21. While rotating the front disc brake hub and rotor, tighten the spindle nut.

22. Loosen the spindle nut two turns.

23. Tighten the spindle nut while rotating the front disc brake hub and rotor.

24. Loosen the spindle nut.

25. Tighten the spindle nut while rotating the front disc brake hub and rotor.

26. Install the following components:

• Install the nut retainer.

• Install the cotter pin.

• Install the hub grease cap.

27. Install the front disc brake caliper anchor plate.

28. Install the wheel and tire assembly.

29. Lower the vehicle.

1999–00 F-250 and F-350 4x4

FRONT

▶ See Figures 57 and 58

1. Raise and safely support the vehicle securely on jackstands.

2. Remove the wheel and tire assembly.

3. Remove the front brake caliper.

4. Remove the front disc brake caliper anchor plate.

5. On single rear wheel (SRW) vehicles, remove the rotor.

6. On dual rear wheel (DRW) vehicles:

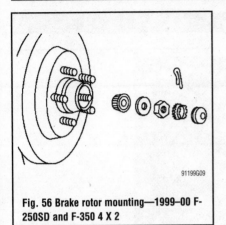

Fig. 56 Brake rotor mounting—1999–00 F-250SD and F-350 4 X 2

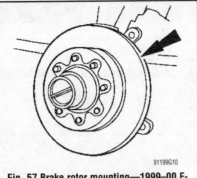

Fig. 57 Brake rotor mounting—1999–00 F-250SD and F-350 4 X 4 with single rear wheels

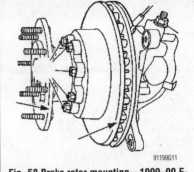

Fig. 58 Brake rotor mounting—1999–00 F-250SD and F-350 4 X 4 with dual rear wheels

a. Remove the eight hub plate nuts.
b. Remove the hub plate.
c. Remove the rotor.

To install:

7. Position the front disc brake rotor to the wheel hub. Make sure the wheel hub and the front disc brake rotor braking and mounting surfaces are clean.

8. On dual rear wheel (DRW) vehicles:

a. Install the front wheel hub plate and nuts. Tighten the hub plate nuts to 130 ft. lbs. (176 Nm).

9. Install the front disc brake caliper anchor plate.
10. Install the brake caliper.
11. Install the wheel and tire assembly.
12. Lower the vehicle.

1999–00 F-Super Duty and Motorhome Chassis

FRONT

1. Raise and safely support the vehicle securely on jackstands.
2. Remove the brake caliper assembly.
3. Remove the front disc brake caliper anchor plate.
4. Remove the hub grease cap screws.
5. Remove the hub grease cap.
6. Remove the cotter pin.
7. Remove the spindle nut.
8. Remove the front wheel outer bearing retainer washer.
9. Remove the outer front wheel bearing.
10. Remove the hub grease cap gasket.
11. Remove the front disc brake hub and rotor.
12. Remove the wheel hub grease seal.
13. Remove the inner front wheel bearing.

To install:

14. Thoroughly clean and inspect the front wheel bearings and the front disc brake hub and rotor.

15. Lubricate the front wheel bearings using premium long-life grease XG-1-C or -K or equivalent meeting Ford specification ESA-M1C75-B.

16. Install the inner front wheel bearing.
17. Install a new wheel hub grease seal.
18. Install the front disc brake hub and rotor.
19. Install the outer front wheel bearing.
20. Install the front wheel outer bearing retainer washer.
21. Install the spindle nut.
22. While rotating the front disc brake hub and rotor, tighten the spindle nut.
23. Loosen the spindle nut two turns.
24. Tighten the spindle nut while rotating the front disc brake hub and rotor.
25. Loosen the spindle nut.
26. Tighten the spindle nut while rotating the front disc brake hub and rotor.
27. Install the cotter pin.
28. Install the hub grease cap gasket and the hub grease cap.
29. Install the hub grease cap screws.
30. Install the front disc brake caliper anchor plate.
31. Install the brake caliper.
32. Install the wheel and tire assembly.
33. Lower the vehicle.

1999–00 F-250SD, F-350 and F-Super Duty

REAR

1. Raise and safely support the vehicle securely on jackstands.
2. Remove the wheel and tire assembly.
3. Remove the axle shaft retaining bolts and remove the axle shaft.
4. Using a suitable hub socket, loosen and remove the hub socket.
5. Remove the outer wheel bearing.
6. Remove the hub and rotor.
7. Remove the rotor-to-hub bolts and separate the hub and rear disc brake rotor.
8. The installation is the reverse of the removal.

INSPECTION

▶ **See Figure 59**

Rotor thickness should be measured any time a brake inspection is done. Rotor thickness can be measured using a brake rotor micrometer or Vernier caliper. Measure the rotor thickness in several places around the rotor. Compare the thickness to the specifications chart found at the end of this section.

The run-out of the brake rotor should be checked any time a vibration during braking occurs. Excessive run-out can be caused by a build-up of rust scale or other particles on the rotor or hub surfaces. Remove the rotor and thoroughly clean the hub and rotor-to-hub mounting surface on the back of the rotor. Mount a dial indicator to a suspension member and zero the indicator stylus on the face of the rotor. Rotate the rotor 360 degrees by hand and record the run-out.

Compare measurements to the brake specifications chart. If the thickness and run-out do not meet specifications, replace the rotor.

Fig. 59 Check brake rotor thickness in several places around the rotor using a Vernier caliper

DRUM BRAKES

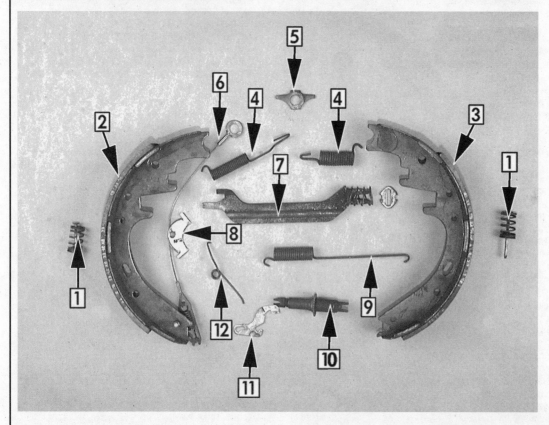

REAR DRUM BRAKE COMPONENTS

1. Shoe hold-down spring and retainer
2. Primary brake shoe
3. Secondary brake shoe
4. Brake shoe retracting springs
5. Anchor pin guide plate
6. Shoe adjusting lever cable
7. Parking brake strut
8. Shoe adjusting lever cable guide
9. Brake shoe adjusting screw spring
10. Brake adjuster screw
11. Brake shoe adjusting lever
12. Adjusting lever return spring
13. Wheel cylinder
14. Parking brake lever retaining clip
15. Parking brake lever

91199P75

Brake Drums

REMOVAL & INSTALLATION

F-150, F-250 and Expedition Models

▶ **See Figure 60**

1. Raise and safely support the vehicle securely on jackstands.
2. Remove the tire and wheel assembly.
3. Remove the three retaining clips (if equipped) and remove the brake drum.

➡ **It may be necessary to back off the brake shoe adjustment in order to remove the brake drum. This is because the drum might be grooved or worn from being in service for an extended period of time.**

➡ **Before installing a new brake drum, be sure to remove any protective coating with brake cleaner or a suitable fast-drying degreaser.**

4. Install the brake drum in the reverse order of removal and adjust the brakes.

1997–98 F-250HD and F-350 Models

▶ **See Figure 61**

1. Raise the vehicle and install jackstands.
2. Remove the tire and wheel assembly.
3. Loosen the rear brake shoe adjustment.
4. Remove the rear axle retaining bolts and lockwashers, axle shaft, and gasket.
5. Remove the wheel bearing lock-nut, lockwasher, and adjusting nut.
6. Remove the hub and drum assembly from the axle.
7. Remove the brake drum-to-hub retaining screws, bolts or bolts and nut. Remove the brake drum from the hub.
   To install:
8. Place the drum on the hub and attach it to the hub with the attaching nuts and bolts.

9. Place the hub and drum assembly on the axle and start the adjusting nut.
10. Adjust the wheel bearing nut and install the wheel bearing lockwasher and lock-nut.
11. Install the axle shaft with a new gasket and install the axle retaining bolts and lockwashers.
12. Install the wheel and adjust the brake shoes. Remove the jackstands and lower the vehicle.

INSPECTION

▶ **See Figures 62 and 63**

Check that there are no cracks or chips in the braking surface. Excessive bluing indicates overheating and a replacement drum is needed. The drum can be machined to remove minor damage and to establish a rounded braking surface on a warped drum. Never exceed the maximum oversize of the drum when machining the braking surface.

The brake drum inside diameter and run-out can be measured using a brake drum micrometer. The drum should be measured every time a brake inspection is performed. Take the inside diameter readings at points 90° apart from each other on the drum to measure the run-out. The maximum inside diameter is stamped on the rim of the drum or on the inside above the lug nut stud holes and is also contained in the brake specifications chart at the end of this section.

Brake Shoes

INSPECTION

▶ **See Figure 64**

Inspect the brake shoes for wear using a ruler or Vernier caliper. Compare measurements to the brake specifications chart. If the lining is thinner than specification or there is evidence of the lining being contaminated by brake fluid

Fig. 60 Lift the brake drum from the shoes and backing plate

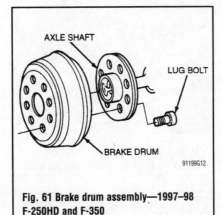

Fig. 61 Brake drum assembly—1997–98 F-250HD and F-350

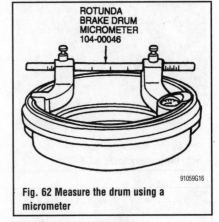

Fig. 62 Measure the drum using a micrometer

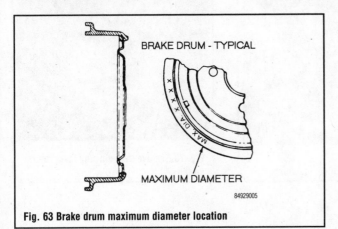

Fig. 63 Brake drum maximum diameter location

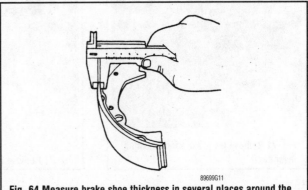

Fig. 64 Measure brake shoe thickness in several places around the shoe

or oil, repair the leak and replace all brake shoe assemblies (a complete axle set). In addition to the shoes inspect all springs and brake shoe hardware for wear and replace as necessary.

REMOVAL & INSTALLATION

F-150, F-250 and Expedition Models

▶ See Figures 65 thru 82

1. Raise and safely support the vehicle securely on jackstands.

➡ **When servicing drum brakes, only dissemble and assemble one side at a time, leaving the remaining side intact for reference.**

2. Contract the brake shoes by pulling the self-adjusting lever away from the starwheel adjustment screw and turn the starwheel up and back until the pivot nut is drawn onto the starwheel as far as it will come.

3. Pull the adjusting lever, cable and automatic adjuster spring down and

Fig. 65 Remove the brake shoe retracting springs . . .

Fig. 66 . . . from both sides

Fig. 67 Rotate the hold down spring retainer and . . .

Fig. 68 . . . remove the hold down spring from the primary brake shoe

Fig. 69 Remove the primary shoe and unhook the adjusting spring from the shoe

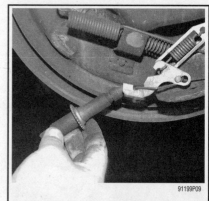

Fig. 70 Remove the adjusting screw

Fig. 71 Remove the brake shoe adjusting lever cable

Fig. 72 Remove the adjusting spring

Fig. 73 Remove the adjusting lever return spring

Fig. 74 Remove the anchor pin guide plate

Fig. 75 Remove the parking brake strut

Fig. 76 Remove the secondary shoe hold down spring

Fig. 77 Lift the secondary shoe from the backing plate

Fig. 78 Remove the parking brake lever horseshoe clip apart and . . .

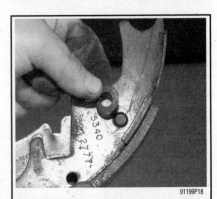

Fig. 79 . . . remove the washer from under the horseshoe clip then . . .

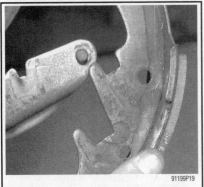

Fig. 80 . . . remove the secondary brake shoe from the parking brake lever

Fig. 81 Thoroughly clean and . . .

Fig. 82 . . . lubricate the shoe contact points on the backing plate

toward the rear to unhook the pivot hook from the large hole in the secondary shoe web. Do not attempt to pry the pivot hook from the hole.

4. Remove the automatic adjuster spring and the adjusting lever.

5. Remove the secondary shoe-to-anchor spring. Remove the primary shoe-to-anchor spring and unhook the cable anchor. Remove the anchor pin plate.

6. Remove the cable guide from the secondary shoe.

7. Remove the shoe hold-down springs, shoes, adjusting screw, pivot nut, and socket. Note the color of each hold-down spring for assembly. To remove the hold-down springs, reach behind the brake backing plate and place one finger on the end of one of the brake hold-down spring mounting pins. Using a pair of pliers, grasp the washer type retainer on top of the hold-down spring that corresponds to the pin which you are holding. Push down on the pliers and turn them 90° to align the slot in the washer with the head on the spring mounting pin. Remove the spring and washer retainer and repeat this operation on the hold down spring on the other shoe.

8. Remove the parking brake link and spring. Disconnect the parking brake cable from the parking brake lever.

9. After removing the rear brake secondary shoe, disassemble the parking brake lever from the shoe by removing the retaining clip and spring washer.

To install:

10. Assemble the parking brake lever to the secondary shoe and secure it with the spring washer and retaining clip.

11. Apply a light coating of Lubriplate®, or equivalent, at the points where the brake shoes contact the backing plate.

12. Position the brake shoes on the backing plate, and install the hold-down spring pins, springs, and spring washer type retainers. On the rear brake, install the parking brake link, spring and washer. Connect the parking brake cable to the parking brake lever.

13. Install the anchor pin plate, and place the cable anchor over the anchor pin with the crimped side toward the backing plate.

14. Install the primary shoe-to-anchor spring with the brake tool.

15. Install the cable guide on the secondary shoe web with the flanged holes fitted into the hole in the secondary shoe web. Thread the cable around the cable guide groove.

16. Install the secondary shoe-to-anchor (long) spring. Be sure that the cable end is not cocked or binding on the anchor pin when installed. All of the parts should be flat on the anchor pin. Remove the wheel cylinder piston clamp.

17. Apply Lubriplate®, or equivalent, to the threads and the socket end of the adjusting starwheel screw. Turn the adjusting screw into the adjusting pivot nut to the limit of the threads and then back off ½ turn.

➡️**Interchanging the brake shoe adjusting screw assemblies from one side of the vehicle to the other would cause the brake shoes to retract rather than expand each time the automatic adjusting mechanism is operated. To prevent this, the socket end of the adjusting screw is stamped with an "R" or an "L" for "RIGHT" or "LEFT". The adjusting pivot nuts can be distinguished by the number of lines machined around the body of the nut; one line indicates left hand nut and two lines indicate a right hand nut.**

18. Place the adjusting socket on the screw and install this assembly between the shoe ends with the adjusting screw nearest to the secondary shoe.

19. Place the cable hook into the hole in the adjusting lever from the backing plate side. The adjusting levers are stamped with an R (right) or a L (left) to indicate their installation on the right or left hand brake assembly.

20. Position the hooked end of the adjuster spring in the primary shoe web and connect the loop end of the spring to the adjuster lever hole.

21. Pull the adjuster lever, cable and automatic adjuster spring down toward the rear to engage the pivot hook in the large hole in the secondary shoe web.

22. After installation, check the action of the adjuster by pulling the section of the cable guide and the adjusting lever toward the secondary shoe web far enough to lift the lever past a tooth on the adjusting screw starwheel. The lever should snap into position behind the next tooth, and release of the cable should cause the adjuster spring to return the lever to its original position. This return action of the lever will turn the adjusting screw starwheel one tooth. The lever should contact the adjusting screw starwheel one tooth above the centerline of the adjusting screw.

If the automatic adjusting mechanism does not perform properly, check the following:

23. Check the cable and fittings. The cable ends should fill or extend slightly beyond the crimped section of the fittings. If this is not the case, replace the cable.

24. Check the cable guide for damage. The cable groove should be parallel to the shoe web, and the body of the guide should lie flat against the web. Replace the cable guide if this is not so.

25. Check the pivot hook on the lever. The hook surfaces should be square with the body on the lever for proper pivoting. Repair or replace the hook as necessary.

26. Make sure that the adjusting screw starwheel is properly seated in the notch in the shoe web.

1997–98 F-250 HD and F-350 Models

▶ **See Figure 83**

1. Raise and support the vehicle.
2. Remove the wheel and drum.
3. Remove the parking brake lever assembly retaining nut from behind the backing plate and remove the parking brake lever assembly.
4. Remove the adjusting cable assembly from the anchor pin, cable guide, and adjusting lever.

❋ CAUTION

Brake shoes may contain asbestos, which has been determined to be a cancer causing agent. Never clean the brake surfaces with compressed air! Avoid inhaling any dust from any brake surface! When cleaning brake surfaces, use a commercially available brake cleaning fluid.

5. Remove the brake shoe retracting springs.
6. Remove the brake shoe hold-down spring from each shoe.
7. Remove the brake shoes and adjusting screw assembly.
8. Disassemble the adjusting screw assembly.
9. Clean the ledge pads on the backing plate. Apply a light coat of Lubriplate®, or equivalent, to the ledge pads (where the brake shoes rub the backing plate).

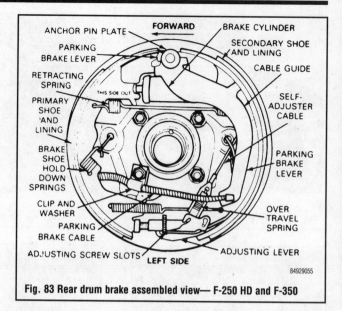

Fig. 83 Rear drum brake assembled view— F-250 HD and F-350

To install:

10. Apply Lubriplate® to the adjusting screw assembly and the hold-down and retracting spring contacts on the brake shoes.

11. Install the upper retracting spring on the primary and secondary shoes and position the shoe assembly on the backing plate with the wheel cylinder pushrods in the shoe slots.

12. Install the brake shoe hold-down springs.

13. Install the brake shoe adjustment screw assembly with the slot in the head of the adjusting screw toward the primary shoe, lower retracting spring, adjusting lever spring, adjusting lever assembly, and connect the adjusting cable to the adjusting lever. Position the cable in the cable guide and install the cable anchor fitting on the anchor pin.

14. Install the adjusting screw assemblies in the same locations from which they were removed. Interchanging the brake shoe adjusting screws from one side of the vehicle to the other will cause the brake shoes to retract rather than expand each time the automatic adjusting mechanism is operated. To prevent incorrect installation, the socket end of each adjusting screw is stamped with an R or an L to indicate their installation on the right or left side of the vehicle. The adjusting pivot nuts can be distinguished by the number of lines machined around the body of the nut. Two lines indicate a right hand nut; one line indicates a left hand nut.

15. Install the parking brake assembly in the anchor pin and secure with the retaining nut behind the backing plate.

16. Adjust the brakes before installing the brake drums and wheels. Install the brake drums and wheels.

17. Lower the vehicle and road test the brakes. New brakes may pull to one side or the other before they are seated. Continued pulling or erratic braking should not occur.

ADJUSTMENTS

▶ **See Figure 84**

The drum brakes are self-adjusting and require a manual adjustment only after the brake shoes have been replaced, or when the length of the adjusting screw has been changed while performing some other service operation, as, for example, when taking off brake drums.

To adjust the brakes, perform the procedures that follow:

Drum Installed

1. Raise and support the rear of the vehicle on jackstands.
2. Remove the rubber plug from the adjusting slot on the backing plate.

❋ CAUTION

Brake shoes may contain asbestos, which has been determined to be a cancer causing agent. Never clean the brake surfaces with compressed air! Avoid inhaling any dust from any brake surface!

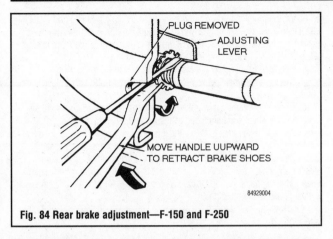

Fig. 84 Rear brake adjustment—F-150 and F-250

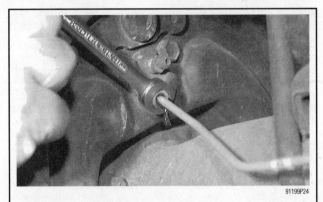

Fig. 85 Loosen the brake line fitting on the wheel cylinder

When cleaning brake surfaces, use a commercially available brake cleaning fluid.

3. Insert a brake adjusting spoon into the slot and engage the lowest possible tooth on the starwheel. Move the end of the brake spoon downward to move the starwheel upward and expand the adjusting screw. Repeat this operation until the brakes lock the wheels.

4. Insert a small screwdriver or piece of firm wire (coat hanger wire) into the adjusting slot and push the automatic adjusting lever out and free of the starwheel on the adjusting screw and hold it there.

5. Engage the topmost tooth possible on the starwheel with the brake adjusting spoon. Move the end of the adjusting spoon upward to move the adjusting screw starwheel downward and contract the adjusting screw. Back off the adjusting screw starwheel until the wheel spins freely with a minimum of drag. Keep track of the number of turns that the starwheel is backed off, or the number of strokes taken with the brake adjusting spoon.

6. Repeat this operation for the other side. When backing off the brakes on the other side, the starwheel adjuster must be backed off the same number of turns to prevent side-to-side brake pull.

7. When the brakes are adjusted make several stops while backing the vehicle, to equalize the brakes at both of the wheels.

8. Remove the jackstands and lower the vehicle. Road test the vehicle.

Drum Removed

> ✳✳ **CAUTION**
>
> **Brake shoes may contain asbestos, which has been determined to be a cancer causing agent. Never clean the brake surfaces with compressed air! Avoid inhaling any dust from any brake surface! When cleaning brake surfaces, use a commercially available brake cleaning fluid.**

1. Make sure that the shoe-to-contact pad areas are clean and properly lubricated.

2. Using an inside caliper check the inside diameter of the drum. Measure across the diameter of the assembled brake shoes, at their widest point.

3. Turn the adjusting screw so that the diameter of the shoes is 0.030 in. (0.76mm) less than the brake drum inner diameter.

4. Install the drum.

Wheel Cylinders

REMOVAL & INSTALLATION

◆ **See Figures 85 and 86**

1. Raise and safely support the vehicle.
2. Remove the rear wheel and tire assembly.
3. Remove the brake drum retainers, if equipped.
4. Grasp the brake drum and remove.
5. If the drum will not slide off with light force, then the brake shoes need to be backed off.

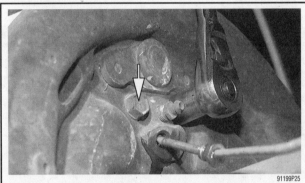

Fig. 86 Remove the wheel cylinder retaining bolts and remove the cylinder

> ✳✳ **CAUTION**
>
> **Brake shoes may contain asbestos, which has been determined to be a cancer causing agent. Never clean the brake surfaces with compressed air! Avoid inhaling any dust from any brake surface! When cleaning brake surfaces, use a commercially available brake cleaning fluid.**

6. Remove the brake drum.
7. Remove the brake shoes.

> ✳✳ **CAUTION**
>
> **Brake fluid contains polyglycol ethers and polyglycols. Avoid contact with the eyes and wash your hands thoroughly after handling brake fluid. If you do get brake fluid in your eyes, flush your eyes with clean, running water for 15 minutes. If eye irritation persists, or if you have taken brake fluid internally, IMMEDIATELY seek medical assistance.**

8. Disconnect the brake line at the wheel cylinder.
9. Remove the 2 bolts securing the wheel cylinder to the backing plate and remove the wheel cylinder.

To install:

10. Reinstall the wheel cylinder to the brake backing plate and install the 2 retaining bolts. Torque the retaining bolts to 84–108 inch. lbs. (10–13 Nm).

11. Reconnect the brake line to the wheel cylinder and torque the fitting to 10–18 ft. lbs. (14–24 Nm).

12. Lubricate the rear brake shoe contact points on the backing plate with an appropriate grease.

13. Install the brake shoes.

14. Make sure that the brake drum and brake shoes are clean of any oils or protective coatings.

15. Reinstall the brake drum.

16. Bleed the brake system of air until a firm pedal is achieved. Top off the brake fluid in the master cylinder.

✳✳ WARNING

Clean, high quality brake fluid is essential to the safe and proper operation of the brake system. You should always buy the highest quality brake fluid that is available. If the brake fluid becomes contaminated, drain and flush the system, then refill the master cylinder with new fluid. Never reuse any brake fluid. Any brake fluid that is removed from the system should be discarded. Also, do not allow any brake fluid to come in contact with a painted surface; it will damage the paint.

17. Reinstall the wheel and tire assembly.
18. Lower the vehicle.
19. Pump the brake pedal several times to assure a good pedal.
20. Road test the vehicle and check the brake system for proper operation.

OVERHAUL

▶ See Figures 87 thru 96

✳✳ CAUTION

Brake fluid contains polyglycol ethers and polyglycols. Avoid contact with the eyes and wash your hands thoroughly after handling brake fluid. If you do get brake fluid in your eyes, flush your eyes with clean, running water for 15 minutes. If eye irritation persists, or if you have taken brake fluid internally, IMMEDIATELY seek medical assistance.

Wheel cylinder overhaul kits may be available, but often at little or no savings over a reconditioned wheel cylinder. It often makes sense with these components to substitute a new or reconditioned part instead of attempting an overhaul.

If no replacement is available, or you would prefer to overhaul your wheel cylinders, the following procedure may be used. When rebuilding and installing wheel cylinders, avoid getting any contaminants into the system. Always use clean, new, high quality brake fluid. If dirty or improper fluid has been used, it will be necessary to drain the entire system, flush the system with proper brake fluid, replace all rubber components, then refill and bleed the system.

1. Remove the wheel cylinder from the vehicle and place on a clean workbench.
2. First remove and discard the old rubber boots, then withdraw the pistons. Piston cylinders are equipped with seals and a spring assembly, all located behind the pistons in the cylinder bore.
3. Remove the remaining inner components, seals and spring assembly. Compressed air may be useful in removing these components. If no compressed air is available, be VERY careful not to score the wheel cylinder bore when removing parts from it. Discard all components for which replacements were supplied in the rebuild kit.
4. Wash the cylinder and metal parts in denatured alcohol or clean brake fluid.

Fig. 87 Remove the outer boots from the wheel cylinder

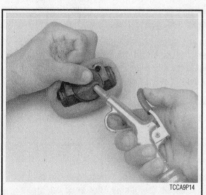
Fig. 88 Compressed air can be used to remove the pistons and seals

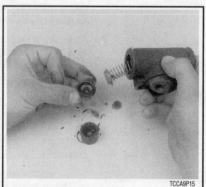
Fig. 89 Remove the pistons, cup seals and spring from the cylinder

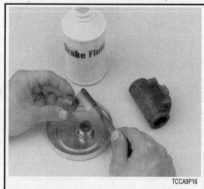
Fig. 90 Use brake fluid and a soft brush to clean the pistons . . .

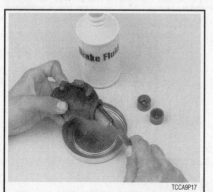
Fig. 91 . . . and the bore of the wheel cylinder

Fig. 92 Once cleaned and inspected, the wheel cylinder is ready for assembly

Fig. 93 Lubricate the cup seals with brake fluid

Fig. 94 Install the spring, then the cup seals in the bore

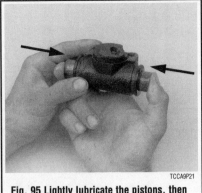

Fig. 95 Lightly lubricate the pistons, then install them

Fig. 96 The boots can now be installed over the wheel cylinder ends

❈❈ WARNING

Never use a mineral-based solvent such as gasoline, kerosene or paint thinner for cleaning purposes. These solvents will swell rubber components and quickly deteriorate them.

5. Allow the parts to air dry or use compressed air. Do not use rags for cleaning, since lint will remain in the cylinder bore.

PARKING BRAKE

Cable(s)

REMOVAL & INSTALLATION

1997–98 F-250HD and F-350

▶ See Figure 97

PARKING BRAKE CONTROL

1. Raise and safely support the vehicle.

6. Inspect the piston and replace it if it shows scratches.
7. Lubricate the cylinder bore and seals using clean brake fluid.
8. Position the spring assembly.
9. Install the inner seals, then the pistons.
10. Insert the new boots into the counterbores by hand. Do not lubricate the boots.
11. Install the wheel cylinder.

2. Loosen the adjusting nut at the equalizer.
3. Working in the engine compartment, remove the nuts attaching the parking brake control to the firewall.
4. Remove the cable from the control assembly clevis by compressing the conduit end prongs.
5. Installation is the reverse of removal. Torque the attaching nuts to 15 ft. lbs. (20 Nm).

EQUALIZER-TO-CONTROL ASSEMBLY CABLE

1. Raise and safely support the vehicle.
2. Back off the equalizer nut and disconnect the cable from the tension limiter.

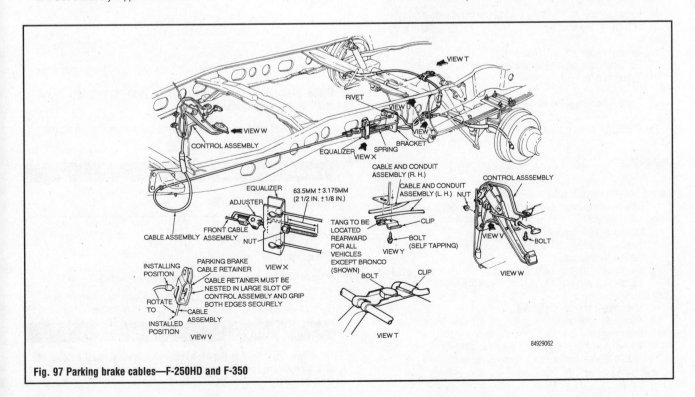

Fig. 97 Parking brake cables—F-250HD and F-350

3. Remove the parking brake cable from the mount.
4. Disconnect the forward end of the cable from the control assembly.
5. Using a cord attached to the upper end of the cable, pull the cable from the vehicle.
6. Installation is the reverse of removal. Adjust the parking brake.

EQUALIZER-TO-REAR WHEEL CABLE

1. Raise and safely support the vehicle.
2. Remove the wheels and brake drums.
3. Remove the tension limiter.
4. Remove the lock-nut from the threaded rod and disconnect the cable from the equalizer.
5. Disconnect the cable housing from the frame bracket and pull the cable and housing out of the bracket.
6. Disconnect the cables from the brake backing plates.
7. With the spring tension removed from the lever, lift the cable out of the slot in the lever and remove the cable through the backing plate hole.
8. Installation is the reverse of removal. On the F-250 and F-350, check the clearance between the parking brake operating lever and the cam plate. Clearance should be 0.015 in. (0.38mm) with the brakes fully released.
9. Adjust the brakes.

F-150, F-250, Expedition and Navigator; 1999–00 F-250SD, F-350 and F-Super Duty Models

FRONT CABLE

1. Raise and safely support the vehicle.
2. While an assistant relieves tension on the system by pulling on the parking brake intermediate cable or the front brake cable insert a 5/32 inch (4mm) steel pin or equivalent drill bit into the hole provided in the parking brake control assembly.
3. Disconnect the front cable from the parking brake cable equalizer.
4. Lower the vehicle.
5. Remove the front door scuff plate and cowl side trim panel.
6. Disconnect the brake cable from the parking brake control.
7. Raise and safely support the vehicle.
8. Pry the rubber seal from the floor pan and compress the cable retainer from the bracket.
9. Remove the front parking brake cable from the vehicle.

To install:

10. Feed the front parking brake cable through the hole in the front floor pan and secure the rubber grommet.
11. Route the cable and conduit around the control assembly pulley and attach the cable to the control assembly. Make sure the connector is locked in place.
12. Raise and safely support the vehicle.
13. Route the cable through the cable bracket and lock cable in place.
14. Connect the front parking brake cable to the parking brake cable equalizer.
15. Remove the steel pin or equivalent from the parking brake control assembly.
16. Operate the parking brake control several times and verify correct parking brake operation.

REAR CABLE

1. While an assistant relieves tension on the system by pulling on the parking brake intermediate cable or the front brake cable insert a 5/32 inch (4mm) steel pin or equivalent drill bit into the hole provided in the parking brake control assembly.
2. Raise and safely support the vehicle.
3. Remove the wheel and tire assembly.
4. Remove the brake drum.
5. Pull down on the front brake cable and disconnect the cable equalizer.
6. Compress the retainer and release the rear brake cable from the bracket.
7. Unclip the cable from the bracket.
8. Remove the brake shoes and lift the parking brake rear cable out of the slot in the parking brake lever (attached to the secondary shoe).
9. On the wheel side of the backing plate, compress the retainer fingers with a 9/16 inch flare nut wrench or equivalent and remove the rear cable through the hole in the backing plate.

To install:

10. Route the cable through the hole in the backing plate. Insert the cable anchor behind the slot in the parking brake lever. Make sure the cable is securely engaged in the parking brake lever so the cable return spring is holding the cable in the parking brake lever.
11. Push the retainer through the hole in the backing plate so the retainer prongs engage the backing plate.
12. Insert the parking brake cable into the rear guide bracket.
13. Connect the cable to the cable bracket ensuring the retainer locks in place.
14. Connect the rear cable to the equalizer.
15. Install rear brake drum and adjust rear brakes, if needed.
16. Install the wheel and tire assembly. Torque the lug nuts to 83–112 ft. lbs. (113–153 Nm).
17. Partially lower the vehicle.
18. Apply and release the parking brake control several times. Rotate both wheels to ensure that the parking brakes apply and release without dragging.
19. Lower the vehicle.
20. Verify proper parking brake operation.

ADJUSTMENT

1997–98 F-250HD and F-350

➡Before making any parking brake adjustment, make sure that the drum brakes are properly adjusted.

BASIC ADJUSTMENT

1. Raise and support the rear end on jackstands.
2. The brake drums should be room temperature.
3. Make sure that the parking brake pedal is fully released.
4. While holding the tension equalizer, tighten the equalizer nut 6 full turns past its original position.
5. Fully depress the parking brake pedal. Using a cable tension gauge, check rear cable tension. Cable tension should be 350 lbs. minimum.
6. Fully release the parking brake. No drag should be noted at the wheels.
7. If drag is noticed, remove the drums and adjust the clearance between the parking brake lever and cam plate. Clearance should be 0.015 in. (0.38mm). Clearance is adjusted at the parking brake equalizer adjusting nut.

INITIAL ADJUSTMENT WHEN THE TENSION LIMITER HAS BEEN REPLACED

1. Raise and support the vehicle on jackstands.
2. Depress the parking brake pedal fully.
3. Hold the tension limiter, install the equalizer nut and tighten it to a point 2½ in. +/- ⅛ in. (63.5mm +/- 3mm) up the rod.
4. Check to make sure that the cinch strap has 1⅜ in. (35mm) remaining.

F-150, F-250, Expedition and Navigator; 1999–00 F-250SD, F-350 and F-Super Duty Models

The parking brake system is self-adjusting and requires no further adjustments.

Parking Brake Shoes

REMOVAL & INSTALLATION

F-250, Expedition and Navigator

▶ See Figure 98

➡Make sure the parking brake control is fully released.

1. Relieve the tension on the parking brake system by pulling the front parking brake cable and conduit and inserting a suitable retainer.

⁂ CAUTION

The electrical power to the air suspension system must be shut off prior to hoisting, jacking or towing an air suspension vehicle. This

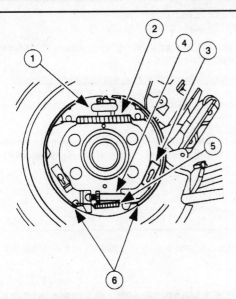

Item	Description
1	Parking Brake Lever
2	Brake Shoe Retracting Spring
3	Brake Shoe Hold-Down Spring
4	Brake Adjuster Screw
5	Brake Shoe Adjusting Screw Spring
6	Rear Brake Shoe and Lining

91199G13

Fig. 98 Parking brake shoes—F-250, Expedition and Navigator

can be accomplished by turning off the air suspension switch located in the rear jack storage area. Failure to do so can result in unexpected inflation or deflation of the air springs, which can result in shifting of the vehicle during these operations.

2. Raise and safely support the vehicle securely on jackstands.
3. Remove the tire and wheel assembly.

☼ WARNING

Do not let the rear disc brake caliper hang from caliper hose, use wire to hang it aside.

4. Remove the rear brake disc caliper bolts.
5. Remove the rear brake disc caliper and position aside.

➡Be sure to remove square cut O-rings from hub before removing rear brake disc.

6. Remove the rear brake disc.
7. Remove the brake shoe retracting spring.
8. Remove the brake shoe adjusting screw spring.
9. Remove the brake adjuster screw.
10. Remove the rear brake shoe hold-down springs.
11. Remove the rear brake shoes and linings along with the inboard brake shoe retracting spring.
12. Inspect the components for excessive wear or damage and install new components as required.

To install:

➡Lubricate the brake shoe contact point before installation of rear brake shoes using Silicone Brake Caliper Grease and Dielectric Compound D7AZ-19A331-A (Motorcraft WA-10) or an equivalent silicone compound meeting Ford specification ESE-M1C171-A.

13. Install the rear brake shoes and linings along with the inboard brake shoe retracting spring.
14. Install the brake shoe hold-down springs.
15. Install the brake adjuster screw.
16. Install the brake shoe adjusting screw spring.
Install the outboard brake shoe retracting spring.
17. Use Brake Adjusting Gauge to measure the inside diameter of the drum portion of the rear brake disc.
18. Use Brake Adjusting Gauge to set the rear brake shoe and lining diameter to 0.020 inch (0.5 mm) less than the inside diameter to the drum portion of the rear brake disc.

➡After rear brake disc has been installed, be sure to install the square cut O-ring in the hub groove.

19. Install the rear brake disc.
20. Install the rear disc brake caliper.
21. Install the rear brake disc caliper-to-rear brake disc caliper anchor plate bolts.
22. Clean the wheel hub mounting surface.
23. Install the wheel and tire assembly.
24. If equipped with air suspension, reactivate the system by turning on the air suspension switch.
25. Lower the vehicle.
26. Apply tension to the parking brake cable system.
27. Hold the front parking brake cable and conduit taut.
28. Remove the retainer from the parking brake control.
29. Check the operation of the parking brake.

1999–00 F-250SD, F-350 and F-Super Duty Models

▶ See Figure 99

1. Raise and safely support the vehicle securely on jackstands.
2. Remove the tire and wheel assembly.

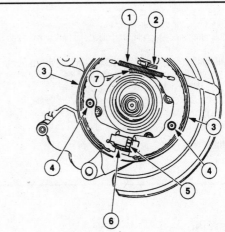

Item	Description
1	Brake Shoe Retracting Spring— (Outboard)
2	Parking Brake Lever
3	Parking Brake Shoe and Linings
4	Brake Shoe Hold-Down Spring
5	Brake Adjuster Screw
6	Brake Shoe Adjusting Screw Spring
7	Brake Shoe Retracting Spring— (Inboard)

91199G14

Fig. 99 Parking brake shoes—1999–00 F-250SD, F-350 and F-Super Duty models

3. Remove the rear disc brake rotor.
4. Disconnect the rear parking brake cable at the parking brake cable equalizer.
5. Disconnect the parking brake cable at the parking brake lever.
6. Remove the outboard brake shoe retracting spring.
7. Remove the brake shoe adjusting screw spring.
8. Remove the brake shoe hold-down springs.
9. Remove the brake adjuster screw.
10. Remove the parking brake shoe and linings along with the inboard brake shoe retracting spring.
11. Inspect the components for excessive wear or damage and replace as required.

To install:

➡**Make sure the inboard brake shoe retracting spring is attached to the parking brake shoe.**

12. Install the LH parking brake shoe and brake shoe hold-down spring, along with the inboard brake shoe retracting spring.
13. Connect the inboard brake shoe retracting spring to the RH parking brake shoe, and install the RH parking brake shoe and the brake shoe hold-down spring.

14. Install the brake adjuster screw.
15. Install the brake shoe adjusting screw spring.

➡**The outboard brake shoe retracting spring mounts above the inboard brake shoe retracting spring.**

16. Install the outboard brake shoe retracting spring.
17. Connect the parking brake cable at the parking brake lever.
18. Connect the rear parking brake cable at the parking brake cable equalizer.
19. Install the rear disc brake rotor.
20. Use the Brake Adjusting Gauge to set the rear brake shoe and lining diameter to 0.030 inch (0.75 mm) less than the inside diameter of the drum portion of the rear disc brake rotor.
21. Install the tire and wheel assembly.
22. Lower the vehicle.

ADJUSTMENT

The parking brake system is self-adjusting and requires no further adjustments.

TRANSMISSION MOUNTED PARKING BRAKE

Parking Brake Assembly

➡**This system is found on F-Super Duty models only. To replace the brake shoes, or any other component, the unit must be disassembled.**

REMOVAL

◆ **See Figures 100, 101 and 102**

1. Place the transmission in gear.
2. Fully release the parking brake pedal.
3. Raise and support the truck on jackstands.
4. Spray penetrating oil on the adjusting clevis, jam nut and threaded end of the cable.
5. Loosen the jam nut and remove the locking pin from the clevis pin.
6. Remove the clevis pin, clevis and jam nut from the cable.
7. Remove the cable from the bracket on the case.
8. Matchmark the driveshaft and disconnect it from the flange.
9. Remove the 6 hex-head bolts securing the parking brake unit to the transmission extension housing and lift off the unit.

➡**The unit is filled with Ford Type H ATF.**

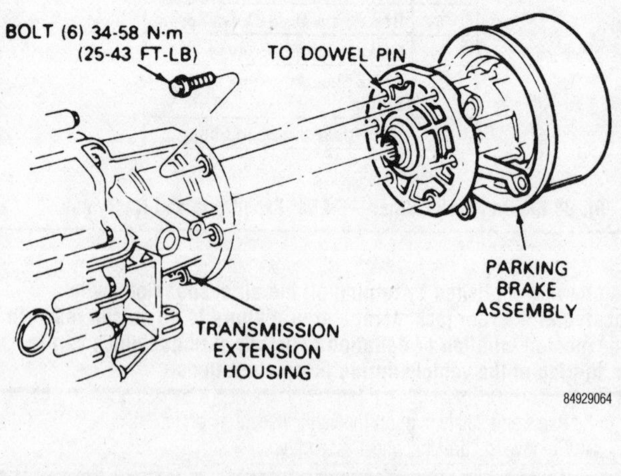

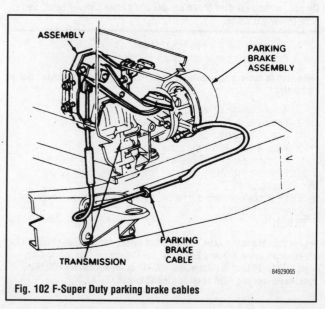

Fig. 101 F-Super Duty parking brake unit removal

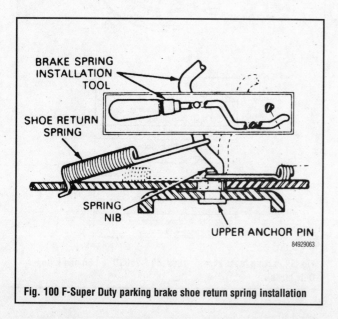

Fig. 100 F-Super Duty parking brake shoe return spring installation

Fig. 102 F-Super Duty parking brake cables

✳✳ CAUTION

Brake shoes may contain asbestos, which has been determined to be a cancer causing agent. Never clean the brake surfaces with compressed air! Avoid inhaling any dust from any brake surface! When cleaning brake surfaces, use a commercially available brake cleaning fluid.

DISASSEMBLY

➡**Several special tools and a hydraulic press are necessary.**

1. Remove the unit from the truck.
2. Remove the 4 bolts securing the yoke flange and drum, and remove the flange and drum.
3. Remove the 75mm hex nut from the mainshaft, using tool T88T–2598–G, or equivalent.
4. Press the mainshaft, drum and output flange from the case.
5. Remove the speedometer drive gear from the case.
6. Using tools D80L–1002–2, D79L–4621–A and D80L–630–6, remove the outer bearing cone from the mainshaft.
7. Place the threaded end of the output shaft in a soft-jawed vise.
8. Matchmark the drum, flange/yoke and mainshaft. Remove the 4 nuts securing the flange and drum to the output shaft and remove the flange and drum.
9. Using tool T77F–1102–A, remove the input shaft oil seal, spacer, O-ring, bearing cone and race from the input shaft end of the case.
10. Remove the 4 bolts securing the splash shield and brake assembly from the case. Remove the brake assembly and splash shield.
11. Remove the brake actuating lever and spring from the case.
12. Using tool T77F–1102–A, remove the outer bearing cup and oil seal.
13. Unscrew the vent from the case.
14. Hold the brake assembly securely and remove the 2 brake sure return springs.
15. Spread the free ends of the shoes and remove the shoes from the lower anchor pin. Remove the shoe-to-shoe spring.

ASSEMBLY

▸ **See Figures 103 and 104**

1. Clean the brake assembly thoroughly with a brake cleaning solvent.
2. Using a brake caliper grease, place a light coating on:
   • Camshaft lugs and ball on the actuating lever
   • Shoe guide lugs and support pads on the support plate
   • Upper and lower anchor pins
   • Brake shoe anchor pin contact points
3. Connect a NEW shoe-to-shoe spring between the brake shoes, spread the shoes and position them on the lower anchor pin.
4. Position the upper ends on the upper anchor pin, inserting the show webs between the shoe guide lugs and the pads on the support plate.
5. Install 2 NEW return springs.
6. Drive a new inner bearing race into place.
7. Drive a new outer bearing race into the case making sure it bottoms evenly.
8. Install a new outer bearing.
9. Coat the outer edge of a new outer oil seal with sealer and drive the seal into place with the lip facing inward. The seal must be flush with the bore surface.
10. Install the actuating lever spring.
11. Apply a light coating of brake grease on the actuating lever ball and install the lever through the coiled end of the spring.
12. Position the brake assembly into the case. Insert the lever into position in the brake assembly.
13. Tighten the 4 brake assembly attaching bolts to 90 ft. lbs. (122 Nm).
14. Attach the retracting spring to the actuating lever while bending the long end to snap over the lever.
15. Place the mainshaft in a soft-jawed vise with the flanged end upward.
16. Install the brake drum and output flange onto the mainshaft, being aware of the matchmarks.
17. Install the 4 nuts and tighten them to 85 ft. lbs. (115 Nm).
18. Turn the mainshaft over and clamp it in the vise.
19. Install the case, with the outer bearing installed loosely on the mainshaft, guiding the mainshaft through the oil seal and bearing cone.

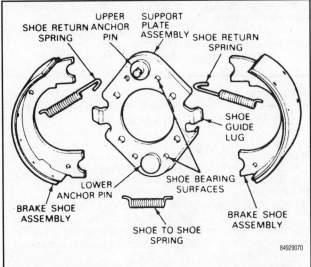

Fig. 103 Exploded view of the F-Super Duty parking brake shoes

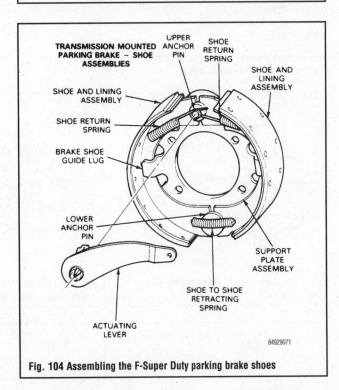

Fig. 104 Assembling the F-Super Duty parking brake shoes

20. Install the outer bearing cone on the mainshaft using tool T88T–2598–F, or equivalent, to seat the bearing on the shaft.
21. Install the speedometer gear and snap-ring.
22. Install the shim on the mainshaft.

➡**This shim determines end-play. It is available in several thickness with variations of 0.0019 in. (0.05mm).**

23. Install the inner bearing cone and spacer on the mainshaft.

➡**To check end-play, first install the inner bearing spacer without the O-ring.**

24. Thread the 75mm nut onto the shaft and tighten it to 215 ft. lbs. (292 Nm).
25. Mount a dial indicator and bracket with the dial indicator between the mainshaft and case to check end-play. While rotating the case assembly on the mainshaft to center the bearings, apply pressure up and down. An end-play reading of 0.0019–0.0039 in. (0.05–0.10mm) is desired. Shim as necessary.
26. Remove the 75mm nut, spacer and bearing to install the shim(s).
27. Install the bearing.

28. Coat the outer edge of a new seal with sealer and seat it in the case bore with the lip facing inward.

29. Install a new O-ring in the spacer and install the spacer on the mainshaft until it butts against the shoulder of the shaft.

30. Install a NEW 75mm nut and tighten it to 215 ft. lbs. (292 Nm).

31. Install the vent.

INSTALLATION

▶ **See Figures 105, 106, 107, 108 and 109**

1. Refill the unit through the filler plug to the bottom of the plug hole. Install the plug and tighten it to 45 ft. lbs. (61 Nm).

2. Position the unit on the extension housing using 2 guide pins.

3. Using 6 NEW hex-bolts, attach the unit and tighten the bolts to 40 ft. lbs. (54 Nm).

4. Connect the driveshaft and tighten the bolts to 20 ft. lbs. (27 Nm).

5. Assemble the cable components. Screw on the clevis until the pin can be inserted while the lever and cable are held tightly in the applied position. Then, remove the pin, let go of the cable and lever, and turn the clevis 10 full turns counterclockwise (loosen).

6. Install the pin.

ADJUSTMENT

▶ **See Figure 110**

➡To replace the brake shoes, or any other component, the parking brake cable must be disconnected.

1. Place the transmission in gear.

2. Fully release the parking brake pedal.

3. Raise and safely support the vehicle.

4. Spray penetrating oil on the adjusting clevis, jam nut and threaded end of the cable.

5. Loosen the jam nut and remove the locking pin from the clevis pin.

6. Remove the clevis pin, clevis and jam nut from the cable.

7. Remove the cable from the bracket on the case.

8. Matchmark the driveshaft and disconnect it from the flange.

9. Remove the 6 hex-head bolts securing the parking brake unit to the transmission extension housing and lift off the unit.

➡The unit is filled with Ford Type H automatic transmission fluid.

To install:

10. Refill the unit through the filler plug to the bottom of the plug hole. Install the plug and tighten it to 45 ft. lbs. (61 Nm).

11. Position the unit on the extension housing using 2 guide pins.

12. Using 6 NEW hex-bolts, attach the unit and torque the bolts to 40 ft. lbs. (54 Nm).

13. Connect the driveshaft and torque the bolts to 20 ft. lbs. (27 Nm).

14. Assemble the cable components. Screw on the clevis until the pin can be inserted while the lever and cable are held tightly in the applied position. Then, remove the pin, let go of the cable and lever and turn the clevis 10 full turns counterclockwise (loosen).

15. Install the pin.

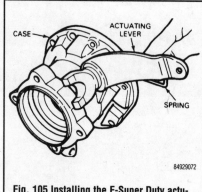

Fig. 105 Installing the F-Super Duty actuating lever

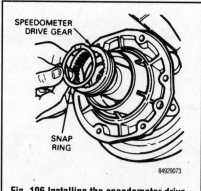

Fig. 106 Installing the speedometer drive gear on the F-Super Duty parking brake

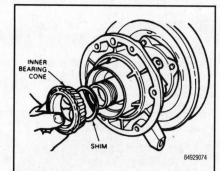

Fig. 107 Installing the inner bearing cone and shim on the F-Super Duty parking brake

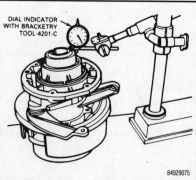

Fig. 108 Measuring end-play on the F-Super Duty parking brake

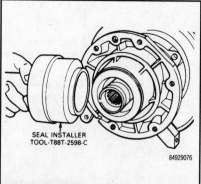

Fig. 109 Installing the inner seal on the F-Super Duty parking brake

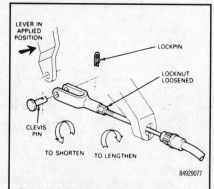

Fig. 110 F-Super Duty parking brake adjustment points

REAR WHEEL ANTI-LOCK BRAKE SYSTEM (RABS)

General Information

The Rear Wheel Anti-lock Brake System (RABS) is an electronically operated, hydraulically controlled rear wheel brake control system. Major components include the vacuum power brake booster, master cylinder, the speed sensor, and the control valve or Hydraulic Control Unit (HCU) and the control module.

The system is designed to retard rear wheel lockup during periods of high wheel slip when braking. Retarding the rear wheel lockup is accomplished by modulating fluid pressure to the rear wheel brake circuit. When the control module detects a variation in voltage across the speed sensor, the RABS is activated. The control module opens and closes various valves located inside the HCU/control unit. These valves, called dump and isolation valves, modulate the hydraulic pressure to the rear wheels by applying and venting the pressure to the brake fluid circuits.

Diagnosis and Testing

DIAGNOSTIC TROUBLE CODE RETRIEVAL

Except 1999–00 Super Duty Models

✳ WARNING

Care must be taken to connect only the black/orange stripe wire to ground. Attaching the mating connector wire to ground will result in a blown fuse.

Verify the ignition switch is in the RUN position (engine does not need to be running). Next, locate the black RABS II diagnostic connector. The diagnostic connector has two mating halves, one of which has a black/orange wire connected to it. Detach the two connector halves. Attach one end of a jumper wire to the black/orange wire side of the diagnostic connector. Ground the opposite end of the jumper wire by connecting it to a ground until the ABS light begins to flash. Grounding this wire should start the yellow ABS warning indicator flashing.

The code consists of a number of short flashes and ends with a long flash. Count the short flashes and include the following long flash in the count to obtain the code number. For example, three short flashes followed by one long flash indicates diagnostic trouble code 4. The code will continue to repeat itself until the key is turned off. It is recommended that the code be verified by reading it several times. This code will be used later for system repair instructions. It should be written down for future use. A diagnostic trouble code 16 is obtained when the anti-lock brake control module detects normal system operation.

1999–00 Super Duty Models

The Diagnostic Trouble Codes (DTC) are retrieved using a scan tool, such as Rotunda NGS Tester 007-00500 or its equivalent. Refer to the manufacturer's instructions for operating the tool and retrieving the codes.

The data link connector (DLC) for the ABS is the OBDII connector located under the driver's side of the instrument panel, underneath the steering column.

Rear Wheel Anti-Lock Brake System (RABS)

Diagnostic Trouble Codes

Diagnostic Trouble Code (DTC) 2 — Open RABS II Isolation Solenoid Circuit

Diagnostic Trouble Code (DTC) 3 — Open RABS II Dump Solenoid Circuit

Diagnostic Trouble Code (DTC) 4 — Open/Grounded RABS Valve Reset Circuit

Diagnostic Trouble Code (DTC) 5 — Excessive Dump Solenoid Activity

Diagnostic Trouble Code (DTC) 6 — Erratic Rear Anti-Lock Brake Sensor Circuit

Diagnostic Trouble Code (DTC) 7 — No Isolation Solenoid During Self-Check

Diagnostic Trouble Code (DTC) 8 — No Dump Solenoid During Self-Check

Diagnostic Trouble Code (DTC) 9 — High Speed Sensor Resistance

Diagnostic Trouble Code (DTC) 10 — Low Speed Sensor Resistance

Diagnostic Trouble Code (DTC) 11 — Brake Pedal Position (BPP) Switch Always Closed

Diagnostic Trouble Code (DTC) 12 — Loss Of Hydraulic Brake Fluid During An Anti-Lock Stop

Diagnostic Trouble Code (DTC) 13 — RABS II Module Failure

Diagnostic Trouble Codes (DTC) 16 — RABS System OK

91199G25

RABS DIAGNOSTIC TROUBLE CODES - 1999-00 SUPER DUTY MODELS

Code	Description
B1342	Anit-lock brake control module failure
C1241	Hydraulic pressure differential switch
C1226	Brake warning lamp output-short-to-ground
C1202/C1204	Rear dump valve
C1206/C1208	Rear isolation valve
C1230	Rear anti-lock brake sensor (electrical/static)
C1229/C1237	Rear anti-lock brake sensor (dynamic)
C1169	Excessive dump time
C1222	Wheel speed error
B2141/B2477	Vehicle speed calibration data not programmed into the control module

91199G26

ERASING DIAGNOSTIC TROUBLE CODES (DTC)

Except 1999–00 Super Duty Models

The last step of the system pre-check always includes clearing the keep alive memory (KAM). Turn off the ignition while the diagnostic connector halves are separated as described in retrieving diagnostic trouble codes in this section. The diagnostic connector should be re-assembled to provide KAM power to the anti-lock brake control module.

1999–00 Super Duty Models

The Diagnostic Trouble Codes (DTC) are cleared using a scan tool, such as Rotunda NGS Tester 007-00500 or its equivalent. Refer to the manufacturer's instructions for operating the tool and clearing the codes.

Speed Sensor

REMOVAL & INSTALLATION

▸ See Figures 111 and 112

The sensor is located on the rear axle housing.
1. Raise and safely support the vehicle securely on jackstands.
2. Carefully clean the axle surface to keep dirt from entering the housing.
3. Detach the connector on the speed sensor.
4. Remove the sensor hold-down bolt.
5. Remove the sensor.
6. If a new sensor is being installed, lubricate the O-ring with clean engine

Fig. 111 Detach the connector on the speed sensor

91199P30

Fig. 112 Remove the sensor hold-down bolt and remove the sensor

91199P31

oil. Carefully push the sensor into the housing aligning the mounting flange hole with the threaded hole in the housing. Tighten the hold-down bolt to 30 ft. lbs. (41 Nm)—If the old sensor is being installed, clean it thoroughly and install a new O-ring coated with clean engine oil.
7. Attach the connector on the speed sensor.
8. Lower the vehicle.

Tone (Exciter) Ring

REMOVAL & INSTALLATION

The exciter ring is located in the differential case inside the axle housing on the rear gear. The rear differential must be disassembled to replace the ring. Refer to Section 7.

Control Valve

REMOVAL & INSTALLATION

1997–98 F-250HD, F-350 and F-Super Duty; F-150 and F-250

▸ See Figure 113

✳✳ CAUTION

Brake fluid contains polyglycol ethers and polyglycols. Avoid contact with the eyes and wash your hands thoroughly after handling

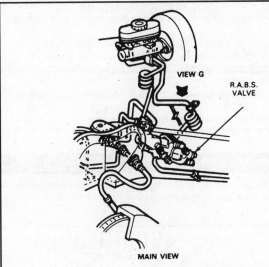

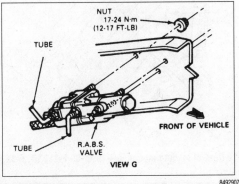

Fig. 113 Rear anti-lock braking system valve—1997–98 F-250HD, F-350 and F-Super Duty

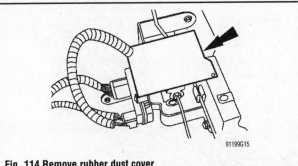

Fig. 114 Remove rubber dust cover

brake fluid. If you do get brake fluid in your eyes, flush your eyes with clean, running water for 15 minutes. If eye irritation persists, or if you have taken brake fluid internally, IMMEDIATELY seek medical assistance.

The valve is located on the frame rail, under the vehicle on the driver's side on the 1997–98 F-250HD, F-350 and F-Super Duty. The valve is located in the brake lines, below the master cylinder.
1. Disconnect the brake lines from the valve and plug the lines.
2. Disconnect the wiring harness at the valve.
3. Remove the 3 nuts retaining the valve to the frame rail and lift out the valve.
4. Installation is the reverse of removal. Don't overtighten the brake lines. Bleed the brakes.

1999–00 F-250SD, F-350 and F-Super Duty
♦ See Figures 114, 115, 116 and 117

✸✸ WARNING

Electronic modules are sensitive to static electrical charges. If exposed to these charges, damage may result.

1. On diesel engine equipped vehicles, remove the battery tray.
2. On gasoline engine equipped vehicles, disconnect the battery tray ground cable.
3. On gasoline engine equipped vehicles, remove the engine air cleaner assembly.
4. On gasoline engine equipped vehicles, remove the EVAP canister.
5. Remove rubber dust cover.
6. Remove pushpin.
7. Detach the anti-lock brake control module electrical connectors.

✸✸ CAUTION

Brake fluid contains polyglycol ethers and polyglycols. Avoid contact with the eyes and wash your hands thoroughly after handling brake fluid. If you do get brake fluid in your eyes, flush your eyes with clean, running water for 15 minutes. If eye irritation persists, or if you have taken brake fluid internally, IMMEDIATELY seek medical assistance.

✸✸ WARNING

Plug each port to prevent brake fluid from spilling.

8. Disconnect the hydraulic brake lines.
9. Remove the HCU bracket
10. Remove the HCU.
11. The installation is the reverse of the removal.
12. Bleed the RABS system.

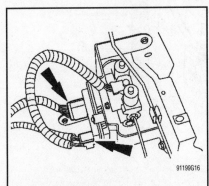

Fig. 115 Detach the anti-lock brake control module electrical connectors

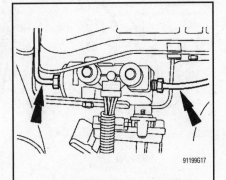

Fig. 116 Disconnect the hydraulic brake lines

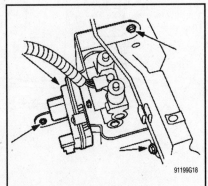

Fig. 117 Remove the HCU bracket and remove the HCU

Control Module

REMOVAL & INSTALLATION

1997–98 F-250HD, F-350 and F-Super Duty

▶ See Figure 118

The module is located on the firewall just inboard of the master cylinder.
1. Disconnect the wiring harness.
2. Remove the 2 attaching screws and lift out the module.
3. Installation is the reverse of removal.

F-150 and F-250

✳✳ WARNING

Electronic modules are sensitive to static electrical charges. If exposed to these charges, damage may result.

1. Disconnect the negative battery cable.
2. Remove the instrument panel cluster panel. Refer to Section 6.
3. Detach the anti-lock brake control module electrical connector.
4. Remove the module retaining bolts.
5. Remove the anti-lock brake control module.
6. The installation is the reverse of the removal.

1999–00 F-250SD, F-350 and F-Super Duty

▶ See Figure 119

✳✳ WARNING

Electronic modules are sensitive to static electrical charges. If exposed to these charges, damage may result.

1. On diesel engine equipped vehicles, remove the battery tray.
2. On gasoline engine equipped vehicles, disconnect the battery ground cable.
3. On gasoline engine equipped vehicles, remove the engine air cleaner.
4. On gasoline engine equipped vehicles, remove the EVAP canister.
5. Remove rubber dust cover.
6. Remove pushpin.
7. Detach the three anti-lock brake control module electrical connectors.
8. Remove the screw.
9. Lift and remove the anti-lock brake control module.
10. The installation is the reverse of the removal.

Bleeding the ABS System

The RABS system is bleed in the same manner as a conventional brake system. Refer to brake bleeding in this section.

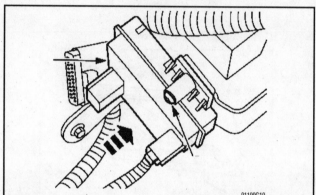

Fig. 119 Control module mounting—1999–00 F-250SD, F-350 and F-Super Duty

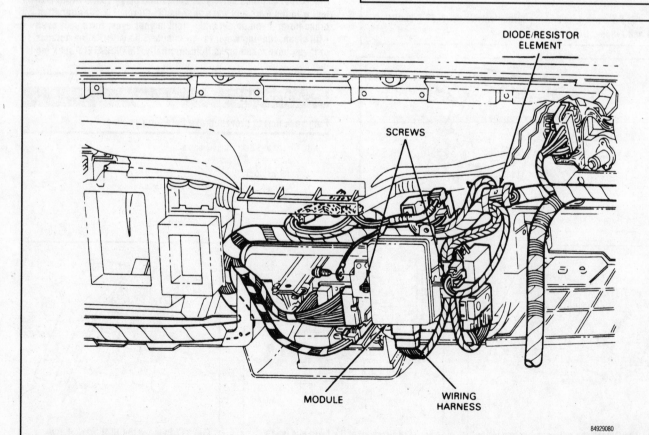

Fig. 118 Rear anti-lock braking system module

4-WHEEL ANTI-LOCK BRAKE SYSTEM (ABS)

General Information

The 4-Wheel Anti-lock Brake System (ABS) is an electronically operated, all wheel brake control system. Major components include the power brake booster, master cylinder, the wheel speed sensors, and the Hydraulic Control Unit (HCU) which contains the control module, a relay, and the pressure control valves.

The system is designed to retard wheel lockup during periods of high wheel slip when braking. Retarding wheel lockup is accomplished by modulating fluid pressure to the wheel brake units. When the control module detects a variation in voltage across the wheel speed sensors, the ABS is activated. The control module opens and closes various valves located inside the HCU. These valves, called dump and isolation valves, modulate the hydraulic pressure to the wheels by applying and venting the pressure to the brake fluid circuits.

Diagnosis and Testing

The ABS module performs system tests and self-tests during startup and normal operation. The valves, wheel sensors and fluid level circuits are monitored for proper operation. If a fault is found, the ABS will be deactivated and the amber ANTI LOCK light will be lit until the ignition is turned OFF. When the light is lit, the Diagnostic Trouble Code (DTC) may be obtained. Under normal operation, the light will stay on for about 2 seconds while the ignition switch is in the ON position and will go out shortly after.

The Diagnostic Trouble Codes (DTC) are an alphanumeric code and a scan tool, such as Rotunda NGS Tester 007-00500 or its equivalent, is required to retrieve the codes. Refer to the manufacturer's instructions for operating the tool and retrieving the codes.

The data link connector (DLC) for the ABS is the OBDII connector located under the driver's side of the instrument panel, underneath the steering column.

Speed Sensors

REMOVAL & INSTALLATION

Front

▶ **See Figures 120 and 121**

1. Raise and safely support the vehicle securely on jackstands.
2. Remove the wheel and tire assembly.
3. On 4 X 4 models except for F-250SD, F-350 and F-Super Duty models, remove the disc brake rotor shield.

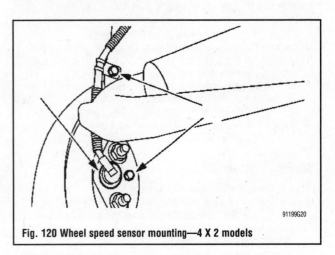

91199G20

Fig. 120 Wheel speed sensor mounting—4 X 2 models

4-WHEEL ABS DIAGNOSTIC TROUBLE CODES

Code	Description
B1342	Anit-lock brake control module failure
C1220	Yellow ABS warning indicator failure
B2141/B2477	Vehicle speed calibration data not programmed into the control module
C1194/C1196	Left front dump valve
C1198/C1200	Left front isolation valve
C1202/C1204	Rear dump valve
C1206/C1208	Rear isolation valve
C1210/C1212	Right front dump valve
C1214/C1216	Right front isolation valve
C1155	Left front anti-lock brake sensor (electrical/static)
C1158/C1233	Left front anti-lock brake sensor (dynamic)
C1145	Right front anti-lock brake sensor (electrical/static)
C1148/C1234	Right front anti-lock brake sensor (dynamic)
C1230	Rear anti-lock brake sensor (electrical/static)
C1095/C1096	Pump motor
C1113/C1115	Internal power relay
C1185	Open internal power relay
C1229/C1237	Rear anti-lock brake sensor (dynamic)
C1169	Excessive dump time
C1184	ABS system timeout
C1222	Wheel speed error

91199G27

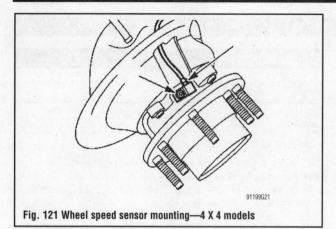

Fig. 121 Wheel speed sensor mounting—4 X 4 models

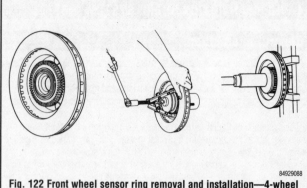

Fig. 122 Front wheel sensor ring removal and installation—4-wheel ABS

4. On 4 X 4 F-250SD, F-350 and F-Super Duty models, remove the disc brake rotor.
5. Detach the front anti-lock brake sensor electrical connector.
6. Separate the sensor cable from the brake hose clips.
7. Remove the front anti-lock brake sensor bolt and the front anti-lock brake sensor.
8. The installation is the reverse of the removal.

Rear

▶ **See Figures 111 and 112**

The sensor is located on the rear axle housing.
1. Raise and safely support the vehicle securely on jackstands.
2. Carefully clean the axle surface to keep dirt from entering the housing.
3. Detach the connector on the speed sensor.
4. Remove the sensor hold-down bolt.
5. Remove the sensor.
6. If a new sensor is being installed, lubricate the O-ring with clean engine oil. Carefully push the sensor into the housing aligning the mounting flange hole with the threaded hole in the housing. Tighten the hold-down bolt to 30 ft. lbs. (41 Nm)—If the old sensor is being installed, clean it thoroughly and install a new O-ring coated with clean engine oil.
7. Attach the connector on the speed sensor.
8. Lower the vehicle.

Tone (Exciter) Ring

REMOVAL & INSTALLATION

Front

4 X 2 MODELS

▶ **See Figure 122**

1. Raise and support the front end on jackstands.
2. Remove the wheels.
3. Remove the caliper, rotor and hub.
4. Using a 3-jawed puller, remove the ring from the hub. The ring cannot be reused; it must be replaced.
To install:
5. Support the hub in a press so that the lug studs do not rest on the work surface.
6. Position the new sensor ring on the hub. Using a cylindrical adapter 98mm IDx106mm OD, press the ring into place. The ring must be fully seated!
7. The remainder of installation is the reverse of removal.

4 X 4 MODELS

The exciter ring is integral to the hub assembly. Refer to Section 7.

Rear

The exciter ring is located in the differential case inside the axle housing on the rear gear. The rear differential must be disassembled to replace the ring. Refer to Section 7.

Hydraulic Control Unit

REMOVAL & INSTALLATION

▶ **See Figures 123 and 124**

1. Disconnect the negative battery cable.
2. On Super Duty models, remove the air cleaner assembly.
3. On Super Duty models, remove the EVAP canister.
4. Detach the anti-lock brake control module electrical connectors.

❋❋ CAUTION

Brake fluid contains polyglycol ethers and polyglycols. Avoid contact with the eyes and wash your hands thoroughly after handling brake fluid. If you do get brake fluid in your eyes, flush your eyes with clean, running water for 15 minutes. If eye irritation persists, or if you have taken brake fluid internally, IMMEDIATELY seek medical assistance.

5. Disconnect and plug the hydraulic brake lines.
6. Remove the HCU retaining bolts and remove the HCU.
7. If necessary, remove the HCU bracket.
To install:
8. If removed, install the HCU bracket.
9. Position the HCU.
10. Install and tighten the retaining bolts.

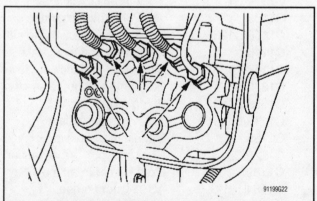

Fig. 123 Disconnect and plug the hydraulic brake lines

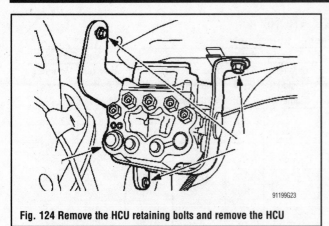

Fig. 124 Remove the HCU retaining bolts and remove the HCU

11. Connect the hydraulic brake lines.
12. Connect the anti-lock brake control module electrical connectors.
13. On Super Duty models, install the EVAP canister.
14. On Super Duty models, install the air cleaner assembly.
15. Connect the negative battery cable.
16. Bleed the 4-wheel ABS.

Control Module

REMOVAL & INSTALLATION

▶ See Figure 125

❊❊ WARNING

Electronic modules are sensitive to static electrical charges. If exposed to these charges, damage may result.

1. Disconnect the negative battery cable.
2. Detach the anti-lock brake control module electrical connectors.
3. Remove the module retaining screws and remove the anti-lock control module.
4. The installation is the reverse of the removal.

Bleeding the ABS System

❊❊ CAUTION

Brake fluid contains polyglycol ethers and polyglycols. Avoid contact with the eyes and wash your hands thoroughly after handling brake fluid. If you do get brake fluid in your eyes, flush your eyes with clean, running water for 15 minutes. If eye irritation persists, or if you have taken brake fluid internally, IMMEDIATELY seek medical assistance.

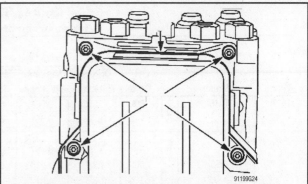

Fig. 125 Remove the module retaining screws and remove the anti-lock brake control module

→If equipped with the 4 wheel anti-lock brake system and the Hydraulic Control Unit (HCU) has been replaced or is suspected of containing trapped air, bleed the brake system using the procedure below. Conventional brake system bleeding cannot remove the air trapped in the lower portion of the HCU.

If a spongy brake pedal is present and air in the hydraulic control unit is suspected, use the following procedure:
1. Bleed the brake system as outlined in the conventional bleeding procedure.
2. Connect a New Generation Star (NGS) tester or equivalent scan tool, to the serial data link connector below the instrument panel as though retrieving codes.
3. Make sure the ignition switch is in the RUN position.
4. Follow the instructions on the NGS screen. Verify correct vehicle and model year go to the "Diagnostic Data Link" menu item, choose ABS Module, choose "Function Tests", and choose "Service Bleed".

❊❊ WARNING

Do not allow the brake master cylinder to run dry of brake fluid during the brake bleeding procedure. Only use new DOT 3 or equivalent brake fluid from a closed container.

5. Bleed the right-front wheel as follows:
   a. Open the caliper bleed screw and pump the brake pedal for 3 seconds. Repeat the procedure again.
   b. When the fluid runs clear, begin the program and continue to pump the brake pedal.
   c. Continue bleeding for approximately 1 to 2 minutes after the program ends and then tighten the bleed screw.
6. Repeat the bleeding procedure to the left-front, left-rear and finally the right-rear wheel.
7. Remove the pressure bleeding device and adjust the brake fluid level.
8. Road test the vehicle and check for proper brake system operation.

BRAKE SPECIFICATIONS
All measurements in inches unless noted

Year	Model		Master Cyl. Bore	Brake Disc			Brake Drum Diameter			Minimum Lining Thickness	Brake Caliper	
				Original Thickness	Minimum Thickness	Maximum Runout	Original Inside Diameter	Max. Wear Limit	Maximum Machine Diameter		Bracket Bolts (ft. lbs.)	Mounting Bolts (ft. lbs.)
1997	F-150	F	1.000	1.023	0.964	0.0025	—	—	—	0.030	136	21-26
		R	—	0.700	0.657	0.0025	11.03	11.12	11.06	0.030	120	20
	F-250	F	1.000	1.023	0.964	0.0025	—	—	—	0.030	136	21-26
		R	—	0.700	0.657	0.0025	11.03	11.12	11.06	0.030	120	20
	F-250HD		1.062	1.220	1.210	0.0025	12.00	12.09	12.06	0.030	141-190	16-30
	F-350		1.125	1.220	1.210	0.0025	12.00	12.09	12.06	0.030	141-190	16-30
	F-Super Duty	F	NA	1.220	1.180	0.0025	—	—	—	0.030	141-190	16-30
		R	—	NA	1.430	0.0025	—	—	—	0.030	74-100	—
	Expedition	F	1.000	1.023	0.964	0.0025	—	—	—	0.030	136	21-26
		R	—	0.700	0.657	0.0025	—	—	—	0.030	120	20
1998	F-150	F	1.000	1.023	0.964	0.0025	—	—	—	0.030	136	21-26
		R	—	0.700	0.657	0.0025	11.03	11.12	11.06	0.030	120	20
	F-250	F	1.000	1.023	0.964	0.0025	—	—	—	0.030	136	21-26
		R	—	0.700	0.657	0.0025	11.03	11.12	11.06	0.030	120	20
	F-250HD		1.062	1.220	1.210	0.0025	12.00	12.09	12.06	0.030	141-190	16-30
	F-350		1.125	1.220	1.210	0.0025	12.00	12.09	12.06	0.030	141-190	16-30
	F-Super Duty	F	NA	1.220	1.180	0.0025	—	—	—	0.030	141-190	16-30
		R	—	NA	1.430	0.0025	—	—	—	0.030	74-100	—
	Expedition	F	1.000	1.023	0.964	0.0025	—	—	—	0.030	136	21-26
		R	—	0.700	0.657	0.0025	—	—	—	0.030	120	20
	Navigator	F	1.000	1.023	0.964	0.0025	—	—	—	0.030	136	21-26
		R	—	0.700	0.657	0.0025	—	—	—	0.030	120	20
1999	F-150	F	1.000	1.023	0.964	0.0025	—	—	—	0.030	136	21-26
		R	—	0.700	0.657	0.0025	11.03	11.12	11.06	0.030	120	20
	F-250	F	1.000	1.023	0.964	0.0025	—	—	—	0.030	136	21-26
		R	—	0.700	0.657	0.0025	11.03	11.12	11.06	0.030	120	20
	F-250SD	F	NA	1.220	1.180	0.0025	—	—	—	0.030	166	42
		R	—	NA	1.430	0.0025	—	—	—	0.030	128	27
	F-350	F	NA	1.220	1.180	0.0025	—	—	—	0.030	166	42
		R	—	NA	1.430	0.0025	—	—	—	0.030	128	27
	F-Super Duty	F	NA	1.220	1.180	0.0025	—	—	—	0.030	166	42
		R	—	NA	1.430	0.0025	—	—	—	0.030	128	27
	Expedition	F	1.000	1.023	0.964	0.0025	—	—	—	0.030	136	21-26
		R	—	0.700	0.657	0.0025	—	—	—	0.030	120	20
	Navigator	F	1.000	1.023	0.964	0.0025	—	—	—	0.030	136	21-26
		R	—	0.700	0.657	0.0025	—	—	—	0.030	120	20
2000	F-150	F	1.000	1.023	0.964	0.0025	—	—	—	0.030	136	21-26
		R	—	0.700	0.657	0.0025	11.03	11.12	11.06	0.030	120	20
	F-250	F	1.000	1.023	0.964	0.0025	—	—	—	0.030	136	21-26
		R	—	0.700	0.657	0.0025	11.03	11.12	11.06	0.030	120	20
	F-250SD	F	NA	1.220	1.180	0.0025	—	—	—	0.030	166	42
		R	—	NA	1.430	0.0025	—	—	—	0.030	128	27
	F-350	F	NA	1.220	1.180	0.0025	—	—	—	0.030	166	42
		R	—	NA	1.430	0.0025	—	—	—	0.030	128	27
	F-Super Duty	F	NA	1.220	1.180	0.0025	—	—	—	0.030	166	42
		R	—	NA	1.430	0.0025	—	—	—	0.030	128	27
	Expedition	F	1.000	1.023	0.964	0.0025	—	—	—	0.030	136	21-26
		R	—	0.700	0.657	0.0025	—	—	—	0.030	120	20
	Navigator	F	1.000	1.023	0.964	0.0025	—	—	—	0.030	136	21-26
		R	—	0.700	0.657	0.0025	—	—	—	0.030	120	20

NA - Not Available
F - Front
R - Rear

91199C01

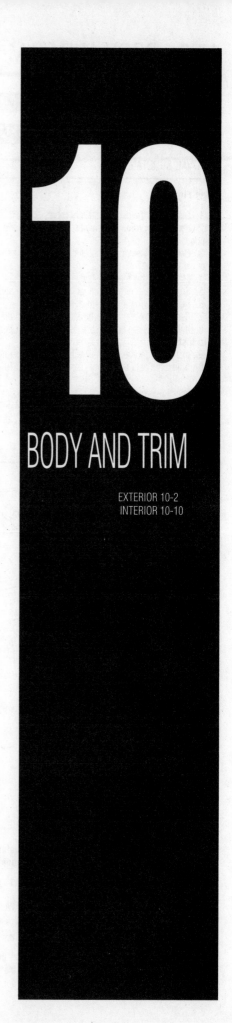

10

BODY AND TRIM

EXTERIOR

Doors

REMOVAL & INSTALLATION

▶ **See Figure 1**

1. Disconnect the negative battery cable.
2. Remove any trim necessary to access the electrical connector inside the front door.
3. Detach the electrical connector inside the door and pull the wire harness out of the front door.
4. Matchmark the hinge-to-body and hinge-to-door locations.
5. Support the door either on jackstands or have somebody hold it for you.
6. Remove the lower hinge-to-door bolts.
7. Remove the upper hinge-to-door bolts and lift the door off the hinges.
8. If the hinges are being replaced, remove them from the door pillar.

To install:

9. Install the door and hinges with the bolts finger tight.
10. Adjust the door and tighten the hinge bolts to 19–25 ft. lbs. (26–35 Nm).
11. Install the wire harness into the door opening.
12. Attach the electrical connector inside the front door.
13. Install any trim removed from the door.
14. Connect the negative battery cable.

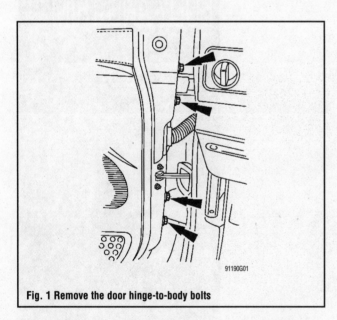

Fig. 1 Remove the door hinge-to-body bolts

ADJUSTMENT

1997–98 F-250HD, F-350 and F-Super Duty

▶ **See Figures 2 and 3**

➡**Loosen the hinge-to-door bolts for lateral adjustment only. Loosen the hinge-to-body bolts for both lateral and vertical adjustment.**

1. Determine which hinge bolts are to be loosened and back them out just enough to allow movement.
2. To move the door safely, use a padded prybar. When the door is in the proper position, tighten the bolts to 19–25 ft. lbs. (26–35 Nm) and check the door operation. There should be no binding or interference when the door is closed and opened.
3. Door closing adjustment can also be affected by the position of the lock striker plate. Loosen the striker plate bolts and move the striker plate just enough to permit proper closing and locking of the door.

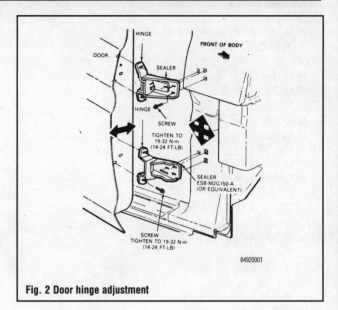

Fig. 2 Door hinge adjustment

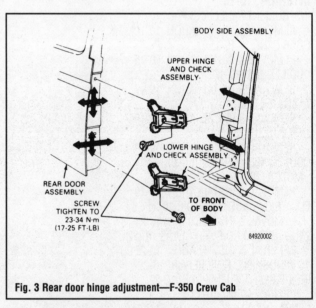

Fig. 3 Rear door hinge adjustment—F-350 Crew Cab

F-150, F-250, Expedition and Navigator

HORIZONTAL AND VERTICAL ADJUSTMENT

▶ **See Figure 1**

1. Loosen the front door hinge to front door bolts.
2. Adjust the front door alignment.
3. Tighten the front door hinge to front door bolts to 19–25 ft. lbs. (26–35 Nm).

FRONT DOOR FORE AND AFT ADJUSTMENT

▶ **See Figure 1**

➡**Check the rear door hinge adjustment before adjusting the front door hinge.**

1. Remove the front fender.
2. Loosen the front door hinge to body bolts.
3. Adjust the front door alignment to specification.
4. Tighten the front door hinge to body bolts.
5. Install the front fender.

1999–00 F-Super Duty Models

DOOR ADJUSTMENT

▶ **See Figure 1**

➡ **The following procedure is for performing fore, aft, up, down and tilt adjustments.**

1. Remove the door striker.
2. Loosen the bolts only enough to allow for slight door movement.
3. Carefully close and adjust the door until flush with the adjacent body panels.
4. Carefully open the door and tighten the bolts.
5. Re-install and adjust the door striker.
6. Check the door for proper operation and alignment.

STRIKER ADJUSTMENT

▶ **See Figure 4**

➡ **Mark the position of the striker before loosening.**

1. Loosen the striker retaining bolts.
2. Adjust the door striker and tighten the striker retaining bolts.

Hood

REMOVAL & INSTALLATION

▶ **See Figures 5, 6 and 7**

➡ **You'll need an assistant for this job.**

1. Open the hood.
2. Disconnect the negative battery cable.
3. Detach any electrical connectors, washer fluid lines, or any other components necessary for hood removal.
4. On all models except for 1997–98 F-250HD, F-350 and F-Super Duty:
   a. Support the hood with a bar, long sturdy handle or have an assistant hold it.

b. Release the hood lift-to-body retaining clips and remove the hood lifts from the pivot ball.
5. Matchmark the hood-to-hinge position.
6. While an assistant supports the hood, remove the hinge bolts from one side of the hood.
7. Repeat the procedure for the other side.
8. Carefully lift and remove the hood taking care not to scratch the paint.
9. Place the hood in a safe place and place rags around the painted surfaces that will make contact with the ground or other surface on which it is placed.
10. The installation is the reverse of the removal. Tighten the hinge bolts to19–25 ft. lbs. (26–35 Nm).

ALIGNMENT

1. Open the hood.
2. Loosen the hinge-to-hood bolts just enough to allow movement of the hood.
3. Move the hood as required to obtain the proper fit and alignment between the hood and the top of the cowl panel.
4. Tighten the hood-to-hinge bolts to 19–25 ft. lbs. (26–35 Nm).
5. Lubricate the latch and hinges and check the hood fit several times.

Tailgate

REMOVAL & INSTALLATION

▶ **See Figures 8 and 9**

1. Remove the tailgate support or strap or cable at the pillar T-head pivot.2. Lift off the tailgate at the right hinge.
3. Pull off the left hinge.
4. Installation is the reverse of removal.

ALIGNMENT

Loosen the striker bolts and move the strikers until the tailgate is aligned. Tighten the striker bolts.

91190G02

Fig. 4 Loosen the striker mounting bolt

91190P05

Fig. 5 Release the hood lift-to-body retaining clips and remove the hood lifts from the pivot ball

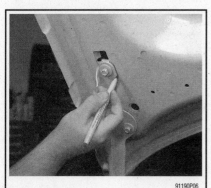

91190P06

Fig. 6 Matchmark the hood-to-hinge position

91190P07

Fig. 7 While an assistant supports the hood, remove the hinge bolts from one side of the hood

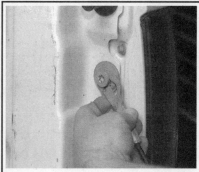

91190P30

Fig. 8 Grasp the tailgate support cable and . . .

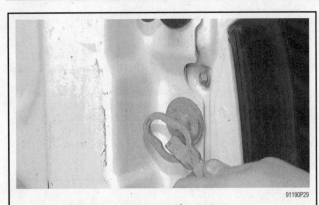

Fig. 9 . . . lift the cable from the pillar T-head pivot

Liftgate

REMOVAL & INSTALLATION

▶ See Figure 10

1. Disconnect the negative battery cable.
2. Remove the trim and detach the harness connector for the liftgate.
3. Have an assistant support the liftgate.
4. Remove the liftgate hinge-to-body bolts.
5. Remove the liftgate from the vehicle.
6. The installation is the reverse of the removal.
7. Tighten the liftgate hinge-to-body bolts to 91–123 inch lbs. (10–14 Nm).

ALIGNMENT

▶ See Figure 10

1. Loosen the liftgate hinge to liftgate bolts.
2. Adjust the liftgate alignment.
3. Tighten the liftgate hinge to liftgate bolts.
4. Tighten the liftgate hinge-to-liftgate bolts to 91–123 inch lbs. (10–14 Nm).

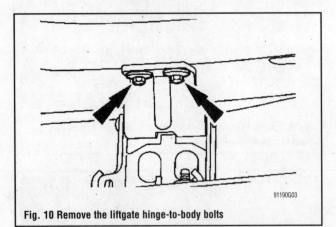

Fig. 10 Remove the liftgate hinge-to-body bolts

Grille

REMOVAL & INSTALLATION

1997–98 F-250HD, F-350 and F-Super Duty

▶ See Figure 11

1. Open the hood.
2. Remove the screws securing the top of the grille to the front valance panel.

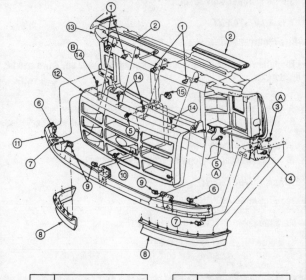

Item	Description	Item	Description
1	Nut (4 Req'd)	9	Nut (3 Req'd)
2	Radiator Air Deflector	10	Screw (1 Req'd)
3	Screw (1 Req'd)	11	Front Valance Panel
4	Screw (1 Req'd Each Side)	12	Radiator Grille
5	Screw (3 Req'd)	13	Radiator Grille Opening Panel Reinforcement
6	Nut (1 Req'd Each Side)	14	Screw (4 Req'd)
7	Nut (1 Req'd Each Side)	A	Tighten to 6.0-8.0 N·m (53-71 Lb-In)
8	Front Bumper Stone (RH) Deflector Filler	B	Tighten to 1.0-2.0 N·m (9-18 Lb-In)
8	Front Bumper Stone (LH) Deflector Filler		

Fig. 11 Grille mounting—1997–98 F-250HD, F-350 and F-Super Duty

3. Remove the screws securing the top of the grille to the radiator grille opening panel reinforcement.
4. Remove the grille.
5. The installation is the reverse of the removal.

F-150, F-250 and Expedition

▶ See Figures 12 and 13

1. Raise and support the hood.
2. Remove the service jack handle.
3. Remove the retaining screws and remove front upper air deflector.
4. Remove the headlamps.
5. Remove the combination lamps.
6. Remove the eight stone guard pin-type retainers (four on each side).
7. Remove the ten radiator grille screws.
8. Release the clips from the radiator grille opening panel reinforcement.
9. Remove the radiator grille.
10. The installation is the reverse of the removal.

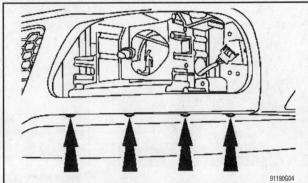

Fig. 12 Remove the eight stone guard pin-type retainers (four on each side)

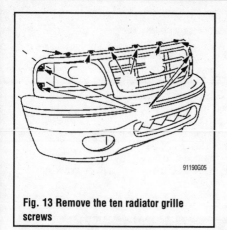

Fig. 13 Remove the ten radiator grille screws

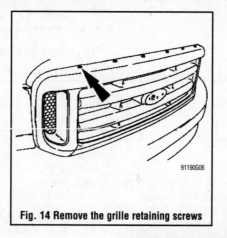

Fig. 14 Remove the grille retaining screws

Fig. 15 Release the lower retainers and remove the grille assembly

Navigator

The grille on the Navigator is integral with the hood assembly.

1999–00 F-Super Duty Models

▶ See Figures 14 and 15

1. Remove the grille retaining screws.
2. Release the lower retainers.
3. Remove the radiator grille.

To install:

4. Position the radiator grille in the grille opening.
5. Secure the radiator grille retainers by pushing into place.
6. Install the retaining screws.

Outside Mirrors

REMOVAL & INSTALLATION

1997–98 F-250HD, F-350 and F-Super Duty

DUAL POSITION RECREATION SWING-OUT MIRROR

▶ See Figure 16

1. Remove the four mirror retaining screws .
2. Remove the mirror from the door.
3. The installation is the reverse of the removal.

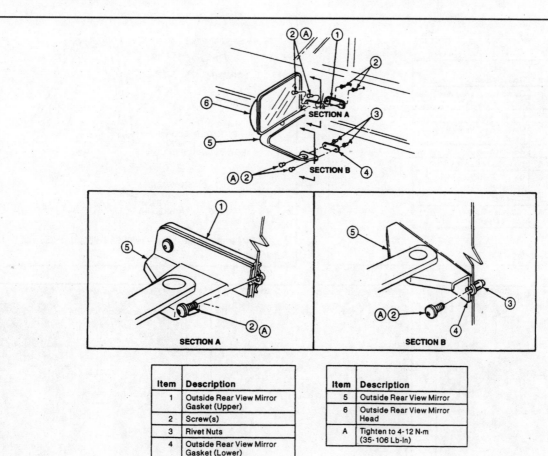

Item	Description
1	Outside Rear View Mirror Gasket (Upper)
2	Screw(s)
3	Rivet Nuts
4	Outside Rear View Mirror Gasket (Lower)

Item	Description
5	Outside Rear View Mirror
6	Outside Rear View Mirror Head
A	Tighten to 4-12 N·m (35-106 Lb-In)

Fig. 16 Dual position recreation swing-out mirror mounting

WESTERN TYPE SWING-AWAY

♦ **See Figure 17**

1. Remove the four mirror retaining screws .
2. Remove the mirror from the door.
3. The installation is the reverse of the removal.

POWER MIRROR

♦ **See Figure 18**

1. Disconnect the negative battery cable.
2. Remove the front door trim panel.
3. Remove the front door watershield.
4. Detach the power mirror electrical connector.
5. Remove the two screws retaining the mirror to the outside of the door.
6. Remove the one screw retaining the mirror to the inside of the door.

7. Remove the mirror from the door.
8. The installation is the reverse of the removal.

Except 1997–98 F-250HD, F-350 and F-Super Duty

♦ **See Figures 19, 20 and 21**

1. Disconnect the negative battery cable.
2. Remove the front door trim panel.
3. Remove the mirror sail cover to gain access to the mirror retaining nuts.
4. If equipped with power mirrors, detach the power mirror electrical connector.
5. Disconnect the power mirror wiring clip.
6. Remove the outside rear view mirror nuts.
7. Remove the outside rear view mirror and feed the power mirror wiring through the opening in the front door.
8. The installation is the reverse of the removal.

Antenna

REPLACEMENT

1997–98 F-250HD, F-350 and F-Super Duty Models

♦ **See Figure 22**

1. Remove the radio from the instrument panel and detach the antenna cable from the radio.
2. Remove the antenna cable from retaining clips along the bottom of the instrument panel.

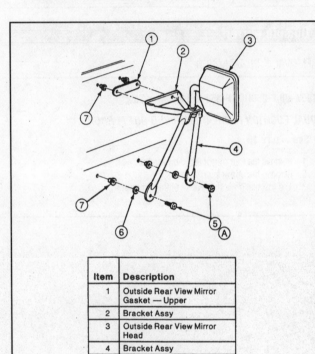

Item	Description
1	Outside Rear View Mirror Gasket — Upper
2	Bracket Assy
3	Outside Rear View Mirror Head
4	Bracket Assy
5	Screw(s) (4 Req'd)
6	Outside Rear View Mirror Gasket — Lower
7	Rivet-Nut (4 Req'd)
A	Tighten to 4-8 N·m (35-71 Lb-In)

91190G08

Fig. 17 Western type swing-away mirror mounting

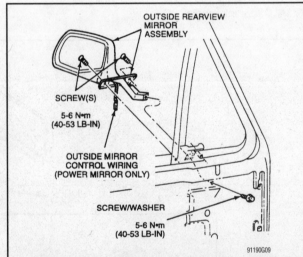

91190G09

Fig. 18 Power mirror mounting—1997–98 F-250HD, F-350 and F-Super Duty

91190P26

Fig. 19 Remove the mirror sail cover to gain access to the mirror retaining nuts

91190P27

Fig. 20 Remove the outside rear view mirror nuts and . . .

91190P28

Fig. 21 . . . remove the outside rear view mirror

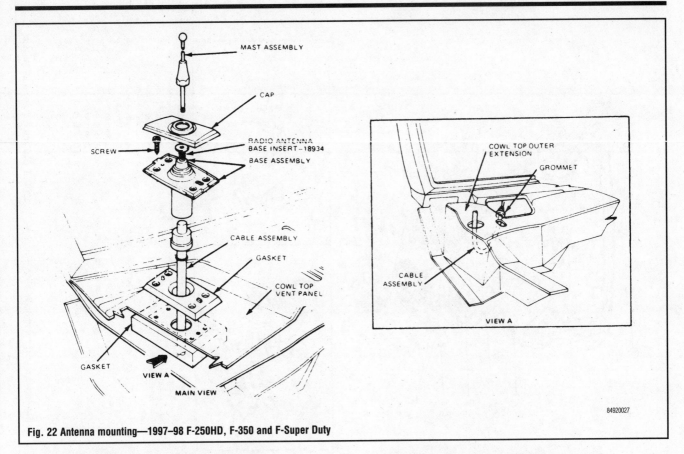

Fig. 22 Antenna mounting—1997–98 F-250HD, F-350 and F-Super Duty

3. Remove the antenna mast from the base by unscrewing it.
4. Unsnap the cap from the antenna base and remove the cap.
5. Remove the 4 screws and lift off the antenna.
6. Detach the antenna cable from the antenna base.
7. Remove the antenna base from the vehicle.
8. Installation is the reverse of removal.

F-150, F-250, Expedition and Navigator

1. Remove the antenna mast from the base by unscrewing it.
2. Remove the 3 screws and lift off the antenna.
3. Detach the antenna cable from the antenna base.
4. Remove the antenna base from the vehicle.
5. Installation is the reverse of removal.

1999–00 F-Super Duty Models

▶ See Figures 23, 24 and 25

1. Remove the passenger side cowl top vent panel cover.

2. Remove the antenna mast from the base by unscrewing it.
3. Remove the 3 screws and lift off the antenna.
4. Detach the antenna cable from the antenna base.
5. Remove the antenna base from the vehicle.
6. Installation is the reverse of removal.

Fenders

REMOVAL & INSTALLATION

1997–98 F-250HD, F-350 and F-Super Duty Models

▶ See Figures 26 and 27

1. Clean all fender fasteners and liberally apply penetrating oil.
2. Remove the headlamp assemblies.
3. Remove the fender-to-radiator support screws.
4. Remove the screw attaching the fender to the lower corner of the cab.

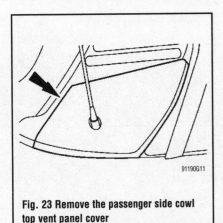

Fig. 23 Remove the passenger side cowl top vent panel cover

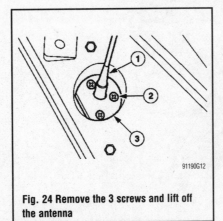

Fig. 24 Remove the 3 screws and lift off the antenna

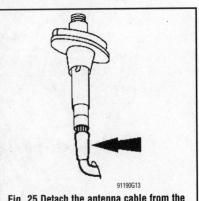

Fig. 25 Detach the antenna cable from the antenna base

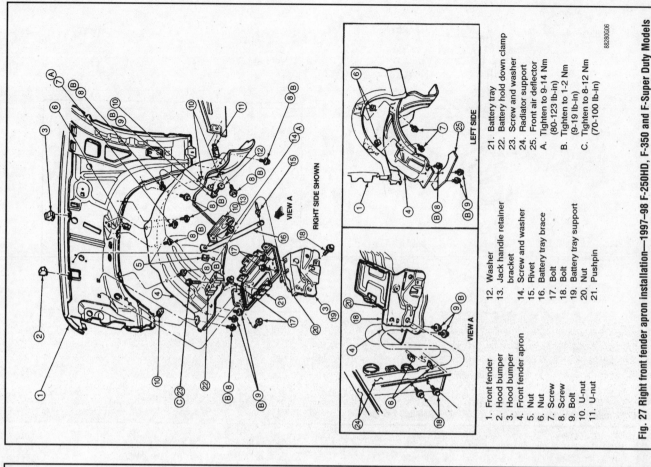

Fig. 27 Right front fender apron installation—1997–98 F-250HD, F-350 and F-Super Duty Models

1. Front fender
2. Hood bumper
3. Hood bumper
4. Front fender apron
5. Nut
6. Nut
7. Screw
8. Screw
9. Bolt
10. U-nut
11. U-nut
12. Washer
13. Jack handle retainer bracket
14. Screw and washer
15. Rivet
16. Battery tray brace
17. Bolt
18. Bolt
19. Battery tray support
20. Nut
21. Pushpin
21. Battery tray
22. Battery hold down clamp
23. Screw and washer
24. Radiator support
25. Front air deflector
A. Tighten to 9-14 Nm (80-123 lb-in)
B. Tighten to 1-2 Nm (9-19 lb-in)
C. Tighten to 8-12 Nm (70-100 lb-in)

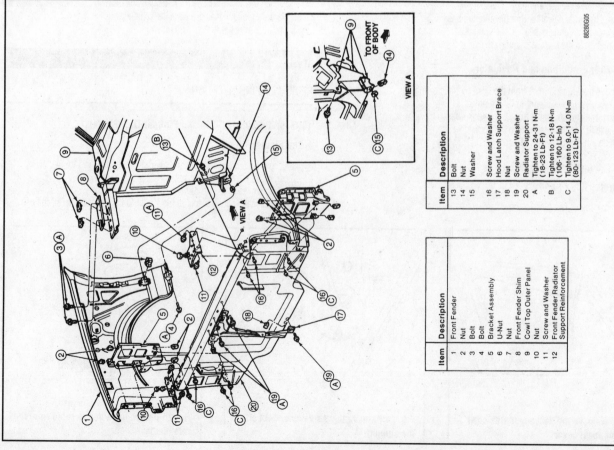

Fig. 26 Right front fender installation—1997–98 F-250HD, F-350 and F-Super Duty Models

Item	Description
1	Front Fender
2	Nut
3	Bolt
4	Bolt
5	Bracket Assembly
6	U-Nut
7	Nut
8	Front Fender Shim
9	Cowl Top Outer Panel
10	Nut
11	Screw and Washer
12	Front Fender Radiator Support Reinforcement

Item	Description
13	Bolt
14	Nut
15	Washer
16	Screw and Washer
17	Hood Latch Support Brace
18	Nut
19	Screw and Washer
20	Radiator Support
A	Tighten to 24-31 N-m (18-23 Lb-Ft)
B	Tighten to 12-18 N-m (106-160 Lb-in)
C	Tighten to 9.0-14.0 N-m (80-123 Lb-Ft)

5. Remove the screw inside the cab attaching the lower end of the fender to the cowl.

6. Remove the screws attaching the top edge of the fender to the cowl extension.

7. Remove the screws that attach the fender to the apron, around the wheel opening.

8. Remove the top fender-to-apron bolts.

9. On the right side, remove the battery and the battery tray.

10. On the driver's side, remove the auxiliary battery and/or tool box (both are options).

11. On the right side, detach the main wiring harness from the fender.

12. On the driver's side, detach the hood latch cable from the fender.

13. Remove the hood prop spring from the fender.

14. Remove the fender.

To install:

15. Apply sealer to the upper edge of the apron.

16. Position the fender on the truck and loosely install all screws nuts and bolts.

17. Go around the fender and check its fit. Position the fender for even fit with all adjoining panels and tighten all the fasteners.

18. Install all parts removed previously.

F-150, F-250 and Expedition

1. Remove the radiator grille opening panel reinforcement.

2. If equipped, remove the front wheel opening moulding.

3. Remove the front fender splash shield.

4. Remove the cowl grille.

5. On the passenger side front fender:

    a. Remove the antenna mast.

    b. Remove the antenna base by gently inserting a thin straight-edged screwdriver underneath the cap and carefully following inside the perimeter until both snaps are free.

    c. Remove the screws and lift the antenna base.

    d. Disconnect the radio antenna lead-in cable and remove the antenna base.

6. Remove the fender stuffer.

7. Remove the stone guard.

8. Remove the front fender retaining bolts.

9. Remove the fender from the body.

10. The installation is the reverse of the removal.

Navigator

1. Remove the cowl top vent panels.

2. Remove the jack handle.

3. Remove the air deflector.

4. Remove the headlamp mounting clips and remove the headlamp.

5. Detach the electrical connectors.

6. Remove the radiator opening cover.

7. Remove the driver's side radiator grille opening panel reinforcement bolts.

8. Remove the center radiator grille opening panel reinforcement bolts.

9. Remove the passenger side radiator grille opening panel reinforcement bolts.

10. Remove the radiator grille opening panel reinforcement-to-front fender bolt.

11. On the passenger side front fender, remove the antenna mast.

12. On passenger side front fender, remove the antenna base by gently inserting a thin straight-edged screwdriver underneath the cap and carefully following inside the perimeter until both snaps are free.

13. Remove the screws and lift the antenna base.

14. Disconnect the radio antenna lead-in cable and remove the antenna base.

15. Remove the lower rear screw from the front wheel opening moulding.

16. Remove the lower rear pushpin from the front wheel opening moulding.

17. Remove the front fender splash shield.

18. Remove the front fender splash shield

19. Remove the front bumper cover to front fender nuts.

20. Remove the concealed radiator grille opening panel reinforcement nut.

21. Carefully position the radiator grille opening panel slightly forward.

22. Remove the inner fender stuffer.

23. Remove the front fender retaining bolts.

24. Remove the fender from the body.

25. The installation is the reverse of the removal.

26. Tighten the fender retaining bolts to 94–120 inch lbs. (11–14 Nm).

1999–00 F-Super Duty Models

♦ **See Figures 28 thru 34**

1. Support the hood using a prop rod.

2. Disconnect the hood lifts.

3. Remove the headlights and turn signals.

4. Remove the screws at the lower edge of the front fender securing the splash shield.

5. If equipped, remove the running board.

Fig. 28 Remove the screws at the lower edge of the front fender securing the splash shield

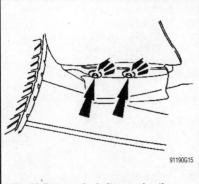

Fig. 29 Remove the bolts securing the lower rear of the front fender

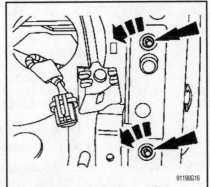

Fig. 30 Remove the fender-to-radiator grille opening support retaining bolts

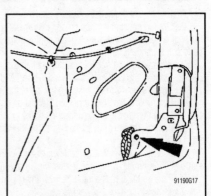

Fig. 31 Remove the fender-to-radiator support retaining screws

6. Remove the pushpins at the rear lower edge of the front fender.
7. Remove the bolts securing the lower rear of the front fender.
8. Remove the fender-to-radiator grille opening support retaining bolts.
9. Remove the fender-to-radiator support retaining screws.
10. Open the door, then remove the fender retaining bolts.
11. Remove the upper fender retaining bolts.
12. Remove the hood support bolt.
13. Remove the front fender.
14. The installation is the reverse of the removal.

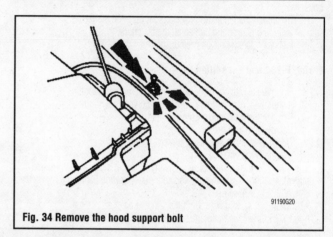

Fig. 33 Remove the upper fender retaining bolts

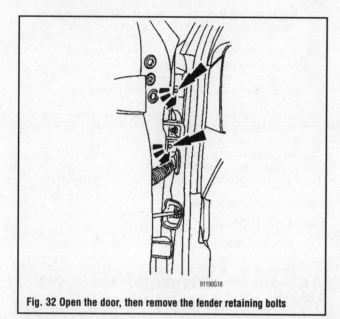

Fig. 32 Open the door, then remove the fender retaining bolts

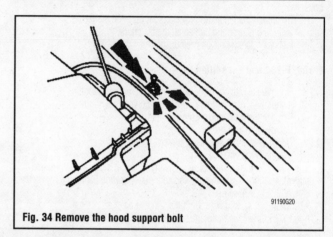

Fig. 34 Remove the hood support bolt

INTERIOR

Instrument Panel and Pad

REMOVAL & INSTALLATION

1997–98 F-250HD, F-350 and F-Super Duty

▶ See Figure 35

⚹⚹ **CAUTION**

On vehicles equipped with air bags, please refer to section 6 for arming, disarming and precautions. Accidental deployment of the air bag system can cause serious personal injury.

1. Disconnect the negative battery cable.
2. Unplug the connectors from the instrument panel rear lamp wiring and the engine control sensor wiring in the engine compartment by loosening the bolts and separating the connectors.
3. Remove the radio as outlined in Section 6.
4. Remove the right and driver's side windshield side garnish moldings.
5. Remove the 4 screws attaching the top of the instrument panel to the cowl.
6. Remove the 2 screws attaching the instrument panel steering column opening cover assembly to the underside of the instrument panel.
7. Remove the cover by pulling up at the top of the cover and unsnapping the 4 retaining clips.
8. Pull the antenna lead-in cable down and unsnap the wire from the bottom of the instrument panel and lay the wire down on the floor out of the way.
9. Remove the bolt attaching the instrument panel to the panel brace. Some vehicles may have 2 lower braces.
10. Remove the screw and washer assembly located at the lower corner on the passenger side of the instrument panel.

11. Unplug the wiring connectors from the main wiring harness at the right cowl side panel.
12. Unplug the wiring connector from the parking brake control.
13. Remove the 3 nuts attaching the parking brake control to the driver's side cowl panel and lay on the floor. Do not disconnect the parking brake cable.
14. On vehicles with column shift; disconnect the shift cable from the steering column shift cable bracket.
15. Unplug the wiring connector from the brake light switch.
16. On vehicles with manual transmission; unplug the wiring connector from the clutch interlock switch.
17. Unplug the wiring connectors from the main wiring harness at the left cowl side panel.
18. Remove the pinch bolt from the steering column to the lower steering column shaft. Move the lower steering column shaft toward the engine and separate from the column U-joint.
19. With the aid of an assistant, support the instrument panel and remove the 3 bolts and 1 nut attaching the driver's side of the instrument panel.
20. With the aid of an assistant, pull the instrument panel rearward and detach the heater controls and air conditioner vacuum line connector, if equipped. Unplug any remaining wiring harnesses.
21. With the aid of an assistant, carefully remove the instrument panel through the front door.
22. Installation is the reverse of removal.

F-150, F-250, Expedition and Navigator

▶ See Figures 36 thru 47

1. Move the seat fully rearward.
2. If equipped with a manual transmission, place the transmission into second gear.
3. Disarm the Air bag system. Refer to Section 6.

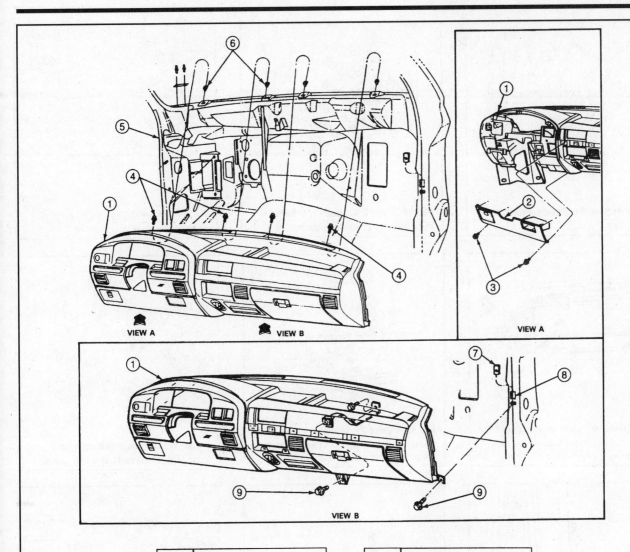

Item	Description	Item	Description
1	Instrument Panel	5	Cowl Side Panel (LH)
2	Steering Column Opening Cover	6	Nut Insert (4 Req'd)
3	Screw(s) 2.0-3.0 N•m (19.0-26.0 In-Lb)	7	U-Nut
		8	Cowl Side Panel (RH)
4	Screw(s) 2.0-2.4 N•m (18.0-21.0 In-Lb)	9	Screw(s) 2.0-2.4 N•m (18.0-21.0 In-Lb)

88280G13

Fig. 35 Instrument panel installation—1997–98 F-250HD, F-350 and F-Super Duty

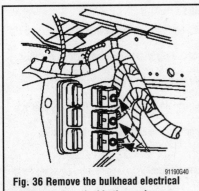

91190G40

Fig. 36 Remove the bulkhead electrical connectors from inside the engine compartment

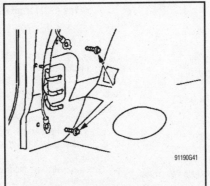

91190G41

Fig. 37 Remove the audio unit ground and the GEM/CTM ground bolts

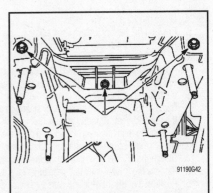

91190G42

Fig. 38 Remove the instrument panel bolts through the steering column opening

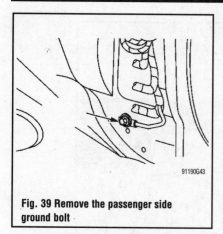

Fig. 39 Remove the passenger side ground bolt

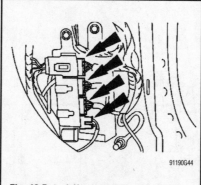

Fig. 40 Detach the passenger side instrument panel main harness connectors

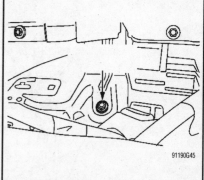

Fig. 41 Remove the instrument panel bolt on the relay bracket

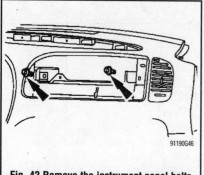

Fig. 42 Remove the instrument panel bolts through the passenger side air bag module opening

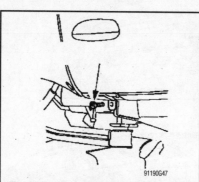

Fig. 43 Remove the instrument panel reinforcement bolt below the driver's side corner of the glove compartment

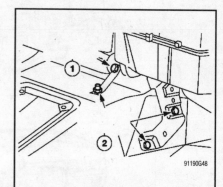

Fig. 44 Position the carpet aside and loosen the instrument panel floor brace

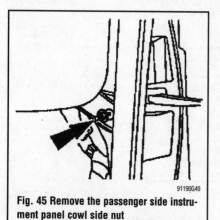

Fig. 45 Remove the passenger side instrument panel cowl side nut

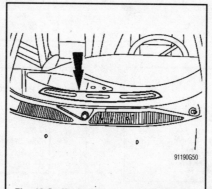

Fig. 46 On Navigator, remove the defroster grille assembly

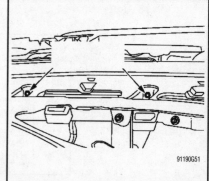

Fig. 47 Remove the cowl panel mounting bolts

4. Disconnect the negative battery cable.
5. Position the battery junction box aside.
6. Remove the bulkhead electrical connectors from inside the engine compartment.
7. Remove the bulkhead electrical connector insulator.
8. Unclip the bulkhead electrical connectors from the dash panel.
9. If equipped, remove the center console.
10. Remove the lower instrument panel steering column cover.
11. If equipped, remove the valance panel.
12. Detach the restraint control module (RCM) electrical connector.
13. Detach the electronic blend door actuator electrical connector.
14. Detach the climate control head vacuum harness connector.
15. Remove the driver's side and passenger side scuff plates.
16. Position the driver's side and passenger side door weatherstrip seals aside.
17. Remove the driver's side and passenger side A-pillar lower trim panels.
18. If equipped, remove the alternative fuel control module (AFCM).

➡The AFCM is attached with velcro.

19. Remove the four covers, the four screws and remove the passenger side assist handle.
20. Remove the driver's side and passenger side windshield side garnish mouldings.
21. Detach the brake pedal position switch electrical connector.
22. If equipped, detach the clutch pedal position switch.
23. On Expedition and Navigator models, detach the adjustable pedal motor connector, if equipped.
24. Remove the audio unit ground and the GEM/CTM ground bolts.
25. Detach the driver's side instrument panel main wiring harness connectors.
26. Remove the instrument panel steering column opening cover reinforcement.
27. Detach the air bag sliding contact electrical connectors and the anti-theft sensor electrical connector.

28. Detach the remaining electrical connectors on the steering column.
29. If equipped, detach the transmission range indicator from the steering column.
30. Lower the steering column.
31. Remove the instrument panel bolts through the steering column opening.
32. Remove the instrument panel reinforcement bolt below the driver's side corner of the cigar lighter and power point.
33. Detach the inertia fuel shutoff switch electrical connector.
34. Remove the passenger side ground bolt.
35. If equipped, detach the air suspension wiring harness electrical connector.
36. Detach the passenger side instrument panel main harness connectors.
37. Release all the wiring harness locators from the cowl side panel.
38. Detach the climate control wiring harness connector.
39. Remove the radio chassis. Refer to Section 6.
40. Disconnect the three cable locators from the lower instrument panel channel and remove the audio unit antenna lead-in cable from the instrument panel.
41. Remove the instrument panel relay cover.
42. Remove the instrument panel bolt on the relay bracket.
43. Remove the glove compartment.

✳✳ CAUTION

Carry a live air bag with the bag and trim cover pointed away from your body. An accidental deployment will then deploy with minimal chance of injury. Place a live air bag on a bench or other surface with the trim cover up.

44. Remove the passenger side air bag module.
45. Remove the instrument panel bolts through the passenger side air bag module opening.
46. Remove the instrument panel reinforcement bolt below the driver's side corner of the glove compartment.
47. Position the carpet aside and loosen the instrument panel floor brace.
48. Remove the passenger side instrument panel cowl side nut.
49. Remove the driver's side instrument panel cowl side nut.
50. On all models except for Navigator, remove the instrument panel cowl top bolts.
51. On Navigator, remove the defroster grille assembly.
52. Remove the cowl panel mounting bolts.

➡Two people are required to perform this step.

53. Remove the instrument panel.
To install:

➡Two people are required to perform this step.

54. Align and position the instrument panel with the clips in the sheet metal.
55. Install the instrument panel cowl top bolts.
56. Install the instrument panel mounting bolts.
57. Install the covers.
58. Install the driver's side instrument panel cowl side nut.
59. Install the passenger side instrument panel cowl side nut.

➡To prevent any squeaks or rattles, install and tighten the upper instrument panel floor brace bolt first, then tighten the floor brace bolts and nut.

60. Install the upper instrument panel floor brace bolt.
61. Install the instrument panel reinforcement bolt below the driver's side corner of the glove compartment.
62. Install the instrument panel bolt on the relay bracket.
63. Install the instrument panel bolts through the passenger side air bag module opening.

➡Install the passenger side bolt first.

✳✳ CAUTION

Never probe the connectors on the air bags. Doing so may result in air bag deployment, which could result in personal injury. Carry a live air bag with the bag and trim cover pointed away from your body. An accidental deployment will then deploy with a minimal chance of injury.

64. Install the passenger side air bag module.
65. Install the glove compartment.
66. Install the instrument panel relay cover.
67. If equipped, attach the autolamp sensor electrical connector.
68. Install the instrument panel relay cover.
69. Position the audio unit antenna lead-in cable into the instrument panel.
70. Connect the cable locators between the instrument panel channel and the audio unit end of the cable.
71. Install the radio chassis. Refer to Section 6.
72. Attach the climate control wiring harness connector.
73. Attach the passenger side instrument panel main harness connectors.
74. If equipped, attach the load leveling control suspension wiring harness electrical connector.
75. Install the passenger side ground bolts.
76. Attach the inertia fuel shutoff switch electrical connector.
77. Install the instrument panel reinforcement bolt below the driver's side corner of the cigar lighter and power point.
78. Install the instrument panel bolts through the steering column opening.
79. Position the steering column.
80. Install the four steering column support nuts.
81. If equipped, connect the transmission range indicator to the steering column.
82. Attach the remaining electrical connectors on the steering column.
83. Attach the air bag sliding contact electrical connectors and the anti-theft sensor electrical connector.
84. Install the instrument panel steering column opening cover reinforcement.
85. Attach the driver's side instrument panel main wiring harness connectors.
86. Connect the audio unit ground and the GEM/CTM ground bolts.
87. If equipped, connect the CPP switch.
88. Attach the BPP switch electrical connector.
89. Install the driver's side and passenger side windshield side garnish mouldings.
90. Install the passenger side assist handle.
91. If equipped, install the alternative fuel control module (AFCM).
92. Attach the electrical connnector.
93. Install the driver's side and passenger side A-pillar lower trim panels.
94. Install the driver's side and passenger side door weatherstrip seals.
95. Install the driver's side and passenger side scuff plates.
96. Attach the climate control head vacuum harness connector.
97. Attach the electronic blend door actuator electrical connector.
98. Attach the RCM electrical connector, engage the locking tab and insert the wiring harness locator.
99. If equipped, install the valance panel.
100. Install the lower instrument panel steering column cover.
101. Clip the bulkhead electrical connectors into the dash panel.
102. Install the bulkhead electrical connector insulator.
103. Attach the bulkhead electrical connectors from inside the engine compartment.
104. Install the battery junction box into the mounting tabs.
105. Connect the negative battery cable.

1999–00 F-Super Duty Models

▶ **See Figures 48 thru 53**

1. Disconnect the negative battery cable.
2. Disarm the air bag system. Refer to Section 6.

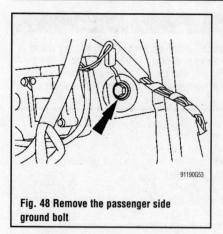

Fig. 48 Remove the passenger side ground bolt

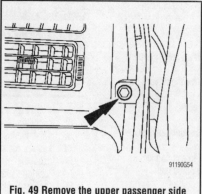

Fig. 49 Remove the upper passenger side cowl side bolt

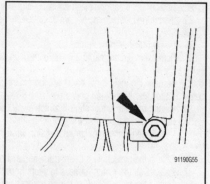

Fig. 50 Remove the lower passenger side cowl side bolt

Fig. 51 Remove the driver's side cowl side bolts

Fig. 52 Remove the driver's side instrument panel center support bolt

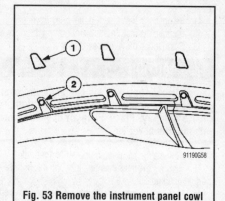

Fig. 53 Remove the instrument panel cowl top bolts

3. Remove the driver side air bag module. Refer to Section 6.
4. Detach the driver's side bulkhead wiring harness connectors.
5. Remove the driver's side bulkhead wiring harness connectors from the dash panel.
6. Remove the driver's side and passenger side scuff plates.
7. Remove the driver's side and passenger side cowl side trim panels.
8. Position the driver's side and passenger side front door weatherstrips aside.

➡The antenna cable will be removed with the instrument panel.

9. Remove the antenna base as outlined in this section.
10. Position the passenger side front fender splash shield away from the dash panel.
11. Unseat the antenna cable grommet from the dash panel.
12. Route the antenna cable into the passenger compartment.

❋❋ WARNING

Use care when removing the instrument panel steering column cover or damage to the cover locating tab may occur.

13. Remove the instrument panel steering column cover.
14. Position the parking brake release handle aside.
15. Detach the parking brake switch electrical connector.
16. Detach the brake pedal position (BPP) switch electrical connector.
17. Through the steering column opening, detach the wiring harness electrical connectors.
18. Separate the intermediate shaft from the steering column.
19. If equipped, disconnect the transmission shift cable from the steering column.
20. Remove the electronic crash sensor (ECS) cover.
21. Detach the ECS electrical connector.
22. While releasing the glove compartment stops, lower the glove compartment.
23. Detach the blend door actuator harness electrical connector.

24. Detach the climate control vacuum harness connector.
25. Depress the glove compartment stops and close the glove compartment.
26. Detach the passenger side cowl side electrical connectors.
27. Remove the passenger side ground bolt.
28. Remove the passenger side cowl side inner panel cover.
29. Remove the upper passenger side instrument panel cowl side bolt.
30. Remove the lower passenger side instrument panel cowl side bolt.
31. Remove the driver's side instrument panel finish end panel.
32. Remove the driver's side instrument panel cowl side bolts.
33. Remove the driver's side instrument panel center support bolt.
34. Remove the instrument panel covers.
35. Remove the instrument panel cowl top bolts.

➡Two people are required to perform this step.

36. Remove the instrument panel.
To install:

➡Two people are required to perform this step.

37. Install the instrument panel.
38. Install the instrument panel cowl top bolts.
39. Install the instrument panel covers.
40. Install the driver's side instrument panel center support bolt.
41. Install the driver's side instrument panel cowl side bolts.
42. Install the driver's side instrument panel finish end panel.
43. Install the lower passenger side instrument panel cowl side bolt.
44. Install the upper passenger side instrument panel cowl side bolt.
45. Install the passenger side cowl side inner panel cover.
46. Install the passenger side ground bolt.
47. Attach the passenger side cowl side electrical connectors.
48. Open the glove compartment and while releasing the glove compartment stops, lower the glove compartment.
49. Attach the climate control vacuum harness connector.
50. Attach the blend door actuator harness electrical connector.
51. Close the glove compartment.

52. Attach the ECS electrical connector.
53. Install the ECS cover.
54. If equipped, connect the transmission shift cable to the steering column.
55. Connect the intermediate shaft to the steering column.
56. Install the steering column shaft pinch bolt.
57. Through the steering column opening, attach the wiring harness electrical connectors.
58. Attach the BPP switch electrical connector.
59. Attach the parking brake switch electrical connector.
60. Install the parking brake release handle.
61. Install the instrument panel steering column cover.
62. Route the antenna cable into the inner fender opening.
63. Seat the antenna cable grommet into the dash panel.
64. Install the antenna base.
65. Install the passenger side front fender splash shield.
66. Install the driver's side and passenger side front door weatherstrips.
67. Install the driver's side and passenger side cowl side trim panels.
68. Install the driver's side and passenger side scuff plates.
69. Install the driver's side bulkhead electrical connectors into the dash panel.
70. Attach the driver's side bulkhead wiring harness connectors.
71. Install the driver side air bag module. Refer to Section 6.

Door Panels

REMOVAL & INSTALLATION

1997–98 F-250HD, F-350 and F-Super Duty

▶ See Figures 54

1. Remove the armrest pad retaining screw.
2. Remove the inside door handle screw and pull off the handle.

3. If equipped with manual windows, remove the window regulator handle screw and pull off the handle and washer. On vehicles with power windows, remove the power window switch housing.
4. If equipped with manual door locks, remove the door lock control. On vehicles with power door locks, remove the power door lock switch housing.
5. On models with electric outside rear view mirrors, remove the power mirror switch housing.
6. Remove the retaining screw and washer from the trim panel lower corner.
7. Using a special door trim panel removal tool or a flat wood spatula, insert it carefully behind the panel and slide it along to find the push-pins. When you encounter a pin, pry the pin outward. Do this until all the pins are out. NEVER PULL ON THE PANEL TO REMOVE THE PINS!
8. Installation is the reverse of removal.

Except 1997–98 F-250HD, F-350 and F-Super Duty

▶ See Figures 55 thru 65

1. Disconnect the negative battery cable.
2. Remove the front door sail panel.
3. Remove the inside door handle finish panel.
4. If equipped with power windows, remove the window regulator switch plate.
5. If equipped with manual windows, remove the window regulator handle by separating the handle cover from the handle.
6. Remove the handle retaining screw and remove the window regulator handle and the spacer.

✳✳ WARNING

Do not pull directly outward on the front door trim panel, as damage may occur.

7. Remove the door panel retaining clips.
8. Remove the door panel retaining screws.

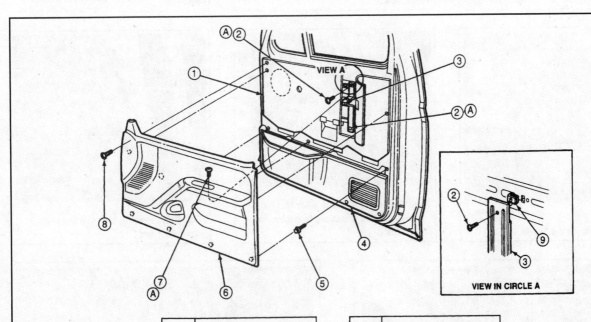

Item	Description
1	Front Door Trim Shield
2	Screw and Washer (2 Req'd Each Side)
3	Armrest Support
4	Map Pocket Assy
5	Pushpin (5 Req'd Each Side)
6	Front Door Trim Panel

Item	Description
7	Screw (1 Req'd Each Side)
8	Screw and Washer (1 Req'd Each Side)
9	Spring Nut (2 Req'd Each Side)
A	Tighten to 1-2 N·m (9-18 Lb-In)

91190G30

Fig. 54 Door panel assembly—standard series

91190P09

Fig. 55 Remove the front door sail panel

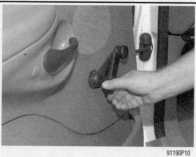

91190P10

Fig. 56 If equipped with manual windows, remove the window regulator handle by separating the handle cover from the handle and . . .

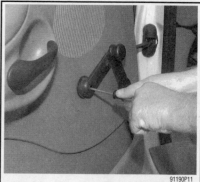

91190P11

Fig. 57 . . . remove the handle retaining screw

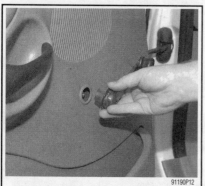

91190P12

Fig. 58 . . . remove the handle and the spacer behind it

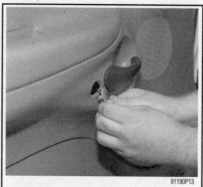

91190P13

Fig. 59 Remove the handle retaining bolt cover and . . .

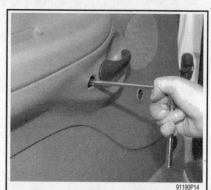

91190P14

Fig. 60 . . . remove the handle retaining bolt and . . .

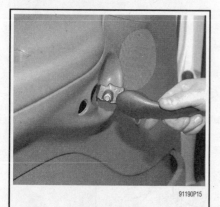

91190P15

Fig. 61 . . . remove the handle

91190P16

Fig. 62 Remove the door pillar trim by carefully puling it outward to release the trim clips

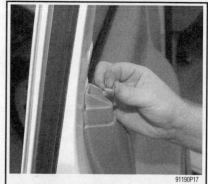

91190P17

Fig. 63 Remove the trim clip under the door pillar and . . .

91190P18

Fig. 64 . . . the sail panel

91190P19

Fig. 65 Remove the door panel by carefully lifting the panel upward to release the retaining clips

9. Lift and remove the front door trim panel.

10. If equipped, twist the courtesy lamp bulb socket one quarter turn and remove the socket from the front door trim panel.

11. The installation is the reverse of the removal.

Door Locks

REMOVAL & INSTALLATION

Front Door Latch

1997–98 F-250HD, F-350 AND F-SUPER DUTY

▶ **See Figure 66**

1. Remove the door trim panel and watershield.

2. Disconnect the rods from the handle and lock cylinder, and from the remote control assembly.

3. Remove the latch assembly attaching screws and remove the latch from the door.

4. Installation is the reverse of removal.

F-150, F-250, EXPEDITION AND NAVIGATOR

➡ **The front door window glass must be completely up.**

1. Remove the door panel.

2. Remove the watershield.

3. Remove the rear glass channel bolt and position the glass channel aside.

4. Disconnect the rods from the door latch.

5. Unclip the locking clip.

6. Remove and discard the door latch retaining screws.

7. Position the latch aside.

8. Detach the electrical connectors and remove the latch.

To install:

➡ **Install the front door latch screw in the small opening first, followed by the large opening.**

9. The installation is the reverse of the removal.

10. If necessary, use Multi-Purpose Grease Spray F5AZ-19G209-AA or equivalent meeting Ford specification ESR-M1C159-A to lubricate the latches.

1999–00 F-SUPER DUTY MODELS

➡ **The window must be in full up position.**

1. Remove the front door trim panel.

2. Remove the outside front door handle.

3. Separate the push button rod from the front door latch.

4. Remove the lock rod clips.

5. Remove the latch retaining screws.

6. Position the front door latch in the inside door access opening.

7. Detach the electrical connector(s).

8. Remove the front door latch cable cover.

9. Remove the remote control cable case from the latch.

10. Remove the remote control cable from the front door latch.

11. Remove the front door latch.

12. The installation is the reverse of the removal.

Rear Door Latch

CREW CAB PICKUPS

1. Remove the door trim panel and watershield.

2. Disconnect the rods from the handle and lock cylinder, and from the remote control assembly.

3. Remove the latch assembly attaching screws and remove the latch from the door.

4. Installation is the reverse of removal.

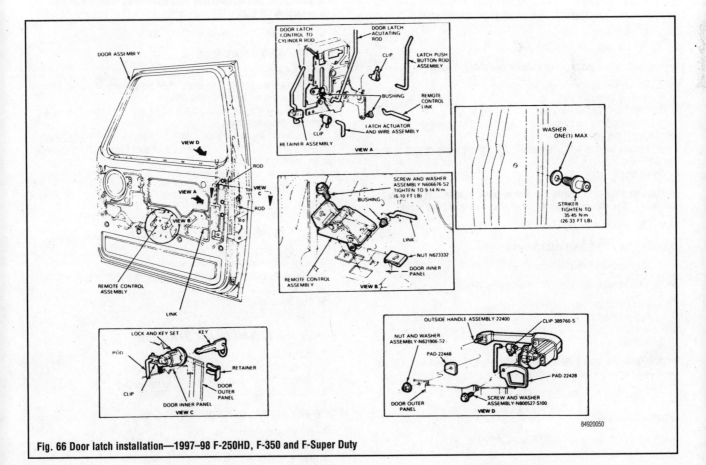

Fig. 66 Door latch installation—1997–98 F-250HD, F-350 and F-Super Duty

84920050

EXPEDITION AND NAVIGATOR

➡The rear door window glass must be completely raised.

1. Remove rear door trim panel.
2. Disconnect the rear door latch rod.
3. Remove the rear door latch remote control screw.
4. Slide the rear door latch remote control forward and remove.
5. Remove the rear door speaker.
6. Remove the rear door watershield.
7. Remove the outside rear door handle.
8. Remove the child safety lock finish panel.
9. If equipped, detach the power door lock actuator electrical connector.
10. If equipped, drill out the power door lock actuator rivet.
11. Drill out the push button rod rivet.
12. Detach the door open warning lamp electrical connector.
13. Remove and discard the latch retaining screws.
14. Remove the rear door latch through the outside rear door handle opening.
15. Disconnect any remaining actuating rods.

To install:

➡Make sure the latch release rod is not preloading the latch. It should be clipped in a relaxed state with no slack.

➡Install the rear door latch screw in the small opening first, followed by the large opening.

16. The installation is the reverse of the removal.
17. If necessary, use Multi-Purpose Grease Spray F5AZ-19G209-AA or equivalent meeting Ford specification ESR-M1C159-A to lubricate the latches.

Inside Handle

1997–98 F-250HD, F-350 AND F-SUPER DUTY; 1999–00 F-SUPER DUTY MODELS

1. Remove the retaining screw/nut and remove the handle.
2. The installation is the reverse of the removal.

F-150, F-250, EXPEDITION AND NAVIGATOR FRONT DOOR

1. Remove the front door trim panel.
2. Remove the front door watershield.

➡The front door window glass must be completely raised.

3. Detach the door handle electrical connector.
4. Remove the door handle nuts.
5. Disconnect the front door latch to lock cylinder rod.
6. Disconnect the front door latch to outside front door handle rod at the handle and at the latch.
7. Remove the door handle by pushing it out from the bottom surface of the handle.

To install:

➡Make sure the door handle and lock cylinder rods are not preloading the latch. They should be clipped in a relaxed state with no slack.

8. The installation is the reverse of the removal.

EXPEDITION AND NAVIGATOR REAR DOOR

1. Remove the rear door trim panel.

➡The rear window glass must be completely raised.

2. Disconnect the rear door latch rod.
3. Remove the screw and slide the rear door latch remote control forward and remove.

To install:

➡Make sure the latch release rod is not preloading the latch. It should be clipped in a relaxed state with no slack.

4. The installation is the reverse of the removal.

Outside Handle

1997–98 F-250HD, F-350 AND F-SUPER DUTY

1. Remove the front door trim panel.

2. Remove the front door watershield.
3. Disconnect the actuating rods from the handle.
4. Remove the one handle retaining nut and screw.
5. Remove the handle from the door.
6. The installation is the reverse of the removal.

F-150, F-250, EXPEDITION AND NAVIGATOR FRONT DOOR

1. Remove the front door trim panel.
2. Remove the front door watershield.

➡The front door window glass must be completely raised.

3. Detach the door handle electrical connector.
4. Remove the door handle retaining nuts.
5. Disconnect the front door latch to lock cylinder rod.
6. Disconnect the front door latch to outside front door handle rod at the handle and at the latch.
7. Remove the door handle by pushing it out from the bottom surface of the handle.

To install:

➡Make sure the door handle and lock cylinder rods are not preloading the latch. They should be clipped in a relaxed state with no slack.

8. The installation is the reverse of the removal.

EXPEDITION AND NAVIGATOR REAR DOOR

1. Remove the front door trim panel.
2. Remove the front door watershield.
3. Remove the door handle retaining nuts.
4. Disconnect the rear door latch-to-lock cylinder rod.
5. Remove the outside rear door handle by pushing it out from the bottom surface of the handle.

To install:

➡Make sure the door handle and the rear door handle rod is in a relaxed position and that the rear door handle rod is all the way up before closing the clips.

6. The installation is the reverse of the removal.

1999–00 F-SUPER DUTY MODELS

1. Remove the front door trim panel.
2. Remove the cover from the side of the door and remove the nut.
3. Remove the nut from inside the door.
4. Pull the outside door handle out of the front door far enough to expose the attached door latch linkage.
5. Disconnect the lock cylinder linkage rod from the outside door handle.
6. Disconnect the release rod from the front door latch by prying open the clip and removing the latch release rod.
7. Remove the outside door handle.
8. The installation is the reverse of the removal.

Door Lock Cylinder

1997–98 F-250HD, F-350 AND F-SUPER DUTY

1. Place the window in the UP position.
2. Remove the trim panel and watershield.
3. Disconnect the actuating rod from the lock control link clip.
4. Slide the retainer away from the lock cylinder.
5. Pull the cylinder from the door.
6. Installation is the reverse of removal.

F-150, F-250, EXPEDITION AND NAVIGATOR

1. Remove the front door outside handle.
2. Remove the front door lock cylinder retainer.
3. Remove the front door lock cylinder.
4. The installation is the reverse of the removal.

1999–00 F-SUPER DUTY MODELS

1. Remove the front door trim panel.
2. Remove the outside door handle.
3. Remove the spring clip and remove the lock cylinder.

To install:
4. The installation is the reverse of the removal.

Actuator Motor

1997–98 F-250HD, F-350 AND F-SUPER DUTY

1. Remove the door trim panel.
2. Disconnect the motor from the door latch.
3. Remove the motor and swivel bracket from the door by drilling out the pop rivet.
4. Disconnect the wiring harness.
5. Installation is the reverse of removal. Make sure that the pop rivet is tight.

EXCEPT 1997–98 F-250HD, F-350 AND F-SUPER DUTY

1. Remove the door latch.
2. Remove the door ajar switch.
3. Pry up on lock actuator tab.
4. Slide the door latch lock actuator off the latch channels using a prying action.
5. Remove the door latch lock actuator.
6. The installation is the reverse of the removal.

Tailgate Lock

REMOVAL & INSTALLATION

Lock Cylinder

1997–98 F-250HD, F-350 AND F-SUPER DUTY

1. Remove the tailgate access cover.
2. Raise the glass. If the glass can't be raised, remove it as described below.
3. Remove the lock cylinder retainer.
4. Disengage the lock cylinder from the switch and remove it from the tailgate.
5. Installation is the reverse of removal.

EXCEPT 1997–98 F-250HD, F-350 AND F-SUPER DUTY

1. Remove the tailgate handle.
2. Remove the lock cylinder retaining clip.
3. Remove the lock cylinder.
4. The installation is the reverse of the removal.

Tailgate Handle

1. Open the tailgate.
2. Remove the tailgate access panel.
3. Disconnect the tailgate latch rods.
4. Remove the tailgate handle retaining nuts.
5. Remove the tailgate handle.

➡ **Make sure the latch release rods are not preloading the latches. They should be clipped in a relaxed state with no slack.**

6. The installation is the reverse of the removal.

Liftgate Lock

REMOVAL & INSTALLATION

Handle

1. Remove the liftgate trim panel.
2. On Navigator models, remove the license plate bracket.
3. Remove the liftgate latch remote control bolts and position aside.
4. On Expedition:
   a. Remove the liftgate handle two retaining nuts.
   b. Remove the reinforcement plate and remove the liftgate handle.

✳✳ WARNING

Use care when removing the liftgate handle to avoid breaking the plastic tangs.

5. On Navigator:
6. Disconnect the liftgate latch remote control rod.
   a. Remove the liftgate handle two retaining nuts.
   b. Remove the liftgate handle.

To install:
7. The installation is the reverse of the removal. Make sure the handle shaft and the driver on the liftgate latch controller are properly aligned. On Navigator, make sure the plastic tangs of the handle fully engage the holes in the sheet metal. On Navigator, make sure the liftgate latch remote control rod is not preloading the liftgate latch. It should be clipped in a relaxed state with no slack.

Lock Cylinder

➡ **Individual lock cylinders are repaired by discarding the inoperative lock cylinder and building a new lock cylinder using the appropriate lock repair package. The lock repair package includes a detailed instruction sheet to build the new lock cylinder to the current code of the vehicle.**

1. Remove the liftgate trim panel.
2. Disconnect the lock cylinder rod.
3. Remove the retaining clip.
4. Remove the lock cylinder.
5. The installation is the reverse of the removal.

Latch

1. Disconnect the negative battery cable.
2. Remove the liftgate trim panel.
3. On Navigator, remove the license plate bracket.
4. Remove the liftgate latch screws.
5. Separate the liftgate latch from the liftgate.
6. Detach the door open warning lamp electrical connector.

✳✳ WARNING

Be careful not to kink the liftgate latch control cable while disconnecting it.

7. Disconnect the liftgate latch control cable.
8. Remove the liftgate latch.
9. The installation is the reverse of the removal.

➡ **If necessary, use Multi-Purpose Grease Spray F5AZ-19G209-AA or equivalent meeting Ford Specification ESR-M1C159-A to lubricate the latch.**

Power Door Lock Actuator

1. Remove the liftgate trim panel.
2. Detach the power door lock actuator electrical connector.
3. Drill out the actuator retaining rivet.
4. Disconnect the power door lock actuator rod and remove the actuator.
5. The installation is the reverse of the removal.

Door Glass and Regulator Motor

REMOVAL & INSTALLATION

1997–98 F-250HD, F-350 and F-Super Duty

FRONT DOOR GLASS

1. Remove the door trim panel.
2. Remove the screw from the vent window division bar.

3. Remove the 2 vent window weatherstrip attaching screws from the front edge of the door.

4. Lower the glass and remove the inside and outside front door front belt line weatherstrips.

5. Pull the door glass top run out of the window opening near the front door vent window division bar enough to allow the removal of the front door vent window and glass assembly.

6. Tilt the door vent window glass and frame assembly and the division bar toward the rear of the door and remove the vent window assembly from the door.

7. Remove the window regulator arm roller from the front door glass channel and retainer.

8. Rotate the front edge of the door window glass downward and lift it and the attached front door glass channel and retainer from the door.

9. The installation is the reverse of the removal.

REAR DOOR GLASS (CREW CAB MODELS)

1. Remove the door panel.
2. Lower the rear door glass and remove the inside and outside weatherstrips.
3. Remove one screw at the top of the rear door glass front lower retainer.
4. Remove the door glass run front lower retainer by pulling up and twisting it so that the retainer bracket clears the window opening and the rear door glass run slides off.
5. Pull the rear door glass run out of the rear door opening.
6. Raise the window glass half-way and remove the window regulator arm from the window glass channel.
7. Lift the rear door window glass up and out of the door opening.
8. The installation is the reverse of the removal.

WINDOW REGULATOR

1. Remove the front door trim panel..
2. Raise and support the front door window glass to the full up position.
3. Drill out the center retaining rivets using a ¼ inch (6.35 mm) drill bit.

✳✳ WARNING

Be careful not to damage sheet metal holes during drilling.

4. Remove the window regulator arm roller from the front door glass channel and retainer and remove the regulator from the door.
5. The installation is the reverse of the removal.

➡ **A ¼–20 X ½ inch bolt and washer and a ¼–20 nut and washer assembly may be used in place of rivets.**

F-150 and F-250

FRONT DOOR GLASS

▶ See Figure 67

1. Remove the front door trim panel.
2. Peel back the front door watershield.
3. Lower the window glass to access the two window glass to regulator nuts.
4. Remove the inside glass weatherstrip.
5. Remove the rear glass channel bolt and lift the channel.
6. Loosen the window glass to regulator nuts.
7. Slide glass channel rearward until the rear glass to regulator nut lines up with the hole in the glass channel.
8. Slide the glass through the outboard side of the door and remove the front door window glass.
9. The installation is the reverse of the removal.

WINDOW REGULATOR

▶ See Figures 68, 69, 70 and 71

1. Remove the front door trim panel.
2. Peel back the front door watershield.
3. Lower the window glass to access the two window glass to regulator nuts.
4. Remove the window glass nuts.
5. Support the front door window glass in the full up position.
6. If equipped, detach the power window electrical connector.
7. Remove the window regulator retaining nuts and drill out the rivets.

8. Remove the window regulator.
9. The installation is the reverse of the removal.

Expedition and Navigator

WINDOW REGULATOR AND MOTOR

➡ **The window regulator and motor are removed as an assembly.**

1. Remove the front door trim panel..
2. Remove the front door radio speaker.
3. Remove the front door watershield.

✳✳ WARNING

Support the window glass to avoid damage.

4. Raise and support the front door window glass to the full up position.
5. Detach the power window motor electrical connector.
6. Remove the window glass to regulator nuts.
7. Drill out the rivets retaining the regulator.
8. Remove the motor and window regulator assembly.

✳✳ WARNING

Prior to motor removal, ensure the regulator arms are in a fixed position to prevent counterbalance spring unwind.

9. Remove the power window motor retaining bolts and remove the power window motor from the regulator.
10. The installation is the reverse of the removal.

1999–00 F-Super Duty Models

FRONT DOOR GLASS

1. Remove the window switch.
2. Remove the window crank handle (manual windows only).
3. Remove the door trim panel, interior sail cover and watershield.
4. Loosen the outside rearview mirror or outside sail cover (if equipped).
5. Temporarily install the window switch or the window crank, and lower the window to access the glass bracket nuts and loosen them.
6. Remove the inner beltline weatherstrip and outer beltline weatherstrip.
7. Loosen the rear glass run bolt.
8. Remove the door glass from the channel by sliding the channel forward, then position the door glass in the bottom of the door.
9. Remove the window glass from the inner door by tilting the window glass forward and lifting the glass out of the door.
10. The installation is the reverse of the removal.

REAR DOOR GLASS (CREW CAB MODELS)

1. Remove the window switch.
2. Remove the window crank handle (manual windows only).
3. Remove the door trim panel and watershield.
4. Temporarily install the window switch or window crank handle, and lower the window to access the glass bracket nuts and loosen the nuts.
5. Remove the inner beltline weatherstrip and outer beltline weatherstrip.
6. Loosen the rear glass run bolt.
7. Remove the door glass from the regulator channel by sliding the channel forward, then position the door glass in the bottom of the door.
8. Remove the front edge of the window glass from the glass run.
9. Lift the window glass up through the belt opening to remove from the door.
10. The installation is the reverse of the removal.

WINDOW REGULATOR

➡ **This procedure also applies to the rear door on Crew Cab models.**

1. Remove the window switch.
2. Remove the window crank handle (manual windows only).
3. Remove the door trim panel and watershield.

➡ **Do not remove the window glass from the door.**

4. Remove the window from the window regulator.
5. Tape the window glass in the full up position.

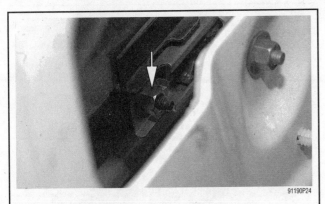

Fig. 67 Loosen the window glass to regulator nuts

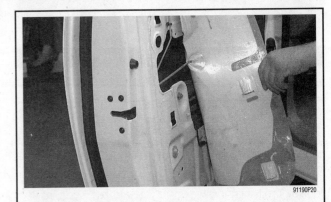

Fig. 68 Peel back the front door watershield

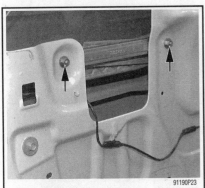

Fig. 69 Remove the regulator retaining nuts and . . .

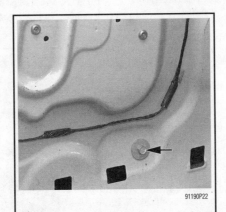

Fig. 70 . . . bolts as shown

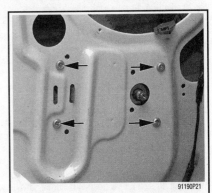

Fig. 71 Drill out the rivets shown to remove the window regulator—F-150 and F-250

6. Detach the window motor electrical connector (power windows only).
7. Loosen the window regulator arm retaining nuts and pull the arm from the mounting position.
8. Loosen the window regulator mounting bolts and remove the window regulator.
9. The installation is the reverse of the removal.

Electric Window Motor

REMOVAL & INSTALLATION

1997–98 F-250HD, F-350 and F-Super Duty

1. Disconnect the battery ground.
2. Remove the door trim panel.
3. Disconnect the window motor wiring harness.
4. There are 2 dimples in the door panel, opposite the 2 concealed motor retaining bolts. Using a ½ in. (13mm) drill bit, drill out these dimples to gain access to the motor bolts. Be careful to avoid damage to the wires.
5. Remove the 3 motor mounting bolts.
6. Push the motor towards the outside of the door to disengage it from the gears. You'll have to support the window glass once the motor is disengaged.
7. Remove the motor from the door.
8. The installation is the reverse of the removal.

➡To avoid rusting in the drilled areas, prime and paint the exposed metal, or, cover the holes with waterproof body tape.

F-150 and F-250

1. Raise the front door window glass to the full up position.
2. Remove the front door trim panel.
3. Peel back the front door watershield.

✳✳ WARNING

Make sure the electrical connector is not in the way before drilling.

4. To access the power window motor bolts, use a ¾ -inch hole saw with a ¼-inch pilot to drill two holes at the existing drill dimples on the door.

✳✳ WARNING

Prior to motor removal, make sure the regulator arms are in a fixed position to prevent counterbalance spring unwind.

5. Remove the motor retaining bolts.
6. Detach the electrical connector.
7. Remove the power window motor.
8. The installation is the reverse of the removal.

Expedition and Navigator

The window regulator and motor are removed as an assembly. Refer to regulator removal and installation in this section.

1999–00 Super Duty Models

➡This procedure also applies to the rear door on Crew Cab models.

1. Remove the window switch.
2. Remove the door trim panel and watershield.
3. Tape the window in the full up position.
4. Detach the window motor electrical connector.

✳✳ WARNING

Support the window motor while removing the window motor retaining screws.

5. Remove the window motor screws and remove the motor.

6. The installation is the reverse of the removal.

Windshield and Fixed Glass

REMOVAL & INSTALLATION

If your windshield, or other fixed window, is cracked or chipped, you may decide to replace it with a new one yourself. However, there are two main reasons why replacement windshields and other window glass should be installed only by a professional automotive glass technician: safety and cost.

The most important reason a professional should install automotive glass is for safety. The glass in the vehicle, especially the windshield, is designed with safety in mind in case of a collision. The windshield is specially manufactured from two panes of specially-tempered glass with a thin layer of transparent plastic between them. This construction allows the glass to "give" in the event that a part of your body hits the windshield during the collision, and prevents the glass from shattering, which could cause lacerations, blinding and other harm to passengers of the vehicle. The other fixed windows are designed to be tempered so that if they break during a collision, they shatter in such a way that there are no large pointed glass pieces. The professional automotive glass technician knows how to install the glass in a vehicle so that it will function optimally during a collision. Without the proper experience, knowledge and tools, installing a piece of automotive glass yourself could lead to additional harm if an accident should ever occur.

Cost is also a factor when deciding to install automotive glass yourself. Performing this could cost you much more than a professional may charge for the same job. Since the windshield is designed to break under stress, an often life saving characteristic, windshields tend to break VERY easily when an inexperienced person attempts to install one. Do-it-yourselfers buying two, three or even four windshields from a salvage yard because they have broken them during installation are common stories. Also, since the automotive glass is designed to prevent the outside elements from entering your vehicle, improper installation can lead to water and air leaks. Annoying whining noises at highway speeds from air leaks or inside body panel rusting from water leaks can add to your stress level and subtract from your wallet. After buying two or three windshields, installing them and ending up with a leak that produces a noise while driving and water damage during rainstorms, the cost of having a professional do it correctly the first time may be much more alluring. We here at Chilton, therefore, advise that you have a professional automotive glass technician service any broken glass on your vehicle.

WINDSHIELD CHIP REPAIR

▶ See Figures 72 and 73

➡Check with your state and local authorities on the laws for state safety inspection. Some states or municipalities may not allow chip repair as a viable option for correcting stone damage to your windshield.

Although severely cracked or damaged windshields must be replaced, there is something that you can do to prolong or even prevent the need for replacement of a chipped windshield. There are many companies which offer windshield chip repair products, such as Loctite's® Bullseye¬ windshield repair kit. These kits usually consist of a syringe, pedestal and a sealing adhesive. The syringe is mounted on the pedestal and is used to create a vacuum which pulls the plastic layer against the glass. This helps make the chip transparent. The adhesive is then injected which seals the chip and helps to prevent further stress cracks from developing

➡Always follow the specific manufacturer's instructions.

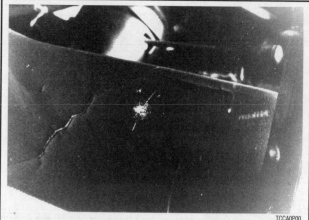

Fig. 72 Small chips on your windshield can be fixed with an aftermarket repair kit, such as the one from Loctite®

Fig. 73 Most kits use a self-stick applicator and syringe to inject the adhesive into the chip or crack

Inside Rear View Mirror

REPLACEMENT

▶ See Figures 74 and 75

1. Perform the following steps if the rear view mirror is still attached.

   a. Insert the Rear View Mirror Remover T91T-17700-A, or equivalent into the mount on the inside rear view mirror.

   b. Use the tool to release the mirror retaining clip while pulling the inside rear view mirror away from the mirror mount.

   c. Remove the inside rear view mirror.

2. Use a wax pencil or other suitable tool to mark the location of the inside rear view mirror bracket on the outside surface of the windshield glass.

3. Perform the following step if the mirror bracket is still attached.

   a. Apply low heat to the windshield glass to soften the adhesive and remove the bracket from the windshield.

4. Remove the remaining adhesive from the windshield glass.

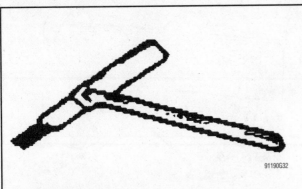

Fig. 74 Rear View Mirror Remover T91T-17700-A or equivalent is required to remove the mirror

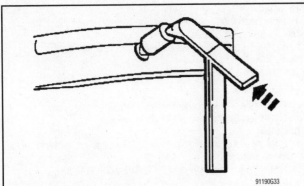

Fig. 75 Use the tool to release the mirror retaining clip while pulling the inside rear view mirror away from the mirror mount

To install:
5. Clean the inside of the windshield glass with isopropyl alcohol to remove any remaining adhesive.
6. Use a fine grit sandpaper on the inside rear view mirror bracket to lightly scuff the bonding surface.
7. Wipe the surface of the bracket clean with a paper towel soaked in isopropyl alcohol.

➡Do not touch the mounting surfaces before installation.

8. Apply Rear View Mirror Adhesive D9AZ-19554-CA or equivalent meeting Ford specification ESB-M2G176-A to the bonding surface of the inside rear view mirror bracket and the windshield glass.
9. Apply the accelerator solution to the bracket and allow the accelerator material to dry for three minutes.
10. Press the inside rear view mirror bracket firmly against the windshield glass for approximately one minute.
11. Allow the adhesive to set for five minutes.
12. Remove any excess adhesive from the windshield glass with a clean, alcohol dampened cloth.
13. Slide the inside rear view mirror downward onto the inside rear view mirror bracket.

Seats

REMOVAL & INSTALLATION

Front Bench Seat

1997–98 F-250HD, F-350 AND F-SUPER DUTY

1. Remove the 4 seat track-to-floor pan bolts or nuts.
2. Carefully lift the seat and remove from the vehicle.

To install:
3. Apply sealer to the mounting hole areas.
4. Install the seat in the vehicle and adjust position.
5. Install the mounting bolts and tighten to 35–46 ft. lbs. (47–63 Nm).

1999–00 F-SUPER DUTY MODELS

▶ **See Figure 76**

1. Disconnect the negative battery cable.
2. Remove the front safety belts from the front seat.

➡Removing the front seat requires more than one person.

3. Remove the two front seat riser support-to-floorpan bolts.
4. Remove the front seat riser-to-floorpan nuts.
5. Detach the safety belt electrical connector.
6. Remove the front seat.
7. The installation is the reverse of the removal.
8. Tighten the nuts to 30–39 ft. lbs. (41–53 Nm). Tighten the bolts to 35–46 ft. lbs. (47–63 Nm).

40/20/40 Split Bench

1. Fold the front seat back forward and remove the screws attaching the center safety belt bracket to the center seat.
2. Remove the 4 seat track-to-floor pan bolts or nuts.
3. Carefully lift the seat and remove from the vehicle.
To install:
4. Apply sealer to the mounting hole areas.
5. Install the seat in the vehicle and adjust position.
6. Install the mounting bolts and tighten to 35–46 ft. lbs. (47–63 Nm).

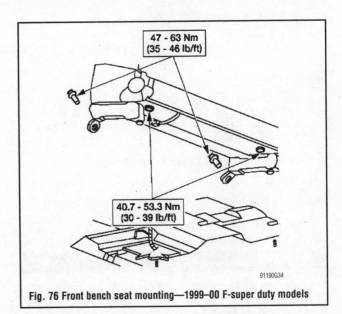

Fig. 76 Front bench seat mounting—1999–00 F-super duty models

60/40 Split Bench

FRONT

▶ **See Figure 77**

➡Removing the 60 percent front bench requires more than one person.

1. Remove the retaining bolts and nuts.
2. Remove the 60 percent front bench.
3. Remove the 40 percent front bench.
4. The installation is the reverse of the removal.
5. Tighten the bolts and nuts to 35–46 ft. lbs. (47–63 Nm).

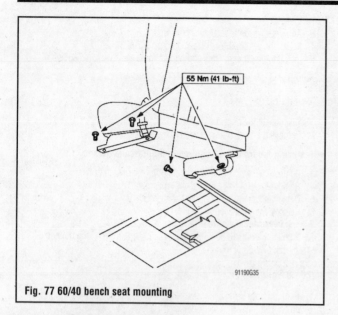

Fig. 77 60/40 bench seat mounting

91190G35

REAR (EXPEDITION AND NAVIGATOR)

➡ Removing the 60 percent front bench requires more than one person.

1. Remove the second row seat riser bolt covers and remove the bolts.
2. Lift the recliner handle and fold the second row seat back forward.
3. Remove the four seat retaining bolts.
4. Remove the 60 percent second row seat.
5. Remove the 40 percent second row seat.
6. The installation is the reverse of the removal.
7. Tighten the bolts to 22–29 ft. lbs. (30–40 Nm).

Captain's Chairs

1. Detach any necessary electrical connectors.
2. Remove the 4 seat track-to-floor pan bolts and lift out the seat.
3. Apply sealer to the hole areas and install the seat. Tighten the bolts to 35–46 ft. lbs. (47–63 Nm).

EZ-Entry Second Row Seats (Expedition and Navigator)

▶ See Figures 78

1. Remove the E-Z seat riser to floor bolt covers and remove the bolts.
2. Fold the seat forward to gain access to the seat strap bolt.
3. Remove the seat strap bolt.

✳✳ WARNING

Do not damage the anti-chuck hook while removing or storing the 40% E-Z entry seat. The weight of the seat should never rest on the anti-chuck hook, as damage to the hook may occur.

4. Remove the seat.
5. The installation is the reverse of the removal.

Rear Bench Seat Cushion (Supercab)

1. Remove the seat cushion retaining screws.
2. Lift the seat cushion and feed the seat belt through the cushion.
3. Lift the cushion up ensuring the retaining hooks are free and remove the cushion.

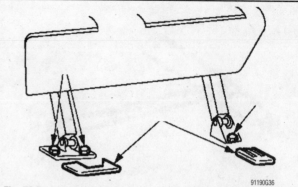

91190G36

Fig. 78 Remove the E-Z seat riser to floor bolt covers and remove the bolts

To install:

4. Place the cushion into place, place the seat belts through the cushion and engage the retaining hooks.
5. Tighten the retaining screws to 19–25 ft. lbs. (26–34 Nm).

Rear Bench Seat Back (Supercab)

1. Remove the seat cushion.
2. Remove the seat back bottom retaining screws.
3. Lift the seat back and remove it from the vehicle.
To install:
4. Place the seat cushion into place ensuring the retainers on the top of the seat back are engaged.
5. tighten the retaining screws to 19–32 ft. lbs. (25–44 Nm).

Rear Bench Seat (Crew Cab)

1. Remove the seat track-to-floor pan bolts and lift the seat and track out of the truck.
2. Installation is the reverse of removal. Apply sealer to the area of the bolt holes. Tighten the bolts to 18–32 ft. lbs. (25–44 Nm).

Side-Mounted Folding Rear Seat (Super Cab)

1. Remove the seat bracket-to-floor screw and washer assemblies.
2. Remove the seat assembly.
3. Remove the bumper screws-to-retainer.
4. Remove the bumper.
5. Remove the trim panel retaining screws.
6. Remove the seat assembly.
7. Tighten the bolts to 22–30 ft. lbs. (30–40 Nm).

Forward Facing Folding Rear Seat (Super Cab)

1. Release the rear seat back latch striker and put the rear seat back frame in the fold down position.
2. Remove the seat belts.
3. Remove the retaining screws attaching the rear seat back cover to the rear seat back frame.
4. Lift up the seat back cover and remove it from the vehicle.
5. Remove the panel and support assembly-to-floor retaining screws.
6. Pull the rear seat back release latch and remove the rear seat cushion frame and rear seat cushion cover.
7. Move the seat cushion so that the bottom panel is toward the front.
8. Remove the retaining screws to the bottom panel and support assembly.
9. Feed the strap-to-rear seat back release latch through the rear seat cushion pad.
10. Remove the rear seat cushion.
11. The installation is the reverse of the removal.

TORQUE SPECIFICATIONS

Components	English	Metric
Captain's chair retaining bolts	35-46 ft. lbs.	47-63 Nm
Door hinge bolts	19-25 ft. lbs.	25-35 Nm
Front bench seat		
1997-98 F-250HD, F-350 and F-Super Duty	35-46 ft. lbs.	47-63 Nm
1999-00 F-Super Duty models		
Retaining nuts	30-39 ft. lbs.	41-53 Nm
Retaining bolts	35-46 ft. lbs.	47-63 Nm
Front 40/20/40 bench seat retaining bolts and nuts	35-46 ft. lbs.	47-63 Nm
Front 60/40 bench seat retaining bolts and nuts	35-46 ft. lbs.	47-63 Nm
Hood hinge bolts	19-25 ft. lbs.	25-35 Nm
Liftgate hinge-to-body bolts	91-123 inch lbs.	10-14 Nm
Rear 60/40 bench seat retaining bolts and nuts	22-29 ft. lbs.	30-40 Nm
Rear bench seat (Crew cab)	19-32 ft. lbs.	25-44 Nm
Rear bench seat back (Supercab)	19-32 ft. lbs.	25-44 Nm
Rear bench seat cushion (Supercab)	19-25 ft. lbs.	25-35 Nm
Rear side mounted folding rear seat (Super cab)	22-30 ft. lbs.	30-40 Nm
Seat motor retaining screws		
Except 1999-00 F-Super Duty models	16-21 ft. lbs.	21-29 Nm

91190C01

AIR/FUEL RATIO: The ratio of air-to-gasoline by weight in the fuel mixture drawn into the engine.

AIR INJECTION: One method of reducing harmful exhaust emissions by injecting air into each of the exhaust ports of an engine. The fresh air entering the hot exhaust manifold causes any remaining fuel to be burned before it can exit the tailpipe.

ALTERNATOR: A device used for converting mechanical energy into electrical energy.

AMMETER: An instrument, calibrated in amperes, used to measure the flow of an electrical current in a circuit. Ammeters are always connected in series with the circuit being tested.

AMPERE: The rate of flow of electrical current present when one volt of electrical pressure is applied against one ohm of electrical resistance.

ANALOG COMPUTER: Any microprocessor that uses similar (analogous) electrical signals to make its calculations.

ARMATURE: A laminated, soft iron core wrapped by a wire that converts electrical energy to mechanical energy as in a motor or relay. When rotated in a magnetic field, it changes mechanical energy into electrical energy as in a generator.

ATMOSPHERIC PRESSURE: The pressure on the Earth's surface caused by the weight of the air in the atmosphere. At sea level, this pressure is 14.7 psi at 32°F (101 kPa at 0°C).

ATOMIZATION: The breaking down of a liquid into a fine mist that can be suspended in air.

AXIAL PLAY: Movement parallel to a shaft or bearing bore.

BACKFIRE: The sudden combustion of gases in the intake or exhaust system that results in a loud explosion.

BACKLASH: The clearance or play between two parts, such as meshed gears.

BACKPRESSURE: Restrictions in the exhaust system that slow the exit of exhaust gases from the combustion chamber.

BAKELITE: A heat resistant, plastic insulator material commonly used in printed circuit boards and transistorized components.

BALL BEARING: A bearing made up of hardened inner and outer races between which hardened steel balls roll.

BALLAST RESISTOR: A resistor in the primary ignition circuit that lowers voltage after the engine is started to reduce wear on ignition components.

BEARING: A friction reducing, supportive device usually located between a stationary part and a moving part.

BIMETAL TEMPERATURE SENSOR: Any sensor or switch made of two dissimilar types of metal that bend when heated or cooled due to the different expansion rates of the alloys. These types of sensors usually function as an on/off switch.

BLOWBY: Combustion gases, composed of water vapor and unburned fuel, that leak past the piston rings into the crankcase during normal engine operation. These gases are removed by the PCV system to prevent the buildup of harmful acids in the crankcase.

BRAKE PAD: A brake shoe and lining assembly used with disc brakes.

BRAKE SHOE: The backing for the brake lining. The term is, however, usually applied to the assembly of the brake backing and lining.

BUSHING: A liner, usually removable, for a bearing; an anti-friction liner used in place of a bearing.

CALIPER: A hydraulically activated device in a disc brake system, which is mounted straddling the brake rotor (disc). The caliper contains at least one piston and two brake pads. Hydraulic pressure on the piston(s) forces the pads against the rotor.

CAMSHAFT: A shaft in the engine on which are the lobes (cams) which operate the valves. The camshaft is driven by the crankshaft, via a belt, chain or gears, at one half the crankshaft speed.

CAPACITOR: A device which stores an electrical charge.

CARBON MONOXIDE (CO): A colorless, odorless gas given off as a normal byproduct of combustion. It is poisonous and extremely dangerous in confined areas, building up slowly to toxic levels without warning if adequate ventilation is not available.

CARBURETOR: A device, usually mounted on the intake manifold of an engine, which mixes the air and fuel in the proper proportion to allow even combustion.

CATALYTIC CONVERTER: A device installed in the exhaust system, like a muffler, that converts harmful byproducts of combustion into carbon dioxide and water vapor by means of a heat-producing chemical reaction.

CENTRIFUGAL ADVANCE: A mechanical method of advancing the spark timing by using flyweights in the distributor that react to centrifugal force generated by the distributor shaft rotation.

CHECK VALVE: Any one-way valve installed to permit the flow of air, fuel or vacuum in one direction only.

CHOKE: A device, usually a moveable valve, placed in the intake path of a carburetor to restrict the flow of air.

CIRCUIT: Any unbroken path through which an electrical current can flow. Also used to describe fuel flow in some instances.

CIRCUIT BREAKER: A switch which protects an electrical circuit from overload by opening the circuit when the current flow exceeds a predetermined level. Some circuit breakers must be reset manually, while most reset automatically.

COIL (IGNITION): A transformer in the ignition circuit which steps up the voltage provided to the spark plugs.

COMBINATION MANIFOLD: An assembly which includes both the intake and exhaust manifolds in one casting.

COMBINATION VALVE: A device used in some fuel systems that routes fuel vapors to a charcoal storage canister instead of venting them into the atmosphere. The valve relieves fuel tank pressure and allows fresh air into the tank as the fuel level drops to prevent a vapor lock situation.

COMPRESSION RATIO: The comparison of the total volume of the cylinder and combustion chamber with the piston at BDC and the piston at TDC.

CONDENSER: 1. An electrical device which acts to store an electrical charge, preventing voltage surges. 2. A radiator-like device in the air conditioning system in which refrigerant gas condenses into a liquid, giving off heat.

CONDUCTOR: Any material through which an electrical current can be transmitted easily.

CONTINUITY: Continuous or complete circuit. Can be checked with an ohmmeter.

COUNTERSHAFT: An intermediate shaft which is rotated by a mainshaft and transmits, in turn, that rotation to a working part.

CRANKCASE: The lower part of an engine in which the crankshaft and related parts operate.

CRANKSHAFT: The main driving shaft of an engine which receives reciprocating motion from the pistons and converts it to rotary motion.

CYLINDER: In an engine, the round hole in the engine block in which the piston(s) ride.

CYLINDER BLOCK: The main structural member of an engine in which is found the cylinders, crankshaft and other principal parts.

CYLINDER HEAD: The detachable portion of the engine, usually fastened to the top of the cylinder block and containing all or most of the combustion chambers. On overhead valve engines, it contains the valves and their operating parts. On overhead cam engines, it contains the camshaft as well.

DEAD CENTER: The extreme top or bottom of the piston stroke.

DETONATION: An unwanted explosion of the air/fuel mixture in the combustion chamber caused by excess heat and compression, advanced timing, or an overly lean mixture. Also referred to as "ping".

DIAPHRAGM: A thin, flexible wall separating two cavities, such as in a vacuum advance unit.

DIESELING: A condition in which hot spots in the combustion chamber cause the engine to run on after the key is turned off.

DIFFERENTIAL: A geared assembly which allows the transmission of motion between drive axles, giving one axle the ability to turn faster than the other.

DIODE: An electrical device that will allow current to flow in one direction only.

DISC BRAKE: A hydraulic braking assembly consisting of a brake disc, or rotor, mounted on an axle, and a caliper assembly containing, usually two brake pads which are activated by hydraulic pressure. The pads are forced against the sides of the disc, creating friction which slows the vehicle.

DISTRIBUTOR: A mechanically driven device on an engine which is responsible for electrically firing the spark plug at a predetermined point of the piston stroke.

DOWEL PIN: A pin, inserted in mating holes in two different parts allowing those parts to maintain a fixed relationship.

DRUM BRAKE: A braking system which consists of two brake shoes and one or two wheel cylinders, mounted on a fixed backing plate, and a brake drum, mounted on an axle, which revolves around the assembly.

DWELL: The rate, measured in degrees of shaft rotation, at which an electrical circuit cycles on and off.

ELECTRONIC CONTROL UNIT (ECU): Ignition module, module, amplifier or igniter. See Module for definition.

ELECTRONIC IGNITION: A system in which the timing and firing of the spark plugs is controlled by an electronic control unit, usually called a module. These systems have no points or condenser.

END-PLAY: The measured amount of axial movement in a shaft.

ENGINE: A device that converts heat into mechanical energy.

EXHAUST MANIFOLD: A set of cast passages or pipes which conduct exhaust gases from the engine.

FEELER GAUGE: A blade, usually metal, or precisely predetermined thickness, used to measure the clearance between two parts.

FIRING ORDER: The order in which combustion occurs in the cylinders of an engine. Also the order in which spark is distributed to the plugs by the distributor.

FLOODING: The presence of too much fuel in the intake manifold and combustion chamber which prevents the air/fuel mixture from firing, thereby causing a no-start situation.

FLYWHEEL: A disc shaped part bolted to the rear end of the crankshaft. Around the outer perimeter is affixed the ring gear. The starter drive engages the ring gear, turning the flywheel, which rotates the crankshaft, imparting the initial starting motion to the engine.

FOOT POUND (ft. lbs. or sometimes, ft.lb.): The amount of energy or work needed to raise an item weighing one pound, a distance of one foot.

FUSE: A protective device in a circuit which prevents circuit overload by breaking the circuit when a specific amperage is present. The device is constructed around a strip or wire of a lower amperage rating than the circuit it is designed to protect. When an amperage higher than that stamped on the fuse is present in the circuit, the strip or wire melts, opening the circuit.

GEAR RATIO: The ratio between the number of teeth on meshing gears.

GENERATOR: A device which converts mechanical energy into electrical energy.

HEAT RANGE: The measure of a spark plug's ability to dissipate heat from its firing end. The higher the heat range, the hotter the plug fires.

HUB: The center part of a wheel or gear.

HYDROCARBON (HC): Any chemical compound made up of hydrogen and carbon. A major pollutant formed by the engine as a byproduct of combustion.

HYDROMETER: An instrument used to measure the specific gravity of a solution.

INCH POUND (inch lbs.; sometimes in.lb. or in. lbs.): One twelfth of a foot pound.

INDUCTION: A means of transferring electrical energy in the form of a magnetic field. Principle used in the ignition coil to increase voltage.

INJECTOR: A device which receives metered fuel under relatively low pressure and is activated to inject the fuel into the engine under relatively high pressure at a predetermined time.

INPUT SHAFT: The shaft to which torque is applied, usually carrying the driving gear or gears.

INTAKE MANIFOLD: A casting of passages or pipes used to conduct air or a fuel/air mixture to the cylinders.

JOURNAL: The bearing surface within which a shaft operates.

KEY: A small block usually fitted in a notch between a shaft and a hub to prevent slippage of the two parts.

MANIFOLD: A casting of passages or set of pipes which connect the cylinders to an inlet or outlet source.

MANIFOLD VACUUM: Low pressure in an engine intake manifold formed just below the throttle plates. Manifold vacuum is highest at idle and drops under acceleration.

MASTER CYLINDER: The primary fluid pressurizing device in a hydraulic system. In automotive use, it is found in brake and hydraulic clutch systems and is pedal activated, either directly or, in a power brake system, through the power booster.

MODULE: Electronic control unit, amplifier or igniter of solid state or integrated design which controls the current flow in the ignition primary circuit based on input from the pick-up coil. When the module opens the primary circuit, high secondary voltage is induced in the coil.

NEEDLE BEARING: A bearing which consists of a number (usually a large number) of long, thin rollers.

OHM: (Ω) The unit used to measure the resistance of conductor-to-electrical flow. One ohm is the amount of resistance that limits current flow to one ampere in a circuit with one volt of pressure.

OHMMETER: An instrument used for measuring the resistance, in ohms, in an electrical circuit.

OUTPUT SHAFT: The shaft which transmits torque from a device, such as a transmission.

OVERDRIVE: A gear assembly which produces more shaft revolutions than that transmitted to it.

OVERHEAD CAMSHAFT (OHC): An engine configuration in which the camshaft is mounted on top of the cylinder head and operates the valve either directly or by means of rocker arms.

OVERHEAD VALVE (OHV): An engine configuration in which all of the valves are located in the cylinder head and the camshaft is located in the cylinder block. The camshaft operates the valves via lifters and pushrods.

OXIDES OF NITROGEN (NOx): Chemical compounds of nitrogen produced as a byproduct of combustion. They combine with hydrocarbons to produce smog.

OXYGEN SENSOR: Use with the feedback system to sense the presence of oxygen in the exhaust gas and signal the computer which can reference the voltage signal to an air/fuel ratio.

PINION: The smaller of two meshing gears.

PISTON RING: An open-ended ring with fits into a groove on the outer diameter of the piston. Its chief function is to form a seal between the piston and cylinder wall. Most automotive pistons have three rings: two for compression sealing; one for oil sealing.

PRELOAD: A predetermined load placed on a bearing during assembly or by adjustment.

PRIMARY CIRCUIT: the low voltage side of the ignition system which consists of the ignition switch, ballast resistor or resistance wire, bypass, coil, electronic control unit and pick-up coil as well as the connecting wires and harnesses.

PRESS FIT: The mating of two parts under pressure, due to the inner diameter of one being smaller than the outer diameter of the other, or vice versa; an interference fit.

RACE: The surface on the inner or outer ring of a bearing on which the balls, needles or rollers move.

REGULATOR: A device which maintains the amperage and/or voltage levels of a circuit at predetermined values.

RELAY: A switch which automatically opens and/or closes a circuit.

RESISTANCE: The opposition to the flow of current through a circuit or electrical device, and is measured in ohms. Resistance is equal to the voltage divided by the amperage.

RESISTOR: A device, usually made of wire, which offers a preset amount of resistance in an electrical circuit.

RING GEAR: The name given to a ring-shaped gear attached to a differential case, or affixed to a flywheel or as part of a planetary gear set.

ROLLER BEARING: A bearing made up of hardened inner and outer races between which hardened steel rollers move.

ROTOR: 1. The disc-shaped part of a disc brake assembly, upon which the brake pads bear; also called, brake disc. 2. The device mounted atop the distributor shaft, which passes current to the distributor cap tower contacts.

SECONDARY CIRCUIT: The high voltage side of the ignition system, usually above 20,000 volts. The secondary includes the ignition coil, coil wire, distributor cap and rotor, spark plug wires and spark plugs.

SENDING UNIT: A mechanical, electrical, hydraulic or electro-magnetic device which transmits information to a gauge.

SENSOR: Any device designed to measure engine operating conditions or ambient pressures and temperatures. Usually electronic in nature and designed to send a voltage signal to an on-board computer, some sensors may operate as a simple on/off switch or they may provide a variable voltage signal (like a potentiometer) as conditions or measured parameters change.

SHIM: Spacers of precise, predetermined thickness used between parts to establish a proper working relationship.

SLAVE CYLINDER: In automotive use, a device in the hydraulic clutch system which is activated by hydraulic force, disengaging the clutch.

SOLENOID: A coil used to produce a magnetic field, the effect of which is to produce work.

SPARK PLUG: A device screwed into the combustion chamber of a spark ignition engine. The basic construction is a conductive core inside of a ceramic insulator, mounted in an outer conductive base. An electrical charge from the spark plug wire travels along the conductive core and jumps a preset air gap to a grounding point or points at the end of the conductive base. The resultant spark ignites the fuel/air mixture in the combustion chamber.

SPLINES: Ridges machined or cast onto the outer diameter of a shaft or inner diameter of a bore to enable parts to mate without rotation.

TACHOMETER: A device used to measure the rotary speed of an engine, shaft, gear, etc., usually in rotations per minute.

THERMOSTAT: A valve, located in the cooling system of an engine, which is closed when cold and opens gradually in response to engine heating, controlling the temperature of the coolant and rate of coolant flow.

TOP DEAD CENTER (TDC): The point at which the piston reaches the top of its travel on the compression stroke.

TORQUE: The twisting force applied to an object.

TORQUE CONVERTER: A turbine used to transmit power from a driving member to a driven member via hydraulic action, providing changes in drive ratio and torque. In automotive use, it links the driveplate at the rear of the engine to the automatic transmission.

TRANSDUCER: A device used to change a force into an electrical signal.

TRANSISTOR: A semi-conductor component which can be actuated by a small voltage to perform an electrical switching function.

TUNE-UP: A regular maintenance function, usually associated with the replacement and adjustment of parts and components in the electrical and fuel systems of a vehicle for the purpose of attaining optimum performance.

TURBOCHARGER: An exhaust driven pump which compresses intake air and forces it into the combustion chambers at higher than atmospheric pressures. The increased air pressure allows more fuel to be burned and results in increased horsepower being produced.

VACUUM ADVANCE: A device which advances the ignition timing in response to increased engine vacuum.

VACUUM GAUGE: An instrument used to measure the presence of vacuum in a chamber.

VALVE: A device which control the pressure, direction of flow or rate of flow of a liquid or gas.

VALVE CLEARANCE: The measured gap between the end of the valve stem and the rocker arm, cam lobe or follower that activates the valve.

VISCOSITY: The rating of a liquid's internal resistance to flow.

VOLTMETER: An instrument used for measuring electrical force in units called volts. Voltmeters are always connected parallel with the circuit being tested.

WHEEL CYLINDER: Found in the automotive drum brake assembly, it is a device, actuated by hydraulic pressure, which, through internal pistons, pushes the brake shoes outward against the drums.

MASTER

INDEX

For information on other titles, visit your local Chilton® Retailer
For a Catalog, for information, or to order call toll-free: **877-4CHILTON.**

 1020 Andrew Drive, Suite 200 • West Chester, PA 19380-4291
www.chiltononline.com